MANAGERIAL ACCOUNTING

MANAGERIAL ACCOUNTING

AN INTRODUCTION TO CONCEPTS, METHODS AND USES

Sidney Davidson, Ph.D., CPA
The University of Chicago

James S. Schindler, Ph.D., CPA
The State University of New York at Buffalo

Clyde P. Stickney, D.B.A., CPA
Dartmouth College

Roman L. Weil, Ph.D., CPA, CMA
The University of Chicago

The Dryden Press
Hinsdale, Illinois

Material from the Uniform CPA Examination,
copyright 1968 by the American Institute of
Certified Public Accountants, Inc., is adapted
with permission.

Material from the Certificate in Management
Accounting Examinations, copyright © 1972,
1973, and 1975 by the National Association of
Accountants, is adapted with permission.

Whatever be the detail with which you cram
your students, the chance of their meeting in
after-life exactly that detail is almost
infinitesimal; and if they do meet it, they
will probably have forgotten what you taught
them about it. The really useful training yields
a comprehension of a few general principles
with a thorough grounding in the way they
apply to a variety of concrete details. In
subsequent practice the students will have
forgotten your particular details; but they will
remember by an unconscious common sense
how to apply principles to immediate
circumstances.

Alfred North Whitehead
The Aims of Education and Other Essays

PREFACE

The study of managerial accounting can be both a rewarding and a frustrating experience. The experience is rewarding because it allows the student to draw upon concepts and techniques studied in economics, statistics, behavioral sciences, and other courses in the solving of managerial problems. This process can give the student a feeling of finally "putting it all together."

At the same time, the experience can be frustrating. We feel the frustration has two primary causes. First, most textbooks, in an effort to foster the synthesizing process, intermingle concepts appropriate for three different uses of accounting information: (1) managerial decision making, (2) managerial planning and control, and (3) external financial reporting. As a result, students attempt inappropriately to transfer concepts between various uses of accounting information. For example, the average unit cost of inventory items is correctly used in external financial reporting but is incorrectly used in deciding whether to accept or reject a special order. Another example: some fixed costs that are correctly ignored in certain decision-making contexts are incorrectly assumed to be irrelevant to managerial performance evaluation. Although allocation of central maintenance costs to divisions is understood to be irrelevant for decision-making purposes, the allocation on the basis of square footage used may be correctly argued to provide the best basis of allocation for the purposes of product costing. In our opinion, the use of a particular concept must be adequately developed prior to discussion of how the concept relates to others.

A second cause of students' frustration in studying managerial accounting results from the lack of a cohesive link between financial and managerial accounting in the typical text. Managerial accounting students have often completed a course in financial accounting just before taking the managerial accounting course. No effort is made, however, to link the two disciplines of accounting. For example, students learn in financial accounting that fixed manufacturing overhead costs are product costs for the purpose of determining net income. On the other hand, when the teacher or managerial accounting text discusses cost-volume-profit analysis, little mention is made of the fact that these manufacturing costs are effectively being treated as period expenses for the analysis. In managerial accounting, students learn that investments should be undertaken only if they are expected to provide a positive net present value. But they learned in financial accounting that certain investments, such as those in a portfolio of research and development efforts, can have an immediate dampening effect on reported profits. Students are then left to wonder what is the relation between the proper decision-making model on the one hand and the proper reporting model on the other.

In writing this book, we have attempted to eliminate these two difficulties. As we describe in more detail in the next section, the text is structured around the three primary uses of accounting information: (1) managerial decision making, (2) managerial planning and control, and (3) external financial reporting. The concepts appropriate to each use are discussed and illustrated, followed by a synthesis in Chapter 14. Second, we have attempted throughout the text to provide links between financial and managerial accounting. Chapter 1 suggests that financial and managerial accounting should be congenial. In later chapters we point out areas in accounting where the two do and do not interact congenially. Chapter 14 summarizes the important similarities and differences.

It should be clear from a reading of the Table of Contents that we have continued the current trend toward deemphasizing traditional "cost accounting" topics and emphasizing the more user-oriented topics of decision making, planning, and control. It should also be clear from reading a few sample chapters that we have attempted to strike a balance between accounting concepts and accounting procedures. We concur with most writers of accounting textbooks that the most effective way for students to learn an accounting concept is for them to work problems and exercises. When too much emphasis is placed on accounting procedures, however, there is a tendency for students to be lulled into the security of thinking they understand an accounting concept fully, merely because they can implement some of its procedures. The mixture of concepts and procedures in this book is one with which we have experimented extensively and which we have found effective in classroom use.

ORGANIZATION OF THE BOOK

This book starts with an introductory chapter; the five major parts of the text are outlined below:

Part	Topic	Chapters
I	External Reporting of Managerial Decisions	2–3
II	Managerial Decision Making	4–7
III	Planning and Control	8–11
IV	Cost Accumulation and Allocation	12–14
V	Special Topics in Managerial Decision Making	15–18

For a course dealing only with managerial accounting topics, Chapter 1 and Parts II, III, and IV provide the core of the course material. Chapter 1 provides a general overview of managerial accounting by discussing the three principal uses of accounting information. Parts II, III, and IV then discuss each of these three uses in greater depth. Part II (Chapters 4 through 7) deals with managerial decision making; Part III (Chapters 8 through 11) discusses managerial planning and control; and Part IV (Chapters 12 through 14) focuses on the process for generating accounting information for external reporting. Chapter 14 ties together much of the material in the book; it considers specific areas where managerial and financial accounting are and are not congenial.

This organization reflects our view that learning occurs most effectively when a course starts with a broad picture then breaks up that broad picture into smaller pieces until the desired depth is achieved. Finally the course synthesizes the pieces so that the student can keep the relationship between the parts and the whole in perspective.

Part I (Chapters 2 and 3) presents a brief overview of financial accounting. Our including this material reflects the view that an understanding of managerial accounting principles requires an awareness of the way in which the results of management's actions will be reported in the external financial statements. This part of the book can be skipped or skimmed if students have previously had a course in financial accounting. If not, we feel it should be covered before beginning Part II.

Part V (Chapters 15 through 18) presents additional managerial accounting materials to supplement earlier chapters in the book. It provides the instructor with flexibility to cover certain topics in greater depth. For example, Chapters 16–18 can be assigned to follow Chapter 7 if the instructor wishes to emphasize present value analysis in managerial decision making.

CHAPTER CONTENTS

Chapter 1 presents a brief discussion of the three principal uses of accounting information. We discuss each use separately and then show how the uses are integrated. We have found that in order to develop an understanding of managerial accounting concepts and the skills necessary to make correct transfers of these concepts, the rather different nature of the three uses of accounting information must be emphasized. In Chapter 1, we argue that financial and managerial accounting should be mutually supportive.

Chapters 2 and 3 provide a brief summary of financial accounting. Chapter 2 describes the purpose, content, and format of the three principal financial statements found in corporate annual reports. The critical concepts underlying these statements are also discussed. We have omitted all procedural aspects of preparing the statements so that end uses can be emphasized. Finally, Chapter 3 summarizes some techniques for analyzing the statements.

Chapters 4 through 7 consider the kinds of accounting information required for managerial decision making and the generation of those data. Chapter 4 is perhaps the most important chapter in this section because it describes and illustrates the principles of incremental analysis. Some students have difficulty switching gears from the historical cost, after-the-fact (ex post) orientation of financial accounting to the before-the-fact (ex ante) orientation of much of managerial accounting. We attempt to help students switch gears early in the course by introducing the incremental principle and showing the irrelevance of sunk cost (past cost) for most decisions. Chapter 5 discusses some techniques for estimating, or predicting, future revenues and costs. These techniques provide data that are necessary inputs for the incremental model. Chapters 6 and 7 then illustrate the application of the incremental principle to short-run and long-run managerial problems. Chapter 6 considers several short-term decisions, including those related to cost–volume–profit, pricing, and inventory management. Chapter 7 focuses on long-run capital budgeting decisions, with emphasis on the net present value model and the impact of income taxes.

Chapters 8 through 11 consider the kinds of accounting information required for managerial planning and control and the generation of those data. Chapter 8 introduces critical planning and control concepts with emphasis on behavioral considerations. Chapter 9 focuses on the planning and budgeting process, and Chapter 10 considers the control process, including analysis of sales and cost variances. Chapter 11 discusses divisional performance measurement and control.

Chapters 12 through 14 deal with (1) the internal accounting problem of generating the data needed for external reporting and (2) the relationship of those data to information needed for managerial decision making and for planning and control. We find that these three chapters, particularly Chapter 14, effectively synthesize the material covered in both financial and managerial accounting courses. Chapter 12 describes the fundamentals of product costing. Chapter 13 discusses the need for common cost allocations in much of accounting and the kinds of misinterpretations which often result. Chapter 14 considers areas where financial and managerial accounting do not provide consistent, coordinated reports and the effect which this lack of congruence can have on users.

Chapters 15 through 18 explore several managerial accounting topics in more depth. Chapter 15 discusses techniques of accounting for price changes, a topic of interest in both managerial and financial accounting. Chapter 16 delves more deeply into capital budgeting by considering decision models other than net present value. Chapters 17 and 18, unique among managerial accounting texts, explore in detail the impact of income taxes on managerial decisions. Included in these chapters are discussions of decisions relating to compensation, capital structure, and organization form as well as the selection of accounting methods for income tax reporting.

The Appendix at the end of the book describes the concepts and techniques of compound interest. If the student has not been exposed previously to this topic, it should be assigned before Chapter 7. A comprehensive glossary of accounting terms is also included at the end of the book. We hope that this glossary will serve as a useful reference tool for accounting and other business terms. It provides additional descriptions of a few topics considered only briefly in the text.

RELATED MATERIALS ACCOMPANYING THE TEXT

The following materials have been prepared for use with the text.

Instructor's Manual Containing Problem Solutions

The manual contains responses to all questions and solutions to all exercises, problems, and cases. We were assisted by James A. Hayssen of Touche Ross & Co. in the compilation of these answers. The instructor's manual also includes some sample course outlines, check figures for various problems in the text, and sample examination questions and solutions. We would like to acknowledge the assistance of Professor Robert G. Ronay of the University of Minnesota in preparation of this item.

Study Guide to Accompany Text

Professor Michael W. Maher of the University of Michigan has prepared a student study guide to accompany this text.

The *Guide* is published by our publisher, Dryden Press, and is available from them. The *Guide* includes for each chapter and the appendix:

1 An outline of the chapter with emphasis on the key points.
2 A set of fill-in-the-blank questions and answers for students' self-help.
3 A set of matching (term and definition) questions and answers for students' self-help.
4 A set of multiple choice questions and answers for students' self-help.
5 Several longer problems and cases for students' self-help with answers or suggested solutions.

Several dozen CMA Examination questions and answers are included among the longer problems and cases. In addition, the *Guide* includes a summary, synthesizing chapter with integrating problems and cases for the text as a whole.

Transparency Masters

A set of masters is available in the instructor's manual for making transparencies for most of the exhibits in the text and problems at the end of each chapter. Additionally, a set of acetate transparencies for selected solutions is available.

ACKNOWLEDGMENTS

We gratefully acknowledge the helpful criticisms and suggestions of the following people who reviewed the manuscript at various stages: K. E. Bailey III, University of Florida; Robert E. Bennett, Northern Illinois University; Charles Carter, University of Missouri–Kansas City; Ronald Copeland, University of South Carolina; James T. Godfrey, University of Michigan; R. E. Jensen, University of Massachusetts; Chris Luneski, University of Oregon; Michael W. Maher, University of Michigan; Robert D. Ronay, University of Minnesota; E. J. Sanders, Corpus Christi State University; Myles Stern, Wayne State University; Gary Sundem, University of Washington; and Ronald C. Waterman, University of Northern Colorado.

Thomas Horton and Daughters, Inc., has given us permission to reproduce material from our *Accounting: The Language of Business,* published by them. The following have consented to let us use problems or cases prepared by them for which we are appreciative: Case Clearing House, David O. Green, David Solomons, George Sorter, and Shyam Sunder. Material from the Uniform CPA Examinations and Unofficial Answers, copyright by the American Institute of Certified Public Accountants, Inc., is adapted with permission. Permission was received from the Institute of Management Accounting of the National Association of Accountants to use problem materials from past Certified Management Accounting Examinations.

We thank the following people for their help in preparing this book: Sylvia Dobray, Sydney Dominick, Phyllis Maxwell, Mardine McReynolds, Mary Lee Peeler, Raymonde Rousselot, Kathy Stickney and Katherine Xenophon-Rybowiak.

Finally, we would like to thank Bruce Frymire, Ray Ashton, and in particular, Sandy Nykerk, of the Dryden Press for their assistance in all phases of the preparation of this book. It was Jere Calmes' idea.

S.D.
J.S.S.
C.P.S.
R.L.W.

CONTENTS

MANAGERIAL ACCOUNTING

CHAPTER 1
THE MANAGEMENT PROCESS AND ACCOUNTING INFORMATION

Accounting is often divided into "financial" and "managerial" accounting. *Financial accounting* typically refers to the preparation of general purpose reports for use by persons outside, or external to, a firm. Such users include shareholders (owners) of a corporation, creditors (those who lend money to a business), financial analysts, labor unions, government regulators, and the like. The primary interest of external users is the review and evaluation of the operations and financial status of the business as a whole.

Managerial accounting typically refers to the preparation of more specific-purpose reports for use by persons within, or internal to, a firm. For example, a production manager may desire a report on the number of units of product manufactured by various workers in order to evaluate their performance. A sales manager might be interested in a report showing the relative profitability of two products in order to decide where selling effort should be directed.

This book focuses primarily on managerial accounting. We shall consider how accounting aids management in making decisions and in planning and controlling operations. Some consideration is also given to the manner in which the results of management's decisions are reported to external users under current financial accounting principles.

MANAGERIAL AND FINANCIAL ACCOUNTING: CONGENIAL DISCIPLINES

For many years, accounting has been recognized as a valuable source of information for both managers and investors. It is highly desirable that the two uses of accounting —internal and external—be complementary rather than competitive. That is, it is desirable that wise decisions by management, based on a careful consideration of probable future consequences and proceeding precisely according to plan, should be reported as being successful in the external financial statements. Unwise managerial actions should likewise be realistically reported.

The logical unity of managerial and financial accounting may be understood by considering the basic goals of financial reporting. It is felt, almost universally, that the primary goal of financial accounting is the periodic determination of net income. The primary responsibility of management is to direct a firm's operations to maximize income. The periodic measure of net income for external reports should be consistent with the measure of income used by management in making decisions. Otherwise, what is a wise decision from management's viewpoint may be reported as a poor decision to external users (or vice versa).

Example 1   A firm plans to expand its operations and must decide whether to establish operations in the East or in the West. If it locates in the East, it will be able to generate $500,000 of sales each year. Manufacturing costs are expected to be $300,000 and selling costs $100,000 annually. If it locates in the West, it will be able to generate $600,000 of sales each year. Manufacturing and selling costs are expected to be $380,000 and $140,000, respectively. In either case, the firm will rent the necessary production and selling facilities in the area selected.

In making this decision, management should compare the additional, or incremental, cash inflows with the incremental cash outflows from each alternative. See Exhibit 1.1. If all other factors (such as potential for further expansion, location preferences of employees) are the same for the two alternatives, management should choose to locate in the East. In this way, it will maximize net cash inflows, or income.

EXHIBIT 1.1
Example 1

	Locate in the East	Locate in the West
Incremental Cash Inflows..............	$500,000	$600,000
Less Incremental Cash Outflows:		
Manufacturing	(300,000)	(380,000)
Selling.............................	(100,000)	(140,000)
Incremental Net Cash Inflows	$100,000	$ 80,000

How will the results of this decision be reported in the external financial statements? If revenues and costs proceed according to plan, the firm will report income from operating in the East of $100,000 each year. If the wrong decision is made (that is, to locate in the West), the firm will report a lower income of $80,000 and the income for the firm as a whole will be correspondingly lower. Thus, managerial and financial accounting report consistent, complementary results.

Certain "generally accepted accounting principles" (required to be followed in preparing external financial statements) do not, however, permit the results of some management decisions to be accurately reported. That is, management can make a good decision that is externally reported as a bad one, at least in the short run. Similarly, management can make a bad decision that is externally reported as a good one, at least in the short run.

Example 2   A machine now owned by a firm has a book value of $20,000. (This means that the original cost of the machine less the depreciation recognized to date is reported in the accounting records as $20,000.) The machine has no current salvage or resale value. It is estimated that the machine will be able to produce 1,000 units of product during each of the next five years if $6,000 is spent each year for materials and labor. A new machine has been developed that costs $15,000, will also last for five years, and will also produce 1,000 units of product each year. The yearly costs of materials and labor on the new machine are expected to be only $2,000. The selling price of the product will be $12 per unit regardless of which machine is used. Management must decide whether to keep the old machine or replace it with the new machine.

As we shall see in Chapter Seven, it probably makes sense to spend $15,000 this year for the new machine in order to save $4,000 (= $6,000 − $2,000) in cash outflows per year for five years. The best decision from management's viewpoint is to acquire the new machine.

How will the results of this decision be reported in the external financial statements? Exhibit 1.2 shows the net income for each of the next five years under both alternatives. If the correct managerial decision is made and the new machine is acquired, financial accounting will report a loss in the first year of $13,000. If the incorrect managerial decision is made and the old machine is continued in use, reported net income will be $2,000 in the first year.

It seems illogical that a wise decision by management, based on a careful consideration of probable future consequences and proceeding precisely according to plan, would have the immediate effect of reducing reported net income. Yet this sometimes happens. It is scant comfort for management to be told that, if the program continues according to plan, reported net income will ultimately be higher, indeed higher by an amount that compensates for the earlier reported loss. Income measures management's effectiveness. Judgments of management's effectiveness are made too frequently for managers to take much comfort from the thought that this year's reported losses will be offset by profits sometime in the future. It is discouraging enough for managers to think of being replaced by a new management as a result of deficient financial reporting. It is even more discouraging to be told that the successor manager will look especially good because of the future profits that will offset losses being reported currently. When managers feel that financial accounting practices inhibit desirable action, financial accounting and managerial accounting are not working together effectively.

There are several areas in financial reporting where accounting may inhibit proper management decisions. Because this is so, it is important that any study of managerial

EXHIBIT 1.2
Example 2: Projected Income from Keeping the Old Machine versus Acquiring the New Machine

	Year					Total
	1	2	3	4	5	
Keeping Old Machine						
Revenues (1,000 × $12)	$ 12,000	$12,000	$12,000	$12,000	$12,000	$60,000
Costs of Materials and Labor	(6,000)	(6,000)	(6,000)	(6,000)	(6,000)	(30,000)
Depreciation on Equipment ($20,000/5)	(4,000)	(4,000)	(4,000)	(4,000)	(4,000)	(20,000)
Income	$ 2,000	$ 2,000	$ 2,000	$ 2,000	$ 2,000	$10,000
Acquiring New Machine						
Revenues (1,000 × $12)	$ 12,000	$12,000	$12,000	$12,000	$12,000	$60,000
Cost of Materials and Labor	(2,000)	(2,000)	(2,000)	(2,000)	(2,000)	(10,000)
Depreciation on Equipment ($15,000/5)	(3,000)	(3,000)	(3,000)	(3,000)	(3,000)	(15,000)
Loss on Retirement of Old Equipment[a]	(20,000)	—	—	—	—	(20,000)
Income (Loss)	$(13,000)	$ 7,000	$ 7,000	$ 7,000	$ 7,000	$15,000

[a] The old machine is currently shown in the accounting records at depreciated historical cost of $20,000. If the machine is retired now, a loss of $20,000 must be recorded.

accounting contain some review of the implications for financial accounting (or external reporting) of managerial decision making. This book, therefore, contains a significant amount of financial accounting, with the primary emphasis on the resulting reporting of management's decisions.

USES OF ACCOUNTING INFORMATION

Accounting provides information for three broad purposes, or uses: (1) managerial decision making, (2) managerial planning, control, and internal performance evaluation, and (3) financial reporting and external performance evaluation.

Managerial Decision Making

Management is continually confronted with the need to make decisions. Some of these decisions affect operations for only a few weeks or months, whereas others may have consequences for many years in the future. For example, what prices should be set for a firm's product during the next year? Should an important component of a firm's product be manufactured by the firm or purchased directly from outsiders? Should existing equipment be replaced with newer, more efficient equipment? Should a more capital-intensive factory be constructed that will result in significant future savings in labor costs? These are just some of the decisions that face management.

The decision-making process can be described as including the following steps:

1 Identifying a problem requiring managerial action.
2 Specifying the objective or goal to be achieved (for example, maximizing income).
3 Listing the possible alternative courses of action.
4 Gathering information about the consequences of each alternative.
5 Making a decision, by selecting one of the alternatives.

Managerial accounting plays a critical role in step 4 of the decision-making process. As the principal source of data on transactions that have already occurred, managerial accounting systems contain a storehouse of valuable information for predicting the results of various courses of action. Managerial accounting systems are designed to provide quantitative measures of performance. Thus, managerial accounting can assist management in formally structuring decision problems as well as placing the alternatives and their consequences in a form that will be easier for management to evaluate.

Example 3 A manufacturer of electronic equipment is considering the introduction of citizens band (CB) radios into its product line. Management wishes to predict the expected costs of manufacturing the CB radios and the expected revenues that might be generated. The managerial accountant has a record of the costs incurred in the past to manufacture similar electronic equipment. These past costs might be classified into various groups (for example, materials, labor, and overhead). An attempt can then be made to project the future costs of manufacturing the CB radios. It is likely that data would also be available concerning the amount of advertising costs required to market similar products and the amount of sales revenue generated. Projections from these data would provide management with the information necessary to decide whether or not to add CB radios to the product line.

The decision-making process might be depicted graphically as in Figure 1.1.

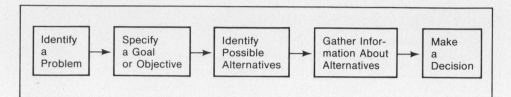

FIGURE 1.1
The Decision-making Process

Managerial Planning, Control, and Internal Performance Evaluation

The planning and control process might be described as including the following steps or components:

1 Specify a criterion (standard or budget) as to what actual performance should be.
2 Measure the results of actual performance.
3 Evaluate performance by comparing actual performance with the criterion. This evaluation aids management in assessing actions already taken and in determining which courses of action should be taken in the future.

Example 4   The firm in Example 1 in this chapter decided to locate in the East. It anticipated sales of $500,000 each year for five years. (Refer to Exhibit 1.1.) This amount might serve as the criterion or standard for evaluating the performance of the sales manager responsible for the eastern territory. If annual sales vary significantly from $500,000, an effort would be made to determine the cause of the variance. If factors or conditions that are not under the control of the sales manager caused the variance, then the sales manager would not be held responsible for it. (For example, a strike by production workers might cause a shortage of products and thereby a loss in sales which would not be controllable by the sales manager.) If the sales manager can control the causes of the variance, then the positive or negative variance would be attributable to the sales manager in evaluating that manager's performance. (For example, good design and implementation of an effective sales incentive program by the sales manager might lead to increased sales. On the other hand, poor coordination of the sales force might lead to reduced sales; the sales manager would be held accountable.) This evaluation process is also useful for planning selling strategies for future periods.

Managerial accounting plays an important role in the planning and control process. By assisting management in the decision-making process, as discussed earlier, it provides information for establishing the expectation or criterion as to what performance

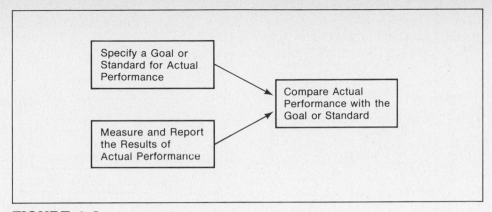

FIGURE 1.2
The Planning and Control Process

should be. All actual transactions are processed by the internal, or managerial, accounting system. Thus it provides management with measures of the results of actual performance. As a part of both the standard-setting stage and the actual performance stage of the planning and control process, managerial accounting helps isolate the causes of variances from planned levels of costs and other activities.

Figure 1.2 illustrates the planning and control process.

Financial Reporting and External Performance Evaluation

A third principal use of accounting information is to assist investors, creditors, and others in evaluating a firm's performance and in making decisions whether or not to allocate their resources to the firm. Unlike reports prepared to assist management in decision making, planning, and control, the financial reports prepared for users external to the firm must follow certain standard formats and measurement rules. For example, a publicly held firm is required to present a statement of financial position (or balance sheet), a statement of net income, and a statement of changes in financial position each year. These statements must be prepared and presented in accordance with "generally accepted accounting principles." Chapters Two and Three consider the format and content of these financial statements. One of the accountant's jobs is to prepare these statements for external users.

Figure 1.3 illustrates the relationships among the three principal uses of accounting information discussed in this section. You will note that the managerial decision-making process and the managerial planning and control process are closely related. As a result of making a decision, management has an expectation as to what the results of actual performance should be if everything goes according to plan. This "expected outcome" becomes the criterion or standard for internal evaluation and control of actual performance. The results of this internal performance evaluation in one period become an input into the planning and decision-making process of the next period.

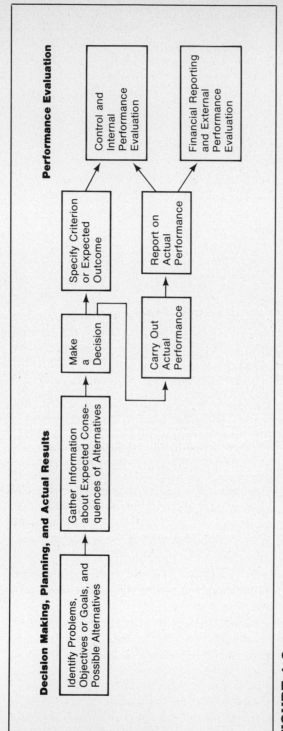

FIGURE 1.3
Managerial Processes and Accounting Information

The managerial control and financial reporting processes are also closely related. Both rely heavily on the results of actual performance. The report on actual performance for internal performance evaluation may be quite different from the report for external performance evaluation. The external report must be prepared in accordance with "generally accepted accounting principles," whereas the internal report may be prepared following whatever measurement procedures management feels will provide the most useful information.

The ideal situation from both a management and an accounting standpoint is

1 For the decision-making process to be based on sound logic and economic reasoning, and
2 For the control process and financial reporting process to be based on measures of performance that realistically reflect the economic consequences of decisions made and actions taken.

In this way,

1 Management will be encouraged to take actions that will maximize income, and
2 A single accounting system can be designed to generate information for
   a Managerial decision making,
   b Managerial planning, control, and internal performance evaluation,
   c Financial reporting and external performance evaluation.

Example 2, concerning the decision whether to keep or replace an old machine, demonstrated that managerial and financial reporting practices are not always compatible in the short run. Any study of accounting, whether managerial or financial, must consider these areas of incompatibility.

OUTLINE OF THE BOOK

The purpose of this book is to help educate effective managers. It is devoted primarily to managerial accounting, but it contains material that is often thought of as financial accounting. The rest of this chapter describes the environment of managerial and financial accounting, including its authorities and the literature. It also considers some desirable characteristics of accounting information prepared for both managers and external users.

Part 1, Chapters Two and Three, presents an overview of financial accounting and reporting. Chapter Two discusses the important concepts and principles underlying the statement of financial position, statement of net income, and the statement of changes in financial position. Chapter Three describes some techniques for analyzing and interpreting external financial statements. Many users of this book will have had some introduction to financial accounting, and Part 1 will serve as a review of that material.

Part 2, Chapters Four through Seven, discusses accounting concepts and techniques useful for managerial decision making. Chapter Four considers incremental analysis, the essential concept for managerial decision making. Although the term *incremental analysis* may be unfamiliar, you have probably already encountered the same concept in economics, where it is called *marginal analysis.* Incremental analysis requires that the decision maker consider only those factors that will change cash flows. If an item does not change cash flows, then it need not be considered in making a decision. A firm grasp of the principles of incremental analysis is necessary for effective decision making. Chapter Five describes some techniques for estimating future cash flows. Chapter Six focuses on short-term profit planning and decision-making. Chapter Seven considers long-term capital investment decisions.

Part 3, Chapters Eight through Eleven, discusses managerial planning, control, and internal performance evaluation. Chapter Eight provides an overview of the planning and control process and discusses some behavioral considerations. Chapter Nine considers the development of budgets as tools for planning. Chapter Ten deals with the use of budgets, or standards, for controlling operations of a firm. Chapter Eleven focuses on the control of decentralized operations.

Part 4, Chapters Twelve through Fourteen, describes the accumulation of data for the internal and external reporting of actual performance. Whereas Parts 2 and 3 treat the questions, "What information do we want and how do we use it?" Part 4 treats the question, "How do we generate the information?" The material in Part 4 is often called *cost accounting.*

Chapters One through Fourteen form the core of a study of managerial accounting. Chapters Fifteen, Sixteen, Seventeen, and Eighteen explore several special topics in managerial decision making.

The Appendix discusses compound interest calculations, which are required for comparing amounts of money to be received or paid at different times. Comparing cash flows that occur at different times is essential for making effective managerial decisions (and understanding much of financial accounting as well). The Appendix is independent of the rest of the book and may be read at any time.

THE ENVIRONMENT OF MANAGERIAL AND FINANCIAL ACCOUNTING

Accounting Authorities and Literature

The managerial accountant prepares reports that provide information to users within the firm. The corporate treasurer might use a budget of estimated cash receipts and disbursements to determine if short-term borrowing is necessary. The production supervisor might use a report on the productivity or efficiency of various individuals in deciding how a special order is to be routed through the factory. A sales manager might use a report on the costs of producing and selling different product lines in recommending the prices that should be charged and the products that should be pushed by the sales staff. In contrast to financial accounting, there are no externally imposed procedures that must be followed in preparing these reports. Users of information within the firm are generally free to specify the type of information they want for their decisions. Accounting reports are prepared to conform to their requests. Managerial accounting is thus more flexible than financial accounting because it is not constrained by "generally accepted accounting principles."

Frequent references are made throughout this book to the "generally accepted accounting principles" that govern financial accounting. These "principles" are the accounting methods used by firms in preparing their external financial statements.

By Congressional enactment, the Securities and Exchange Commission (SEC) has been granted the legal authority to prescribe accounting principles to be followed by most corporations. The SEC has used its power sparingly, however, and the real authority over accounting principles has been vested in the financial community. Generally accepted accounting principles are not all codified, and they are not all promulgated by a single governmental, private, or professional authority. Rather they are found in the literature of the field, including pronouncements of interested professional organizations and security exchanges, governmental regulations, articles, and textbooks. Thus management, the accounting profession, the users of financial statements, and governmental agencies contribute to the continued development of generally accepted principles of accounting. Some of the leading organizations and sources of accounting literature that influence the development of accounting principles are discussed below.

The Securities and Exchange Commission has a considerable responsibility assigned to it with respect to financial accounting under the Securities Act of 1933, the Securities Exchange Act of 1934, and their amendments. The SEC has decided to rely primarily on the accounting profession for the establishment of accounting principles on most topics. The SEC prescribes the form of financial statements to be submitted to it and has issued rulings in certain areas. Among its publications are the following:

Regulation S-X. A document pertaining to the form and content of financial statements required to be filed with the SEC.

Accounting Series Releases. A series of opinions on accounting principles which together with *Regulation S-X* are the primary statements on the form and content of financial statements filed with the Commission.

Staff Accounting Bulletins. A series of bulletins issued by the staff of the Chief Accountant's Office interpreting Accounting Series Releases and explaining their enforcement.

Since 1973, the *Financial Accounting Standards Board* (FASB) has been the highest nongovernmental authority on generally accepted accounting principles. The FASB issues *Statements of Financial Accounting Standards* (and *Interpretations* of these statements) from time to time establishing or clarifying generally accepted accounting principles.

The *American Institute of Certified Public Accountants* (AICPA) is the national organization of certified public accountants. Its publications and committees are influential in the development of accounting principles and practices. It actively promulgates standards of ethics and reviews conduct within the profession. Among its influential publications are the following:

Journal of Accountancy. A monthly periodical containing articles, pronouncements, announcements, and practical sections of direct interest to the practicing members of the profession.

Accounting Research Bulletins Nos. 1–51 (1939–1959). A series of statements on accounting problems that contributed greatly to the narrowing of differences and inconsistencies in accounting practice and to the development and recognition of generally accepted accounting principles.

Opinions of the Accounting Principles Board Nos. 1–31 (1962–1973). A series of statements on accounting problems and generally accepted accounting principles. These pronouncements remain in effect unless superseded by statements of the Financial Accounting Standards Board.

Accounting Research Studies. A series of monographs on accounting problems that provide a basis for further development of generally accepted accounting principles in the particular area.

Statements on Auditing Standards. No. 1 (1973) of this series is a codification of all statements on auditing standards previously issued by the AICPA. Later numbers of the series deal with specific auditing procedures.

The *American Accounting Association* is an organization primarily for accountants in academic work, but it is open to all who are interested in accounting. It participates in the development of generally accepted accounting principles and practice, and it promotes the academic phases of accounting theory, research, and instruction. Among its influential publications are:

The Accounting Review. A quarterly periodical containing articles and sections covering a broad span of subjects related to accounting practice, research, and instruction for purposes of both external and internal reporting.

Statement on Accounting Theory and Theory Acceptance. An integrated statement for educators, practitioners, and others interested in accounting. The statement seeks to identify the field of accounting, to establish standards by which accounting information can be judged, to point out possible improvements in accounting practice, and to present a useful framework for scholars who wish to extend the uses of accounting.

The *National Association of Accountants* is a national society generally open to all engaged in activities closely associated with managerial accounting. Among its publications are the following:

Management Accounting. A monthly periodical.

Research Series. A series of monographs on subjects of internal and external accounting.

Accounting Practice Reports. A series of summaries of surveys on current practice in a limited area of accounting.

The *Financial Executives Institute* is an organization of financial executives of large businesses, such as chief accountants, controllers, treasurers, and financial vice-presidents. Among its publications are the *Financial Executive,* a monthly periodical, and a number of studies on problems confronting accounting and financial management.

Income tax legislation and administration have had a substantial impact on the practice of accounting. Although income tax requirements in themselves do not establish principles and practices for external reporting, their influence on the choice of acceptable procedures is substantial. At the federal level, in addition to the *Internal*

Revenue Code passed by the Congress, there are the *Regulations* and *Rulings* of the Internal Revenue Service, and the opinions of the U.S. Tax Court.

The *Cost Accounting Standards Board* (CASB) has been authorized by the U.S. Congress to set accounting standards for cost determination by defense contractors under federal contracts. The increasing complexity of government buying procedures, coupled with a need to negotiate cost-based contracts, have resulted in increasing reliance on cost accounting data to determine contract prices. The former diversity in cost accounting systems used by contractors made it difficult for the government to evaluate proposals and to determine the payments due contractors. Congress recognized this difficulty and after several preliminary actions established the CASB in 1970. The CASB attempts to set standards to achieve uniformity and consistency in contract proposals and cost reporting. Most of the work of the CASB does not directly affect the form of financial statements, but its requirements have considerable weight in many areas of practice, especially those dealing with the measurement and allocation of costs.

Accounting Terminology

Accounting terminology generally follows common usage. Occasionally, however, commonly used words are given restricted technical meanings. For example, the word *reserve* in common usage indicates that a pool of something is earmarked or set aside, but in accounting terminology its meaning is altogether different. The term *surplus* may mean "too much" in commonly used terminology, but this is not its meaning when used in accounting. Students of accounting can generally use the vocabulary that has been developed for general communication. You will find it necessary, however, to learn a rather limited vocabulary of new technical terms and to become aware of technical meanings assigned to a few common words such as *allowance, cost,* and *credit.* Moreover, you must understand the difference in accounting between words that often mean the same thing in everyday language, such as *revenue* and *receipt, expense* and *expenditure, cost* and *value.* A *Glossary* of accounting terms and other terms with special meanings in accounting appears at the back of this book. Questions at the end of each chapter list the important accounting terms used in that chapter. Use the glossary to aid in reviewing the meaning of those terms.

CRITERIA FOR EVALUATING THE USEFULNESS OF ACCOUNTING INFORMATION

Before studying the concepts and methods of accounting, it may be worthwhile to set out some criteria for evaluating the usefulness of the information which is generated. Throughout this text, we consider the data required to make decisions and various procedures for reporting the effects of a given event or transaction. It will be helpful if we are armed with some criteria for choosing among alternative sets of data and alternative accounting methods. The criteria discussed in this section are potentially useful for this purpose.

Relevance to Decisions

To be useful, accounting information should be helpful in choosing among alternatives faced by the decision maker. For example, a manager who wishes to decide whether or not to replace an old machine must have reliable estimates of the future cash flows resulting from keeping the asset and those from replacing it.

If investors wish to estimate the return and risk from purchasing a firm's shares of common stock and are to use accounting reports to make their decisions, then financial statements should present information on the various factors affecting overall return and risk. There are several practical problems in applying the relevance criterion in financial accounting. One is the difficulty in determining the types of information desired by various users. The information required by bankers or security analysts is not necessarily the same as that required by the small investor. A second uncertainty is how much detail to present. Too much condensation will limit the usefulness of the reports to some users, whereas excessive detail may obscure the major facts for others.

Accuracy of Presentation

The accuracy of presentation criterion suggests that accounting should present realistic descriptions of the events or transactions that are disclosed in the report. Accounting measurements serve as descriptions for the decisions made and events that have taken place, or are expected to take place. The closer the correspondence between the event and the report, the better.

Verifiability

The criterion of verifiability suggests that the results of decisions or events should not be included in accounting reports unless they can be verified with reasonable confidence. Verification serves as a check on processing and measurement errors that might have occurred. Verification may also be helpful in reducing bias that the managers of a firm, in their own interests, might have injected into the report.

Comparability: Through Time

The need for comparability through time suggests that the procedures used by a firm in processing accounting data should be followed consistently from period to period. In this way, accounting reports of a particular division, or the firm as a whole, can be more easily compared from one period to the next.

Comparability: Among Firms and Divisions

The need for comparability among firms and divisions suggests that the accounting procedures used by all firms within an industry or by all divisions within a company be the same. Then, accounting reports of various firms and divisions can be more easily compared with each other.

Efficiency

When the benefits of information to users exceed the costs of providing it, the information generating process is said to be *efficient*. This criterion might be used in determining the type of information included in accounting reports and the precision of the accounting measurements.

Timeliness

To be useful, the information must be available sufficiently early so that appropriate changes in resource allocations can be made. Application of this criterion has led to quarterly, rather than merely annual, reporting by publicly held corporations and to weekly, or even daily, reporting to managers.

Conflicts among Criteria

In selecting the foregoing or other sets of criteria for assessing the usefulness of accounting reports, conflicts will often arise. For example, investors might feel that the most relevant valuation basis for land, buildings, and equipment is the current selling price of each asset. If there is no ready secondhand market, however, current selling prices for used, specialized assets may be difficult to determine and verify. Trade-offs between relevancy and verifiability are therefore required. Another conflict might arise in attempting to achieve efficiency and timeliness. A production manager might desire hourly information on the number of units produced by every worker in order to keep a close watch on their performance. The costs of gathering and recording hourly production data may, however, exceed the benefits of such timely information. Trade-offs are therefore necessary between efficiency and timeliness.

SUMMARY

This chapter provides an overview of the three principal uses of accounting information: (1) for managerial decision making, (2) for managerial planning, control, and internal performance evaluation, and (3) for financial reporting and external performance evaluation. Perhaps more questions have been raised than have been answered. It is helpful, however, to see how the various uses of accounting information are interrelated before separately considering each use in depth.

Now we turn to the study of managerial accounting. We recognize that most readers of this book will not choose careers in the field of accounting. Accordingly, emphasis is placed primarily on the uses of accounting data for those who will receive it in the form of various reports and secondarily on the compilation of the accounting data. Whatever the reader's interest in accounting, we have found that the most effective means of comprehending the concepts and procedures discussed in this book is the careful study of the numerical examples presented in the chapters and the diligent working of several problems at the end of each chapter. Keep this in mind as you proceed with your study.

QUESTIONS AND PROBLEMS

1 Review the meaning of the following concepts or terms introduced in this chapter.
  a Managerial accounting.
  b Financial accounting.
  c SEC.
  d FASB.
  e CASB.

2 Distinguish between financial accounting and managerial accounting.

3 Generally accepted accounting principles are the methods of accounting used by publicly held firms in preparing their financial statements. A principle in physics, such as the law of gravity, serves as a basis for developing theories and explaining the relationships among physical objects. In what ways are generally accepted accounting principles similar to and different from principles in physics?

4 Assets such as buildings and equipment generally decrease in value or depreciate over time as those assets are used. Accountants measure depreciation by recognizing as an expense each period a portion of the acquisition cost of these assets based on some systematic procedure (for example, an equal amount each year of the asset's useful life). Economists measure depreciation as the decrease in the amount at which the building or equipment could be sold between the beginning and end of the period.

  You are planning to acquire the assets of a steel company and must determine the price you are willing to pay. Using either the criteria discussed in the chapter or others you consider desirable, which of these two methods of measuring depreciation and asset values do you think provides the more useful information for this decision?

5 An existing machine has a net book value of $10,000 and can be used for four more years to produce a given quantity of output if $1,800 of labor and materials are used each year. The existing machine has no net resale value—the costs of removing the machine from the factory just offset the proceeds receivable from disposing of it. A new machine is available that costs $10,000 and can be used for four years to produce the same given quantity of product. The new machine, however, requires only $1,000 a year in labor and materials. Ignore income taxes.
  a Prepare an income statement (similar to that shown in Exhibit 1.2) for each of the four years, assuming that the new machine is acquired. Recognize the loss of $10,000 on retirement of the old machine in the first year.
  b Prepare a corresponding income statement for each of the four years, assuming that the old machine is kept in use.
  c Should the new machine be acquired? Why?

6 Refer to the data in the preceding problem.
  a What amount of annual depreciation on the existing machine would make total annual expenses from using the existing machine equal to those from using the new machine?
  b What loss should be recognized on the old machine in the first year so that other operating profits in years 1 through 4 would be the same under both alternatives?

7 Diversified Industries, Incorporated, operates through 30 divisions and associated companies located throughout the United States, Canada, and Europe. It manufactures and sells a broad line of industrial and consumer products. It is currently faced with a decision whether or not to establish a new division in Belgium.

a Prepare a list of the most important quantitative and nonquantitative information that top management would need in making this decision.

b Assume that a decision has been made to establish a new division in Belgium. Identify the types of information that top management would be likely to need in order to evaluate the performance of the Belgian division each year.

c Identify the types of information that stockholders and potential investors would need for evaluating Diversified Industries' decision to invest in Belgium. How, if at all, would the information needed by stockholders and potential investors differ from that needed by top management for internal performance evaluation?

d Discuss briefly similarities and differences in the data sets identified in parts **a, b,** and **c.**

PART ONE
EXTERNAL REPORTING AND MANAGERIAL DECISIONS

CHAPTER 2
OVERVIEW OF FINANCIAL STATEMENTS

In this chapter, we shall consider the manner in which information about a firm's operations and financial position is presented in external accounting reports. The discussion and illustrations concentrate on the financial statements presented in annual reports to stockholders, although similar reporting practices are followed in preparing financial statements for creditors, stock exchanges, and governmental agencies. In Chapter Three, we describe some techniques for analyzing these financial statements.

COMPONENTS OF ANNUAL REPORTS

The section of the annual report presenting the firm's financial statements generally includes the following items:

1 Auditor's opinion,
2 Comparative financial statements and supporting schedules,
3 A summary of significant accounting policies, and
4 A series of notes elaborating more fully on items reported upon in the financial statements.

Auditor's Opinion

An important section of the annual report to the stockholders is the opinion of the independent certified public accountant on the financial statements, supporting schedules, and notes. Exhibit 2.1 illustrates an auditor's opinion.

The opinion usually follows a standard format and contains two paragraphs—a *scope* paragraph and an *opinion* paragraph. The scope paragraph indicates the finan-

---

EXHIBIT 2.1
Example of Auditor's Opinion

Report of Independent Accountants
To the Board of Directors and
Stockholders of
International Corporation

We have examined the statement of financial position of International Corporation and consolidated subsidiaries as of December 31, 19X0 and 19X1, and the related statements of current and retained earnings and changes in financial position for the years then ended. Our examination was made in accordance with generally accepted auditing standards, and accordingly included such tests of the accounting records and such other auditing procedures as we considered necessary in the circumstances.

In our opinion, the aforementioned financial statements present fairly the financial position of International Corporation and consolidated subsidiaries at December 31, 19X0 and 19X1, and the results of their operations and the changes in their financial position for the years then ended, in conformity with generally accepted accounting principles applied on a consistent basis.

Stuckey Wells & Co.

5836 South Greenwood Avenue
Chicago, Illinois 60637

February 11, 19X2

---

cial presentations covered by the opinion and affirms that auditing standards and practices generally accepted by the accounting profession have been adhered to unless otherwise noted and described. Exceptions to the statement that the auditor's "examination was made in accordance with generally accepted auditing standards" are seldom, if ever, seen in published annual reports. There are occasional references to the auditor's having relied on financial statements examined by other auditors, particularly for subsidiaries or for data from prior periods.

The opinion expressed by the auditor in the second paragraph is the heart of the independent auditor's report. The opinion may be *unqualified* or *qualified*. The great majority of opinions are unqualified; that is, there are no exceptions or qualifications to the auditor's opinion that the statements "present fairly the financial position . . . and the results of operations and the changes in financial position . . . in conformity with generally accepted accounting principles applied on a consistent basis."

Qualifications to the opinion result primarily from material uncertainties regarding valuation or realization of assets, outstanding litigation or tax liabilities, or accounting inconsistencies between periods caused by changes in the application of accounting principles. An opinion qualified as to fair presentation is usually noted by the phrase *subject to;* an opinion qualified as to consistency in application of accounting principles is usually noted by *except for,* with an indication of the auditor's approval of the change.

A qualification so material that the auditor feels an opinion cannot be expressed as to the fairness of the financial statements as a whole must result in either a *disclaimer of opinion* or an *adverse opinion.* Adverse opinions and disclaimers of opinion are extremely rare in published reports.

Comparative Statements, Schedules, and Notes

The principal financial statements included in the annual report are (1) a statement of financial position, or balance sheet, (2) a statement of net income, and (3) a statement of changes in financial position. We discuss the purpose and content of each of these statements later in this chapter.

With few exceptions, the primary financial statements are presented in comparative form, usually for the current year and the preceding year. Comparative reports make clearer the nature and trend of changes in operations, assets, and financing than would a set of statements for a single year. The principal financial statements also contain a series of notes that explain more fully various items in the body of the statements.

Summary of Significant Accounting Policies

A summary of significant accounting policies is required as an integral part of the financial statement presentation.[1] The disclosure of accounting policies identifies the accounting principles adopted by the reporting enterprise and the methods of applying those principles that substantially affect the determination of income, financial position, and changes in financial position. The summary statement may be given either in a separate "Summary of Significant Accounting Policies" preceding the notes to the financial statements, or in the first note to the statements.

The following list indicates the areas of accounting principles and methods of application frequently presented in a summary statement of accounting policies:

Basis for consolidation
Basis for foreign currency translation
Method of recognizing income on long-term construction contracts
Method of recognizing revenue from franchising and leasing operations
Basis for valuation of inventory
Methods of accounting for:
    Investments
    Property, plant, and equipment
    Intangibles, such as patents and goodwill
    Retirement and pension plans
    Leases and rentals
    Income taxes and investment tax credits
    Earnings per share

---

[1]   *Opinion No. 22,* Accounting Principles Board, AICPA, April 1972.

THE BALANCE SHEET—MEASURING FINANCIAL POSITION

The statement of financial position, or balance sheet, presents a snapshot of the resources of a firm (assets) and claims on those resources (liabilities and owners' equity) as of a specific moment in time. Exhibit 3.1 on page 69 presents a balance sheet for Solinger Electric Corporation. The balance sheet derives its name from the fact that it shows the following balance, or equality:

$$\text{Assets} = \text{Liabilities} + \text{Owners' Equity}$$

That is, a firm's assets or resources are in balance with, or equal to, the claims on those resources by creditors and owners. The balance sheet views resources from two angles: a listing of the specific forms in which they are held (for example, cash, inventory, equipment) and a listing of the persons or interests that have claims on them (for example, suppliers, employees, governments, stockholders). Several important questions must be answered before a balance sheet can be understood:

1 Which resources of a firm are recognized as assets?
2 What valuations are placed on these assets?
3 How are assets classified, or grouped, within the balance sheet?
4 Which claims against a firm's assets are recognized as liabilities?
5 What valuations are placed on these liabilities?
6 How are liabilities classified within the balance sheet?
7 What valuation is placed on the owners' equity in a firm, and how is the owners' equity disclosed?

In seeking answers to these questions, we explore briefly several accounting concepts and conventions that underlie the balance sheet.

Asset Recognition

Assets are resources that have the potential for providing a firm with future economic services or benefits. In short, *an asset is a future benefit.* The resources that are recognized as assets are those (1) for which the firm has acquired rights to their future use as a result of a past transaction or exchange and (2) for which the value of the future benefits can be measured, or quantified, with a reasonable degree of precision.

Example 1 Miller Corporation sold merchandise and received a note from the customer who agreed to pay $1,000 within three months. This note receivable is an asset of Miller Corporation, because a right has been established to receive a definite amount of cash in the future as a result of the sale of merchandise.

Example 2 Miller Corporation acquired manufacturing equipment costing $20,000 and agreed to pay the seller over two years. After the final payment, legal title to the equipment will be transferred to Miller Corporation. The equipment is Miller's asset, even though Miller does not possess legal title, because it has obtained the rights and responsibilities of ownership and can sustain those rights as long as the payments are made on schedule.

Example 3   Miller Corporation plans to acquire a fleet of new trucks next year to replace those wearing out. These new trucks are not now assets, because no exchange between Miller Corporation and a supplier has taken place and, therefore, no right to the future use of the trucks has been established.

Example 4   Miller Corporation has developed a good reputation with its employees, customers, and citizens of the community. This good reputation is expected to provide benefits to the firm in its future business activities. A good reputation, however, is generally *not* recognized as an asset, because the future benefits are difficult to quantify.

Most of the difficulties in deciding which items to recognize as assets are caused by uncertainties concerning the type and extent of future rights necessary to justify classification as an asset. In Example 3, suppose that Miller Corporation entered into a contract with a local truck dealer to acquire the trucks next year at a cash price of $50,000. Miller Corporation has acquired rights to future benefits, but the contract has not been executed. Unexecuted contracts of this nature are generally not recognized as assets in accounting. Miller Corporation will recognize an asset for the trucks when they are received next year.

Asset Valuation Methods

A dollar amount must be assigned to each asset in the balance sheet. The financial statements currently prepared by publicly held firms are based on one of two valuation methods—one for monetary assets and one for nonmonetary assets.

Monetary assets, such as cash and accounts receivable, are generally shown on the balance sheet at their current cash, or cash-equivalent, values. Cash is stated at the amount of cash on hand or in the bank. Accounts receivable from customers are stated at the amount of cash expected to be collected in the future. If the period of time until a receivable is to be collected spans more than one year, then the expected future cash receipt is discounted to a present value. (This kind of calculation is explained in the Appendix at the back of the book.) Most accounts receivable, however, are collected within one to three months. The amount of future cash flows is approximately equal to the present value of these flows, and the discounting process is ignored.

Nonmonetary assets, such as merchandise inventory, land, buildings, and equipment, are stated at acquisition cost, in some cases adjusted downward for depreciation to reflect services of the assets that have been consumed.

The acquisition cost of an asset may include more than its invoice price. Cost includes all expenditures made or obligations incurred in order to put the asset into a usable condition. Transportation costs, costs of installation, handling charges, and any other necessary and reasonable costs incurred in connection with the asset up to the time it is put into service should be considered as part of the total cost assigned to the asset. For example, the cost of an item of equipment might be calculated as follows:

Invoice Price of Equipment.	$8,000
Less: 2 Percent Discount for Prompt Cash Payment	160
Net Invoice Price.	$7,840
Transportation Cost.	232
Installation Costs	694
Total Cost of Equipment.	$8,766

Instead of disbursing cash or incurring a liability, other forms of consideration (for example, common stock, merchandise inventory, land) may be given in exchange. In these cases, acquisition cost is measured by the market value of the consideration given or the market value of the asset received, depending on which market value is more objectively determinable.

Accounting's use of acquisition-cost valuations for nonmonetary assets rests on three important concepts or conventions. First, a firm is assumed to be a *going concern*. Liquidation, or selling, prices of the individual assets are assumed to be largely unimportant. Second, acquisition cost is relatively easy to measure, because an "arm's length" *exchange* between the firm and some other entity has taken place. Third, a *common monetary measuring unit* is assumed, so that the cost of assets acquired at different times can be aggregated to determine total assets. This third assumption has questionable validity during periods of rapid price changes. We consider the effects of changing prices on accounting reports in Chapter Fifteen.

Asset Classification

The classification of assets within the balance sheet varies widely in published annual reports. The principal asset categories are described below.

Current Assets   The term *current assets* "is used to designate cash and other assets or resources commonly identified as those which are reasonably expected to be realized in cash or sold or consumed during the normal operating cycle of the business." [2] Included in this category are cash, marketable securities held as short-term investments, accounts and notes receivable net of allowances for uncollectible accounts, inventories of merchandise, raw materials, supplies, work in process, and finished goods and prepaid operating costs. Prepaid costs, or prepayments, are current assets to the extent that if they were not paid in advance, then current assets would be required to be used to acquire them within the next operating cycle.

Investments   The section of the balance sheet labeled "Investments" includes primarily the investments in securities of other firms where the purpose of the investment is long term in nature. For example, shares of common stock of a supplier might be

---

[2]   *Accounting Research Bulletin No. 43*, AICPA, June 1953, chap. 3.A.

purchased to help assure continued availability of raw materials. Or shares of common stock of a firm in another area of business activity might be acquired to permit the acquiring firm to diversify its operations. When one corporation (the parent) owns more than 50 percent of the voting stock in another corporation (the subsidiary), consolidated financial statements are usually prepared. That is, the specific assets, liabilities, revenues, and expenses of the subsidiary are merged, or consolidated, with those of the parent corporation. When consolidated financial statements are prepared, the account, Investment in Subsidiary, is eliminated as part of the consolidation process. Intercorporate investments in securities shown in the Investments section of the balance sheet are therefore investments in firms whose financial statements have not been consolidated with the parent or investor firm.

Property, Plant, and Equipment   Property, plant, and equipment (sometimes called *plant assets* or *fixed assets*) includes the tangible, long-lived assets used in a firm's operations over a period of years and generally not acquired for resale. This category includes land, buildings, machinery, automobiles, furniture, fixtures, computers, and other equipment. The amount shown on the balance sheet for each of these items (except land) is acquisition cost less accumulated depreciation. Frequently, only the net balance, or book value, is disclosed on the balance sheet. Land is presented at acquisition cost.

Intangible Assets   Intangible assets include such items as patents, trademarks, franchises, and goodwill. When presented on the balance sheet, these items are sometimes referred to as *deferred charges.* The expenditures made by the firm in developing intangible assets are usually recognized as an expense as incurred, because of the difficulty of determining the existence of future benefits necessary to warrant treatment of the costs as assets.[3]

Liability Recognition

A liability represents an obligation of a firm to make payment of a reasonably definite amount at a reasonably definite future time for benefits or services received currently or in the past.

Example 1   Miller Corporation acquired merchandise inventory from a supplier and promised to pay $10,000 by the end of the following month. This obligation is a liability, because Miller Corporation has received the goods and must pay a definite amount at a reasonably definite future time.

Example 2   Miller Corporation borrowed $100,000 from its local bank, agreeing to repay the loan plus 8 percent interest at the end of one year. This obligation is a liability, because Miller has received the cash and must repay the loan in a definite amount at a definite future time.

---

[3]   Financial Accounting Standards Board, "Accounting for Research and Development Costs," *Statement of Financial Accounting Standards No. 2,* 1974.

Example 3 Miller Corporation provides a three-year warranty on its products. The obligation renders the warranty plan a liability. The selling price for its products implicitly includes a charge for the future warranty services. As customers pay the selling price, Miller Corporation receives a benefit (that is, the cash received). Past experience should provide a basis for estimating the proportion of customers that will return goods under the warranty agreement and the expected cost of providing warranty services. Thus, the amount of the liability can be estimated with a reasonable degree of accuracy.

Example 4 Miller Corporation has signed an agreement with its employees' labor union, promising to increase wages 6 percent and to provide for medical and life insurance. This agreement does not immediately give rise to a liability, because services have not yet been received from employees that would require any payments for wages and insurance. As labor services are received, a liability will arise.

The most troublesome questions of liability recognition relate to unexecuted contracts. The labor union agreement in Example 4 above is an unexecuted contract. Other examples include leases, pension agreements, and purchase-order commitments. Whether unexecuted contracts should be recognized as liabilities has been and continues to be controversial.

Liability Valuation

Most liabilities are monetary in nature. Those due within one year or less are stated at the amount of cash expected to be paid to discharge the obligation. If the payment date extends more than one year into the future, the liability is stated at the present value of the future cash outflow. (This kind of calculation is explained in the Appendix at the back of the book.)

A liability that is discharged by delivering goods or rendering services, rather than by paying cash, is nonmonetary. The warranty obligation in Example 3 above is a nonmonetary liability. These liabilities are stated at the expected future cost of the materials and labor necessary to satisfy the warranty obligation.

Liability Classification

Liabilities in the balance sheet are typically classified in one of the following categories.

Current Liabilities The term *current liabilities* "is used principally to designate obligations whose liquidation is reasonably expected to require the use of existing resources properly classified as current assets, or the creation of other current liabilities."[4] Included in this category are liabilities to merchandise suppliers, employees, and governmental units. Notes and bonds payable are also included to the extent that they will require the use of current assets within a relatively short period of time, typically during the next 12 months.

---

[4] *Accounting Research Bulletin No. 43,* AICPA, June 1953, chap. 3.A.

Long-Term Debt   Obligations having due dates, or maturities, more than one year after the balance sheet date are generally classified as long-term debt. Included are bonds, mortgages, and similar debts, as well as some obligations under long-term leases.

Other Long-Term Liabilities   Obligations not properly considered as current liabilities or long-term debt are classfied as *other long-term liabilities,* or *indeterminate-term liabilities.* Included are such items as deferred pension obligations and deferred income taxes.

Owners' Equity Valuation and Disclosure

The owners' equity in a firm is a residual interest. That is, the owners have a claim on all assets not required to meet the claims of creditors. The valuation of the assets and liabilities included in the balance sheet therefore determines the valuation of total owners' equity.

The remaining question concerns the manner of disclosing this total owners' equity. In preparing the balance sheet for a corporation, the amounts contributed directly by stockholders for an interest in the firm (that is, common stock) are generally separated from the subsequent earnings realized by the firm in excess of dividends declared (that is, retained earnings).

In addition, the amount received from stockholders is usually further disaggregated into the *par* or *stated value* of the shares and *amounts contributed in excess of par value or stated value.* The par or stated value of a share of stock is a somewhat arbitrary amount assigned to comply with corporation laws of each state. As a result, the distinction between par or stated value and amounts contributed in excess of par or stated value is of questionable informational value, but is typically shown nonetheless.

Example 1   Lorlace Corporation was formed on January 1, 19X0. It issued 15,000 shares of $10 par value common stock for $10 cash per share. During 19X0, Lorlace Corporation had net income of $30,000 and paid dividends of $10,000 to stockholders. The stockholders' equity section of the balance sheet of Lorlace Corporation on December 31, 19X0, is

Common Stock (par value of $10 per share, 15,000 shares issued and outstanding)	$150,000
Retained Earnings	20,000
Total Stockholders' Equity	$170,000

Example 2   Instead of issuing $10 par value common stock as in Example 1, assume that Lorlace Corporation issued 15,000 shares of $1 par value common stock for $10 cash per share. (The market price of a share of common stock depends on the economic value of the firm and not on the par value of the shares.) The stockholders' equity section of the balance sheet of Lorlace Corporation on December 31, 19X0, is

Common Stock (par value of $1 per share, 15,000 shares issued
   and outstanding) . . . . $ 15,000
Capital Contributed in Excess of Par Value. 135,000
Retained Earnings. 20,000
   Total Stockholders' Equity $170,000

Balance Sheet Account Titles

The following list shows balance sheet account titles that are commonly used. The descriptions should help in understanding the nature of various assets, liabilities, and owners' equities. Alternative account titles can be easily devised. The list is not intended to exhaust all the account titles used in this book or appearing in the financial statements of publicly held firms. Certain items are shown for the sake of completeness although an explanation of them is deferred until later.

Assets

Cash. Coins and currency, and such items as bank checks and money orders. The latter items are merely claims against individuals or institutions, but by custom are called "cash." Cash in the bank consists of demand deposits, against which checks can be drawn, and time deposits, usually savings accounts and certificates of deposit.

Marketable Securities. Government bonds, or stocks and bonds of corporations. The word *marketable* implies that they can be bought and sold readily through a security exchange such as the New York Stock Exchange. The firm holding securities classified under this title generally intends to sell them within a relatively short time as cash is needed.

Accounts Receivable. Amounts due from customers of a business from the sale of goods or services.

Notes Receivable. Amounts due from customers or from others to whom loans have been made or credit extended, when the claim has been put into writing in the form of a promissory note.

Interest Receivable. Interest on assets such as promissory notes or bonds that has accrued, or come into existence, through the passing of time but that has not been collected as of the date of the balance sheet.

Merchandise Inventory. Goods on hand that have been purchased for resale.

Finished Goods Inventory. Completed but unsold manufactured products.

Work-in-Process Inventory. Partially completed manufactured products.

Raw Materials Inventory. Unused materials from which manufactured products are to be made.

Prepaid Insurance. Insurance premiums paid for future coverage. An alternative title is *Unexpired Insurance.*

Prepaid Rent. Rent paid in advance of future use of land, buildings, or equipment.

Land. Land occupied by buildings or used in operations.

Buildings. Factory buildings, store buildings, garages, warehouses, and so forth.

Machinery and Equipment. Lathes, ovens, tools, boilers, computers, motors, bins, cranes, conveyors, and so forth.

Furniture and Fixtures. Desks, tables, chairs, counters, showcases, scales, and other such store and office equipment.

Office Machines. Typewriters, adding machines, bookkeeping equipment, calculators, and so forth. Sometimes combined with Furniture and Fixtures.

Automobiles. Delivery trucks, sales staff's cars, and so forth.

Investments. The cost of shares of stock in other companies, where the firm's purpose is to hold the shares for relatively long periods of time.

Leasehold. The right to use property owned by someone else.

Accumulated Depreciation. This account shows the cumulative amount of the cost of long-term assets (such as buildings and machinery) that has been allocated to prior periods in measuring net income or the costs of production. The amount in this account is subtracted from the acquisition cost of the long-term asset to which it relates in determining the *net book value* of the asset to be shown in the balance sheet.

Organization Costs. Amounts paid for legal and incorporation fees, for printing the certificates for the shares of stock, and for accounting and any other costs incurred in organizing the business so it can begin to function. This asset is seen most commonly on the balance sheets of newly formed corporations.

Patents. A right granted for 17 years by the federal government for exclusive use of a certain process or device. Under current generally accepted accounting principles, research and development costs must be treated as an expense in the year incurred rather than being recognized as an asset with future benefits.[5] (This treatment seems to us to be at odds with good accounting theory.) As a result, a firm that develops and owns a patent will not normally show it as an asset. On the other hand, a firm that purchases a patent from another firm or from an individual will recognize the patent as an asset.

Goodwill. An amount paid by one firm in acquiring another business enterprise that is greater than the sum of the values assignable to other assets. A good reputation and other desirable attributes are generally not recognized as assets by the firm that creates or develops them. However, when one firm acquires another firm, these desirable attributes are recognized as assets, because they are a factor in determining the valuation of goodwill.

Liabilities

Accounts Payable. Amounts owed for goods or services acquired under an informal credit agreement. These accounts are usually payable within one or two months. The same items appear as Accounts Receivable on the creditors' books.

Notes Payable. The face amount of promissory notes given in connection with loans

---

[5] Financial Accounting Standards Board, "Accounting for Research and Development Costs," *Statement of Financial Accounting Standards No. 2*, 1974.

from the bank or the purchase of goods or services. The same items appear as Notes Receivable on the creditors' books.

Withheld Income Taxes. Amounts withheld from wages and salaries of employees for income taxes that have not yet been remitted to the taxing authority. This is a tentative income tax on the earnings of employees, and the employer merely acts as a tax-collecting agent for the federal and state governments. A few cities also levy income taxes, which the employer must withhold from wages.

Payroll Taxes Payable. Amounts withheld from wages and salaries of employees for federal and state payroll taxes and the employer's share of such taxes.

Interest Payable. Interest on obligations that has accrued or accumulated with the passage of time but that has not been paid as of the date of the balance sheet. The liability for interest is customarily shown separately from the face amount of the obligation.

Income Taxes Payable. The estimated liability for income taxes, accumulated and unpaid, based on the taxable income of the business from the beginning of the taxable year to the date of the balance sheet.

Deferred Income Taxes. Certain income tax payments are delayed beyond the current accounting period. This item appears on the balance sheet of most U.S. corporations. Its nature is discussed in financial accounting texts.

Rent Received in Advance. An example of a nonmonetary liability. The business owns a building that it rents to a tenant. The tenant has prepaid the rental charge for several months in advance. The amount applicable to future months cannot be considered a component of income until the rent is earned as service is rendered with the passage of time. Meanwhile the advance payment results in a liability payable in services (that is, in the use of the building). On the records of the tenant the same amount would appear as an asset, Prepaid Rent. Other similar advance payments include deposits from customers for goods to be delivered later and payments received by a publisher for newspaper or magazine subscriptions.

Mortgage Payable. Long-term promissory notes that have been given greater protection by the pledge of specific pieces of property as security for their payment. If the loan or interest is not paid according to the agreement, the property can be sold for the benefit of the creditor.

Bonds Payable. Amounts borrowed by the business for a relatively long period of time under a formal written contract or indenture. The loan is usually obtained from a number of lenders, each of whom receives one or more bond certificates as written evidence of his or her share of the loan.

Debenture Bonds. The most common type of bond, except in the railroad and public utility industries. This type of bond carries no specific security or collateral; instead it is issued on the basis of the general credit of the business. If other bonds have a prior claim on the assets of the business, then the debenture is called *subordinated.*

Convertible Bonds. A bond which the holder can *convert* into or "trade in" for shares of common stock. The number of shares to be received when the bond is converted into stock, the dates when conversion can occur, and other details are specified in the bond indenture.

Capitalized Lease Obligations. The present value of future commitments for cash payments to be made in return for the right to use property owned by someone else.

Owners' Equity

Common Stock. Amounts received for the par or stated value of a firm's principal class of voting stock.

Preferred Stock. Amounts received for the par value of a class of a firm's stock that has some preference relative to the common stock. This preference is usually with respect to dividends and to assets in the event the corporation is liquidated. Sometimes preferred stock is convertible into common stock.

Capital Contributed in Excess of Par or Stated Value. Amounts received from the issuance of common or preferred stock in excess of such shares' par value or stated value. This account is also referred to as *Additional Paid-in Capital.*

Stock Warrants. The amount in this account represents the amount the firm received for issuing certificates that permit the holders to purchase shares of stock at a specified price. The rights contained in stock warrants are usually exercisable for only a limited period.

Retained Earnings. An account reflecting the increase in net assets since the business was organized as a result of generating earnings in excess of dividend declarations. When dividends are declared, net assets are distributed, and retained earnings are reduced by an equal amount.

Treasury Shares. This account shows the cost of shares of stock originally issued but subsequently reacquired by the corporation for one of several reasons. The firm may reacquire its own shares for later distributions under stock option plans, for stock dividends, or for issuance to holders of convertible bonds or convertible preferred stock when they convert their holdings into common stock. The firm may also consider treasury stock as a worthwhile use for idle funds. Treasury shares are not entitled to dividends and are not considered to be "outstanding" shares. The cost of treasury shares is almost always shown on the balance sheet as a deduction from the total of the other shareholders' equity accounts.

Summary of Balance Sheet Concepts

The balance sheet, or statement of financial position, is composed of three major classes of items—assets, liabilities, and owners' equity.

Resources are recognized as assets when a firm has acquired rights to their future use as a result of a past transaction or exchange and when the value of the future benefits can be measured with a reasonable degree of precision. Monetary assets are, in general, stated at their current cash, or cash-equivalent, values. Nonmonetary assets are stated at acquisition cost, in some cases adjusted downward for the cost of services that have been consumed.

Liabilities represent obligations of a firm to make payments of a reasonably definite amount at a reasonably definite future time for benefits already received. Owners' equity is the difference between total assets and total liabilities and, for corporations, is typically segregated into contributed capital and retained earnings.

THE INCOME STATEMENT—
MEASURING OPERATING PERFORMANCE

The second principal financial statement is the income statement. Exhibit 3.2 on page 70 presents an income statement for Solinger Electric Corporation. This statement provides a measure of the earnings performance of a firm for some particular period of time. Net income, or earnings, is equal to revenues minus expenses. Revenues measure the inflow of net assets (assets less liabilities) from selling goods and providing services. Expenses measure the outflow of net assets that are used up, or consumed, in the process of generating revenues. As a measure of earnings performance, revenues reflect the services rendered by the firm and expenses indicate the related efforts required or expended.

The Accounting Period Convention

The income statement is a report on earnings performance over a specified period of time. Years ago, the length of this period varied substantially among firms. Income statements were prepared at the completion of some activity, such as after the round-trip voyage of a ship between England and the colonies or at the completion of a construction project.

The earnings activities of most modern firms are not so easily separated into distinguishable projects. Instead, the income-generating activity is carried on continually. For example, a plant is acquired and used in manufacturing products for a period of 40 years or more. Delivery equipment is purchased and used in transporting merchandise to customers for five, six, or more years. If the preparation of the income statement were postponed until all earnings activities were completed, the report might never be prepared and, in any case, would be too late to help a reader appraise performance and make decisions. An accounting period of uniform length is used to facilitate timely comparisons and analyses across firms.

An accounting period of *one year* underlies the principal financial statements distributed to stockholders and potential investors. Most firms prepare their annual reports using the calendar year as the accounting period. A growing number of firms, however, use a *natural business year*. The use of a natural business year is an attempt to measure performance at a time when most earnings activities have been substantially concluded. The ending date of a natural business year varies from one firm to another. For example, Sears uses a natural business year ending on January 31, which comes after completion of the Christmas shopping season. American Motors uses a year ending September 30, the end of its model year. A. C. Nielsen (producers of television ratings and other surveys) uses a year ending August 31, just prior to the beginning of the new television season.

In order to provide even more timely information, most publicly held firms also report earnings data for interim periods within the regular annual accounting period. These interim reports generally cover three-month periods, or "quarters."

The Accounting Basis for Recognizing Revenues and Expenses

When measuring earnings performance for the accounting period, some activities will have been started and completed within the period. For example, during a particular accounting period, merchandise might be purchased from a supplier, sold to a customer on account, and the account collected in cash. Few difficulties are encountered in measuring performance in these cases. The difference between the cash received from customers and the cash disbursed to acquire, sell, and deliver the merchandise represents earnings from this series of transactions.

Many earnings activities, however, are started in one accounting period and completed in another. Buildings and equipment are acquired in one period but used over a period of several years. Merchandise is sometimes purchased in one accounting period and sold during the next period, whereas cash is collected from customers during a third period. A significant problem in measuring performance for specific accounting periods concerns the determination of the amount of revenues and expenses to be recognized from earnings activities that are in process as of the beginning of the period or are incomplete as of the end of the period. Two approaches to measuring earnings performance are (1) the cash basis of accounting, and (2) the accrual basis of accounting.

Cash Basis of Accounting   Under the *cash basis of accounting*, revenues from selling goods and providing services are recognized in the period when cash is received from customers. Expenses are typically reported in the period in which expenditures are made for merchandise, salaries, insurance, taxes, and similar items. To illustrate the determination of net income under the cash basis of accounting, consider the following example.

Donald and Joanne Allens open a hardware store on January 1, 19X0. They contribute $10,000 in cash and borrow $6,000 from a local bank. The loan is repayable on June 30, 19X0, with interest charged at the rate of 10 percent per year. A store building is rented on January 1, and two months' rent of $2,000 is paid in advance. The premium of $1,200 for property and liability insurance coverage for the year ending December 31, 19X0, is paid on January 1. During January, merchandise costing $20,000 is acquired, of which $13,000 is purchased for cash and $7,000 is purchased on account. Sales to customers during January total $25,000, of which $17,000 is sold for cash and $8,000 is sold on account. The acquisition cost of merchandise sold during January is $16,000, while various employees are paid $2,500 in salaries.

Exhibit 2.2 presents an income statement for Allens' Hardware Store for the month of January 19X0 under the cash basis of accounting. Sales revenue of $17,000 reflects the portion of the total sales of $25,000 made during January that was collected in cash. Although merchandise costing $20,000 was acquired during January, only $13,000 cash was disbursed to suppliers, and this amount is therefore recognized as an expense of the period. Expenses recognized for salaries, rent, and insurance reflect the amounts of cash disbursements during January for these services, without regard to whether or not the services were fully consumed by the end of January. The net loss for January under the cash basis of accounting is $1,700.

As a basis for measuring performance for a particular accounting period (for example, January 19X0 for Allens' Hardware Store), the cash basis of accounting is subject to two important and somewhat related criticisms. First, revenues are not adequately matched with the cost of the efforts required in generating the revenues. Performance of one period therefore gets mingled with the performance of preceding and succeeding periods. The store rental payment of $2,000 provides rental services for both January and February, but under the cash basis, the full amount is recognized as an expense during January. Likewise, the annual insurance premium provides coverage for the full year, whereas under the cash basis of accounting, none of this insurance cost will be recognized as an expense during the months of February through December. The longer the period over which future benefits are received, the more serious is this criticism of the cash basis of accounting. Consider, for example, the investments of a capital-intensive firm in buildings and equipment that might be used for 10, 20, or more years. The length of time between the purchase of these assets and the collection of cash for goods produced and sold can span many years.

A second, and probably less serious, criticism of the cash basis of accounting is that it postpones unnecessarily the time when revenue is recognized. In most cases, the sale (delivery) of goods or rendering of services is the critical event in generating revenue. The collection of cash is relatively routine, or at least highly predictable. In these cases, recognizing revenue at the time of cash collection may result in reporting the effects of earnings activities one or more periods after the critical revenue-generating activity has occurred. For example, sales to customers during January by Allens' Hardware Store totaled $25,000. Under the cash basis of accounting, $8,000 of this amount will not be recognized until February or later, when the cash is collected. If the credit standings of customers have been checked prior to making sales on account, it is highly probable that cash will be collected, and there is little reason to postpone recognition of the revenue.

The cash basis of accounting is principally used by lawyers, accountants, and other professional people who have relatively small investments in multiperiod assets, such as buildings and equipment, and who tend to collect cash from their clients soon after services are rendered. Some firms use a *modified cash basis of accounting*, under which the costs of buildings, equipment, and similar items are treated as assets when purchased. A portion of the acquisition cost is then recognized as an expense when services of these assets are consumed. Except for the treatment of these long-lived assets, revenues are recognized at the time cash is received and expenses are reported when cash disbursements are made. Some physicians and dentists with relatively heavy investments in equipment use the modified cash basis of accounting.

Most individuals use the cash basis of accounting for the purpose of computing personal income and personal income taxes. Where inventories are an important factor in generating revenues, such as for a manufacturing or merchandising firm, the Internal Revenue Code prohibits a firm from using the cash basis of accounting in its income tax returns.

Accrual Basis of Accounting   Under the *accrual* basis of accounting, revenue is recognized when some critical event or transaction occurs that is related to the earnings process. In most cases, this critical event is the sale (delivery) of goods or the rendering

EXHIBIT 2.2
Allens' Hardware Store
Income Statement
for the Month of January 19X0
(Cash Basis of Accounting)

Cash Receipts from Sales of Merchandise		$17,000
Less Cash Expenditures for Merchandise and Services:		
Merchandise	$13,000	
Salaries	2,500	
Rental	2,000	
Insurance	1,200	
Total Cash Expenditures		18,700
Net Loss		($1,700)

of services. The nature and significance of this critical event are discussed later in the chapter. Under the accrual basis of accounting, costs incurred are reported as expenses in the period when the revenues to which they relate are recognized. Thus, an attempt is made to *match* expenses with associated revenues. When particular types of costs incurred cannot be closely identified with specific revenue streams, they are treated as expenses of the period in which services of an asset are consumed or future benefits of an asset disappear.

Exhibit 2.3 presents an income statement for Allens' Hardware Store for January 19X0 using the accrual basis of accounting. The entire $25,000 of sales during January is recognized as revenue even though cash in that amount has not yet been received. Because of the high probability that outstanding accounts receivable will be collected, the critical revenue-generating event is the sale of the goods rather than the collection of cash from customers. The acquisition cost of the merchandise sold during January is $16,000. Recognizing this amount as cost of goods sold expense leads to an appropriate matching of sales revenue and merchandise expense in the income statement. Of the advance rental payment of $2,000, only $1,000 applies to the cost of services consumed during January. The remaining rental of $1,000 applies to the month of February. Likewise, only $100 of the $1,200 insurance premium represents coverage for January. The remaining $1,100 of the insurance premium provides coverage for February through December and will be recognized as an expense during those months. The interest expense of $50 represents one month's interest on the $6,000 bank loan at an annual rate of 10 percent ($= \$6,000 \times .10 \times \frac{1}{12}$). Although the interest will not be paid until the loan becomes due on June 30, 19X0, the firm benefited from having the funds available for its use during January and an appropriate portion of the total interest cost on the loan should be recognized as a January expense. The salaries, rental, insurance, and interest expenses, unlike the cost of merchandise sold, cannot be associated directly with revenues recognized during the period. These costs are therefore reported as expenses of January.

EXHIBIT 2.3
Allens' Hardware Store
Income Statement
for the Month of January 19X0
(Accrual Basis of Accounting)

Sales Revenue		$25,000
Less Expenses:		
Cost of Merchandise Sold	$16,000	
Salaries Expense	2,500	
Rent Expense	1,000	
Insurance Expense	100	
Interest Expense	50	
Total Expenses		19,650
Net Income		$ 5,350

The accrual basis of accounting provides a better measure of earnings performance for Allens' Hardware Store for the month of January than does the cash basis, both because revenues are measured more accurately and because expenses are associated more closely with reported revenues. Likewise, the accrual basis will provide a superior measure of performance for future periods, because activities of those periods will be charged with their share of the costs of rental, insurance, and other services to be consumed.

Several important questions regarding the recognition of revenues and expenses have not yet been considered:

1 When, or at what point(s), within the earnings process is revenue recognized (that is, what is the nature of the critical revenue-generating event)?
2 How do we measure or determine the amount of revenue to be recognized?
3 When, or at what point(s), within the earnings process are expenses reported (that is, what is the nature of the matching convention)?
4 How do we measure or determine the amount of expenses to be reported?

We consider the principles employed in measuring revenues and expenses in the next two sections.

Revenue Recognition and Measurement Principles

In reporting revenue, we are concerned with *when* it arises (a timing question) and *how much* is recognized (a measurement question).

Timing of Revenue Recognition   The earnings process for the acquisition and sale of merchandise might be depicted as shown in Figure 2.1. Revenue could conceivably be recognized at the time of purchase, sale, or cash collection, at some point(s) between

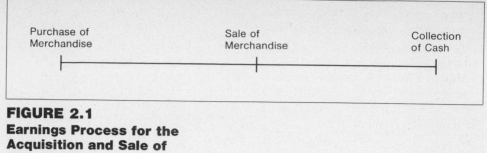

FIGURE 2.1
Earnings Process for the
Acquisition and Sale of
Merchandise

these events, or even continuously. To answer the timing question, we must have a set of criteria for revenue recognition.

Criteria for revenue recognition   The criteria currently required to be met before revenue is recognized are as follows:

1 All, or a substantial portion, of the services to be provided have been performed.
2 Cash, receivables, or some other asset susceptible to objective measurement has been received.

Recognition at the point of sale   For the vast majority of firms involved in selling goods and services, revenue is recognized at the time of sale (delivery). This method of recognizing revenues is called the *completed sale,* or in some contexts the *completed contract,* method of revenue recognition. The goods have been transferred to the buyer or the services have been performed. Future services, such as for warranties, are likely to be insignificant, or if significant, can be estimated with reasonable precision. An exchange between an independent buyer and seller has occurred that provides an objective measure of the amount of revenue. If the sale is made on account, past experience and an assessment of customers' credit standings provide a basis for predicting the amount of cash that will be collected. The sale of the goods or services is therefore the critical revenue-generating event. Under the accrual basis of accounting, revenue is typically recognized at the time of sale.

Recognition at the time of production   On some long-term construction projects, the buyer and the seller agree in advance on the contract price and the timing of cash payments. Revenue from these long-term contracts is often recognized during the period of production. The earnings process for a particular long-term construction project may span several years. If the firm waited until the project was completed to recognize revenue, the efforts and accomplishments of several accounting periods would be recognized in the one period when the contract was completed. This approach would give an unsatisfactory measure of performance for each period during the contract. In these cases, some firms use the *percentage-of-completion method* of recognizing revenue. A portion of the total contract price, based on the degree of completion of the work, is recognized as revenue each period. This proportion is determined using either engineers' estimates of the degree of completion or the ratio of costs incurred to date to the total expected costs for the contract.

Although future services required on these long-term construction contracts can be substantial at any given time, the costs to be incurred in providing these services can often be estimated with reasonable precision. The existence of a contract indicates that a buyer has been obtained and a price for the construction services has been set. Cash is usually collected from the buyer as construction progresses or the assessment of the customer's credit standing leads to a reasonable expectation that the contract price will be received in cash after construction is completed. Construction activities are therefore the critical revenue-generating events. The actual schedule of cash collections is *not* significant for the revenue-recognition process when the percentage-of-completion method is used.

Some firms involved with construction contracts postpone the recognition of revenue until the construction project and the sale are completed. This method is the same as the completed-sale basis, but is often referred to as the *completed-contract method* of recognizing revenue. In some cases, the completed-contract method is used because the contracts are of such short duration (such as three or six months) that earnings reported with the percentage-of-completion method and the completed-contract method are not significantly different. In these cases, the completed-contract method is used because it is generally easier to implement. Some firms use the completed-contract method in situations when a specific buyer has not been obtained during the periods while construction is progressing, as is sometimes the case in constructing residential housing. In these cases, future selling efforts are required and substantial uncertainty may exist regarding the contract price ultimately to be established and the amount of cash to be received.

The primary reason for a contractor's not using the percentage-of-completion method when a contract exists is the uncertainty of total costs to be incurred in carrying out the project. If total costs cannot be reasonably estimated, the percentage of total costs incurred by a given date also cannot be estimated, and the percentage of services already rendered (revenue) cannot be determined.

Recognition at the point of cash collection   Occasionally, estimating the amount of cash or other assets that will be received from customers is extremely difficult. Therefore, an objective measure of the services rendered and the benefits to be received cannot be made at the time of sale. Under these circumstances, revenue is recognized at the times cash is collected.

This basis of revenue recognition is sometimes used by land development companies. These companies typically sell undeveloped land and promise to develop it over several future years. The buyer makes a nominal down payment and agrees to pay the remainder of the purchase price in installments over 10, 20, or more years. In these cases, future development of the land is a significant aspect of the earnings process. Also, substantial uncertainty often exists as to the ultimate collectibility of the installment notes, particularly those not due until several years in the future. The critical revenue-generating event in this case is the collection of cash. When revenue is recognized as the periodic cash collections are received and costs incurred in generating the revenue are matched as closely as possible with the revenue, the firm is using the *installment method* of accounting. The installment method is similar to the cash basis of accounting, because revenue is recognized as cash is received. The installment method, however, is an accrual method of accounting, because an effort is made to match expenses with associated revenues.

For most sales of goods and services, past experience and an assessment of customers' credit standings provide a sufficient basis for predicting the amount of cash to be received. The installment method is therefore not used in these situations, and revenue is recognized at the time of sale.

Recognition between purchase and sale   The period between the acquisition, or production, and the sale of merchandise and other salable goods is referred to as a *holding period*. The current market prices of these assets could change during this holding period. Such changes are described as *unrealized holding gains and losses*, because a transaction or exchange has not taken place.

Unrealized holding gains could be recognized as they occur. Accountants typically wait, however, until the asset is sold or exchanged before recognizing the gain. At that time, an inflow of net assets subject to objective measurement is presumed to have taken place. Because the accountant assumes that the firm is a going concern, the unrealized gain will be recognized as revenue in a future period in the ordinary course of business. Thus, the recognition of revenue and the valuation of assets are closely associated. Nonmonetary assets are typically stated at acquisition cost until sold. At the time of sale, an inflow of net assets occurs (for example, cash, accounts receivable), and revenue reflecting the previously unreported unrealized gain is recognized. This treatment of unrealized holding gains has the effect of shifting income from periods when the asset is held and the market price increases to the later period of sale. The longer the holding period (as, for example, land used for several decades), the more is income likely to be shifted forward in time by the process of requiring an arm's length transaction before recognizing the gain.

Current accounting practices do not treat unrealized holding losses in the same way as unrealized holding gains, particularly on inventory items. If the current market prices of inventory items decrease below the acquisition cost during the holding period, the asset is usually written down and the unrealized loss is recognized. This treatment of losses rests on the convention that earnings should be reported conservatively. Considering the estimates and predictions required in measuring revenues and expenses, some accountants feel it is desirable to provide a conservative measure of earnings so that statement users will not be misled into thinking the firm is doing better than it really is.

The inconsistent treatment of unrealized gains and unrealized losses does not seem warranted. The arguments used against recognizing unrealized gains apply equally well to unrealized losses. If gains cannot be determined objectively prior to sale, then how can losses be measured prior to sale? If losses can be measured objectively prior to sale, then why cannot gains? We consider the accounting treatment of unrealized holding gains and losses further in Chapter Fifteen.

Measurement of Revenue   The amount of revenue recognized is generally measured by the cash or cash-equivalent value of other assets received from customers. As a starting point, this amount is the agreed-upon price between buyer and seller at the time of sale. Some adjustments to this amount may be necessary, however, if revenue is recognized in a period prior to the collection of cash.

Uncollectible accounts   If some of the cash for a period's sales is not expected to be collected, the amount of revenue recognized for that period must be adjusted for estimated uncollectible accounts arising from those sales. Logic suggests that this adjustment of revenue should occur in the period when revenue is recognized and not in a later period when specific customers' accounts are declared to be uncollectible. If the adjustment is postponed, reported income of subsequent periods will be affected by earlier decisions to extend credit to customers. Thus, the performance of the firm for both the period of sale and the period when the account is judged uncollectible would be measured inaccurately. Income in the period of sale is overstated. Income in the period when the uncollectible becomes apparent is understated. The two errors cancel each other out; but here, as elsewhere, two wrongs do not make a right.

Delayed payments   If the period between the sale of the goods or services and the time of cash collection extends over several years, it is likely that the selling price includes an interest charge for the loan conveying the right to delay payment. Under the accrual basis of accounting, this interest element should be recognized as interest revenue during the periods between sale and collection when the loan is outstanding. To recognize all potential revenue entirely in the period of sale would be to recognize too soon the return for services rendered over time in lending money. Thus, when cash collection is to be delayed, the measure of current revenue should be the selling price reduced to account for the interest element applicable to future periods. Only the *present value* of the amount to be received should be recognized as revenue during the period of sale. For most accounts receivable, the period between sale and collection spans only two to three months. The interest element is likely to be relatively insignificant in these cases. As a result, in accounting practice no reduction for interest on delayed payments is made for receivables to be collected within one year or less. This procedure is a practical expedient rather than a strict following of the underlying accounting theory.

Expense Recognition and Measurement Principles

Analogous to the questions raised regarding revenue recognition, we are confronted with the questions of *when* expenses are recognized and at *what amount* they are stated.

Timing of Expense Recognition   Recall that assets represent resources providing future benefits to the firm. *Expenses* are a measurement of the assets consumed in generating revenue. Assets may be referred to as *unexpired* (or *deferred*) *costs* and expenses as *expired costs* or "gone assets." Our attention focuses on the question of when the asset expiration takes place. The critical question is "When have asset bene-fits expired—leaving the balance sheet—and become expenses—entering the income statement as reductions in owners' equity?" Thus:

Balance Sheet   *Income Statement*

Assets or Unexpired Costs → Expenses or Expired Costs

Expense recognition criteria   The criteria presently employed by accountants in making the timing decision may be summarized as follows:

1 Asset expirations, or expenses, directly associated with particular types of revenue are recognized as expenses in the period in which the revenues are recognized. This treatment is called the *matching convention,* because cost expirations are matched with revenues.
2 Asset expirations, or expenses, not directly or easily associated with revenues are treated as expenses of the period in which services are consumed in operations.

Product or production costs   The cost of goods or merchandise sold is perhaps the easiest expense to associate with revenue. At the time of sale, the asset physically changes hands. Revenue is recognized, and the cost of the merchandise transferred is treated as an expense.

A *merchandising firm* purchases inventory and later sells it without changing its physical form. The inventory is shown as an asset stated at acquisition cost on the balance sheet. Later, when the inventory is sold, the same amount of acquisition cost is shown as an expense (cost of goods sold) on the income statement.

A *manufacturing firm,* on the other hand, incurs various costs in changing the physi-cal form of the goods it produces. These costs are typically of three types: (1) direct material, (2) direct labor, and (3) manufacturing overhead (sometimes called indirect manufacturing costs). Direct material and direct labor costs can be directly associated with particular products manufactured. Manufacturing overhead includes a mixture of costs that provide a firm with a capacity to produce. Examples of manufacturing overhead costs are expenditures for utilities, property taxes, and insurance on the fac-tory, as well as depreciation on manufacturing plant and equipment. The services of each of these items are used, or consumed, during the period while the firm is creating new assets, the inventory of goods being worked upon or held for sale. Benefits from direct material, direct labor, and manufacturing overhead are, in a sense, transferred to, or become embodied in, the asset represented by units of inventory. Because the inventory items are assets until sales are made to customers, the various direct ma-terial, direct labor, and manufacturing overhead costs incurred in producing the goods are treated as unexpired costs and included in the valuation of the inventory. Such costs, which are assets transformed from one form to another, are called *product costs.* Product costs are assets; they become expenses only when the goods in which they are embodied are sold.

Selling costs   In most cases, the costs incurred in selling, or marketing, a firm's prod-ucts relate to the units sold during the period. For example, salaries and commissions of the sales staff, sales literature used, and most advertising costs are incurred in generating revenue currently. Because these selling costs are associated with the revenues of the period, they are reported as expenses in the period when the services provided by these costs are consumed. It can be argued that some selling costs, such as advertising and other sales promotion, provide future-period benefits for a firm and should continue to be treated as assets. However, distinguishing what portion of the cost relates to the current period to be recognized as an expense and what portion relates to future periods to be treated as an asset can be extremely difficult. Therefore, accountants typically treat selling and other marketing activity costs as expenses of the period when the services are used. These selling costs are treated as *period expenses* rather than as assets, even though they may enhance the future marketability of a firm's products.

Administrative costs   The costs incurred in administering, or directing, the activities of the firm cannot be closely associated with units produced and sold and are, therefore, like selling costs, treated as period expenses. Examples include the president's salary, accounting and data-processing costs, and the costs of conducting various supportive activities such as legal services and corporate planning.

Measurement of Expenses   Expenses are costs expired, or assets consumed, during the period. The amount of an expense is therefore the amount of the expired asset. Thus, the basis for expense measurement is the same as for asset valuation. Because assets are primarily stated at acquisition cost on the balance sheet, expenses are primarily measured by the acquisition cost of assets.

Format and Classification within the Income Statement

The income statement might contain some or all of the following sections or categories, depending on the nature of the firm's income for the period:

1 Income from continuing operations,
2 Income, gains, and losses from discontinued operations,
3 Adjustments for changes in accounting principles, and
4 Extraordinary gains and losses.

The great majority of income statements include only the first section. The other sections are added if necessary.

Income from Continuing Operations   Revenues, gains, expenses, and losses from the continuing areas of business activity of a firm are presented in the first section of the income statement. A heading such as "Income from Continuing Operations" is used if there are other sections in the income statement.

Income, Gains, and Losses from Discontinued Operations   If a firm sells a major division or segment of its business during the year or contemplates its sale within a short time after the end of the accounting period, Accounting Principles Board *Opinion No. 30* requires that any income, gains, and losses related to that segment be disclosed separately from ordinary, continuing operations in a section of the income statement entitled "Income, Gains, and Losses from Discontinued Operations."[6] This section follows the section presenting Income from Continuing Operations.

Adjustments for Changes in Accounting Principles   A firm that changes its principles, or methods, of accounting during the period is required in most cases to disclose the effects of the change on current and prior years' net income.[7] This information is presented in a separate section, after Income, Gains, and Losses from Discontinued Operations.

Extraordinary Gains and Losses   Extraordinary gains and losses are presented in a separate section of the income statement. For an item to be classified as *extraordinary*, it must generally meet all three of the following criteria (one exception is the gain or loss on bond retirement, which is considered to be extraordinary):

1 Unusual in nature,
2 Infrequent in occurrence, and
3 Material in amount.[8]

These criteria are applied as they relate to a specific firm and similar firms in the same industry, taking into consideration the environment in which the entities operate. Thus, an item might be extraordinary for some firms and ordinary for others. Examples of items likely to be extraordinary for most firms are losses from hurricanes and tornadoes, and expropriation or confiscation of assets by foreign governments. Since 1973, when Accounting Principles Board *Opinion No. 30* was issued, extraordinary items are seldom seen in published annual reports except for gain or loss on bond retirements.

Earnings per Share   Earnings per share data must be shown in the body of the income statement in order to receive an unqualified accountant's opinion.[9] Earnings per common share is conventionally calculated by dividing net income minus preferred stock dividends by the average number of outstanding common shares during the accounting period. For example, assume that a firm had net income of $500,000 during the year 19X0. Dividends declared and paid on outstanding preferred stock were $100,000. The average number of shares of outstanding common stock during 19X0 was 1 million shares. Earnings per common share would be $.40 [= ($500,000 − $100,000)/1,000,000].

If a firm has securities outstanding that can be converted into or exchanged for common stock, it may be required to present two sets of earnings-per-share amounts: *primary earnings per share* and *fully diluted earnings per share.* For example, some firms issue convertible bonds or convertible preferred stock that can be exchanged

---

6   *Opinion No. 30,* Accounting Principles Board, AICPA, June 1973.
7   *Opinion No. 20,* Accounting Principles Board, AICPA, July 1971.
8   *Opinion No. 30,* Accounting Principles Board, AICPA, June 1973; *Statement of Financial Accounting Standards No. 4,* FASB, March 1975.
9   *Opinion No. 15,* Accounting Principles Board, AICPA, May 1969.

directly for shares of common stock. Also, many firms have employee stock option plans under which shares of the company's common stock may be acquired by employees under special arrangements. If these convertible securities were converted or stock options were exercised and additional shares of common stock were issued, the amount conventionally shown as earnings per share would probably decrease, or become *diluted.* When a firm has outstanding securities that, if exchanged for shares of common stock, would decrease earnings per share by 3 percent or more, a dual presentation of primary and fully diluted earnings per share is required.[10]

Summary of Income Statement Concepts

Net income is determined for discrete accounting periods in order to facilitate appraisals of earnings performance among firms and over time for a given firm. Most business firms use the accrual basis of accounting for measuring earnings and financial position. A few firms use the cash basis or modified cash basis.

Under the cash basis, revenue is recognized when cash is received, and expenses are reported when cash disbursements for merchandise, salaries, taxes, and similar items are made. The cash basis suffers from two weaknesses: (1) it unnecessarily defers the recognition of revenue, and (2) it recognizes expenses in periods that may differ from those when economic benefits are received as revenues.

The accrual basis of accounting is not subject to these important weaknesses of the cash basis. Revenue is generally recognized when merchandise is sold or services are rendered to customers. Costs incurred in generating revenues are recognized as expenses of the period in which the associated revenues are recognized. Costs incurred that cannot be closely associated with particular revenue items are treated as expenses of the period in which the services of assets are consumed. Factory costs for labor, material, and overhead, called product costs, do not become expenses until the goods in which these costs are embodied are sold.

Firms involved in selling goods and services under long-term contracts sometimes recognize revenue on a percentage-of-completion, or production, basis. A portion of the contract price is recognized as revenue for each accounting period during the contract, and an appropriate amount of the costs incurred in generating the revenue is recognized as expense.

When substantial uncertainty exists regarding the amount of cash to be collected from customers for goods sold or services rendered, some firms recognize revenue on a cash-collection, or installment, basis. Revenue is recognized when cash is received, and appropriate amounts of the costs incurred are recognized as expenses.

Unless information is provided to the contrary, all illustrations and problems in this book assume that the accrual basis of accounting is used and that revenue is recognized at the time goods are sold or services are rendered.

THE STATEMENT OF CHANGES IN FINANCIAL POSITION

The third principal financial statement is the statement of changes in financial position. Exhibit 3.3 (page 71) presents the statement of changes in financial position for

---

[10] *Ibid.*

Solinger Electric Corporation. This statement usually explains the change in working capital (current assets minus current liabilities) during a period. The statement also discloses other significant changes in financial position, even though the transactions or events do not affect working capital directly. For example, the issuance of common stock in the acquisition of land would be an event disclosed in the statement.

Rationale for the Statement of Changes in Financial Position

Solinger Electric Corporation was formed during January 19X6 to operate a retail electrical supply business. The net income from operating the business has increased each year since opening, from $3,000 in 19X6 to $20,000 in 19X9. The firm has had increasing difficulty, however, paying its monthly bills as they become due. Management is puzzled as to how net income could be increasing while at the same time the firm continually finds itself strapped for cash.

The experience of Solinger Electric Corporation is not unusual. Many firms, particularly those experiencing rapid growth, discover that their cash position is deteriorating despite an excellent earnings record. The statement of changes in financial position provides information that is useful in assessing changes in a firm's *liquidity* (its holdings of cash and other assets that could be readily turned into cash), by reporting on the flows of funds into and out of the business during a period.

Income Flows and Cash Flows   The revenues and expenses reported in the income statement differ from the cash receipts and disbursements during a period for two principal reasons:

1 The accrual basis of accounting is used in determining net income, so that the recognition of revenues does not necessarily coincide with the receipts of cash from customers, and the recognition of expenses does not necessarily coincide with the disbursements of cash to suppliers, employees, and other creditors.
2 The firm has cash receipts and disbursements not directly related to the process of generating earnings, such as from issuing capital stock or bonds, paying dividends, or purchasing buildings and equipment.

Exhibit 2.2 showed receipts and disbursements for Allens' Hardware Store while Exhibit 2.3 showed revenues and expenses. We noted earlier the difference between the two exhibits and discussed why Exhibit 2.3 measures performance better. Next we consider a more complicated example.

Exhibit 2.4 shows the relationship between the revenues and expenses and the cash receipts and disbursements of Solinger Electric Corporation during 19X9. Although sales revenue was $125,000, only $90,000 was collected from customers. The remaining amount of sales was not collected by the end of the year and is reflected in the Accounts Receivable account on the balance sheet. Likewise, the cost of goods sold was $60,000, but only $50,000 was disbursed to suppliers during the year. Similar differences between income flows and cash flows can be seen for salaries and for other expenses. Note that there is no specific cash flow associated with depreciation expense. Although the operating activities generated $20,000 in net income, these activities led

EXHIBIT 2.4
Solinger Electric Corporation
Income Statement and Statement
of Cash Receipts and Disbursements
for the Year 19X9

	Income Statement	Statement of Cash Receipts and Disbursements	
Sales Revenue	$125,000	Collections from Customers	$ 90,000
Less Expenses:		Less Disbursements:	
Cost of Goods Sold	$ 60,000	To Merchandise Suppliers	$ 50,000
Salaries	20,000	To Employees	19,000
Depreciation	10,000	—	0
Other	15,000	To Other Suppliers	13,000
Total Expenses	$105,000	Total Disbursements to Suppliers and Employees	$ 82,000
Net Income	$ 20,000	Net Cash Inflow from Operations	$ 8,000
		Receipts from Issuing Long-Term Bonds	100,000
		Total Receipts from Operations and Bond Issue	$108,000
		Disbursements for Dividends	$ 10,000
		Disbursements for Equipment	125,000
		Total Disbursements for Dividends and Equipment	$135,000
		Net Decrease in Cash	$ 27,000

to only an $8,000 increase in cash during 19X9. The firm's cash balance decreased by $27,000 between the beginning and end of 19X9 because the cash inflows from operations ($8,000) and from issuing long-term bonds ($100,000) were less than the cash required to pay dividends ($10,000) and purchase equipment ($125,000).

Cash Flows and Working Capital Flows   The statement of changes in financial position reports on the flows of funds into and out of a business during a period. Funds were viewed as "cash" in Exhibit 2.4 in which the Statement of Changes in Financial Position was essentially a statement of cash receipts and disbursements. The term "funds," however, is a general one, which can have different meanings depending on the circumstances. Consider the following two questions, which the management of Solinger Electric Corporation might raise:

1 Does the firm have sufficient funds to acquire new equipment immediately?
2 Will the firm have sufficient funds to acquire new equipment within the next six months?

In answering the first question, management is likely to consider the amount of cash on hand and in its bank account. It would also consider if the equipment could be acquired on account from one of its regular suppliers. In answering the second question, management would, in addition, consider if the firm had marketable securities or other assets that could be sold for cash during the next six months. It should be clear, however, that *time is the important factor* in answering the questions about available funds. When the time horizon is short, the meaning of funds is more restrictive than when the time horizon is longer.

The statements of changes in financial position of most publicly held firms use a definition of funds broader than cash. In most instances, the statements explain the change in the net current asset position, or *working capital*, of the firm. That is, funds are defined as the difference between current assets (cash, readily marketable securities, accounts receivable, inventories, and current prepayments) and current liabilities (accounts payable, salaries payable, and other short-term debt). Current assets are those assets that are either cash or are expected to be turned into cash, or sold, or consumed within the operating cycle, usually one year. Current liabilities are obligations expected to be discharged or paid within approximately one year. Thus, the amount of working capital at a particular time represents the excess of cash and cash-like assets over short-term claims on these liquid assets. This broader definition of funds is considered to provide more useful information to investors and other users of a firm's financial statements than does the more restrictive definition of funds as cash alone.

Exhibit 2.5 shows the relationship between the cash receipts and disbursements and the increases (sources) and decreases (uses) of working capital of Solinger Electric Corporation during 19X9. Revenues led to only a $90,000 increase in cash but to a $125,000 increase in cash and accounts receivable. Because accounts receivable are likely to be collected within a short period, the working capital definition of funds gives a better indication of the effect of revenues on liquidity. Salaries Expense and Other Operating Expenses resulted in a $32,000 (= $19,000 + $13,000) decrease in cash but a $35,000 reduction in working capital. Current liabilities (for example, Sala-

EXHIBIT 2.5
Solinger Electric Corporation
Statements of Cash Receipts and Disbursements and Increases and Decreases in Working Capital for the Year 19X9

Statement of Cash Receipts and Disbursements

Cash Receipts:	
Collections from Customers	$ 90,000
Less Disbursements:	
To Merchandise Suppliers	$ 50,000
To Employees	19,000
To Other Suppliers	13,000
Total Disbursements to Suppliers and Employees	$ 82,000
Net Cash Inflow from Operations	$ 8,000
Receipts from Issuing Long-Term Bonds	100,000
Total Receipts from Operations and Bond Issue	$108,000
Disbursements for Dividends	$ 10,000
Disbursements for Equipment	125,000
Total Disbursements for Dividends and Equipment	$135,000
Net Decrease in Cash	$ 27,000

Statement of Increases and Decreases in Working Capital

Increase in Working Capital from Operations:	
Sales Revenue	$125,000
Less Decreases in Working Capital from Operations:	
Inventory Sold	$ 60,000
Salaries Paid or Earned and Accrued	20,000
Other Expenses Paid or Accrued	15,000
Total Decreases in Working Capital from Operations	$ 95,000
Net Increase in Working Capital from Operations	$ 30,000
Increase in Working Capital from Issuing Long-Term Bonds	100,000
Total Increase in Working Capital from Operations and Bond Issue	$130,000
Decrease in Working Capital for Dividends Declared	$ 10,000
Decrease in Working Capital for Equipment Acquired	125,000
Total Decrease in Working Capital for Dividends Declared and Equipment Acquired	$135,000
Net Decrease in Working Capital	$ 5,000

ries Payable, Accounts Payable) must therefore have *increased* by $3,000 (= $35,000 − $32,000). The firm's liquidity is affected by the need to pay these $35,000 of obligations in the near future, and the obligation should be considered in assessing liquidity. Note that depreciation expense does not affect either cash flows or working capital flows. Operations generated a net cash inflow of $8,000 but an increase in net working capital of $30,000. The $22,000 difference is caused largely by an increase in accounts receivable, which is a part of working capital but is not cash.

Objective of the Statement of Changes in Financial Position

The statement of changes in financial position presents information on the sources (increases) and uses (decreases) of working capital during a period. Figure 2.2 shows the major sources and uses. These are described below.

1 *Sources—Operations.* The excess of revenues increasing working capital over expenses using working capital is the most important source of funds. When assessed over several years, working capital from operations indicates the extent to which the operating or earnings activities have generated more working capital than is used. The excess from operations can then be used for dividends, acquisition of buildings and equipment, or repayment of long-term debt if necessary.

2 *Sources—Issuance of Long-Term Debt or Capital Stock.* In contrast to the short-term nature of working capital from operations, increases in long-term debt or capital stock represent longer-term sources of financing for a firm.

3 *Sources—Sale of Noncurrent Assets.* The sale of buildings, equipment, and other noncurrent assets results in an increase in working capital. These sales generally cannot be viewed as a major source of financing for a firm, because the amounts received from the sales are not likely to be sufficient to replace the assets sold.

4 *Uses—Dividends.* Dividends are generally a recurring use of working capital, because most publicly held firms are reluctant to reduce or omit the payment of dividends, even during a year of poor earnings performance.

5 *Uses—Redemption of Long-Term Debt or Capital Stock.* In most instances, publicly held firms redeem or pay long-term debt at maturity with the proceeds of another bond issue. Thus, these redemptions often have little effect on the *net* change in working capital. Some firms also occasionally reacquire or redeem their own capital stock for various reasons.

6 *Uses—Acquisition of Noncurrent Assets.* The acquisition of noncurrent assets such as building and equipment usually represents an important use of working capital. These assets must be replaced as they wear out, and additional noncurrent assets must be acquired if a firm is to grow.

Firms sometimes issue long-term debt or capital stock directly to the vendor, or seller, in acquiring buildings, equipment, or other noncurrent assets. These transactions technically do not affect a working capital account. However, the transaction is reported in the statement of changes in financial position as though two transactions took place: the issuance of long-term debt or capital stock for cash and the immediate use of the cash in the acquisition of noncurrent assets. This is called the *dual trans-*

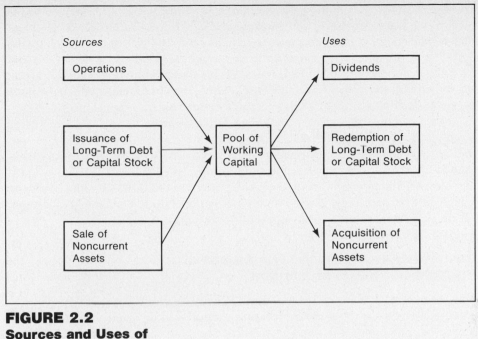

FIGURE 2.2
Sources and Uses of
Working Capital

actions assumption. Such a transaction would normally be disclosed in the statement of changes in financial position as both a source and use of working capital of equal amounts.

Uses of Information in the Statement of Changes in Financial Position

The statement of changes in financial position provides information that may be used in:

1 Assessing changes in a firm's liquidity, and
2 Assessing changes in the structure of a firm's assets and equities.

Liquidity Perhaps the most important factor not reported on the balance sheet and income statement alone is how the operations of a period affect the liquidity of a firm. It is easy to assume that increased earnings mean increased cash or other liquid assets. However, a new plant may have been acquired and other similar events could have occurred. On the other hand, increased liquidity can accompany reduced earnings, if cash is allowed to accumulate rather than being used to replace plant and equipment.

When one uses information from the statement of changes in financial position in assessing changes in liquidity, the definition of funds as working capital must be kept in mind. If near-term liquidity is of interest, then funds should be redefined as cash.

Structure of Assets and Equities   In addition to providing information about changes in a firm's liquidity during a period, the statement of changes in financial position also indicates the major transactions causing changes in the structure of a firm's assets and equities. For example, acquisitions and sales of specific types of noncurrent assets (buildings, equipment, patents) are reported. Likewise, issues and redemptions of long-term debt and capital stock are disclosed. These transactions are difficult to observe by looking at either the income statement or balance sheet alone. For example, the change in the account, "Buildings and Equipment—Net of Accumulated Depreciation," could be attributable to depreciation charges, to acquisition of new buildings and equipment, to disposition of old buildings and equipment, or to a combination of these. The income statement and comparative balance sheets do not provide sufficient information about these three items individually for the reader to disaggregate the net change in the account during the period. A statement of changes in financial position is required to report this information.

Classification Within the Statement of Changes in Financial Position

The statement of changes in financial position is divided into two sections. The first section contains a listing of the sources and uses of working capital or financial resources for the period. The items in this first section might be classified as being related to:

1 Earnings activities,
2 Income distributions of the firm,
3 Financing activities, and
4 Investing activities.

The first item generally reported on the statement is the amount of working capital provided (or used) by operations. This item indicates whether the earnings activities of the firm (that is, acquiring and selling goods or services) have resulted in an increase or decrease in working capital. Working capital provided by operations is the source of income distributions (dividends). Frequently, expansion of the firm's activities are financed with working capital provided by operations. Working capital provided (or used) by operations is therefore an important indicator of the firm's financial health, particularly when working capital flows are assessed over several years.

The derivation of the amount of working capital provided (or used) by operations is typically shown in the statement by beginning with the amount of net income for the period and adjusting net income for expenses not using working capital and revenues not providing working capital. The amount of working capital provided or used from operations might better be disclosed by listing revenues that provide working capital and then subtracting only those expenses that use working capital. The end result is the same under both methods of presentation. The first procedure leads some statement readers to the mistaken conclusion that depreciation is a source of working capital.

The sources and uses of working capital from financing activities include the issuance and redemption of common or preferred stock or long-term bonds. The sources and uses of working capital from investing activities include the purchase and sale of land, buildings, equipment, and other noncurrent assets. The declaration of dividends (income distribution) is a use of working capital.

Whereas the first section of the statement of changes in financial position presents the sources and uses of working capital or financial resources, the second section summarizes the change in each of the working capital accounts.

OTHER ITEMS IN ANNUAL REPORTS

Several additional schedules or statements, which supplement the three principal financial statements, are often presented in the annual report. In most cases, these items are covered by the auditor's opinion.

Reconciliation of Retained Earnings

The beginning and ending balances in retained earnings must be reconciled in the financial statements. The reconciliation can appear either in a separate statement or as the lower section in a combined statement of income and retained earnings. In most instances, net income and dividends are the only reconciling items. Occasionally an adjustment or correction of prior years' income statements will appear as an addition to or a subtraction from the beginning balance in retained earnings. Examples of such items are settlements of litigation and income tax disputes, corrections of accounting errors in past reports, and retroactive restatements for certain changes in accounting principles or procedures.

Statement of Changes in Contributed Capital

As with retained earnings, a reconciliation of changes in the capital stock and additional paid-in capital accounts must be presented. This reconciliation includes the effects of financing by issuing capital stock, conversion of debt or preferred shares into common shares, issue of shares to employees under stock option plans, issue of shares to shareholders as a stock dividend, and reacquisitions of the firm's shares on the market and held as treasury shares.

Historical Summary

It is common reporting practice to include a 5- or 10-year historical summary of important financial statement information in the annual report. Items usually included in the historical summary are net sales revenue, income taxes, net income, earnings per share, dividends per share, working capital, total assets, long-term debt, and stockholders' equity. To enhance comparability of the data, restatements of previously reported amounts may be required for changes in accounting procedures, acquisitions of other companies, and changes in the number of outstanding shares caused by stock dividends and stock splits.

Line of Business or Segment Reports

The growing number of conglomerate firms that have segments or divisions operating in widely different industries has led to the requirement for information concerning the performance of each segment.[11] The segments are typically classified by product or industry groupings. Other definitions of segments include geographical location of markets (domestic and foreign) and type of customer (consumer, industry, government).

Two common accounting problems encountered in preparing segment earnings reports concern the treatment of sales and other transactions between divisions and the allocation of central corporate expenses. Should sales between divisions be included in the segment sales, or should only sales to parties outside the firm be disclosed? If sales or transfers to other divisions are included, what transfer price should be used (for example, cost to the selling division, outside market price, negotiated price between the segments)? Likewise, should central corporate expenses recognized during the period (for example, the president's salary, research and development or data-processing expenses, interest, and income tax expenses) be allocated to each segment, or left unallocated? If these expenses are allocated, what basis should be used (for example, number of employees, square feet of floor space used, segment sales revenue)? The accounting profession's answers to these questions are discussed in financial accounting books and in the FASB Statement on the subject.[12]

ASSESSING CURRENT EXTERNAL REPORTING PRACTICES

In Chapter One we discussed several possible criteria for assessing the usefulness of accounting information, including relevance to decisions, accuracy in presentation, and others. In recent years, the usefulness of financial statements has been questioned on three broad fronts.

Some critics have complained that the information disclosed is too aggregated, or condensed, to be of much help to readers in assessing operating performance and financial position. The presentation of earnings data by segments or lines of business is one response to this criticism. Another response is in the expanded use of notes to the financial statements, providing further elaboration on items in the body of the statements.

Perhaps the easiest way to satisfy these critics is to provide more data and let each user decide what is or is not relevant information. The incremental benefits of more data must be compared, though, with the incremental costs of generating the data. Some point will be reached where the incremental costs will exceed the incremental benefits. Further, the managers of some firms argue that expanded disclosure will help competitors and thus will harm shareholders.

---

[11] Financial Accounting Standards Board, "Financial Reporting for Segments of a Business Enterprise," *Statement of Financial Accounting Standards No. 14,* December 1976.
[12] *Ibid.*

A second major criticism is aimed at the diversity of generally accepted accounting principles and the flexibility permitted firms in choosing the accounting methods used in preparing financial statements. The use of different accounting procedures, it is suggested, makes it difficult to compare performance and financial position among firms. The counterargument is that alternative accounting methods are necessary so that the firm can select the methods that most fairly present the underlying transactions or events to which it is a party.

A third criticism of current accounting reports is that too much emphasis is placed on verifiability, or auditability, and not enough on relevancy to the user. This criticism has been directed primarily at the use of acquisition cost as the valuation basis for many assets rather than some type of current valuation, such as replacement cost or net realizable value. The interest among accountants in disclosing current values for assets as supplements to acquisition cost amounts has been increasing in recent years. We consider this topic further in Chapter Fifteen.

SUMMARY

This chapter has provided an overview of the manner in which information generated as part of the accounting process is disclosed in published accounting reports. The relationships among the three principal financial statements might be depicted as follows.

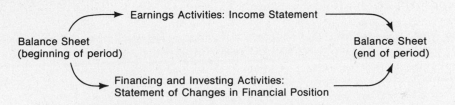

Perhaps the most effective overview of external financial reporting is obtained by reading and studying carefully the annual reports of several publicly held companies.

QUESTIONS AND PROBLEMS

1 Review the meaning of the following concepts or terms discussed in this chapter.
   a Auditor's opinion.
   b Unqualified opinion.
   c Summary of significant accounting policies.
   d Balance sheet.
   e Asset.
   f Liability.
   g Owners' equity.
   h Monetary assets.

    i   Nonmonetary assets.
    j   Acquisition cost.
    k   Current assets.
    l   Current liability.
    m Net income.
    n   Revenue.
    o   Expense.
    p   Product cost.
    q   Period expense.
    r   Cash basis of accounting.
    s   Accrual basis of accounting.
    t   Income from continuing operations.
    u   Income from discontinued operations.
    v   Extraordinary items.
    w Earnings per share.
    x   Working capital.
    y   Historical summary.
    z   Line of business report.

2 Prepare a balance sheet of your personal assets, liabilities, and owner's equity. How does the presentation of owner's equity on your balance sheet differ from that in Exhibit 3.1?

3 Suggest procedures you would follow in determining the amounts at which the following resources would be stated on a balance sheet if they were to be recognized as assets.
    a   Well-known trademark or other product symbol.
    b   Well-trained employee labor force.

4 What factors give rise to the need for generating accounting information on a time, or accounting period, basis rather than on a project basis?

5 What factors would a firm be likely to consider in its decision to use the calendar year versus a fiscal year as its accounting period?

6 Conservatism is generally regarded as a convention in accounting. Indicate who might be hurt by conservatively stated accounting reports.

7 Distinguish between a revenue and a cash receipt. Under what conditions will they be the same?

8 Distinguish between an expense and a cash disbursement. Under what conditions will they be the same?

9 What is the purpose of the independent accountant's audit and expression of opinion on a firm's financial statements?

10 If an item is considered important enough to warrant disclosure in a note to the financial statements, why is it not disclosed in the body of the statements?

11 Why are investments in the securities of some companies shown among current assets and those in other companies included among long-term investments?

12 Define dilution and describe its significance in measuring earnings per share.

13 Explain the difference, if any, between the items referred to by the following pairs of terms:
  a Qualified opinion and unqualified opinion.
  b "Subject to" opinion and "except for" opinion.
  c Statement of financial position and statement of changes in financial position.
  d Income from continuing operations and income from discontinued operations.
  e Extraordinary items and prior-period adjustments.
  f Income from continuing operations and working capital provided by operations.
  g Statement of changes in financial position and funds statement.

14 Indicate whether or not each of the following items would be recognized as assets by a firm according to the definition in the text.
  a The cash received from a customer for goods to be delivered in a future accounting period.
  b A contract signed by a customer to purchase $1,000 of goods next year.
  c A favorable reputation.
  d A patent on a new invention developed by a firm.
  e A good credit standing.
  f A delivery truck.
  g A degree in engineering from a reputable university, awarded to the firm's chief engineer.

15 Indicate whether or not each of the following events immediately gives rise to an asset. If an asset is recognized, state an account title and amount.
  a An investment of $8,000 is made in a government bond. The bond will have a maturity value of $10,000 in three years.
  b An order for $600 of merchandise is received from a customer.
  c Merchandise inventory with a list price of $300 is purchased, with payment being made in time to secure a 2-percent discount for prompt payment.
  d Notice has been received from a manufacturer that materials billed at $4,000, with payment due within 30 days, have been shipped by freight. The seller retains title to the materials until they are received by the buyer.
  e A contract is signed for the construction of a specially designed piece of machinery. The terms are $5,000 down upon signing the contract and the balance of $8,000 upon delivery of the equipment. Consider this question from the standpoint of the purchaser.
  f A check for $900 is sent to a landlord for two months' rent in advance (consider from the standpoint of the tenant, often called the *lessee*).
  g A check for $1,000 is written to obtain an option to purchase a tract of land. The price of the land is $32,500.
  h Bonds with a face value of $100,000 are purchased for $96,000. The bonds mature in 25 years. Interest is payable by the issuer of the bonds at the rate of 8 percent annually.

16 Indicate whether or not each of the following items is recognized as a liability.
  a Unpaid wages of employees.
  b An obligation to maintain a rented office building in good repair.
  c The amount payable by a firm for a newspaper advertisement that has appeared but for which payment is not due for 30 days.
  d An incompetent brother-in-law of the firm's president, who is employed in the business.
  e The reputation for not paying bills promptly.
  f The outstanding common stock of a corporation.

g   An obligation to deliver merchandise to a customer next year for which cash has been received.

h   An obligation to provide rental services to a tenant who has paid three months' rent in advance.

17 Indicate whether or not each of the following events immediately gives rise to the recognition of a liability. If a liability is recognized, state the account title and amount.

a   A landscaper agrees to improve land owned by the company. The agreed price for the work is $425. Consider from the standpoint of the company.

b   Additional common stock with a par value of $50,000 is issued for $62,500.

c   A check for $12 for a two-year future subscription to a magazine is received.

d   A construction company agrees to build a bridge for $2 million. A down payment of $200,000 is received upon signing the contract, and the remainder is due when the bridge is completed.

e   During the last pay period, employees earned wages amounting to $24,500 for which they have not been paid. The employer is also liable for payroll taxes of 8 percent of the wages earned.

f   A landlord received $900 for three months' rent in advance.

g   A 60-day, 8-percent loan for $10,000 is obtained at a bank.

h   A firm signs a contract to purchase at least $5,000 worth of merchandise during the next three months.

18 Accounts might be classified in the balance sheet and income statement in one of the following categories:
   (1) Current assets.
   (2) Investments.
   (3) Fixed assets.
   (4) Intangibles.
   (5) Current liabilities.
   (6) Long-term liabilities.
   (7) Stockholders' equity.
   (8) Income statement items.
   (9) Items excluded from the balance sheet and income statement under present generally accepted accounting principles.

Various accounts that might be presented in the financial statements are listed below. Using the numbers above, indicate the appropriate classification of each account. Use an X before the number if the account is a contra account. For example, Allowance for Uncollectible Accounts is X-1. State any assumptions that you feel are necessary.

a   Accounts payable.
b   Accounts receivable.
c   Accumulated depreciation.
d   Advances by customers.
e   Advances to suppliers.
f   Advertising expenses.
g   Allowance for uncollectibles.
h   Bond sinking fund.
i   Building.
j   Cash.
k   Certificate of deposit.
l   Common stock.

m Construction in progress.
n Current maturities of bonds payable (to be paid from general cash account).
o Current maturities of bonds payable (to be paid from cash in bond sinking fund).
p Customers' deposits.
q Deposits on equipment purchases.
r Depreciation expense.
s Dividends payable.
t Estimated liabilities under warranty contracts.
u Finished goods inventory.
v Furniture and fixtures.
w Gain on sale of equipment.
x General and administrative expenses.
y Goodwill.

19 Accounts might be classified in the balance sheet and income statement in one of the following categories:
   (1) Current assets.
   (2) Investments.
   (3) Fixed assets.
   (4) Intangibles.
   (5) Current liabilities.
   (6) Long-term liabilities.
   (7) Stockholders' equity.
   (8) Income statement items.
   (9) Items excluded from the balance sheet and income statement under present generally accepted accounting principles.
   Various accounts that might be presented in the financial statements are listed below. Using the numbers above, indicate the appropriate classification of each account. Use an X before the number if the account is a contra account. For example, Allowance for Uncollectible Accounts is X-1. State any assumptions that you feel are necessary.
   a Income taxes withheld.
   b Interest expense.
   c Interest payable.
   d Interest receivable.
   e Investment in General Motors stock.
   f U.S. Treasury Notes.
   g Investment in unconsolidated subsidiary.
   h Land.
   i Machinery.
   j Marketable securities.
   k Merchandise inventory.
   l Mortgage payable (noncurrent).
   m Notes payable (due in three months).
   n Notes receivable (due in six months).
   o Patents.
   p Plant.
   q Preferred stock.
   r Prepaid insurance.
   s Raw materials inventory.
   t Rental revenue.

    u Retained earnings.

    v Sales discounts and allowances.

    w Tools and dies.

    x Unexpired insurance.

    y Work in process.

20 J. Thompson opened a hardware store on January 1, 19X0. Thompson invested $5,000 and borrowed $6,000 from the local bank. The loan is repayable on March 31, 19X0, with interest at the rate of 8 percent per year.

    Thompson rented a building on January 1, 19X0, and paid two months' rent in advance in the amount of $800. Property and liability insurance coverage for the year ending December 31, 19X0, was paid on January 1 in the amount of $600.

    Thompson purchased $20,000 of merchandise inventory on account on January 2 and paid $4,000 of this amount on January 25. The cost of merchandise on hand on January 31 was $12,000.

    During January, cash sales to customers totaled $7,000 and sales on account totaled $3,000. Of the sales on account, $2,000 were collected as of January 31.

    Other costs incurred and paid in cash during January were as follows: utilities, $200; salaries, $650; taxes, $150.

    a Prepare an income statement for January, assuming that Thompson uses the accrual basis of accounting with revenue recognized at the time goods are sold (delivered).

    b Prepare an income statement for January, assuming that Thompson uses the cash basis of accounting.

    c Which basis of accounting do you feel provides a better indication of the operating performance of the hardware store during January? Why?

21 Management Consultants, Inc., opened a consulting business on July 1, 19X1. Roy Bean and Sarah Bower each contributed $5,000 cash for shares of the firm's common stock. The corporation borrowed $6,000 from a local bank on August 1, 19X1. The loan is repayable on July 31, 19X2, with interest at the rate of 10 percent per year.

    Office space was rented on August 1, with two months' rent paid in advance. The remaining monthly rental fees of $600 per month were made on the first of each month beginning October 1. Office equipment with a three-year life was purchased for cash on August 1 for $3,600.

    Consulting services rendered for clients between August 1 and December 31, 19X1 were billed at $11,000. Of this amount, $7,000 was collected by year-end.

    Other costs incurred and paid in cash by the end of the year were as follows: utilities, $250; salary of secretary, $5,000; supplies used, $150. Unpaid bills at year-end are as follows: utilities, $50; salary of secretary, $800; supplies used, $40.

    a Prepare an income statement for the five months ended December 31, 19X1, assuming that the corporation uses the accrual basis of accounting, with revenue recognized at the time services are rendered.

    b Prepare an income statement for the five months ended December 31, 19X1, assuming that the corporation uses the cash basis of accounting.

    c Which basis of accounting do you feel provides a better indication of operating performance of the consulting business for the five months ended December 31, 19X1? Why?

22 Indicate which of the following transactions involve the immediate recognition of revenue under the accrual basis of accounting:

    a The delivery of an issue of a magazine to subscribers.

    b The sale of an automobile by an automobile agency.

c A collection of cash from accounts receivable debtors.
d The borrowing of money at a bank.
e The sale of merchandise on account.
f The collection of cash by a barber for a haircut.
g The rendering of dry-cleaning services on account.
h The issue of shares of preferred stock.
i The sale of tickets for a concert to be given in two weeks.

23 Assume that the accrual basis of accounting is used and that revenue is recognized at the time goods are sold or services are rendered. How much revenue is recognized during the month of May in each of the following transactions?

a Collection of cash from customers during May for merchandise sold and delivered in April, $5,200.
b Sales of merchandise during May for cash, $3,600.
c Sales of merchandise during May to customers to be collected in June, $5,400.
d A store building is rented to a toy shop for $600 a month, effective May 1. A check for $1,200 for two months' rent is received on May 1.
e Data of **d**, except that collection is received from the tenant in June.

24 Assume that the accrual basis of accounting is used and that revenue is recognized at the time goods are sold or services are rendered. Indicate the amount of expense recognized during March, if any, in each of the following situations:

a Rent is paid on March 1, $1,800, for the three months starting at that time.
b An advance on the April salary is paid to an employee on March 28, $100.
c Property taxes on a store building of $1,200 for the year were paid in January.
d An employee earned $800 of commissions during March, but has not yet been paid.
e The cost of equipment purchased on March 26, to be put into operation on April 1, is $5,000.
f $800 of supplies were purchased during March. On March 1, supplies were on hand that cost $300. At March 31, supplies that cost $400 were still on hand.
g Data of **f**, except that $200 of supplies were on hand at March 1.
h At March 1, the balance in the Prepaid Insurance account was $4,800. The insurance policy had 24 months to run at that time.

25 Three ways of recognizing revenue are as follows:
(1) Recognition of revenue as production is carried on.
(2) Recognition of revenue when goods are furnished or services are rendered to customers.
(3) Recognition of revenue only as cash is collected from customers, if that time differs from (2).
Indicate the method likely to be used by each of the following types of businesses:

a A drug store.
b A manufacturer of umbrellas.
c A bridge-building firm.
d A real estate developer selling lots on long-term contracts with small down payments.
e A wholesale tobacco distributor.
f A dentist.
g A clothing manufacturer.
h A shipbuilding firm constructing an aircraft carrier.
i A shoe store.
j A citrus-growing firm.

26 Feltham Company acquired used machine tools costing $75,000 from various sources. These machine tools were then sold to Mock Corporation. Delivery costs paid by Feltham Company totaled $4,500. Mock Corporation had agreed to pay $100,000 cash for these tools. Finding itself short of cash, however, Mock Corporation offered $110,000 of its par value bonds to Feltham Company. These bonds promised 8 percent interest per year. At the time the offer was made, the bonds could have been sold in public bond markets for $98,000.

Feltham Company accepted the offer and held the bonds for three years. During the three years, it received interest payments of $8,800 per year, or $26,400 total. At the end of the third year, Feltham Company sold the bonds for $95,500.

  a What profit or loss did Feltham Company recognize on the sale of machine tools to Mock Corporation?

  b What profit or loss would Feltham Company have recognized on the sale of machine tools if it had sold the bonds for $98,000 immediately upon receiving them?

  c What profit or loss would Feltham Company have recognized on the sale of machine tools if it had held the bonds to maturity, receiving $8,800 each year for another five years and $110,000 at the time the bonds matured?

27 The Webster Corporation produces a single product at a cost of $5 each, all of which is paid in cash when the unit is produced. The selling cost consists of a sales commission of $3 a unit and is paid in cash at the time of shipment. The selling price is $10 a unit; all sales are made on account. No uncollectible accounts are expected, and no costs are incurred at the time of collection.

During 19X0, the firm produced 200,000 units, shipped 150,000 units, and collected $1 million from customers. During 19X1, the firm produced 125,000 units, shipped 160,000 units and collected $2 million from customers.

Determine the amount of net income for 19X0 and for 19X1 (ignoring income taxes):

  a If revenue and expense are recognized at the time of production.

  b If revenue and expense are recognized at the time of shipment.

  c If revenue and expense are recognized at the time of cash collection.

  d A firm experiencing growth in its sales volume will often produce more units during a particular period than it sells. In this way, inventories can be built up in anticipation of an even larger sales volume during the next period. Under these circumstances, will recognition of revenue and expense at the time of production, shipment, or cash collection generally result in the largest reported net income for the period? Explain.

  e A firm experiencing decreases in its sales volume will often produce fewer units during a period than it sells in an effort to reduce the amount of inventory on hand for the next period. Under these circumstances, will recognition of revenue and expense at the time of production, shipment, or cash collection generally result in the largest reported net income for a period? Explain.

28 The Humbolt Electric Company received a contract late in 19X0 to build a small electricity-generating unit. The contract price was $700,000 and it was estimated that total costs would be $600,000. Estimated and actual construction time was 15 months and it was agreed that payments would be made by the purchaser as follows:

March 31, 19X1.	$ 70,000
June 30, 19X1	105,000
September 30, 19X1	203,000
December 31, 19X1.	161,000
March 31, 19X2.	161,000
	$700,000

Estimated and actual costs of construction incurred by the Humbolt Electric Company were as follows:

January 1–March 31, 19X1	$120,000
April 1–June 30, 19X1	120,000
July 1–September 30, 19X1	180,000
October 1–December 31, 19X1	120,000
January 1–March 31, 19X2	60,000
	$600,000

The Humbolt Electric Company prepares financial statements quarterly at March 31, June 30, and so forth. Determine the amount of revenue, expense, and net income for each quarter under each of the following methods of revenue recognition:

a Production (percentage-of-completion) method.
b Sales (completed-contract) method.
c Cash-collection (installment) method.
d Which method do you feel provides the best measure of Humbolt's performance under this contract? Why?
e Under what circumstances would the methods not selected in **d** provide a better measure of performance?

29 The results of various transactions and events are classified within the income statement in one of the following three sections: (1) income from continuing operations, (2) income, gains, and losses from discontinued operations, and (3) extraordinary items. Using the appropriate number, identify the classification of each of the transactions or events below. State any assumptions that you feel are necessary.

a Depreciation expense for the year on a company's automobile used by its president.
b Uninsured loss of a factory complex in Louisiana as a result of a hurricane.
c Gain from the sale of marketable securities.
d Loss from the sale of a delivery truck.
e Loss from the sale of a division that conducted all of the firm's research activities.
f Earnings during the year up to the time of sale of the division in e.
g Loss in excess of insurance proceeds on an automobile destroyed during an accident.
h Loss of plant, equipment, and inventory held in a South American country when confiscated by the government of that country.

30 B. Stephens, L. Harris, and G. Winkle, recent business school graduates, set up a management consulting practice on December 31, 19X0, by issuing common stock for $750,000. The accounting records of the S, H, & W Corporation as of December 31, 19X1, reveal the following:

Balance Sheet Items

Cash	$ 50,000
Accounts Receivable from Clients	165,000
Supplies Inventory	5,000
Office Equipment (net of depreciation)	85,000
Office Building (net of depreciation)	500,000
Accounts Payable to Suppliers	10,000
Payroll Taxes Payable	5,000
Income Taxes Payable	20,000
Common Stock	750,000

Income Statement Items

Revenue from Consulting Services	$300,000
Rental Revenue (from renting part of building)	30,000
Property Taxes and Insurance Expense	40,000
Salaries Expense	215,000
Depreciation Expense	25,000
Income Tax Expense	20,000

Dividend Information

Dividends Declared and Paid	$ 10,000

a Prepare an income statement for S, H, & W Corporation for the year ending December 31, 19X1.

b Prepare a comparative balance sheet for S, H, & W Corporation as of December 31, 19X0, and December 31, 19X1.

c Prepare an analysis of the change in retained earnings during 19X1.

31 Comment on any unusual features of the following balance sheet of the Western Sales Corporation.

Western Sales Corporation
Balance Sheet for the Year Ended
December 31, 19X0

ASSETS

Current Assets

Cash and Certificates of Deposit	$ 86,500	
Accounts Receivable—Net	193,600	
Merchandise Inventory	322,900	$ 603,000

Investments (substantially at cost)

Investment in U.S. Treasury Notes	$ 60,000	
Investment in Eastern Sales Corp.	196,500	256,500

Fixed Assets (at cost)

Land	$225,000	
Buildings and Equipment—Net	842,600	1,067,600

Intangibles and Deferred Charges

Prepaid Insurance	$ 1,200	
Prepaid Rent	1,500	
Goodwill	2	2,702
Total Assets		$1,929,802

LIABILITIES AND STOCKHOLDERS' EQUITY

Current Liabilities

Accounts Payable	$225,300	
Accrued Expenses	10,900	
Income Taxes Payable	89,200	$ 325,400

Long-Term Liabilities

Bonds Payable	$500,000	
Pensions Payable	40,600	
Contingent Liability	100,000	640,600

Stockholder's Equity

Common Stock—$10 par value, 50,000 shares issued and outstanding	$625,000	
Earned Surplus	338,802	963,802
Total Liabilities and Stockholders' Equity		$1,929,802

32 Comment on any unusual features of the following income statement of Nordic Enterprises, Inc.

Nordic Enterprises, Inc.
Income Statement December 31, 19X0

Revenues and Gains

Sales Revenue	$1,964,800	
Rental Revenue	366,900	
Interest Revenue	4,600	
Gain on Sale of Equipment	2,500	
Gain on Sale of Subsidiary	643,200	$2,982,000

Expenses and Losses

Cost of Goods Sold	$1,432,900	
Depreciation Expense	226,800	
Salaries Expense	296,900	
Interest Expense	6,600	
Loss of Plant Due to Fire	246,800	
Additional Income Taxes for Prior Years	122,000	
Income Tax Expense	200,000	
Dividends Expense	100,000	2,632,000
Net Income		$ 350,000

33 Comment on any unusual features of the following statement of changes in financial position of Elasco Enterprises, Incorporated.

Elasco Enterprises, Inc.
Statement of Changes in Financial Position
December 31, 19X1

Sources of Working Capital

Net Income	$500,000
Less Depreciation Expense	250,000
Working Capital Provided by Operations	$250,000
Sale of Land	100,000
Acquisition of Treasury Stock	60,000
Issuance of Common Stock to Acquire Building	200,000
Total Sources	$610,000

Uses of Working Capital

Dividends.	$300,000
Issuance of Bonds	150,000
Acquisition of Building from Issuance of Common Stock	200,000
Total Uses	$650,000
Decrease in Working Capital	$ 40,000

34 The segment earnings report for Norton Products, Inc., for the years 19X0 to 19X4 appears below:

Norton Products, Inc.
Segment Earnings Statement
for the Years Ending December 31, 19X0 to 19X4

The following table reflects the respective contributions in excess of 10 percent of certain product lines to sales and net income before taxes. The compilation has been prepared by management, predicated on the present marketing pattern for the various groups of products and has not been subject to independent verification by the Company's auditors.

	Percent				
	19X0	**19X1**	**19X2**	**19X3**	**19X4**
Sales and Net Income Before Taxes by Product Lines					
Sales					
Domestic					
Drugs and Cosmetics	26%	27%	26%	26%	25%
Household Products	20	21	23	22	22
Food Products	20	19	19	19	17
Specialty Chemicals	12	12	11	11	11
Industrial and Ice Control Salt. . .	8	7	8	7	8
International.	14	14	13	15	17
	100%	100%	100%	100%	100%
Net Income Before Taxes					
Domestic					
Drugs and Cosmetics	52%	64%	56%	55%	55%
Household Products	7	6	12	10	2
Food Products	18	15	16	13	12
Specialty Chemicals	(4)	(7)	(5)	—	5
Industrial and Ice Control Salt. . .	11	9	9	9	9
International.	16	13	12	13	17
	100%	100%	100%	100%	100%

What questions might be raised regarding the manner in which the segment earnings data are disclosed in this report?

CHAPTER 3
FINANCIAL STATEMENT ANALYSIS

Chapter Two provided an overview of the three principal financial statements prepared by business firms for external users. One of the major purposes of financial accounting is to provide information useful for making investment decisions. Financial statement analysis embraces the methods used in assessing and interpreting the results of past performance and current financial position as they relate to particular factors of interest in investment decisions.

OBJECTIVES OF FINANCIAL STATEMENT ANALYSIS

When comparing investment alternatives, the decision maker is interested in the expected return to be realized from each investment and the risk or uncertainty of that return. The decision maker is concerned with the future. Financial statements, based on the results of past activities, are analyzed and interpreted as a basis for predicting future rates of return and for assessing risk.

The factors affecting the assessment of rates of return and risk depend on the type of investment. For example, an investor might purchase a firm's common or preferred stock, acquire its long-term bonds, or extend short-term credit through an open account, note, or similar debt instrument.

The return from an investment in common or preferred stock consists of dividends plus capital gains (or minus capital losses) from changes in market prices of the shares. One of the principal factors affecting future dividends and market price changes is the expected *profitability* of a company. The past profitability of a firm is, therefore, one basis for predicting future profitability and rates of return.

An investor in long-term bonds is interested in a firm's ability to make periodic interest and principal payments as they become due. A firm that is unable to make its required payments is insolvent. An investor in long-term debt is therefore interested in assessing the long-term *solvency* of a firm.

A bank that makes a three- or six-month loan to a firm is more interested in short-term *liquidity*. That is, the bank is concerned with whether or not the firm will have sufficient cash available to repay the loan and interest within a few months.

Before analyzing a set of financial statements, it is important that the objective of the analysis be clearly specified. The analytical techniques used will differ, as we show in this chapter, depending on the purpose of the analysis.

USEFULNESS OF RATIOS

The various items in financial statements may be difficult to interpret in the form in which they are presented. For example, the profitability of a firm may be difficult to assess by looking at the amount of net income alone. It is helpful to compare earnings with the assets or capital required to generate those earnings. This relationship, and other important ones between various items in the financial statements, can be expressed in the form of ratios. Some ratios compare items within the income statement only; some use only balance sheet data; others relate items from both statements. Ratios are useful tools of financial statement analysis because they conveniently summarize data in a form that is more easily understood, interpreted, and compared.

Ratios are, by themselves, difficult to interpret. For example, does a rate of return on common stock of 8.6 percent reflect a good performance? Once calculated, the ratios must be compared with some standard. Several possible standards might be used:

1 The planned or budgeted ratio for the period being analyzed.
2 The corresponding ratio during the preceding period for the same firm.
3 The corresponding ratio for a similar firm in the same industry.
4 The average ratio for other firms in the same industry.

Difficulties encountered in using each of these bases for comparison are discussed later.

The number of ratios that could be calculated between various items in the financial statements is quite large. Many of these ratios have limited usefulness. In the sections that follow, we describe several ratios that are useful for assessing profitability, liquidity, and solvency. Some of the ratios, however, may be used in assessing more than one of these factors. To demonstrate the calculation of various ratios, we shall use data for Solinger Electric Corporation as shown in Exhibit 3.1 (balance sheet), Exhibit 3.2 (income statement), and Exhibit 3.3 (statement of changes in financial position).

MEASURES OF PROFITABILITY

Usually the most important question asked about a business is "How profitable is it?" Most financial statement analysis is directed at various aspects of this question. Some measures of profitability relate earnings to resources or capital employed, other com-

EXHIBIT 3.1
Solinger Electric Corporation
Comparative Balance Sheets
for December 31, 19X8 and 19X9

	December 31, 19X8	December 31, 19X9
ASSETS		
Current Assets		
Cash	$ 30,000	$ 3,000
Accounts Receivable.	20,000	55,000
Merchandise Inventory	40,000	50,000
Total Current Assets	$ 90,000	$108,000
Noncurrent Assets		
Buildings and Equipment		
(Cost).	$100,000	$225,000
Accumulated Depreciation	(30,000)	(40,000)
Total Noncurrent Assets. . . .	$ 70,000	$185,000
Total Assets	$160,000	$293,000
EQUITIES		
Current Liabilities		
Accounts Payable—		
Merchandise Suppliers	$ 30,000	$ 50,000
Accounts Payable—		
Other Suppliers	10,000	12,000
Salaries Payable	5,000	6,000
Total Current Liabilities	$ 45,000	$ 68,000
Noncurrent Liabilities		
Bonds Payable	0	100,000
Total Liabilities	$ 45,000	$168,000
Owners' Equity		
Capital Stock ($10 par value) . .	$100,000	$100,000
Retained Earnings.	15,000	25,000
Total Owners' Equity	$115,000	$125,000
Total Equities	$160,000	$293,000

putations relate earnings and various expenses to sales, while a third group seeks to explain profitability by measuring the efficiency with which inventories, receivables, or other assets have been administered.

EXHIBIT 3.2
Solinger Electric Corporation
Income Statement
for the Year 19X9

Sales Revenue	$125,000
Less Expenses:	
Cost of Goods Sold	$ 60,000
Salaries	19,667
Depreciation	10,000
Interest	2,000
Income Taxes	13,333
Total Expenses	$105,000
Net Income	$ 20,000

Rate of Return on Total Capital

One of the most important profitability ratios, particularly in assessing management's performance, is the *rate of return earned on total capital* or resources employed by the firm. This rate is often called the *return on investment* or *ROI*. The "capital employed" is indicated by the total of either side of the balance sheet, the total assets or the total equities (liabilities plus owners' equity). Because the earnings rate *during the year* is being determined, the measure of investment should reflect the average amount of capital invested during the year. A crude, but usually satisfactory, figure for average capital invested is the sum of the total assets (or equities) at the beginning and end of the year divided by 2.

In order to assess management's operating performance independently of financing decisions, the earnings figure to be compared with total capital employed should be net income before deducting any distributions to the providers of capital. Because interest is a payment to a source of capital, interest expense should be added back to net income to measure the return on total capital employed. The amount added back to net income, however, is not equal to interest expense shown on the income statement. Because interest expense is deductible in determining taxable income, interest expense does not reduce *aftertax* net income by the full amount of interest expense. The amount added back to net income is, therefore, interest expense reduced by income tax effects.

For example, interest expense of Solinger Electric Corporation as shown in Exhibit 3.2 is $2,000. The income tax rate is assumed to be 40 percent of pretax income. The income tax saved because interest is deductible in determining taxable income is $800 (= .40 × $2,000). The amount of interest expense net of income tax savings that is added back to net income is therefore $1,200 (= $2,000 − $800). There is no need to add back dividends to stockholders, because they are not deducted as an expense in calculating net income.

EXHIBIT 3.3
Solinger Electric Corporation
Statement of Changes in
Financial Position
for the Year 19X9

SECTION I. SOURCES AND USES OF WORKING CAPITAL

Sources of Working Capital
Operations
Net Income $20,000
   Add Back Expenses Not Using Working Capital:
Depreciation.   10,000
   Total Sources from Operations . . . . $ 30,000
Proceeds from Long-Term Bonds Issued   100,000
   Total Sources of Working Capital $130,000

Uses of Working Capital
Dividends. . . . . $ 10,000
Acquisition of Buildings and Equipment.   125,000
   Total Uses of Working Capital $135,000
Net Decrease in Working Capital During the Year
   (Sources Minus Uses). . . . . $ 5,000

SECTION II. ANALYSIS OF CHANGES IN WORKING CAPITAL ACCOUNTS

Current Asset Item Increases (Decreases)
Cash . . . . $(27,000)
Accounts Receivable.   35,000
Merchandise Inventory   10,000
Net Increase (Decrease) in Current Asset Items . . . . $ 18,000

Current Liability Increases (Decreases)
Accounts Payable—Merchandise Suppliers $20,000
Accounts Payable—Other Suppliers   2,000
Salaries Payable   1,000
Net Increase (Decrease) in Current Liability Items   23,000
Net Decrease in Working Capital During the Year
   (Net Increase in Current Liability Items Minus Net
   Increase in Current Asset Items) . . . . $ 5,000

The calculation of rate of return on total capital is as follows:

$$\frac{\text{Net Income Plus Aftertax Interest Expense}}{\text{Average Total Assets}} = \frac{\$20,000 + (1 - .40) \times \$2,000}{\frac{1}{2}(\$160,000 + \$293,000)}$$

$$= 9.4 \text{ percent}$$

Thus, for each dollar of capital invested, Solinger Electric Corporation was able to earn 9.4 cents before payments to the suppliers of capital. The rate of return on total capital is sometimes called the *all-capital earnings rate*.

Disaggregating the All-Capital Earnings Rate   The all-capital earnings rate might be disaggregated into two other ratios as follows:

$$\begin{matrix} \text{All-Capital} \\ \text{Earnings Rate} \end{matrix} = \begin{matrix} \text{Profit Margin Ratio} \\ \text{(before interest} \\ \text{expense and related} \\ \text{income tax effects)} \end{matrix} \times \begin{matrix} \text{Total Assets} \\ \text{Turnover Ratio} \end{matrix}$$

$$\frac{\begin{matrix}\text{Net Income Plus} \\ \text{Aftertax Interest} \\ \text{Expense}\end{matrix}}{\begin{matrix}\text{Average} \\ \text{Total Assets}\end{matrix}} = \frac{\begin{matrix}\text{Net Income Plus} \\ \text{Aftertax Interest} \\ \text{Expense}\end{matrix}}{\text{Total Revenue}} \times \frac{\text{Total Revenue}}{\begin{matrix}\text{Average Total} \\ \text{Assets}\end{matrix}}$$

The profit margin ratio is a measure of a firm's ability to control the level of costs, or expenses, relative to revenues generated. By holding down costs, a firm will be able to increase the profits from a given amount of revenue and thereby improve its profit margin ratio. The total assets turnover ratio is a measure of a firm's ability to generate revenues from a particular level of investment in assets.

The rate of return on total capital of 9.4 percent for Solinger Electric Corporation is disaggregated into profit margin and total assets turnover ratios as follows:

$$9.4\% = \frac{\$\,21,200}{\$125,000} \times \frac{\$125,000}{\frac{1}{2}(\$160,000 + \$293,000)}$$

$$9.4\% = 17.0\% \times .552$$

For every dollar invested in assets, Solinger Electric Corporation was able to generate, on average, 55.2 cents of revenue. It was able to earn 17 cents per dollar of revenue generated (before payments to the suppliers of capital). Thus, its overall earnings rate on capital is 9.4 percent (= 17.0% × .552).

Improving the all-capital earnings rate can be accomplished by increasing the profit margin ratio, the rate of asset turnover, or both. Some firms, however, may have little flexibility in altering some of these components. For example, a firm committed under a three-year labor union contract may have little control over the wage paid. Or a firm operating under market- or government-imposed price controls may not be able to increase the prices of its products. In these cases, the opportunities for improving the profit margin ratio are limited. In order to increase the rate of return on capital employed, the level of investment in assets such as inventory, plant, and equipment must be reduced or, to put it another way, revenues per dollar of assets must be increased.

Rate of Return on Common Stock Equity

The investor in a firm's common stock is probably more interested in the *rate of return on common stock equity* than the rate of return on total capital. To determine the amount of earnings assignable to common stock equity, the earnings allocable to any preferred stock equity, usually the dividends on preferred stock declared during the period, must be deducted from net income. The capital provided during the period by common stockholders can be determined by averaging the aggregate par value of common stock, capital contributed in excess of par value on common stock, and retained earnings (or by deducting the equity of preferred stockholders from total stockholders' equity) at the beginning and end of the period.

The rate of return on common stock equity of Solinger Electric Corporation is calculated as:

$$\frac{\text{Net Income} - \text{Dividends on Preferred Stock}}{\text{Average Common Stockholders' Equity}} = \frac{\$20,000 - \$0}{\frac{1}{2}(\$115,000 + \$125,000)}$$

$$= 16.7 \text{ percent}$$

The rate of return on common stock equity of Solinger Electric Corporation, 16.7 percent, is larger in this case than the rate of return on the total capital (9.4 percent). The return to the common stock equity is larger than the rate of return on all capital because the payments to the other suppliers of capital (for example, creditors and preferred stockholders) are less than the overall 9.4 percent rate of return generated from capital that they provided. For example, the current liabilities carry no explicit interest payment. The common stock equity group benefited because capital contributed by others earned 9.4 percent but required a lower rate of interest payments or income distributions. This phenomenon is called *leverage* and is described next.

Leverage: Trading on the Equity Financing with debt and preferred stock to increase the return to the residual common shareholders' equity is referred to as *leverage* or *trading on the equity*. So long as a higher rate of return can be earned on capital than is paid for the use of that capital, then the rate of return to owners can be increased. Exhibit 3.4 explores this phenomenon. Leveraged Company and No-Debt Company both have $100,000 of assets. Leveraged Company borrows $40,000 at a 10-percent annual rate. No-Debt Company raises all its capital from owners. Both companies pay income taxes at the rate of 40 percent. In the "good" year, both companies earn $10,000 before interest charges (but after taxes except for tax effects of interest charges).[1] Leveraged Company's net income is $7,600 [= $10,000 − (1 − .40 tax rate) × 10 percent × $40,000 borrowed], which represents a rate of return of 12.7 percent on shareholders' equity. No-Debt Company's net income of $10,000 represents only a 10-percent return on shareholders' equity. In the "bad" year, income before interest charges is $4,000.[2] Leveraged Company's overall rate of return on assets is lower than

---

[1] That is, income before taxes and before interest charges is $16,667; $10,000 = (1 − .40) × $16,667.
[2] That is, income before taxes and before interest charges is $6,667; $4,000 = (1 − .40) × $6,667.

EXHIBIT 3.4
Effects of Leverage on Rate of Return of Shareholders' Equity (Income Tax Rate Is 40 Percent of Pretax Income)

	Long-Term Equities		Income after Taxes but before Interest Charges[a]	Aftertax Interest Charges[b]	Net Income	Rate of Return on Common Shareholders' Equity (Percent)	Rate of Return on Total Capital[c] (Percent)
	Long-Term Borrowing at 10 Percent Per Year	Shareholders' Equity					
Good Earnings Year							
Leveraged Company. . .	$40,000	$ 60,000	$10,000	$2,400	$ 7,600	12.7%	10.0%
No-Debt Company	—	100,000	10,000	—	10,000	10.0	10.0
Neutral Earnings Year							
Leveraged Company. . .	40,000	60,000	6,000	2,400	3,600	6.0	6.0
No-Debt Company	—	100,000	6,000	—	6,000	6.0	6.0
Bad Earnings Year							
Leveraged Company. . .	40,000	60,000	4,000	2,400	1,600	2.7	4.0
No-Debt Company	—	100,000	4,000	—	4,000	4.0	4.0

a But not including any income tax savings caused by interest charges. Income before taxes and interest for *good* year is $16,667; for *neutral* year is $10,000; for *bad* year is $6,667.
b $40,000 (borrowed) × .10 (interest rate) × [1 − .40 (income tax rate)]. The numbers shown in the preceding column for aftertax income do not include the effects of interest charges on taxes.
c In each year, the rate of return of total capital (all-capital earnings rate) is the same for both companies as the rate of return on common shareholders' equity for No-Debt Company, 10 percent, 6 percent, and 4 percent, respectively.

the rate of interest paid for borrowing so that the rate of return to owners drops below that of No-Debt Company. Clearly, leverage can work two ways. It can enhance owners' rates of return in good years but will make bad years worse than they would be without the borrowing.

Earnings per Share of Common Stock

Earnings per share of common stock is determined by dividing net income applicable to common shareholders by the average number of common shares outstanding during the period.

Earnings per share for Solinger Electric Corporation is calculated as follows:

$$\frac{\text{Net Income} - \text{Preferred Stock Dividend}}{\text{Weighted Average Number of Shares Outstanding During the Period}} = \frac{\$20,000 - \$0}{10,000 \text{ Shares}}$$

$$= \$2 \text{ per Share}$$

If a firm has securities outstanding that can be converted into or exchanged for common stock, it may be required to present two earnings-per-share amounts: *primary earnings per share* and *fully diluted earnings per share.* For example, some firms issue convertible bonds or convertible preferred stock that can be exchanged directly for shares of common stock. Also, many firms have employee stock option plans under which shares of the company's common stock may be acquired by employees under special arrangements. If these convertible securities were converted or stock options were exercised and additional shares of common stock were issued, the amount conventionally shown as earnings per share would probably decrease, or become *diluted.* When a firm has outstanding securities that, if exchanged for shares of common stock, would decrease earnings per share by 3 percent or more, a dual presentation of primary and fully diluted earnings per share is required.[3]

Primary Earnings per Share   In determining earnings per share, adjustments may be made to the conventionally determined amount for securities that are nearly the same as common stock. These securities are called *common stock equivalents.* Common stock equivalents are securities whose principal value arises from their capability of being exchanged for, or converted into, common stock rather than only for their own periodic cash yields over time. Stock options and warrants are always common stock equivalents. Convertible bonds and convertible preferred stock may or may not be common stock equivalents. A test is employed to determine if the return from these convertible securities at the date of their issue is substantially below the

---

[3]   Accounting Principles Board, "Earnings Per Share," *Opinion No. 15,* AICPA, 1969.

return available from other debt or preferred stock investments. If so, the presumption is that the securities derived their value primarily from their conversion privileges and are therefore common stock equivalents. Adjustments are made in calculating primary earnings per share for the dilutive effects of securities classified as common stock equivalents.

Fully Diluted Earnings per Share   As the title implies, fully diluted earnings per share indicates the maximum possible dilution that would occur if all options, warrants, and convertible securities outstanding at the end of the accounting period were exchanged for common stock. This amount, therefore, represents the maximum limit of possible dilution that could take place on the date of the balance sheet. All securities convertible into or exchangeable for common stock, whether or not classified as common stock equivalents, enter into the determination of fully diluted earnings per share.

Firms that do not have convertible or other potentially dilutive securities outstanding compute earnings per share in the conventional manner. Firms with outstanding securities that have the potential for materially diluting earnings per share as conventionally determined must present dual earnings-per-share amounts.

Earnings-per-share amounts are often compared with the market price of the stock to determine the rate of return currently being earned on the investment. This return is the starting point in investors' estimates of the rate that may be earned in the future. For example, assume that the common stock of Solinger Electric Corporation is selling for $25.00 per share at the end of 19X9. The earnings yield is 8 percent (= $2/$25). The *price-earnings ratio* (called the P/E ratio) is the reciprocal of the earnings yield: 12.5 to 1. The latter ratio is often presented in tables of stock market prices and in financial periodicals. The relationship is sometimes expressed by saying that "the stock is selling at 12.5 times earnings."

Comparisons of Earnings per Share Among Companies   Comparisons of rates of growth over time in earnings per share among companies can often be misleading. Assume, for example, that two companies earn identical rates of return on shareholders' equity, but one company declares and pays dividends equal to net income each year whereas the other retains all its earnings, paying no dividends. Assume that the number of common shares outstanding does not change for either company. Then, the earnings per share of the first company, the one paying dividends, will remain level, whereas the earnings per share amounts of the second company, the one retaining earnings, will grow over time (at a rate equal to the rate of return on shareholders' equity). The second company may appear to be doing better, but the earnings-per-share data indicate merely that the management of the second company has more assets per share with which to work. Problem **13** at the end of the chapter explores this phenomenon.

Inventory Turnover

In an effort to judge the efficiency of using various classes of assets, the turnover of these assets can be calculated. For example, a significant indicator of the efficiency of the operations of many businesses is the *inventory turnover ratio,* or the number of times the average inventory has been sold during the period. The calculation divides cost of goods sold by the average inventory during the period. The inventory turnover for Solinger Electric Corporation is calculated as follows:

$$\frac{\text{Cost of Goods Sold}}{\text{Average Inventory}} = \frac{\$60,000}{\frac{1}{2}(\$40,000 + \$50,000)} = 1.33 \text{ times per period}$$

The interpretation of the inventory turnover figure involves two opposing considerations. Management would like to sell as many goods as possible with a minimum of capital tied up in inventories. An increase in the rate of inventory turnover between periods would seem to indicate more profitable use of the investment in inventory. On the other hand, management does not want to have so little inventory on hand that shortages result and customers are turned away. An increase in the rate of inventory turnover in this case may mean a loss of customers and thereby offset any advantage gained by decreased investment in inventory. Some trade-offs are therefore required in deciding the optimum level of inventory for each firm and thus the desirable rate of inventory turnover.

The inventory turnover ratio is often expressed in terms of the average number of days inventory is on hand by dividing the inventory turnover ratio into 365 days. For Solinger Electric Corporation, the average number of days inventory is held is 274 days (= 365/1.33). Thus, inventory is held on average slightly over nine months before it is sold.

MEASURES OF SHORT-TERM LIQUIDITY

Investors or creditors whose claims will become payable in the near future are interested in the liquidity or "nearness to cash" of a firm's assets. One tool for predicting whether or not cash will be available when the claims become due is a budget of cash receipts and disbursements for several months or quarters in the future. Such budgets are often prepared for management and used internally for planning cash requirements. Chapter Nine discusses cash budgeting. Budgets of cash receipts and disbursements are not generally available for use by persons outside a firm. Investors must therefore use other tools in assessing liquidity.

The statement of changes in financial position is one published source of information for assessing liquidity. The amount of working capital provided by operations indicates the extent to which the operating activities have generated sufficient working capital to replace fixed assets and pay dividends. The statement also discloses the extent to which additional financing has been required for these purposes. For Solinger Electric Corporation, working capital provided by operations of $30,000 fell short of the uses of working capital needed for paying dividends and acquiring buildings and equipment. Therefore, additional long-term financing was necessary during the period.

Several ratios are also useful in assessing the current liquidity of the firm. The most popular are the current ratio, the quick ratio, and the accounts receivable turnover ratio.

Current Ratio

The *current ratio* is calculated by dividing current assets by current liabilities. It is commonly expressed as a ratio such as "2 to 1" or "2 : 1" meaning that current assets are twice as large as current liabilities. The current ratio of Solinger Electric Corporation on December 31, 19X9, is 1.59 to 1 (= $108,000/$68,000). A year earlier, on December 31, 19X8, the current ratio was 2.0 to 1 (= $90,000/$45,000).

This ratio is presumed to indicate the ability of the concern to meet its current obligations, and is therefore of particular significance to short-term creditors. Although an excess of current assets over current liabilities is generally considered desirable from the creditor's viewpoint, changes in the trend of the ratio may be difficult to interpret. For example, when the current ratio is larger than 1 to 1, an increase of equal amount in both current assets and current liabilities results in a decline in the ratio, while equal decreases result in an increased current ratio.

If a corporation has a particularly profitable year, the large current liability for income taxes may cause a decline in the current ratio. In a recession period, business is contracting, current liabilities are paid, and even though the current assets may be at a low point, the ratio will often go to high levels. In a boom period, just the reverse effect might occur. In other words, a very high current ratio may accompany unsatisfactory business conditions, whereas a falling ratio may accompany profitable operations.

Furthermore, the current ratio is susceptible to "window dressing"; that is, management can take deliberate steps to produce a financial statement that presents a better current ratio at the balance sheet date than the average or normal current ratio. For example, toward the close of a fiscal year normal purchases on account may be delayed. Or loans to officers, classified as noncurrent assets, may be collected and the proceeds used to reduce current liabilities. These actions may be taken so that the current ratio will appear as favorable as possible in the annual financial statements at the balance sheet date.

Although the current ratio is probably the most common ratio presented in statement analysis, there are limitations in its use as discussed above. Its trends are difficult to interpret and, if overemphasized, it can easily lead to undesirable business practices as well as misinterpretation of financial condition.

Quick Ratio

A variation of the current ratio, usually known as the *quick ratio* or *acid-test ratio,* is computed by including in the numerator of the fraction only those current assets that could be converted quickly into cash. The items customarily included are cash, marketable securities, and receivables, but it would be better to make a study of the facts in each case before deciding whether or not to include receivables and to exclude inventories. In some businesses the inventory of merchandise might be converted into cash more quickly than the receivables of other businesses.

Assuming that the accounts receivable of Solinger Electric Corporation are included but that merchandise inventory is excluded, the quick ratio is .85 to 1

($= \$58,000/\$68,000$) on December 31, 19X9, as compared to 1.11 to 1 ($= \$50,000/\$45,000$) on December 31, 19X8. Thus, both the current and the quick ratios indicate a decline in liquidity between the end of 19X8 and the end of 19X9.

Accounts Receivable Turnover

The rate at which accounts receivable turn over gives an indication of their nearness to being converted into cash. The accounts receivable turnover is calculated by dividing net sales on account by average accounts receivable. For Solinger Electric Corporation, the accounts receivable turnover assuming all sales are on account (that is, none are for immediate cash) is calculated as follows:

$$\frac{\text{Net Sales on Account}}{\text{Average Accounts Receivable}} = \frac{\$125,000}{\frac{1}{2}(\$20,000 + \$55,000)} = 3.33$$

The average number of days that accounts receivable are outstanding is 109.5 days ($= 365/3.33$). Thus, on average, accounts receivable are collected approximately three and one-half months after the date of sale. The interpretation of this average collection period depends on the terms of sale. If the terms of sale are "net 30 days," the accounts receivable turnover indicates that collections are not being made in accordance with the stated terms. Such a ratio would warrant a review of the credit and collection activity for an explanation and for possible corrective action. If, however, the firm offers terms of "net 6 months," the results indicate that accounts receivable are being handled well.

MEASURES OF LONG-TERM SOLVENCY

Measures of long-term solvency are used in assessing the firm's ability to meet interest and principal payments on long-term debt and similar obligations as they become due. If the payments cannot be made on time, the firm becomes *insolvent* and may have to be reorganized or liquidated.

Perhaps the best indicator of long-term solvency is a firm's ability to generate profits over a period of years. If a firm is profitable, it will either generate sufficient capital from operations or be able to obtain needed capital from creditors and owners. The measures of profitability discussed previously are therefore applicable for this purpose as well. Two other commonly used measures of long-term solvency are equity ratios and the number of times that interest charges are earned.

Equity Ratios

There are several variations in the equity ratio, but the one most commonly encountered is the *debt-equity* ratio. This ratio is calculated by dividing total liabilities (current and noncurrent) by total equities (liabilities plus shareholders' equity).

The debt-equity ratio of Solinger Electric Corporation was .57 (= $168,000/ $293,000) on December 31, 19X9, as compared to .28 (= $45,000/$160,000) on December 31, 19X8.

This ratio indicates the proportion of total capital supplied by creditors. In general, the higher the ratio, the higher the likelihood the firm may be unable to meet fixed interest and principal payments in the future. The decision for most firms is how much financial risk they can afford to assume. Funds obtained from issuing bonds or borrowing from a bank have a relatively low interest cost but require fixed, periodic payments.

In assessing the debt-equity ratio, analysts customarily vary the standard in direct relation to the stability of the firm's earnings. The more stable the earnings, the higher the debt-equity ratio that is considered acceptable or safe. The debt-equity ratios of public utilities are customarily high, on the order of 60 to 70 percent. The stability of public utility earnings makes these ratios acceptable to many investors who would be dissatisfied with such large leverage for firms with less stable earnings.

One variation of the equity ratio relates total stockholders' equity to total equities. This is, of course, the complement of the debt-equity ratio. Another variation of the equity ratio relates total long-term debt to total long-term financing (long-term debt plus stockholders' equity). Because several variations of the equity ratio appear in corporate annual reports, care in making comparisons of equity ratios among firms is necessary.

Interest Coverage: Times Interest Charges Earned

Another measure of long-term solvency is the *number of times that interest charges are earned,* or covered. This ratio is calculated by dividing net income before interest and income tax expenses by interest expense. For Solinger Electric Corporation, the times interest earned ratio is calculated as follows:

$$\frac{\text{Net Income Before Interest and Income Taxes}}{\text{Interest Expense}} = \frac{\$20,000 + \$2,000 + \$13,333}{\$2,000}$$

$$= 17.7 \text{ times}$$

The purpose of this ratio is to indicate the relative protection of bondholders and to assess the probability that the firm will be forced into receivership by a failure to meet required interest payments. If periodic repayments of principal on long-term liabilities are also required, the repayments might also be included in the denominator of the ratio. The ratio would then be described as the *number of times that fixed charges were earned,* or covered.

The times interest or fixed charges earned ratios can be criticized as measures for assessing solvency because the ratios use earnings rather than cash flows in the numerator. Interest and other fixed payment obligations are paid with cash, and not with earnings. When the value of the ratio is relatively low (for example, two to three times), some measure of cash flows, such as cash flows from operations, may be preferable in the numerator.

For convenient reference, Exhibit 3.5 summarizes the calculation of the ratios discussed in this chapter.

EXHIBIT 3.5
Summary of Important Financial Ratios and Sample Computations for Solinger Electric Corporation for 19X9

Ratio	Numerator	Denominator	Calculations for Solinger Electric Company
Rate of Return on Total Capital	Net Income + Interest Expense (net of tax effects)[a]	Average Total Assets or Equities During the Period	$\dfrac{\$20,000 + (1 - .40) \times \$2,000}{\frac{1}{2} \times (\$160,000 + \$293,000)} = 9.4$ percent[d] Note d
Rate of Return on Common Stock Equity	Net Income − Preferred Stock Dividends	Average Common Stockholders' Equity During the Period	$\dfrac{\$20,000 - \$0}{\frac{1}{2} \times (\$115,000 + \$125,000)} = 16.7$ percent Note e
Earnings per Share of Stock[b]	Net Income − Preferred Stock Dividends	Weighted Average Number of Common Shares Outstanding During the Period	$\dfrac{\$20,000 - \$0}{10,000 \text{ shares}} = \$2$ per share[e]
Inventory Turnover	Cost of Goods Sold	Average Inventory During the Period	$\dfrac{\$60,000}{\frac{1}{2} \times (\$40,000 + \$50,000)} = 1.33$ times
Current Ratio	Current Assets	Current Liabilities	$\dfrac{\$108,000}{\$68,000} = 1.59$ to 1 at year-end 19X9
Quick or Acid-Test Ratio	Highly Liquid Assets (ordinarily, cash, marketable securities, and receivables)[c]	Current Liabilities	$\dfrac{\$58,000}{\$68,000} = .85$ to 1 at year-end 19X9
Accounts Receivable Turnover	Net Sales on Account	Average Accounts Receivable During the Period	$\dfrac{\$125,000}{\frac{1}{2}(\$20,000 + \$55,000)} = 2.63$ times
Debt-Equity Ratio	Total Liabilities	Total Equities (liabilities plus stockholders' equity)	$\dfrac{\$168,000}{\$293,000} = 57.3$ percent at year-end 19X9 Note f
Times Interest Charges Earned	Net Income Before Interest and Income Taxes	Interest Expense	$\dfrac{\$20,000 + \$2,000 + \$13,333}{\$2,000} = 17.7$ times[f]

[a] If a consolidated subsidiary is not owned entirely by the parent corporation, the minority interest share of earnings must also be added back to net income.

[b] This calculation can be more complicated when there are convertible securities, options, or warrants outstanding.

[c] Receivables could conceivably be excluded for some firms and inventories included for others. Such refinements are seldom employed in practice.

[d] Assumes interest expense of $2,000 and an income tax rate of 40 percent of pretax income.

[e] Assumes that capital stock has par value of $10 per share and that 10,000 shares were outstanding throughout 19X9.

[f] If income tax rate is 40 percent and net income is $20,000, then income taxes are $20,000 [.40/(1 − .40)] = $13,333. Interest expenses (Note d) is $2,000.

LIMITATIONS OF RATIO ANALYSIS

The analytical computations discussed in this section have a number of limitations that should be kept in mind by anyone preparing or using them. Several of the more important limitations are:

1 The ratios are based on financial statement data and are therefore subject to the same criticisms as the financial statements (for example: use of acquisition cost rather than current replacement cost or net realizable value; the latitude permitted firms in selecting from among various generally accepted accounting principles).
2 Changes in many ratios are highly associated, or correlated, with each other. For example, the changes in the current ratio and quick ratio between two different times are generally in the same direction and approximately proportional. It is therefore not necessary to compute all the ratios to assess a particular factor.
3 When comparing the size of a ratio between periods for the same firm, one must recognize conditions that have changed between the periods being compared (for example, different product lines or geographical markets served, changes in economic conditions, changes in prices).
4 When comparing ratios of a particular firm with those of similar firms, one must recognize differences between the firms (for example, use of different methods of accounting, differences in the method of operations, type of financing, and so on).

Results of financial statement analyses cannot be used by themselves as direct indications of good or poor management. Such analyses merely indicate areas that might be investigated further. For example, a decrease in the turnover of raw materials inventory, ordinarily considered to be an undesirable trend, may reflect the accumulation of scarce materials that will keep the plant operating at full capacity during shortages when competitors have been forced to restrict operations or to close down. Ratios derived from financial statements must be combined with an investigation of the facts before valid conclusions can be drawn.

SUMMARY

Financial statement analysis assesses past performance and current financial position as a basis for predicting future rates of return and for estimating the risk or uncertainty of that return. Ratios are useful tools for expressing important financial relationships between items in the financial statements.

The relative weight given to measurements of profitability, liquidity, and solvency in assessing return and risk differs, however, depending on the nature of the investment. For many investors, the firm's profitability is the most important concern. The rates of return on total capital and on common stock equity provide useful measures of profitability. For relatively short-term lenders, liquidity is of paramount interest. The current and quick ratios are useful tools in this situation, although an analysis of cash or working capital flows is also helpful. Relatively long-term lenders are more concerned with a firm's ability to meet its obligations for fixed payments as they come due. The debt-equity ratio and the times interest (fixed charges) earned ratio are useful for assessing long-term solvency.

The potential limitations inherent in ratio analysis cannot be overemphasized. Ratios are used principally for detecting significant changes or unusual relationships between financial statement items. They serve as signals for further investigation. Particular caution must be exercised when comparing the size of a ratio with the corresponding ratio of an earlier period or with that of a similar firm in the same industry. Changed conditions or different operating environments may limit the comparability of the ratios in these, and other, cases.

QUESTIONS AND PROBLEMS

1 Review the meaning of the following concepts or terms discussed in this chapter.
  a Risk and return.
  b Profitability.
  c Liquidity.
  d Solvency.
  e Rate of return on total capital.
  f Rate of return on common stock equity.
  g Leverage.
  h Earnings per share.
  i Price-earnings ratio.
  j Current ratio.
  k Quick ratio.
  l Debt-equity ratio.
  m Times interest charges earned.

2 Is rate of return on common stock equity a measure for assessing the return from investing in a firm's common stock or for assessing the risk or uncertainty of that return? Explain.

3 Distinguish between liquidity and solvency.

4 Describe several factors that might limit the comparability of a firm's current ratio over several years.

5 Describe several factors that might limit the comparability of one firm's current ratio with that of another firm in the same industry.

6 Net income attributable to common stockholders' equity of Florida Corporation during 19X1 was $250,000. Earnings per share were $.50 during the period. The average common stockholders' equity during 19X1 was $2,500,000. The market price at year-end was $6.00 per share.
  a Determine the rate of return on common stockholders' equity for 19X1.
  b Determine the rate of return currently being earned on the market price of the stock (the ratio of earnings per common share to market price per common share).
  c Why is there a difference between the rates of return determined in a and b?

7 Under what circumstances will the rate of return on the common stock equity be more than the return on total capital? Under what circumstances will it be less?

8 The following comparative percentages were obtained from the financial statements of Companies M and N:

	Co. M	Co. N
Net Income to Sales	4%	6%
Net Income to Stockholders' Equity.	13%	10%

On the basis of this limited data, which company would appear to be more profitable? Explain.

9 The following data are taken from the 19X2 annual reports of the Alabama Company and Carolina Company:

	Alabama Co.	Carolina Co.
Sales.	$2,000,000	$2,400,000
Net Income	120,000	120,000
Average Total Assets During the Year	1,500,000	1,000,000

a Determine the rate of return on total assets for each company (assume that interest expenses and preferred dividends are zero).
b Disaggregate the rate of return in **a** into profit margin percentages and asset turnover ratios.
c Comment on the relative performance of the two companies.

10 The following data are taken from the financial statements of the Press Company:

	Dec. 31, 19X1	Dec. 31, 19X0
Current Assets	$210,000	$180,000
Noncurrent Assets	275,000	255,000
Current Liabilities	78,000	85,000
Long-Term Liabilities.	75,000	30,000
Common Stock (10,000 shares)	300,000	300,000
Retained Earnings.	32,000	20,000

	19X1 Operations
Net Income	$72,000
Interest Expense.	3,000
Income Taxes (40% rate)	48,000
Dividends Declared	60,000

Calculate the following ratios:
a Rate of return on total capital.
b Rate of return on stockholders' equity.
c Earnings per share of common stock.
d Current ratio (both dates).

e Times interest earned.

f Debt-equity ratio (both dates).

11 The Borrowing Company has total assets of $100,000 during the year. It has borrowed $20,000 at a 10 percent annual rate and pays income taxes at a rate of 40 percent of pretax income. Shareholders' equity is $80,000.

a What must net income be for the rate of return on shareholders' equity to equal the rate of return on total assets (the all-capital earnings rate)?

b What is the rate of return on shareholders' equity for the net income determined above in **a**?

c What must income before interest and income taxes be to achieve this net income?

d Repeat parts **a, b,** and **c** assuming borrowing of $80,000 and shareholders' equity of $20,000.

e Compare the results from the two different debt-equity relations. What generalizations can be made?

12 (CMA adapted) The Virgil Company is planning to invest $10 million in an expansion program that is expected to increase income before interest and taxes by $2.5 million. Currently, Virgil Company has total equities of $40 million, 25 percent of which is debt and 75 percent of which is shareholders' equity, represented by 1 million shares. The expansion can be financed with the issuance of 200,000 new shares at $50 each or by issuing long-term debt at an annual interest rate of 10 percent. The following is an excerpt from the most recent income statement.

Earnings Before Interest and Taxes	$10,500,000
Less: Interest Charges	500,000
Earnings Before Income Taxes	$10,000,000
Income Taxes (at 40 percent)	4,000,000
Net Income	$ 6,000,000

Assume that Virgil Company maintains its current earnings on its present assets, achieves the planned earnings from the new program, and that the tax rate remains at 40 percent.

a What will be earnings per share if the expansion is financed with debt?

b What will be earnings per share if the expansion is financed by issuing new shares?

c At what level of earnings before interest and taxes will earnings per share be the same, whichever of the two financing programs is used?

d At what level of earnings before interest and taxes will the rate of return on shareholders' equity be the same, whichever of the two financing plans is used?

13 Company A and Company B both start the year 19X0 with $1 million of shareholders' equity and 100,000 shares of common stock outstanding. During 19X0 both companies earn net income of $100,000, a rate of return of 10 percent on shareholders' equity. Company A declares and pays $100,000 of dividends to common shareholders at the end of 19X0, while Company B retains all its earnings, declaring no dividends. During 19X1, both companies earn net income equal to 10 percent of shareholders' equity at the beginning of 19X1.

a Compute earnings per share for Company A and for Company B for 19X0 and for 19X1.

b Compute the rate of growth in earnings per share for Company A and Company B, comparing earnings per share in 19X1 with earnings per share in 19X0.

   c Using the rate of growth in earnings per share as the criterion, which company's management appears to be doing a better job for its shareholders? Comment on this result.

   d Repeat parts **a, b,** and **c** assuming that during 19X1 Company B earns only 5 percent on the extra $100,000 investment while continuing to earn a 10-percent return on the initial $1 million investment.

14 The income statements and balance sheets of Illinois Corporation and Ohio Corporation are presented below:

Income Statements for the Year 19X0

	Illinois Corp.	Ohio Corp.
Sales.	$4,300,000	$3,000,000
Less Expenses:		
Cost of Goods Sold	$2,800,000	$1,400,000
Selling and Administrative Expenses	330,000	580,000
Interest Expense	100,000	200,000
Income Tax Expense	428,000	328,000
Total Expenses	$3,658,000	$2,508,000
Net Income.	$ 642,000	$ 492,000

Balance Sheets December 31, 19X0

	Illinois Corp.	Ohio Corp.
ASSETS		
Cash	$ 100,000	$ 50,000
Accounts Receivable (Net)	700,000	400,000
Merchandise Inventory	1,200,000	750,000
Plant and Equipment (Net)	4,000,000	4,800,000
Total Assets.	$6,000,000	$6,000,000
EQUITIES		
Accounts Payable	$ 572,000	$ 172,000
Income Taxes Payable	428,000	328,000
Long-Term Bonds Payable (10 percent)	1,000,000	2,000,000
Capital Stock	2,000,000	2,000,000
Retained Earnings.	2,000,000	1,500,000
Total Equities.	$6,000,000	$6,000,000

Assume that the balances in asset and equity accounts at year-end approximate the average balances during the period. The income tax rate is 40 percent. On the basis of this information, which company is:

a More profitable?
b More liquid?
c More secure in terms of long-term solvency?
Use financial ratios, as appropriate, in doing your analysis.

15 Presented below are comparative balance sheets, income statements, and statements of changes in financial position for Nykerk Electronics Corporation. You are asked to assess changes in the relative profitability, liquidity, and solvency of the firm over the three years 19X1 to 19X3. Point out areas of the firm's operations that you feel may be sources of trouble and should be explored further. The firm's marginal tax rate is 40 percent.

Nykerk Electronics Corporation
Comparative Balance Sheets
(Dollar Amounts in Millions)

	December 31			
	19X0	**19X1**	**19X2**	**19X3**
ASSETS				
Cash	$ 10	$ 10	$ 8	$10
Marketable Securities	—	4	—	2
Accounts Receivable (net)	26	36	46	76
Inventories	14	30	46	83
Total Current Assets	$ 50	$ 80	$100	$171
Land	$ 20	$ 30	$ 60	$ 60
Building	150	150	150	190
Equipment	70	192	276	313
Less Accumulated Depreciation	(40)	(52)	(66)	(84)
Total Noncurrent Assets	$200	$320	$420	$479
Total Assets	$250	$400	$520	$650
LIABILITIES AND STOCKHOLDERS' EQUITY				
Accounts Payable	$ 25	$ 30	$ 35	$ 50
Salaries Payable	10	13	15	20
Income Taxes Payable	5	7	10	20
Total Current Liabilities	$ 40	$ 50	$ 60	$ 90
Bonds Payable	50	50	100	150
Total Liabilities	$ 90	$100	$160	$240
Common Stock	$100	$150	$160	$160
Additional Paid-in Capital	20	100	120	120
Retained Earnings	40	50	80	130
Total Stockholders' Equity	$160	$300	$360	$410
Total Liabilities and Stockholders' Equity	$250	$400	$520	$650

Nykerk Electronics Corporation
Comparative Statements of
Changes in Financial Position
(Dollar Amounts in Millions)

	For the Year Ended December 31		
	19X1	19X2	19X3
Sources of Working Capital			
Operations:			
Net Income	$ 16	$ 40	$ 60
Add Back Expenses Not Using Working Capital:			
Depreciation	12	14	18
Working Capital Provided by Operations	$ 28	$ 54	$ 78
Other Sources:			
Issuance of Bonds	—	50	50
Issuance of Common Stock	130	30	—
Total Sources	$158	$134	$128
Uses of Working Capital			
Dividends	$ 6	$ 10	$ 10
Purchase of Land	10	30	—
Purchase of Building	—	—	40
Purchase of Equipment	122	84	37
Total Uses	$138	$124	$ 87
Net Change in Working Capital	$ 20	$ 10	$ 41

Analysis of Effects of Increases
(Decreases) in Working Capital

Cash	$ —	$ (2)	$ 2
Marketable Securities	4	(4)	2
Accounts Receivable	10	10	30
Inventories	16	16	37
Accounts Payable	(5)	(5)	(15)
Salaries Payable	(3)	(2)	(5)
Income Taxes Payable	(2)	(3)	(10)
Net Changes in Working Capital	$ 20	$ 10	$ 41

Nykerk Electronics Corporation
Comparative Income Statements
(Dollar Amounts in Millions)

	For the Year Ended December 31		
	19X1	**19X2**	**19X3**
Sales.	$210	$310	$475
Less Expenses:			
Cost of Goods Sold.	$121	$175	$280
Selling.	35	38	46
Administrative.	11	13	15
Depreciation.	12	14	18
Interest	5	10	16
Total	$184	$250	$375
Net Income Before Taxes.	$ 26	$ 60	$100
Income Tax Expense.	10	20	40
Net Income	$ 16	$ 40	$ 60

PART TWO
MANAGERIAL DECISION MAKING

CHAPTER 4
FUNDAMENTALS OF MANAGERIAL DECISION MAKING: INCREMENTAL ANALYSIS

Have you ever heard a manager of a retail store say, "February is always a terrible month for us; we always lose money in February?" If you were to ask such a manager why the store is kept open during February, the response is typically that "It would be bad business practice to shut down." The manager who responds in this fashion implicitly recognizes that the financial accounting statements, which report a loss for February, do not provide the appropriate information for making decisions of this kind. In making the decision to remain open, the manager must expect the cash taken in from sales to exceed the cash to be paid out to keep the store open that month. The decision to remain open is correct. The financial accounting statements that show losses are potentially misleading and, if improperly used, could result in incorrect decisions.

To make effective decisions, managers need to know two basic things: **(1)** the appropriate basis for making decisions and **(2)** the types of data to use and the types of data to ignore. This part of the book explores these two basic needs. In this chapter we discuss the principle of incremental analysis, which is required for most business decisions. In Chapter Five we consider some techniques for gathering information useful for decision making. Chapters Six and Seven illustrate the application of incremental analysis to a variety of business decisions. Part 3 of the book explores still further some techniques for gathering data, particularly cost data, in a business.

THE INCREMENTAL PRINCIPLE

Managerial decision making can be described as the process of making choices. If there are no alternatives, then there are no decisions to be made. If a choice is to be made between alternatives, then there must be differences between the alternatives. The analysis of the differences between alternatives is called *incremental analysis*.

To illustrate the important dimensions of incremental analysis, assume that the owner of a bowling alley must decide whether or not to reopen a pool room on the side of the bowling alley. The pool tables are in usable condition even though they have not been used for several years and have a book value of zero. Columns 1 and 3 of Exhibit 4.1 show the estimated monthly cash inflows and cash outflows for each of the two alternatives: operate and do not operate the pool room. In the sections that follow, we discuss the important dimensions of incremental analysis as they are illustrated in Exhibit 4.1. We shall ignore the effects of income taxes in this illustration. The impact of income taxes on business decisions is discussed in Chapters Seventeen and Eighteen.

EXHIBIT 4.1
Comparison of Monthly Cash Flows of Operating Bowling Alley With and Without Pool Room

	(1) Do Not Operate the Pool Room	(2) Incremental Cash Flows	(3) Operate the Pool Room
Cash Inflows			
Pool Table Rentals	—	$1,900	$1,900
Bowling Lane Fees	$8,000	(500)	7,500
Concessions	500	50	550
Total Inflows	$8,500	$1,450	$9,950
Cash Outflows			
Labor	$2,400	$ 800	$3,200
Supplies	200	100	300
Utilities	160	30	190
Rent[a]	1,000	—	1,000
Insurance[a]	100	—	100
Miscellaneous	140	70	210
Total Outflows	$4,000	$1,000	$5,000
Net Cash Inflows	$4,500	$ 450	$4,950

[a] Because these cash flows do not change, they can be ignored.

Focus on Cash Flows

The most difficult part of decision making is estimating the benefits and costs of each alternative. Although benefits and costs have several dimensions, the important dimensions for business decisions are the amounts and timing of cash flows. The emphasis on cash flow is fundamental for two reasons:

1 Cash is the medium of exchange. It can be used immediately to pay debts or dividends or to purchase equipment. Noncash assets can eventually be converted into cash, but this takes time and perhaps some additional costs.

2 Cash serves as a common, highly objective, measure of the benefits and costs of alternatives. If one alternative is stated in terms of units or inventory to be produced and another in terms of the number of machines to be acquired, then the alternatives are not expressed in a common measuring unit. Before these alternatives can be compared, their benefits and costs must be reexpressed in a common measuring unit. Cash flows are used as the common measuring unit because they represent the most objective and quantifiable measure of benefits and costs.

Net cash flow for a period is not the same as net income for the period (this point is discussed in Chapter Two). Net income is affected by sometimes arbitrary decisions concerning when revenue is recognized (for example, at time of production, at time of sale, at time of cash collection) and when and how expenses are recognized (for example, inventory cost flow assumption for determining costs of goods sold, depreciable life and depreciation method for determining depreciation expense).

Focus on Future Amounts

The cash flows of interest in decisions are those expected to occur in the future. These include the expected cash inflows from pool table and bowling lane rentals, and the expected cash outflows for labor, supplies, utilities, and similar operating costs. The amount of a past cash outflow, called a *sunk cost,* is never directly relevant to a decision. This concept is a difficult one for many decision makers to understand. For example, assume that one year ago the manager of the bowling alley paid $3,000 to refinish the pool tables in anticipation of reopening the pool room at some time in the future. Should this cash flow now be considered in the decision? The answer is *no,* because the past cash outflow represents a sunk cost. The firm should select the alternative with the greatest incremental effect on net cash inflows *from its given current cash position.* That current cash position is less than it otherwise might be had the pool tables not been refinished (that is, had the past cash outflow not have taken place). Nonetheless, it is the current cash position from which we measure the incremental cash flows. Current cash position is the same regardless of which alternative is selected. Some managers, in an effort to overcome the results of unwise investment decisions in the past, will attempt to "recover their investment" and include sunk costs in their analyses. Such behavior often leads to incorrect decisions.

The amounts of past cash flows, although not relevant to decisions, may provide useful information for estimating the amounts of future cash flows. For example, if the pool tables must be refinished once each year, the cost incurred last year might be helpful in predicting the required cash outflow for refinishing the tables in the future. The past cash outflow is useful for prediction but, by itself, is not relevant to the decision.

Focus on Cash Flows That Will Differ

The future cash flows that will affect a decision are those that will differ between alternatives. In Exhibit 4.1, these are referred to as *incremental cash flows.* The cash outflows for rent and insurance, although they are future cash flows, do not affect the decision because they are the same regardless of which alternative is selected. The remaining cash outflows, as well as the cash inflows, are all relevant to the decision because they differ between the alternatives. The correct decision in this case is to operate the pool room, because that action will lead to incremental net cash inflows of $450 more than the alternative of not operating the pool room.

Figure 4.1 summarizes the types of cash flows relevant to decisions. The cash flows of interest are those in the southeast quadrant, those future cash flows that will differ between alternatives.

Opportunity Costs

One concept frequently encountered, particularly in economics, is that of *opportunity cost*. The opportunity cost of an asset already owned by a company is a measure of the amount of cash foregone, or given up, by using the asset for its intended use rather than for its best alternative use. In the pool room example, we assume that the pool tables had no resale value or alternative uses. The opportunity cost of using the pool tables is therefore zero. Suppose, however, that the pool tables could be rented to

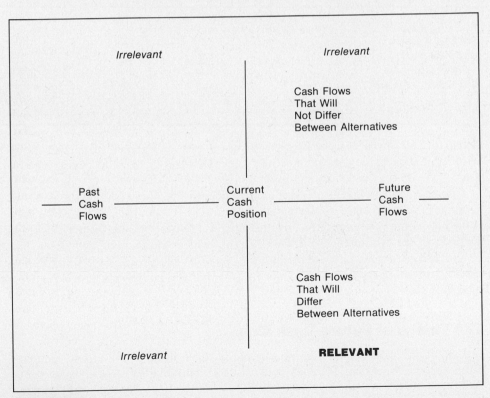

FIGURE 4.1
Cash Flows Relevant
to Decisions

EXHIBIT 4.2
Comparison of Monthly Cash
Flows of Operating Bowling Alley
With and Without Pool Room
(Pool Tables Can be Leased for $600 a Year)

	(1) Do Not Operate the Pool Room	(2) Incremental Cash Flows	(3) Operate the Pool Room
Cash Inflows			
Pool Table Rentals	—	$1,900	$1,900
Bowling Lane Rentals	$8,000	(500)	7,500
Concessions	500	50	550
Rental of Pool Tables.	600	(600)	—
Total Inflows.	$9,100	$ 850	$9,950
Cash Outflows			
Labor	$2,400	$ 800	$3,200
Supplies	200	100	300
Utilities	160	30	190
Rent	1,000	—	1,000
Insurance	100	—	100
Miscellaneous	140	70	210
Total Outflows	$4,000	$1,000	$5,000
Net Cash Inflows	$5,100	$ (150)	$4,950

others for $600 a year if a decision is made not to operate the pool room. The opportunity cost of using the pool tables is $600, the cash foregone from the best alternative use.

Opportunity costs can be analyzed in the same way as other cash flows. Exhibit 4.2 compares the two pool room alternatives assuming that the tables are leased for $600 if the pool room is not operated.[1] By operating the pool room, the incorrect decision in this case, the firm foregoes the $600 cash inflow from renting the pool tables. This is reflected as a negative incremental cash flow in column (2). Opportunity costs are important factors to be taken into consideration in comparing cash flows from alternatives.

The Timing of Future Cash Flows

In Exhibit 4.1, we assumed that the incremental cash flows of $450 from operating, rather than not operating, the pool room would remain roughly constant each month.

---

[1]   We assume here that the pool tables will have zero salvage value after several years of leasing if the pool room is reopened. This unrealistic assumption allows us to illustrate a relatively simple analysis.

We therefore did not need to be concerned with the timing of the cash flows. For many alternatives, we must analyze differences in both the *amounts* and the *timing* of cash flows.

Suppose that a manager must decide what kind of new company car to purchase. The alternatives have been narrowed to buying from a certain manufacturer who offers the same car either with a gasoline or with a diesel engine. The gasoline model costs less. However, diesel fuel is cheaper than gasoline and the diesel model gets more miles per gallon than does the gasoline model. Specifically, the gasoline model costs $6,000 and gets 25 miles per gallon, whereas the diesel model costs $7,200 and gets 30 miles per gallon. Gasoline is expected to cost $.70 a gallon and diesel fuel is expected to cost $.50 a gallon. The cars will be used for four years and will be driven a total of 120,000 miles in that four-year period. The mileage is not expected to be the same each year. Rather, it is expected that 36,000 miles will be driven in the first year, 30,000 miles will be driven in the second and third years, and 24,000 miles will be driven in the fourth year. To simplify the analysis, we assume that the cars will have no salvage value at the end of the four-year period and that all other operating costs of the cars will be identical.

Exhibit 4.3 shows the derivation of all cost and cash flow data required for making the purchase decision and also shows the depreciation that will be recorded each year in the financial statements. Computing the periodic cash flows correctly for each alternative presents no conceptual difficulties, but does require clear thinking and careful work.

Exhibit 4.4 shows the effects both on the income statement and on cash outflows of the two alternatives. First note that *total* expense over the four-year period for each alternative is exactly the same as *total* cash outflow. There is, however, a significant difference in the *timing* of the expenses and the *timing* of the cash flow expenditures within the four years. In each year the gasoline model shows higher expenses than does the diesel model, with total expenses being $160 larger over the four-year period. A manager who looks only at effects on the income statement would probably conclude that the diesel model should be acquired because it results in lower reported expenses each year. The pattern of cash outflows is, however, much different from the pattern of expenses. The diesel model requires an additional $1,200 expenditure at the start of the first year but saves $1,360 in fuel outlays over the life of the car. Over the four years, the diesel requires $160 less cash.

All that is required to make the correct managerial decision is proper analysis of column (6) in Exhibit 4.4. After some effort is devoted to deriving the costs and expenditures in Exhibit 4.3 and the other columns of Exhibit 4.4, the alternatives are completely summarized in column (6): if an incremental $1,200 is spent initially, then incremental cash savings in each of the next four years will be $408, $340, $340, and $272, respectively.

Which car should be acquired? This turns out to be the same question as "Does it make sense to spend $1,200 today in order to save $408, $340, $340, and $272, respectively, over the next four years?" Chapter Seven presents the method for deriving the analytical answer to this question. We shall see that under realistic conditions, the firm should prefer to buy the gasoline model. Even though the total costs are $160 larger

EXHIBIT 4.3
Costs of Acquiring and Operating
Gasoline and Diesel Automobiles
(Ignoring Income Taxes)

GASOLINE AUTOMOBILE
ACQUISITION COST: $6,000

Year	Miles Driven (1)	Fuel Consumption at 25 mpg (in gal) (2)	Fuel Cost at $.70/gal (3)	Depreciation Shown in Income in Statement[a] (4)
1........	36,000	1,440	$1,008	$1,800
2........	30,000	1,200	840	1,500
3........	30,000	1,200	840	1,500
4........	24,000	960	672	1,200
	120,000	4,800	$3,360	$6,000

DIESEL AUTOMOBILE
ACQUISITION COST: $7,200

Year	Miles Driven	Fuel Consumption at 30 mpg (in gal)	Fuel Cost at $.50/gal	Depreciation Shown in Income in Statement[a]
1........	36,000	1,200	$ 600	$2,160
2........	30,000	1,000	500	1,800
3........	30,000	1,000	500	1,800
4........	24,000	800	400	1,440
	120,000	4,000	$2,000	$7,200

[a] Units of Production (Mileage) Basis = [Amount in Column (1)/120,000 miles] × Acquisition Cost.

over the life of the gasoline car, the pattern of cash outflows favors its purchase so long as the firm can earn 5.5 percent or more per year for its cash investments. To see this, assume that cash can be invested at 5.5 percent or more per year. Then this firm should acquire the gasoline model and can invest the $1,200 extra cash it saved by not acquiring the diesel. The $1,200 and the interest earned on it will more than pay for the extra fuel costs over the four years of $1,360 (= $3,360 − $2,000).

COST BEHAVIOR

Identifying the ways that various cost items[2] behave in response to changes in levels of activities facilitates the estimation of the effects of various alternatives on future cash flows. The response of costs to levels of activity can be described in one of four basic ways. These are illustrated in Figure 4.2.

[2]   We use the terms *cash outflow* and *cost* synonymously in this section. The latter term is more commonly used in discussions of cost behavior patterns.

EXHIBIT 4.4
**Comparison of Income Statement
and Cash Flow Effects of Gasoline
and Diesel Automobiles
(Ignoring Income Taxes)**

	Expenses for Income Statement (Fuel + Depreciation)			Cash Outflows for Managerial Decisions (Fuel Costs Only After Outlay to Purchase)		
	Gasoline Model[a] (1)	Diesel Model[a] (2)	Excess of Expenses for Gasoline over Diesel Model (3) = (1) − (2)	Gasoline[b] (4)	Diesel[b] (5)	Excess (or Savings) of Cash Flows for Gasoline over Diesel Model (6) = (4) − (5)
Initial Outlay	—	—	—	$6,000	$7,200	($1,200)
1	$2,808	$2,760	$ 48	1,008	600	408
2	2,340	2,300	40	840	500	340
3	2,340	2,300	40	840	500	340
4	1,872	1,840	32	672	400	272
Total . . .	$9,360	$9,200	$160	$9,360	$9,200	$ 160

[a] Sum of columns (3) and (4) in Exhibit 4.3.
[b] Column (3) in Exhibit 4.3 after initial outlay to purchase.

Variable Costs

Variable costs change as the volume of activity changes and are zero when production is zero. Raw materials costs are typically variable costs. When workers are paid on an hourly basis, labor costs are also a variable cost. In accounting, variable costs are usually assumed to be linear, such as shown by the line $0A$ in Figure 4.2(A). Strictly speaking, variable costs can be nonlinear such as in lines $0B$ and $0C$, but nonlinear costs curves are seldom used by accountants or managers. Thus, for convenience, a *variable cost,* in accounting, typically means a cost that is constant per unit of activity or one that is strictly proportional to output. For example, if raw materials cost is variable and one unit of final product requires $5 of raw material, then 10 units of final product should require $50 of raw material and, in general, X units of final product should require $5X$ of raw material costs.

Example Miller Corporation is a manufacturer of umbrellas. A special order for 10,000 umbrellas has been received and Miller Corporation must decide whether to accept or reject the order. Past experience indicates that each umbrella requires $.60 of raw materials and $1.40 of labor costs. These variable costs of $2.00 per unit are expected to continue in the near future. Knowing that raw materials and labor costs are variable permits Miller Corporation to estimate the amount, $20,000, of future cash outflows if the special order is accepted. That is, $20,000 is 10,000 units times $2.00 per unit.

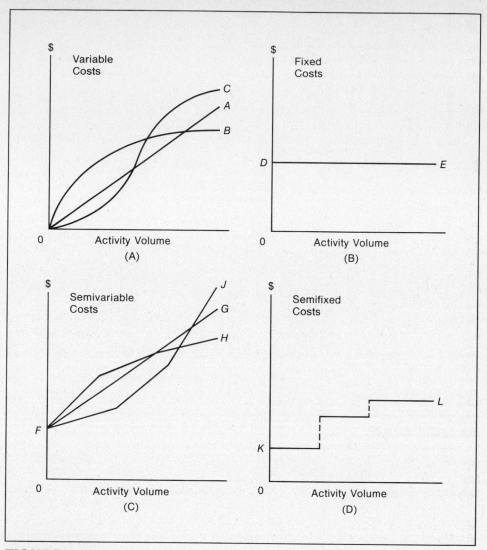

FIGURE 4.2
Patterns of
Cost Behavior

Fixed Costs

Fixed costs remain constant during an accounting period within a reasonable range of activity (sometimes called the *relevant range*). Costs quoted as a price per unit of time, such as rent per month, insurance premiums per year, and supervisors' salaries per week, are typical examples of costs fixed for a period. Fixed costs are represented in Figure 4.2(B) by line *DE*.

Example   Miller Corporation in the example above rents its factory facilities for $10,000 per month. The rental fee is the same regardless of the level of activity. Knowing that the rent behaves in a fixed cost pattern for any level of activity permits Miller Corporation to exclude rent from the analysis of incremental cash flows. Whether the special order is accepted or not, the cash outflow for rent will be $10,000 per month.

Fixed costs are not fixed forever, merely for the specific period. Many "fixed" costs will change if the plant is expanded or an extra production shift is added. Chapter Five discusses fixed costs at greater length.

Semivariable Costs

Semivariable costs, by convention, refer to costs that have fixed and variable components such as represented by lines *FG*, *FH*, and *FJ* in Figure 4.2(C). Repair and maintenance costs or utility costs exemplify semivariable cost behavior. There is a fixed cost (0*F*) to provide a minimum repair service capability within a plant, such as for regular salaries of repair personnel. As repairs are actually performed, costs increase as materials are used and overtime wages are paid. Utility companies typically charge a fixed minimum per month (0*F*) for providing service and an extra charge for uses of the service above some minimum amount. If the charge per unit of, say, electricity decreases at certain stages as consumption increases, then the cost curve would look like line *FH*. If the per unit charge increases at certain stages as usage increases, then the costs would look like *FJ*. Semivariable costs are often called *mixed costs*.

Example   Miller Corporation has a highly automated plant. There is a direct relationship between the hours of electricity used and the number of units produced. Past experience suggests that electricity costs behave in a semivariable pattern as follows:

Up to 50,000 units.	$300
Next 20,000 units	.006/unit
Next 20,000 units	.005/unit

Miller Corporation expects to produce 65,000 units if a special order is not accepted. The expected cash outflow for electricity would be $390 [= $300 + (15,000 × $.006)]. If the special order is accepted, production will be 75,000 units (= 65,000 + 10,000). Electricity costs will therefore be $445 [= $300 + (20,000 × $.006) + (5,000 × $.005)]. The incremental cash outflow for electricity from accepting the special order is $55 (= $445 − $390).

Semifixed Costs

The term *semifixed costs,* by convention, refers to costs that increase in steps, such as shown by the broken line *KL* in Figure 4.2(D). If a quality control inspector can examine 1,000 units per day, then inspection costs will be semifixed with a break for every 1,000 units per day examined. Neither the vertical nor horizontal breaks, or steps, need be of equal size. Semifixed costs are sometimes described as *step costs*.

Example   Miller Corporation hires one quality control inspector for each 25,000 units produced. The annual salary is $12,000 per inspector. Acceptance of the special order will increase production from 65,000 to 75,000 units. Because inspection of the additional 10,000 units can be handled with the three inspectors already hired, there are no incremental cash flows from quality control inspection if the special order is accepted.

Cost Behavior and Decisions

While it is often true that variable costs are relevant to decisions while fixed costs are not, it is not always true. For example, acceptance of a special order may require the rental of additional manufacturing and warehousing facilities for $3,000 per month. The rental cost behaves in a semifixed, or step, pattern. It is relevant to the decision because the required cash outflow will increase if the special order is accepted. The behavior of various cost items must be studied carefully to determine the *incremental effect* of various alternatives on cash flows.

USING DATA IN MAKING DECISIONS

The distinction between cash flows that will change (incremental flows) and those that will not change as a result of an action is essential for managerial decisions. Most of the data developed in a business are, however, developed for several different purposes. The data are used in financial reports to shareholders, in income tax reports to governments, in reviewing performance of various divisions or departments, as well as for management's decisions. No one method of organizing data will work best for all these different uses. Decision makers must often adapt reported data to the task at hand. In this section, we examine some recurring managerial decisions and illustrate how the incremental principle is used in making decisions.

Abandonment Decisions

Managers must decide when to drop products from the product line and when to abandon sales territories. The incremental principle implies the following analysis. If the cash inflow from the sale of a product is greater than the incremental cash outlay required to produce the sales, then the product generates a positive net cash inflow and should be continued. This is the correct decision even though it may show a loss in financial statements because of the allocation of various overhead costs. Many items of overhead, such as utilities and executive salaries, will not be affected by abandoning a single product. If the product more than covers its incremental costs, and if no other alternative use of the production and sales facilities exists, then the product should be retained.

Consider the data in Exhibit 4.5 on three product lines. Fixed costs (rent and executive salaries) of the entire company are $28,000 per month. For purposes of calculating net income, these costs are allocated to product lines on the basis of sales. Because fixed costs ($28,000) are 20 percent of sales ($140,000), each product line is charged with 20

EXHIBIT 4.5
Data for Abandonment Decision

INCOME STATEMENT ANALYSIS

	Product R	Product S	Product T	Total
Sales.	$10,000	$80,000	$50,000	$140,000
Less Variable Costs.	8,500	51,000	31,500	91,000
Total Contribution Margin	$ 1,500	$29,000	$18,500	$ 49,000
Less Allocated Portion of Fixed Costs[a].	2,000	16,000	10,000	28,000
Net Income (Loss).	($ 500)	$13,000	$ 8,500	$ 21,000

INCREMENTAL CASH FLOW ANALYSIS

	Products S and T Only	Incremental Cash Flows	Products R, S, and T
Cash Inflows from Sales. .	$130,000	$10,000	$140,000
Cash Outflows for Variable Costs	(82,500)	(8,500)	(91,000)
Cash Outflows for Fixed Costs.	(28,000)	—	(28,000)
Net Cash Flows.	$ 19,500	$ 1,500	$ 21,000

[a] Allocations of the $28,000 of fixed costs made in proportion to sales: 20 percent (= $28,000/$140,000) of sales dollars charged to each product as fixed costs.

percent of its dollar sales as fixed costs. Thus, for example, product R is charged with $2,000 (= .20 × $10,000 sales) of fixed costs.

Product R shows a reported loss of $500 for the month, and unsophisticated managers might want to drop it from the line. If product R is dropped, net cash inflows will be $1,500 less than the $21,000 total shown if product R is retained, because the incremental cash inflows from product R are $1,500 larger than the incremental outlays required to produce it. The firm might want to investigate more profitable uses of the facilities used in producing and selling product R because its contribution margin appears to be the weakest of the three products. Until such alternatives emerge, it pays to continue producing and selling product R.

Note the arrangement of costs in the Income Statement Analysis portion of Exhibit 4.5. Rather than classifying the costs by their nature (for example, cost of goods sold, selling and administrative), we classified them according to their behavior patterns. An important subtotal results from this arrangement: the contribution margin. The *total contribution margin* is equal to sales less variable costs. It indicates the amount of sales dollars left over after variable costs are paid; it is the contribution to covering fixed costs and to providing a profit. More important for our purposes, the total contribution margin for product R of $1,500 is equal to the incremental cash flows from keeping product R in the product line as shown in the lower part of Exhibit 4.5. For many decision situations, the total contribution margin will be equal to the incremental cash flows. We shall often find it useful, therefore, to focus on total contribution margin amounts.

Replacement Decisions

Chapter One illustrated a problem that arises when financial accounting does not accurately report the effects of sound managerial decisions. The example concerned machine replacement. A new machine is available that costs $15,000. The book value of a machine now owned is $20,000. Both machines will produce 1,000 units of product each year for the next five years. The new machine is so much more efficient than the old one that it is expected to save $4,000 per year in variable costs over the next five years in producing the 1,000 units each year. We observed that it will pay to spend $15,000 today for the new machine in order to save $4,000 a year for five years. In making a replacement decision, the book value of the old machine, $20,000 in this case, is a sunk cost and should not be considered. The incremental cash flows are all that matter.

Rationing Scarce Capacity

Firms often find that, at least in the short run, there is insufficient capacity in the manufacturing plant to produce all that could be profitably sold. Suppose, for example, that machine A is used to produce products L, M, and N. Only 100 hours of time is available on machine A this period. The time requirements for each of the three products, their selling prices and variable costs are shown in Exhibit 4.6. Even though product N has a per-unit contribution margin percentage of 63 percent (contribution margin per unit is 63 percent of selling price per unit), and product L has a per-unit contribution margin percentage of only 40 percent, product L is still the best product to produce given the capacity constraint on machine A. Product L contributes $4.00 per hour (= $2.00 per unit/.5 hours per unit) of time used on machine A, whereas product N contributes only $2.50 per hour of time used on machine A. Incremental analysis indicates that the total contribution margin from using machine A to produce product L is $400, whereas the contribution from producing product M is $350 and from producing product N is $250.

When there is only one scarce resource, time on machine A in this example, the decision is easy to make: choose the product that gives the largest contribution per unit of the scarce resource used. When there are several scarce resources and each product uses different proportions of each of them, then the computational problem becomes more difficult. *Mathematical programming* is the name of the tool used to solve such constrained decision problems.

Acceptance of Special Orders

Sometimes, a firm has unused capacity and is confronted by an opportunity to sell a special order of goods at a price lower than average total cost. Should such an order be accepted? As the previous discussion suggests, if the price offered is greater than the

EXHIBIT 4.6
Rationing Scarce Capacity
(Machine A Is Available only 100
Hours per Week)

	Product		
	L	**M**	**N**
Time Required on Machine A per Unit Produced	0.5 hr	2.0 hr	4.0 hr
Selling Price per Unit.	$5.00	$12.00	$16.00
Variable Costs to Produce One Unit.	3.00	5.00	6.00
Contribution Margin per Unit	$2.00	$ 7.00	$10.00
Contribution Margin Percentage (Contribution Margin/Selling Price)	40%[a]	58%	63%
Contribution Margin Per Hour on Machine A (Contribution Margin Per Unit/Time Requirement in Hours). . .	$4.00/hr[b]	$3.50/hr	$2.50/hr
Total Contribution Margin from Using 100 Hours on Machine A	$400	$350	$250

[a] $2.00/$5.00 = 40%.
[b] $2.00/.5 hour = $4.00 per hour.

incremental cost of producing the order, the firm increases profits by accepting the order. Here again, only the incremental or differential costs must be considered. In this case, the incremental costs would be the change in total costs associated with accepting this order.

In special order decisions, the manager must also consider the effect of the special order on current sales of the primary product. To accept the special order at the lower price and thereby to lose equal sales at a higher unit price clearly would not be a good decision. Only if the two markets are separate, or can be separated, is the special order worthwhile. There must also be idle capacity so that the new order can be produced with facilities that would otherwise be unused. In general, correct short-run decisions result from undertaking projects where incremental cash inflows exceed incremental cash outflows.

The Value of Information

What is additional information worth? This question often arises in business, and its answer requires incremental analysis. For example, should an additional marketing study based on expanded sampling of a new product by consumers be undertaken, or should the company discontinue its marketing tests and proceed directly to full-scale production? In the absence of the other information, the manager uses incremental cash flow analysis, perhaps in an uncertain environment, to decide on the best course of action and the expected payoff (net cash flows) to that decision. Call that expected payoff P. Now assume that new information becomes available. The manager again uses incremental cash flow analysis to decide the best course of action using that information and the expected payoff to that decision. Let Q represent the present expected payoff before the decision is made but with the new information available at the time the decision is made. The only difference between the two cases is the absence of the additional information in the first case with expected payoff P and its availability in the second case with expected payoff Q. Thus the expected value of the additional information is the difference $Q - P$. If the information costs less than $Q - P$, then it is worth acquiring. Otherwise, the manager expects to be better off acting without acquiring the new information.

To illustrate, suppose that Bulloch sells hot dogs at football games. Hot dogs cost $.30 each and are sold for $.50 each. Bulloch buys either 10,000 or 20,000 for each game. If it rains, Bulloch can sell 10,000; and if the weather is clear, Bulloch can sell 20,000. Any hot dogs left over at the end of the day are worthless. In the absence of a weather forecast, Bulloch assumes that rain and clear weather are equally probable. That is, it rains half the time and it is clear half the time. How much should Bulloch be willing to pay for a perfect weather forecast on the day of a football game?

EXHIBIT 4.7
Payoff to Bulloch Depending on Weather from Two Purchasing Strategies

Purchases		Clear Weather		
		Sales		
in Units	**Cost in Dollars**	**Units**	**Dollars**	**Contribution Margin**
10,000	$3,000	10,000	$ 5,000	$2,000
20,000	$6,000	20,000	$10,000	$4,000

Purchases		Rainy Weather		
		Sales		
In Units	**Cost in Dollars**	**Units**	**Dollars**	**Contribution Margin**
10,000	$3,000	10,000	$5,000	$2,000
20,000	$6,000	10,000	$5,000	($1,000)

Exhibit 4.7 analyzes Bulloch's cash flows for all possible combinations of weather conditions and numbers of hot dogs purchased. Buying 10,000 hot dogs per game always yields a contribution margin of $2,000 (= $5,000 − $3,000). Buying 20,000 hot dogs yields a negative contribution margin of $1,000 (= $5,000 − $6,000) when it rains and a positive contribution margin of $4,000 (= $10,000 − $6,000) when it is clear. In the absence of a weather forecast, Bulloch believes that rainy weather and clear weather are equally likely, so that the expected contribution margin if 20,000 hot dogs are purchased is $1,500 (= .5 × $1,000 negative + .5 × $4,000 positive). Because the expected payoff from buying 20,000 hot dogs, $1,500, is less than that from buying 10,000 hot dogs, Bulloch would always buy 10,000 hot dogs and expect to have a $2,000 contribution margin.

If a perfect weather forecast is available, Bulloch will learn the days (half the time) when it will rain for sure; on those days Bulloch will purchase 10,000 hot dogs and the contribution margin will be $2,000. The other half of the time, Bulloch will learn that the weather will be clear so that 20,000 hot dogs will be purchased and the contribution margin will be $4,000. On average, the expected contribution margin is $3,000 (= .5 × $2,000 + .5 × $4,000). Because the expected payoff with the forecast is $3,000 and the expected payoff without the forecast is $2,000, the expected value of the new information from the forecast is $1,000 (= $3,000 − $2,000). Bulloch could pay up to $1,000 per game for a perfect weather forecast and expect to be better off in the long run as a result.

The maximum value of information can thus be calculated as the incremental change in the expected contribution margin resulting from the use of the information.

SUMMARY

Decision makers must understand which costs are relevant for a specific decision. To be relevant for a given decision, a cost must affect a future cash flow and must differ between alternatives being considered. All past costs are sunk costs and are irrelevant. Incremental cash flows are the difference in total future cash flows between alternatives. In making decisions, managers should choose the alternative with the largest excess of benefits measured by cash inflows over costs measured by cash outflows. When the inflows and outflows do not occur at the same times for the considered alternatives, then compound interest techniques are used to make the flows comparable. These techniques are discussed in Chapter Seven.

QUESTIONS AND PROBLEMS

1 Review the meaning of the following concepts or terms introduced in this chapter.
  a Incremental principle.
  b Net cash flow versus net income.
  c Opportunity cost.
  d Sunk cost.
  e Variable cost.
  f Fixed cost.
  g Semivariable (mixed) cost.
  h Semifixed (step) cost.
  i Value of information.
  j Relevant range.
  k Relevant cost.
  l Total contribution margin.

2 Assuming that there are no income taxes, how should each of the following costs enter into a decision to replace old equipment?
  a Book value of old equipment.
  b Disposal value of old equipment.
  c Cost of new equipment.

3 Solve Problem **5** in Chapter One.

4 Below is a list of costs. **(1)** Classify each of them as (strictly) variable, fixed, semivariable, semifixed (step) costs, or some combination of these. **(2)** Refer to Figure 4.2. Which of the lines shown there is most representative of the costs? If none is, sketch an appropriate line. Be sure to label the horizontal axis in the graph with the name of the variable causing, or most closely related to, the cost. **(3)** For each cost with a fixed component—all but strictly variable—attempt to judge the time period over which the cost is fixed.
  a Depreciation of an office building.
  b Costs of raw materials used in producing a firm's products.
  c Wages of delivery truck drivers. One driver is required, on average, for each $1 million of sales.
  d Leasing costs of a delivery truck, which is $250 per month and $.18 per mile.
  e Costs of advertising in the local newspaper.
  f Fees paid to a management consulting firm that is advising the company on a new internal reporting system to take into account rapidly changing prices in the industry.
  g Costs of internal programs for teaching recent business school graduates about the operating procedures and policies of the firm.
  h Local property taxes on land and buildings.
  i Compensation of sales staff on straight commission.
  j Compensation of sales staff on salary plus commission.
  k Compensation of sales staff with commission rates that increase as sales increase: 4 percent of the first $100,000 of annual sales and 6 percent of all sales in excess of $100,000. If total commissions earned by a salesperson are less than $10,000, then the salary for the year is $10,000, in lieu of commissions.
  l A book publisher agrees to pay an author $1,000 when a manuscript is submitted to the publisher. When the book is published, the author will receive royalties equal to 10 percent of the publisher's receipts from bookstores.
  m Same data as **l**, but the first $1,000 of royalties, if any, is not paid to the author but is used to repay the publisher for the $1,000 advance paid to the author earlier.
  n Fees paid to an independent firm of CPAs for auditing and attesting to financial statements.

5 Data from the shipping department of Weston Company for the last two months are as follows:

	Number of Packages Shipped	Shipping Department Costs
November	3,000	$4,500
December	4,500	6,000

  a Using graph paper, or carefully drawing on other paper, sketch a line describing these costs as a function of the number of packages shipped.

b The graph should indicate that these shipping costs are semivariable. What is the apparent fixed cost per month of running the shipping department during November and December?

c What is the apparent variable cost per package shipped?

6 Data from the shipping department of Kennelly Company for the last three months are as follows:

	Number of Packages Shipped	Shipping Department Costs
June	2,000	$3,500
July.	2,500	4,000
August.	1,500	2,900

What is the apparent relation between shipping department costs and the number of packages shipped? (Hint: Your analysis should find that costs are semivariable: there are both fixed costs and variable cost components.)

7 The management of the Glide-Rite Company, which manufactures No-Stick spray starch, plans to increase sales by cutting the sales price in 19X1. You are given the following data for 19X0 and estimates for 19X1.

	500,000 Cans (19X0 Sales)	750,000 Cans (Projected 19X1 Sales)
Sales Price per Can.	$.890	$.790
Cost per Can	.675	.600

a Compute the incremental cash inflows and cash outflows if the price cut takes place.

b Should the selling price be cut for 19X1? Explain.

8. The Brunson Grain Company has four large milling machines of approximately equal capacity. Each was run at close to its full capacity during 19X5. Each machine is depreciated separately using an accelerated method. Data for each machine are as follows:

	No. 1	No. 2	No. 3	No. 4
Date Acquired	1/1/X0	1/1/X1	1/1/X3	1/1/X4
Cost	$50,000	$60,000	$75,000	$80,000
Operating Costs: 19X5				
Labor	$20,000	$18,000	$22,000	$21,500
Materials	5,000	6,000	4,500	3,000
Maintenance	1,000	1,000	700	550
Depreciation.	3,363	5,454	10,910	13,091
Total	$29,363	$30,454	$38,110	$38,141

Activity in 19X6 is expected to be less than in 19X5 so that one machine is to be dropped from service. It has been proposed that No. 4 should be that machine on the grounds that it has the highest operating cost. Do you agree or disagree with this proposal? Why or why not?

9 The Dodd Manufacturing Company produces machinery of which part No. 301 is a sub-assembly. Part No. 301 is presently being produced by the Dodd Manufacturing Company in its own shops, but the West Products Company offers to supply it at a cost of $200 per 500 units. An analysis of the costs of producing part No. 301 by the Dodd Manufacturing Company reveals the following information:

	Cost per 500 Units
Direct (Variable) Material	$ 65
Direct (Variable) Labor.	90
Other Variable Costs	22
Fixed Costs[a]	110
Total	$287

[a] Fixed overhead consists largely of depreciation on general purpose equipment and factory buildings.

a Should the offer by the West Products Company be accepted if the plant is operating well below capacity?

b Should the offer be accepted if the price is reduced to $165 per 500 units?

c If other profitable uses can be found for the facilities now used in turning out part No. 301, what maximum purchase price should be accepted?

10 The Exton Company is considering making a bid on a contract to supply the Defense Department with 500,000 gallons of chemicals. The capacity of the plant is 10,000,000 gallons a year, and Exton is currently producing and selling at the rate of 8,500,000 gallons a year. The fixed costs of the plant total $5,400,000 per year regardless of the level of operations. The variable costs of chemicals of this type is approximately $2 per gallon. The sales manager says that a bid of no more than $1,200,000 would probably enable the company to get the contract.

a Should a bid of $1,200,000 be made? Explain.

b Assume that the present production is being sold at an average price of $3 per gallon and average variable costs equal $2 per gallon. Present income statements as they would appear **(i)** if the government contract were not obtained and **(ii)** if the government contract were obtained at a bid of $1,200,000.

11 The Milky Way Company produces a precision part for use in rockets, missiles, and a variety of other products. In the first half of 19X0, it operated at 80 percent of capacity and produced 160,000 units. Manufacturing costs in that period were as follows:

Raw Material	$430,000
Direct Labor.	770,000
Other Variable Costs	150,000
Fixed Costs	450,000

The parts were all sold at a price of $14 per unit.

The AMF Aircraft Company offers to buy as many units of the part as the Milky Way Company can supply at a price of $10 per unit. It is estimated that to increase operations to a 100-percent capacity level would increase office and administrative costs by $50,000 for a six-month period. Management feels that sales to AMF at this price will not affect their ability to reach the previous level of sales at the regular price and that there are no legal restrictions on selling at the lower price.

Present a schedule indicating if it would be worthwhile to accept the AMF offer. (Show your calculations.)

12 On the last day of last year Oliver bought a new, special-purpose machine for $150,000 for use during a project that will last for three years. One week after purchase of the machine a salesperson from another company showed Oliver a different machine that costs $180,000. The latter machine is technically superior. Neither machine will have any salvage or disposal value in three years. As compared to the "old machine," the new machine will save $55,000 per year in operating costs—raw materials and labor. The "old" machine can be sold now for only $50,000.

Oliver is confident that the new machine would save $55,000 each year for three years but hesitates to recognize a loss on the old machine by selling it now. "I will use the old machine for three years and I will have no loss; by using the machine for three years, I'll get my money out of it."

Annual cash operating costs for the old machine are $80,000; this amount does not include any charge for depreciation. Sales, all for cash, will be $1 million each year. All other expenses will amount to $700,000 each year and will be paid for in cash. The amount of all other cash expenses is independent of the machine used. The machine in question is the only long-term asset that Oliver uses. Ignore income taxes and compound interest considerations.

  a Prepare a statement of cash receipts and disbursements for each of the three years assuming that the old machine is kept.

  b Repeat **a** assuming that the new machine is acquired.

  c What is the total net difference between cash flows over the three years of the alternatives? Which one has the higher cash flows?

  d Prepare an income statement for each of the three years assuming that the old machine is kept and straight-line depreciation is used.

  e Repeat **d** assuming that the new machine is acquired and straight-line depreciation is used.

  f What is the total net difference between incomes over the three years of the two alternatives, and which one has the larger total income?

  g How would the answers to parts **c** and **f** differ if the old machine had cost $200,000 instead of $150,000? $300,000 instead of $150,000?

  h What is the name for the kind of cost represented by the $150,000 cost of the old machine just after its purchase?

13 The Norwood Printing Company operates a medium-sized printing shop. In May, it received an inquiry from a prospective customer about its prices for furnishing an advertising booklet in quantities of 2,000 copies, 8,000 copies, and 15,000 copies. After analyzing the job, the estimating staff furnished the following estimates of cost:

Setup Costs for Job.	$500
Material Cost per 100 Booklets	50
Direct Labor Cost per 100 Booklets	45

In the company's cost accounting records, fixed costs are allocated to jobs on a direct-labor-cost basis, at a rate of 80 percent of direct labor costs. Thus, for example, if direct labor costs for a job are $100, the job would also be charged with $80 of fixed costs. The company seeks to make a profit of 10 percent of the bid price on each order. The printing shop was operating with sufficient excess capacity to fill the orders up to 15,000 copies.

  a Assuming that the bid was to be based on average *total* cost (including fixed costs charged to products at the rate of 80 percent of direct labor costs) and a 10-percent profit margin, what price would be quoted for each quantity? (Show computations for this and all other parts of the question.)

b By how much would income of the firm increase if the price quoted in part **a** for 8,000 copies were accepted?

c Repeat part **b** for 15,000 copies.

d What is the minimum bid that should be accepted for 2,000 copies? For 8,000 copies?

14 The Able Bakery now purchases frozen precut cookie dough at a cost of $.03 per cookie. Management is considering purchasing either an automatic or semiautomatic cookie cutter. If the automatic machine is purchased, the annual fixed costs will be $8,000. In addition, there will be a $.010 variable cost per cookie cut. Use of a semiautomatic machine will lead to $4,500 in fixed costs per year, plus $.015 of variable cost per cookie.

a At what volume of operations will the total annual costs incurred by using the semi-automatic machine equal outside purchase costs?

b At what volume of operations will the total annual costs incurred by using the automatic machine equal outside purchase costs?

c Which of the three alternatives is least costly if annual production volume is 600,000 cookies?

d Which of the three alternatives is least costly if annual production volume is 800,000 cookies?

e At which level of production volume are the costs incurred by using the two machines equal?

15 The Brozen Manufacturing Company maintains a fleet of 300 automobiles for use by its sales staff. It has determined that buying the cars is cheaper than leasing them. The automobiles cost $5,000 each and are depreciated using the double-declining-balance method over three years. Various cost data are given in the schedule below. Cars are driven about 10,000 miles a year. At the beginning of the fifth year, the cars can be sold for $1,575. The Brozen Manufacturing Company has to choose a replacement policy: should it sell cars and buy new ones every year, every two years, every three years, or every four years? It wishes to choose the policy that implies the lowest annual cash outlay per year. The age structure of the fleet is constant. That is, under a two-year replacement policy, 150 cars will be sold and re-

Brozen Manufacturing Company
Assumed Cost Data for
Each Year of Life

	Year			
	1	**2**	**3**	**4**
Market Value at Beginning of Year. . . .	$5,000	$3,750	$2,800	$2,100
Depreciation Expenses for Year	$3,333	$1,111	$ 556	—
Gas and Oil Costs.	2,000	2,200	2,400	$2,600
Maintenance Costs	75	75	75	75
Repair Costs	25	100	200	300
Tire Costs	0	100	150	175
Insurance	160	140	110	80
	$5,593	$3,726	$3,491	$3,230

placed every year, under a three-year replacement policy 100 cars will be sold and replaced every year, or under a four-year policy, 75 cars will be sold and replaced every year. All gains realized on sale of used cars are taxed at 40 percent, as is all other income. There is sufficient other income that all depreciation and operating expenses reduce taxable income for the year of the expense.

a What is the replacement policy that leads to lowest net cash outflow, taking taxes into account?

b Why can we ignore the time value of money in this case?

16 The Eastern States Railroad (ESRR) has four locomotives, each of approximately equal capability. Each was run full time during the past year. Each locomotive is depreciated separately using an accelerated method. Operating data for each locomotive for the past year are as follows:

	Locomotive			
	A	**B**	**C**	**D**
Operating Costs:				
Labor	$15,500	$15,800	$15,900	$15,900
Maintenance and Repairs.	5,000	3,500	3,500	4,200
Depreciation.	13,250	15,750	15,000	20,500
Total	$33,750	$35,050	$34,400	$40,600

Locomotive A originally cost $220,000; locomotive B cost $250,000; locomotives C and D were purchased for $240,000 each.

Rail traffic is expected to decrease so that one locomotive will be put on a standby basis. The vice-president in charge of operations has suggested that locomotive D be put on standby because it has the highest operating costs. Do you agree? If not, which one should be put on standby and why?

17 The Jamie Company bought a machine 10 years ago for $42,000 and has been depreciating it on a straight-line basis. The book value of the machine now is $12,000. The machine can be sold today for $7,000. The Jamie Company must decide whether to keep the machine, sell it and purchase a new machine, or trade it in on a new machine. The income tax rate paid by the Jamie Company is 40 percent.

If the Jamie Company sells the machine today, the loss of disposal can be used to offset other income.

a What is the relevant opportunity cost of keeping the machine rather than selling it?

b Suppose that the new machine can be bought for $50,000 cash or for $40,000 cash and the old machine (traded in). What is the opportunity cost of the new machine?

18 The Horwell Company is considering accepting an order for a product that is not in its present product line. The machinery and labor needed to fill the order are available, but there is some question concerning the incremental materials and labor costs. The data available to management are summarized below.

(1) The order requires 5,000 units of Halcyon. Although Halcyon is no longer used in Horwell's regular manufacturing process, some 20,000 units are presently on hand. These units were acquired for $100,000 as part of a special purchase. Replacement costs would amount to $220,000, but the best offer Horwell has received for the 20,000 units of Halcyon is $80,000.

(2) The order requires 7,000 units of Miserly. Because Horwell uses Miserly regularly, there is a large inventory on hand. Although the average price per unit of Miserly in inventory is $3, the price has recently risen to $3.80. If 7,000 units are used to fill a special order, the purchasing department will have to reorder two months earlier than planned, incurring an expected cost per unit of $2.90. The drop in price is due to seasonal factors, which should drive the price of Miserly down to $2.50 about six weeks or two months after the price falls to $2.90.

(3) One thousand units of Sludge, a by-product of a present Horwell manufacturing process, are needed. Generally, it costs Horwell $.02 per unit to dispose of Sludge.

(4) The order will require 15 hours of supervisory time at $12 per hour. At present, the 10 workers who would be involved in filling the orders are working 37 hours per week at $6 and being paid $4 per hour standby wages for three hours per week. The order should require 90 hours of worker time and must be filled within two weeks. Overtime rates are 150 percent of the regular wage rate.

What is the relevant cost for the special order of:

a Halcyon?
b Miserly?
c Sludge?
d Labor?

19 The value of information is defined as the payoff of the optimal action taken in the presence of information (available before a decision is made) minus the payoff to the optimal action taken in the absence of information. To show that this definition has application outside the business environment, the next two problems consider a medical context.

Suppose that a patient visits a doctor's office and that the doctor decides on the basis of the signs that the patient's appendix should be removed immediately. Meanwhile the doctor orders a white-cell blood count. The doctor decides that the appendix must be removed no matter what the blood count happens to be.

a What is the value of the information (in the cost/benefit sense discussed in this chapter) about the blood count to the doctor?
b Why might the doctor order the test anyway?

20 (Refer to the first paragraph of the preceding question.) If a mother with Rh negative blood bears a child whose father is Rh positive, then there may be complications (the medical name is *erythroblastosis foetalis*) in subsequent pregnancies unless a shot of Rhogam is given to the mother soon after the first child is born. Assume that 87 percent of all people have Rh positive blood, that 13 percent have Rh negative blood, and that matings occur randomly among blood types. Assume that the complications occur in 5 percent of the matings where the mother is negative and the father is positive and that the cost of the complications is $12,000.

a In what percentage of matings could the complication arise?
b What is the expected cost per mating from the complication if the Rhogam shot is not given to any mothers?
c What is the cost per mating if every mother is given the shot, which costs $50?
d Comparing your answers to b and c, what is the optimal action in the absence of information about blood types and what is the expected cost per mating from following that action?
e Suppose that information on blood types is known. What is the expected cost per mating if the Rhogam shot is given only in matings with Rh negative mothers and Rh positive fathers?

    f Comparing your answers in **d** and **e,** what is the value of perfect information about blood types?

    g How does your answer depend on the (arbitrary) cost of $12,000 assigned to the discomfort and possible death that may result if the complications arise?

21 The pathology laboratory at Presbyterian University Hospital is staffed by a medical doctor (pathologist) and several laboratory technicians. The lab contains equipment of two basic kinds: microscopes and the like for doing individual tests, and sophisticated testing equipment for doing 12 tests simultaneously on batches of specimens from several patients. Below is a list of costs. **(1)** Classify each of them as (strictly) variable, fixed, semivariable, semifixed (step) costs, or a combination of these. **(2)** Refer to Figure 4.2. Which of the lines shown there is most representative of the costs? If none is, sketch an appropriate line. Be sure to label the horizontal axis in the graph with the name of the variable causing, or most closely related to, the cost. **(3)** For each cost with a fixed component—all but strictly variable—attempt to judge the time period over which the cost is fixed.

    a Salary of the pathologist.

    b Hourly wages of the lab technicians.

    c Depreciation of a microscope.

    d Leasing costs of sophisticated testing equipment. The equipment is leased for $2,000 per month plus a charge of $1 per batch of specimens run plus a charge of $.10 per specimen in each batch.

    e Malpractice insurance premiums for the workers in the lab.

    f Repair services for owned equipment. (The specialists perform repair services in all sections of the hospital and work where necessary.)

    g Supplies for tests.

    h Costs incurred in on-the-job training of new technicians.

    i Fees paid to a local university professor of accounting who has been helping the hospital director to understand the causes of total costs shown for each month.

22 The sales representatives of the Piney Paper Company have secured two orders, either of which, in addition to regular orders, will keep the plant operating at capacity through the slack season. One order is for 200,000 printed placemats and the other is for 300,000 sheets of engraved office stationery. The proposed prices are $.0070 per mat for the placemats and $.0062 per sheet for the stationery. Cost estimates are as follows:

	Mats Cost per 100 Mats	Stationery Cost per 100 Sheets
Raw Materials.	$0.3550	$0.2775
Labor costs:		
Variable	0.1100	0.0993
Fixed.	0.0300	0.0089
Manufacturing Overhead Costs:		
Variable	0.0430	0.0330
Fixed.	0.0370	0.0523
Selling expense (to procure order)	0.0900	0.0912
Administrative expense (to procure order)	0.0950	0.0878
Total cost per 100 items.	$0.7600	$0.6500
Selling price per 100 items	$0.7000	$0.6200

Based on the above data, prepare schedules to assist the management of Piney Paper Company in making its decision.

23 In the mid-1970s, Peugeot offered its automobile Model 504 in two versions—one with a gasoline engine and one with a diesel engine. The gasoline version had a list price of $6,270 and the diesel version, a list price of $6,986. Assume for the purposes of this exercise that the list prices were actually charged in purchase transactions. According to federal EPA mileage tests, the gasoline version gets, on average, 23 miles per gallon of gasoline, which costs $.60 per gallon. The diesel version gets, on average, 30 miles per gallon of diesel fuel, which costs $.45 per gallon. Assume that a purchaser had decided to acquire one of these two cars and that other operating costs of the two models of cars are identical. The purchaser expects to drive 12,000 miles a year for five years before disposing of the car. The gasoline version is expected to have a resale value five years hence of $1,500 and the diesel, a resale value of $1,675.

Assume that costs per gallon of gasoline and diesel fuel are expected to remain constant over the five years.

a Compile a list of incremental cash flows for each year relevant to the purchaser who wants to decide which of the two models of Peugeot cars to buy.

b Assume that each of the cars can be purchased for a 10-percent discount from list price. Repeat the instructions in **a**.

c Assume that fuel costs increase at the rate of 10 percent per year and that full list price is paid. Repeat part **a**.

24 The Vancil Company has one machine on which it can produce either of two products, Y or Z. Sales demand for both products is such that the machine could operate at full capacity on either of the products and all output could be sold at current prices. Product Y requires 2 hours of machine time per unit of output and Product Z requires 4 hours of machine time per unit of output. Machine time (depreciation) is charged to products at the rate of $8 per hour.

The following information summarizes the per-unit cash inflows and costs of Products Y and Z.

	Per Unit	
	Product Y	**Product Z**
Selling Price.	$60	$110
Materials	$ 9	$ 11
Labor	3	5
Machine Depreciation[a].	16	32
Allocated Portion of Fixed Factory Costs[b].	12	20
Total Cost of Unit Sold.	$40	$ 68
Gross Margin per Unit	$20	$ 42

[a] This item under these circumstances could be referred to as "variable factory costs."
[b] Allocated in proportion to (direct) labor costs.

Selling costs are the same whether product Y or Z, or both, are produced, and can be ignored. Should Vancil Company plan to produce product Y, product Z, or some mixture of both? Why?

25 Prior to 19X0, Kahn Wholesalers Company had not kept departmental income statements. In order to achieve better management control, the Company decided to install department-by-department accounts. At the end of 19X0, the new accounts showed that although the business as a whole was profitable, the Dry Goods Department had shown a substantial loss. The income statement for the Dry Goods Department, shown here, reports on operations for 19X0.

Kahn Wholesalers Company
Dry Goods Department
Partial Income Statement for 19X0

Net Sales.	$500,000	
Cost of Goods Sold.	375,000	
Gross Margin		$125,000
Expenses:		
Payroll, Direct Labor, and Supervision	$ 33,000	
Commissions of Sales Staff[a]	30,000	
Rent[b]	26,000	
State Taxes[c]	3,000	
Insurance on Inventory	4,000	
Depreciation[d]	7,000	
Administration and General Office[e]	22,000	
Interest for Inventory Carrying Costs[f]	5,000	
Total Expenses.		130,000
Loss Before Allocation of Income Taxes.		($ 5,000)

[a] All sales staff are compensated on straight commission, at a uniform 6 percent of all sales.
[b] Rent is charged to departments on a square-foot basis. The Company rents an entire building, and the Dry Goods Department occupies 15 percent of the building.
[c] Assessed annually on the basis of average inventory on hand each month.
[d] Eight and one-half percent of cost of departmental equipment.
[e] Allocated on basis of departmental sales as a fraction of total Company sales.
[f] Based on average inventory quantity multiplied by the Company's borrowing rate for three-month loans.

Analysis of these results has led to a suggestion that the Dry Goods Department be closed down. Members of the management team agree that keeping the Dry Goods Department is not essential to maintaining good customer relations and supporting the rest of the Company's business. That is, eliminating the Dry Goods Department is expected to have no effect on the amount of business done by the other departments.

What action do you recommend to management of Kahn Wholesalers Company and why?

26 (CMA adapted.) Vendo Company operates the concession stands at the University football stadium. Records of past sales indicate that there are basically four kinds of football weather, that sales of hot dogs depend on the weather, and that the percentage of football games played in each kind of weather is as follows:

Weather	Percentage of Game Days	Hot Dogs Sold
Snow.	10%	10,000
Rain	20	20,000
Clear/Warm	40	30,000
Clear/Cold.	30	40,000

Hot dogs cost Vendo Company $.30 each and are sold for $.50. Hot dogs unsold at the end of each game are worthless. Ignore income taxes.

    a Prepare a table with four rows and four columns showing the contribution margin from each of the four purchasing strategies of buying 10,000, 20,000, 30,000, or 40,000 hot dogs and the four weather conditions, snow, rain, clear/warm, and clear/cold.

    b Assuming that the chances of snow, rain, clear/warm, and clear/cold are 10 percent, 20 percent, 40 percent, and 30 percent, respectively, compute the expected contribution margin from each of the following purchasing strategies:

        (i)   Buy 10,000 hot dogs.

        (ii)   Buy 20,000 hot dogs.

        (iii) Buy 30,000 hot dogs.

        (iv) Buy 40,000 hot dogs.

    c What is the optimal purchasing strategy in the absence of a weather forecast, and what is the expected contribution margin from following this strategy? (This answer will be the largest of the four expected payoffs computed in **b**.)

    d If Vendo had a perfect weather forecast for each game, it would buy 10,000 hot dogs when snow is predicted, 20,000 when rain is predicted, 30,000 when clear/warm is predicted, and 40,000 when clear/cold is predicted. What is the expected average contribution margin per football game assuming the availability of a perfect weather forecast and that the four kinds of weather will occur in the frequencies 10, 20, 40, and 30 percent?

    e What is the expected dollar value to Vendo Company of a perfect weather forecast per football game? That is, what is the expected dollar value of the information from a perfect weather forecast?

27 Refer to the data in Problem **22** of Chapter Fifteen for the Pepper River Electric Company. Assume that the current oil-burning plant has a book value of $4 million, but no net salvage value—the costs of abandoning the plant are just offset by the proceeds from selling scrap materials. Assume that the Company pays income taxes at the rate of 40 percent of taxable income and can use the loss from disposal of the oil-burning plant to offset other taxable income and reduce current tax payments. What is the incremental cost of scrapping the oil-burning plant, building a coal-burning plant, and using the coal-burning plant to generate electricity?

28*The Liquid Chemical Company manufactured and sold a range of high-grade products throughout Great Britain. Many of these products required careful packing, and the company had always made a feature of the special properties of the containers used. They had a special patented lining, made from a material known as GHL, and the firm operated a department especially to maintain its containers in good condition and to make new ones to replace those that were past repair.

    Mr. Walsh, the general manager, had for some time suspected that the firm might save money, and get equally good service, by buying its containers from an outside source. After careful inquiries, he approached a firm specializing in container production, Packages, Ltd., and asked for a quotation from it. At the same time he asked Mr. Dyer, his chief accountant, to let him have an up-to-date statement of the cost of operating the container department.

    Within a few days, the quotation from Packages, Ltd., came in. The firm was prepared to supply all the new containers required—at that time running at the rate of 3,000 a year—for £12,500** a year, the contract to run for a guaranteed term of five years and thereafter to be renewable from year to year. If the required number of containers increased, the contract price would be increased proportionally. Additionally, and irrespective of whether the

---

** At the time of this case, one British pound (£) was worth about $2.35.

above contract was concluded or not, Packages, Ltd., undertook to carry out purely maintenance work on containers, short of replacement, for a sum of £3,750 a year, on the same contract terms.

Mr. Walsh compared these figures with the cost figures prepared by Mr. Dyer, covering a year's operations of the container department of the Liquid Chemical Company, which were as follows:

Materials		£7,000
Labour		5,000
Department Overheads:		
Manager's Salary	£ 800	
Rent	450	
Depreciation of Machinery	1,500	
Maintenance of Machinery	360	
Other Expenses	1,575	
		4,685
		£16,685
Proportion of General Administrative Overheads		2,250
Total Cost of Department for Year		£18,935

Walsh's conclusion was that no time should be lost in closing the department and in entering into the contracts offered by Packages, Ltd. However, he felt bound to give the manager of the department, Mr. Duffy, an opportunity to question this conclusion before he acted on it. He therefore called him in and put the facts before him, at the same time making it clear that Duffy's own position was not in jeopardy; for even if his department were closed, there was another managerial position shortly becoming vacant to which he could be moved without loss of pay or prospects.

Mr. Duffy looked thoughtful and asked for time to think the matter over. The next morning, he asked to speak to Mr. Walsh again, and said he thought there were a number of considerations that ought to be borne in mind before his department was closed. "For instance," he said, "what will you do with the machinery? It cost £12,000 four years ago, but you'd be lucky if you got £2,000 for it now, even though it's good for another four years at least. And then there's the stock of GHL (a special chemical) we bought a year ago. That cost us £10,000, and at the rate we're using it now, it'll last us another four years or so. We used up about one fifth of it last year. Dyer's figure of £7,000 for materials probably includes about £2,000 for GHL. But it'll be tricky stuff to handle if we don't use it up. We bought it for £50 a ton, and you couldn't buy it today for less than £60. But you wouldn't have more than £40 a ton left if you sold it, after you'd covered all the handling expenses."

Walsh thought that Dyer ought to be present during this discussion. He called him in and put Duffy's points to him. "I don't much like all this conjecture," Dyer said. "I think my figures are pretty conclusive. Besides, if we are going to have all this talk about 'what will happen if,' don't forget the problem of space we're faced with. We're paying £850 a year in rent for a warehouse a couple of miles away. If we closed Duffy's department, we'd have all the warehouse space we need without renting."

"That's a good point," said Walsh. "Though I must say, I'm a bit worried about the workers if we close the department. I don't think we can find room for any of them elsewhere in the firm. I could see whether Packages can take any of them. But some of them are getting on. There's Walters and Hines, for example. They've been with us since they left school 40 years ago. I'd feel bound to give them a small pension—£150 a year each, say."

Duffy showed some relief at this. "But I still don't like Dyer's figures," he said. "What about this £2,250 for general administrative overheads? You surely don't expect to sack anyone in the general office if I'm closed, do you?" "Probably not," said Dyer, "but someone has to pay for these costs. We can't ignore them when we look at an individual department, because if we do that with each department in turn, we shall finish up by convincing ourselves that directors, accountants, typists, stationery, and the like don't have to be paid for. And they do, believe me."

"Well, I think we've thrashed this out pretty fully," said Walsh, "but I've been turning over in my mind the possibility of perhaps keeping on the maintenance work ourselves. What are your views on that, Duffy?"

"I don't know," said Duffy, "but it's worth looking into. We shouldn't need any machinery for that, and I could hand the supervision over to a foreman. You'd save £300 a year there, say. You'd only need about one fifth of the workers, but you could keep on the oldest. You wouldn't save any space, so I suppose the rent would be the same. I shouldn't think the other expenses would be more than £650 a year." "What about materials?" asked Walsh. "We use about 10 percent of the total on maintenance," Duffy replied.

"Well, I've told Packages, Ltd., that I'd let them know my decision within a week," said Walsh. "I'll let you know what I decide to do before I write to them."

a Assuming that no additional information can be readily obtained, what action should be taken?

b What, if any, additional information do you think is necessary for a sound decision?

CHAPTER 5
COST ESTIMATION

Managerial decision making requires estimates of the incremental future cash flows for each alternative under consideration. As we discussed in Chapter Four, the estimation of future cash flows is made easier if the behavior of cost items can be identified. The cash flow associated with a variable cost item changes as the level of activity changes, whereas the cash flow associated with a fixed cost item remains constant regardless of the level of activity. In this chapter we consider several techniques for estimating the total amounts for various cost items and the portions of the total costs that are variable and fixed. Once the behavior of costs is determined and cost estimates are made, the manager can begin to evaluate alternatives and make decisions. Chapters Six and Seven discuss several decision-making models, or tools, that rely on estimates of variable and fixed costs.

THE NATURE OF FIXED AND VARIABLE COSTS

Short Run versus Long Run

Variable costs are those costs that will change as the level of activity is changed. Fixed costs are those costs that will be incurred whatever level of activity is carried on during the period. If the accounting period were long enough—many years would be required—there would be no fixed costs. Salaried personnel could be hired and fired, buildings and equipment could be bought or sold, and so on. But a business can change the general nature of its activities only slowly. Capacity can be expanded, but it takes time to plan for new facilities, to arrange financing to acquire new facilities, to acquire them, to staff them, and to put them to work. Capacity can be expanded or reduced, but it takes time.

During any time span short enough to serve the purpose of being an accounting period, the firm must operate with a relatively fixed set of productive facilities, sales force, and managerial staff. This fact provides the basis for the distinction drawn in economics between the short run and the long run and in accounting between variable costs and fixed costs. To the economist, the *short run* is a time period long enough to allow management to change the level of production or other activity within the constraints of current total productive capacity. Total productive capacity can be changed only in the *long run*.

To the manager, costs that vary with activity levels in the short run are variable costs; costs that will not vary in the short run no matter what the level of activity are fixed costs. The accounting concepts of variable and fixed costs are, then, short-run concepts. They must be defined in terms of a particular period of time and relate to a particular level of productive capacity.

Consider for example the total costs (both variable and fixed) for a firm as shown in Figure 5.1. The graph on the left shows the total costs in the long run. If the productive capacity of the firm is 10,000 units per year, total costs will be measured by line *AB*. If new production facilities are acquired in order to increase capacity to 20,000 units, then total costs will be measured by line *CD*. An increase in capacity to 30,000

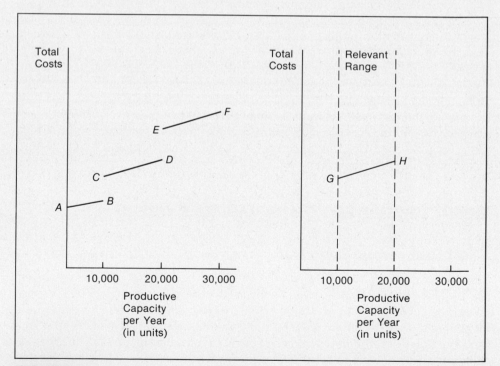

FIGURE 5.1
Long-run versus Short-run Nature of Costs

units will increase the total costs to that shown by line *EF*. These shifts in capacity can occur only in the long run.

In the short run, there is only one capacity level, that of the existing plant. The total costs in the short run are shown in the graph at the right on the assumption that the capacity of the existing plant is 20,000 units per year. Note that line *GH* (which is equivalent to line *CD* in the long run) represents costs for the production level of 10,000 units to 20,000 units only. For production levels outside of this range, a different plant capacity is needed and the total costs line will shift up or down. The level of activity likely to be undertaken with existing plant is referred to as the *relevant range* of activity. Estimates of variable and fixed costs are applicable only if the contemplated level of activity is within the relevant range. If an alternative under consideration requires a level outside the relevant range, then new plant facilities must be acquired and the total cost line will be different than that for current production facilities.

Types of Fixed Costs

Where the short run stops and the long run starts is a fuzzy distinction in practice. Thus, the accounting concept of fixed costs contains several subclassifications that are helpful in understanding the relationship between particular types of fixed costs and current capacity.

Capacity Costs   Many resources used during a period provide a firm with the capacity to produce or to sell or both. These fixed costs are called *capacity costs*. Capacity costs are sometimes further disaggregated into *standby* costs and *enabling* costs.

Standby costs are those costs that will be incurred even if operations are temporarily shut down completely. Examples include property taxes and some executive salaries. Management typically has no control over standby costs in the short run.

Enabling costs are those that will cease if operations are shut down completely, but must be incurred in fixed amounts if operations are carried out at any level. A security force can be laid off if production ceases, but once the force is employed, it guards the plant no matter how little or how much activity is going on inside the plant. Management can control enabling costs in the short run only to the extent that it can decide to shut down completely.

Many costs usually thought of as enabling, such as the wages of quality-control inspectors, are really semifixed, or step, costs. [See Figure 4.2(D) on page 100.] One inspector may be all that is required for a one-shift operation, but two would be required for two shifts. But if the inspector can handle the entire output during a shift, the costs incurred for inspection do not vary with output during a shift.

Programmed Costs   In contrast to fixed capacity costs, there are other fixed costs that are not required for production activities. Activities such as research, development, and advertising designed to generate new business are fixed in the sense that once a commitment is made, the amount of cost incurred does not vary with production activity. These costs are, however, controllable by management in the short run. These costs are usually called *programmed costs,* but the terms *discretionary costs* and *managed costs* are sometimes used. Programmed costs are often incurred to generate business, whereas capacity costs are incurred to produce goods.

COST ESTIMATION

The purpose of cost estimation is to estimate the fixed cost amount and the variable cost amount for various types of total costs (for examples, raw material, labor, utilities, insurance). Of course, some costs, such as rent and insurance, will have only a fixed portion. Others, such as raw materials and direct labor, will have only a variable portion. Many costs, however, are mixed, having both fixed and variable components.

The total cost of an item can be expressed as

$$\begin{pmatrix} \text{Total} \\ \text{Cost} \\ \text{During} \\ \text{Period} \end{pmatrix} = \begin{pmatrix} \text{Fixed} \\ \text{Cost} \\ \text{During} \\ \text{Period} \end{pmatrix} + \begin{pmatrix} \text{Variable} \\ \text{Cost per} \\ \text{Unit of} \\ \text{Activity} \end{pmatrix} \times \begin{pmatrix} \text{Units of} \\ \text{Activity} \\ \text{Carried Out} \\ \text{During Period} \end{pmatrix}$$

or, using briefer but fairly standard notation,

$$TC = a + bx$$

where a is total fixed cost, b is variable cost per unit of activity, and x is the number of units of activity carried out. For example, assume that the total cost of utilities per month is determined to be $400 plus $.05 per kilowatt-hour used. If the use of 100,000 kilowatt-hours is anticipated next month, utilities cost is estimated to be $5,400 (= $400 + $.05 per kilowatt-hour × 100,000 kilowatt-hours).

The activity represented by x is often called the *independent variable* and the amount of total costs is the *dependent variable*. In some sophisticated analyses, more than one activity or independent variable is presumed to influence total cost. The symbolic representation of such a relation might be

$$TC = a + bx_1 + cx_2 + \text{etc.}$$

where a is total fixed cost, b is the variable cost per unit of activity x_1 carried out, c is the variable cost per unit of activity x_2 carried out, and so on. The activities might be direct labor hours worked and number of units produced. In this discussion of cost estimation, we assume only one activity, or independent, variable.

There are two basic approaches to estimating costs—engineering estimates of what costs *should be* and analysis of historical data showing what costs *have been*. Both approaches can be useful; both are used in practice.

Engineering Method of Estimating Costs

The engineering method is probably so named because it was first used in estimating manufacturing costs from engineer's specifications of the required inputs to the manufacturing process for a unit of manufactured output. The method is not, however, confined to manufacturing, as the frequent use of time-and-motion studies of certain administrative or selling activities attests.

Virtually all business activities are designed to produce a defined output from a variety of labor, material, and capital equipment inputs. The engineers' cost estimates are based on a study of the physical relation between the quantities of these inputs and each unit of output (what economists call the "production function"). It is then a relatively simple matter to assign costs to each of the physical inputs (wages, material prices, insurance charges, etc.) in order to estimate the cost of the outputs.

There are several difficulties in using the engineering method to estimate costs. The cost estimate will be of low quality to the extent that the actual amounts of inputs used, such as materials and labor, vary during the production process because of waste, spoilage, and varying labor efficiency. Another difficulty of this method is that workers have varying degrees of skill with correspondingly varying wage rates. The engineering estimate of the appropriate skill level and wage rate may be subject to large errors. Using the engineering method it is usually difficult to estimate the indirect costs of production—the cost of utilities, supervision, maintenance, security—so that the method tends to be reliable only when most costs have a direct relation to output, such as for labor and materials. Finally, the engineering method is surprisingly costly to use. Analysis of time, motion, materials, operating characteristics of equipment, and the ability of labor with varying skills requires an expert. Expert engineers are costly.

The engineering method of estimating costs is reliably used only when direct costs are a large proportion of total costs and when input-output relationships are fairly stable over time. The engineering method must be used, however, when there are no historical data to analyze.

Estimation of Costs Using Historical Data

When a firm has been carrying out activities for some time and future activities are expected to be similar to those of the past, then the firm can analyze the historical data to estimate the variable and fixed components of total cost and to determine likely future costs. There are several methods used to estimate costs from historical data; these range from the simple to the sophisticated. Whatever method is used, the manager should take some preliminary steps before relying on cost estimates based on historical data.

PRELIMINARY STEPS IN ANALYZING HISTORICAL COST DATA

In the several decades since computers have become a cost-effective tool for analysis, the expression GIGO, "garbage-in, garbage-out," has become well known to data analysts. GIGO means that the results of an analysis cannot be better than the input data. Before using cost estimates, the analyst should be confident that the estimates make sense and are based on valid assumptions.

Keep in mind that we are trying to determine fixed costs per period, a, and variable cost, b, per unit of some activity or independent variable in the relation

$$TC = a + bx$$

The historical data will consist of several observations. An observation is the amount of total costs for a period and the level of activity carried out during that period. Thus, we might have total labor costs by months (the dependent variable) and the number of units produced during each of the months or the number of direct labor hours worked during each of the months (the independent variable). We do not provide here an exhaustive list of all the steps to take in analyzing historical data, but the following are some of the more important.

(1) Review Alternative Activity Bases (Independent Variables)

In deciding which measure of activity to use, there are often several alternatives. The activity base chosen should have some logical relation to the cost item. The total cost for an item might be a function of number of units produced, labor hours used, labor costs incurred, machine hours used, quantities of materials used, cost of materials used, and so on. The objective in selecting an activity base is to find one whose variation is closely associated with the cost item being estimated. In principle, there is no reason not to use more than one activity base or independent variable, but a given cost estimation usually focuses on just one. (In order to have more than one independent variable, the number of observations must be large if the statistical relations are to be robust and reliable.)

(2) Plot the Data

One of the simplest procedures, but one often omitted by careless analysts, is to plot each of the observations of total costs against activity levels. Such plots can indicate an "outlier" observation—one that is unlike the others. Such outliers may indicate faulty data collection, incorrect arithmetic, or merely a time period when production was so far out of control that it would make sense to ignore the observation in determining the average relationships among total, fixed, and variable costs. Moreover, plotting the data may make it clear that no relation or only a nonlinear relation exists between the activity base and actual costs.[1]

(3) Examine the Data and Method of Accumulation

Do the time periods for the cost data and the activity correspond? Occasionally, accounting systems will record costs actually incurred late on a given day as occurring on

---

[1]   The cost estimation methods discussed in this chapter assume that a linear relationship exists between the dependent and independent variables. If a nonlinear relationship is found to exist, more sophisticated estimation methods are required.

the following day. It is difficult to deduce valid relations when the data for the dependent variable (total costs, in our case) are not compiled for the same period as the data for the independent variable (activity base, in our case). Are the time periods covered by each observation of total costs and the activity base long enough to be meaningful, but short enough to allow for variations in activity levels? If, for example, observations are collected by the hour, the time of day may obscure the relationship between the dependent and independent variables. Workers may be more efficient in the morning and less so in the late afternoon. On the other hand, observations collected by month may smooth over meaningful variations of activity level and cost that could be observed if the data were based on weekly observations.

(4) Examine the Constancy of the Production Process

Do the observations (of total cost and activity level) all refer to times when production processes were approximately the same? Comparisons of total costs and activity level are not likely to be meaningful if there have been technological changes in production processes, changes in the skill level or wage rate of the labor force, or changes in the prices of materials. The data analyst must make trade-offs between having more observations, which increases the reliability of the cost estimates, and keeping the total time span covered by the observations short enough so that the production process remains relatively unchanged.

Once the activity base is chosen for the independent variable, the data have been gathered and plotted to see if there are outlier observations that should be discarded, and the production process is determined to have been fairly constant over the time of the observations, the actual cost estimation procedure can begin.

METHODS OF COST ESTIMATION USING HISTORICAL DATA

This section presents some of the methods used in estimating historical relationships between total costs and activity levels. The methods are illustrated for the data shown in Exhibit 5.1 and plotted in Figure 5.2. These data show the total manufacturing overhead costs of the Chicago Manufacturing Company for each month during the previous year. Manufacturing overhead costs include all manufacturing costs except those for direct materials and direct labor. The overhead costs include utility costs, property taxes on the factory building, supervisors' wages, wages for security and maintenance staff, insurance on the factory building and depreciation on factory buildings, machinery, and equipment. The problem here is to determine the relationship between total overhead costs and activity for the Chicago Manufacturing Company.[2] The activity base that is suspected to correlate best with total overhead costs per

---

[2]   Alternatively, we could estimate the amount of each of these overhead costs individually and aggregate the fixed and variable cost components to obtain an estimate of total overhead costs. These alternative approaches normally yield approximately the same results.

EXHIBIT 5.1
Chicago Manufacturing Company
Overhead Cost Data by Month

Month	Total Overhead Costs Incurred During Month	Direct Labor Hours Worked During Month
January	$ 5,580	6,000
February	4,330	5,500
March	4,080	3,500
April	2,830	3,000
May	2,455	2,500
June	3,080	2,000
July	3,580	4,000
August	4,455	4,500
September	5,330	5,000
October	6,580	6,500
November	5,580	7,000
December	6,930	7,500
	$54,810	57,000

---

month is the number of direct hours worked during the month. Exhibit 5.1 shows total overhead costs and direct labor hours worked during the month.

The cost relationship to be estimated is

$$\begin{array}{ccc} \text{Total Overhead} & & \text{Fixed} \\ \text{Costs per} & = & \text{Costs} \\ \text{Month} & & \text{per Month} \end{array} + \left(\begin{array}{ccc} \text{Variable Overhead} & & \text{Direct Labor} \\ \text{Cost per Direct} & \times & \text{Hours} \\ \text{Labor Hour} & & \text{Worked During Month} \end{array} \right)$$

$$\text{TC} = a + bx$$

Before estimating the cost relationship, we plot the data, as in Figure 5.2. There are no apparent outliers for the twelve observation pairs in Exhibit 5.1. Two outliers are drawn on the plot so that you can see what we mean by an outlier.[3] If there were one or two months with outliers such as those shown, we should investigate what happened during those months and possibly discard the observations once we understood their cause.

Three common methods of estimating the cost relationship, that is, identifying *a* and *b* in the above equation, are illustrated next.

---

[3] One of the outliers, the one corresponding roughly to 7,000 hours and $3,000 of total costs, is a "good" outlier in the sense that total costs are much less than they apparently should be. We suspect that the cause here is faulty recording of data, but if not, then we would want to know what happened that month. Then we might change operations to incur costs each month that are this small relative to activity levels. Investigation of outliers illustrates the concept called "management by exception." Understanding the cause of outlier observations is particularly important for managerial control.

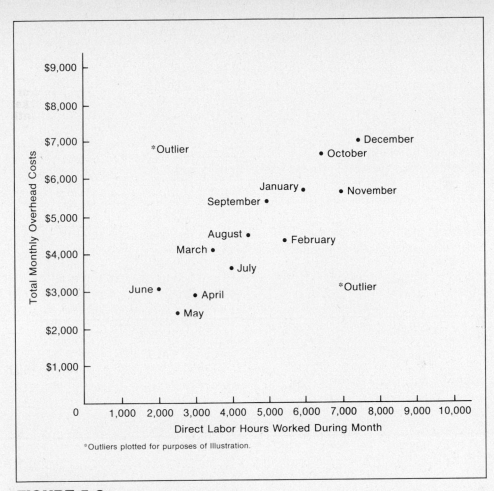

FIGURE 5.2
Chicago Manufacturing Company
Scatter Plot of Total Monthly
Overhead Costs and Direct Labor
Hours Used During Month

High-Low Method

The high-low method is easy to use. It estimates the fixed and variable cost components using the observations with the highest and lowest total costs (ignoring outliers). Although this method is easy to apply, its principal weakness is that it uses only two of the observations.

First, identify the observation with the largest total cost, December in this example. Then identify the observation with the smallest total cost, May in this example. Next compute the difference in total costs between these two extreme observations, $4,475 (= $6,930 − $2,455) in the example. Then compute the change in activity base levels between the two extreme observations, 5,000 hours (= 7,500 hours − 2,500 hours) in the example. Then estimate b, the variable cost per unit of activity base by dividing the cost difference by the activity difference. In our example, the variable cost would be estimated at $.895 (= \$4,475/5,000$ hours) per direct labor hour worked. The general formula, using subscript h and l to represent high and low, respectively, is

$$b = \frac{TC_h - TC_l}{x_h - x_l}$$

The estimate of the fixed cost, a, can then be determined from either of the following two relationships (both will give the same estimate of a):

$$\text{Fixed Costs} = a = TC_h - bx_h \quad \text{or} \quad \text{Fixed Costs} = a = TC_l - bx_l$$

In the example, the high-low method would estimate the fixed cost to be \$217.50. The calculation of this amount is as follows (subtracting the second equation from the first):

Total Costs =		a	+	bx
\$6,930	=	a	+	b (7,500 hours)
$-$ [2,455	=	a	+	b (2,500 hours)]
\$4,475	=	0	+	b (5,000 hours)

$$b = \frac{\$4,475}{5,000 \text{ hours}} = \$.895 \text{ per hour}$$

$$a = \$6,930 - (\$.895 \text{ per hour} \times 7,500 \text{ hours}) = \underline{\$217.50}$$

or

$$a = \$2,455 - (\$.895 \text{ per hour} \times 2,500 \text{ hours}) = \underline{\$217.50}$$

Thus, in the example, we estimate fixed overhead costs to be \$217.50 per month and variable overhead costs to be \$.895 per direct labor hour worked. This relationship is drawn in Figure 5.3. The line seems to fit the data points reasonably well but, as we shall see when we examine a line fit with statistical methods, the results are quite different. The main shortcoming of this method is that it uses only two of the observations, the highest and the lowest. The accuracy of the estimates of a and b depends on how representative the high and low data points are of all the data. The highest and lowest cost observations may by their very nature be atypical.

Visual Curve-Fitting Method

Another method of estimating cost from data such as those in Exhibit 5.1 is visual curve fitting. In contrast to the high-low method, visual curve fitting uses all of the available observations. In visual curve fitting a straight line is drawn through the data points that seems to "fit" well. By "fit," we mean a straight line that goes through the

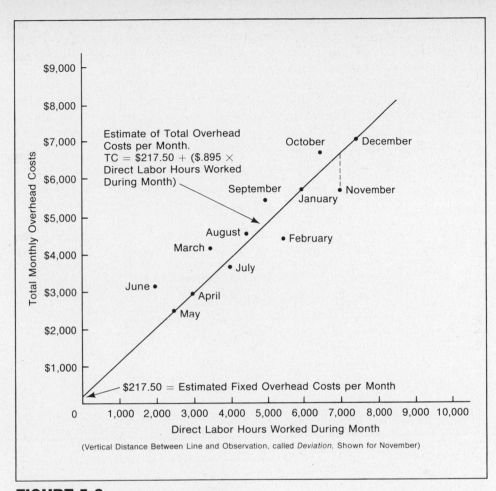

FIGURE 5.3
Chicago Manufacturing Company High-Low Method of Estimating Fixed Overhead Costs per Month and Variable Overhead Costs per Direct Labor Hour Worked (Based on Data in Exhibit 5.1)

middle of data points as closely as possible. Draw in such a line in Figure 5.2. The line we visually fit to these data intercepts the vertical axis at $1,000 and has a slope of $.75 per hour.[4] The chances are that the line you drew is not exactly the same as ours. Yours and ours would each give roughly the same estimate of total costs for 3,000 hours to 6,000 direct labor hours per month, but probably give significantly different estimates

---

[4] That is, we drew a line indicating $1,000 per month of fixed costs, *a*, and variable costs, *b*, of $.75 per direct labor hour. (You may reproduce our visually fit line by drawing a line on Figure 5.2 between the point $1,000 on the vertical axis and a total cost of $7,000 for 8,000 hours.)

of total costs for 2,000 or 8,000 direct labor hours per month. The shortcoming of this method has, we hope, been demonstrated by the difference between your visually fit line and ours. The visually fit line is subjective, and different analysts may reach different conclusions from examining the same data.

Once you have drawn a line to fit the data, the estimate of the fixed cost component, a, is the total cost for a zero level of activity, the amount at the point where the line crosses the vertical axis. The estimate of the variable cost per unit of activity can be found by reading the numbers for any two points *on the line*. The relation is as follows, where subscripts *1* and *2* refer to the two points:

$$\text{Variable Cost per Unit of Base Activity} = b = \frac{TC_1 - TC_2}{x_1 - x_2} = \frac{\text{Change in Costs Between Two Points}}{\text{Change in Activity Between the Two Points}}$$

In our case, we use the points

Point 1:   8,000 hours; $7,000 total costs

Point 2:   0 hours; $1,000 total costs

Using the formula above, we find that

$$b = \frac{\$7,000 - \$1,000}{8,000 \text{ hours} - 0 \text{ hours}} = \frac{\$6,000}{8,000 \text{ hours}} = \$.75 \text{ per hour}$$

Thus, total overhead cost is estimated as:

$$\text{Total Overhead Costs per Month} = \$1,000 + \$.75 \text{ per direct labor hour}$$

Statistical Methods

When computing facilities are available, by far the most cost-effective and accurate method for determining cost relations is *regression analysis.* Rather than estimating the cost relationship by the high-low or visual curve-fitting methods, the regression analysis "fits" a line to the data by the method of least squares. That is, a line is fit to the observations in such a way that the sum of the squares of the vertical distance of the observation points from the point on the regression line is minimized. (See November in Figure 5.3 for an illustration of the "vertical distance.") The statistical regression locates the line that best goes through the data points using the least-squares criterion. (The sum of the absolute deviations might just as well be minimized, but the computational problems are somewhat more difficult. Nearly all "canned" computer library programs use the least-squares criterion.)

In our example, an observed value of total overhead cost is y and the line we fit by the least-squares regression will be of the form

$$\hat{y} = a + bx$$

where $\hat{y}$ is the predicted or fitted value for any x. The right-hand side of the equation should already be familiar to you. The vertical distance between the actual and the fitted values, $y - \hat{y}$, is called the *residual*. The method of least squares therefore fits a line to the data so as to minimize the sum of all the squared residuals.

It is beyond the scope of this text to do more than introduce the methods of regression analysis, but virtually every computer system has a program in its library that will perform the calculations. Furthermore, pocket calculators commercially available for under $100 will perform the calculations automatically. Our purpose here is to show the results of using the statistical methods and give a brief introduction to interpreting the results. You should be aware, however, that entire books have been devoted to these methods and their use.

Running the data in Exhibit 5.1 through a computer "least-squares regression" program gives the following results, which will be explained.

$$\begin{array}{c} \text{Total} \\ \text{Overhead} \\ \text{Costs} \\ \text{per Month} \end{array} = \begin{array}{l} \$1,002 \\ (\$470) \end{array} + \begin{array}{l} \$.751 \\ (\$.093) \end{array} \times \text{Direct Labor Hours Worked During Month}$$

Adjusted $R^2 = 0.85$
Standard Deviation of Total Costs (y) = $1,453.50
Mean of Total Costs ($\bar{y}$) = $4,567.50
Standard Deviation of the Residuals = $556

By now, you should be able to interpret only the $1,002 and $.751 amounts. The first is the estimate of the fixed overhead cost per month and the second is the estimate of the variable overhead cost per unit of base activity, direct labor hours worked during the month. The two numbers $1,002 (for fixed costs) and $.751 (for variable costs) are called *coefficients* of the regression equation.

The numbers shown in parentheses below these coefficients are called "standard errors of the coefficients." These standard errors are measures of variation and give a rough idea of the confidence we can have in the above fixed and variable cost coefficients. The smaller the standard error relative to its coefficient, the better. For example, the standard error of the fixed overhead cost per month is $470; the estimate of fixed costs of $1,002 is 2.13 times (= $1,002/$470) as large as the standard error. The ratio between an estimated regression coefficient and its standard error is called the "t-value" or "t-statistic." If the t-value is approximately 2 or larger, then a commonly used rule of thumb is that we can be relatively confident that the actual coefficient is different from zero. The larger the t-value, the more confidence we can have in our estimate of the coefficient. On the other hand, when the standard error of the fixed cost coefficient is large relative to the estimated coefficient (which is the same thing as saying that the t-value is small), then the fixed cost coefficient is not statistically different from zero. In such a case we would conclude that the fixed costs per period are not significantly different from zero (which we would expect for a strictly variable cost such as direct materials or direct labor).

The standard error of the variable cost estimate is relatively small; the t-value is relatively large: $0.751/$.093 = 8.08. We conclude, therefore, that there is a statistically significant relationship between changes in total overhead costs and changes in direct labor hours: larger amounts of direct labor hours worked per month are correlated with larger amounts of total overhead costs. In cases where the standard error of the variable cost coefficient is large relative to the coefficient (small t-value), the variable cost coefficient is not significantly different from zero. We would conclude, then, that there is no statistical relationship between total costs and this particular activity (or independent variable), and that there is no apparent linear relationship between these independent and dependent variables.

Adjusted R^2   The "adjusted R^2" attempts to measure how well the line fits the data (that is, how closely the data points cluster about the fitted line). If all the data points were on the same straight line, then the adjusted R^2 would be 1.00—a perfect fit. If the data points formed a circle or disk, then the adjusted R^2 would be zero, indicating that no line passing through the center of the circle or disk fits the data better than any other.[5] Technically, the adjusted R^2 is a measure of the fraction of the total variance of the dependent variable about its mean that is explained by the fitted line.[6] An R^2 of one means that all of the variance is explained; an R^2 of zero means that none of the variance is explained. Many users of statistical regression analysis believe that low R^2's indicate a weak relation between the total costs (dependent variable) and the activity base (independent variable). Whether or not the activity base is a good explanatory variable for total costs is signalled by a low standard error (or high t-value) for the estimated coefficient b. If there are sufficiently many data observations, there can be both low R^2 and significant regression coefficients. This possibility is shown graphically in Figure 5.4. In general, the R^2 number is difficult and tricky to interpret. In most instances, the information that the R^2 statistic gives can also be acquired from the standard deviation of the residuals, but without the possibility of incorrect inferences.

Standard Deviation of the Residuals   The "standard deviation of the residual" gives us an indication of the degree of certainty we have with regard to predictions made from using the fitted line (and its regression equation). The standard deviation of the residuals is merely the square root of the following quantity: the sum of the squared residuals divided by the number of the residuals minus two.[7] In effect, the standard deviation of the residuals is a measure of the dispersion of the actual y's around the

---

[5]   Other situations can also lead to an R^2 of zero.

[6]   Many books and computer outputs report merely an R^2 that is not labeled "adjusted" or otherwise. The more sophisticated programs report both an "adjusted" and an "unadjusted" R^2. The adjustment takes into account the number of coefficients that have been fit to the data—two in a linear regression of the kind illustrated here: one for the constant (fixed costs in our applications) and one for the coefficient of the activity variable. An adjusted R^2 is a better measure than an unadjusted R^2 because the "score" is appropriately penalized for the use of more independent variables. (If you used as many independent variables as you have observations, you would always get an unadjusted R^2 of 1.00.) The unadjusted R^2 for a simple linear regression is merely the square of the correlation coefficient between the independent and dependent variables.

[7]   The standard deviation of the residuals is

$$\sqrt{\frac{\sum_{i=1}^{n} (\hat{y}_i - y_i)^2}{n-2}} = \sqrt{\frac{\sum_{i=1}^{n} (a + bx_i - y_i)^2}{n-2}}$$

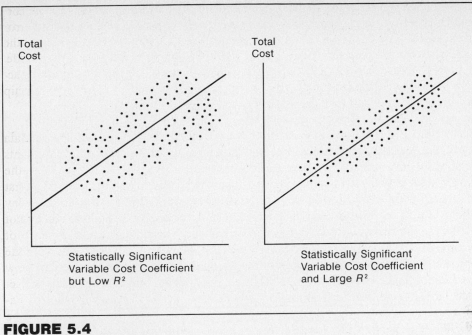

FIGURE 5.4
Relationship Between
Statistical Significance of
Regression Coefficient and R^2

fitted line. A standard deviation of zero would mean that all the residuals were zero and hence our predicted values would equal the observed values and the regression line would be a perfect "fit." This would be analogous to an R^2 value of 1.00.

The standard deviation of y (total cost) is similar to the standard deviation of residuals. The difference is that the standard deviation of y measures the dispersion of y about its own mean, rather than around the regression line. The calculation of the standard deviation of y is the same as that of the residuals except that instead of using the residuals we use the difference between each y and its mean, and the denominator would be one less than the number of observations.[8]

The smaller the standard deviation of residuals relative to the standard deviation of y, the more confident we can be of a prediction made by using the regression line. More specifically, the standard deviation of the residuals divided by the standard deviation of y indicates the degree of success of our regression equation in predicting y values from x values. In our example we have a ratio between the two standard deviations of .3825 ($= \$556/\$1,453.50$). That is, the dispersion of y about the regression

---

[8] The standard deviation of y is

$$\sqrt{\frac{\sum\limits_{i=1}^{n} (y_i - \bar{y})^2}{n-1}} = \sqrt{\frac{\sum\limits_{i=1}^{n} \left[y_i - \left(\sum\limits_{i=1}^{n} y_i \Big/ n \right) \right]^2}{n-1}}$$

line is only 38 percent of the dispersion of y about its own mean. To put it another way, the dispersion of the residuals around the regression line is 62 percent less than the dispersion of y about its own mean. If the standard deviation of the residuals had been larger than the standard deviation of y, we would be able to make more accurate predictions of future values of y by making the average value of y our prediction rather than using the regression equation.

Predicting Costs with Regression Equations   Using the regression line to predict total cost, we proceed as follows. If total direct hours worked during the month were 4,750 hours, the equation would predict total overhead costs of $1,002 + $.751 × 4,750 hours = $4,569. The standard deviation of the residuals of $556 tells us that we would expect to see actual total overhead costs within the range $4,569 plus or minus $556 about 68 percent of the months when 4,750 hours are worked. We expect to see actual total overhead cost within the range of $4,569 plus or minus 2 × $556 about 95 percent of the months when 4,750 hours are worked and within the range of $4,569 plus or minus 3 × $556 about 99.7 percent of the months when 4,750 hours are worked.[9] The smaller the "standard deviation of the residuals," the more certain we can be of a prediction made by using the line. The standard deviation of the residuals will be small when the R^2 is large and vice versa.

The Relevant Range   The least-squares regression equation

$$TC = \$1,002 + \$.751 \times \text{Direct Labor Hours Worked}$$

is graphed as a heavy straight line in Figure 5.5 with the underlying observations shown and identified by month. We can be relatively confident about this linear cost relationship in the range between 2,000 and 8,000 direct labor hours worked per month because of the low standard errors and good t-statistics. The dashed line graphed on Figure 5.5 shows that these same data observations may have been generated by a nonlinear relation between costs and activity that appears to be linear in the range of observations. We should be wary of predicting total costs for direct labor hours worked less than about 2,000 per month or more than about 8,000 per month. If the true relation between costs and activity is that shown by the dashed line, not the assumed straight line, then we would make substantial errors in predicting costs when 10,000 direct labor hours are worked during a month. The range of activity levels over which we can be reasonably confident of an estimated relationship between activity levels and associated total costs is the *relevant range* for that relationship.

Warning   Probably the major difficulty of using statistical estimating techniques is that they are so easy to do in this day of inexpensive computing devices, but the neces-

---

[9]   The standard deviation of the residuals can be used in precisely this way to attain a range for the dependent variable only when the independent variable is equal to the arithmetic mean of the observed independent variable. In our example, the arithmetic mean number of direct labor hours used for the month is 4,750 hours per month (= 57,000 hours annual total/12 months).
  As the value of the independent variable used for making the prediction gets farther away from the mean, the range of the predicted dependent variable for any given degree of confidence gets larger.

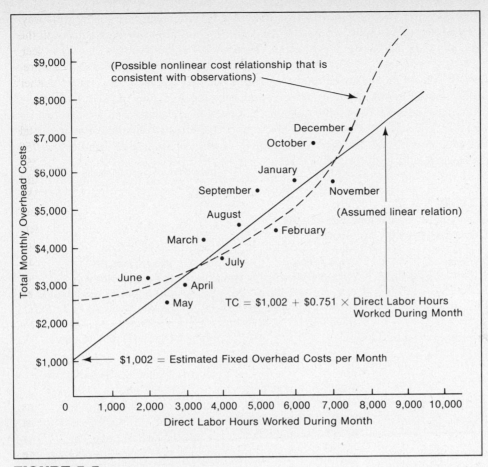

FIGURE 5.5
Chicago Manufacturing Company
Statistical (Least-Squares Regression)
Method of Estimating Fixed
Overhead Costs per Month and
Variable Overhead Costs per
Direct Labor Hour Worked
(Based on Data in Exhibit 5.1)

sary warnings are not printed on the package as they are for cigarettes. We conclude this section by providing two warnings. First, a relationship achieved in a regression analysis does not imply a causal relationship. That is, a correlation between two variables does not imply that changes in one will cause changes in the other. An assertion of causality must be based on either *a priori* knowledge or some analysis other than a regression analysis.

Second, until you become more familiar with the meaning of the terms *multicollinearity, autocorrelation,* and *heteroscedasticity,* you should be wary of drawing too many inferences from the results of canned computer programs for statistical estimation.[10]

In the rest of this book, we assume that the cost estimates have been validly derived from the data, without going into the mechanics of the derivation.

When we wish to explain total costs using more than one activity base simultaneously, the techniques of *multiple* regression analysis are used. The interpretations of the standard error of coefficients, *t*-value, adjusted R^2's, and the standard error of estimates are identical with those of the regression model using a single independent variable. The statistical methods are even more cost-effective than the visual or high-low methods, mostly because humans find it hard to draw graphs in more than two dimensions and to think about them.

EXHIBIT 5.2
Strengths and Weaknesses of
Cost Estimation Methods

Method	Strengths	Weaknesses
Engineering Method	Based on studies of what future costs should be rather than what past costs have been.	Not particularly useful when the physical relationship between inputs and outputs is indirect. Can be costly to use.
High-Low Method	Easy to understand and apply. Provides reasonably good cost estimates when the high and low observations are representative.	Uses only two of the available observations of cost data.
Visual Curve-Fitting Method	Uses all of the observations of cost data. Relatively easy to understand and apply.	The fitting of the line to the observations is subjective. Difficult to do where several independent variables are to be used.
Regression Method	Uses all of the observations of cost data. The line is statistically fit to the observations. A measure of the goodness of fit of the line to the observations is provided. Relatively easy to apply with "canned" regression program.	The regression model requires that several relatively strict assumptions be satisfied in order for the results to be valid. More difficult to understand than the preceding methods.

---

[10]   We use these words, not to intimidate you, but because they are the words actually used. Briefly, *multicollinearity* refers to the problem caused in multiple linear regression (more than one independent variable)

SUMMARY

Exhibit 5.2 summarizes the strengths and weaknesses of the four methods of cost estimation discussed in this chapter.

QUESTIONS AND PROBLEMS

1 Review the meaning of the following terms or concepts discussed in this chapter.
  a Fixed costs.
  b Variable costs.
  c The short run and the long run.
  d Capacity costs.
  e Standby costs.
  f Enabling costs.
  g Programmed (discretionary, managed) costs.
  h Activity base.
  i Independent variable.
  j Dependent variable.
  k Engineering method of cost estimation.
  l Garbage-in, garbage-out.
  m Observation.
  n Outlier.
  o High-low method.
  p Visual curve fitting.
  q Least-squares regression.
  r Standard error of regression coefficient.
  s *t*-value.
  t Adjusted R^2.
  u Standard deviation of the residuals.
  v Multiple linear regression.
  w Relevant range.

2 Each of the costs listed below is to be considered as a fixed cost rather than a variable cost.

---

when the independent variables are not independent of each other but are correlated. When there is severe multicollinearity, the regression coefficients are unreliable. For example, direct labor hours worked during a month are likely to be strongly correlated with direct labor costs during the month, even when wage rates change over time. If both direct labor hours and direct labor costs are used in a multiple linear regression, we would expect to have a problem of multicollinearity. *Autocorrelation* refers to the phenomenon that occurs when, for example, a linear regression is fit to data where there is actually a nonlinear relation between the dependent and independent variables. In that case, the deviation of one observation from the fitted line can be predicted, to one degree or another, from the deviation of the prior observation(s). For example, if there is seasonal demand for a product and production is also seasonal, then a month of large total costs is more likely to be followed by another month of large total costs than by a month of small total costs. In such a case, we would have autocorrelation in the deviations of the data points from a fitted straight line. *Heteroscedasticity* refers to the phenomenon that occurs when the average deviation of the dependent variable from the best-fitting linear relationship is systematically larger in one part of the range of independent variable(s) than in others. For example, if less reliable equipment and less-skilled labor are brought into use in months of large total production, then there is likely to be more variation in total costs during months of large total production than in months of small total production.

For each of the costs, indicate whether it is a *programmed cost* or a *capacity cost;* if a capacity cost, indicate whether it is an *enabling cost* or a *standby cost.*

a Factory rent.
b Superintendent's salary.
c Fire insurance on equipment.
d Depreciation on equipment.
e Property taxes on equipment.
f Salary of chief scientist in research laboratory.
g Fees paid to the independent certified public accountant.
h Costs of the internal accounting department.
i Hourly wages of finished goods warehouse clerk.
j Entertainment costs of customers incurred by sales force.
k Hourly wages of clean-up staff in the factory.
l Hourly wages of clean-up staff in the office building.
m Electric bill for factory lighting.
n Amortization of patents.
o Salaries of sales force.
p Advertising of company's products.

3 Weekly manufacturing costs of the Coda Company are believed to be semivariable; that is, they have a fixed component and a component that varies with the number of units produced. When 80,000 units were produced in a week, total manufacturing costs were $70,000; when 40,000 units were produced in a week, total manufacturing costs were $40,000.
a Using the data above, determine the apparent variable cost per unit produced.
b Determine the apparent fixed cost per week.
c What are the apparent total costs if total weekly production is 50,000 units?

4 The highest and lowest cost observations for three manufacturing cost items for a month are shown below.

Cost Item	10,000 Units Produced	15,000 Units Produced
A	$50,000	$ 75,000
B	20,000	20,000
C	4,000	5,000
Total Cost	$74,000	$100,000

a Using the high-low method, determine the fixed cost per month and the variable cost per unit for each of the three cost items.
b Using the high-low method, determine the fixed cost per month and the variable cost per unit based on the total cost of the three cost items combined.

5 Data on total manufacturing costs and production output of the Anwell Company for the past six months are shown below.
a Estimate fixed cost per month and variable cost per unit produced from the above data using the high-low method.
b Estimate fixed costs per month and variable cost per unit produced from the above data using a straight line visually fit to a plot of the above data.
c Estimate total monthly costs for a month when 250 units are produced using the estimates of fixed and variable costs from a and from b.

Anwell Company

Month	Units Produced	Total Costs
March	200	$16,000
April	280	19,200
May.	300	19,800
June	260	19,000
July.	260	18,600
August.	240	16,400

6 An analysis of repair costs by month in the Baiman Company was made using linear regression analysis. The equation fit was of the form

$$\text{Total Repair Costs} = \text{Fixed Costs} + \left(\begin{array}{c} \text{Variable Repair Costs} \\ \text{per Machine Hour Used} \\ \text{During Month} \end{array} \times \begin{array}{c} \text{Machine Hours} \\ \text{Actually Used} \\ \text{During Month} \end{array} \right)$$

$$\text{TRC} = a + bx$$

The results were as follows (standard error of coefficients shown in parentheses):

$$\text{TRC} = \$20,000 - \$.75x$$
$$(\$7,000) \quad (\$.25)$$

The adjusted R^2 was 0.90 and the standard deviation of the residuals was $1,500.

Average monthly repair costs have been $18,800 and machine hours used have averaged 1,600 hours per month. Management is concerned about the ability of the analyst who carried out this work because of the *negative* coefficient for variable cost. How do you evaluate these results?

7 F. R. Oliver has reported the results of a study of the cost of issuing driver and vehicle licenses in England and Wales.* This problem involves a discussion of the methodology used and an interpretation of the results.

Oliver studied the cost of issuing licenses at county borough offices in England and Wales. There were 83 such offices, ranging in size from Merthyr Tydfil's 16,600 licenses issued during the year studied to Birmingham's 465,200 licenses issued. About 70 percent of the total license-issuing costs for the year represent labor costs, and salary scales are set nationally. The results reported below show dollar measures, although the original results were reported in pounds sterling. The average cost of issuing licenses was $.344 per license.

TC represents the total cost for a year in issuing licenses for a given office.
x_1 represents the total number of driver's licenses issued by an office.
x_2 represents the total number of vehicle licenses issued by an office.
x represents the total number of licenses, whether for vehicles or for drivers in an office.
$\quad x = x_1 + x_2$

Two regressions were run, with the results indicated in the accompanying table which uses the above notations.

* F. R. Oliver. "A Cross-Section Study of Marginal Cost," *Applied Statistics,* 11, 2 (June 1962), pp. 69–78.

Cost Estimates of Issuing Licenses

Regression Form	Coefficient (Standard Error in Parentheses)			Adjusted R^2	Standard Deviation of Residuals
	a	**b**	**c**		
1. TC = a + bx	$ 78	$.34	—	.972	$3,800
	($423)	($.0065)	—		
2. TC = a + bx_1 + cx_2	$290	$.60	$.21	.973	$3,750
	($418)	($.16)	($.08)		

In answering the following questions, use either of the regression results, or both, as appropriate.

a The apparent fixed cost per year of running a license-issuing office is zero. Which of the regression results enables us to reach this conclusion? What factors might cause this to be true?

b What is the apparent variable cost of issuing a license, whether driver or vehicle? How confident are we of this estimate? How does it compare to the average total cost of issuing a license?

c If we had to predict the total cost of issuing licenses for the Birmingham office, what estimate would we make? If we wanted a range of estimates for the Birmingham office that would have a 95 percent probability of including the actual cost, what would that range be?

d Are there apparent differences in cost of issuing vehicle and driver licenses? How confident can you be of your answer?

e Oliver wanted to analyze the data to find out if there were increasing, decreasing, or constant variable costs of issuing licenses as the issuing offices increased in size. (The economist would say that we want to see if there were increasing, decreasing, or constant returns to scale.) What form of regression equation might Oliver fit to the data to answer this question?

8 The cost analyst of the Jensen Company has gathered activity and total cost data in two separate manufacturing departments, A and B, of the organization. The data span the preceding 39 weeks and are plotted in the accompanying figure. Fitted regression lines are shown in Figure 5.6.

a In which department does there appear to be a greater variance in the total costs? For which regression equation do you expect to see the larger R^2? Explain.

b Which department do you expect will have a smaller standard deviation of the residuals? Explain.

9 (Adapted from material by George Benston, *The Accounting Review,* October 1966, pp. 657–672.) The Benston Company manufactures widgets and digits. The widgets are assembled in batches, whereas digits are made one at a time. The cost of producing widgets is believed to be independent of the number of digits produced in a week. Cost data were gathered for 156 weeks. The following notation is used:

C = total manufacturing costs per week,
N = number of widgets produced during a week,

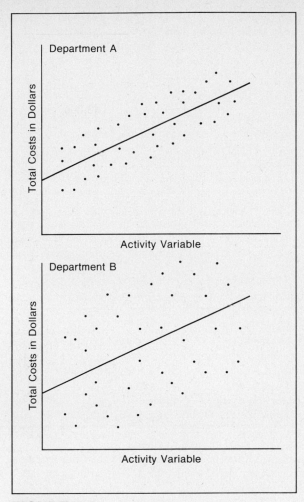

FIGURE 5.6

B = average number of widgets in a batch during the week, and
D = number of digits produced during the week.

A multiple linear regression was fit to the observations, with the following results (standard errors of estimated coefficients are shown in parentheses under the coefficients):

$$C = \$265.80 + \$8.21N - \$7.83B + \$12.32D$$
$$(\$110.80) \quad (\$.53) \quad (\$1.69) \quad (\$2.10)$$

The adjusted R^2 was .89, and the standard deviation of the residuals was \$420.83.

a According to the regression results, by how much are weekly costs expected to increase if the number of widgets is increased by one?

b What are the expected costs for the week if 500 widgets are produced in batches of 20 each and the number of digits produced during the week is 300?

c Refer to the answer in **b.** What is the range of costs for that production plan with a 95 percent probability of containing the actual cost for the week?

d Interpret the negative coefficient ($-\$7.83$) estimated for the variable B.

e As stated above, the cost of producing widgets is believed to be independent of the number of digits produced per week. What, if anything, do the regression results indicate about the validity of that belief?

10 (Comprehensive problem in estimating costs from historical data.) The internal accounting department at Ling Company is attempting to set overhead standards for the coming year. (Standard cost systems are discussed in Chapter Ten.) The accounting department has available the data shown in the accompanying table: observations by month for the last three years on total overhead costs for the month, on direct labor hours worked for the month, and on direct labor costs for the month in dollars. The problem is to estimate the fixed overhead costs per month and the variable overhead costs per unit of base activity. Analysis of the overhead costs indicates that direct labor hours required and direct labor costs are both closely related to variable overhead costs. The procedures and questions below mirror the steps taken by the accountants at Ling Company in determining estimates of fixed and variable overhead costs.

a Before the data are used in establishing estimated costs, what questions should be raised and answered about how data shown in the accompanying table were processed through the accounting system? Assume that these questions have been satisfactorily answered before the following steps are taken.

b Prepare a graph with total overhead costs on the vertical axis and direct labor *hours* on the horizontal axis. Plot the 36 monthly observations.

c Prepare a graph with total overhead costs on the vertical axis and direct labor *costs* in dollars on the horizontal axis. Plot the 36 monthly observations.

d Use the high-low method to fit linear cost relationships for each of the graphs and determine both the fixed cost and variable cost coefficients derived by this method.

e Visually fit a linear cost relation to the graphs drawn in **b** and **c,** and determine the fixed cost and variable cost coefficients from your visually fit lines.

f The data were run through a computer linear regression program. The first regression used total overhead costs as the dependent variable and direct labor hours as the independent variable. The results were as follows:

	Coefficient	Standard Error	*t*-Value
Fixed Costs	$9,553	$558.10	17.1
Direct Labor Hours	$.03527	$.00226	15.6

Adjusted $R^2 = 0.87$
Standard Deviation of the Residuals = $861

Second, a regression was run using total overhead costs as the dependent variable and direct labor costs in dollars as the independent variable. The results were as follows:

	Coefficient	Standard Error	*t*-Value
Fixed Costs	$5,706.70	$542.50	10.5
Direct Labor Costs	$.00723	$.00031	23.0

Adjusted $R^2 = 0.94$
Standard Deviation of the Residuals = $605

Ling Company
Observations by Month of Total Overhead Costs, Direct Labor Hours, and Direct Labor Costs

		Direct Labor Hours Worked During Month	Direct Labor Costs Incurred During Month	Total Overhead Costs for Month
19X0:	January	300,000	$1,920,000	$19,200
	February	300,000	1,920,000	20,000
	March	315,000	2,016,000	20,000
	April	285,000	1,824,000	19,200
	May	315,000	2,016,000	19,600
	June	330,000	2,112,000	20,000
	July	330,000	2,112,000	20,800
	August	345,000	2,208,000	22,000
	September	360,000	2,304,000	22,000
	October	345,000	2,208,000	21,600
	November	300,000	1,920,000	22,000
	December	315,000	2,268,000	22,400
19X1:	January	285,000	2,052,000	20,000
	February	225,000	1,620,000	18,000
	March	240,000	1,728,000	18,400
	April	210,000	1,512,000	16,800
	May	225,000	1,620,000	17,200
	June	210,000	1,512,000	16,400
	July	225,000	1,620,000	17,600
	August	225,000	1,620,000	16,800
	September	150,000	1,080,000	12,800
	October	195,000	1,404,000	15,200
	November	180,000	1,296,000	15,200
	December	180,000	1,440,000	15,600
19X2:	January	165,000	1,320,000	15,200
	February	150,000	1,200,000	14,800
	March	180,000	1,440,000	16,400
	April	180,000	1,440,000	16,000
	May	195,000	1,572,000	16,800
	June	195,000	1,572,000	17,200
	July	210,000	1,692,000	18,000
	August	210,000	1,692,000	18,400
	September	150,000	1,200,000	14,400
	October	180,000	1,452,000	16,800
	November	195,000	1,572,000	17,600
	December	210,000	1,704,000	17,200

Third, a *multiple* linear regression was run using total overhead costs as the dependent variable and both direct labor hours and direct labor dollars as independent variables. The results were as follows:

	Coefficient	Standard Error	t-Value
Fixed Costs	$5,703	$772	7.40
Direct Labor Hours	−$.000046	$.00628	.01
Direct Labor Costs	$.00724	$.00124	5.80

Adjusted R^2 = 0.94
Standard Deviation of the Residuals = $614

Interpret the results of these regressions. Which appears to be the most useful? What cost estimates result?

g Assess the difference between the simple estimates of costs based on the high-low method and visual curve fitting and the more sophisticated estimates resulting from the statistical regressions. (This is a general question, not specifically related to the data for the Ling Company.)

CHAPTER 6
SHORT-RUN OPERATING DECISIONS

In Chapter Four we discussed the incremental principle, the appropriate basis for most management decisions. In Chapter Five, we considered several methods for estimating fixed and variable costs. We are now ready to demonstrate the application of the incremental principle to a variety of managerial problems. In this chapter, we focus on short-run operating decisions, including cost-volume-profit decisions, pricing decisions, and inventory management decisions. In Chapter Seven, we consider long-run capacity decisions.

COST-VOLUME-PROFIT DECISIONS

Management's performance is usually judged on the basis of a firm's success in generating profits. The criterion for many of management's decisions, therefore, is the incremental effect of various alternatives on profits. This section introduces the cost-volume-profit model, a useful tool for analyzing relationships among revenues, cost or expenses, activity levels, and profits. As will be demonstrated, the cost-volume-profit model aids management in making several important short-run operating decisions.

The "profits" in the cost-volume-profit model are not precisely the same as the "net income" shown in financial accounting reports. First, profits in the cost-volume-profit model are largely defined in terms of an excess of cash inflows over cash outflows plus depreciation[1] from operations, whereas net income under the accrual basis is defined

---

[1] Because depreciation is an expense in determining net income, it is included as a fixed cost in the cost-volume-profit model. When the cost-volume-profit model is used as a tool of decision making, however, depreciation is irrelevant, because it represents the allocation of a past, sunk cost that will not differ among alternatives.

as an excess of revenues over expenses. We shall momentarily avoid these differences by assuming that cash inflows from operations and revenues are the same and cash outflows for operating costs (other than depreciation) and expenses are the same. Second, the cost-volume-profit model assumes that all fixed manufacturing costs are expenses of the period in which the costs are incurred. As we shall see in Chapter Fourteen, net income as computed in external financial reports assumes that fixed manufacturing costs are treated as part of the cost of goods manufactured during the period. Fixed manufacturing costs do not become expenses in external financial reports until the manufactured goods are sold. This may be in a later period than the period of production. We shall also temporarily avoid this difference between "profits" and "net income" by assuming that there is no change in inventory between the beginning and end of the period being considered. Thus, the amount of manufacturing *costs* for a period will be equal to the amount of manufacturing *expenses* for the period. Because all manufacturing costs are, in effect, expenses for the period, and because most of the standard terminology for the cost-volume-profit model is stated in terms of costs, we use the terms *costs* and *expenses* as synonyms in this discussion.

These two differences between the cost-volume-profit model for internal decision making and the net income model for external financial reporting are not unimportant. As we demonstrated in Chapter One, basing decisions on the net income model can lead management to make incorrect decisions. We consider the difference between these two income models more fully in Chapter Fourteen.

The Cost-Volume-Profit Equation

We shall continue to use the notation introduced in Chapter Five:

$$TC = a + bx$$

This equation represents the relationship stating that total cost is equal to fixed costs, a, plus variable costs per unit of base activity, b, times the units of base activity carried out during the period, x. Throughout this discussion, the unit of base activity is assumed to be units produced and sold.

If we let Y stand for profit and P for selling price per unit, we can write:

$$Profit = Revenues - Expenses$$

$$Profit = Revenues - (Fixed\ Expenses + Variable\ Expenses)$$

$$Y = Px - (a + bx)$$

The cost-volume-profit model is used to study the relationships among profit (Y), selling price (P), volume (x), and costs (fixed costs, a, and variable costs, b). The model is used to answer questions such as:

1   For a given price, at what volume, x, will we break even, that is, have exactly zero profit?

2 For a given price, what level of sales must we achieve to have a profit of, say, $100,000?

3 For a given level of sales, what price must be charged for profit to be $100,000?

4 Given actual sales and prices, what was the *margin of safety,* the excess of actual revenues over revenues at the breakeven point, the point of zero profit?

If you are familiar with algebra and comfortable with algebraic manipulation, it will be apparent that each of these questions can be answered from the equation

$$Y = Px - (a + bx)$$

Most managers are not, however, comfortable with algebra; the cost-volume-profit model with its related graphs has been developed to make an understanding of the relationships easier.

The discussion in this section is developed around the illustrative data for the Baltimore Manufacturing Company presented in Exhibit 6.1. From Exhibit 6.1, we can see that total variable cost per unit produced and sold is $22 and total fixed cost per month is $4,800. In terms of our notation, then, a, is $4,800 and b is $22 per unit produced. The selling price, P, is $30 per unit. Revenue is equal to total sales in units times $30; revenues = $30x.

The Cost-Volume-Profit Graph

Figure 6.1(A), the top panel of Figure 6.1, presents two linear relationships. First, total revenues, $Px = \$30x$, are plotted. Because revenues are zero when sales, x, are zero, the revenue line goes through the origin (the zero, zero point) of the graph. It has a slope of $30; for each increase in units sold, the revenues go up by $30 so that, for ex-

---

EXHIBIT 6.1
Baltimore Manufacturing Company
Data for Cost-Volume-Profit
Illustrations
(Selling Price = $30 per Unit)

Cost Classification	Variable Cost (per Unit)	Fixed Cost (per Month)
Manufacturing Costs:		
Direct Material	$ 4	—
Direct Labor.	9	—
Other Manufacturing Costs	4	$3,060
Total Manufacturing Costs	$17	$3,060
Selling, General, and Administrative Costs	5	1,740
Total Costs.	$22	$4,800

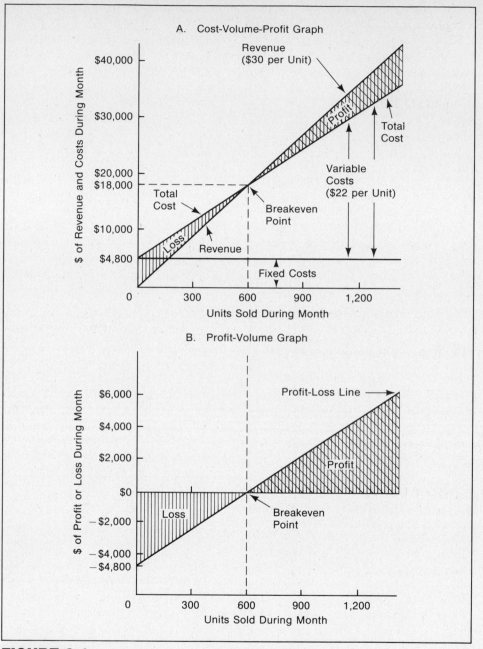

FIGURE 6.1
Profit Graphs for the
Baltimore Manufacturing Company

ample, at 600 units sold, total revenues are $18,000. The second linear relation graphed in Figure 6.1(A) is total cost as a function of activity (units produced): TC = $4,800 + $22x. Because the fixed costs are $4,800 per month, the total cost line goes through the vertical axis at $4,800. Because variable costs per unit produced are $22 per unit, the total cost line increases $22 for each increase in units produced during the month. At 600 units produced during the month, for example, total costs are $4,800 of fixed costs plus $13,200 (= $22 per unit × 600 units) of variable costs, or $18,000 total costs.

The point where total costs and total revenues are equal, 600 units in Figure 6.1, is called the *breakeven point*. At sales volumes less than 600 units per month, the firm incurs a loss equal to the vertical distance between the total cost line and the revenue line. The amount of the loss decreases as volume increases, because the variable cost of $22 per unit is less than the revenue per unit of $30. At sales volume greater than 600 units per month, the firm makes a profit equal to the vertical distance between the revenue line and the total cost line.

Without resorting to a graph such as the one in Figure 6.1(A), you can determine the breakeven point by using the equation

$$Y = Px - (a + bx)$$

At the breakeven point, profit, Y, must be zero. In our example, we know that $P = 30, $a = $4,800$ and $b = 22. Thus the breakeven sales quantity is represented by x in the equation

$$0 = $30x - ($4,800 + $22x)$$

or

$$0 = $8x - $4,800$$

$$$8x = $4,800$$

$$x = \frac{$4,800}{$8}$$

$$= 600 \text{ Units}$$

The Profit-Volume Graph

The cost-volume-profit graph shown in the top panel of Exhibit 6.1 is convenient enough for finding the breakeven point or getting a rough idea of profit or loss at various sales levels. However, because the profit or loss is measured as the vertical distance between two lines, neither of which is horizontal, it is not convenient for precisely observing the profit or loss as a function of sales volume. Consequently, the relation between profit and volume is often graphed as in Figure 6.1(B), the *profit-volume graph*. The vertical axis of the profit-volume graph shows the amount of profit or loss for the period, one month in the example. At zero sales, the loss is equal to the fixed costs, *a*. At the breakeven point, 600 units sold in the example, the profit is zero. The slope of the profit line is equal to the *contribution margin per unit sold,* $8 (= $30 − $22) in this example, which is discussed next.

The Contribution Margin

Many of the questions that can be answered with the cost-volume-profit model are easier to answer by use of the contribution concept. Each unit sold makes a contribution to fixed costs and the earning of profit. The *contribution margin* per unit is the excess of unit selling price over unit variable cost.[2] In terms of our symbols, the contribution margin is defined by

$$\text{Contribution Margin per Unit} = P - b$$

For the Baltimore Manufacturing Company, the contribution margin is

$$\$8 = \$30 \text{ Selling Price per Unit} - \$22 \text{ Variable Cost per Unit}$$

Recall the basic equation relating profit and sales volume:

$$Y = Px - (a + bx)$$

If we rearrange the terms in that equation we obtain

$$Y = (P - b)x - a$$
$$= (\text{Contribution Margin per Unit} \times \text{Units}) - \text{Fixed Costs per Period}$$

For the Baltimore Manufacturing Company, we have

$$\text{Profit} = \$8 \times \text{Number of Units Sold} - \$4{,}800 \text{ Fixed Costs per Month}$$

This is the relation shown in the profit-volume graph, Figure 6.1(B).

The relationship between the breakeven point and the contribution margin is particularly simple:

$$\text{Breakeven Point in Units} = \frac{\text{Fixed Costs per Period}}{\text{Contribution Margin per Unit}}$$

The equation relating contribution margin and profit is convenient for answering cost-volume-profit questions when both selling prices and variable costs per unit are

---

[2]   The concepts of "sales revenue less total variable cost" and "sales revenue per unit less variable cost per unit" are both often called *contribution margin.* The former is actually *total contribution margin,* whereas the later is *contribution margin per unit.* We, and others, often use the term *contribution margin* to mean one or the other, depending on the context.

known. For example, if Baltimore Manufacturing Company wants to know the sales required in a month to achieve a profit of $5,000, it can solve the following:

$$\$5,000 = \$8x - \$4,800$$

$$\$8x = \$9,800$$

$$x = 1,225 \text{ Units per Month}$$

Applications of the Cost-Volume-Profit Model

In this section, we illustrate several uses of the cost-volume-profit model.

Example 1   The manager of Baltimore Manufacturing Company wants to know what price must be charged if sales are 800 units per month and profit is to be $4,000 per month. Because the selling price is the unknown and to draw the profit charts requires knowing the selling price, it is more convenient to solve the following equation than to draw a series of profit charts assuming different prices:

$$\text{Profit} = \text{Revenues} - \text{Expenses}$$

$$\$4,000 = 800P - [(800 \times \$22) + \$4,800]$$

$$800P = \$17,600 + \$4,800 + \$4,000$$

$$800P = \$26,400$$

$$P = \$33 \text{ Required Selling Price per Unit}$$

Example 2   The manager of Baltimore Manufacturing Company wants to know what sales in units per month are required to break even under the following conditions: fixed costs increase to $5,600 per month, but variable costs remain at $22 per unit and selling price remains at $30 per unit. As before, x represents the number of units produced and sold.

$$\text{Profit} = \text{Revenues} - \text{Expenses}$$

$$\$0 = \$30x - (\$22x + \$5,600)$$

$$\$8x = \$5,600$$

$$x = 700 \text{ Units Required to Break Even}$$

Example 3   The manager of Baltimore Manufacturing Company is considering two alternatives to increase profits. Under alternative A, machinery will be substituted for work currently done by workers. This action will increase fixed costs to $6,000 per month but reduce variable cost to $18 per unit. Under alternative B, higher-quality raw materials will be purchased, increasing variable cost to $25 per unit. The cost of inspection and quality control should decrease, resulting in a reduction in fixed cost to $4,000 per month. Under both alternatives, the selling price will be $30 per unit and 2,000 units will be sold each month. The expected profit under alternative A is

$$\text{Profit} = \text{Revenues} - \text{Expenses}$$
$$= (\$30 \times 2,000 \text{ Units}) - [\$6,000 + (\$18 \times 2,000 \text{ Units})]$$
$$= \$60,000 - \$6,000 - \$36,000$$
$$= \$18,000$$

The expected profit under alternative B is

$$\text{Profit} = \text{Revenues} - \text{Expenses}$$
$$= (\$30 \times 2,000 \text{ Units}) - [\$4,000 + (\$25 \times 2,000 \text{ Units})]$$
$$= \$60,000 - \$4,000 - \$50,000$$
$$= \$6,000$$

The analysis indicates that alternative A should be selected, because it results in the larger incremental profit.

Three Warnings

Three warnings should be kept in mind when using graphs such as those in Figure 6.1. Although the line showing total cost in Figure 6.1(A) and the line showing total profits or loss in Figure 6.1(B) are drawn as straight lines for their entire length, it is likely that at very low or very high levels of output (outside the relevant range), variable cost would be different from $22 per unit. The variable cost figures are probably estimated by studies of operations when the variation in sales was in a relatively narrow range, such as from 300 to 1,000 units per month. For production levels outside the relevant range, the linear relationship may not be valid. For this reason, the total cost curve, as in Figure 6.1(A) and the total profit curve, as in Figure 6.1(B), are sometimes shown as dotted lines at activity levels outside the range, where the linear relationships are suspected to be invalid.

Second, these charts have been vastly simplified by our assuming a single-product firm. For a multiproduct firm, the activity base to be shown on the horizontal axis may be difficult to define. Assume, for example, a two-product firm. Product X sells for $6 per unit and product Y sells for $4 per unit. The firm has been selling three units of product Y for every two units of product X. A convenient way to construct a single "product" for this firm is to define a composite "commodity" consisting of two units of product X and three units of product Y with a composite selling price of $24 = [(2 \times \$6) + (3 \times \$4)]$. Then the activity base axis (the horizontal axis) of the profit graphs can represent sales of the composite product bundle. The graphs will be valid so long as the ratio of sales of product X to product Y remains stable at two for three. When that ratio changes, however, the entire picture changes. In most multiproduct firms, the several products use common production facilities, but in different proportions. One of the problems of the multiproduct firm is to find the optimal proportions of units to sell. This problem is most easily solved with the techniques of linear programming. Once a firm uses linear programming, it will find that the information generated by the linear programming solution contains all the information in the profit graphs and will not find the profit graphs worth analyzing. The linear program will produce all the information the manager needs to know about breakeven, relative profit ratios, proper product mixes, and how the optimal mix of products changes as prices or technology change. We hasten to add, however, that the cost-volume-profit model and the breakeven point are much more often used by managers than is linear programming.

Third, the cost-volume-profit model considers only those factors in a decision that can be quantified. Managers should use the results of cost-volume-profit analysis as only one input into their decisions. In some cases, nonquantitative factors may play a much larger role in the decision than those that can be quantified.

Summary of the Cost-Volume-Profit Model

Listed below are the most important assumptions of the cost-volume-profit model. Because the required assumptions differ depending on the use made of the model, we have grouped the assumptions according to intended uses of the model.

Analysis of the Effects of Alternatives on Operations   The cost-volume-profit model is most powerful when used as a tool for analyzing the effects of various alternatives on operations. This is because the model captures most of the important operating relationships of the firm in a single equation. We can analyze the effects of changes in any of the following variables on the remaining variables: selling price, number of units sold, variable cost, fixed cost, sales mix, and production mix. Only one assumption is required by the model: *total costs can be broken down into fixed and variable components.*

Our illustrations in this chapter assumed that there was a linear relationship between revenues and volume and between costs and volume. It is possible, however, to apply the model with nonlinear revenue and cost functions. We also implicitly assumed that the variables in the model could be predicted with certainty. This assumption is likewise not required. Techniques have been developed for applying the cost-volume-profit model under conditions of uncertainty.[3] (See Problem **21** at the end of the chapter.)

Determination of a Unique Breakeven Point   This use of the cost-volume-profit model is more limited than the uses described earlier in this chapter and requires several more assumptions. In addition to the assumption of only fixed and variable costs described above, the following assumptions are required:

1 Selling price per unit, total fixed costs, and variable costs per unit will not change as the level of activity is changed.
2 The production mix and sales mix are constant.

---

[3]   Robert K. Jaedicke and Alexander A. Robichek, "Cost-Volume-Profit Analysis Under Conditions of Uncertainty," *The Accounting Review*, XXXIX (October 1964), pp. 917–926.

Predicting the Effects of Alternatives on Net Income   In order to use the cost-volume-profit model to predict the effect of various alternatives on net income reported to readers of external financial statements, the following assumptions are required:

1   Revenues are equal to cash inflows and expenses (other than depreciation) are equal to cash outflows.
2   There is no change in inventory between the beginning and end of the period.

PRICING DECISIONS

Decisions regarding the prices to be charged for a firm's products are complex, involving such factors as a firm's costs, competitors' actions, market conditions, and others. In many cases a firm will not be in a competitive position to set prices. The more highly competitive the market, the more likely that the market price will have to be accepted as given. In some situations, however, firms do have at least some control over the prices charged. In this section, we briefly consider pricing decisions to show that correct pricing decisions involve the principles of incremental analysis.

Cost-Based Approach to Pricing

One approach to setting prices is to add a markup to the total cost of producing and selling a product. For example, assume that product A requires manufacturing costs of $10 per unit and selling and administrative costs of $5 per unit. If a firm feels that a reasonable markup for this product is 20 percent on cost, then a price of $18 [= $15 + (.20 × $15)] will be set.

If a firm is to remain in business in the long run, it must recover all of its cost plus provide an adequate return to its owners. It is desirable, then, that long-run *average* prices approximate the amount derived from a cost-based approach to pricing. There are several shortcomings, however, to using this approach in making pricing decisions.

First, the "costs" attributable to a particular product are affected by several questionable accounting practices and conventions. For example, the cost of using plant and machinery is based on the acquisition cost of these assets. No recognition is given to the current opportunity cost of using the plant and machinery in manufacturing the product. Also, the portion of the acquisition cost of these assets attributable, or allocated, to each period is affected by the depreciable life and depreciation method used. The allocation of various costs to specific products becomes particularly questionable as the cost items become more and more indirect with respect to the product. Consider, for example, the allocation of the president's salary to each of a firm's products. Accounting practices such as these raise questions about the validity of product "cost" amounts.

Second, there is a circularity in pricing decisions when the cost-based approach is used. The per-unit cost of a product is critically affected by the number of units produced. As the number of units is increased, the amount of fixed cost allocated to each unit decreases. Thus, the per-unit cost of a product if 50,000 units are produced is different than when 60,000 units are produced. The number of units produced and sold, however, is affected by the price set. The quantity sold can be increased only if the price is decreased (that is, there is a downward-sloping demand curve). Thus,

Price is related to per-unit costs;
Per-unit cost is related to volume;
Volume is related to price.

There is a constant interplay among price, costs, and volume that makes it difficult to set prices on a cost-based approach.

Third, cost-based pricing can lead to incorrect decisions, particularly in the short run. For example, assume that the $15 per-unit cost of product A was composed of $5 variable cost and $10 fixed cost. The firm has received a special order for 10,000 units of product A for $8 a unit. This order will have no effect on the firm's regular market. Also, the firm has excess capacity to produce this product. If a cost-based approach to pricing were used, this special order would probably be rejected because the $8 price is less than the $15 per-unit cost. As we demonstrate below, rejection of this order would be an incorrect decision. Applying the incremental approach to pricing results in the correct decision.

Incremental Approach to Pricing

The incremental approach to pricing is based on the premise that the price must at least be equal to the *incremental* cost of producing and selling the product. In the short run, this will result in a positive contribution to the coverage of fixed costs, and generation of profit. In the long run, this will result in the coverage of all costs, because both fixed and variable costs become incremental costs in the long run.

The incremental approach is particularly useful in special-order decisions. Consider the special order for 10,000 units of product A discussed above. Exhibit 6.2 presents an analysis of the effects of not accepting and of accepting the special order, assuming that the regular market for product A consists of 100,000 units sold at a price of $20 a unit. As Exhibit 6.2 demonstrates, the special order at $8 per unit should be accepted, because that price permits the firm to cover the incremental costs of $5 per unit and provide a contribution of $3 per unit to coverage of fixed costs and profit.

The incremental approach to pricing works well for special orders but has been criticized for pricing a firm's regular products. It is suggested that following the incremental approach in the short run (that is, setting prices equal to variable cost) will lead to underpricing in the long run, because there will be no contribution to the coverage of fixed costs or generation of profit.

There are two responses to this criticism. First, the incremental approach does lead to correct short-run pricing decisions. Once plant capacity has been set and fixed costs have been incurred, the fixed costs become irrelevant to the short-run pricing decision. The firm must attempt to set a price at least equal to the incremental, or variable, costs. Second, both in the short and long run, the incremental approach only provides an indicator of the *minimum* acceptable price. The actual price charged will be some higher amount, taking market demand, competitors' actions, and similar factors into

EXHIBIT 6.2
Incremental Analysis for
Special-Order Decision

	Do Not Accept Special Order	Incremental Effect	Accept Special Order
Cash Inflows:			
100,000 × $20.	$2,000,000	—	$2,000,000
10,000 × $ 8.	—	$80,000	80,000
Cash Outflows			
Variable Costs:			
100,000 × $5	(500,000)	—	(500,000)
10,000 × $5	—	(50,000)	(50,000)
Fixed Costs.	(1,000,000)[a]	—	(1,000,000)[a]
Net Cash Inflow	$ 500,000	$30,000	$ 530,000

[a] If fixed costs are $10 per unit for 100,000 units, then the total fixed costs must be $1,000,000.

consideration. Consider the data for product A in Exhibit 6.3. The minimum acceptable price in the short run is the incremental cost of $5 per unit. In the long run, the
minimum acceptable price is $15 per unit, because both variable and fixed costs must
be covered. The desired long-run price is $18, which includes a profit of 20 percent of
cost. Between the $5 short-run minimum price and the $18 long-run desired price lies
the range of price flexibility for the firm. A price slightly larger than the variable cost
might be set for a special order as long as there is excess capacity and the firm's regular
market will not be affected. If extensive market competition exists for the firm's regular
product, a price slightly higher than the $5 minimum might be set. The firm hopes to
underprice competitors and to capture a larger share of the market. The increase in
quantity sold may more than offset the reduction in the contribution margin per unit
from a lower selling price, resulting in a larger *total* contribution margin. If a firm is
the only supplier of this product, it will be in a position to charge a price close to the
$18 long-run desired price. In this case, however, the earning of high profits may in-
duce other firms to manufacture the product, thereby reducing the initial firm's
market share. Thus, the pricing decision should begin with an analysis of short-run
and long-run incremental costs and then consider market conditions and competitors'
actions.

INVENTORY MANAGEMENT DECISIONS

Thus far in this chapter, we have considered cost-volume-profit decisions and pricing
decisions. In this section, we discuss inventory management decisions. Among the
questions faced by management of a merchandising or manufacturing firm are the
following:

1 How many units of inventory should be on hand and available for use or sale at various times during the year?
2 For a merchandising firm, what is the optimal number of times a particular item
should be ordered during the year, and what is the optimal size of the order?

EXHIBIT 6.3
Data for Pricing Product A

Short-Run Incremental Costs (Variable Costs) . . .	$ 5 =	Short-Run Minimum Price
Fixed Costs	10	
Long-Run Incremental Costs	$15 =	Long-Run Minimum Price
Desired Profit (.20 × $15)	3	
Target Selling Price.	$18 =	Long-Run Desired Price

3 For a manufacturing firm, what is the optimal number of production runs during the year, and what is the optimal number of units that should be produced in each production run?

The Inventory Management Problem

Inventory management decisions involve two types of opposing costs. There are fixed costs incurred each time an order is placed or a production run is made (for example, cost of processing each purchase order or cost of preparing machinery for each production run). The incurrence of these fixed costs suggests a strategy of minimizing the number of orders placed or production runs made. However, by ordering or producing less frequently, each order or production run must be for a larger number of units. The firm must carry a larger inventory so that sufficient inventory will be on hand between orders or production runs. A carrying cost is thereby incurred (for example, cost of maintaining warehouse facilities) that varies with the number of units on hand.

Thus, the inventory management problem is to find the optimal trade-off between these two types of opposing costs. The problem translates into a question of determining the optimal number of orders or production runs each year and the optimal number of units to be ordered or produced. For example, suppose that a firm sells 120,000 items per year, spread evenly throughout the year, that an item costs $1 to produce, that the setup cost per production run is $1,000, and that the cost of carrying an item in inventory for a year is 15 percent of the item's cost to produce. That is, if $1 is carried in inventory for a year, carrying costs for the year will be $.15. The firm could manufacture an entire year's production of 120,000 units in one batch, but if it did, it would carry, *on average,* 60,000 units in inventory during the year and the total carrying cost for the year would be $9,000 (= 60,000 × $.15). The firm could manufacture 10,000 units a month and then its average inventory on hand would be only 5,000 units, but there would be 12 separate incurrences of the setup cost, $12,000 in total. Exhibit 6.4 presents the setup costs, inventory carrying costs, and total costs as the number of batches increases. As the number of batches goes up, the setup costs increase and the carrying costs decrease.

The Inventory Management Solution

The selection of the optimal number of production runs per year or, equivalently, the number of units in a production run (because the number of production runs times the number of units per production run must equal 120,000 units per year) is essentially a problem requiring incremental analysis. The inventory carrying costs in column (4) of Exhibit 6.4 decrease as the number of production runs increase. The setup costs increase as the number of production runs increase. The optimal choice occurs when the decrease in carrying costs is equal to (or slightly greater than) the increase in setup costs. For example, when two production runs are made per year rather than just one, there is a decrease in carrying costs of $4,500 (= $9,000 − $4,500) and an increase in setup cost of $1,000 (= $2,000 − $1,000). Because the change in carrying cost exceeds the change in setup cost, it is desirable to increase the number of production runs to at least two per year. Now compare two production runs to three production runs per year. There is a decrease in carrying cost of $1,500 (= $4,500 − $3,000) and an increase in setup cost of $1,000 (= $3,000 − $2,000). Three production runs are therefore better than two. Now consider the alternatives of three versus four production runs per year. The decrease in carrying cost of $750 (= $3,000 − $2,250) is less than the increase in setup costs of $1,000 (= $4,000 − $3,000). It is therefore not desirable to go to four production runs per year. The optimal choice in this situation is three production runs per year with 40,000 units produced in each run.

In general, the optimal number of production runs per year and the optimal number of items per production run can be determined by using the following formula:[4]

$$N = \frac{D}{Q}, \quad \text{where} \quad Q = \sqrt{\frac{2SD}{H}}$$

In this formula, D is the annual demand in units (120,000 in the example), S is the setup cost per production run ($1,000 in the example), H is the cost of holding one unit in inventory for a year ($1 \times .15 = \$.15$ in the example), Q is the *economic order quantity*, or the optimal number of items in a production run (or order), and N is the optimal number of production runs (orders) per year. The two equations above are often referred to as the *EOQ model*.

In the example,

$$Q = \sqrt{\frac{2 \times \$1,000 \times 120,000}{\$.15}} = 40,000 \text{ Units per Production Run}$$

$$N = \frac{120,000}{40,000} = 3 \text{ Production Runs per Year}$$

Although the optimal number of production runs per year was an integer, 3, in the example, the result of the calculation will not usually lead to an integer answer. If the

---

[4] Using differential calculus, we can derive this formula by noting that

$$\frac{\text{Total Costs}}{\text{per Year}} = \frac{\text{Setup Costs}}{\text{per Year}} + \frac{\text{Holding Costs}}{\text{per Year}}$$

$$= \frac{SD}{Q} + \frac{HQ}{2}$$

Total costs are then a function of Q, whose minimum can be found by differentiating the expression on the right with respect to Q, setting the result equal to zero, and solving for Q.

EXHIBIT 6.4
Economic Order Quantity
Calculation

Setup Costs per Run are $1,000.
Annual Requirement is 120,000 Units.
Inventory Carrying Costs are 15 Percent per Year.
Manufacturing Cost per Unit is $1.00.

Production Runs (1)	Units in a Production Run[a] (2)	Average Number of Units in Inventory[b] (3)	Inventory Carrying Costs[c] (4)	Setup Costs[d] (5)	Total Costs[e] (6)
1	120,000	60,000	$9,000	$1,000	$10,000
2	60,000	30,000	4,500	2,000	6,500
3	40,000	20,000	3,000	3,000	6,000
4	30,000	15,000	2,250	4,000	6,250
5	24,000	12,000	1,800	5,000	6,800
6	20,000	10,000	1,500	6,000	7,500
12	10,000	5,000	750	12,000	12,750

[a] 120,000 units/number of production runs from column (1).
[b] Number of units in a production run from column (2)/2.
[c] Amount in column (3) $\times$ $1 cost per unit $\times$ .15.
[d] $1,000 $\times$ number of production runs from Column (1).
[e] Amount in column (4) + amount in column (5).

answer were, say, 3.50, we could carry out the optimal policy by producing 34,286 (= 120,000 units/3.50 production runs per year) items in each production run. We would find at the end of the year that there would be some items left over to start the next year. In two years, we would have a total of seven production runs.

Estimating Inventory Costs

The management scientist loses interest in the inventory management problem at this point, because a formula has been found that will always provide the optimal solution. The management accountant, however, must estimate the various costs for the formula to be used. This step is the most important as well as the most difficult. Incremental *setup* costs include wages (and payroll taxes on wages), the lost time of not running the equipment while the equipment is being set up, and so on. Incremental holding costs include wages, utilities, and other costs that vary with the number of units held in inventory. The carrying costs should not include an allocated portion of warehouse depreciation or rent if these costs are fixed regardless of the number of units in inventory. In this case, the depreciation and rent do not represent *incremental* holding costs.

Our discussion of the inventory management decision has been kept simple in order to demonstrate that it represents another area where incremental analysis is required. Applications of EOQ models by business firms require estimates of several costs in addition to those mentioned here. For example, by minimizing the number of orders or production runs per year, a firm incurs possible out-of-stock costs. This cost, essentially representing lost customer goodwill, occurs when a customer wants to purchase an item, finds the firm's inventory of that item has been depleted, and purchases the item from a competitor. This cost is extremely difficult to estimate. These refinements of the EOQ model are discussed in advanced management accounting texts.

QUESTIONS AND PROBLEMS

1 Review the meaning of the following terms and concepts discussed in this chapter.
  a Activity base.
  b Breakeven point.
  c Margin of safety.
  d Cost-volume-profit graph.
  e Profit-volume graph.
  f Contribution margin per unit.
  g Cost-based approach to pricing.
  h Incremental approach to pricing.
  i Short-run minimum price.
  j Long-run minimum price.
  k Inventory order.
  l Production run.
  m Setup cost.
  n Holding or carrying cost of inventory.
  o Economic order quantity.
  p EOQ model.
  q Out-of-stock cost.

2 Refer to the profit graph shown in Figure 6.2. Use the following list of concepts in answering each of the questions.
  (1) Variable expense.
  (2) Fixed expense.
  (3) Revenue.
  (4) Contribution margin per unit.
  (5) Margin of safety.
  (6) Breakeven sales in units.
  (7) None of the above.
  For each of the following segments on the graph, identify the concept from the list above that corresponds to the line segment.

  a $0A$ **c** $0D$ **e** $HE - DC$ **g** $HF + HG$
  b IG **d** $B0$ **f** $B0/0D$

3 Refer to the graph in Figure 6.2. Answer each of the following as "true" or "false."
  a If revenue is CD, then the margin of safety is zero.
  b If revenue is HE, then the margin of safety is GE.
  c Total profit could never be larger than total expense.
  d If selling price is increased, breakeven sales in units would increase.
  e If selling price is increased, HF would increase.
  f $FE = HG$.

4 What effect could the following changes, occurring independently, have on **(1)** the breakeven point, **(2)** the contribution margin, and **(3)** the expected profit?

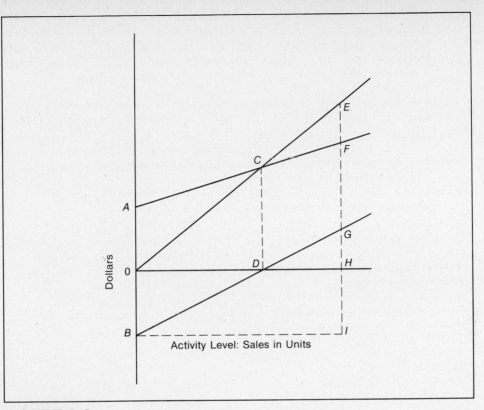

FIGURE 6.2

a An increase in fixed costs.
b A decrease in wage rates applicable to direct, strictly variable labor.
c An increase in the selling price of the product.
d An increase in production volume.
e An increase in insurance rates.

5 Assume the linear cost relationships of the cost-volume-profit model for a single-product firm and use the following answer key:
(1) More than double.
(2) Double.
(3) Increase, but less than double.
(4) Remain the same.
(5) Decrease.
Complete each of the following statements, assuming that all other quantities remain constant.
a If price is doubled, revenue will _____.
b If price is doubled, the total contribution margin (contribution margin per unit times number of units) will _____.
c If price is doubled, profit will _____.
d If contribution margin per unit is doubled, profit will _____.
e If fixed costs are doubled, the total contribution margin will _____.
f If fixed costs are doubled, profit will _____.

g   If fixed costs are doubled, the breakeven point of units sold will _____.

h   If total sales of units are doubled, profit will _____.

i   If total sales dollars are doubled, the breakeven point will _____.

j   If the contribution margin per unit is doubled, the breakeven point will _____.

k   If both variable costs per unit and selling price per unit are doubled, profit will _____.

6 Analysis of the operations of the Homes Company shows the fixed costs to be $100,000 and the variable costs to be $4 per unit. Selling price is $8 per unit.

a   Determine the breakeven point expressed in units.

b   How many units would have to be sold to earn a profit of $140,000?

c   What would profits be if revenue from sales were $1,000,000?

7 An excerpt from the income statement of the Wooster and Valley Company is shown below.

Wooster and Valley Company
Income Statement
Year Ended December 31, 19X1

Sales.		$2,000,000
Operating Expenses:		
Cost of Goods Sold.	$950,000	
Selling Expenses	300,000	
Administrative Expenses	150,000	
Total Operating Expenses		1,400,000
Profit.		$ 600,000

It was estimated that fixed expenses in 19X1 were $440,000.

a   What percentage of sales revenue is variable cost?

b   What is the breakeven point for Wooster and Valley Company?

c   Prepare a profit-volume graph for Wooster and Valley Company.

d   If sales revenue falls to $1,800,000, what will be the estimated amount of profit?

e   What volume of sales would be required to produce a profit of $1,120,000?

8 The operating data of the Snavely Company for April are as follows:

	Fixed	Variable	Total
Sales.			$2,200,000
Operating Expenses:			
Cost of Goods Sold.	$550,000	$610,000	$1,160,000
Administrative Expenses	110,000	30,000	140,000
Selling Expenses	185,000	42,000	227,000
Total Expenses.	$845,000	$682,000	$1,527,000
Profit.			$ 673,000

There were 110,000 units sold during April.

a What is the breakeven point in terms of units of product?
b If sales can be increased to 200,000 units, determine the amount of profits.
c For a revenue of $1,800,000, estimate the amount of profits.

9 The estimate of operating costs of the Tarmin Company for the year is that fixed costs will total $300,000 and that variable costs will be $2 per unit.
a Determine the breakeven point in sales at a selling price of $3 per unit.
b Determine the breakeven point in sales at a selling price of $4 per unit.
c How many units must be sold at a price of $5 per unit in order to generate a profit of $150,000?

10 In the last year, the sales of the Woodward Company were $1,200,000, fixed costs were $400,000, and variable costs were $600,000.
a At what sales volume would the company break even?
b If sales volume increased by 15 percent but prices are unchanged, by how much will profit increase?
c If fixed costs were reduced by 10 percent, by how much would profit increase?
d If variable costs were reduced by 10 percent, by how much would profit increase?

11 (This problem and the next three are adapted from problems by David O. Green.) When Britain's auto business slumped in 1921, William R. Morris (the "Henry Ford of Britain") gambled on cost saving from his new assembly lines and cut prices to a point where his expected loss per car in 1922 would be $240 if sales were the same as in 1921, 1,500 cars. However, sales in 1922 rose to 60,000 cars, and profits for the year were $810,000. For 1922, calculate:
a The contribution margin per car.
b Total fixed costs.
c Breakeven point in cars.

12 During 1963 Studebaker sold 90,000 cars for $250 million and realized a loss for the year of $24 million. The breakeven point was 120,000 cars. For 1963, calculate:
a The contribution margin per car.
b Total fixed costs.
c Profits for 1963 had sales been twice as large.

13 In 1967, reported *Time* magazine, the future of the American Motor Company seemed so shaky that its creditors, a consortium of banks headed by Chase Manhattan, examined the books every 10 days. The new management trimmed fixed costs by $20 million to cut the breakeven point from 350,000 cars in 1967 to 250,000 cars in 1968. From this information, calculate:
a The contribution margin per car (assumed constant for 1967 and 1968).
b Fixed costs for 1967 and 1968.
c 1967 losses assuming sales of 300,000 cars.
d 1968 profits assuming sales of 400,000 cars.

14 Reporting on Chrysler Corporation's performance for 1969, the *Wall Street Journal* pointed out that Chrysler had boosted its market share from 10 percent in 1962 to 18 percent in 1968. In 1969, however, countermeasures by Ford and General Motors, coupled with a 10-percent decline, or 1 million cars, in industry sales, created problems for Chrysler. Chrysler cut prices and increased advertising so that the contribution margin per car was $100 less in

1969 than in 1968. Fixed costs were reduced 20 percent in 1969 from what they had been in 1968. Nevertheless, Chrysler's 1969 profits were only $80 million on sales of 1.4 million autos, whereas 1968 profits had been $300 million. From this information, calculate:

a Industry sales (in autos) for 1968 and 1969.
b Chrysler's total fixed costs for 1968 and 1969.
c Chrysler's contribution margin per car in 1968 and 1969.

15 The Multiproduct Company produces and sells three different products. Operating data for the three products are shown below.

	Selling Price per Unit	Variable Cost per Unit	Fixed Cost per Month
Product P	$3	$2	—
Product Q	5	3	—
Product R	8	5	—
Entire Company	—	—	$48,000

For every unit of product R sold, the Company sells two units of product Q and three units of product P.

a Draw a cost-volume-profit graph for the Multiproduct Company.
b At what sales revenue does the Multiproduct Company break even?
c If the Company sells two units of product P for every two units of product Q and one unit of product R, at what sales revenue does it break even?

16 The Unitec Corporation had 19X0 revenues of $400,000 and profit equal to $4 per unit sold. Early in 19X1, the president of Unitec learned that a rival firm had contracted for a nation-wide advertising program of extraordinary proportions to launch a competing product. Thereupon, the president of Unitec Corporation ordered a price cut for Unitec's single product. At the start of 19X1, the president ordered an increase of $48,000 in advertising expenditures to publicize the price cut. The price cut and increased advertising produced 19X1 sales in units double the 19X0 sales in units, but left profit unchanged in 19X1 compared to 19X0.

Had the new, 19X1 price been in effect during 19X0, revenues on its actual 19X0 sales volume would have been $96,000 less than actual 19X0 revenues and the loss would have been equal to $2 per unit sold.

Compute each of the following quantities for 19X1.

a Sales volume in units.
b Revenues.
c Profit.
d Contribution margin per unit.
e Fixed costs.

17 Lecarla Company increased its market share from 12 percent in 19X0 to 36 percent in 19X5. By 19X6, however, actions by competitors and a 10-percent decline of 1,000 units in total industry sales from their 19X5 level created severe problems for Lecarla Company. In an unsuccessful effort to maintain its market share, the Company reduced selling prices during 19X6, resulting in a decrease in contribution margin of $10 per unit compared to 19X5. Cutbacks in administrative activities reduced total fixed costs by 20 percent in 19X6. Net income in 19X6 was only $12,000 on sales of 2,800 units, whereas 19X5 net income was $54,000.

Compute each of the following:

a Fixed costs during 19X5.
b Fixed costs during 19X6.
c Contribution margin per unit during 19X5.
d Contribution margin per unit during 19X6.
e Breakeven sales in units during 19X5.
f Breakeven sales in units during 19X6.

18 Despite an increase in sales revenue from $4,704,000 in 19X8 to $4,725,000 in 19X9, the American Steel Corporation recently reported a decline in net income of $129,500 from 19X8 to an amount equal to 2 percent of sales revenue in 19X9. Among other factors, an increase in average total cost per unit of $2.05 from the average total cost per unit of $20 in 19X8 was provided as an explanation.

a Determine the changes, if any, in average selling price and sales in units from 19X8 to 19X9.
b Determine the total fixed costs and variable cost per unit during 19X9. Assuming that such a calculation is improper given the above information, illustrate why with a graph and discuss any important assumptions of the cost-volume-profit model that have apparently been violated.

19 The Ronald Tool Corporation operated near the breakeven point of $1,125,000 during 19X1, while incurring fixed costs of $450,000. Management is considering two alternatives to reduce the breakeven level. Alternative A trims fixed costs by $100,000 annually; doing so will, however, reduce the quality of the product and result in a 10-percent decrease in selling price, although no change in the number of units sold. Alternative B substitutes automatized processing equipment for certain operations now performed manually. Alternative B will result in an annual increase in $150,000 in fixed costs, but will lead to a 5-percent decrease in variable costs per unit produced.

a What was the total contribution margin (contribution margin per unit times number of units sold) during 19X1?
b What is the breakeven sales in dollars under alternative A?
c What is the breakeven sales in dollars under alternative B?
d What should the company do?

20 Partial income statements of the Ford Corporation for the first two quarters of 19X2 appear below.

Ford Corporation
Partial Income Statements
for First and Second Quarters of 19X2

	First Quarter	**Second Quarter**
Sales at $0.90 per unit	$36,000	$63,000
Total expenses	49,000	67,000
(Loss)	($13,000)	($ 4,000)

Each dollar of variable cost per unit comprises $.50 of direct labor, $.25 of direct materials, and $.25 of variable overhead costs. Sales during the third quarter are expected to remain at the same level as during the second quarter, 70,000 units.

a What is the breakeven point in units?

b The company has just received a special order from the government for 30,000 units at a price of $.80 per unit. The company's regular market for 70,000 units in the third quarter would be unaffected if the order is accepted. The additional units can be produced with existing capacity, but if they are, direct labor costs will increase by 10 percent for *all* units produced because of the need to hire and use new labor. Additional insurance and administrative costs will result in an increase in fixed costs of $3,000 if the new order is accepted. Should the government order be accepted?

c Assume the order in **b** is accepted. What level of sales to nongovernment customers would be required for third-quarter profit to be $6,800?

21 (This problem should be assigned only to students who have had some introduction to statistics and access to tables for the normal distribution.) The Brown Corporation provides the following estimates of quantities relating to its business operations:

Selling Price.	$2.00 per Unit
Variable Costs	$1.50 per Unit
Fixed Costs	$5,000 per Month
Expected (Mean) Level of Sales, Which Are Normally Distributed.	16,000 Units per Month
Standard Deviation of Monthly Sales	4,000 Units

a What is the breakeven level of sales?

b What is the profit at the expected level of sales?

c Determine the probability of the company's at least breaking even in a given month.

d Determine the probability of profit being at least $5,000 for a given month.

22 United Instruments Corporation follows a cost-based approach to pricing. Prices are set equal to 120 percent of cost. The annual cost of producing one of its products is as follows:

Variable Manufacturing Costs.	$40 per Unit
Fixed Manufacturing Costs.	$100,000 per Year
Variable Selling and Administrative Costs.	$10 per Unit
Fixed Selling and Administrative Costs.	$60,000 per Year

a Assuming that 10,000 units are produced and sold, calculate the selling price per unit.

b Assuming that 20,000 units are produced and sold, calculate the selling price per unit.

23 Western Electronics Company follows a cost-based approach to pricing. Prices are set equal to 110 percent of cost. The company has annual fixed costs of $600,000. The variable costs of the company's products are as follows:

Product	**Variable Cost per Unit**
A	$10
B	20
C	30

The company expects to produce and sell 10,000 units of product A, 40,000 units of product B, and 10,000 units of product C.

a Compute the selling price of each product if fixed costs are allocated to products on the basis of the number of units produced.

b Compute the selling price of each product if fixed costs are allocated to products on the basis of total variable costs.

24 Eastern Furniture Company has a capacity of 100,000 tables per year. The company is currently producing and selling 80,000 tables per year at a selling price of $200 per table. The cost of producing and selling one table at the 80,000-unit level of activity is as follows:

Variable Manufacturing Costs.	$ 80
Fixed Manufacturing Costs.	20
Variable Selling and Administrative Costs.	40
Fixed Selling and Administrative Costs.	10
Total Costs.	$150

The company has received a special order for 10,000 tables at a price of $130. Because no sales commission would be paid on the special order, the variable selling and administrative costs would be only $25 per table. The company has rejected the offer based on the following computations:

Selling Price per Table.	$130
Variable Manufacturing Costs.	(80)
Fixed Manufacturing Costs.	(20)
Variable Selling and Administrative Costs.	(25)
Fixed Selling and Administrative Costs.	(10)
Net Loss per Table	$ (5)

Should Eastern Furniture Company have accepted the special order? Show your computations.

25 MacInnes Electronics Corporation manufactures citizens band radios. Early in 1976 it invested $20 million in manufacturing facilites that could produce 23-channel CB radios. Data for 1976 are as follows:

Number of Radios Produced and Sold.	40,000
Variable Cost per Radio.	$30
Fixed Cost per Radio.	25
Selling Price per Radio	80

Early in 1977, the federal government increased the number of channels permitted from 23 to 40. The result was that market demand for 23-channel radios decreased significantly and market price dropped to $50 a radio. Management has decided to close down its production facilities. The president stated, "We are hurt no matter what we do. We cannot adapt our current production facilities to manufacture 40-channel radios. However, if we continue manufacturing 23-channel radios, we will lose $5 on each unit produced and sold. We are, therefore, better off just to close down."

a Show how the president calculated the $5 loss on each 23-channel radio.

b Do you agree with the president's decision? If not, explain why and show your computations.

26 Whitley Electronics Company produces precision instruments for airplanes. It is currently operating at capacity. It has received an invitation to bid on a government contract for 1,000 specially designed precision instruments. The company has estimated its costs for the contract to be as follows:

Variable Manufacturing Costs.	$20,000
Allocated Fixed Manufacturing Costs.	15,000
Special Design and Production Setup Costs.	10,000
Shipping Costs.	5,000
Special Administrative Costs. . . . . :	5,000
Total Costs.	$55,000
Cost per Precision Instrument ($55,000/1,000)	$ 55

If Whitley accepts the government contract, it will have to forego regular sales of 1,000 units. These 1,000 units would have a selling price of $80 each, variable costs of $40 each, and fixed costs of $20 each.

a What is the lowest per-unit price that Whitley can bid on this contract without sacrificing profits?

b Whitley has learned that it will receive the contract if it bids $78 or less per unit. What action should Whitley take?

27 The Culler Company is introducing a new product and must decide what price should be set. An estimated demand schedule for the product is as follows:

Price	Quantity Demanded (in Units)
$10	40,000
12	36,000
14	28,000
16	24,000
18	18,000
20	15,000

Estimated costs are as follows:

Variable Manufacturing Costs.	$4 per Unit
Fixed Manufacturing Costs.	$40,000 per Year
Variable Selling and Administrative Costs.	$2 per Unit
Fixed Selling and Administrative Costs.	$10,000 per Year

a Prepare a schedule showing the total revenue, total cost, and total profit or loss for each selling price.

b Which price should be selected? Explain.

28 The purchasing agent responsible for ordering cotton underwear for Soares Retail Stores estimates that 10,000 packages of cotton underwear are sold evenly throughout each year, that each order costs $24 to place, and that it costs $.12 to hold a package of underwear in inventory for a year.

a How many packages of underwear should be ordered in each order?

b How many times per year should underwear be ordered?

29 The Lewis Company sells 3,000 medium-priced stereo sets per year in addition to many other items. The medium-priced stereo sets cost Lewis Company $100 each. Total costs of holding inventory for a year are 16 percent of an item's cost. A single purchasing department processes all purchase orders. Data on purchasing department costs for each of the last several years is shown below.

**Lewis Company
Total Orders Placed and
Costs Incurred in Purchasing Department**

Year	Orders Placed	Total Ordering Costs
1............................	5	$3,997
2............................	75	4,000
3............................	98	4,002
4............................	130	4,595
5............................	200	6,010
6............................	350	6,995

The purchasing department will be placing about 130 orders during the next year for items other than medium-priced stereo sets.

a What is the apparent relation between orders placed and total order costs? What is the incremental cost of placing an order for medium-priced stereo sets?

b What is the optimal number of medium-priced stereo sets to order at a time?

c What is the optimal number of orders to place each year for medium-priced stereo sets?

30 The Magee Foundry regularly uses 1,000 bolts per day, 250 days per year. Bolts can be purchased in lots of 1,000 for $10 per lot or in lots of 10,000 for $96.10 per lot. Ordering costs are $10 per order and the holding cost of items in inventory is estimated to be 20 percent of cost per year.

a What is the economic order quantity and associated annual costs assuming that only lots of 1,000 items are available?

b What is the economic order quantity and associated annual costs assuming that only lots of 10,000 items are available?

c Compare the costs of the two answers above and state the optimal ordering policy for these bolts assuming that lots of 1,000 or of 10,000 items can be ordered.

31* Bill French picked up the phone and called his boss, Wes Davidson, controller of Duo-Products Corporation. "Say, Wes, I'm all set for the meeting this afternoon. I've put together a set of breakeven statements that should really make the boys sit up and take notice — and I think they'll be able to understand them, too." After a brief conversation about other matters, the call was concluded and French turned to his charts for one last check-out before the meeting.

French had been hired six months earlier as a staff accountant. He was directly responsible to Davidson and, up to the time of this case, had been doing routine types of analysis work. French was an alumnus of a liberal arts undergraduate school and graduate business school, and was considered by his associates to be quite capable and unusually conscientious. It was this latter characteristic that had apparently caused him to "rub some of the working guys the wrong way," as one of his co-workers put it. French was well aware of his

---

* Copyright (1959) by the President and Fellows of Harvard College and reproduced by permission.

capabilities and took advantage of every opportunity that arose to try to educate those around him. Wes Davidson's invitation for French to attend an informal manager's meeting had come as some surprise to others in the accounting group. However, when French requested permission to make a presentation of some breakeven data, Davidson acquiesced. The Duo-Products Corporation had not been making use of this type of analysis in its review or planning programs.

Basically, what French had done was to determine the level at which the company must operate in order to break even. As he phrased it,

> The company must be able at least to sell a sufficient volume of goods so that it will cover all the variable costs of producing and selling the goods; further, it will not make a profit unless it covers the fixed, or nonvariable, costs as well. The level of operation at which total costs (that is, variable plus nonvariable) are just covered is the breakeven volume. This should be the lower limit in all our planning.

The accounting records had provided the following information that French used in constructing his chart:

Plant capacity—2 million units.
Past year's level of operations—1.5 million units.
Average unit selling price—$1.20.
Total fixed costs—$520,000.
Average variable unit cost—$.75.

From this information, French observed that each unit contributed $.45 to fixed overhead after covering the variable costs. Given total fixed costs of $520,000, he calculated that 1,155,556 units must be sold in order to break even. He verified this conclusion by calculating the dollar sales volume that was required to break even. Because the variable costs per unit were 62.5 percent of the selling price, French reasoned that 37.5 percent of every sales dollar was left available to cover fixed costs. Thus, fixed costs of $520,000 require sales of $1,386,667 in order to break even.

When he constructed a breakeven chart to present the information graphically, his conclusions were further verified. The chart also made it clear that the firm was operating at a fair margin over the breakeven requirements, and that the profits accruing (at the rate of 37.5 percent of every sales dollar over breakeven) increased rapidly as volume increased (see Figure 6.3).

Shortly after lunch, French and Davidson left for the meeting. Several representatives of the manufacturing departments were present, as well as the general sales manager, two assistant sales managers, the purchasing officer, and two people from the product engineering office. Davidson introduced French to the few people whom he had not already met, and then the meeting got under way. French's presentation was the last item on Davidson's agenda, and in due time the controller introduced French, explaining his interest in cost control and analysis.

French had prepared enough copies of his chart and supporting calculations for everyone at the meeting. He described carefully what he had done and explained how the chart pointed to a profitable year, dependent on meeting the volume of sales activity that had been maintained in the past. It soon became apparent that some of the participants had known in advance what French planned to discuss; they had come prepared to challenge him and soon had taken control of the meeting. The following exchange ensued (see Exhibit 6.5 for a checklist of participants with their titles):

COOPER (production control): You know, Bill, I'm really concerned that you haven't allowed for our planned changes in volume next year. It seems to me that you should have

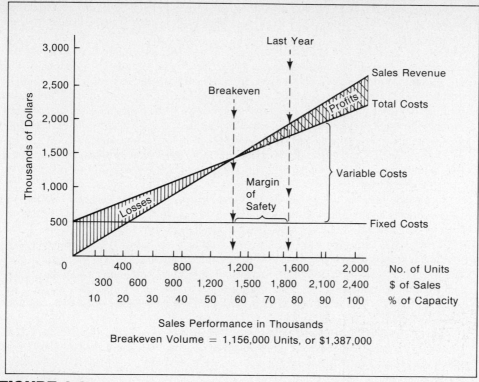

FIGURE 6.3

allowed for the sales department's guess that we'll boost sales by 20 percent, unit-wise. We'll be pushing 90 percent of what we call capacity then. It sure seems that this would make quite a difference in your figuring.

FRENCH: That might be true, but as you can see, all you have to do is read the cost and profit relationship right off the chart for the new volume. Let's see—at a million-eight units we'd. . . .

WILLIAMS (manufacturing): Wait a minute, now!!! If you're going to talk in terms of 90 percent of capacity, and it looks like that's what it will be, you had better note that we'll be shelling out some more for the plant. We've already got okays on investment money that will

---

EXHIBIT 6.5
List of Participants in the Meeting

Bill French	Staff Accountant
Wes Davidson	Controller
John Cooper	Production Control
Fred Williams	Manufacturing
Ray Bradshaw	Assistant Sales Manager
Arnie Winetki	General Sales Manager
Anne Fraser	Administrative Assistant to the President

boost your fixed costs by $10,000 a month, easy. And that may not be all. We may call it 90 percent of plant capacity, but there are a lot of places where we're just full up and we can't put things up any tighter.

COOPER: See, Bill? Fred Williams is right, but I'm not finished on this bit about volume changes. According to the information that I've got here—and it came from your office—I'm not sure that your breakeven chart can really be used even if there were to be no changes next year. Looks to me like you've got average figures that don't allow for the fact that we're dealing with three basic products. Your report here (see Exhibit 6.6) on costs, according to product lines, for last year makes it pretty clear that the "average" is way out of line. How would the breakeven point look if we took this on an individual product basis?

FRENCH: Well, I'm not sure. Seems to me that there is only one breakeven point for the firm. Whether we take it product by product or in total, we've got to hit that point. I'll be glad to check for you if you want, but. . . .

BRADSHAW (assistant sales manager): Guess I may as well get in on this one, Bill. If you're going to do anything with individual products, you ought to know that we're looking for a big swing in our product mix. Might even start before we get into the new season. The "A" line is really losing out and I imagine that we'll be lucky to hold two-thirds of the volume there next year. Wouldn't you buy that, Arnie? [Agreement from the general sales manager.] That's not too bad, though, because we expect that we should pick up the 200,000 that we lose, and about a quarter million units more, over in "C" production. We don't see anything that shows much of a change in "B." That's been solid for years and shouldn't change much now.

WINETKI (general sales manager): Bradshaw's called it about as we figure it, but there's something else here too. We've talked about our pricing on "C" enough, and now I'm really going to push our side of it. Ray's estimate of maybe half a million—450,000 I guess it was—up on "C" for next year is on the basis of doubling the price with no change in cost. We've been priced so low on this item that it's been a crime—we've got to raise, but good, for two reasons. First, for our reputation; the price is out of line class-wise and is completely incon-

EXHIBIT 6.6
Product Class Cost Analysis
(Normal Year)

	Aggregate	"A"	"B"	"C"
Sales at Full Capacity (Units)	2,000,000			
Actual Sales Volume (Units)	1,500,000	600,000	400,000	500,000
Unit Sales Price	$ 1.20	$ 1.67	$ 1.50	$ .40
Total Sales Revenue	$1,800,000	$1,000,000	$600,000	$200,000
Variable Cost per Unit	$ .75	$ 1.25	$ .625	$ .25
Total Variable Cost	$1,125,000	$ 750,000	$250,000	$125,000
Fixed Costs	$ 520,000	$ 170,000	$275,000	$ 75,000
Net Profit	$ 155,000	$ 80,000	$ 75,000	—
Ratios:				
Variable Costs to Sales	.63	.75	.42	.63
Variable Income to Sales	.37	.25	.58	.37
Utilization of Capacity	75.0%	30.0%	20.0%	25.0%

sistent with our quality reputation. Second, if we don't raise the price, we'll be swamped and we can't handle it. You heard what Williams said about capacity. The way the whole "C" field is exploding, we'll have to answer to another half-million units in unsatisfied orders if we don't jack the price up. We can't afford to expand that much for this product.

At this point, Anne Fraser (administrative assistant to the president) walked up toward the front of the room from where she had been standing near the rear door. The discussion broke for a minute, and she took advantage of the lull to interject a few comments.

FRASER: This has certainly been enlightening. Looks like you fellows are pretty well up on this whole operation. As long as you're going to try to get all the things together that you ought to pin down for next year, let's see what I can add to help you:

Number One: Let's remember that everything that shows in the profit area here on Bill's chart is divided just about evenly between the government and us. Now, for last year we can read a profit of about $150,000. Well, that's right. But we were left with half of that, and then paid our dividends of $50,000 to the stockholders. Since we've got an anniversary year coming up, we'd like to put out a special dividend of about 50 percent extra. We ought to hold $25,000 in for the business, too. This means that we'd like to hit $100,000 *after* the costs of being governed.

Number Two: From where I sit, it looks like we're going to have a talk with the union again, and this time it's liable to cost us. All the indications are—and this isn't public—that we may have to meet demands that will boost our production costs—what do you call them here, Bill—variable costs—by 10 percent across the board. This may kill the bonus-dividend plans, but we've got to hold the line on past profits. This means that we can give that much to the union only if we can make it in added revenues. I guess you'd say that that raises your breakeven point, Bill—and for that one I'd consider the company's profit to be a fixed cost.

Number Three: Maybe this is the time to think about switching our product emphasis. Arnie Winetki may know better than I which of the products is more profitable. You check me out on this Arnie—and it might be a good idea for you and Bill French to get together on this one, too. These figures that I have (Exhibit 6.6) make it look like the percentage contribution on line "A" is the lowest of the bunch. If we're losing volume there as rapidly as you sales folks say, and if we're as hard pressed for space as Fred Williams has indicated, maybe we'd be better off grabbing some of that big demand for "C" by shifting some of the facilities over there from "A."

That's all I've got to say. Looks to me like you've all got plenty to think about.

DAVIDSON: Thanks, Anne. I sort of figured that we'd get wound up here as soon as Bill brought out his charts. This is an approach that we've barely touched, but, as you can see, you've all got ideas that have got to be made to fit here somewhere. I'll tell you what let's do. Bill, suppose you rework your chart and try to bring into it some of the points that were made here today. I'll see if I can summarize what everyone seems to be looking for.

First of all, I have the idea buzzing around in the back of my mind that your presentation is based on a rather important series of assumptions. Most of the questions that were raised were really about those assumptions; it might help us all if you try to set the assumptions down in black and white so that we can see just how they influence the analysis.

Then, I think that Cooper would like to see the unit sales increase taken up, and he'd also like to see whether there's any difference if you base the calculations on an analysis of individual product lines. Also, as Bradshaw suggested, since the product mix is bound to change, why not see how things look if the shift materializes as sales has forecast?

Arnie Winetki would like to see the influence of a price increase in the "C" line; Fred Williams looks toward an increase in fixed manufacturing costs of $10,000 a month, and Anne Fraser has suggested that we should consider taxes, dividends, expected union demands, and the question of product emphasis.

I think that ties it all together. Let's hold off on our next meeting, fellows, until Bill has time to work this all into shape.

With that, the participants broke off into small groups and the meeting disbanded. French and Wes Davidson headed back to their offices and French, in a tone of concern asked Davidson, "Why didn't you warn me about the hornet's nest I was walking into?"

"Bill, you didn't ask!"

a What are the assumptions implicit in Bill French's determination of his company's break-even point?

b On the basis of French's revised information, what does next year look like:

   (1) What is the breakeven point?

   (2) What level of operations must be achieved to pay the extra dividend, ignoring union demands?

   (3) What level of operations must be achieved to meet the union demands, ignoring bonus dividends?

   (4) What level of operations must be achieved to meet both dividends and expected union requirements?

c Can the breakeven analysis help the company decide whether to alter the existing product emphasis? What can the company afford to invest for additional "C" capacity?

d Is this type of analysis of any value? For what can it be used?

CHAPTER 7
LONG-RUN CAPACITY DECISIONS: INTRODUCTION TO CAPITAL BUDGETING

In Chapter Six, we considered the application of the incremental principle to several kinds of short-run operating decisions. In each of the cases discussed, the firm's plant capacity was fixed. The objective was to decide how best to use that fixed capacity in the short run, for example: How many units should be produced? What price should be charged? How much inventory should be kept on hand? In this chapter, we shift our attention to the long run. We focus on decisions to change plant or operating capacity. Should a larger plant be built? Should new machinery be acquired to replace older, less efficient machinery? Should machinery be acquired that will perform services currently performed by workers? No decision is more important to the long-run success of a firm than deciding which investment projects to undertake.

Short-run operating decisions and long-run capacity decisions are similar in that both rely on an incremental analysis of cash inflows and cash outflows. There is one important difference, however. Long-run capacity decisions involve cash flows over several future periods, whereas the typical operating decisions involve only short-range cash flows. When the cash flows extend over several future periods in different patterns for various alternatives, some technique must be employed for making the cash flows comparable. This technique is *present value analysis*. The Appendix discusses present value analysis. You should be familar with it before studying this chapter.

INDEPENDENCE OF INVESTMENT AND FINANCING DECISIONS

A firm faced with a decision to acquire new plant or equipment must decide (1) whether to acquire the new asset (the investment decision), and (2) how to raise the capital required to obtain the new asset (the financing decision). The capital might be raised through borrowing, by retaining earnings (through a curtailing of dividends), or by issuing additional capital stock.

One of the most significant contributions to the theory of finance in recent years is the principle that the investment decision should be made independently of the financing decision. That is, the investment decision should be made first, and only after a project gets the go-ahead should management begin to consider how to finance it.

The rationale for separating investment and financing decisions rests on the premise that all of a firm's assets are financed by all of a firm's equities (that is, liabilities plus owners' equity). A new asset will involve investing capital, but once the asset is added to the firm's portfolio of assets, it is financed by all of the firm's equities. Specific assets do not match specific types of equities.

Raising capital is an important problem, but it does not concern us here. This chapter discusses only the investment decision.

THE NET PRESENT VALUE METHOD

There are several methods used by business firms for making investment decisions that are discussed in the accounting and finance literature. In this chapter, we present the preferred method, which relies on net present value analysis. Chapter Sixteen discusses several alternative methods used and their shortcomings.

The net present value method involves the following steps:

1 Estimating the amounts of future cash inflows and future cash outflows for each alternative under consideration.
2 Discounting the future cash flow to the present using the firm's cost of capital.
3 Accepting or rejecting the proposed project.

If the net present value of the future cash inflows and outflows is positive, then the alternative should be accepted. If the net present value of the future cash flows is negative, then the alternative should be rejected.

This three-step procedure is a simplified description of a complex process involving many estimates and predictions. These complexities are considered later in this chapter. For now, however, let us look at two illustrations of the net present value method, the first ignoring income taxes and the second considering income taxes.

Illustration Ignoring Income Taxes

Garden Winery Company is contemplating the acquisition of equipment that will allow it to bring a new variety of wine to the market. The equipment costs $10,000 and is expected to last four years. Exhibit 7.1 shows the cash inflows and cash outflows expected from this equipment during each of the four years of its useful life. At the end of year 0, that is, at the start of the project, the equipment is purchased for $10,000. The decreasing pattern of cash inflows over the four years results in part from the equipment becoming less productive over time and in part from the expected reaction of other wine sellers, who will copy the new wine variety and force down the selling price.

EXHIBIT 7.1
Garden Winery Company
Cash Flows Associated with a
New Wine Project
(Ignoring Income Taxes)

End of Year (1)	Cash Inflows (2)	Cash Outflows (3)	Net Cash Inflow (Outflows) (4)	Present Value Factor at 20% (5)	Present Value of Cash Flows (6)
0	—	$10,000	$ (10,000)	1.00000	$ (10,000)
1	$ 6,000	1,000	5,000	.83333	4,167
2	5,500	1,000	4,500	.69444	3,125
3	5,000	1,000	4,000	.57870	2,315
4	4,000	1,000	3,000	.48225	1,447
Total . .	$20,500	$14,000	$ 6,500		$ 1,054

(2), (3): given.
(4) = (2) − (3).
(5) Based on the factors in Table 2 at the back of the book.
(6) = (4) × (5).

The cash outflows for each of the four years are for labor, grapes, bottles, and similar costs. Note that we do not consider depreciation on the equipment, because it does not affect cash flows. (Cash flows are affected only when the equipment is acquired, not later.) We have also assumed that the equipment has a zero salvage value at the end of four years. Column (4) shows the net cash flow for each year.

The cash flows in column (4) are not directly comparable. Because cash can be invested over time to earn interest, cash received or paid today has a higher present value than cash to be received or paid at some time in the future. To put these cash flows on a comparable basis, they are discounted to their present value. The discount rate used in this illustration is 20 percent (we discuss the selection of an appropriate discount rate later in this chapter). If cash can be invested to earn 20 percent, the right to receive $5,000 at the end of year 1 is equivalent to receiving $4,167 today. Column (5) shows the discount factors for the present value of $1 for various periods at 20 percent. Column (6) shows the present value of each cash flow.

This project results in a positive net present value of $1,054. That is, the present value of the net future cash inflows exceeds the initial investment by $1,054. This project should therefore be accepted and the equipment acquired.

Illustration Considering Income Taxes

Income taxes are a major expense of doing business. Income taxes affect both the *amounts* of cash flows and the *timing* of cash flows, and, consequently, must be considered in making investment decisions. Chapters Seventeen and Eighteen discuss many of the managerial implications of income taxes, but here we briefly introduce this important topic.

EXHIBIT 7.2
Garden Winery Company
Cash Flows Associated with a
New Wine Project
(Considering Income Taxes)

(A) STRAIGHT-LINE DEPRECIATION METHOD

End of Year (1)	Cash Inflows (2)	Cash Outflows (3)	Pretax Net Cash Flow (4)	Depreciation Expense (5)	Taxable Income (6)	Income Tax Expense (7)	Net Cash Inflow (Outflow) (8)	Present Value Factor at 10% (9)	Present Value of Cash Flows (10)
0	—	$10,000	$ (10,000)	—	—	—	$ (10,000)	1.00000	$ (10,000)
1	$ 6,000	1,000	5,000	$ 2,500	$2,500	$1,000	4,000	.90909	3,636
2	5,500	1,000	4,500	2,500	2,000	800	3,700	.82645	3,058
3	5,000	1,000	4,000	2,500	1,500	600	3,400	.75131	2,554
4	4,000	1,000	3,000	2,500	500	200	2,800	.68301	1,912
Total	$20,500	$14,000	$ 6,500	$10,000	$6,500	$2,600	$ 3,900		$ 1,160

(B) DOUBLE-DECLINING-BALANCE DEPRECIATION METHOD

End of Year (1)	Cash Inflows (2)	Cash Outflows (3)	Pretax Net Cash Flow (4)	Depreciation Expense (5)	Taxable Income (6)	Income Tax Expense (7)	Net Cash Inflow (Outflow) (8)	Present Value Factor at 10% (9)	Present Value of Cash Flows (10)
0	—	$10,000	$ (10,000)	—	—	—	$ (10,000)	1.00000	$ (10,000)
1	$ 6,000	1,000	5,000	$ 5,000	$ 0	$ 0	5,000	.90909	4,545
2	5,500	1,000	4,500	2,500	2,000	800	3,700	.82645	3,058
3	5,000	1,000	4,000	1,250	2,750	1,100	2,900	.75131	2,179
4	4,000	1,000	3,000	1,250	1,750	700	2,300	.68301	1,571
Total	$20,500	$14,000	$ 6,500	$10,000	$6,500	$2,600	$ 3,900		$ 1,353

(2), (3): given.
(4) = (2) − (3).
(5)(A) = $10,000/4.

(5) (B) = $10,000 × .5 = $5,000.
 5,000 × .5 = 2,500.
 2,500 × .5 = 1,250.
 1,250 × 1.0 = 1,250.

(6) = (4) − (5).
(7) = .40 × (6).
(8) = (4) − (7).

(9) Based on the factors from Table 2 at the back of the book.
(10) = (8) × (9).

Reconsider the proposed equipment acquisition for Garden Winery Company. In this case, assume an income tax rate of 40 percent and a discount rate for aftertax cash flows of 10 percent. Also assume that straight-line depreciation is used. The top panel of Exhibit 7.2 shows the calculation of the net present value of the proposed project, assuming that the equipment is depreciated using the straight-line method for income tax purposes. Note that depreciation expense in column (5) is not a cash flow. It does represent an expense, however, in determining taxable income. Income taxes require cash. Depreciation expense, therefore, *indirectly* affects cash flows by way of its effect on taxable income and the income taxes paid. Using a 10-percent discount rate, the project has a positive net present value and should be accepted.

Accelerated Depreciation   One of the most important effects of income tax laws on investment decisions arises from the ability to use accelerated depreciation methods. Accelerated depreciation methods (such as double-declining-balance and sum-of-the-years'-digits) shift depreciation charges from later to earlier years as compared to the straight-line method. This has the effect of shifting taxable income and tax payments from earlier to later years. Although accelerated depreciation does not change the total tax liability generated by a project over its life, it does influence the desirability of the project by affecting the timing of cash flows.

The lower panel of Exhibit 7.2 shows the calculation of the net present value of the project, assuming that the double-declining-balance method of depreciation is used. Note that the total depreciation expense in column (5) is $10,000 under both the straight-line and double-declining-balance methods. In the latter case, however, the deductions are more accelerated. The net cash flows in column (8) total $3,900 in both cases, but they occur in a different pattern. The net present value of the project is greater if the double-declining-balance depreciation method is used for tax purposes as compared to the use of the straight-line method.

The Cost of Capital

The appropriate discount rate to use in evaluating investment projects is the firm's *cost of capital.* The cost of capital is easy to define but, in practice, is difficult to measure. Two common definitions of the cost of capital are as follows:

1 The average rate a firm must pay for funds invested in that firm.
2 The rate of return for new investment projects such that, if all projects undertaken by a firm yield that rate, then the market value of the firm's shares will remain unchanged.

These definitions may not appear to be saying the same thing, but the modern theory of finance can demonstrate their equivalence. The easiest of these definitions to consider is the first. It says, essentially, that a project must generate a return at least equal to the *average* cost to the firm of obtaining its capital. The equities side of the balance sheet (liabilities and stockholders' equity) shows the sources of capital to the firm. Each of the components of capital provided to the firm has a price. Current liabilities, such as accounts payable, provide capital to the firm at no explicit cost. Notes and bonds payable have an explicit, or contractual, interest cost. Because interest on bonds and notes is deductible from otherwise taxable income, the aftertax cost to the firm for interest on notes and bonds is less than the quoted interest rate. The effective price to the firm for preferred stock is the actual dividend rate, because preferred stock dividends are not expenses in determining taxable income. The price for capital in the form of common stockholders' equity (common stock, additional paid-in capital, and retained earnings) is the rate of discount that equates the present value of the total dividend stream the market expects the firm to distribute over its life to the current market price of the firm's stock. The rate of return on the common stock accounts is, of course, the hardest to compute in practice.

Because we separate the investment and financing decisions, we expect each investment project to earn a rate of return equal to at least the *average* cost of capital for the firm. If the project earns just the cost of capital (that is, the project has a zero net present value), then the market value of the firm's shares will remain unchanged as a result of the new investment project. If a project has a positive net present value, then the market value of the firm's shares should increase when that project is undertaken. This occurs because the firm is able to generate a higher rate of return than the average rate required by the suppliers of capital. Because the returns to creditors and preferred stockholders are fixed, this excess return accrues to the benefit of the common stockholders.

The subtleties of computing the cost of capital rate are properly the subject of finance courses. Here, the emphasis is on using that rate. The decision rule is: *A firm should undertake an investment project if the net present value of the cash flows is positive when the cash flows are discounted at the cost of capital rate.*

Sensitivity of Net Present Value to Estimates

The calculation of the net present value of a proposed project requires three types of predictions or estimates:

1 The amount of future cash flows.
2 The timing of future cash flows.
3 The cost of capital rate.

There is likely to be some error in the amount predicted or estimated for each of these three items. The net present value model exhibits different degrees of sensitivity to such errors.

Amounts of Future Cash Flows   Errors in predicting the amounts of future cash flows are likely to have the largest impact of the three items. Exhibit 7.2 indicated that the proposed project for Garden Winery Company had a net present value (using the straight-line depreciation method) of $1,160 based on the cash flows initially predicated. Suppose that there is a 10 percent error in these predictions and that the estimate of future cash flows each year should have been 10 percent less than the amounts shown in column (4) of Exhibit 7.2. The net present value of the proposed project using the same 10 percent discount rate is $362. The total error in present value dollars is $798 (= $1,160 − $362), which is about 8 percent of the initial investment, $10,000. Thus, a 10 percent error in predicted cash flows caused about a 10 percent error in the measurement of the net present value. Given the sensitivity of the net present value model to errors in the predictions of cash flows, it is desirable that the predictions be as accurate as possible. Statistical techniques have recently been developed for dealing with the uncertainty inherent in predictions of cash flows. These techniques, which build on the net present value model, are beyond the scope of this book.[1]

Timing of Future Cash Flows   The degree of sensitivity of the net present value model to shifts in the pattern, but not in the total amount, of cash flows depends on the extent of the shifting. Column (8) of Exhibit 7.2 shows net cash flows for years 1 through 4 of $4,000, $3,700, $3,400, and $2,800, or $13,900 in total when the straight-line depreciation method is used. Suppose that the pattern of cash flows should have been estimated to be relatively stable as follows: $3,500, $3,500, $3,500, $3,400, again a total of $13,900. The net present value in the latter case would be $1,027, as compared to $1,160 in Exhibit 7.2. The error is $133 (= $1,160 − $1,027) in present value terms, or just over 1 percent of the initial investment. Other examples could be constructed that would result in a different percentage effect. It seems clear, however, that errors in predicting the amount of cash flows tend to be more serious than in predicting their pattern.

Calculation of Cost of Capital   A third uncertain factor in the net present value calculation is the cost of capital. The difficulty here lies not in predicting a future cash flow but in estimating returns required currently by various suppliers of capital, particularly common stockholders. No satisfactory techniques have yet been developed for empirically verifying a firm's estimate of its cost of capital rate.

What loss does a firm suffer if it incorrectly calculates its cost of capital? Using the 10 percent cost of capital for Garden Winery Company in Exhibit 7.2 results in a net present value of $1,160 for the proposed project (using the straight-line depreciation method). If the cost of capital should have been estimated to be 15 percent, the net present value for this project would have been + $113. Management miscalculated the cost of capital by 50 percent [= (.15 − .10)/.10]. That large error resulted in a misestimate of the net present value by $1,047 (= $1,160 − $113), or only 10 percent of the initial investment. In general, if a project is marginally desirable for a given cost of capital, it will ordinarily not be grossly undesirable for slightly higher rates. If a project is clearly worthwhile when the cost of capital is 10 percent (that is, has a positive net present value), it is likely to be worthwhile even when the cost of capital is 15 percent.

EVALUATING ALTERNATIVE INVESTMENT PROJECTS

Two problems frequently encountered in capital budgeting decisions concern mutually exclusive projects and capital rationing. These two topics are considered briefly here.

---

[1]   Interested readers might consult the following books for additional discussion of capital budgeting under uncertainty: Harold Bierman, Jr., and Seymour Smidt, *The Capital Budgeting Decision,* 4th ed. (New York: Macmillan Company, 1975); J. Fred Weston and Eugene F. Brigham, *Managerial Finance* (Hinsdale, Ill.: Dryden Press, 1975), chap. 11.

Mutually Exclusive Projects

Mutually exclusive projects are projects where acceptance of one alternative eliminates the need to consider further the rejected alternatives. For example, a firm needing a new truck might prepare a net present value analysis for trucks meeting the firm's specifications from each of four different suppliers. After one of the trucks is selected there is no need to consider the other three trucks as viable investment alternatives. Only one truck is needed. The decision rule for choosing among mutually exclusive projects is to accept the project with the largest net present value and reject the others.

In Chapter Sixteen we consider other decision rules for evaluating investment projects. There we see that several of the other rules can give wrong answers when projects are mutually exclusive.

Capital Rationing

Another problem arises in connection with capital rationing. Suppose that a manager is faced with a set of investment alternatives, each of which requires current cash outlays and has a positive net present value. Altogether they require more funds this year than have been made available by higher management. For example, assume that a manager has $20,000 to invest in projects, is told to use a 12 percent cost of capital, and may choose from the set of four projects shown in Exhibit 7.3. Aside from the capital constraint, each of the four projects is independent of the others (that is, they are not mutually exclusive projects).

EXHIBIT 7.3
Data for Capital Rationing
Illustration

	At Cost of Capital of 12 Percent		
Project Name (1)	Initial Cash Outlay Required (2)	Present Value of Cash Inflows (3)	Net Present Value of Cash Flows (4) = (3) − (2)
A	$12,000	$17,000	$5,000
B	11,000	15,000	4,000
C	7,000	10,000	3,000
D	3,000	5,500	2,500

All four projects represent worthwhile investments but the manager, given a $20,000 constraint on first-year cash outlays, may not undertake all of them. Juggling the possibilities, we can see from Exhibit 7.4 that the manager must choose one from several combinations of projects.

What is the manager to do? To maximize the net present values of the cash flows to the firm, the manager must choose the combination of projects A and C and reject the others. (Any funds not invested in these four projects must be used elsewhere in the firm and will, presumably, earn the cost of capital.)

EXHIBIT 7.4
Dilemma Caused by
Capital Rationing

Project Combinations (1)	For Each Project Combination, the Sum of		
	Initial Cash Outlays (2)	Present Value of Cash Inflows (3)	Net Present Values (4) = (3) − (2)
A, C	$19,000	$27,000	$8,000
A, D	15,000	22,500	7,500
B, C	18,000	25,000	7,000
B, D	14,000	20,500	6,500
C, D	10,000	15,500	5,500

The problem of capital rationing arises from the inherent contradiction in telling a manager to use a cost of capital of, say, 12 percent while simultaneously limiting the capital budget. A limited capital budget implies a high, if not infinite, cost of capital. With a budget constraint, the firm is implicitly telling the manager that the cost of capital for funds in excess of $20,000 per year is so large that capital expenditures in excess of $20,000 per year should not be considered. But because all the firm's capital finances all its projects, the larger cost of capital is the rate the manager (and the firm) should use for evaluating *all* potential investment projects. For these purposes, the cost of capital is not a number that necessarily increases as more capital is used.

Using the cost of capital to calculate net present values of cash flows contains the only needed budgeting device: managers will not invest funds in projects returning less than the cost of capital because the net present values of such projects will be negative. Capital rationing has no place in a profit-seeking firm that chooses between investment alternatives by taking the time value of money into account.

If management perceives a constraint on funds available for investment, then all managers should be told to use a higher cost of capital than had been used before. If, when the higher discount rate is used by managers in evaluating projects, the total funds required still exceed the perceived constraints, then the discount rate should be increased to still a higher level. If at the higher discount rate not all of the "available funds" would be used, the rate should be reduced. By a series of successive approximations, the discount rate to allocate available funds will be optimally determined.

Although capital rationing logically should not occur, it is nonetheless a problem commonly encountered in business practices. Techniques similar to those shown in Exhibit 7.4 are generally used for allocating the capital budget each period.

SUMMARY

The capital budgeting problem consists of two decisions that should be kept separate: Should a project be undertaken? If so, how should it be financed? This chapter treats the first of these questions and leaves the second to finance courses. The time value of money should be taken into account in evaluating investment proposals so that cash flows, not accounting income figures, are the basic data to be analyzed. The appropriate discount rate for evaluating investment projects is the firm's cost of capital. The decision rule that will maximize the expected wealth of the firms' owners is to accept a project if and only if the net present value of its cash flows is positive.

QUESTIONS AND PROBLEMS

1 Review the meaning of the following concepts or terms discussed in this chapter:
  a Investment decision versus financing decision.
  b Net present value of cash flows.
  c Cost of capital.
  d Effect of depreciation expense on cash flows.
  e Mutually exclusive projects.
  f Irrationality of capital rationing.

2 Chapter Two states, "Depreciation is not a source of funds." This chapter states that accelerated depreciation methods result in larger cash flows than does the straight-line method. Reconcile these two statements.

3 There is no contractual obligation to pay anything to common stockholders. How can the capital they provide be said to have a cost other than zero?

4 "But Mr. Miller, you have said that one conceptual measure of the cost of capital is the rate of return on the marginal investment project available to the firm. So long as the firm has debt outstanding, one opportunity for idle funds will be to retire debt. Therefore, the cost of capital cannot be higher than the debt rate for any firm with debt outstanding." How should Mr. Miller reply?

5 A firm has a cost of capital of 10 percent. Compute the net present value of each of the five projects listed below.

Project	Aftertax Cash Flow End of Year			
	0	1	2	3
A	$(10,000)	$4,000	$4,000	$4,000
B	(10,000)	6,000	4,000	2,000
C	(10,000)	2,000	4,000	6,000
D	(10,000)	4,400	4,400	4,400
E	(10,000)	3,600	3,600	3,600

6 The aftertax net cash flows associated with two mutually exclusive projects, G and H, are as follows:

Project	Cash Flow End of Year		
	0	1	2
G	$(100)	$125	—
H	(100)	50	$84

a Calculate the net present value for each project using discount rates of 0, .04, .08, .12, .16, .20, and .24. The present value factors for discount rates not given in the table at the back of the book are as follows:

Number of Years to Elapse Before Cash Flow Occurs	Discount Rate	
	r = .16	r = .24
0..	1.000	1.000
1..	.862	.806
2..	.743	.650

b Prepare a graph as follows. The vertical axis should be labeled "Net Present Value in Dollars" and the horizontal axis should be labeled "Discount Rate in Percent per Year." Plot the net present value amounts calculated in part **a** for project G and project H.

c State the decision rule for choosing between projects G and H as a function of the firm's cost of capital.

7 Refer to the data in Chapter Four, in Exhibits 4.3 and 4.4, which derive the incremental cash flows arising from a choice between a gasoline and a diesel automobile. Notice, in column (6) of Exhibit 4.4, that the choice between the two automobiles reduced to the question of whether it makes sense to spend $1,200 cash today in order to save cash outflows of $408, $340, $340, and $272, respectively, at the end of each of the next four years. Ignore income taxes in all parts of the problem.

a Calculate the net present value of each of the automobiles at discount rates of 0, 2, 4, 5, 6, and 8 percent per year.

b Prepare a graph as follows: The vertical axis should be labeled "Net Present Value in Dollars" and the horizontal axis should be labeled "Discount Rate in Percent per Year." Plot the net present value amounts calculated in part **a** for each of the two automobiles.

c State the decision rule for choosing between the gasoline and diesel automobiles as a function of the firm's cost of capital.

8 The Wisher Washer Company purchased a made-to-order machine tool for grinding washing machine parts. The machine cost $100,000 and was installed yesterday. Today, a salesperson offers to sell the company a machine tool that will do exactly the same work but costs only $50,000. Assume that the cost of capital is 12 percent, that both machines will last for five years, that both machines will be depreciated on a straight-line basis with no salvage value, that the income tax rate is and will continue to be 40 percent, and that Wisher Washer Company earns sufficient income that any loss from disposing of or depreciating the "old" machine can be used to offset other taxable income.

How much, at a minimum, must the "old" machine fetch on resale at this time to make purchasing the new machine worthwhile?

9 The Jamie Company must decide whether or not to continue selling a line of children's shoes manufactured on a machine that can be used for no other purpose by the company. The machine is capable of producing 6,500 pairs of shoes a year. The machine has a current book value of $12,000 and can be sold today for $7,000. The machine is being depreciated on a straight-line basis assuming no salvage value and could continue in use for four more years. If the machine is kept in use, it can be disposed of at the end of four years for $600, although this will not affect the depreciation charge for the next four years. The variable costs of producing a pair of shoes on the machine are $5, and the shoes are sold to customers for $7. To produce and sell the children's shoes requires cash outlays of $10,000 per year for administrative and overhead expenditures as well. The tax rate paid by Jamie Company is 40 percent. The rate applies to any gain or loss on disposal of the machine as well as to other income. From its other activities, Jamie Company earns more income than any losses from the line of children's shoes or from disposal of the machine.

a Prepare a schedule showing all the cash and cost flows that Jamie Company needs to consider to decide whether to keep the machine.

b Should Jamie Company keep the machine if its cost of capital is 10 percent?

c Repeat step **b** assuming a cost of capital of 12 percent. (Round discount factors to three decimal places.)

10 The Double D Company has a cost of capital of 10 percent. It has just purchased two new machines, each with no salvage value. Machine A cost $20,000 and has a depreciable life of four years. Machine B cost $21,000 and has a depreciable life of six years.

For both machines calculate the present value of depreciation charges assuming:

a Sum-of-the-years'-digits depreciation.

b Double-declining-balance depreciation (assume a switch to straight-line after two years for A and after three years for B).

c Which depreciation method should be used if different methods can be used for each machine?

d Which depreciation method should be used if the same method must be used for both machines? (Round calculations to the nearest dollar and discount factors to three decimal places.)

11 (Adapted from a problem by David O. Green.) The Precisely Made Company set up a capital budgeting committee to review investment proposals. The committee applies a cost of capital rate of 12 percent to aftertax cash flows in making its decisions. The production manager proposes a project that involves an initial outlay of $12,000 for a machine and that recovers $4,200 before taxes at the end of each of the next four years (cash inflows less cash outflows). The salvage value of the asset is zero. Precisely Made uses the sum-of-the-years' digits depreciation method when accelerated depreciation is allowed.

Consider initiating this project from the point of view of the capital budgeting committee at five different times—1953, 1954, 1962, 1964, and 1977—when the tax laws were different from what they were during the other four years. The applicable tax laws were as follows:

1953   Straight-line depreciation was required.

1954   Accelerated depreciation was allowed.

1962   An investment tax credit of one-third of 7 percent of the cost of capital outlays with a depreciable life of between three and five years was granted. That is, at the time the four-year asset is purchased, an amount equal to one-third of 7 percent of its cost is subtracted from the income taxes payable at the time of purchase. Accelerated depreciation was allowed. The portion of the cost of the asset subject to depreciation was the initial outlay less the amount of the investment tax credit.

1964   The same conditions as 1962 but depreciable cost is the full cost, unreduced by the amount of the investment tax credit.

1977   The same conditions as 1964, that is, depreciable cost is the full cost, except that the investment tax credit for assets with the four-year lives is one-third of 10 percent, rather than 7 percent, of the asset's cost.

For each of the five different times of initiating the project, determine the net present value of the production manager's proposal. Assume that a tax rate of 40 percent of taxable income is applicable and that the Precisely Made Company generates more income from other projects than any loss computed for this particular project. (Round calculations to the nearest dollar.) Notice how the same project can appear more or less attractive as the tax laws change. (Round discount factors to three decimal places.)

12 The Dopuch Company purchases a machine for $12,000 that has no salvage value at the end of its useful life. The machine is to be depreciated on a straight-line basis for tax purposes. If the depreciable life is chosen to be three years, then Dopuch Company will receive an investment tax credit of $400 ($= $12,000 \times \frac{1}{3} \times 10\%$; see Problem **11** above and assume the 1977 treatment) but if a five-year depreciable life is chosen, two-thirds of 10 percent of the cost of the machine, or $800 will be granted as a credit toward Dopuch Company's income tax bill at the time of purchase.

Calculate the present value of the tax savings for three- and five-year depreciable lives of the machine. Assume a 40 percent marginal tax rate and a cost of capital of:
a 10 percent compounded annually.
b 20 percent compounded annually.
c Which depreciable life should be chosen?
(Round calculations to the nearest dollar. Use five-decimal-place discount factors.)

13 The Eastern States Railroad (ESRR) is considering replacing its power jack tamper, used to maintain track and roadbed, with a new automatic-raising power tamper. The present power jack tamper cost $36,000 five years ago and was estimated to have a total life of 12 years. If it is kept, it will require an overhaul two years from now that is estimated to cost $10,000. It can be sold for $5,000 now; it will be worthless seven years from now.

A new automatic-raising tamper costs $46,000 delivered and has an estimated physical life of 12 years. ESRR anticipates, however, that because of developments in maintenance machines, the new machine should be disposed of at the end of the seventh year for $10,000. Furthermore, the new machine will require an overhaul costing $14,000 at the end of the fourth year. The new equipment will eliminate the need for one machine operator, who costs $16,000 per year in wages and fringe benefits.

Track maintenance work is seasonal, so the equipment is normally used only from May 1 through October 31 of each year. Track maintenance employees are transferred to other work and receive the same rate of pay for the rest of the year.

The new machine will require $2,000 per year of maintenance, whereas the old machine requires $2,400 per year. Fuel consumption for the two machines is identical. ESRR's cost of capital is 12 percent per year and, because of operating losses, ESRR pays no income tax.

Should the new machine be purchased? (Round discount factors to three decimal places and round periodic calculations to the nearest hundred dollars.)

14 Refer to the data in Problem **23** of Chapter Four concerning the Peugeot automobile Model 504, in gasoline and diesel versions. Assume that the automobile is purchased and the first year's gasoline payments are made on January 1 of year 1. Subsequent cash payments are made on January 1 of each year and the automobile is sold on January 1 of year 6.
a If the purchaser uses a discount rate of 12 percent per year, which version should the purchaser acquire, and what is the net present value of the savings from buying this version rather than the other?
b At what mileage driven each year, assuming equal annual mileage per year for five years and constant resale values, is the purchaser indifferent between the two versions?
c Assuming that 12,000 miles are driven each year, at what discount rate is the purchaser indifferent between the two versions? Find the approximate answer, using the tables at the back of the book.

15 (This problem and the next are adapted from problems by David O. Green.) Brogan Company must buy a crane. It can buy a new one from the factory for $150,000. Cromwell Company, a competitor, bought an identical model last week for $150,000, finds that it needs a larger crane, and offers to sell its crane to Brogan. The new factory crane and the Cromwell crane have five-year lives with no salvage value. Ignore the investment credit.

Brogan uses the sum-of-the-years'-digits depreciation method where it is allowed, but the regulations do not permit accelerated depreciation for used assets acquired.

Brogan's cost of capital is 10 percent, and its marginal tax rate is 40 percent. Tax payments occur at the end of the first and subsequent years. What is the maximum price Brogan can pay Cromwell and be as well off as buying from the factory?

16 Cromwell Company can sell its crane to Brogan (see Problem **15**) or can trade in the crane on the larger model, which also has a five-year life with no salvage value. The cash price of the larger model is $300,000, and the factory will give Cromwell an allowance of $135,000 if the "old" crane is traded in. If an asset is traded in, there is no tax loss recognizable at the time of trade-in, and the depreciable cost of the new asset is the book value of the old plus any cash paid at the time the new asset is purchased. Cromwell uses the sum-of-the-years'-digits depreciation method, has a cost of capital of 10 percent, and is taxed at a marginal rate of 40 percent. If Cromwell sells to Brogan, any loss is fully deductible from taxable income at the time of sale, that is, immediately.

a What is the lowest price Cromwell can get from Brogan and be as well off as if trading in?

b (Note: this part requires that Problem **15** has been worked.) At what price will the two parties agree for Cromwell to sell to Brogan? (Round calculations to the nearest hundred dollars.)

17 The Hornbeer Company issued $1 million of callable 10-year, 8-percent, annual coupon bonds on January 1, 19X0, to mature on December 31, 19X9. The bonds were issued at par, so that proceeds to the company were exactly $1 million. Late in 19X4, when interest rates had dropped so that Hornbeer Company could borrow for 6 percent, it decided to call the outstanding bonds at 106 percent of par, the price required by the bond indenture. That is, the Company was required to pay $1.06 million (plus any interest accrued at that time) to the holders of the bonds. On December 31, 19X4, the Company borrowed $1 million from an insurance company at 6 percent interest, payable annually through December 31, 19X9. The proceeds of the loan and $60,000 additional cash were used to retire the bond issue after the interest payment for 19X4 was made. Compute the net present value of these bond refunding transactions assuming a discount rate of 6 percent per year. (Ignore income tax considerations and use three decimal places in discount factors.)

18 Refer to the data in the preceding problem for the Hornbeer Company. Assume that the original 8 percent bond issue had been issued at 96 percent of par and that discount is being amortized on a straight-line basis. At the time the 8 percent issue is called at the end of 19X4, the book value of the bonds is 98 percent of par. The loss on bond retirement is deductible for tax purposes in the year 19X4 and is shown as an extraordinary item on the financial statements for 19X4. Compute the net present value of these bond refunding transactions assuming a discount rate of 6 percent per year, a marginal income tax rate of 40 percent per year, and that a loss on bond retirement can be used to reduce otherwise taxable income.

19 Refer to Problem **22** in Chapter Fifteen, the Pepper River Electric Company. Assume a cost of capital of 1 percent per month and that all costs are incurred at the end of each month.

a   What is the net present value of the cash savings from using a coal-burning, rather than an oil-burning, plant?

b   What is the current replacement cost of the Company's current ability to produce 1 million kilowatt-hours of electricity per month?

20 The Largay Corporation is contemplating selling a new product. The equipment necessary to market the product can be acquired for $100,000. It has an estimated life of 10 years and no salvage value. In addition, it will be eligible for an immediate 10-percent investment tax credit. That is, if the asset is acquired, the income taxes otherwise payable in the year of acquisition will be reduced by $10,000 (= .10 × $100,000). The following schedule shows the expected sales volume, selling price, and variable cost per unit of production.

Year	Sales Volume	Selling Price	Variable Cost of Production
1	10,000 units	$5.00	$3.00
2	12,000	5.00	3.10
3	13,000	5.50	3.25
4	15,000	5.75	3.25
5	20,000	6.00	3.30
6	25,000	6.00	3.40
7	20,000	6.10	3.50
8	18,000	6.10	3.50
9	15,000	6.25	3.50
10	15,000	6.30	3.75

Production in each year must be sufficient to meet each year's sales. In addition, 5,000 extra units will be produced in year 1 to provide a continuing inventory of 5,000 units. Thus, production in year 1 will be 15,000 units but in year 10 will be only 10,000 units so that at the end of year 10, ending inventory is zero. Inventory will be accounted for using the LIFO (last-in, first-out) cost flow assumption. The corporation's income tax rate is 40 percent and its cost of capital is 10 percent per year. Cash is received at the end of the year when sales are made and expended at the end of the year when costs are incurred. Variable selling expenses are estimated at $1 per unit sold. Depreciation on the new equipment is an expense each period. (You may assume that the Largay Corporation generates sufficient cash flows from other operations so that the investment tax credit can all be used to reduce tax payments in year 1.)

a   Prepare a schedule of cash flows for this project.

b   Verify that the new present value of the project is approximately $11,134.

PART THREE
PLANNING AND CONTROL

CHAPTER 8

THE PLANNING AND CONTROL PROCESS

Part 2 of this book, Chapters Four through Seven, focused on managerial decision making. If management applies the principles of incremental analysis, it should make economically sound decisions. Once management has made a decision, its job is only partially complete. The alternatives selected must be translated into action. Then the actions, once taken, must be evaluated to ensure that performance coincides as closely as possible with expectations. These latter tasks comprise the planning and control process. In Part 3, Chapters Eight through Eleven, we consider important concepts and useful techniques for managerial planning and control.

As initially developed, the concept of control in business firms concerned the safeguarding of assets. Elaborate procedures were developed for controlling the receipt and disbursement of cash, the protection of inventories from theft, and so on. These procedures comprised what is called a firm's *internal control system*. The task of the internal auditing staff within firms has been to check on the functioning of this internal control system. The concept of control has evolved and broadened, however, so that the focus is more and more on performance appraisal in addition to safeguarding assets. The internal auditing function is likewise beginning to expand to include management audits, a topic discussed later in this chapter. The discussion of planning and control systems in this chapter focuses primarily on performance appraisal rather than on safeguarding assets. The latter is generally considered in depth in auditing texts.

COMPONENTS OF THE PLANNING AND CONTROL PROCESS

The planning and control process comprises three phases:

1 Standard-setting phase—the specification of a criterion as to what actual performance should be.

2 Operating phase—the carrying out of actual performance and the measuring of results.

3 Feedback phase—the comparison of actual performance with the standard or criterion as a basis for evaluating past performance and guiding future action.

Standard-Setting Phase

The standard-setting phase is closely linked to the decision-making process. As a result of analyzing the incremental cash flows for an alternative, management generates an expectation as to what actual performance should be. For example, in deciding to manufacture internally a given component rather than purchase the component from an outside supplier, management generates an expectation as to the manufacturing costs to be incurred. In deciding on the optimum amount and frequency of merchandise to be purchased, management bases its decision on expected demand, carrying costs, and ordering costs. The standard-setting stage essentially involves formalizing the results of the decision-making process into a plan for action. In many instances, the plan is expressed in the form of a *budget*. In other instances, which we discuss later in this chapter, it may be desirable not to formalize explicit standards.

Operating Phase

The operating phase represents the carrying out of actual performance. Actual performance should be measured in terms consistent with the measure used in the standard-setting phase. Lack of consistency in the performance measure causes many control systems to fail. For example, standards are set based on expected incremental cash flows. Actual performance, however, is reported in terms of "generally accepted accounting principles" for external purposes. Because measures of performance derived from cash flows and from accounting principles are not always the same, the comparison of actual performance as externally reported with the standard can be misleading. In some instances, then, it is necessary to measure performance differently for control purposes than for external reporting purposes. Chapter Fourteen discusses some of these instances in more detail.

Feedback Phase

The feedback phase serves two purposes. By comparing actual performance with the standard and investigating the reasons for any variances, management has a basis for evaluating past performance. For example, a production supervisor might compare the actual number of units produced by various workers with the standard for a period to determine which workers should receive bonuses or be promoted. A company president might compare the rate of return on assets of an operating division with a standard to assess the division manager's performance.

A second use of the information from the feedback phase is to guide management in assessing changes to be made in the future. It is virtually impossible for managers to keep a close watch on all the activities for which they are responsible. They depend on planning and control systems to do a large part of the surveillance. In this way they can focus only on those areas where there is a large variance between actual performance and the standard. Then, they can take corrective actions where necessary. Basing action on reported variances is referred to as *management by exception.*

CRITERIA FOR EVALUATING PLANNING AND CONTROL SYSTEMS

A planning and control system is established for an activity (for example, production, selling, research and development) to increase the probability that the objective or goal of that activity will be achieved. In designing a planning and control system, it is essential that the objective of an activity be clearly defined and properly integrated with the overall goals of the firm. It is equally important, however, that the objectives of the individuals performing various tasks be considered. Management involves "getting things done through people." A well-designed planning and control system requires that the behavioral reactions of employees to levels of standards, measures of actual performance, and form and frequency of feedback be given careful consideration. It is desirable that the planning and control system lead the firm to the attainment of its goals and lead employees to the attainment of their personal goals. Such *goal congruence* increases the effectiveness of the planning and control system. In this section, we discuss several characteristics of an effective planning and control system. We give consideration to behavioral concerns where appropriate.

Responsibility Is Fixed

It is desirable that planning and control systems be designed so that responsibility for performing an activity is fixed. Then, managers and other employees will know what is expected of them. More importantly, particular managers and employees can more easily be held accountable for variances of actual performance from the standard. Planning and control systems should therefore be developed around *responsibility centers* within a firm. A responsibility center is a unit of activity within a firm that has control over, or responsibility for, an activity during a particular time period. Where the responsibility center has control only over costs incurred, such as a production department, it is referred to as a *cost center.* Where the responsibility center controls only revenues generated, as in some retailing departments, it is referred to as a *revenue center.* Where the responsibility center has control over both revenues and costs, as with an autonomous division, it is referred to as a *profit center.*

There are two important dimensions to the concept of a responsibility center. The first one is the notion that a particular manager or group of employees has control over an activity. Control is relatively easy to define in principle but difficult to identify precisely in practice. The difficulty arises because there are different degrees of control depending on the particular circumstances.

Example 1   Horton Corporation maintains a purchasing department that is responsible for the acquisition of raw materials for the production departments. Production supervisors inform the purchasing department of the quantities and qualities of raw materials that will be needed at various times. The purchasing department then searches for suppliers that will provide the needed raw materials at the best price. The purchasing department is held accountable for variances of the actual prices paid from the standard prices.

The purchasing department in this case is a responsibility center with respect to the price paid for raw materials. Suppose, however, that, due to poor production planning, a production foreman places a rush order for raw materials that must be received within three days. In order to obtain the raw materials on time, the purchasing department agrees to pay a higher price to expedite the order. As a consequence, the actual price paid is significantly higher than the standard price. Should the purchasing department be held accountable for this unfavorable price variance? This is a difficult question to answer. The response depends heavily on the behavioral reactions of employees in the purchasing and producing departments of having the variance assigned to them.

The main point of this example is that control is not always easily determinable. Control runs along a continuum from absolute control to no control. Most cases fall in between these extremes. The guideline generally followed is that the unit in the firm with the most influence over the item is held accountable for it. In the rush order example, the production department would probably be held responsible for the unfavorable price variance even though price variances are normally the responsibility of the purchasing department.

The second dimension of the responsibility center concept is that control must be defined in terms of a particular time period. Most variable costs tend to be controllable by some unit within the firm each time period. Some fixed costs are also controllable in the short run. Most fixed costs are, however, controllable only in the long run. Once capacity level decisions have been made, managers are generally locked into a particular level of fixed costs. For purposes of evaluating performance in the short run, the question arises as to whether or not managers should be held accountable for fixed cost variances.

Example 2   The producing departments of Horton Corporation submit capital budgeting proposals to central corporate headquarters. Given various constraints on growth (for example, market demand and availability of managerial talent), personnel in central corporate headquarters decide which capital investment proposals will be accepted and which will be rejected. In the long run, then, the producing departments, which generate capital investment proposals, and central corporate headquarters, which selects particular proposals, share the responsibility for fixed capacity costs (for example, depreciation on building and equipment, property taxes and insurance on the manufacturing facilities). In the short run, however, neither of these two units controls fixed capacity costs.

Suppose that property tax rates or insurance premiums are increased so that during a particular time period there is an unfavorable fixed cost variance with respect to these costs. Who should be held accountable for the variance? A response is again difficult, because it depends on who can control the costs. The main point is that control must be defined in terms of a particular time period. In this case, the producing departments do not control property taxes and insurance in the short run and probably should not be held accountable for any cost variances. (It may be desirable to show the variances on the cost report for the producing departments, however, to make the producing departments' employees more aware of these costs, which they can partially and indirectly control in the long run.)

The identification of responsibility centers within a firm is an important first step in designing planning and control systems. Setting the boundaries of control for a particular responsibility center is far from precise. Nonetheless, an attempt must be made if the planning and control system is to be effective.

Performance Measure Is Relevant to Objectives

A second desirable attribute of planning and control systems is the following: the measures used for evaluating performance should be relevant to the objectives or purposes of the responsibility centers. If the purpose of a producing department is to manufacture products of a particular quality at the lowest cost, then manufacturing cost per unit passing quality inspection might be used as the performance measure. If the objective of a secretarial typing pool is to type quality copy at the lowest cost, then the evaluation measure might be correct lines typed per dollar of cost in the pool.

An improperly designed performance measure will provide data of questionable usefulness to the firm. It may also misdirect the efforts of employees who attempt to perform so that they look good relative to the measure. For example, a performance measure for the traveling sales staff that relates revenue generated to the number of calls made to customers (that is, sales divided by calls made) may lead salespersons to *reduce* the number of calls made in order to improve their performance report. If the development of a good relationship between the salespeople and the customers is critical and depends on frequent calls by the sales staff, then this performance measure could lead to action (reduced numbers of sales calls) that is clearly not in the best interest of a firm.

One problem in designing planning and control systems for some activities is that it is often difficult to design a quantitative measure for evaluating performance. In most cases this occurs because there is no clear-cut relationship between inputs and outputs. For example, consider the order-procuring activities of the sales staff. The amount of revenue generated by a particular salesperson cannot be related directly to the hours of time worked or the cost of promotional materials developed. There are too many intervening variables, such as general economic conditions, the behavior of competitors, and geographical diversity.

As another example, consider the research and development activity. The desired output is a set of new inventions and developments that will permit a firm to maintain or improve its market position. There is no precise relationship, however, between the salaries of research scientists or the cost of supplies used (inputs) and the value of new discoveries and developments. It is difficult, therefore, to design a quantitative measure that captures the relevant aspects of performance for this activity.

More effective control generally results when a quantitative performance measure can be designed and the planning and control system can be formalized. In cases where this is not possible, the planning and control systems tend to be less formalized and more intuitive. Different methods for controlling performance must therefore be used. Some of the methods that might be employed are described below. These serve essentially as substitutes for an effective quantitative measure of performance.

1. Plan of Organization   A plan of organization is essential so that responsibility for performance can be fixed. The plan of organization should indicate the persons with authority to make various kinds of decisions. For example, the control system for the internal legal staff should indicate the kinds of questions for which the internal staff has authority to determine the firm's legal position and the situations where external counsel is required. Formalized job descriptions should be prepared whenever possible.

2. Quality and Training of Personnel   An important control tool, particularly when judgmental skills are required, is the hiring of capable personnel. This is particularly important, for example, in the case of scientists for the research and development staff and attorneys for the legal staff. These individuals often work unsupervised for long periods. If the employees are capable and conscientious, there is less need for continuous monitoring of their work. It is also important that adequate resources be provided so that employees' skills can be maintained and improved through continuing professional development.

3. Budgeting of Costs   We noted earlier that there is often no direct, or observable, relationship between the amount of cost incurred and the amount or quality of output. Even when this is the case, it is desirable that the level of input costs be budgeted, that actual costs be compared with budget, and that corrective action be taken when necessary. The process of setting budgeted amounts and the existence of a control system for these costs should make the personnel involved more aware of the need to use resources wisely.

4. Periodic Performance Evaluation   Employees need to know how their supervisors feel they are performing. This need is largely satisfied in more formal control systems as actual performance is compared with the standards. In less formalized control systems, this need must be satisfied through other means, such as an annual or semi-annual review session with an employee's supervisor.

5. Management Audits   An increasingly popular control tool is a management audit. Although this term has been used by various writers to mean different things, we use it to refer to a qualitative assessment of an activity relative to a set of objectives. For example, a management audit of a firm's legal staff would begin with an explicit statement of objectives for that activity. These might include expectations with respect to the quality of assistance given to operating departments in executing contracts, the degree of interaction with the firm's external attorneys in handling damage and other suits, and the continuing professional development of the personnel on the legal staff. Interviews and other means would then be used to form a judgment as to how effectively these objectives were being met. Management audits are particularly useful for activities where more formalized control methods cannot be employed.

Performance Standards Are Properly Set

Once responsibility centers have been identified and performance measures have been designed, the next step is to set the standard or criterion as to what performance should be for a particular period. There are two principal factors of concern in this process: (1) the extent of employee participation in setting standards, and (2) the tightness of the standards.

Employee Participation   There is an extensive literature, both theoretical and empirical, on the question of if, and to what extent, employees should participate in the setting of standards against which their performance will be evaluated. No clear-cut conclusions can be drawn from the literature to date. An appreciation might be obtained of the issues involved by considering some of the questions that have been addressed in this research.

1 Does participation lead employees to feel that they are a more integral part of an organization and, because of this ego involvement, result in improved performance?
2 Does participation merely lead to greater group cohesiveness among employees, which can then work either to the advantage or disadvantage of the firm depending on the group's feeling about the benefits of the participation?
3 Are the results of participation different in the following two situations?
   a Employees merely provide inputs to the standard-setting process but have no voice in the actual standards setting.
   b Employees both supply inputs and participate in setting specific standards.
4 Are the results of participation different depending on the managerial style of supervisors (authoritarian, democratic) and the personality characteristics of employees?
5 Are the results of participation different depending on the educational backgrounds and technical skills of employees and the nature of the tasks (production versus research and development or legal services)?
6 How is participation related to the creation of slack in organizations (a term referring to the difference between the resources available to a firm and the amount necessary to maintain the organization coalition of individuals and groups)?

Interested readers might consult the references listed below to explore these questions more fully.[1]

Tightness of Standards   Standards for performance may be set very loose and be met a large percentage of the time or set very tight and be met only a small percentage of the time. Empirical research tends to suggest that employees underperform when

---

[1]   Andrew C. Stedry, *Budget Control and Cost Behavior* (Englewood Cliffs, N.J.: Prentice-Hall, 1960); Chris Argyris, "Organizational Leadership and Participative Management," *Journal of Business,* XXVII (January 1955), pp. 1–7; Selwyn Becker and David Green, Jr., "Budgeting and Employee Behavior," *Journal of Business,* XXXV (October 1962), pp. 392–402; Michael Schiff and Arie Y. Lewin, "The Impact of Budgets on People," *The Accounting Review,* XLV (April 1970), pp. 259–268; Ken Milani, "The Relationship of Participation in Budget-Setting to Industrial Supervisor Performance and Attitudes: A Field Study," *The Accounting Review,* L (April 1975), pp. 274–284.

standards are set too loose. Introducing a moderate level of tension by way of tighter standards leads to higher employee motivation and thereby better performance. The principal question, then, is just how tight the standards should be. Two types of standards have been described in the literature: (1) ideal standards, and (2) normal or currently attainable standards.

Ideal standards are those that can be met under the most efficient operating conditions for existing resources (plant, equipment, employees). Ideal standards are used when management feels that such standards provide the best incentive to good performance. Generally, however, empirical research tends to show that standards do not provide an incentive to perform well unless the employee, whose performance is measured against the standard, perceives the standard to be reasonable and attainable.[2] Ideal standards can be criticized, then, because employees may lose initiative for seeking more efficient performance and become discouraged because the standards are seldom achievable.

Normal or *currently attainable standards* are those that can be met under reasonably efficient operating conditions with provision for normal spoilage, rest periods, and other time that is lost because of, for example, normal machine breakdowns. Normal standards are, by definition, those that management can reasonably expect, but stringent enough so that workers who achieve them have reason to be satisfied with their performance.

It is difficult to generalize as to how tight standards should be. All that can be said is that there are dangers in setting the standards too loose or too tight. Standards that are currently attainable but sufficiently tight to motivate employees are probably best. Such standards are easy to define in principle. It takes a wise and capable management to translate them into effective performance norms in practice.

Feedback Is Timely

A control system requires timely feedback if it is to be effective. Management needs to be aware of significant variances of actual performance from the standards in time to take corrective action. Employees need to know whether their performance is judged to be satisfactory or unsatisfactory. Satisfactory performance tends to reinforce employee behavior and leads to greater employee motivation. Unsatisfactory performance may lead to greater employee motivation (if standards are still considered to be attainable) or to withdrawal (when the standards are not considered attainable or the employee no longer feels a part of the management-employee coalition in the firm).[3]

The frequency of feedback differs depending on the nature of the activity. For an automated production line, feedback may be required within seconds or minutes so

---

[2]   Stedry, *Budget Control and Cost Behavior*; also see Gary L. Holstrum, "The Effect of Budget Adaptiveness and Tightness on Managerial Decision Behavior," *Journal of Accounting Research,* 9 (Autumn 1971), pp. 268–277.

[3]   Doris M. Cook, "The Effect of Frequency of Feedback on Attitudes and Performance," *Empirical Research in Accounting: Selected Studies* (*Journal of Accounting Research, Supplement* 1967), pp. 213–224; James E. Sorensen and David D. Franks, "The Relative Contribution of Ability, Self-Esteem and Evaluative Feedback to Performance: Implications for Accounting Systems," *The Accounting Review,* XLVII (October 1972), pp. 735–746.

that corrective action can be taken quickly. For purposes of evaluating the overall performance of a division of a firm, monthly or quarterly feedback is probably sufficient.

Benefits Exceed Costs

One of the most important criteria for evaluating a planning and control system is that the benefits of the system exceed the costs of designing and implementing it. For example, the benefits of a sophisticated system for the acquisition and use of paper clips is not likely to justify the costs to be incurred.

The benefits of planning and control systems are usually more difficult to measure than the costs. Benefits tend to be indirect or not easily quantified. A continual assessment of planning and control systems is necessary, however difficult that might be, if they are to accomplish their purpose.

CLASSIFICATION OF PLANNING AND CONTROL SYSTEMS

We shall study several examples of planning and control systems in Chapters Nine through Eleven. The discussion is structured around three broad types or groups of planning and control systems: (1) operational; (2) divisional; and (3) company-wide.[4] To understand the distinction better, refer to the organization chart in Figure 8.1.

Operational Planning and Control Systems

Operational planning and control systems are designed for activities closest to day-to-day operations. A different system is designed for each type of activity. For example, an operational control system might be designed for raw materials acquisition and storage, office typing and record keeping, and order-getting activities of the sales staff. The most common example of an operational planning and control system is the standard costing system for manufacturing. In most cases, these planning and control systems are formalized and documented in the firm's record-keeping and reporting system. Feedback and evaluation occur monthly, weekly, or even daily. Chapters Nine and Ten discuss operational planning and control systems.

Divisional Planning and Control Systems

Divisional planning and control systems are designed for the next major level above operational control in the organization chart. They result from the need to have some common basis for planning, comparing, and evaluating the performance of divisions selling different goods and services and operating in widely different environments. These planning and control systems typically focus on the profit performance of the

---

[4]   This classification is somewhat analogous to operational control, management control, and strategic planning control used previously. See Robert N. Anthony, John Dearden, and Richard F. Vancil, *Management Control Systems, Text, Cases, and Readings,* rev. ed. (Homewood, Ill.: Richard D. Irwin, 1972).

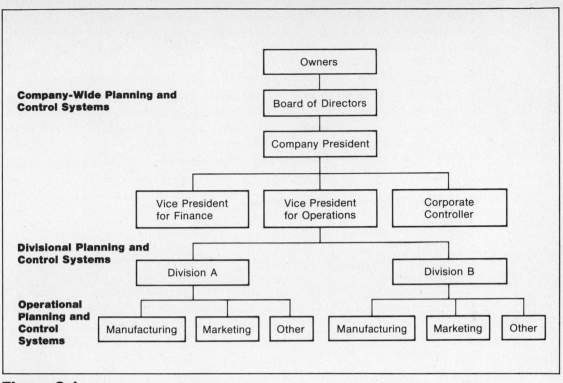

Figure 8.1
Organization Chart for a Typical
Company and Types of Planning
and Control Systems

divisions and tend to be formalized as part of the firm's reporting system. Feedback and evaluation typically occur monthly or quarterly. Divisional performance measurement and control are discussed in Chapter Eleven.

Company-Wide Planning and Control Systems

Company-wide planning and control systems tend to be much less formalized than in the preceding two cases. These planning and control systems essentially involve a periodic review of the company's activities by a board of directors or other group of owners. The comparison of actual with the expected level of performance may occur quarterly or perhaps only once a year. There is an increasing trend to formalize some of these company-wide control systems.

In recent years, a number of large companies have established corporate audit committees. These committees are typically comprised of members of the board of directors of the corporation and report to the chairman of the board. One of their functions has been to oversee the activities of the firm's external auditors. The audit committee sometimes requests the external auditors to extend the usual audit of the financial statements to search for management fraud or illegal payoffs. As these audit committees have become established, they have increased the scope of their activities. Greater attention is given to other aspects of the firm's activities, such as community relations, employee morale, and environmental protection. Management consulting firms have been hired to study various aspects of a company's operations and make recommendations for changes. The scope of activities of corporate audit committees is expected to continue to broaden in the future. The New York Stock Exchange requires audit committees of all companies whose stock is traded on the exchange.

QUESTIONS AND PROBLEMS

1 Review the meaning of the following concepts or terms discussed in this chapter.
  a Planning and control process.
  b Standard-setting phase.
  c Operating phase.
  d Feedback phase.
  e Budget.
  f Management by exception.
  g Goal congruence.
  h Responsibility center.
  i Cost center.
  j Revenue center.
  k Profit center.
  l Quantitative performance measure.
  m Ideal standards.
  n Normal or currently attainable standards.
  o Operational control.
  p Divisional control.
  q Company-wide control.
  r Management audit.
  s Audit committee.

2 Discuss briefly how each of the following might be viewed as a control system:
  a The automatic sprinkling system in a factory building.
  b The inspection system for discovering defective products as they move off the production line.
  c The policing system for regulation of pollutant emissions from a factory.
  d The moral obligation of a large firm to maintain a stable work force in small communities.

3 Reflect upon your performance in this accounting course. Identify the standard-setting, operating, and feedback phases.

4 You are the manager of the assembling division of a manufacturing firm. A report on the division's performance for February shows the following:

Cost Item	Standard	Actual	Variance
Raw Materials.	$ 3,500	$4,000	$500 Unfavorable
Direct Labor.	3,500	3,000	500 Favorable
Supplies	400	300	100 Favorable
Insurance	600	500	100 Favorable
Depreciation.	2,000	2,000	—
Total	$10,000	$9,800	$200 Favorable

What action would you take next? Explain.

5 Who, among management personnel, is most likely to be able to control each of the following?
a Raw materials used (quantity).
b Electricity for machinery.
c Charge for floor space.
d Machinery depreciation.
e Unit price of materials.
f Insurance on machinery.
g Direct labor (quantity).

6 The Dominick Manufacturing Company is organized into two divisions, Assembling and Finishing. The Assembling Division combines raw materials into a semifinished product. The product is then sent to the Finishing Division for painting, polishing, and packing.

During May, the Assembling Division incurred significantly higher raw materials costs than expected because poor-quality raw materials required extensive rework. Because of the rework, fewer units than expected were transferred to the Finishing Division. The Finishing Division incurred higher labor costs per unit of finished product because workers had substantial idle time.
a Who should be held responsible for the raw materials variance in the Assembling Department? Explain.
b Who should be held responsible for the labor (idle time) variance in the Finishing Department? Explain.

7 Cameron and MacInnes, Certified Public Accountants, employ 30 staff accountants. The accountants are primarily involved in auditing the financial statements of the firm's clients. At the completion of each audit assignment, the supervisor evaluates the performance of each staff accountant using a numerical scoring system. The quantitative measures are then used for promotion and compensation decisions. The scoring system involves assignment of a 0, 1, or 2 for each of the following factors scored:
1 General physical appearance.
2 Impression made on client.
3 Ability to work with other staff accountants.
4 Meeting, surpassing, or falling short of last year's audit time on each assigned task.
5 Potential for advancement to partnership.
Evaluate the strengths and weaknesses of this numerical scoring system as a tool for evaluating and controlling performance.

8 The Langston Advertising Agency maintains a petty cash fund of $500 in its office. The fund is used to make cash payments for postage, freight, business luncheons, and other costs that do not exceed $25 per expenditure. Before cash can be distributed, an invoice or other evidence must be submitted to the petty cash custodian. The initials of two people other than the custodian are required to authorize the payment. At the end of each day, the petty cash fund is counted to ensure that the custodian has cash and authorized receipts totaling $500. The fund is then replenished with cash equal in amount to the authorized receipts. As a further check on the custodian, surprise counts are made of the fund during the day approximately twice each week.

Evaluate the strengths and weaknesses of these control procedures for the petty cash fund.

9 Trans Union Airlines is a large domestic airline servicing all major cities throughout the United States. It employs rather sophisticated control systems for many of its activities, including airplane maintenance, baggage handling, customer check-in, and others. One such control system, for telephone reservation services, is described below.

The objective of the control system is to increase the likelihood that customers will receive prompt, courteous, and efficient service when they phone in for reservations. The standards for performance are stated in terms of a list of quantitative and qualitative attributes regarding the telephone conversation.

(1) The telephone call should be answered no later than the third ring.
(2) If a customer is placed "on hold" because of a backlog of calls, the hold period should be no longer than one minute.
(3) The reservation clerk should present a pleasant and helpful disposition to the customer.
(4) In cases where a requested flight is full, the reservation clerk should make an effort to place the customer on other Trans Union flights before offering information on flights of other airlines.
(5) After the flight reservations have been made, the reservation clerk should read the flight numbers and times back to the customer.

The company uses two methods of monitoring the telephone reservation service. First, personnel in the controller's department listen to the telephone conversations by way of telephone taps located in central corporate headquarters. They then prepare a written evaluation of the reservation clerk's performance using the above standards. Because the clerks are unaware that their conversations are being heard, they do not act unnaturally. The second monitoring method involves a periodic call to customers to have them evaluate the conversation.

Evaluate the strengths and weaknesses of this control system as a basis for evaluating the performance of the reservation clerks.

10 An Atlanta-based textile firm employs 30,000 workers in its local plant. A personnel department has been set up to handle hiring and some aspects of training. Before a worker is hired, the personnel department checks his or her credit standing, previous job experience references, and any other factors felt to have a bearing on performance. If the "checker" is satisfied, the applicant is hired immediately or placed on a short waiting list.

Ten individuals are involved in this initial processing in the personnel department. The department supervisor allocates new employment applications to one of the ten checkers and carries out other personnel department activities.

Outline what you feel would be an effective control system for this initial processing activity. Note important strengths and weaknesses as you proceed.

11 United Manufacturing Corporation has recently set up an independent planning department at the central corporate level. This department is responsible for most aspects of budgeting (revenue forecasting, production scheduling, profit planning, capital investment). Planning department personnel are responsible to the vice-president for administration. The resulting budgets are incorporated into the control system designed and administered by the controller's department.

Outline what you feel would be an effective control system for the planning department's activities (that is, how the performance of the planning department is to be evaluated).

12 Consolidated Electronics Corporation conducts its research and development activities in a separate building near the central corporate headquarters. The research staff consists of 20 scientists and engineers and 30 research assistants. Approximately 60 percent of the staff's time is devoted to improvement of existing products and processes. Most of this work is performed at the request of personnel in the firm's operating divisions. The remaining 40 percent of the staff's time is devoted to projects of particular interest to the scientists and engineers. In some cases these efforts result in patents for new products or processes that are either used by Consolidated or sold to other companies. In other cases these research efforts lead to publishable papers in professional journals. In some instances no usable results are obtained and the projects are discontinued.

Design what you feel would be an effective control system for this research and development activity.

13 Stedry (*Budget Control and Cost Behavior,* Prentice-Hall, 1960) studied the relationships among **(1)** participation in standard setting, **(2)** tightness of standards, and **(3)** performance. The task performed by a group of students was the solving of a series of short numerical problems. Performance was measured in terms of the number of correct solutions in a 7-minute period.

Students operated under one of three types of budgeting arrangements:

(1) Imposed budgets—students were told how many correct solutions were expected of them in each 7-minute period with no participation on their part.

(2) Pseudoparticipation budgets—students were asked to write down the number of solutions they aspired to get correct in each 7-minute period. After doing this, the students were given a *preset* budgeted amount. The students were not aware that their input was not considered in setting the budget amounts.

(3) Imposed/aspiration-level budgets—students were told how many correct solutions were expected of them in each 7-minute period. They were then asked to write down the number of solutions they aspired to get correct.

Students operated under one of three types of standards with respect to tightness: **(1)** low, **(2)** medium, or **(3)** high. These amounts were set based on performance during the preceding 7-minute period but were adjusted to reflect the different degrees of tightness. Everyone started with a budget of five correct solutions.

Shown below are the average number of correct solutions for students in each of the nine combinations of budgeting arrangements and tightness of standards.

Budgeting Arrangement

Tightness of Standard	Imposed Budget	Pseudoparticipation Budget	Imposed/ Aspiration-Level Budget
Low.............	4.09	4.70	4.56
Medium........	4.35	5.45	5.50
High	5.13	4.04	5.85

a What observations can be made from these results regarding the relationship between participation in setting standards and performance?

b What observations can be made from these results regarding the relationship between tightness of standards and performance?

CHAPTER 9
PERIOD BUDGETING: ESTABLISHING PLANS FOR ACTION AND STANDARDS FOR CONTROL

A former President of the United States is reputed to have said, "The trouble is that the future lies ahead." The future does indeed lie ahead, and none of us is gifted with prophetic powers. Yet every business manager in making decisions and translating the decisions into action must consider, implicitly or explicitly, what the future will be like. A period budget is simply a formal quantitative statement of management's objectives and plan of action for the future. In this chapter, we consider the principal uses of such budgets and demonstrate how they are developed for a typical business firm.

MANAGERIAL USES OF BUDGETS

Budgets are useful tools for (1) planning, (2) control, and (3) employee motivation.

Tool for Planning

Applying the principles of incremental analysis, management selects the best alternatives with respect to products, prices, levels of output, production techniques, and so on. These choices, once made, must be translated into a formal, integrated plan of action for a firm and its various subunits. This is one of the most important purposes of the budgeting process. It forces management to take each of the choices made and to make sure that it coordinates with other alternatives selected. It also presents management with a comprehensive picture of the expected effects of its decisions on the firm as a whole. Put another way, budgets are estimates of financial statements prepared before the actual transactions occur.

When used as a tool for planning, budgets are generally static. That is, the budgets are developed for a particular expected level of activity, usually sales or production in units. A single set of estimates is derived for sales, manufacturing costs, selling and administrative expenses, and profit. Such budgets are referred to as *static budgets.*

209

Tool for Control

Budgets provide estimates of what performance is expected to be. As such, they serve as criteria or standards for evaluating performance. A comparison of budgeted and actual amounts provides a basis for evaluating past performance and guiding future action. To be effective as tools for control, the budgets must be initially developed for individual responsibility centers. Budgets will be developed for production, marketing, purchasing, administration, and so on. They will then be integrated into a master budget for the firm as a whole. In this way, the performance of each responsibility center can be evaluated with respect to those activities over which it had control during a particular period.

When used as tools for control, budgets are generally *flexible*. That is, the budget for each responsibility center is expressed in the form of a particular level of fixed cost that is expected to be incurred regardless of the level of activity and a variable cost per unit of activity that can change *in total* as the level of activity changes (that is, the $y = a + bx$ formulation studied in Chapter Five). The "flex" in a flexible budget is with respect to variable costs. The budget for fixed costs is static.

Example 1   Studies of past cost behavior indicate that the Assembling Division of Standard Manufacturing Corporation should incur total fixed costs of $100,000 and variable costs of $10 per unit next period. For planning purposes, Standard estimates that 50,000 units will be produced by the Assembling Division. The static cost budget for the division used for planning purposes is therefore $600,000 [= $100,000 + ($10 × 50,000)]. Suppose, however, that due to unexpected demand during the period, the Assembling Division produced 70,000 units. It is not particularly useful *for control purposes* to compare the actual cost of producing 70,000 units with the expected cost of producing 50,000 units. The underlying levels of activity are different. To evaluate actual performance, the budget, or standard, must be expressed in terms of what costs should have been to produce 70,000 units. This is where the flexible budget comes in. It indicates that manufacturing costs should have been $800,000 [= $100,000 + ($10 × 70,000)] during the period. This is the most appropriate standard for control. Note that the estimates of fixed and variable costs form the inputs into both the static budget for planning and the flexible budget for control.

Tool for Employee Motivation

In Chapter Eight, we discussed the importance of the human factor in the planning and control process. We noted that standards, or budgets, can serve as motivating devices for employees if the standards are set at levels that are tight but currently attainable with reasonably efficient performance. It is desirable that the budgets used for planning and control also serve as tools for employee motivation. In this way, a single budgeting and accounting system can be designed that will serve multiple purposes. In some instances, however, the budget of what costs are *expected to be* for planning purposes may be different from the level of costs that, when used as a standard for evaluating performance, will best motivate employees. In these cases, the budgeting and accounting system must be adaptable if it is to serve all purposes.

THE MASTER BUDGET

The master budget, sometimes called the *comprehensive budget,* is a complete blueprint of the planned operations of the firm for a period. It emphasizes the relationship of the various inputs in all areas of the company to final output and sales. Its preparation requires a recognition of the interrelationships among the various units of a firm. For example, to prepare a master budget requires knowing how a projected increase in sales of product A affects each of the following: the several producing departments, the selling, general, and administrative effort, and the financial position of the company.

Preparation of a master budget is a difficult, complex process that requires much time and effort by management at all levels. The difficulties of fitting all pieces together may be great, especially the first few times a master budget is prepared. Despite these difficulties, or perhaps because of them, the master budget is an effective instrument for planning and control. Its value has been proved so often that almost all firms of any size recognize master budget preparation as a vital task of management.

No simple example can effectively convey the complexity of the process, but the illustration in the following pages is designed to indicate some of the problems and possible solutions.

A word of caution about uniformity may be in order before beginning the illustration. Budgets, like most of the other schedules illustrated in this book, are designed to assist management in carrying out its functions. Managements are highly individualistic in their choices of budget titles, order of arrangement, number of supporting schedules, and similar stylistic matters. Many corporate budgets, as well as other texts and budget manuals, will differ in format from the illustration that follows, but all will have as their goal helping management to plan and control operations more effectively.

The budget preparation process will be illustrated for Victoria Corporation for a single period. The period could be a month, a quarter, or a full year. Victoria Corporation produces two products, product A and product B. Product A sells for $4 per unit; product B is a deluxe version of product A and sells for $5 per unit. An organization chart of Victoria Corporation is presented in Figure 9.1. Each box in the organization chart is viewed as a responsibility center. The production, marketing, and corporate staff departments should probably be broken down further into additional responsibility centers. In order to keep the illustrations simple, we shall not do this.

Knowing where to start in preparing a master budget may be a problem, but generally there is one crucial factor that determines the level of activity. For most firms the crucial factor is the volume of anticipated sales, but it could also be the availability of certain raw materials, of the supply of labor, or of factory capacity. In the case of the Victoria Corporation, we assume that budgeted sales is the crucial factor. We start with the sales budget; the other budgets build on the sales budget and relate to one another.

Sales Budget

The sales budget is presented in Exhibit 9.1. Responsibility for preparing this budget usually falls on the chief marketing officer of the firm. The marketing official will rely

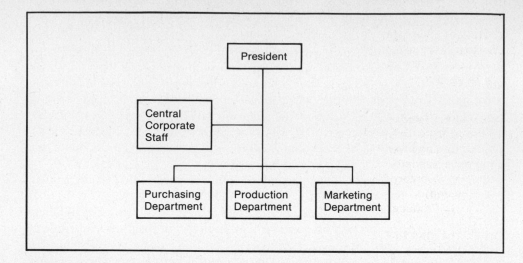

Figure 9.1
Organization Chart for Victoria
Corporation

on inputs from the market research group as well as from salespersons or district managers in the field. The discussions among sales groups in budget preparation frequently serve to bring out problems in the firm's selling and advertising programs and to broaden the participants' thinking about the firm's place in the market.

Previous sales experience is usually the starting point for sales budget estimates. These historical data are then modified to recognize market trends, anticipated changes in general economic conditions, altered advertising plans, and any other factors deemed relevant. In the end, it is the sales executive, relying on experience and knowledge, who must make the final decisions on the precise quantities and dollar amounts to be shown in the sales budget for each product.

EXHIBIT 9.1
Victoria Corporation
Sales Budget
for Period 1

	Units	Amount
Product A (at $4)	30,000	$120,000
Product B (at $5)	60,000	300,000
Total	90,000	$420,000

EXHIBIT 9.2
Victoria Corporation
Production Budget
for Period 1

	Product A	Product B	Total
Units to Be Produced			
Budgeted Sales, in Units (see Sales Budget)........	30,000	60,000	90,000
Desired Ending Inventory (assumed)	3,000	5,000	8,000
Total Units Needed	33,000	65,000	98,000
Beginning Inventory (known at the time budget			
is prepared)........................	2,000	4,000	6,000
Units to Be Produced	31,000	61,000	92,000
Cost Expected to Be Incurred			
Direct Materials:			
Plastic (1 lb per unit @ $.50 per lb)	$15,500	$ 30,500	$ 46,000
Gleemy (1 oz per unit of product A @			
$.30 per oz).......................	9,300	—	9,300
Glowy (1 oz per unit of product B @			
$.50 per oz).......................	—	30,500	30,500
Direct Labor ($\frac{1}{4}$ hour per unit @ $5 per hour)	38,750	76,250	115,000
Manufacturing Overhead:			
Indirect Labor ($.10 per unit)	3,100	6,100	9,200
Supplies ($.04 per unit)	1,240	2,440	3,680
Power ($1,000 per period plus $.03 per unit)......	930[a]	1,830[a]	3,760[a]
Maintenance ($13,830 per period).............	—	—	13,830[a]
Rent ($6,000 per period)	—	—	6,000[a]
Insurance ($1,000 per period)...............	—	—	1,000[a]
Depreciation ($10,160 per period).............	—	—	10,160[a]
Total	$68,820[a]	$147,620[a]	$248,430[a]
Total Cash Outlays			
Direct Materials (see Raw Materials Purchases			
Budget, Exhibit 9.3)			$ 87,100
Direct Labor (from above)			$115,000
Manufacturing Overhead (total less depreciation)			$ 37,470

[a] The amounts attributable to product A and product B represent the variable cost component only. Fixed costs are included only in the total column. For power, $1,000 of periodic fixed costs are included in the total column.

Production Budget

The sales budget plus estimates of desired ending inventories form the basis of the production budget for the Victoria Corporation shown in the top panel of Exhibit 9.2. The number of units desired in the ending inventory usually reflects some early estimates of sales to be made in the next period beyond the one being budgeted. The number of units in ending inventory may differ from the quantity considered optimum by sales projections for next period as the indirect result of efforts to keep production balanced period by period and thereby keep the basic labor force employed on a regular basis.

The quantity of each product to be produced is budgeted by using a variant of the familiar inventory equation:

$$\frac{\text{Beginning}}{\text{Inventory}} + \text{Purchases} - \frac{\text{Ending}}{\text{Inventory}} = \frac{\text{Cost of}}{\text{Goods Sold}}$$

Transposing the factors in this equation leads to:

$$\frac{\text{Cost of}}{\text{Goods Sold}} + \frac{\text{Ending}}{\text{Inventory}} - \frac{\text{Beginning}}{\text{Inventory}} = \text{Purchases}$$

Substituting units of product for dollars and substituting production for purchases in the equation leads to:

$$\frac{\text{Number of}}{\text{Units Sold}} + \frac{\text{Units in}}{\substack{\text{Ending} \\ \text{Inventory}}} - \frac{\text{Units in}}{\substack{\text{Beginning} \\ \text{Inventory}}} = \frac{\text{Units to}}{\text{Be Produced}}$$

The costs to be incurred in producing the desired number of units of product A and product B are shown in the lower panel of Exhibit 9.2. The costs are divided into three categories: (1) direct material, (2) direct labor, and (3) manufacturing overhead.

Direct Materials   Direct materials are raw materials that are traceable to, or directly associated with, individual units produced. Direct materials are almost always a variable cost item. Both product A and product B require 1 pound of plastic per finished unit. Product A is decorated with 1 ounce of Gleemy, whereas Product B relies on 1 ounce of Glowy for decoration. The quantities of raw material required per unit are based on engineering studies of material usage. The cost per pound or per ounce of the raw materials used is based on studies of past cost behavior and current price lists of suppliers.

Direct Labor   Direct labor represents work performed that is directly traceable to particular units of product. Relying on engineering time and motion studies and studies of past cost behavior, it is estimated that a unit of product A or product B requires 15 minutes of labor time. This estimate allows for periodic rest periods but is sufficiently tight so that employees are motivated to perform efficiently. The standard wage rate for production workers in Victoria Corporation's plant is $5.00 per hour and is set by negotiation with the local labor union.

Manufacturing Overhead   Unlike direct material and direct labor, manufacturing overhead costs are not directly traceable to particular units produced. Rather, these costs either give a firm the capacity to produce (fixed manufacturing overhead costs) or represent costs that vary with, but are not directly traceable to, the units produced (variable manufacturing overhead costs). As shown in Exhibit 9.2, indirect labor and supplies are variable manufacturing overhead costs. Power is a semivariable, or mixed, cost, having both variable and fixed components. The amounts shown for power cost for product A and product B are the variable portion. The fixed cost component is shown only in the total column. Maintenance, rent, insurance, and depreciation are fixed manufacturing overhead costs.

Summary of Production Budget The Production Budget shown in Exhibit 9.2 serves as a plan of action for the Production Department for the period. The production manager must schedule production so that 31,000 units of product A and 61,000 units of product B are manufactured. The production budget also serves as a gauge for evaluating the performance of the production department at the end of the period. If production in units proceeds according to plan, then the production department should incur costs of $248,430 during the period. If the level of production differs from the projected amounts, then the flexible budget amounts must be applied to determine the amount of costs which should have been incurred. The flexible budget for the Production Department is

$$\begin{array}{l}\text{Total Cost} \\ \text{for Production} \\ \text{Department}\end{array} = \$31,990 + \left(\$2.22 \times \begin{array}{c}\text{Units of} \\ \text{Product A} \\ \text{Produced}\end{array}\right) + \left(\$2.42 \times \begin{array}{c}\text{Units of} \\ \text{Product B} \\ \text{Produced}\end{array}\right)$$

The fixed cost amount is the sum of the estimates for power, maintenance, rent, insurance, and depreciation ($31,990 = $1,000 + $13,830 + $6,000 + $1,000 + $10,160). The variable cost amount for product A is the sum of the estimates for plastic, Gleemy, direct labor, indirect labor, supplies, and power ($2.22 = $.50 + $.30 + $1.25 + $.10 + $.04 + $.03). For product B, the variable cost amount is composed of the same costs as for product A except that Glowy is substituted for Gleemy.

Raw Materials Purchases Budget

The purchasing of raw materials is the responsibility of the Purchasing Department in Victoria Corporation. Exhibit 9.3 presents the Raw Materials Purchases Budget. The Production Budget along with the estimates of beginning and ending inventories of raw materials serve as the basis for the Raw Materials Purchases Budget. The quantity of each class of materials to be purchased is budgeted by multiplying the quantity of that class of raw material in each unit of product to be produced by the same variant of the familiar inventory formula that was used in deriving the Production Budget. The number of units of each class of raw materials to be purchased each period is shown in the top panel of Exhibit 9.3. The budget indicating the estimated cost of those purchases is shown in the lower panel of Exhibit 9.3. For simplicity in presentation, it is assumed in Exhibit 9.3 that payments to suppliers equal purchases each period. That assumption is probably unrealistic. A procedure for dealing with time lags in payments is illustrated later in the receivables and collections budget (see Exhibit 9.8). The same procedure could have been used for accounts payable to suppliers.

EXHIBIT 9.3
Victoria Corporation
Raw Materials Purchases Budget
for Period 1

Quantities to Be Purchased	Plastic (lb)	Gleemy (oz)	Glowy (oz)
Units to Be Used (see Production Budget)	92,000	31,000	61,000
Planned Ending Inventory (assumed).	10,000	4,000	5,000
Units Needed	102,000	35,000	66,000
Beginning Inventory (known at the time the budget is prepared). . . .	8,000	3,000	5,000
Units to Be Purchased	94,000	32,000	61,000

Cost to Be Incurred			
Plastic: $.50 per pound	$ 47,000		
Gleemy: $.30 per ounce		$ 9,600	
Glowy: $.50 per ounce			$30,500

(Total Costs and Total Cash Outlay:
$47,000 + $9,600 + $30,500 = $87,100)

Selling Expense Budget

The budget for selling expenses for the Victoria Corporation's Marketing Department is shown in Exhibit 9.4. All of the items except commissions and shipping costs are estimated to be fixed. Commissions are 2 percent of sales dollars and shipping costs are $.02 per unit shipped. Note that variable selling costs vary with sales dollars and shipments made, whereas variable manufacturing costs vary with units produced.

EXHIBIT 9.4
Victoria Corporation
Selling Expense Budget

	Period 1
Salaries ($25,000 per period).	$25,000
Commissions (2% of sales; see Exhibit 9.1 Sales Budget).	8,400
Advertising ($30,000 per period)	30,000
Sales Office Costs ($8,400 per period)	8,400
Shipping Costs ($.02 per unit shipped; see Exhibit 9.1, Sales Budget) . .	1,800
Travel ($2,000 per period)	2,000
Total Selling Expense Budget (= Cash Outlay).	$75,600

Central Corporate Administrative Expense Budget

All of the central corporate administrative expenses shown in Exhibit 9.5 are fixed, but not all of them require current cash outlays. Depreciation of office equipment is an expense that does not require a current expenditure but is the allocation of part of the cost of a long-term asset to the current period.

EXHIBIT 9.5
Victoria Corporation
Central Corporate Administrative Expense Budget

	Period 1
President's Salary	$20,000
Salaries of Other Staff Personnel	27,000
Supplies	2,000
Heat and Light	1,400
Rent	4,000
Donations and Contributions	1,000
General Corporate Taxes	8,000
Depreciation—Staff Office Equipment	1,400
Total Central Corporate Administrative Budget	$64,800
Less: Depreciation[a]	1,400
Budgeted Cash Outlays	$63,400

[a] Note that all items except depreciation are fixed costs requiring current cash outlays.

Capital Budget

The capital budget, Exhibit 9.6, shows the Victoria Corporation's plan for acquisition of depreciable, long-term assets during the next period. The company plans to purchase major items of equipment. Part of the costs will be financed by the issuance of

---

EXHIBIT 9.6
Victoria Corporation
Capital Budget

	Period 1
Acquisition of New Factory Machinery	$12,000
Miscellaneous Capital Additions	2,000
Total Capital Budget	$14,000
Borrowings for New Machinery (notes payable)[a]	10,000
Current Cash Outlay	$ 4,000

[a] Notes payable to be repaid at the rate of $4,000 per year.

notes that are payable in a later period to equipment suppliers. The note issuance is deducted from the cost of the acquisitions to determine current cash outlays for equipment. An alternative, accepted treatment would have viewed the note issuance as a cash inflow with the entire cost of the equipment included in cash outflows.

Cash Outlays Budget

A schedule of the planned cash outlays for Period 1 is presented in Exhibit 9.7. The first six items are taken from the cash outlay lines of earlier exhibits. The agreement with the equipment suppliers calls for payment of $4,000 per period plus interest. The amount shown for interest also includes interest on the short-term notes. Each period the Victoria Corporation pays the income taxes accrued in the previous period. Income taxes payable at the start of period 1 are shown on the actual balance sheet (Column 1 of Exhibit 9.11). Dividends at the rate of $.50 per share are declared and paid each period.

EXHIBIT 9.7
Victoria Corporation
Cash Outlays Budget

	Period 1
Materials (Exhibit 9.3)	$ 87,100
Labor (Exhibit 9.2)	115,000
Manufacturing Overhead (Exhibit 9.2)	37,470
Selling Expenses (Exhibit 9.4)	75,600
Central Corporate Administrative Expenses (Exhibit 9.5)	63,400
Capital Expenditures (Exhibit 9.6)	4,000
Payments on Equipment Notes[a]	4,000
Interest[b]	3,000
Income Taxes[c]	19,200
Dividends[d]	10,000
Total Cash Outlays	$418,770

---

[a] Equipment notes are repayable at the rate of $4,000 per period.
[b] Assumed for purposes of illustration.
[c] Income taxes on earnings of previous period are paid in current period. The amount is assumed in this case.
[d] Dividends at the rate of $.50 per share are declared and paid each period.

Receivables and Collections Budget

Most of the sales of each period are collected in the period of sale, but there is some lag in collections. The budget for cash collections from customers is shown in Exhibit 9.8. Collections for sales of a given period normally occur as follows: 85 percent in the period of sale, 12 percent in the next period, and 3 percent in the second period after the period of sale. It would be possible to introduce sales discounts and estimates of uncollectible accounts into the illustration, but they are omitted for simplicity. The accounts receivable at the start of period 1 of $71,400 are shown on the actual balance

EXHIBIT 9.8
Victoria Corporation
Receivables and Collections Budget

	Period 1
Accounts Receivable, Start of Period:	
From Immediately Preceding Period (15% of $400,000)............	$ 60,000
From Second Previous Period (3% of $380,000)	11,400
Total.....................................	$ 71,400
Sales of This Period	420,000
Total Receivables.....................................	$491,400
Collections:	
Current Period (85% of $420,000)........................	$357,000
Previous Period (12% of $400,000)........................	48,000
Second Previous Period (3% of $380,000)	11,400
Total Collections.....................................	$416,400
Accounts Receivable, End of Period	$ 75,000

sheet (column 1 of Exhibit 9.11). The amount represents 15 percent of the sales of $400,000 of the previous period ($60,000 = .15 × $400,000) and 3 percent of the sales of $380,000 of the second previous period ($11,400 = .03 × $380,000). Collections in period 1 are budgeted at 85 percent of that period's sales ($357,000 = .85 × $420,000, see Exhibit 9.1), plus 12 percent of the previous period's sales ($48,000 = .12 × $400,000, leaving 3 percent to be collected in period 2), plus 3 percent of the sales of the second previous period ($11,400 = .03 × $380,000).

Cash Budget

Cash flow is the lifeblood of any business. No budget is more important for planning purposes than the cash budget, illustrated in Exhibit 9.9. This budget is significant

EXHIBIT 9.9
Victoria Corporation
Cash Budget

	Period 1
Cash Receipts:	
Collections from Customers (Exhibit 9.8).....................	$416,400
Other Income.....................................	2,000
Total Receipts	$418,400
Cash Outflows (Exhibit 9.7).............................	418,770
Increase (Decrease) in Cash during Period....................	($ 370)
Cash Balance at Start of Period.........................	39,800
Cash Balance at End of Period	$ 39,430

because it helps management in planning to avoid unnecessary idle cash balances on the one hand, or unneeded, expensive borrowing on the other. Most companies prepare a cash budget rather than a budgeted statement of changes in financial position.

The budgeted amounts for cash outflows and collections from customers are taken from Exhibits 9.7 and 9.8, respectively. The other income is made up of interest and miscellaneous revenues. It is estimated to be $2,000 for the period.

Budgeted (*Pro Forma*) Income and Retained Earnings Statement

All of the previous budget information is pulled together in the Budgeted Income and Retained Earnings Statement and the Budgeted Balance Sheet. The former is illustrated in Exhibit 9.10. It is at this stage in the budgeting process that management's attention switches from decision making, planning, and control to external reporting to stockholders. That is, management becomes particularly interested in how the results of its decisions will be reflected in the income statement and balance sheet. Accordingly, the budgeted income statement and balance sheet should be prepared in accordance with generally accepted accounting principles.

EXHIBIT 9.10
Victoria Corporation
Budgeted (*Pro Forma*) Income and Retained Earnings Statement

	Period 1
Sales.	$420,000
Cost of Goods Sold:	
Product A (at $2.55 per unit sold)	$ 76,500
Product B (at $2.75 per unit sold)	165,000
Underabsorbed (Overabsorbed) Overhead.	1,630
Total Cost of Goods Sold	$243,130
Gross Margin	$176,870
Selling Expense	$ 75,600
Central Corporate Administrative Expense.	64,800
Total Other Operating Expenses	$140,400
Operating Income.	$ 36,470
Other Income.	2,000
	$ 38,470
Interest Expense.	3,000
Pretax Income	$ 35,470
Income Taxes[a]	13,790
Net Income	$ 21,680
Dividends.	10,000
Increase in Retained Earnings	$ 11,680
Retained Earnings at Start of Period.	56,500
Retained Earnings at End of Period	$ 68,180

---

[a] Income taxes average approximately 39 percent of pretax income.

There is one major item that is likely to be treated differently for decision making, planning, and control purposes as compared to the treatment required under generally accepted accounting principles: the accounting for fixed manufacturing overhead costs. Generally accepted accounting principles require that fixed manufacturing overhead costs be allocated to the units produced. These costs do not become expenses until the period in which the units are sold. When studying decision making, planning, and control up to this point in the book, we have treated fixed manufacturing overhead costs as expenses of the period in which the costs were incurred. We shall discuss the techniques for allocating fixed costs to products more fully in Chapters Twelve and Thirteen.

In order to prepare a Budgeted Income and Retained Earnings Statement for Victoria Corporation, we assume that each unit of product A and product B is allocated $.33 of fixed manufacturing overhead cost. The cost of goods sold of product A is therefore $2.55 per unit (= $2.22 variable cost plus $.33 fixed cost) and of product B is $2.75 (= $2.42 variable cost plus $.33 fixed cost). The budgeted fixed manufacturing overhead cost for the period is $31,990 (see Exhibit 9.2). The fixed manufacturing overhead cost expected to be applied to units produced during the period is $30,360 (= 92,000 units × $.33). Victoria Corporation will underapply the fixed cost by $1,630 (= $31,990 − $30,360) if production proceeds according to the plans. Victoria Corporation treats under or overapplied fixed manufacturing overhead costs as an expense of the period with an adjustment to cost of goods sold.

Compilation of all of the data for the period indicates a budgeted net income of $21,680. If top management finds this budgeted result satisfactory, and adequate cash can be made available to carry out the operations as indicated by Exhibit 9.9, the master budget will be approved. If the budgeted results are not considered satisfactory, much additional thought and many additional meetings will be devoted to considering ways in which the budgeted results might be improved through cost reductions.

Budgeted Balance Sheet

The final exhibit of this series, Exhibit 9.11, shows the actual balance sheet at the start of the period and the budgeted balance sheet at the end of the period. Here, as in the budgeted income statement, management will have to decide whether the budgeted overall results will be acceptable. Will cash balances be satisfactory? Is the receivables turnover up to plan? Will the final capital structure and debt-to-equity ratio conform to management's desires? If the budgeted balance sheet and income statement are satisfactory, they will become the initial benchmarks against which actual performance in the ensuing period is checked.

Summary of the Master Budget

The master budget is a summary of management's plans for the period covered. Preparing the master budget is usually a complex, dynamic process requiring the participation of all managerial groups from local plant and sales managers to the top executives of the company. Once the budget is prepared and adopted, it becomes a major planning and control instrument. Master budgets are almost always static

EXHIBIT 9.11
Victoria Corporation
Budgeted Balance Sheet

	Start of Period 1 (actual)	End of Period 1 (projected)
Assets		
Current Assets:		
Cash	$ 39,800	$ 39,430
Accounts Receivable	71,400	75,000
Finished Goods	16,100	21,400
Raw Materials	7,400	8,700
Total Current Assets	$134,700	$144,530
Plant Assets:		
Equipment	460,000	474,000
Accumulated Depreciation	(162,000)	(173,560)
Total Assets	$432,700	$444,970
Equities		
Current Liabilities:		
Accounts Payable	$ 47,000	$ 47,000
Short-Term Notes and Other Payables	28,000	28,000
Income Taxes Payable	19,200	13,790
Total Current Liabilities	$ 94,200	$ 88,790
Long-Term Liabilities:		
Long-Term Equipment Notes	82,000	88,000
Total Liabilities	$176,200	$176,790
Stockholders' Equity:		
Capital Stock ($10 par value)	$200,000	$200,000
Retained Earnings	56,500	68,180
Total Stockholders' Equity	$256,500	$268,180
Total Equities	$432,700	$444,970

budgets; that is, they consider the likely results of operations at the one level of operations specified in the budget. This may facilitate the planning process, but it weakens the effectiveness of the budget as a control device if the scale of operations deviates from the planned level. Under those circumstances, flexible budgets are necessary. Flexible budgets consider the varying amounts of revenues and costs that are appropriate at various levels of operations.

Any accounting report that can be compiled at the end of a period from actual data can be matched by a similar statement compiled at the beginning of the period from projected data. A budget is merely a financial report prepared in advance from data that are expected to reflect operations of the period. A budget is a plan of operations expressed in financial terms. Budgets make possible a comparison of results with plans and thereby help management to control operations.

QUESTIONS AND PROBLEMS

1 Review the meaning of the following concepts or terms discussed in this chapter.
 a Budgets as planning tools.
 b Budgets as control tools.
 c Static budget.
 d Flexible budget.
 e Master budget.

2 Bala Company expects to sell 84,000 units of finished goods over the next three-month period. The Company currently has 44,000 units of finished goods on hand and wishes to have an inventory of 48,000 units at the end of the three-month period. To produce one unit of finished goods requires 4 units of raw materials. The company currently has 200,000 units of raw materials on hand and wishes to have an inventory of 220,000 units of raw materials on hand at the end of the three-month period.

 How many units of raw materials must the Bala Company purchase during the three-month period?

3 PQR Company expects to sell 100,000 units of product during the current year. Budgeted costs per unit are $120 for direct materials, $100 for direct labor, and $50 (all variable) for manufacturing overhead. PQR Company began the period with 30,000 units of finished goods on hand and wants to end the period with 10,000 units of finished goods on hand.

 Compute the budgeted manufacturing costs of the PQR Company for the current period. Assume no beginning or ending inventory of work in process.

4 Jones Corporation normally collects cash from credit customers as follows: 50 percent in the month of sale, 30 percent in the first month after sale, 18 percent in the second month after sale, and 2 percent are never collected. Sales, all on credit, of Jones Corporation are expected to be as follows:

January	$500,000
February	600,000
March	400,000
April	500,000

 a Calculate the amount of cash expected to be received from customers during March.
 b Calculate the amount of cash expected to be received from customers during April.

5 Wallace Corporation purchases raw materials on account from various suppliers. It normally pays for 60 percent of these in the month purchased, 30 percent in the first month after purchase, and the remaining 10 percent in the second month after purchase. Raw materials purchases during the last five months of the year were as follows:

August	$1,400,000
September	1,800,000
October	2,000,000
November	3,500,000
December	1,500,000

Determine the budgeted amount of cash payments to suppliers for the months of October, November, and December.

6 Prepare a cash budget for the month of June using the following information.

    (1) Cash balance, June 1, $120,000.

    (2) Sales are collected as follows: 50 percent in the month of sale, 40 percent in the next month, 8 percent in the next following month, and 2 percent are uncollectible.

    (3) Budgeted sales for June are $1.6 million, sales for May were $1.4 million, and for April were $1.8 million.

    (4) Merchandise purchase invoices are paid as follows: 60 percent in the month of purchase and 40 percent in the following month.

    (5) Merchandise purchases for May were $1 million and budgeted purchases for June are $1.2 million.

    (6) Wages and salaries to be paid in June amount to $175,000.

    (7) A two-year insurance policy requires payment in June. The policy costs $4,800. Insurance coverage starts June 1.

    (8) Depreciation for June amounts to $5,000.

    (9) Taxes estimated to accrue in June amount to $6,000; these will be paid in September.

    (10) A note payable to the bank is due June 20: $200,000 face amount plus $15,000 interest.

    (11) Other cash expenditures for June are estimated to be $80,000.

7 The Cash Poor Company has a balance in its cash account on March 1 of $10,000. In order to maintain a minimum balance in its account of $20,000, the company borrowed $10,000 from the bank on March 2.

    Actual sales of the firm's product (which it purchases for $6 per unit and sells for $10 per unit) for January through April were as follows:

January	5,000 units
February	8,000
March	14,000
April	10,000

Of the sales made, 50 percent are for cash (collected in the period of sale) and subject to a discount of 5 percent, 30 percent are collected in the month after sale and subject to a 2 percent discount, 15 percent are collected in the second month after sale but not subject to a discount, and 5 percent are ultimately considered uncollectible.

    The desired inventory level at the end of each month is equal to the number of units expected to be sold during the following month. Beginning inventory on January 1 was 5,000 units. One-half of the units purchased in a month are paid for in the month of purchase and subject to a 5 percent discount, whereas the other half are paid during the following month, but not subject to a discount.

    Other cash requirements are $12,500 per month for fixed cash expenses and 10 percent of sales dollars for variable selling expenses.

a Prepare a cash budget for the period January through March. Disregard any purchases or sales that may have occurred prior to January 1.

b What is the maximum annual rate of interest that Cash Poor Company can pay on the $10,000 loan so that, after the interest payment for March, the balance in the cash account will be $20,000?

c Now assume that the unit sales in the last two months of the preceding year were:

November	10,000 units
December	20,000

Assume that the cash balance on January 1 is $10,000. Current receivables and current payables on January 1 are $103,800 and $15,000, respectively. Prepare monthly cash budgets for January through March. Determine the amount of required borrowing, if any.

8 J. Cash started a new record shop on July 1, 19X0. Expected sales for the first six months of operations are as follows:

July.	12,000 units
August.	10,000
September	8,000
October.	5,000
November	6,000
December	7,000

Selling prices are twice as large as the costs; 35 percent of all sales are for cash; 5 percent of all sales are expected to be uncollectible. Of the 60 percent of sales made on account and considered collectible, two-thirds will be subject to a discount of 4 percent. Of those accounts taking the discount, 75 percent will be collected in the month of sale and 25 percent in the following month. All other accounts that are collectible are collected by the end of the month after sale.

Purchases of inventory are made on account and paid during the first ten days after the month of purchase without advantage of a discount. J. Cash desires an ending quantity in inventory at the end of each month equal to the next two months' sales. The balance in accounts payable on August 31 is $20,000 and represents the cost of units purchased in August in accordance with the firm's inventory policy.

Other cash requirements include $15,000 per month for fixed expenses and 5 percent of gross sales for variable selling expenses. A dividend of $2,000 is to be paid in September and a single payment note of $5,000 (including interest) is to be paid to a bank on October 31. The balance in the cash account on September 1 is $5,000.

a Prepare a budgeted statement of cash receipts and disbursements for September.

b Prepare a budgeted statement of cash receipts and disbursements for October.

9 As a result of studying past cost behavior and adjusting for expected price increases in the future, Wilson Corporation estimates its manufacturing costs will be as follows:

Direct Materials	$2.00 per unit
Direct Labor.	$1.50 per unit
Manufacturing Overhead:	
Variable.	$ .50 per unit
Fixed.	$50,000 per period

Wilson adopts these estimates for planning and control purposes.

a Wilson Corporation expects to produce 10,000 units during the next period. Prepare a schedule of the expected manufacturing costs.

b Suppose that Wilson Corporation produces only 8,000 units during the next period. Prepare a flexible budget of manufacturing costs for the 8,000-unit level of activity.

c Suppose that Wilson Corporation produces 13,000 units during the next period. Prepare a flexible budget of manufacturing costs for the 13,000-unit level of activity.

10 Refer to the Selling Expense Budget of the Victoria Corporation shown in Exhibit 9.4. Prepare a flexible selling expense budget for the period assuming the following levels of sales and shipments.

	Case 1	Case 2	Case 3
Product A (in units)	30,000	34,000	30,000
Product B (in units)	60,000	60,000	64,000

11 Refer to the Central Corporate Administrative Expense Budget of the Victoria Corporation in Exhibit 9.5. Prepare a flexible central corporate administrative expense budget for the period assuming that production and sales were 100,000 units. Is the term "flexible budget" a misnomer in this case? Explain.

12 (Adapted from a CMA Examination Question.) The Melcher Co. produces farm equipment at several plants. The business is seasonal and cyclical in nature. The company has attempted to use budgeting for planning and controlling activities, but the fluctuating nature of the business has caused some company officials to be skeptical about the usefulness of budgeting to the company. The accountant for the Adrian plant has been using flexible budgeting to help the plant management control operations. The accountant presents the following data.

Planned Level of Production for January 19X0 (in units).	**4,000**
Budgeted Cost Data:	
Direct Materials ($9.00 per unit)	$36,000
Direct Labor ($6.00 per unit)	$24,000
Variable (with production):	
Indirect Labor.	$ 6,650
Indirect Materials	600
Repairs	750
Total Variable	$ 8,000
Fixed:	
Depreciation.	$ 3,250
Supervision	3,000
Total Fixed	$ 6,250
Total Manufacturing Costs	$74,250

Actual Data for January 19X0	
Units Produced.	3,800
Costs Incurred:	
Material	$36,000
Direct Labor.	25,200
Indirect Labor	6,000
Indirect Materials	600
Repairs	1,800
Depreciation.	3,250
Supervision	3,000
Total	$75,850

a Prepare a flexible budget for January based on planned production levels of 3,800 units and of 4,000 units.

b Prepare a report for January comparing actual and budgeted costs based on the actual level of production for the month.

13 (Adapted from a CMA Examination Question.) The Barker Corporation manufactures and distributes wooden baseball bats. The bats are manufactured in Georgia at its only plant. This is a seasonal business with a large portion of its sales occurring in late winter and early spring. The production schedule for the last quarter of the year is heavy in order to build up inventory to meet expected sales volume.

The company experiences a temporary cash strain during this heavy production period. Payroll costs rise during the last quarter because overtime is scheduled to meet the increased production needs. Collections from customers are low because the fall season produces only modest sales. This year the company concern is intensified because of the rapid increases in prices during the current inflationary period. In addition, the sales department forecasts sales of less than 1 million bats for the first time in three years. This decrease in sales appears to be caused by the popularity of aluminum bats.

The cash account builds up during the first and second quarters as sales exceed production. The excess cash is invested in U.S. Treasury bills and other commercial paper. During the last half of the year the temporary investments are liquidated to meet the cash needs. In the early years of the company, short-term borrowing was used to supplement the funds released by selling investments, but this has not been necessary in recent years. Because costs are higher this year, the treasurer asks for a forecast for the month of December to judge if the $40,000 in temporary investments will be adequate to carry the company through the month with a minimum balance at the end of the month of $10,000. Should this amount ($40,000) be insufficient, the treasurer wants to begin negotiations for a short-term loan.

The unit sales volume for the past two months and the estimate for the next four months are

October (actual)	70,000
November (actual)	50,000
December (estimated)	50,000
January (estimated)	90,000
February (estimated)	90,000
March (estimated)	120,000

The bats are sold for $3 each. All sales are made on account. One-half of the accounts are collected in the month of the sale, 40 percent are collected in the month following the sale, and the remaining 10 percent in the second month following the sale. Customers who pay in the month of the sale receive a 2-percent cash discount.

The production schedule for the six-month period beginning with October reflects the company's policy of maintaining a stable year-round work force by scheduling overtime to meet production schedules:

October (actual)	90,000
November (actual)	90,000
December (estimated)	90,000
January (estimated)	90,000
February (estimated)	100,000
March (estimated)	100,000

The bats are made from wooden blocks that cost $6 each. Ten bats can be produced from each block. The blocks are acquired one year in advance so that they can be properly aged. Barker pays the supplier one-twelfth of the cost of this material each month until the obligation is retired. The monthly payment is $60,000.

The plant is normally scheduled for a 40-hour, five-day work week. During the busy production season, however, the work week may be increased to six 10-hour days. Workers can produce 7.5 bats per hour. Normal monthly output is 75,000 bats. Factory employees are paid $4.00 per hour for regular time and time and one-half for overtime.

Other manufacturing costs include variable overhead of $.30 per unit and annual fixed overhead of $280,000. Depreciation charges totalling $40,000 are included in the fixed manufacturing overhead. Selling expenses include variable costs of $.20 per unit and annual fixed costs of $60,000. Fixed administrative costs are $120,000 annually. All fixed costs are incurred uniformly throughout the year.

The controller has accumulated the following additional information:

(1) The balances of selected accounts as of November 30, 19X0, are as follows:

Cash	$ 12,000
Marketable Securities (cost and market are the same)	40,000
Accounts Receivable	96,000
Prepayments	4,800
Accounts Payable (arising from raw material purchases)	300,000
Equipment Note Payable	102,000
Accrued Income Taxes Payable	50,000

(2) Interest to be received from the company's temporary investments is estimated at $500 for December.

(3) Prepayments of $3,600 will expire during December, and the balance of the prepayments account is estimated to be $4,200 at the end of December.

(4) Barker purchased new machinery in 19X0 as part of a plant modernization program. The machinery was financed by a 24-month note of $144,000. The terms call for equal principal payments over the next 24 months with interest paid at the rate of 1 percent per month on the unpaid balance at the first of the month. The first payment was made May 1, 19X0.

(5) Old equipment, which has a book value of $8,000, is to be sold during December for $7,500.

(6) Quarterly dividends of $.20 per share will be paid on December 15 to stockholders of record. Barker Corporation has 7,000 shares outstanding.

(7) The quarterly income taxes payment of $50,000 is due on December 15, 19X0.

a Prepare a schedule that forecasts the cash position at December 31, 19X0.
b What action, if any, will be required to maintain a $10,000 cash balance?

14 (Adapted from a CPA Examination Question.*) Modern Products Corporation, a manufacturer of molded plastic containers, determined in October, 19X0, that it needed cash to continue operations. The Corporation began negotiating for a one-month bank loan of $100,000 starting November 1, 19X0. The loan would carry interest at the rate of 1 percent

---

*   Material from the Uniform CPA Examinations, copyright by the American Institute of Certified Public Accountants, Inc., is adapted with permission.

per month. Interest and principal would be repaid on November 30, 19X0. In considering the loan, the bank requested a projected income statement and a cash budget for the month of November.

The following information is available:

(1) Sales were budgeted at 120,000 units per month in October 19X0, December 19X0, and January 19X1, and at 90,000 units in November 19X0.

The selling price is $2 per unit. Sales are billed on the 15th and last day of each month on terms of 2/10, net 30. (That is, a 2-percent discount is offered for payment within 10 days. Payment is due, in any case, within 30 days.) Experience indicates that sales occur evenly throughout the month and that 50 percent of the customers pay the billed amount within the discount period. The remainder pay at the end of 30 days, except for uncollectible amounts which average $\frac{1}{2}$ percent of gross sales. On its income statement the corporation deducts the estimated amounts for cash discounts on sales and expected uncollectibles from sales.

(2) The inventory of finished goods on October 1 was 24,000 units. The finished goods inventory at the end of each month is to be maintained at 20 percent of sales anticipated for the following month. There is no work in process.

(3) The inventory of raw materials on October 1 was 22,800 pounds. At the end of each month the raw materials inventory is to be maintained at not less than 40 percent of production requirements for the following month. Materials are purchased as needed in minimum quantities of 25,000 pounds per shipment. Raw material purchases of each month are paid in the next succeeding month on terms of net 30 days.

(4) All salaries and wages are paid on the 15th and last day of each month for the period ending on the date of payment.

(5) All manufacturing overhead and selling and administrative expenses are paid on the 10th of the month following the month in which incurred. Selling expenses are 10 percent of gross sales. Administrative expenses, which include depreciation of $500 per month on office furniture and fixtures, total $33,000 per month.

(6) The manufacturing budget for molded plastic containers, based on expected production of 100,000 units per month, is as follows:

Materials (50,000 lb, $1.00 each).	$ 50,000
Labor	40,000
Variable Overhead	20,000
Fixed Overhead (includes depreciation of $4,000)	10,000
Total	$120,000

(7) The cash balance on November 1 is expected to be $10,000.

Prepare the following for Modern Products Corporation, assuming that the bank loan is granted. Ignore income taxes.

a Schedules computing inventory budgets by months for
(i) Finished goods production in units for October, November, and December.
(ii) Raw material purchases in pounds for October and November.

b A projected income statement for the month of November. Cost of goods sold should be equal to the variable manufacturing cost per unit times the number of units sold plus the total fixed manufacturing cost budgeted for the period.

c A cash forecast for the month of November showing the opening balance, receipts (itemized by dates of collection), disbursements, and balance at end of month.

15 The Norwood Corporation has patented a new household product and is now actively marketing it. Its income statement for the first quarter of 19X2 is shown below.

The $7 per unit manufacturing cost is presently made up of material cost, $2; direct labor cost, $4; and overhead costs, $1. The productive capacity of the present plant, working one eight-hour shift per day, is 50,000 units per quarter. The sales manager is certain that additional units could be sold if they were available. Top management is reluctant to increase the size of the plant and, instead, decides to consider the advisability of adding a second, and perhaps a third, shift.

The production manager estimates the following:

(1) That each additional shift would increase output by 50,000 units per quarter; and
(2) That if a second shift were added, labor costs per unit on the output of that shift would be 10 percent higher and total overhead cost would be increased 25 percent.
(3) If a third shift were added, labor costs per unit for the output of that shift would be 25 percent higher than for one-shift operations and total overhead would be 75 percent higher than for one-shift operations. With three-shift operations, it is estimated that material costs of all units could be reduced 4 percent due to larger quantity purchases.

The sales manager estimates the following:

(1) That 100,000 units a quarter could be sold at the current price, but that to sell 150,000 units each quarter the unit price would have to be reduced by 5 percent; and
(2) That selling expenses for 100,000 units per quarter will be 50 percent higher and for 150,000 units will be 90 percent higher than for 50,000 units.

Total administrative expenses are expected to increase by 20 percent and by 40 percent from the 50,000 unit figure for sales of 100,000 units and 150,000 units, respectively.

Prepare projected second-quarter income statements assuming:
a Two-shift operations.
b Three-shift operations.

The Norwood Corporation
Partial Income Statement
January 1 to March 31, 19X2

Sales (50,000 units at $10 per unit)		$500,000
Operating Expenses:		
Cost of Goods Sold ($7 per unit).	$350,000	
Selling Expenses	45,000	
Administrative Expenses	30,000	
Total Expenses.		425,000
Operating Income.		$ 75,000

16 (Adapted from a problem by David O. Green.) A partial income statement for 19X0 of Baines Manufacturing Corporation appears below.

Inventories are usually kept at minimal levels and production each year is equal to sales. Each dollar of finished product produced in 19X0 contained $.50 of direct materials, $.33⅓ of direct labor, and $.16⅔ of overhead costs. During 19X0, fixed overhead costs were $40,000. No changes in production methods or credit policies are anticipated for 19X1.

Baines Manufacturing Corporation
Partial Income Statement for 19X0

Sales (100,000 units at $10)........................		$1,000,000
Cost of Goods Sold		600,000
Gross Margin....................................		$ 400,000
Selling Expenses	$150,000	
Administrative Expenses	100,000	250,000
Operating Income Before Taxes................		$ 150,000

Management has estimated the following changes for 19X1:

30 percent increase in number of units sold.
20 percent increase in unit cost of materials.
15 percent increase in direct labor cost per unit.
10 percent increase in variable overhead cost per unit.
5 percent increase in fixed overhead costs.
8 percent increase in selling expenses because of increased volume.
6 percent increase in administrative expenses arising solely because of increased wages.
There are no other changes.

a What must the unit sales price be in 19X1 for Baines Manufacturing Corporation to earn $200,000 before taxes?

b What will be the 19X1 income before taxes if selling prices are increased, as above, but unit sales increase by 10 percent, rather than 30 percent? (Selling expense would go up by only one-third of the amount projected above.)

c If selling price in 19X1 were to remain at $10 per unit, how many units must be sold in 19X1 for pretax income to be $200,000?

17 The Monmouth Company is preparing its budget for the year 19X1. If the same selling policies that were in effect in 19X0 are continued in 19X1, the budget officer estimates that the income statement will appear as shown below.

All variable expenses vary with the number of units sold. The company could increase its output to 1 million units per year without increasing its fixed manufacturing and administrative costs. In order to increase its income, the company is seeking to utilize the presently unused capacity. Two plans have been suggested to improve the income picture.

Plan A. It is estimated that unit sales could be increased by 25 percent if **(1)** selling price per unit is reduced by 5 percent, and **(2)** an additional advertising campaign is instituted which would increase fixed selling expenses by $15,000.

Plan B. The company has an opportunity to obtain a government contract for an additional 200,000 units if it quotes a low enough price. If the government contract were obtained, it would have no effect on the regular sales of 800,000 units.

a Assuming that plan A were adopted and the results are as anticipated, present the income statement for 19X1.

b If it is anticipated that plan A will function as planned, what is the lowest price the company should bid on the government contract? (Show your computations.)

c If it is decided that plan A is not feasible, what is the lowest price the company should bid on the government contract? (Show your computations.)

The Monmouth Company
Projected Partial Income Statement
Year 19X1

Sales (800,000 units at $2 per unit)		$1,600,000
Operating Expenses:		
Cost of Goods Sold:		
Variable.	$600,000	
Fixed.	300,000	
Total Cost of Goods Sold		$900,000
Administrative Expenses:		
Variable.	$ 20,000	
Fixed.	100,000	
Total Administrative Expenses		120,000
Selling Expenses:		
Variable.	$ 30,000	
Fixed.	120,000	
Total Selling Expenses	150,000	
Total Operating Expenses		1,170,000
Operating Income.		$ 430,000

18 This problem extends the illustration for Victoria Corporation presented in this chapter to period 2. Given the information below, you are asked to prepare a complete master budget with supporting schedules and financial statements for period 2 following the format in Exhibits 9.1 through 9.11. Your instructor may want you to create an additional row or column in each of the exhibits in the chapter text and place your answer directly on the printed page. The following information pertains to period 2.

(1) Sales—It is anticipated that 35,000 units of product A and 70,000 units of product B will be sold. Selling prices are to remain unchanged.

(2) Production—Victoria Corporation desires an ending inventory of 3,000 units of product A and 4,000 units of product B at the end of period 2. The per unit material, labor, and overhead costs are to remain unchanged.

(3) Materials Purchased—Victoria Corporation desires an ending inventory of 15,000 pounds of plastic, 5,000 ounces of Gleemy, and 6,000 ounces of Glowy at the end of period 2. Purchase prices per unit are to remain unchanged. Purchases are paid for in the period when they are acquired.

(4) Manufacturing Overhead—Indirect labor and supplies costs are to remain variable at the same amounts per unit as in period 1. Power cost is to remain a mixed cost with the same amount for fixed and variable cost per unit as in period 1. Fixed manufacturing overhead costs for period 2 are

Maintenance	$14,180
Rent	6,000
Insurance	1,000
Depreciation.	10,460

(5) Selling Expenses—There are no changes expected in the fixed selling expenses in period 2 or in the variable selling expense rate per sales dollar or per unit shipped (as appropriate). The amounts are all paid for in period 2.

(6) Central Corporate Administrative Expenses—Central corporate administrative expenses are not expected to change in period 2. These amounts are all paid for in period 2.

(7) Capital Additions—It is anticipated that $18,000 of new factory machinery will be acquired and $2,000 of miscellaneous capital additions will be made in period 2. The additions will be financed with new borrowings of $15,000.

(8) Other Cash Outlays—Other cash outlays in period 2 will be

Payment on Equipment Notes.	$ 4,000
Interest	3,400
Income Taxes.	13,790
Dividends.	10,000

(9) Collections on Receivables—The collections rate on accounts receivable will remain unchanged in period 2. Cash collections from other income is expected to be $3,000.

(10) Income tax expense of period 2 is $26,570.

CHAPTER 10
MEASURING AND INTERPRETING VARIANCES FROM STANDARD

In Chapter Nine, we considered the first phase of the control process: the setting of budgets or standards. In this chapter, we focus on the second and third phases of the control process: measuring actual results and evaluating performance by comparing actual results with the standards. In particular, we illustrate the calculation of several revenue and expense variances (the difference between actual results and the standard) and discuss appropriate interpretations of these variances. The variances are calculated for individual responsiblity centers having control over the specific revenue, cost, and expense items.

VARIANCE CALCULATIONS IN GENERAL

The standards for most revenue, cost, and expense items are based on both physical measures and dollar measures. Materials usage standards are initially measured, for example, in pounds, units, or gallons. Labor standards are grounded in some measure of time, perhaps minutes or hours of a given skill level. For accounting purposes, the physical standards are then converted into dollars so that the various inputs to a process or product can be measured on a comparable basis. For example, a standard amount of 3 pounds of material, at $1.50 per pound, may be required to manufacture one unit of product. The standard material cost per unit of product is $4.50. The standard labor cost might be calculated similarly. The conversion of raw material into finished product is expected to take five hours of labor time per unit. If the usual employee doing the work earns $6 per hour, the standard labor cost per unit of product is $30 (= $6 per hour × 5 hours).

Because the standards are based on physical and dollar measures, two general types of variances can be calculated for most items: (1) a price variance, and (2) a quantity variance. Consider Figure 10.1. The figure shows two types of prices (actual and standard) and two types of quantities (actual and standard). The difference between the

	Actual Price			Standard Price
Actual Quantity	Actual Revenue, Cost, or Expense (actual quantity at actual price) 1		2	Actual Quantity at Standard Price
Standard Quantity	Standard Quantity at Actual Price 3		4	Standard Revenue, Cost, or Expense (standard quantity at standard price)

FIGURE 10.1
Actual and Standard
Price/Quantity Relationships

actual revenue, cost, or expense (quadrant 1: actual quantity times actual price) and the standard revenue, cost, or expense (quadrant 4: standard quantity times standard price) represents the total variance to be explained. This variance can be explained by first calculating a price variance (the difference between quadrants 1 and 2) and then calculating a quantity variance (the difference between quadrants 2 and 4). Alternatively, the total variance could be explained by first calculating a quantity variance (the difference between quadrants 1 and 3) and then calculating a price variance (the difference between quadrants 3 and 4). By convention, the first approach is generally followed in practice, so that the price variance is calculated as follows:

$$\text{Price Variance} = \text{Actual Quantity} \times \left(\text{Actual Price} - \text{Standard Price} \right)$$

The quantity variance is calculated as follows:

$$\text{Quantity Variance} = \left(\text{Actual Quantity} - \text{Standard Quantity} \right) \times \text{Standard Price}$$

Price and quantity variances are calculated for revenues, raw materials, direct labor, and other costs as will be illustrated in the sections that follow. In the illustrations we use the data for Victoria Corporation discussed in Chapter Nine.

SALES REVENUE VARIANCES

The marketing department has the responsibility for generating sales. Sales for the period, as shown in Exhibit 9.1, were expected to be

Product A: 30,000 units @ $4 per unit $120,000
Product B: 60,000 units @ $5 per unit   300,000
    Total Sales Revenue @ Standard. $420,000

Accounting records show that actual sales for the period were

Product A: 28,000 units @ $4.20 per unit $117,600
Product B: 61,500 units @ $4.90 per unit   301,350
    Total Actual Sales Revenue $418,950

Thus, there is a total unfavorable sales revenue variance of $1,050 (= $420,000 − $418,950). This total variance can be broken down into a sales price variance and a sales quantity variance.

The actual selling prices of the units sold differed from the standard price. The sales price variance is calculated as follows:

$$\begin{matrix} \text{Sales} \\ \text{Price} \\ \text{Variance} \end{matrix} = \begin{matrix} \text{Actual} \\ \text{Quantity} \\ \text{Sold} \end{matrix} \times \left(\begin{matrix} \text{Actual} \\ \text{Selling} \\ \text{Price} \end{matrix} - \begin{matrix} \text{Standard} \\ \text{Selling} \\ \text{Price} \end{matrix} \right)$$

For products A and B, the sales price variances are

Product A = 28,000 × ($4.20 − $4.00) = $5,600 Favorable
Product B = 61,500 × ($4.90 − $5.00) =   6,150 Unfavorable
   Net Sales Price Variance . . . . $ 550 Unfavorable

The quantity of units sold also differed from the standard or expected amounts. The sales quantity variance is calculated as follows:

$$\begin{matrix} \text{Sales} \\ \text{Quantity} \\ \text{Variance} \end{matrix} = \left(\begin{matrix} \text{Actual} \\ \text{Quantity} \\ \text{Sold} \end{matrix} - \begin{matrix} \text{Standard} \\ \text{Quantity Expected} \\ \text{to Be Sold} \end{matrix} \right) \times \begin{matrix} \text{Standard} \\ \text{Selling} \\ \text{Price} \end{matrix}$$

For products A and B, the sales quantity variances are

Product A = (28,000 − 30,000) × $4.00 = $8,000 Unfavorable
Product B = (61,500 − 60,000) × $5.00 =   7,500 Favorable
   Net Sales Quantity Variance . . . . $ 500 Unfavorable

Thus, the total sales revenue variance is explained as follows:

Sales Price Variance . . . . $ 550 Unfavorable
Sales Quantity Variance . . . .   500 Unfavorable
   Total Sales Revenue Variance . . . . $1,050 Unfavorable

The market manager must now consider two questions:

1 Is the variance large enough to warrant additional investigation?
2 If the response to the first question is yes, then what are the reasons or explanations for the variances which occurred?

As we discussed in Chapter Eight, management cannot maintain active surveillance over all of the activities under its control. It must rely on control systems to indicate unusual conditions requiring attention. This is the principle of management by exception. The total sales revenue variance of $1,050 on budgeted sales of $420,000 would probably be considered insignificant by most marketing managers and not investigated further.

Suppose, however, that the variance was considered to be large enough to warrant further investigation. A starting point would be to study the price and quantity variances for each of the products to see if a pattern emerges. It appears that an effort was made by the sales staff to get some customers to switch from product A to product B. This was apparently done by raising the price of product A to an average of $4.20 and reducing the price of product B to an average of $4.90. There was some switching by customers from product A (sales in units were 2,000 less than expected) to product B (sales in units were 1,500 more than expected). If this is the explanation for the variance, then the marketing manager would want to take corrective action, because the net result was a loss in revenue. There are other possible explanations that the marketing manager might want to explore, such as changes in the prices of competitors' products, the introduction of new competing products, and improved general economic conditions causing customers to switch products.

MATERIALS PURCHASE VARIANCES

The purchasing department of Victoria Corporation is responsible for acquiring needed raw materials at the best possible price. Any materials price variances are therefore its responsiblity. Exhibit 9.3 indicates that the budget or standard for the purchasing department for the period was as follows:

Plastic: 94,000 lb @ $.50 per lb	$47,000
Gleemy: 32,000 oz @ $.30 per oz	9,600
Glowy: 61,000 oz @ $.50 per oz	30,500
Total Purchases @ Standard	$87,100

Accounting records for the period show purchases as follows:

Plastic: 94,000 lb @ $.53 per lb	$49,820
Gleemy: 32,000 oz @ $.32 per oz	10,240
Glowy: 61,000 oz @ $.52 per oz	31,720
Total Actual Purchases	$91,780

The total materials purchase variance is \$4,680 unfavorable (= \$91,780 − \$87,100). This variance can likewise be broken down into price and quantity components.

The purchase price variance is calculated as follows:

$$\begin{matrix} \text{Materials} \\ \text{Price} \\ \text{Variance} \end{matrix} = \begin{matrix} \text{Actual} \\ \text{Quantity} \\ \text{Purchased} \end{matrix} \times \left(\begin{matrix} \text{Actual} \\ \text{Price} \\ \text{Paid} \end{matrix} - \begin{matrix} \text{Standard} \\ \text{Purchase} \\ \text{Price} \end{matrix} \right)$$

The materials price variances for Victoria Corporation are

Plastic = 94,000 × (\$.53 − \$.50) = \$2,820 Unfavorable
Gleemy = 32,000 × (\$.32 − \$.30) =   640 Unfavorable
Glowy = 61,000 × (\$.52 − \$.50) =   1,220 Unfavorable
Total Materials Price Variance. . . \$4,680 Unfavorable

A materials purchase quantity variance could likewise be calculated.

$$\begin{matrix} \text{Materials} \\ \text{Purchase} \\ \text{Quantity} \\ \text{Variance} \end{matrix} = \left(\begin{matrix} \text{Actual} \\ \text{Quantity} \\ \text{Purchased} \end{matrix} - \begin{matrix} \text{Standard} \\ \text{Quantity Expected} \\ \text{to Be Purchased} \end{matrix} \right) \times \begin{matrix} \text{Standard} \\ \text{Purchase} \\ \text{Price} \end{matrix}$$

In this and many cases, the materials purchase quantity variance is zero. This is because the purchasing department acquired the raw materials it was required to purchase during the period. However, during a period of severe raw materials shortages, purchasing departments may not be able to acquire raw materials as needed. A material purchases quantity variance would be particularly important in these cases as a signal of the need to closely monitor raw materials purchases. Note that it would be inappropriate to calculate a materials *usage* variance and attribute it to the purchasing department. The purchasing department controls only the price paid. The production department is responsible for the quantity used. As will be illustrated later, a materials usage variance is calculated for the production department. Note also that the materials price variance is calculated at the time raw materials are purchased, not when they are used. If the control system is to be effective, the purchasing manager needs timely feedback so that corrective action can be taken. This may be too late if calculation of the price variance is delayed until the raw materials are used.

The purchasing manager must also consider whether the materials price variance is significant and, if so, the reasons it occurred. The fact that the variance for all three raw materials is unfavorable in this case signals the need for further investigation. Perhaps market prices have increased for these products but the price increases have not yet been reflected in the standards. If this is the case, an effort should be made to change the standards for future periods. On the other hand, the unfavorable variance could be due to lost quantity discounts as a result of purchasing raw materials in quantities that were too small. When standards assume that quantity discounts will be obtained, unfavorable variances result from losing the discounts. If this occurred during the period, the purchasing manager will want to investigate to determine which employees were responsible for the lost discounts and take corrective action.

PRODUCTION COST VARIANCES

The production department of Victoria Corporation has responsibility for the amounts of direct materials, direct labor, and manufacturing overhead costs incurred in manufacturing product A and product B. We consider separately the calculation of variances for each of these cost components.

Direct Materials

As discussed above, the purchasing department of Victoria Corporation is responsible for any raw materials price variances that might occur. These price variances are determined at the time raw materials are acquired. Thus, it is not appropriate to calculate a price variance for the production department. If the production department were responsible for both purchasing and usage of raw materials, then it would be appropriate to calculate a raw materials price variance for the production department.

The production department is responsible for the usage of raw materials. Exhibit 9.2 indicates that the standard raw materials per unit of output, product A and product B, are as follows:

	Product A	**Product B**
Plastic: 1 lb @ $.50 per lb	$.50	$ .50
Gleemy: 1 oz @ $.30 per oz	.30	—
Glowy: 1 oz @ $.50 per oz	—	.50
Total Raw Material per Unit @ Standard	$.80	$1.00

During the period, the production department planned to produce 31,000 units of product A and 61,000 units of product B. The standard cost for these units of output should have been

	Product A	**Product B**
Plastic: 31,000 units × 1 lb × $.50.	$15,500	—
61,000 units × 1 lb × $.50.	—	$30,500
Gleemy: 31,000 units × 1 oz × $.30.	9,300	—
Glowy: 61,000 units × 1 oz × $.50.	—	30,500
Total	$24,800	$61,000

Accounting records show that 31,000 units of product A and 61,000 units of product B were produced as planned and that the actual raw materials used were as follows:

Plastic	91,000 lb
Gleemy	30,000 oz
Glowy	59,500 oz

The raw materials quantity (usage) variance is calculated as follows:

$$
\begin{array}{c}
\text{Materials} \\
\text{Quantity} \\
\text{(Usage)} \\
\text{Variance}
\end{array}
=
\left(
\begin{array}{c}
\text{Actual} \\
\text{Quantity} \\
\text{Used}
\end{array}
-
\begin{array}{c}
\text{Standard Quantity} \\
\text{That Should Have} \\
\text{Been Used}
\end{array}
\right)
\times
\begin{array}{c}
\text{Standard} \\
\text{Purchase} \\
\text{Price}
\end{array}
$$

For the production department, the materials quantity variance is

$$
\begin{aligned}
\text{Plastic} &= (91{,}000 - 92{,}000) \times \$.50 = \$\ \ 500 \text{ Favorable} \\
\text{Gleemy} &= (30{,}000 - 31{,}000) \times \$.30 = \ \ \ \ 300 \text{ Favorable} \\
\text{Glowy} &= (59{,}500 - 61{,}000) \times \$.50 = \underline{\ \ \ \ 750} \text{ Favorable}
\end{aligned}
$$

Total Materials Quantity
(Usage) Variance . . . . $\underline{\$1{,}550}$ Favorable

Note that the "actual quantity" here is the actual quantity used, not the quantity purchased. Note also the calculation of the standard quantity. We begin with the *actual number of units of output* and determine the raw materials (inputs) that should have been used if the units had been produced at standard. For example, a total of 92,000 units of product A and product B were actually produced. Each unit should have received 1 pound of plastic if the units were produced according to the standards. The standard quantity for plastic is therefore 92,000 pounds. Similarly, 31,000 units of product A were actually produced. Each unit of product A should have received 1 ounce of Gleemy. The standard quantity is therefore 31,000 ounces. The "standard quantity" title in the case of production operations might be expanded to "standard input quantity that should have been used for the actual output units produced."

The raw materials usage variances for Victoria Corporation are consistently favorable for the period. The production manager would probably want to explore the reasons for this pattern of variances. Perhaps the raw materials used were of higher quality than those provided for in establishing standards for raw materials usage. If so, there is likely to be less scrap and waste and, therefore, fewer raw materials used. The favorable usage variance coupled with the purchasing department's unfavorable price variance is consistent with the possibility that higher-quality raw materials have been acquired and used. Another possible explanation for the favorable materials usage variances is that the usage standards are outdated. For example, new machinery could have been acquired that reduces raw materials scrap and waste. If the standards have not been changed to reflect the more efficient raw materials usage resulting from the new machinery, then favorable usage variances would be expected. In this case, the production manager would want to see that the usage standards are changed for future periods.

Direct Labor

The production department is responsible for both the prices paid for labor services and the quantity of labor services used. We shall, therefore, calculate a direct labor price variance and a direct labor quantity variance.

The production department was budgeted to produce, and actually produced,

31,000 units of product A and 61,000 units of product B during the period. The standard labor cost for these 92,000 units of output is $115,000 (= 92,000 units × .25 hours per unit × $5.00 per hour). Accounting records show that 25,000 hours were worked at an average wage rate of $4.80 per hour for a total actual labor cost of $120,000. The total direct labor variance of $5,000 unfavorable (= $120,000 − $115,000) can be broken down into price and quantity variances.

The direct labor price (rate) variance is calculated as follows:

$$\begin{array}{c} \text{Labor} \\ \text{Price (Rate)} \\ \text{Variance} \end{array} = \begin{array}{c} \text{Actual} \\ \text{Labor Hours} \\ \text{Worked} \end{array} \times \left(\begin{array}{cc} \text{Actual} & \text{Standard} \\ \text{Wage Rate} - & \text{Wage} \\ \text{Paid} & \text{Rate} \end{array} \right)$$

The direct labor price (rate) variance is $5,000 favorable [= 25,000 × ($4.80 − $5.00)]. The direct labor quantity (efficiency) variance is calculated as follows:

$$\begin{array}{c} \text{Labor} \\ \text{Quantity} \\ \text{(Efficiency)} \\ \text{Variance} \end{array} = \left(\begin{array}{cc} \text{Actual} & \text{Standard Labor} \\ \text{Labor Hours} - & \text{Hours That Should} \\ \text{Worked} & \text{Have Been Worked} \end{array} \right) \times \begin{array}{c} \text{Standard} \\ \text{Wage} \\ \text{Rate} \end{array}$$

The direct labor quantity (efficiency) variance is $10,000 unfavorable [= (25,000 − 23,000) × $5.00]. The 23,000 standard hours is equal to the 92,000 units of output times the standard one-quarter hour per unit.

The total direct labor variance of $5,000 unfavorable is explained as follows:

Price (Rate) Variance . . . . $ 5,000 Favorable
Quantity (Efficiency) Variance. . . . . 10,000 Unfavorable
    Net Direct Labor Variance . . . . $ 5,000 Unfavorable

This pattern of variances suggests several explanations that the production manager might explore. Perhaps workers of lower skills were used on certain tasks than allowed for in the standards. This would explain the lower average wage rate paid and the higher than standard number of labor hours worked. The variance may also be indicative of management/labor problems. For example, management might have reduced the labor rate paid for overtime work and employees responded with a work slowdown. There are, of course, many other possible explanations. The variances may be caused by independent, rather than related, factors. The production manager, being close to the day-to-day operations of the factory, is in a position to suggest the most likely causes that should be investigated.

Manufacturing Overhead

The control system for manufacturing overhead costs is somewhat different from that for direct materials and direct labor for the following reasons:

1 Manufacturing overhead is composed of numerous individual cost items (for example, supplies, rent, insurance, and depreciation) which by themselves do not justify

an elaborate cost control system but in the aggregate are often large enough to necessitate some means of cost control.

2 Unlike direct materials and direct labor, manufacturing overhead costs cannot be directly traced to, or identified with, specific units of product.

3 Unlike direct materials and direct labor, manufacturing overhead is composed of costs that are variable, fixed, semivariable, and semifixed.

The control system for manufacturing overhead is typically designed as follows:

1 Studies of past manufacturing overhead costs are made in an effort to determine their behavior. This is typically done for all overhead costs in the aggregate, although separate studies might be done for the larger overhead cost items. The result of these studies will be a flexible overhead cost budget in the form:

$$\begin{matrix} \text{Budgeted} \\ \text{Manufacturing} \\ \text{Overhead} \\ \text{Cost} \end{matrix} = \begin{matrix} \text{Fixed Overhead} \\ \text{Cost per Period} \end{matrix} + \left(\begin{matrix} \text{Variable Overhead} \\ \text{Cost per Unit} \\ \text{of Activity} \end{matrix} \times \begin{matrix} \text{Activity} \\ \text{Level} \end{matrix} \right)$$

The unit of activity might be units produced, direct labor hours, machine hours, or some other basis.

2 Actual manufacturing overhead costs are accumulated for the period in a single account.

3 At the end of the period, the total actual overhead cost is compared to the flexible budget allowance for the actual level of activity encountered. If the variance is insignificant, it is seldom investigated further. A decision not to investigate further must be made cautiously, however, because a small total overhead variance might be the result of netting several large but offsetting variances for individual cost items. If the total variance is considered large enough to warrant additional investigation, the individual overhead cost items will be studied in relation to their historical amounts and with regard to current price information. The objective of such an investigation is to determine if any individual cost items appear highly unusual. Typically, less time is spent investigating overhead cost variances than is spent with direct materials and direct labor variances because the dollar amounts involved with overhead costs are smaller. Also, whereas direct materials and direct labor variances might be investigated daily or weekly for timely feedback, manufacturing overhead variances are usually investigated monthly or even quarterly.

The budgeted manufacturing overhead costs for Victoria Corporation as shown in Exhibit 9.2 are summarized below. They are based on the assumption that 92,000 units are budgeted to be produced during the period.

Indirect labor ($.10 per unit)	$ 9,200
Supplies ($.04 per unit)	3,680
Power ($1,000 per period plus $.03 per unit)	3,760
Maintenance ($13,830 per period)	13,830
Rent ($6,000 per period)	6,000
Insurance ($1,000 per period)	1,000
Depreciation ($10,160 per period)	10,160
Total Budgeted Overhead Costs	$47,630

The flexible budget for overhead is

$$\begin{matrix} \text{Flexible} \\ \text{Budget for} \\ \text{Manufacturing} \\ \text{Overhead} \\ \text{Cost} \end{matrix} = \$31,990 + \left(\begin{matrix} \$.17 \text{ per Unit} \\ \text{Produced} \end{matrix} \times \begin{matrix} \text{Number of Units} \\ \text{Produced} \end{matrix} \right)$$

The $31,990 fixed cost component is the sum of the fixed costs for power, maintenance, rent, insurance, and depreciation. The $.17 variable cost per unit produced is the sum of the variable costs for indirect labor, supplies, and power.

Accounting records for the period show that the following actual overhead costs were incurred:

Indirect Labor	$10,000
Supplies	3,000
Power	3,800
Maintenance	15,000
Rent	5,500
Insurance	950
Depreciation	10,160
Total Overhead Costs Incurred	$48,410

The flexible budget for 92,000 units, the actual level of output, is $47,630 [= $31,990 + ($.17 × 92,000)]. The total overhead variance is therefore $780 unfavorable (= $48,410 − $47,630). This would probably be considered an insignificant variance. If the production manager suspected, however, that some individual overhead cost items might be out of control, further investigation would be carried out. Exhibit 10.1 presents a comparison of the actual cost and the flexible budget allowance

EXHIBIT 10.1
Victoria Corporation
Comparison of Actual Overhead Costs with the Flexible Budget

Cost Item	Flexible Budget Allowance for 92,000 Units	Actual Cost Incurred	Variance Favorable or Unfavorable
Indirect Labor	$ 9,200	$10,000	$ 800 Unfavorable
Supplies	3,680	3,000	680 Favorable
Power	3,760	3,800	40 Unfavorable
Maintenance	13,830	15,000	1,170 Unfavorable
Rent	6,000	5,500	500 Favorable
Insurance	1,000	950	50 Favorable
Depreciation	10,160	10,160	—
Total	$47,630	$48,410	$ 780 Unfavorable

for each overhead cost item. Indirect labor, supplies, maintenance, and rent are possibilities for further investigation.

It is difficult to categorize the overhead variance as a price variance or a quantity variance as was done with direct materials and direct labor. The difficulty arises because the variance is caused by a combination of price, quantity, and other factors. We prefer to label it simply as the total overhead variance.

When the independent variable in the flexible budget (that is, x in $y = a + bx$) is direct labor hours rather than units of output, some firms break down the total overhead variance for variable cost items into a price (spending) variance and a quantity (efficiency) variance, analogous to the rate and efficiency variances for direct labor. These variances are calculated as follows:

$$
\begin{array}{c}
\text{Variable} \\
\text{Overhead} \\
\text{Price (Spending)} \\
\text{Variance}
\end{array}
=
\begin{array}{c}
\text{Actual} \\
\text{Variable} \\
\text{Overhead Costs} \\
\text{Incurred}
\end{array}
-
\left(
\begin{array}{c}
\text{Actual} \\
\text{Direct} \\
\text{Labor Hours} \\
\text{Worked}
\end{array}
\times
\begin{array}{c}
\text{Budgeted} \\
\text{Variable} \\
\text{Overhead Cost per} \\
\text{Direct Labor Hour}
\end{array}
\right)
$$

$$
\begin{array}{c}
\text{Variable} \\
\text{Overhead} \\
\text{Quantity (Efficiency)} \\
\text{Variance}
\end{array}
=
\left(
\begin{array}{c}
\text{Actual} \\
\text{Direct} \\
\text{Labor Hours} \\
\text{Worked}
\end{array}
-
\begin{array}{c}
\text{Standard Direct} \\
\text{Labor Hours} \\
\text{That Should Have} \\
\text{Been Worked}
\end{array}
\right)
\times
\begin{array}{c}
\text{Budgeted} \\
\text{Variable} \\
\text{Overhead Cost per} \\
\text{Direct Labor Hour}
\end{array}
$$

We do not find this refinement particularly useful. Most overhead cost items that have a variable component also have a fixed component (that is, they are mixed costs). It is virtually impossible to break down the *actual* overhead cost into variable and fixed portions as required for the calculation of the variable overhead price (spending) variances. The breakdown of the overhead variance into a spending and efficiency variance is therefore of questionable usefulness except where the cost item behaves in a strictly variable pattern.[1]

SELLING EXPENSE VARIANCES

The sophistication of the cost control system for selling expenses depends in large part on the relative magnitude of selling expenses as compared to revenues, other costs, or net income. Control of selling expenses for a firm manufacturing a standard line of products for a small group of established customers is probably not as important as in a firm that manufactures custom products in a highly competitive market. In the latter case, extensive advertising and personal selling are required.

Control systems have historically been developed for manufacturing operations. Only in recent years have applications of these same techniques been carried over to the marketing area. We again use the data for Victoria Corporation to demonstrate the

---

[1] Some firms also calculate a fixed overhead quantity (volume) variance. This variance is virtually meaningless for control purposes and thus is not discussed here. We consider this variance in connection with the discussion of product costing in Chapter Twelve.

calculation of cost variances for selling expenses. Exhibit 10.2 presents the relevant data. The flexible budget data for selling expenses is taken from Exhibit 9.4 and summarized in the second column of Exhibit 10.2. The flexible budget is

$$\begin{matrix} \text{Flexible} \\ \text{Budget for} \\ \text{Selling} \\ \text{Expenses} \end{matrix} = \$65{,}400 + (.02 \times \text{Sales Revenue}) + (\$.02 \times \text{Units Shipped})$$

During the period sales revenue was $418,950 and 89,500 units of product A and product B were shipped (see page 236). At these levels of activity, commissions and shipping costs should be $8,379 (= .02 × $418,950) and $1,790 (= $.02 × 89,500), respectively. These amounts are shown in column (3) of Exhibit 10.2. The remaining amounts in column (3) are for the budgeted fixed costs. The flexible budget indicates that $75,569 of selling expenses should have been incurred during the period. Actual selling expenses totaled $80,000 as shown in column (4).

Column (5) shows the selling expense variances for the period. Advertising and travel probably warrant additional investigation. These costs are generally viewed as discretionary; that is, they can be altered quickly at the discretion of management. An explanation should, therefore, be obtained. The variances for commissions and shipping costs are not large enough to warrant additional investigation. It is possible to break down these variances into price and quantity components as was done with sales, direct material, and direct labor. Such a breakdown might be useful if the variances are large and investigation is required.

CENTRAL CORPORATE ADMINISTRATIVE EXPENSE VARIANCES

Central corporate administrative expenses tend to be primarily fixed cost items, including executives' salaries, depreciation, insurance and taxes on central corporate offices, and interest on corporate debt. Because of the preponderance of fixed cost items, there is little need for a continual monitoring of these costs. Most firms compare budgeted and actual costs once each quarter or perhaps only once a year. The variances are primarily important as a basis for estimating fixed costs to be incurred during future periods. It is only with regard to discretionary fixed cost that there is much opportunity for altering the amount of a fixed cost once the period has started.

Exhibit 10.3 presents the budgeted central corporate administrative expenses for Victoria Corporation (as shown in Exhibit 9.5) and the actual costs incurred. The unfavorable variance for other staff salaries probably reflects the hiring of a new or temporary staff member. The variances for supplies and heat and light are insignificant and are probably attributable to treating costs as fixed that are essentially mixed costs. The favorable variance in donations and contributions should be investigated. The sales manager may be postponing contributions in order to offset otherwise unfavorable variances. Such actions may hurt the reputation of the company in the community.

EXHIBIT 10.2
Victoria Corporation
Comparison of Actual Selling Expenses with the Flexible Budget

Cost Item (1)	Flexible Budget Amount (2)	Flexible Budget Allowance for 89,500 Units (3)	Actual Cost Incurred (4)	Variance Favorable or Unfavorable (5)
Salaries	$25,000 per Period	$25,000	$25,000	$ —
Advertising	$30,000 per Period	30,000	33,000	3,000 Unfavorable
Sales Office Costs	$ 8,400 per Period	8,400	8,200	200 Favorable
Travel	$ 2,000 per Period	2,000	3,300	1,300 Unfavorable
Commissions	2 Percent of Sales Revenue	8,379[a]	8,500	121 Unfavorable
Shipping Costs	$.02 per Unit Shipped	1,790[b]	2,000	210 Unfavorable
Total		$75,569[c]	$80,000	$4,431 Unfavorable

[a] .02 × $418,950 = $8,379.
[b] $.02 × 89,500 = $1,790.
[c] $65,400 + (.02 × $418,950) + ($.02 × 89,500).

EXHIBIT 10.3
Victoria Corporation
**Comparison of Actual Central Corporate Administrative Expenses
with the Budget**

Cost Item	Budget	Actual	Variance: Favorable or Unfavorable
President's Salary	$20,000	$20,000	$ —
Other Staff Salaries	27,000	28,000	1,000 Unfavorable
Supplies	2,000	2,200	200 Unfavorable
Heat and Light	1,400	1,500	100 Unfavorable
Rent	4,000	4,000	—
Donations and Contributions	1,000	—	1,000 Favorable
General Corporate Taxes.	8,000	8,000	—
Depreciation.	1,400	1,400	—
Total	$64,800	$65,100	$ 300 Unfavorable

STANDARD COSTS AND INCOME DETERMINATION

We have focused on the use of budgeted or standard revenues and costs as tools for
planning and for control. Standard costs can also be used in calculating the valuation
of ending inventory and measuring the amount of cost of goods sold for purposes of
external reporting to stockholders. If standard costs are used for external reporting,
a decision must be made regarding the disposition of variances. Should the variances
be treated as (1) adjustments to cost of goods sold or (2) allocated to both units in ending inventory and units sold? We consider these issues in Chapter Twelve.

SUMMARY OF VARIANCE ANALYSIS

Exhibit 10.4 summarizes the variances discussed in this chapter. The number of variances and the details of their calculation are perhaps overwhelming to you at this point.
After working several problems at the end of this chapter, you will discover a common
pattern to these variances. For sales revenue, material purchases, material usage, and
direct labor, standards are set for both prices and quantities. A price variance and a
quantity variance are then calculated. The price variance is

$$\frac{\text{Price}}{\text{Variance}} = \frac{\text{Actual}}{\text{Quantity}} \times \left(\frac{\text{Actual}}{\text{Price}} - \frac{\text{Standard}}{\text{Price}} \right)$$

The quantity variance is

$$\frac{\text{Quantity}}{\text{Variance}} = \left(\frac{\text{Actual}}{\text{Quantity}} - \frac{\text{Standard}}{\text{Quantity}} \right) \times \frac{\text{Standard}}{\text{Price}}$$

EXHIBIT 10.4
Summary of Revenue, Cost, and Expense Variances

Each variance is obtained by subtracting the amount on the right of the arrow from the amount on the left. Price variances are (2) − (1); quantity variances are (3) − (2).

	(1)		(2)		(3)
Sales Revenue	Actual Quantity Sold × Actual Price	→ **Sales Price Variance** →	Actual Quantity Sold × Standard Price	→ **Sales Quantity Variance** →	Budgeted Quantity to Be Sold × Standard Price
Materials Purchase	Actual Quantity Purchased × Actual Price	→ **Material Purchase Price Variance** →	Actual Quantity Purchased × Standard Price	→ **Material Purchase Quantity Variance** →	Budgeted Quantity to Be Purchased × Standard Price
Material Usage	(Not Generally Applicable)		Actual Quantity Used × Standard Price	→ **Material Quantity (Usage) Variance** →	Standard Quantity to Be Used × Standard Price
Direct Labor	Actual Quantity Used × Actual Rate	→ **Labor Price (Rate) Variance** →	Actual Quantity Used × Standard Price	→ **Labor Quantity (Efficiency) Variance** →	Standard Quantity to Be Used × Standard Price
Manufacturing Overhead[a]	Actual Overhead Costs Incurred	→ **Total Manufacturing Overhead Variance** →			Flexible Budget Allowance for Actual Level of Activity
Selling Expenses	Actual Selling Expenses Incurred	→ **Total Selling Expense Variance** →			Flexible Budget Allowance for Actual Level of Activity
Administrative Expenses	Actual Administrative Expenses Incurred	→ **Total Administrative Expense Variance** →			Flexible Budget Allowance for Actual Level of Activity

[a] The total manufacturing overhead variance can be split into variable and fixed portions if the variable overhead rate in the flexible budget varies with an input, such as direct labor hours, rather than with output:

Variable Manufacturing Overhead	Actual Variable Overhead Cost Incurred	→ **Variable Overhead Price (Spending) Variance** →	Actual Input Quantity × Flexible Budget Rate	→ **Variable Overhead Quantity (Efficiency) Variance** →	Standard Input Quantity × Flexible Budget Rate
Fixed Manufacturing Overhead	Actual Fixed Overhead Cost Incurred	→————— **Total Fixed Overhead Variance** —————→			Flexible Budget for Fixed Cost

For manufacturing overhead, selling expenses, and administrative expenses, standards are expressed in the form of a flexible budget, $y = a + bx$. The variance for each of these items is calculated as follows:

$$\begin{matrix}\text{Total} \\ \text{Cost} \\ \text{Variance}\end{matrix} = \begin{matrix}\text{Total} \\ \text{Actual Cost} \\ \text{Incurred}\end{matrix} - \left[\begin{matrix}\text{Budgeted} \\ \text{Fixed} \\ \text{Cost}\end{matrix} + \left(\begin{matrix}\text{Budgeted} \\ \text{Variable} \\ \text{Cost Rate}\end{matrix} \times \begin{matrix}\text{Actual} \\ \text{Level of} \\ \text{Activity}\end{matrix}\right)\right]$$

QUESTIONS AND PROBLEMS

1 Review the meaning of the following concepts or terms discussed in this chapter.
  a Price variance.
  b Quantity variance.
  c Standard quantity.
  d Flexible budget allowance.
  e Sales price variance.
  f Sales quantity variance.
  g Materials purchase price variance.
  h Materials purchase quantity variance.
  i Materials quantity (usage) variance.
  j Direct labor price (rate) variance.
  k Direct labor quantity (efficiency) variance.
  l Total manufacturing overhead variance.
  m Variable overhead price (spending) variance.
  n Variable overhead quantity (efficiency) variance.
  o Total fixed overhead variance.
  p Total selling expense variance.
  q Total administrative expense variance.

2 Why is a materials quantity variance typically not calculated for the purchasing activity?

3 Why is a materials price variance typically not calculated for the production activity?

4 Comment on the following statement: "If both materials purchase and materials usage are the responsiblity of the production department, it is just as well to calculate materials price variances at the time materials are used."

5 The total direct labor variance (price variance plus quantity variance) is the difference between the actual cost of labor services acquired and the standard cost of labor services that should have been used to produce the actual level of output. The total materials variance, however, is not simply the difference between the actual cost of materials purchased and the standard cost of material that should have been used to produce the actual level of output. Why is there a difference?

6 Why is a price and quantity variance typically not calculated for variable manufacturing overhead?

7 For control purposes, why is a quantity variance not calculated for fixed manufacturing overhead?

8 "Timely feedback means different things for different types of costs." Explain.

9 "The control systems for manufacturing overhead and selling and administrative expenses are not nearly as sophisticated as those for direct material and direct labor." Explain.

10 "A standard costing system involves more work than a cost accounting system based on actual prices and amounts, but the standard costing system may produce data that are worth the effort." Explain.

11 Budgeted sales of Holt Electronics Corporation for 19X0 were as follows:

Product X (5,000 units) $100,000
Product Y (200 units).   20,000
Product Z (50,000 units)   250,000
    Total Budgeted Sales $370,000

Actual sales for the period were as follows:

Product X (5,300 units) $111,300
Product Y (240 units)   23,040
Product Z (48,000 units)   192,000
    Total Actual Sales. $326,340

Calculate the sales price and quantity variances for each of the three products.

12 The Rubber Duckie Company produces toys. Recently established standard costs are as follows:

Materials: 5 pieces per unit @ $.20 per piece
Labor: .50 hours per unit @ $4.50 per hour

In November, 28,000 pieces of material were purchased for $5,040. Twenty-seven thousand pieces of material were used in producing 5,000 units of finished product. Labor costs were $12,015 for 2,700 hours worked.
a Determine the materials price variance.
b Determine the materials quantity (usage) variance.
c Determine the labor price (rate) variance.
d Determine the labor quantity (efficiency) variance.

13 The Tidy Box Company's budget contains these standards for materials and direct labor for a unit of 10 boxes:

Material—2 lb @ $.50 . . . . $1.00
Direct Labor—1 hr @ $4.50 . . . .   4.50

Although 100,000 units were budgeted for September, only 97,810 were produced. Two hundred thousand pounds of materials were purchased for $105,500. Materials weighing 193,880 pounds were issued to production. Direct labor costs were $396,800 for 99,200 hours.
a Determine the materials price variance.

b Determine the materials quantity (usage) variance.
c Determine the labor price (rate) variance.
d Determine the labor quantity (efficiency) variance.

14 Jonathan Company presents the following data for October:

	Standards per Batch	Actual
Materials	2 lb at $5 per lb	195,000 lb
Labor	3 hours at $6 per hour	280,000 hours
Units Produced.		96,000 batches

During the month, 100,000 pounds of materials were purchased for $505,500. Wages earned were $1,708,000. Compute all labor and material variances.

15 Weda Company presents the following variance data for the month: (F indicates favorable variance; U indicates unfavorable variance.)

	Material A	Material B	Material C
Material Price Variance	$ 42,000F	$ 25,000F	$ 21,000U
Material Quantity Variance	40,000U	30,000U	48,000U
Net Material Variance	$ 2,000F	$ 5,000U	$ 69,000U
Units Produced Requiring			
This Material	100,000	11,000	125,000

Two pounds of each kind of material are allowed for each unit of output requiring that kind of material. For material A, the average price paid was $.20 per pound less than standard; for material B, $.10 less; for material C, $.07 greater. There are no opening or closing inventories of any kind of material (that is, materials are purchased and used in the same period).

For each of the three materials, calculate the following:
a Number of pounds of material purchased.
b Standard cost per pound of material.
c Total standard material cost.

16 Castle Products Company uses a flexible budgeting system for controlling manufacturing overhead costs. As a result of studying past overhead cost data, it has established a flexible budget for overhead as follows:

Fixed Overhead: $500,000 per month
Variable Overhead: $2 per unit

Actual data for January, February, and March are as follows:

	Units Produced	Total Overhead Costs
January	50,000	$650,000
February	60,000	610,000
March	40,000	570,000

Determine the total overhead cost variance for each month.

17 The manufacturing overhead costs of Windum Industries, Incorporated, are separable into fixed and variable components. The flexible budget for overhead costs is

Fixed Costs: $100,000 per period
Variable Costs: $10 per unit

During the period, 20,000 units were produced. Actual manufacturing overhead costs were $350,000.

a Determine the total manufacturing overhead variance.

b Assume that of the $350,000 total overhead costs incurred, $120,000 were fixed costs and $230,000 were variable costs. Determine the total fixed cost variance and the total variable cost variance.

c Assume that each unit of output requires two hours of labor and that variable overhead costs vary both with labor hours and units of output. Thus, variable overhead costs are expected to be $10 per unit or $5 per direct labor hour. During the period 42,000 labor hours were worked in producing the 20,000 units of output. Disaggregate the total variable overhead variance determined in **b** into a price (spending) variance and a quantity (efficiency) variance.

18 Direct labor and variable overhead standards per finished unit for Columbia Metals Company are as follows:

Direct Labor: 10 hours at $5.00 per hour
Variable Overhead: 10 hours at $2.00 per hour

During July, 5,000 finished units were produced. Direct labor costs were $234,000 (52,000 hours). Actual variable overhead costs where $103,000.

a Determine the total variance (price and quantity) for direct labor and the total variance for variable overhead.

b Determine the price (rate) and quantity (efficiency) variances for direct labor.

c Determine the price (spending) and quantity (efficiency) variances for variable overhead.

d What similarities are there likely to be between the factors that cause the direct labor price variance and the variable overhead price variance?

e What similarities are there likely to be between the factors that cause the direct labor quantity variance and the variable overhead quantity variance?

19 Reynolds Products, Incorporated, estimates that the following selling expenses will be incurred next period:

Salaries (fixed)	$ 20,000
Commissions (.05 of sales revenue).	15,000
Travel (.03 of sales revenue).	9,000
Advertising (fixed).	50,000
Sales Office Costs ($4,000 plus $.05 per unit sold).	7,000
Shipping Cost ($.10 per unit sold)	6,000
Total Selling Expenses.	$107,000

a Determine the flexible budget ($y = a + bx$) for selling expenses.

b Assume that 50,000 units are sold during the period at an average price of $6 per unit. Determine the sales revenue price and quantity variances.

c The actual selling expenses incurred during the period were $110,000. Assuming that sales were as given in part **b**, calculate the total selling expense variance.

20 The standard costs for product K are as follows:

Material: 2 lb @ $3.00 per lb
Labor: 1 hour @ $5.00 per hour
Overhead: $10,000 per month plus $3 per unit produced

During October, 25,000 pounds of material were purchased for $74,750 and 20,750 pounds of material were used in producing 10,000 units of finished product. Direct labor costs incurred were $49,896 (10,080 direct labor hours) and overhead costs incurred were $39,800.
Compute the following:
a Materials price variance.
b Materials quantity (usage) variance.
c Labor price (rate) variance.
d Labor quantity (efficiency) variance.
e Total overhead variance.

21 The standard cost of product A of the Acme Company is composed of the following items:

Material: 6 lb @ $.75 per lb
Labor: 1 hour @ $5.00 per hour
Overhead: $2,500 per month plus $2.50 per unit

During January, 30,000 pounds of material were purchased at an average cost of $.76 a pound and 29,000 pounds were used; 5,000 direct labor hours were worked at an average rate of $5.05 per hour; and actual overhead costs were $15,500. There were 5,000 units started and completed during the month.
Compute the amount of each of the following variances:
a Materials price variance.
b Materials quantity (usage) variance.
c Labor price (rate) variance.
d Labor quantity (efficiency) variance.
e Total overhead variance.

22 Alger Company manufactures salad bowls. The company makes two types of bowls, A and B, from the same material. The company has no fixed overhead. The following are the standards and production data for November:

Standard Costs

	Bowl A	**Bowl B**
Raw Materials.	$ .25 (.05 lb @ $5.00)	$ .50 (.10 lb @ $5.00)
Labor	$ .40 (6 min @ $4.00)	$ .45 (6 min @ $4.50)
Overhead.	$1.60 per direct labor hour	$1.50 per direct labor hour

Production Data for November

	Bowl A	**Bowl B**
Units	5,000	3,000
Pounds of Raw Materials Used.	250	305
Direct Labor Hours Used	500	299
Labor Costs Incurred. .	$2,060.00	$1,330.55

Total overhead was $1,236. This amount is to be allocated proportionately to the total costs of the two products on the basis of standard direct labor hours. One thousand pounds of raw materials were purchased for $5,020. The labor quantity variance for bowl A was zero.

a Compute the raw material purchase price variance.

b Compute the raw material quantity (usage) variance for bowl A and for bowl B.

c Compute the direct labor price (rate) and quantity (efficiency) variances for bowl A and for bowl B.

d Compute the overhead price (spending) and quantity (efficiency) variances for bowl A and for bowl B.

23 Under the flexible budget of the Ceramic Tile Company, budgeted variable overhead is $60,000 when 60,000 direct labor hours are worked, whereas budgeted direct labor costs are $300,000. All data apply to the month of February.

The following are some of the variances for February (F denotes Favorable; U denotes Unfavorable):

Variable Overhead Price Variance	$12,000U
Variable Overhead Quantity Variance.	10,000U
Materials Price Variance	15,000F
Materials Quantity (Usage) Variance	8,000U

$325,500 of direct labor costs were incurred in February. According to the standards, 1 pound of material should cost $2.00. One pound of material is the standard for each unit of product. One hundred thousand units were produced in February. The unit materials price variance was $.20 per pound, whereas the average wage rate exceeded the standard average rate by $.25.

Compute the following for February, assuming that there are no opening or closing inventories of materials:

a Pounds of materials purchased.

b Pounds of material usage over standard.

c Standard hourly wage rate.

d Standard direct labor hours for the total February production.

24 The Old Style Company mass produces pseudo-antique roll-top desks. The standard costs are

Wood	25 lb @ $3.20 per lb
Trim	8 lb @ $5.00 per lb
Direct Labor.	5 hrs @ $6.00 per hr
Variable Overhead.	$15 per unit
Fixed Overhead	$62,000 per period

Transactions during February were as follows:

(1) Eighty tons of wood were purchased at $3.25 per pound; 155,000 pounds were issued to production.

(2) Twenty-five tons of trim were purchased at $4.80 per pound. 48,500 pounds were issued to production.

(3) The direct labor payroll was 31,000 hours at $5.75.

(4) Overhead costs were $151,000.

(5) Six thousand desks were produced during February.

Calculate all variances to the extent permitted by the data.

25 The Seasonal Company manufactures Christmas cards and other greeting cards. Fixed overhead is budgeted at $6,000 per month. Variable overhead is budgeted at $9,500 when 10,000 direct labor hours are worked per month.

The following data are available for April (F denotes Favorable; U denotes Unfavorable):

Materials Purchased	20,000 units
Direct Labor Costs Incurred	$36,000
Total of Direct Labor Rate and Quantity Variances.	$500F
Average Actual Wage Rate ($.20 less than the standard wage rate)	$4.80
Variable Overhead Costs Incurred.	$8,000
Total Fixed and Variable Overhead Costs Incurred	$13,875
Materials Price Variance	$200F
Materials Quantity Usage Variance	$610F
Price of Purchased Materials	$.60 per unit
Materials Used	15,000 units

Using the above data, identify and present computations for all variances.

26 The standard materials and labor cost per unit for the manufacturing departments of the Davis Company are as follows:

Material, 2 lb of material A @ $3.00.	$6.00
Labor, 4 standard hr @ $2.00 per hr	8.00

The flexible budget shows the following monthly allowances for manufacturing overhead costs:

Units Produced.	8,000 units	10,000 units	12,000 units
Manufacturing Overhead Costs:			
Fixed.	$30,000	$30,000	$30,000
Variable.	32,000	40,000	48,000
Total Manufacturing Overhead Costs	$62,000	$70,000	$78,000

During the month of December, 8,000 units were completed at the following costs:

Materials Purchased and Used, 16,200 lb at $3.20.	$51,840
Direct Labor, 31,800 hr at $2.10	66,780
Manufacturing Overhead Costs.	63,000

a Compute the price and quantity variances for both material and labor for the month of December.

b Compute the total overhead cost variance for the month of December.

27 The L & S Company produces a single product and uses a standard cost system for control. Direct materials variances are determined at the time of purchase. Standard costs for materials and labor are shown below.

L & S Company
Standard Material and Labor Costs per Unit

Direct Material, 5 lb @ $40/lb. $200
Direct Labor, 10 hr @ $3/hr.   30

A report of operations for March is as follows (F denotes favorable, U denotes unfavorable):

L & S Company
Operations for March

	Actual Costs Incurred	Standard Cost for Actual Output	Price or Rate Variance	Quantity or Efficiency Variance
Direct Material	$42,000[a]	$30,000	$?	$ 1,200F
Direct Labor.	4,785	4,500	165F	450U

[a] This is the cost of the 1,000 lb of direct materials purchased.

a Determine the number of units produced during March.
b Determine the number of pounds of direct material used during March.
c Determine the actual average wage rate for March.
d Determine the amount of the direct material price variance.

28 The Buffalo Manufacturing Company produces a single product. The standard cost system data are as follows:

Standard Quantity of Materials per Finished Unit of Product . . . . . 3 lb
Standard Materials Costs per Pound . . . . $1.50 per lb
Standard Direct Labor Hours per Finished Unit of Product . . . . . . 5 hours
Standard Direct Labor Cost per Hour. $6 per hr
Variable Overhead Rate Applied per Standard Direct
    Labor Hour . . . . $1.35 per hr
Budgeted Fixed Costs per Month $9,375

The information on actual events for the month of September is as follows:

Raw Materials Purchased (10,000 lb @ $1.60 per lb) $16,000
Raw Materials Used. . . . . 5,400 lb
Direct Labor Costs Incurred (11,000 hr @ $5.70 per hr) $62,700
Variable Overhead Costs Incurred. $14,300
Fixed Overhead Costs Incurred. . . . . $ 9,525
Number of Finished Units Produced in September. 2,000

Determine all variances to the extent permitted by the data.

29 Refer to Problem 18 in Chapter Nine. Assume that the amounts determined in that problem represent the budgets or standards for period 2. Actual results for period 2 are as follows:

Sales:

Product A (36,500 units)	$149,650
Product B (68,000 units)	343,400
Total	$493,050

Materials Purchased:

Plastic (94,000 lb)	$ 49,820
Gleemy (32,000 oz)	10,240
Glowy (61,000 oz)	31,720
Total	$ 91,780

Materials Used:

Plastic	106,000 lb
Gleemy	34,000 oz
Glowy	68,000 oz

Direct Labor Costs (28,000 hr)	$134,400

Overhead Costs:

Indirect Labor	$ 10,200
Supplies	4,300
Power	4,010
Maintenance	13,500
Rent	6,000
Insurance	1,200
Depreciation	10,460
Total	$ 49,670

Selling Expenses:

Salaries	$ 26,000
Commissions	9,820
Advertising	32,000
Sales Office Costs	8,200
Shipping Costs	2,300
Travel	1,000
Total	$ 79,320

Central Corporate Expenses:

Executive's Salary	$ 23,000
Salaries of Other Office Personnel	27,000
Supplies	2,100
Heat and Light	1,300
Rent	4,000
Donations and Contributions	1,500
General Corporate Taxes	9,000
Depreciation	1,400
Total	$ 69,300

Units Produced: Product A	35,000
Product B	69,000

Determine all variances to the extent permitted by the data.

CHAPTER 11

DIVISIO AL PERFORMA CE MEASUREMENT AND CONTROL

The General Electric Company is a broadly diversified company. Its central corporate management determines broad corporate policies, establishes long-range plans, raises capital, and conducts other coordinating activities. It also oversees the operations of approximately 150 corporate affiliates and divisions, manufacturing products ranging from industrial power equipment to consumer appliances and operating throughout the United States and the world. How does a company like GE measure and control the performance of its divisions in such a widely diversified and geographically dispersed operating environment? In this chapter, we attempt to answer this question by considering some techinques for designing and implementing control systems for divisionalized firms.

DIVISIONAL ORGANIZATION AND PERFORMANCE

The term "division" is used by different companies to mean different things. Some companies use the term to refer to segments organized according to product groupings, whereas other companies use it in reference to geographical areas served. We use the term "division" to refer to a segment that conducts both manufacturing and marketing activities. It therefore constitutes a *profit center* because it has responsibility for both revenues and expenses.

The essence of divisionalization is the delegation, or decentralization, of decision-making authority and responsibility. The division, therefore, has responsibility, within limits to be discussed later, for directing the use of a portion of the company's resources in generating profit.

There are at least three advantages of a divisional type of organization as compared to an organization where decision-making authority and responsibility are retained by central corporate headquarters. First, better decisions are likely to result because the individuals making the decisions are closer to the scene of action than personnel at central corporate headquarters. Second, divisional managers should be more highly motivated because they will feel that they are running their own shop. Third, the experience gained in running a division provides excellent training for higher-level managerial positions.[1]

The divisional type of organization has some disadvantages, however. Probably foremost among these is the possibility that the divisional managers will take a myopic view of their divisions, making decisions that are beneficial to their divisions but detrimental to the company as a whole. For example, a division manager might decide to purchase materials from an outside supplier even though another division of the firm could produce the raw materials at a lower incremental cost using currently idle facilities. Top management must be continually alert to situations where trade-offs are required between the benefits of decentralized decision-making authority in a divisionalized company and the possible conflicts between the goals of a division and those of the firm as a whole.

CRITERIA FOR DIVISIONAL PERFORMANCE MEASUREMENT

In discussing planning and control systems in Chapter Eight, we pointed out that control systems are likely to be more effective if a quantitative measure can be designed that captures the relevant aspects of performance. This statement is equally applicable in the case of divisional performance control. What are the desirable dimensions of a divisional performance measure?

One desirable attribute is that the measure provides a common basis for comparing and evaluating the performance of divisions operating in widely different geographical and product markets. This is critical from the standpoint of top management. Because a principal goal of all divisions is the generation of profits, the measure commonly used is based on divisional income or profits.

A second desirable attribute is that the divisional performance measure be as independent as possible from performance achieved in other parts of the company. This attribute is desirable so that responsibility can be pinpointed and divisional managers can be held accountable only for activities over which they have some degree of control. A divisional performance measure will not be independent if a portion of one division's costs or part of the central corporate headquarters costs are allocated to another division. If the division had no control over these costs, then they should not affect top management's evaluation of the division's performance.

A third desirable attribute is that the divisional performance measure indicate as closely as possible the contribution the division makes to company-wide results. This contribution may be somewhat different from the amount over which the division has control. One obvious example is the salary of the divisional manager. The amount of the salary is likely to be determined by top management and therefore not be controllable by the division manager. However, it is a necessary cost that must

---

[1] For an expanded discussion, see David Solomons, *Divisional Performance Measurement and Control* (Homewood, Ill.: Richard D. Irwin, 1968).

be covered before the division can contribute to the profits of the company and should, therefore, be included in any performance measure. Another example relates to interdivisional conflict. Recall the earlier example where a division purchased materials externally rather than buying from a division having idle capacity. By purchasing externally, the profits of the two divisions together are less than if the materials had been purchased internally. Should the performance measure for each division reflect the results of its actual transactions? Or should the cost of idle capacity in the one division be charged against the profits of the other division? There are no easy answers to these questions. Top management needs to be informed of situations where actions of individual divisions are detrimental to overall company performance.

RETURN ON INVESTMENT AS THE PERFORMANCE MEASURE

Given that one of the principal goals of the divisions is to contribute to the profits of the company, it is not surprising that divisional net income is commonly used as a measure of performance. Divisional net income by itself, however, does not provide a basis for comparing the performance of various divisions. For example, the fact that Division A had net income of $50,000 does not necessarily mean that it was more successful than Division B, which had net income of $40,000. The difference between these profit levels could be attributable entirely to a difference in the size of the divisions. Some means must therefore be used to scale the divisional profit amounts. The most common approach is to divide divisional net income by some measure of the amount of capital invested in the division. The result is referred to as divisional return on investment, or ROI, and is calculated as follows:

$$\text{Divisional Return on Investment (ROI)} = \frac{\text{Divisional Net Income}}{\text{Divisional Investment}}$$

If the investments of Division A and Division B in the preceding example were $500,000 and $250,000, respectively, then the ROIs would be 10 percent ($= \$50,000/\$500,000$) and 16 percent ($= \$40,000/\$250,000$). Thus, Division B was more successful given its investment base than was Division A, even though Division A generated a larger absolute amount of profit.

There are several important questions that must be answered before ROI can be applied as a control measure:

1 How are revenues measured, particularly when part of a division's output is transferred to another division rather than being sold externally?
2 Which expenses are deducted in determining divisional net income—only those that are controllable by the division or also a portion of central corporate expenses?

3 How is investment to be measured—total assets or net assets, at historical cost or current replacement cost?

These questions are considered in the sections that follow.

Measuring Divisional Revenues

In cases where, because of the nature of the product, none of a division's output can be sold to another division and all of the output is therefore sold externally, there are few unique revenue measurement problems beyond those encountered in financial accounting. That is, accounting policy questions must be made regarding whether revenue will be recognized as production takes place, at the point of sale, or as cash is collected. The only concern with the measurement of divisional revenues in this case is that all divisions follow the same accounting methods, thereby enhancing the comparability of the measures of ROI.

In cases where one division's output can be or is sold to another division, we are confronted with what is called the *transfer pricing problem.* The "price" assigned to the interdivisional transfer of goods or services represents a revenue of the selling division and a cost of the buying division.[2] Should the transfer price be set equal to the manufacturing cost of the selling division? Or should the transfer price be the amount at which the selling (buying) division could sell (purchase) the good or service externally? Or should the transfer price be a negotiated amount somewhere between the selling division's cost of manufacturing and the external market price?

A superficial consideration of the transfer pricing problem might suggest that the selection of a transfer price is of little consequence. After all, what comes out of one corporate pocket goes into another. This simplistic viewpoint ignores the fact that the amount of the transfer price may affect certain divisional decisions which in turn affect the overall profitability of the company. For example, suppose that a transfer price is set at $10 per unit and there is no external market for the product. If the buying division feels that this price is too high, it may take less than it would at a lower price. In this case the buying division may be doing what is best from the standpoint of its own profitability, but the actions of the two divisions together may not be best for the company as a whole. The simplistic view of the transfer pricing problem also ignores the real possibility that a transfer price arbitrarily set by central corporate headquarters may undermine the entire divisional organizational structure. Division managers are supposed to be free, within limits, to make manufacturing and marketing decisions as if they were separate companies. If the return, or profit, from a significant portion of its operations is dictated by the transfer price imposed by top management, the division manager may become frustrated and the benefits of divisionalization will be lost. The selection of an appropriate transfer price can therefore have a significant impact.

---

[2] Only rarely will cash equal to the transfer price actually change hands. Transfer prices are set primarily so that performance of the selling division can be assessed as of the time of the transfer rather than waiting several periods until all manufacturing is completed and the good is sold to someone outside of the company.

On what basis should a transfer price be selected? The goal should be the selection of a transfer price that has, as its end result, the maximization of the profits for the firm as a whole. It is hoped that this transfer pricing scheme will also lead to maximization of divisional profits. Where company-wide and divisional profitability are in conflict, the best interests of the company's owners require attending to overall company profits.

In the sections that follow, we consider several types of transfer prices and discuss the conditions when each type might be appropriate. It is sufficient to point out here that there is no single type of transfer price that satisfies the goal, or ideal, in all cases.

Cost-Based Transfer Prices   One possibility is to base the transfer price on the actual average unit cost of the selling division. This measure is subject to numerous criticisms, however. First, average unit costs will fluctuate from month to month in response to changes in costs. This will require the buying division continually to reassess how much it is willing to purchase from the selling divisions, making production planning decisions more difficult. Second, for a highly automated division, average cost can fluctuate widely in response to changes in volume. This is because the fixed costs are spread over a varying number of units. Thus, production-level decisions by the selling division will affect the profitability of the buying division. Third, transfer prices will be affected by changes in efficiency in the selling division, so that gains and losses in efficiency will be passed on to other divisions. For example, suppose that the selling division is able to reduce average unit cost by more efficient routing of work through the manufacturing process. The benefits of this reduction are passed on to the buying division by way of a lower acquisition cost (that is, transfer price), with a related improvement in the buying division's ROI. The improved efficiency would not be reflected in the selling division's ROI. There is an even more important criticism of average unit cost in the case of losses in efficiency. If management of the selling division knows that all costs can be passed on in the transfer price, there may be little incentive to control costs or improve efficiency. A fourth criticism of using average unit cost as a transfer price is that it does not permit the selling division to show a return, or profit, on goods or services sold to other divisions (that is, revenue = costs). This creates an incentive for the selling division to market its products externally rather than supplying them to another division. It also creates incomparability in the ROIs across divisions, depending on the extent that interdivisional transfers of goods or services take place.

The use of standard, rather than actual, costs will minimize the effects of the first three criticisms above. Standard costs will be less volatile so that transfer prices can remain constant for longer periods. Also, gains and losses in efficiency are not passed on to the buying division. However, the selling division will report a profit only if it is able to produce at less than standard cost. Thus, the use of standard cost as a transfer price is subject to the fourth criticism above.

There are some benefits of using a cost-based transfer price. In situations where there is no external market, it may be the only objective basis for setting a transfer price. This might occur, for example, where the output of one division is a semiprocessed product requiring additional work by a buying division. Information on the cost of manufacturing a product also provides a basis on which the buying and selling divisions can negotiate a transfer price, an approach to be discussed after the use of market prices is considered.

Market Prices as Transfer Prices   The use of an external competitive market price meets most of the requirements of an ideal system. First, use of a market price implies the existence of an external market. Divisions are free to transact either among themselves or in the external market, thereby increasing the freedom of the divisions. Use of a market price also helps assure profit independence of the divisions. Any gains or losses in efficiency of the selling division do not get passed on to the buying division. Use of competitive market prices is also relatively free from argument, thereby saving administrative costs.

Market prices, however, are not always the ideal transfer prices. In some instances, perfectly competitive market prices do not exist. Some of the benefits mentioned above, such as profit independence and attribution of gains and losses in efficiency to the selling division, will therefore be reduced. This is likely to be the case for unique products passing between divisions in semiprocessed form.

Probably the most important criticism of a policy of using market prices is that it may lead to decisions by divisions that are not in the best interests of the company as a whole. Permitting divisions to sell and purchase externally rather than internally results in additional transaction costs from entering the market twice. These costs would be saved if the divisions dealt with each other. To reflect these additional transaction costs, some firms set the transfer price equal to the external market price but reduce it by an estimate of the normal transaction costs. Another case where use of market prices can lead to less than optimal decisions occurs when short-run market demand exceeds the supply available at prevailing prices. For example, assume that a selling division has the capacity for producing 100,000 units per year and can sell these units either to another division within the firm or on the external market. Market demand is such that if the buying division does not purchase at least 75,000 units from the selling division, it will have to curtail its operations significantly. In this situation it is in the best interests of the firm for the selling division to supply the needed units to the buying division rather than to have the selling division indifferent as to its customer. The external market price must be adjusted somehow to induce the intercompany transfer.

A major problem in using market prices arises when market price exceeds variable cost of the selling division and the selling division has unused capacity. Under these circumstances, firm-wide profits can be maximized only if the buying division buys all of its needs from the selling division. If there is no cost-saving advantage in buying from the selling division, the motivation of the buying division to do so is reduced. Under these circumstances, negotiated transfer prices may be required.

Negotiated Transfer Prices   Transfer prices based on cost represent a lower limit on the price that selling divisions are willing to accept. Transfer prices based on market prices represent an upper limit on the price that buying divisions are willing to absorb. The difference between these two prices is the total margin on the transfer. Many firms permit divisional managers to negotiate among themselves as to how the margin is to be split. If both divisions are free to deal either with each other or in the external market, then the negotiated price will likely be close to the external market price. If all of a selling division's output cannot be sold on the external market (that is, a portion must be sold to the buying division), then the negotiated price will likely be less than the market price and the total margin will be shared by the divisions. The use of negotiated transfer prices is consistent with the concept of decentralized decision making in divisionalized firms.

One of the principal disadvantages of negotiated transfer prices is that significant time may be required by the divisions to carry out the negotiating process. Also, interdivision hostility may result, which could hurt overall company performance.

As we mentioned previously, no particular transfer pricing scheme is best in all circumstances. The choice revolves around such factors as the degree of market competition, the relationship between short-run supply and demand, the extent top management chooses to interfere in divisional decisions, and other factors.

Measuring Divisional Expenses

The computation of divisional ROI requires that certain expenses be deducted from divisional revenues to obtain divisional net income. Four types of expenses are considered: (1) controllable direct expenses, (2) noncontrollable direct expenses, (3) controllable indirect expenses, and (4) noncontrollable indirect expenses.

Controllable Direct Expenses   Expenses in the first category include those that are directly traceable to, and are controllable by, the division. Raw materials used in manufacturing the division products, salaries and wages of manufacturing and marketing personnel within the division, and depreciation on the division's equipment are examples of expenses that are likely to be controllable and direct. There is little question that these expenses should be deducted from revenues in determining divisional net income. It may be desirable, however, to report variable and fixed expenses separately on the divisional income statement. This possibility is discussed later in the chapter.

Noncontrollable Direct Expenses   The salary of the divisional manager is an example of a noncontrollable direct expense. Top management generally controls the amount of this expense item. From the standpoint of top management, this expense is a necessary incremental cost of operating a division and one that must be covered if a division is to contribute to the profits of the whole company. These expenses should therefore be deducted in determining divisional net income.

Controllable Indirect Expenses   Costs incurred at central corporate headquarters, called common costs, indirectly benefit all divisions within the firm. These common costs can be classified into two groups: (1) costs of central corporate administration, such as the president's salary; and (2) costs of providing centralized services, such as data processing, product development, and training. Costs in the first group are largely beyond the control of the divisions. Costs in the second group are at least partially controllable by the divisions to the extent that they have discretionary use of the services of these centralized service departments.

A response to the question about whether or not the costs of centralized service departments should be allocated to the divisions will likely revolve around the extent to which the divisions have the choice of either using the centralized services or acquiring similar services from an external source. If decision making is fully decentralized, the divisions will have this choice. In this case, the divisions should be "charged" for the use of centralized services just as if the services were purchased externally. The divisional net income of one division should not be higher than another simply because the first division uses centralized services and the second division acquires the services externally.

In situations where divisional managers are required to use centralized services, the question of whether the costs of providing these services should be allocated to the divisions becomes more complex. The division manager may resent such an allocation because there is no opportunity for going outside if the "charges" become too high. Also, the total amount of centralized costs to be allocated to the divisions depends on the amount of services required by other divisions, as well as certain top-management decisions as to minimum levels of service capacity that will be maintained regardless of demand. Thus, the costs are largely noncontrollable by the division manager. From the viewpoint of top management, the centralized service departments are maintained for the benefit of the divisions. The decision to operate such departments was probably made after considering the costs of decentralizing these services into the divisions as well as the costs of acquiring the services externally. Centralization was selected because it was the least costly or most efficient alternative for the company as a whole. Because these are incremental, although somewhat indirect, costs of operating divisions, top management will argue that these costs should be allocated to the divisions.

Whether or not these costs are allocated will likely revolve around the behavioral reactions of division managers. Top management must communicate the reasons for such allocations to the division managers and indicate just how assessments of divisional performance will be affected by the allocations. Some companies calculate divisional net income both before and after allocations of centralized service department costs. The preallocation figure plays a heavier role in evaluating the month-to-month performance of the divisions. The divisions, however, are expected over longer periods to have a positive margin after allocation to ensure that the central service costs are being adequately covered.

Once a decision has been made to "charge" the divisions for centralized services, the next question concerns the amount to be charged. Most companies do not treat their centralized service departments as profit centers. That is, the amount charged to the division is based on the costs incurred by the service departments. Treating the service departments as cost centers, rather than as profit centers, is based on the rationale that the service departments are operated to provide support to the divisions and not to generate profit. The amount charged, or the transfer price, is therefore based on cost. The costs are allocated to the divisions using an allocation base that varies most closely with the cost item. For example, data processing costs may be allocated based on computer time used. Training costs may be allocated based on the number of employees hired per year. Use of a cost-based transfer price here is subject to many of the same criticisms as the transfer pricing scheme discussed earlier. As a means of inducing service departments to control the amount of costs incurred, some companies charge the divisions for the standard, rather than actual, costs of the services.

Noncontrollable Indirect Expenses   The considerations that bear on the question of allocating centralized service department costs have little relevance in the case of noncontrollable indirect expenses. Divisions cannot control the amount of top management's attention that is given to individual divisions, general corporate policy, and external relations. There are no equivalent "acquire internally–acquire externally" decisions that divisions must make. Different arguments must be offered for and against allocation of central corporate expenses.

The most frequently cited arguments against allocation relate to the divisions' inability to control the amount of costs incurred and to the arbitrary allocation bases that must be used. For example, on what basis should the president's salary be allocated to the divisions—sales, number of employees, square footage of space used? Any allocation base is likely to be meaningless. It will be difficult for top management to evaluate division managers effectively if the divisional net income figure includes elements that are both controllable and noncontrollable by the managers being evaluated.

The most frequently cited argument for allocation is that, unless these costs are allocated to the divisions, the divisions will underprice their products and cause the firm as a whole to operate at a loss. That is, the revenues generated by the divisions will be insufficient to cover both the direct expenses of the divisions and the indirect expenses incurred at central headquarters. This argument is not particularly convincing in the short run. Prices are likely to be determined by competitive market conditions. These prices will be the same whether central corporate expenses are allocated or not. Over the long run, these central corporate expenses must be covered by the divisions and a stronger case can therefore be made for allocation. As a basis for evaluating the month-to-month performance of divisional managers, however, attention should be directed to the divisional contribution to coverage of central corporate expenses and profit (that is, divisional net income before allocation of central corporate expenses). If divisions seek to optimize this divisional contribution amount, they will also optimize divisional net income after allocation of central corporate expenses, however they may be allocated.

Measuring Divisional Investment

As we pointed out earlier, it is inappropriate for top management to evaluate divisional performance by simply comparing net income across divisions. If this is done, the larger divisions are likely to look better. It is desirable to scale the divisional net income amounts to recognize differences in the size of the divisions. Most companies use some measure of capital employed, or invested, in each division. Our concerns in this section are (1) what assets are to be included in the investment base; and (2) what basis of valuation is to be used?

Assets Included in the Investment Base   Two guidelines can be suggested in selecting assets to be included in the investment base. First, consistent with the use of divisional net income as the numerator of ROI, the assets included should be those for which divisions have significant control. For assets physically located in a division and used only in the division's operations, there is little question that they should be included. More difficult problems arise with respect to assets shared with other divisions (for example, a manufacturing plant) and assets acquired by centralized services departments (for example, equipment used in personnel training). Where reasonable bases can be obtained for allocating shared assets, they should be included in the investment base. For example, the cost of a shared manufacturing plant might be allocated between divisions based on square footage used. Where only highly arbitrary allocation bases are possible, it is best not to attribute common investment facilities to the divisions. For example, equipment used in personnel training is probably best left unallocated.

The second general guideline for selecting assets to be included in the investment base is consistency. Whatever base a firm selects, it should follow it consistently across time and across divisions. This will at least stabilize the effects of any biases in the investment base.

Valuation of Assets in the Investment Base   Once a decision has been made regarding which assets are to be included in the investment base, a monetary amount must be assigned. Most firms use acquisition cost as the valuation basis. The necessary amounts can be obtained directly from the company's records and accounts. Also, this valuation basis is consistent with the measurement of cost of goods sold and depreciation expense in the numerator of ROI.

The use of book values of assets, particularly fixed assets, in the denominator of ROI can have undesirable results. A division with old, low-cost, and almost fully depreciated assets may be reluctant to replace the assets with newer, more efficient, but more costly assets. (Replacing old assets with new ones decreases the numerator —income—of the ROI calculation because of increased depreciation charges. It also increases the denominator—cost of total assets—of the ROI calculation. These two effects combine to reduce calculated ROI.) If use of book values in the investment base does have this effect on divisional investment behavior, there are at least two possible ways to deal with the problem. One is to state all assets gross, rather than net, of accumulated depreciation. Assets will therefore be stated at their full acquisition cost regardless of age. Another approach is to state assets at their current replacement cost in new condition (see the discussion in Chapter Fifteen). In this case, the investment base will be stated at the same amount whether or not the division replaces the old assets. Use of either acquisition cost or current replacement cost of assets in new condition, however, does not provide an accurate measure of the capital invested in the division. The best approach here, as in previous cases, is to select the measurement methods that most accurately reflect performance, effectively communicate the reasons for using these measurement methods to divisional personnel, and then apply them consistently over time.

INTERPRETING DIVISIONAL ROI

In previous sections, we have discussed some of the factors to be considered in calculating ROI. In this section, we discuss several additional considerations in using and interpreting ROI as a basis for evaluating divisional performance.

Single Versus Multiple ROIs

We suggested that a firm should settle on the way it is going to calculate ROI and then use it consistently. There is a tendency, however, to place too much emphasis on this single statistic. This is particularly a problem when the divisional performance report is being used for several different purposes. In this section, we suggest a format for a divisional performance report based on the ROI measure that can be used for several different purposes. Exhibit 11.1 presents a divisional performance report in the suggested format.

EXHIBIT 11.1
Suggested Format for a Divisional Performance Report[a]

		Dollars	ROI
Revenues:			
Sales to Outside Customers		$XXX	
Sales to Other Divisions		XXX	
Total Revenues		$XXX	
Less Controllable Expenses:			
Variable Direct	$XXX		
Variable Indirect	XXX	XXX	
Contribution Margin		$XXX	
Fixed Direct	$XXX		
Fixed Indirect	XXX	XXX	
Equals Controllable Profit Margin		$XXX	XX.X%
Less Noncontrollable Direct Expenses		XXX	
Equals Divisional Contribution to Central			
Corporate Expenses		$XXX	XX.X%
Less Allocated Share of Central Corporate			
Expenses		XXX	
Income Before Income Taxes		$XXX	b
Less Income Taxes		XXX	
Net Income After Income Taxes		$XXX	b

---

a The actual performance report should include columns for both budgeted and actual amounts.
b An ROI measure is inappropriate here, because it is difficult to allocate the cost of shared central corporate facilities to each of the divisions in a meaningful way.

Sales and Divisional Expenses   The statement distinguishes between sales to outsiders and those to other divisions. The purpose of this distinction is to show the extent to which the division is dependent on orders from other divisions for its business. The statement also indicates the variable and fixed cost structure under the control of the division. This information might be used for breakeven and other cost-volume-profit analysis.

Profit Margins   The controllable profit margin and the corresponding ROI are measures of the return generated from decisions made within the division. The controllable profit margin and its corresponding ROI are the best measure for evaluating the performance of the division manager. When noncontrollable direct expenses, such as the division manager's salary, are deducted from the controllable profit margin, we obtain the division's contribution to central corporate expenses and its corresponding ROI. These are the best measures for top management to use in evaluating a division (as contrasted to the division manager) in relation to other divisions and to the company as a whole.

Allocation of Central Corporate Expenses   We suggested earlier that it is undesirable to allocate central corporate expenses to divisions if the purpose is to obtain a measure for evaluating divisional performance. Divisions do not have control over these costs and, therefore, should not be held accountable for them. However, divisional personnel must be conscious of the need to provide a positive contribution margin to the coverage of central corporate expenses and to profits. One means of communicating this to divisional personnel is to show on the performance report the relationship between the division's contribution and the amount which top management feels is an equitable share of central corporate expenses.

In addition to subtracting a share of central corporate expenses, some firms also deduct an amount for interest on the capital used by the division. This is typically a charge for implicit, rather than explicit, interest, because no cash payments are made by the division. Instead, the charge represents a minimum desired rate of return that the division should generate. Inclusion of this implicit interest indicates to the division the relationship between the divisional return, or contribution, and the amount expected by top management.[3]

To illustrate, assume that the divisional contributions to profit earned by Division A and Division B are $100,000 and $120,000, respectively, and that the investment of both divisions is $500,000. If top management expected a return of 14 percent on the capital employed, the divisions' net income after interest on capital would be determined as in Exhibit 11.2. After interest imputation, the relative performance of divisions can appear somewhat different from before the imputation.

Allocation of Income Taxes   One question that has not been considered is the treatment of income taxes. In the vast majority of cases, income taxes are assessed on the taxable income of the company as a whole rather than on each division. Should these income taxes be allocated to individual divisions?

---

[3]   Solomons refers to divisional income after subtracting a charge for the use of capital as "residual income." See David Solomons, *Divisional Performance Measurement and Control*, New York: Financial Executives Research Foundation, 1965, pp. 63ff.

EXHIBIT 11.2
Inclusion of Implicit Interest Charge in
Divisional ROI Calculation

	Division A	Division B
Divisional Contribution to Profits.	$100,000	$120,000
Interest on Capital Employed, .14 × $500,000	(70,000)	(70,000)
Divisional Net Income (= Residual Income)	$ 30,000	$ 50,000
Return on Investment after Interest Imputation:		
$30,000/$500,000	6%	
$50,000/$500,000		10%
Return on Investment without Interest Imputation:		
$100,000/$500,000	20%	
$120,000/$500,000		24%

There are two principal arguments for interdivisional allocation of income taxes. First, managers should be encouraged to make decisions keeping in mind the income tax consequences. For example, consideration should be given to the investment tax credit, the tax savings from depreciation deductions, and the tax consequences of selling versus trading in old equipment in capital budgeting decisions (see the discussion in Chapter Seventeen). To the extent that division managers have authority to make these types of decisions, they should be held accountable for the income tax consequences. Second, the Congress has granted income tax incentives for firms to invest in certain risky industries (for example, oil exploration). The decision by a firm to organize a division to operate in such an industry must have taken these income tax incentives into consideration. Because these income tax benefits were considered by top management when it developed its expectations about the profitability of the division, they should be considered when management evaluates the division's performance.

The arguments against allocation are similar to those against allocating central corporate expenses. The amount of income taxes assessed is often beyond the control of divisional managers. In addition, the amount of income taxes that would be paid on divisional income if it were a separate taxable entity may be different from the amount actually assessed when it is aggregated with income of other divisions. For example, a limit is placed on the amount that can be deducted for charitable contributions. If one division contributes more than the maximum in a given year, and income taxes are assessed on the division, it will be unable to deduct the excess contributions in determining taxable income. However, as long as other divisions contribute less than the maximum, the full amount of the division's contributions will be deductible when aggregated at the company-wide level. Thus, the income taxes of one division are not independent of income generated by other divisions.

If, for a particular firm, the arguments against allocation are stronger, our suggested divisional performance report would end with "Income Before Income Taxes."

If, on the other hand, the arguments for allocation are stronger, the income taxes would probably be placed under controllable expenses. Our placement of income taxes at the bottom of the report is a compromise between the two positions. Recognition is given to the fact that allocation of income taxes is as difficult as that for central corporate expenses. However, it emphasizes to division managers the importance of income taxes in decisions and the need that they be covered before profits are generated for the owners.

Disaggregating Return on Investments

Recall from Chapter Three that the rate of return on assets can be disaggregated into profit margin and asset turnover components. A similar disaggregation can be performed for ROI.

Return on Investment = Profit Margin Percentage × Investment Turnover Ratio

$$\frac{\text{Controllable Profit Margin (or other divisional income measure)}}{\text{Divisional Investment}} = \frac{\text{Controllable Profit Margin (or other divisional income measure)}}{\text{Divisional Revenues}} \times \frac{\text{Divisional Revenues}}{\text{Divisional Investment}}$$

To illustrate the usefulness of disaggregating the ROI, assume the following information about Division A:

Year	Sales	Net Income	Investment
19X0	$1,000,000	$100,000	$ 500,000
19X1	2,000,000	160,000	1,000,000
19X2	4,000,000	400,000	2,500,000

The ROI for each of the three years and the associated profit margin percentages and investment turnover ratios are shown below.

Year	ROI =	Profit Margin Percentage	Investment × Turnover Ratio
19X0	20% =	10%	× 2.0
19X1	16% =	8%	× 2.0
19X2	16% =	10%	× 1.6

The profit margin percentage provides information for assessing divisional management's ability to combine inputs to generate outputs. That is, various cost inputs (materials, labor, depreciation) are combined to generate revenue outputs (sales of goods and services). The profit margin percentage indicates the portion of each dollar of revenue that is in excess of the costs incurred. It is often used as a measure for assessing efficiency in producing and selling goods and services. The profit margin percentage for Division A in the example above decreased from 10 percent to 8 percent between 19X0 and 19X1. Because the investment turnover ratio remained the same between the two years, it appears that the decrease in ROI is caused by an inability to control costs or an inability to raise selling prices as costs have increased, or both.

We indicated earlier that divisional income is divided by investment as a means of scaling divisions of different size so that their performance measures are more comparable. When ROI is disaggregated, however, useful information can be obtained on how effectively the capital invested in the division has been used. The investment turnover ratio indicates the dollars of revenue that the division was able to generate for each dollar of invested capital. Returning to the example above, Division A was unable to increase its ROI between 19X1 and 19X2, despite an increase in its profit margin percentage, because its investment turnover ratio decreased. The division was unable to generate $2 of revenue for each dollar invested in 19X2 as it had done in previous years.

More useful information is likely to be provided by studying profit margin percentages and investment turnover ratios for a given division over several periods than by looking at these ratios for all divisions in a particular period. This is caused by the fact that some divisions, because of the nature of their activities, require more capital than others. For example, a division involved in manufacturing and selling heavy equipment is likely to require more capital than one selling management consulting or advertising and promotion services. The investment turnover ratios of these two divisions are inherently likely to be quite different and not a cause of concern for top management. A significant change in the ratio of either division between two periods, however, may signal the need for corrective action. For example, a significant decrease in investment turnover for the manufacturing division may indicate excess capacity and suggest disposal of some facilities.

Setting Minimum Desired ROIs

If the ROI is to serve as an effective measure for controlling divisional performance, a standard, or desired, rate must be set each period. Some firms merely use the actual ROI of the preceding period as the standard. This is common practice where top management emphasizes trends or changes in ROI over time. Use of the actual ROI of a preceding period as a standard is subject to several important criticisms. Past performance might have been poorer than it should have been. Improvement on poor performance may still not be satisfactory. Moreover, even if past performance was considered satisfactory, conditions might have changed in such a way that what was satisfactory for the last period may not be satisfactory for this period.

Another approach is to specify a minimum desired ROI for each division, given their particular operating characteristics. One company,[4] for example, computes a minimum rate of return for various classes of divisional assets and then aggregates to obtain a required ROI. Fixed assets are required to generate a return of 22 percent, inventories 14 percent, and accounts receivable 7 percent. If a division had

---

[4] See Donald R. Hughes, "The Behavioral Aspects of Accounting Data for Performance Evaluation at Burlington Industries, Inc.," in *The Behavioral Aspects of Accounting Data for Performance Evaluation,* ed. Thomas J. Burns (Columbus: Ohio State College of Administrative Science, 1970), p. 56.

$500,000, $400,000, and $100,000 invested on average in these three types of assets, respectively, its minimum required ROI would be 17.3 percent [= (.22 × $500,000) + (.14 × $400,000) + (.07 × $100,000)]/[$500,000 + $400,000 + $100,000]. Specifying a different rate of return is an attempt to adjust for different degrees of risk from investing in each type of asset.

SUMMARY OF DIVISIONAL CONTROL SYSTEMS

We have discussed the most important factors to be considered in designing a divisional control system. The variety of ways of treating transfer prices, central corporate expenses, income taxes, the investment base, investment valuation, and other variables may be unsettling. It must be emphasized, however, that there is no single "correct" way to calculate ROI or any other divisional performance measure. Each firm must design the performance measure to suit its particular needs. The most critical factor to keep in mind is that a balance must be maintained between divisional decision-making autonomy and top management concern for the welfare of the company as a whole.

QUESTIONS AND PROBLEMS

1 Review the meaning of the following concepts or terms discussed in this chapter.
  a Divisionalization.
  b Decentralized decision making.
  c Profit center.
  d Return on investment.
  e Transfer pricing problem.
  f Cost-based transfer price.
  g Market-based transfer price.
  h Negotiated transfer price.
  i Common costs.
  j Centralized service department costs.
  k Central administration costs.
  l Profit margin percentage.
  m Investment turnover ratio.

2 "It may be desirable to use a different ROI measure for evaluating the performance of a division and the performance of the division's manager." Explain.

3 "An action that is optimal for a division may not be optimal for the company as a whole." Explain.

4 Why are transfer prices necessary?

5 In what sense is the term "transfer price" a misnomer?

6 "The case for allocating central service department costs is stronger than the case for allocating central administration costs to divisions." Explain.

7 "The return on investment measure may be biased in favor of divisions with older plant and equipment." Explain.

8 Whitmyer Chemical Company began business in January 19X0. It produces various chemical products that pass through two divisions. Division A refines the basic chemicals. These refined chemicals are then immediately transfered to Division B, which combines them into several chemical products. During 19X0, Division A refined 12,000 pounds of chemicals at a cost of $180,000. Its administration and other expenses amounted to $40,000. Division B incurred $120,000 of additional manufacturing costs in completing 10,000 pounds. No work was done on the remaining 2,000 pounds received from Division A. Division B sold the 10,000 pounds of completed units for $500,000. Its selling and administration expenses for 19X0 were $80,000.

a Prepare divisional income statements for each of these two divisions for 19X0 assuming the transfer price is equal to Division A's total cost.

b Repeat part **a,** assuming that the transfer price is based on the external market price of $20 per pound.

c Repeat part **a,** assuming that the transfer price is based on a negotiated price of $19 per pound.

d Respond to the following statement: "It is immaterial to the company as a whole which transfer price is used."

9 The following information relates to the operating performance of three divisions of Langston Products Corporation for 19X0.

	Division A	**Division B**	**Division C**
Divisional Contribution to Central Corporate Expenses	$ 500,000	$ 500,000	$ 500,000
Divisional Investment.	$ 4,000,000	$ 5,000,000	$ 6,000,000
Divisional Sales	$24,000,000	$20,000,000	$16,000,000
Divisional Employees.	22,500	12,000	10,500

Langston evaluates divisional performance using rate of return on investment (ROI) after allocating a portion of the central corporate expenses to each division. Central corporate expenses for 19X0 were $900,000.

a Determine the ROI of each division before allocation of central corporate expenses.

b Determine the ROI of each division assuming central corporate expenses are allocated based on divisional investments (that is, allocate 4/15 to Division A, 5/15 to Division B, and 6/15 to Division C).

c Repeat step **b,** assuming that central corporate expenses are allocated based on divisional sales.

d Repeat step **b,** assuming that central corporate expenses are allocated based on the number of employees.

e Assume that you are the corporate controller of Langston Products Corporation. The manager of Division A states: "I don't know why I am working so hard. You people at central corporate headquarters make the performance of my division and the other divisions come out any way you want." How would you respond to this statement?

10 The following information relates to the operating performance of three divisions of Dees Manufacturing Company for 19X0.

	Division A	Division B	Division C
Net Income	$ 640,000	$ 3,000,000	$ 6,000,000
Investment	8,000,000	15,000,000	37,500,000

a Determine the rate of return on investment (ROI) of each division for 19X0.

b Assume that a charge is levied on each division for the use of capital. The charge is 10 percent on investment and is deducted in determining divisional net income. Recalculate ROI using divisional net income after deduction of the use of capital charge in the numerator.

c Which of these two measures do you feel gives the better indication of operating performance? Explain your reasoning.

11 The following information relates to the operating performance of two divisions of Pratt Electronics Corporation for 19X0.

	Division A	Division B
Net Income	$ 400,000	$ 600,000
Total Assets (based on acquisition cost)	4,000,000	7,500,000
Total Assets (based on current replacement costs)	6,000,000	8,000,000

a Determine the return on investment (ROI) of each division using total assets stated at acquisition cost as the investment base.

b Determine the ROI of each division using total assets based on current replacement cost as the investment base.

c Which of the two measures do you feel gives the better indication of operating performance? Explain your reasoning.

12 The following information relates to the operating performance of two divisions of the Hargrave Company for 19X0.

	Division A	Division B
Net Income	$ 500,000	$ 800,000
Total Assets (at gross acquisition cost)	6,250,000	20,000,000
Total Assets (net of accumulated depreciation)	5,000,000	5,000,000

a Determine the return on investment (ROI) of each division using total assets at gross acquisition cost as the investment base.

b Determine the ROI of each division using total assets net of acccumulated depreciation as the investment base.

c Which of the two measures do you feel gives the better indication of operating performance? Explain your reasoning.

13 The operating performance of the three divisions of Bobel Corporation for 19X0 is as as follows:

	Division A	Division B	Division C
Sales	$3,800,000	$17,000,000	$20,000,000
Net Income	200,000	500,000	1,000,000
Investment	2,000,000	6,250,000	8,000,000

a Using the profit margin percentage as the criterion, which is the most profitable division?

b Using the rate of return on investment as the criterion, which is the most profitable division?

c Which of the two measures do you feel gives the better indication of overall operating performance? Explain your reasoning.

14 The Assembly Division of the Whitley Manufacturing Company had a rate of return on investment (ROI) of 10 percent (= $200,000/$2,000,000) during 19X0 based on sales of $4,000,000. In an effort to improve its performance during 19X1, the division instituted several cost-saving programs, including the substitution of automatic equipment for work previously done by workers and the purchase of raw materials in large quantities to obtain quantity discounts. Despite these cost-saving programs, the division's ROI for 19X1 was 8 percent (= $220,000/$2,750,000) based on sales of $4,000,000.

a Disaggregate the ROI for 19X0 and 19X1 into profit margin and asset turnover ratios.

b Explain the reason for the decrease in ROI between the two years using results from part a.

15 Robinson Manufacturing Company produces heavy-duty equipment used in construction work. The company is organized into several divisions that operate essentially as autonomous companies. Division managers are permitted to make capital investment and production-level decisions. They can also decide whether to sell to other divisions or to outside customers.

Division A produces a critical component in the construction of cranes manufactured by Division B. It has been selling this component to Division B for $1,500 per unit. Division A recently purchased new equipment for producing the component. To offset its higher depreciation charges, Division A increased its price to $1,600 per unit. The manager of Division A has asked the president to instruct Division B to purchase the component for the $1,600 price rather than permit Division B to purchase externally for $1,500 per unit. The following information is obtained from the company's records:

Division B's Annual Purchases of the Component . . . . 100 units
Division A's Variable Costs per Unit. $1,200
Division A's Fixed Costs per Unit. . . . . $ 300

a Assume that there are no alternative uses for Division A's idle capacity. Will the company as a whole benefit if Division B purchases the component externally for $1,500? Explain.

b Assume that the idle capacity of Division A can be used for other purposes, resulting in cash operating savings of $20,000. Will the company as a whole benefit if Division B purchases the component externally for $1,500? Explain.

c Assume the same facts as in b except that the outside market price drops to $1,350 per unit. Will the company as a whole benefit if Division B purchases the component externally for $1,350? Explain.

d As president, how would you respond to the manager of Division A?

16 The Champion Manufacturing Company uses rate of return on investment (ROI) as a basis for determining the annual bonus of divisional managers. Before calculating ROI at year-end, all manufacturing cost variances are assigned to units produced, whether sold or in ending inventory, so that standard costs are converted into actual costs. Central corporate expenses are allocated to the divisions based on total sales. The calculation of ROI for 19X0 for two independent manufacturing divisions is as follows:

	Division A	Division B
Division Contribution to Central Corporate Expenses and Net Income...............	$100,000	$ 500,000
Share of Central Corporate Expenses	(10,000)	(25,000)
Divisional Net Income	$ 90,000	$ 475,000
Divisional Investment (assets)...............	$600,000	$4,750,000
ROI....................................	15%	10%

Indicate several factors that, if present, would bias the ROI measure as calculated by Champion and lead to possible inequities in determining the annual bonus.

17 The Domestic Corporation manufactures and sells a patented electronic device for detecting burglaries. "Return on Investment" is used as a measure for the control of operations for each of its 16 U.S. divisions.

A new division has been recently organized in Brazil. Domestic contributed the necessary capital for the construction of manufacturing and sales facilities in Brazil while debt financing was obtained locally for working capital requirements. The new division will remit the following amounts annually to the U.S. central corporate office: **(1)** a royalty of $10 for each burglary device sold in Brazil, **(2)** a fee of $40 per hour plus traveling expenses for central corporate engineering services used by the division, and **(3)** a dividend equal to 10 percent of the capital committed by Domestic. Remaining funds generated by operations will be retained by the division for its own use. The division will receive the right to produce and market in Brazil any future electronic devices developed by the central corporate research and development staff.

List some of the questions that must be addressed in designing an ROI measure for this division.

18 Durham Industries is one of the largest and most diversified textile companies in the world. Its products are manufactured and sold through 25 individual divisions which operate much like autonomous companies. Each division has its own manufacturing plants for making the division's products, a sales staff to market them, and an administrative staff to provide financial assistance and control. Broad policy and financial guidance are received from corporate management, and technical assistance can be obtained from the corporate staff. The latter includes treasurer, legal, personnel, advertising, engineering, and purchasing groups.

Although several measures of divisional performance are used, the most significant yardstick is return on investment. The numerator of ROI is calculated as follows:

Divisional Revenues (sales to outsiders plus sales to other divisions based on a negotiated transfer price)
Less Direct Divisional Expenses (excluding income taxes)
Less Charge for Central Corporate Expenses (the costs of central administration and service departments are allocated to the divisions according to each division's investment as a percentage of the total of all of the divisions' investments)
Equals Divisional Net Income.

The investment measure in the denominator of ROI is based on the book value of the following assets: **(1)** accounts receivable net of accounts payable, **(2)** inventories, including supplies, raw materials, work in process, and finished goods, and **(3)** long-term depreciable assets (net of accumulated depreciation). Accounting methods are set by the central corporate controller's staff and used uniformly by all divisions.

The actual ROI is calculated monthly for each division. In evaluating ROI, corporate management uses two bases. First, management pays great attention to trends rather than absolute goals or standards. Maximum interest centers on divisions that are either improving or getting worse. Second, management sets a minimum satisfactory ROI for each division. This represents a lower limit below which the division manager's job is in jeopardy. The minimum is set rather loosely and is easily attainable in almost all cases. The minimum ROI is determined by applying different weights to the three investment components: 20 percent for depreciable assets, 12 percent for inventories, and 6 percent for accounts receivable net of accounts payable.

Discuss the strengths and weaknesses of the return on investment measure as used by Durham as a basis for controlling divisional performance.

*19"If I were to price these boxes any lower than $480 a thousand," said Mr. Brunner, manager of Birch Paper Company's Thompson division, "I'd be countermanding my order of last month for our salesmen to stop shaving their bids and to bid full cost quotations. I've been trying for weeks to improve the quality of our business, and if I turn around now and accept this job at $430 or $450 or something less than $480, I'll be tearing down this program I've been working so hard to build up. The division can't very well show a profit by putting in bids which don't even cover a fair share of overhead costs, let alone give us a profit."

Birch Paper Company was a medium-sized, partly integrated paper company, producing white and kraft papers and paperboard. A portion of its paperboard output was converted into corrugated boxes by the Thompson division, which also printed and colored the outside surface of the boxes. Including Thompson, the company had four producing divisions and a timberland division, which supplied part of the company's pulp requirements.

For several years each division had been judged independently on the basis of its profit and return on investment. Top management had been working to gain effective results from a policy of decentralizing responsibility and authority for all decisions except those relating to overall company policy. The company's top officials felt that in the past few years the concept of decentralization had been successfully applied and that the company's profits and competitive position had definitely improved.

Early in 19X0 the Northern division designed a special display box for one of its papers in conjunction with the Thompson division, which was equipped to make the box. Thompson's package design and development staff spent several months perfecting the design, production methods, and materials that were to be used; because of the unusual color and shape, these were far from standard. According to an agreement between the two divisions, the Thompson division was reimbursed by the Northern division for the cost of its design and development work.

When the specifications were all prepared, the Northern division asked for bids on the box from the Thompson division and from two outside companies, West Paper Company and Erie Papers, Ltd. Each division manager normally was free to buy from whichever supplier he wished, and even on sales within the company, divisions were expected to meet the going market price if they wanted the business.

Early in 19X0 the profit margins of converters such as the Thompson division were being squeezed. Thompson, as did many other similar converters, bought its board, liner, or paper; and its function was to print, cut, and shape it into boxes. Though it bought most of its materials from other Birch divisions, most of Thompson's sales were to outside customers. If

---

Thompson got the order from Northern, it probably would buy its liner, board, and corrugating medium from the Southern division of Birch. The walls of a corrugated box consist of outside and inside sheets of linerboard sandwiching the corrugating medium.

About 70 percent of Thompson's out-of-pocket cost of $400 a thousand for the order represented the cost of linerboard and corrugating medium. Though Southern division had been running below capacity and had excess inventory, it quoted the market price, which had not noticeably weakened as a result of the oversupply. Its out-of-pocket costs on both liner and corrugating medium were about 60 percent of the selling price.

The Northern division received bids on the boxes of $480 a thousand from the Thompson division, $430 a thousand from West Paper Company, and $432 a thousand from Erie Papers, Ltd. Erie Papers offered to buy from Birch the outside linerboard with the special printing already on it, but would supply its own inside liner and corrugating medium. The outside liner would be supplied by the Southern division at a price equivalent to $90 a thousand boxes, and would be printed for $30 a thousand by the Thompson division. Of the $30, about $25 would be out-of-pocket costs.

Since this situation appeared to be a little unusual, Mr. Kenton, manager of the Northern division, discussed the wide discrepancy of bids with Birch's commercial vice-president. He told the commercial vice-president, "We sell in a very competitive market, where higher costs cannot be passed on. How can we be expected to show a decent profit and return on investment if we have to buy our supplies at more than 10 percent over the going market?"

Knowing that Mr. Brunner had on occasion in the past few months been unable to operate the Thompson division at capacity, the commercial vice-president thought it odd that Mr. Brunner would add the full 20 percent overhead and profit charge to his out-of-pocket costs. When he asked Mr. Brunner about this over the telephone, his answer was the statement that appears at the beginning of the case. Mr. Brunner went on to say that having done the developmental work on the box, and having received no profit on that, he felt entitled to a good markup on the production of the box itself.

The vice-president explored further the cost structures of the various divisions. He remembered a comment the controller had made at a meeting the week before to the effect that costs that for one division were variable could be largely fixed for the company as a whole. He knew that in the absence of specific orders from top management, Mr. Kenton would accept the lowest bid, namely, that of the West Paper Company for $430. However, it would be possible for top management to order the acceptance of another bid if the situation warranted such action. And though the volume represented by the transactions in question was less than 5 percent of the volume of any of the divisions involved, other transactions could conceivably raise similar problems later.

a Does the system motivate Mr. Brunner in such a way that actions he takes in the best interest of the Thompson division are also in the best interest of the Birch Paper Company? If your answer is "no," give some specific instances related as closely as possible to the type of situation described in the case. Would the managers of *other* divisions be correctly motivated?

b What should the vice-president do?

20 The home office staff of The Nomram Group evaluates managers of the Nomram divisions by keeping track of the rate of return earned by each division on the average level of assets invested at the division. The home office staff considers 20 percent, which is the aftertax cost of capital of The Nomram Group, to be the minimum acceptable annual rate of return on average investment. When a division's rate of return drops below 20 percent, then division management can expect an unpleasant investigation by the home office and, perhaps, some firings. When the rate of return exceeds 20 percent and grows through time, then the

home office staff is invariably pleased and rewards division management. When the rate of return exceeds 20 percent but declines over time, then the home office staff sends out unpleasant memorandums and cuts the profit-sharing bonuses of the division managers.

In Division A, average assets employed during the year amount to $60,000. Division A has been earning 40 percent per year on its average investment for several years. Management of Division A is proud of its extraordinary record—earning a steady 40 percent per year.

In Division B, average assets employed during the year also amount to $60,000. Division B has been earning 25 percent per year on its average investment. In the preceding three years, the rate of return on investment was 20 percent, 22 percent, and 23 percent, respectively. Management of Division B is proud of its record of steadily boosting earnings.

New investment opportunities have arisen at both Division A and Division B. In both cases, the new investment opportunity will require a cash outlay today of $30,000 and will provide a rate of return on investment of 30 percent for each of the next eight years. The average amount of assets invested in the project will be $30,000 for each of the next eight years. Both new investment opportunities have positive net present values when the discount rate is 20 percent per year (the aftertax cost of capital of The Nomram Group).

When word of the new opportunities reached the home office staff, it was pleased at the prospects of the two new investments because both of them would yield a better return than the average for The Nomram Group.

Management of Division A computed its rate of return on investment both with and without the new investment project and decided not to undertake the project. Management of Division B computed its rate of return on investment both with and without the new investment project and decided to undertake it.

When word of the actions taken by the two divisions reached the home office staff, it was perplexed. Why did Division A's management turn down such a good opportunity? What was it about the behavior of the home office staff that induced Division A's management to reject the new project? Is management of Division B doing a better job than management of Division A? What might the home office do to give Division A an incentive to act in a way more consistent with the well-being of The Nomram Group?

PART FOUR
COST ACCUMULATION AND ALLOCATION

CHAPTER 12
FUNDAMENTALS OF PRODUCT COSTING

Accounting data are used for a variety of purposes. In Chapters Four through Seven we considered their use in short-term operating decisions and long-term capacity decisions. In Chapters Eight through Eleven we considered their use in planning and control. A third important use for accounting data is *product costing*. Information on the cost of manufacturing products is needed primarily for the periodic determination of net income. Cost information may also be used as a guide to pricing, as a basis for cost studies to improve efficiency of manufacturing processes, as helpful data in government contract and labor negotiations, and for other purposes. The use of accounting data for product costing is often referred to as *cost accounting*.

This chapter describes the fundamental concepts and procedures of product costing. Chapter Thirteen focuses on problems of allocating common costs to products and to periods. Chapter Fourteen links financial accounting and managerial accounting by showing how the results of some of management's decisions are reported in the external financial statements.

COST ACCUMULATION AND COST ALLOCATION

As we discussed above, the managerial accounting system must be designed to serve several purposes. For planning and control, costs are accumulated by responsibility centers. Costs are then allocated to products for the purpose of product costing. This relationship between cost accumulation and cost allocation for a typical manufacturing concern is shown in Figure 12.1. A separate purchasing department is responsible for the acquisition of raw materials. There are two manufacturing departments, assembling and finishing. The accounting system is designed so that, for control purposes, costs are initially accumulated for these three responsibility centers. The actual cost of raw materials purchased is accumulated in a separate account for the Purchasing Department. The costs of raw materials, direct labor, and manufacturing overhead

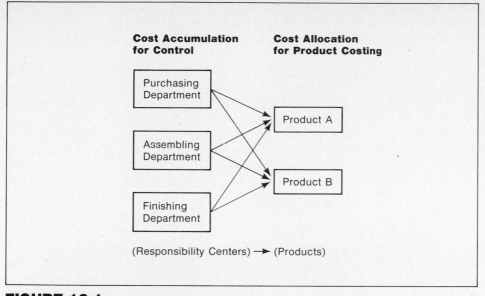

FIGURE 12.1
Relationship Between Cost
Accumulation and Cost Allocation

incurred in production are accumulated in separate accounts for the Assembling and Finishing Departments. The actual costs incurred are then compared with the standard or budgeted amounts and significant variances are investigated. At this point the accounting system has served its function of providing data for control.

For the accounting system to provide product cost information, the data must be reassembled, in a sense, along product lines rather than by responsibility centers. The reassembling process takes the form of allocating costs from responsibility centers to products. This allocation process is the primary focus of Chapters Twelve and Thirteen. It should be kept in mind that the costs allocated to products have initially been collected by responsibility centers for control purposes. Once the costs have been allocated to products, the cost data are generally of little value for control. Their primary uses at this stage are for the purposes of determining the cost of goods manufactured and cost of goods sold, and for valuing ending inventory.

COMPONENTS OF PRODUCT COST

Financial accounting makes an important distinction between a *product cost* and a *period expense*. Costs incurred in changing the physical form of goods being manufactured are product costs. These costs are included in the valuation of inventory and, until the goods are sold, are shown on the balance sheet as assets. When the inventory items are sold, these product costs become expenses of the period of sale. Period expenses, on the other hand, are treated as expenses in the same period in which the costs are incurred (for example, selling and administrative expenses). Thus, period expenses do not become part of the cost of products being manufactured. The question of interest is this: Which costs, or expenditures, are product costs, and which are period expenses?

Generally accepted accounting principles and the income tax law specify the types of costs that are to be treated as product costs. Because a primary purpose of computing product cost is periodic income determination, we center our attention on these provisions. (In Chapter Fourteen, however, we show that use of product cost information based on generally accepted accounting principles can lead management to make incorrect decisions.)

Product cost is composed of three elements: (1) direct material, (2) direct labor, and (3) manufacturing overhead. Direct material and direct labor costs can be closely associated with, or traced to, particular units of product.[1] Manufacturing overhead costs, on the other hand, are not usually traceable directly to specific units manufactured. Instead, these costs give a firm the capacity to produce. Examples of costs that fall into this last category are indirect *factory* rent, insurance, taxes, depreciation, and manufacturing materials and labor. In practice, it is often difficult to draw the line as to how indirect a cost can be to the manufacturing activity and still be considered part of manufacturing overhead (for example, costs of running an employee cafeteria or a maintenance department). Firms typically set their own guidelines and follow them consistently from period to period.

Considerable controversy has arisen as to whether or not fixed manufacturing overhead costs should be considered as product costs. Generally accepted accounting principles and the income tax regulations require that such costs be treated as product costs. This approach to product costing is referred to as *absorption costing,* because fixed manufacturing overhead costs get absorbed into, or included in, the cost of units produced. Opponents of this approach argue that only variable manufacturing costs (that is, direct material, direct labor, and variable manufacturing overhead) should be included in a product's cost. They say that fixed manufacturing overhead costs should be treated as period expenses. This latter approach to product costing is generally referred to as *direct costing,* although *variable costing* is a more appropriate title. We consider the absorption versus direct costing controversy in more depth in Chapter Fourteen. The discussion in this chapter and in Chapter Thirteen is based on absorption costing.

ALLOCATION OF MANUFACTURING COSTS TO PRODUCTS

Direct Material and Direct Labor

The allocation of direct material and direct labor costs from responsibility centers to specific products is a relatively easy task (an exception occurs in the case of joint products, to be discussed in Chapter Thirteen). Because these costs can usually be traced to particular products, there are few allocation problems.

---

[1]   The sum of direct material and direct labor costs is sometimes called *prime costs.*

Manufacturing Overhead

Manufacturing overhead costs are more difficult to allocate for two reasons. First, the costs cannot be traced directly to particular units manufactured. Thus, some basis for allocating these indirect costs must be developed. Second, the incurrence of manufacturing overhead costs, particularly fixed costs, tends to occur unevenly over the year. Property taxes and insurance premiums may be paid once each year. Depreciation may be recognized only quarterly. Production, however, often takes place at a relatively smooth rate during the year. If manufacturing overhead costs were allocated each month as incurred to products manufactured during the month, then the cost of products manufactured during different months of the year could vary significantly depending on whether they were manufactured in a month of high or of low overhead costs.

Example 1   Bowen Corporation produced 10,000 units during each of the months of January and February. The manufacturing overhead costs incurred were as follows:

Type of Overhead Costs	January	February
Variable	$20,000	$20,000
Fixed	50,000	10,000
Total	$70,000	$30,000

Allocation of overhead costs based on the actual level of production and actual amount of overhead costs incurred would result in an overhead cost of $7 per unit (= $70,000/10,000 units) produced in January and $3 per unit (= $30,000/10,000 units) produced in February. Because these units are physically identical, it is illogical to allocate substantially different amounts of overhead costs to them.

The procedure usually followed for allocating manufacturing overhead costs to products is as follows:

1. The amount of manufacturing overhead costs expected to be incurred during the next year is estimated. This information is obtained from cost estimation and budgeting studies done for planning and control purposes. The estimated overhead costs are expressed in the form of a fixed cost per year plus a variable cost per unit of activity (that is, $y = a + bx$).

2. The level of activity at which the firm expects to operate during the next year is estimated. For this purpose, activity may be measured in terms of units to be produced, labor hours to be worked, labor cost to be incurred, or some other activity base. The base generally used is x in the overhead budget equation, $y = a + bx$.

3. A fixed overhead rate and a variable overhead rate are determined. These are sometimes called *predetermined overhead rates*. The fixed overhead rate is:

$$\text{Fixed Overhead Rate} = \frac{\text{Budgeted Fixed Cost}}{\text{Estimated Level of Activity for the Year}}$$

The variable overhead rate per unit of activity is as given in the cost estimation equation (that is, the b in the equation $y = a + bx$).

4. Actual fixed and variable overhead costs are accumulated for the appropriate responsibility centers as they are incurred during the year.

5. As units are produced, they receive an allocation of fixed and variable overhead costs using the *predetermined* overhead rates. See step **3**.

6. If actual overhead costs coincide with the budget and the actual level of activity coincides with the estimated level, then the overhead costs allocated to units produced should be equal to the actual costs incurred. If estimates of overhead costs or the level of activity turn out to have been incorrect, then there will be variances that might need to be investigated.

Example 2   Bowen Corporation, using studies of past cost behavior, estimated its manufacturing overhead costs for 19X0 to be as follows: fixed $100,000; variable, $5 per unit. During 19X0, Bowen expects to produce 50,000 units. Its fixed overhead rate is therefore $2 per unit ($= \$100,000/50,000$ units) and its variable overhead rate is $5 per unit. Assume that actual costs and the actual level of activity coincided with the budget. The variable overhead costs incurred would be $250,000, and the amount allocated to the units produced would also be $250,000 ($= 50,000$ units $\times$ $5 per unit). The actual fixed cost incurred would be $100,000 and the amount allocated to units produced would be $100,000 ($= 50,000$ units $\times$ $2 per unit).

Example 3   Assume the same information as in Example 2 except that the actual variable overhead costs incurred were $260,000. There would be a $10,000 unfavorable variable overhead (budget) variance calculated as follows (see the discussion in Chapter Ten):

$$\begin{matrix} \text{Variable} \\ \text{Overhead} \\ \text{(Budget)} \\ \text{Variance} \end{matrix} = \begin{matrix} \text{Actual Variable} \\ \text{Overhead Costs} \\ \text{Incurred} \end{matrix} - \left(\begin{matrix} \text{Budgeted} \\ \text{Variable} \\ \text{Overhead Rate} \end{matrix} \times \begin{matrix} \text{Actual Number} \\ \text{of Units} \\ \text{Produced} \end{matrix} \right)$$

$$\begin{matrix} \$10,000 \\ \text{(Unfavorable)} \end{matrix} = \$260,000 - (\$5 \times 50,000)$$

If this variance were considered significant in amount, the reasons for its occurrence would be explored.

Example 4   Assume the same information as in Example 2 except that actual fixed costs were $80,000. There would be a $20,000 favorable fixed overhead (budget) variance calculated as follows:

$$\begin{matrix} \text{Fixed} \\ \text{Overhead} \\ \text{(Budget)} \\ \text{Variance} \end{matrix} = \begin{matrix} \text{Actual Fixed} \\ \text{Overhead Cost} \\ \text{Incurred} \end{matrix} - \begin{matrix} \text{Budgeted} \\ \text{Fixed} \\ \text{Cost} \end{matrix}$$

$$\begin{matrix} -\$20,000 \\ \text{(Favorable)} \end{matrix} = \$80,000 - \$100,000$$

If this variance was considered significant, it would likewise be investigated for control purposes.

Example 5 Assume that all costs coincided with the budgeted amounts as given in Example 2 but that actual production was only 40,000 units, not 50,000 units as expected. Variable overhead cost incurred as well as allocated to the units produced would be $200,000 (= 40,000 units × $5) and there would be no variable overhead (budget) variance. Fixed overhead costs incurred of $100,000 would exactly coincide with the budget and there would likewise be no fixed overhead (budget) variance. Overhead costs would be considered "in control" because actual costs coincided with the budget.

In Example 5, however, only $80,000 of fixed overhead costs would be allocated to the 40,000 units produced, $20,000 less than the amount budgeted for the year. What is the nature of this variance, called a *volume variance?* It is caused by an inability to forecast accurately the level of production for the period. If management had accurately forecasted that 40,000 units would be produced, it would have used that quantity in establishing a fixed overhead rate of $2.50 per unit (= $100,000/40,000 units). Thus, the volume variance is caused by estimation errors in most cases. The variance provides some information about management's forecasting abilities. Beyond this, the variance is virtually meaningless for control purposes. The control of fixed overhead costs focuses on the fixed overhead (budget) variance.

Some disposition must be made of overhead variances at the end of the period. The ideal approach under normal circumstances is to allocate the variances to the units in production during the period, whether or not they are sold. In this way the cost of the units will be stated at the actual costs incurred for material, labor, and overhead. Some firms simply treat the variances as an adjustment to cost of goods sold for the period. This procedure is an expedient and justified only if virtually all units produced are also sold during the period.

FLOW OF MANUFACTURING COSTS

Manufacturing costs are incurred to change the physical form of products. The specific form that units being manufactured take at any particular time depends on where they are in the production process. In some cases, raw materials will have been purchased but no labor services yet expended to change their physical form. In other cases work will have been started on units of product but the units will not have been completed as of the end of the period. In still other cases, units will have been finished and be sitting in the storeroom waiting to be sold. We stated earlier that product costs are considered assets until the time the units are sold. Manufacturing costs then flow with the units produced, starting with the time raw materials are taken from inventory and ending with the sale to customers.

Figure 12.2 presents a diagram of the flow of costs and relates this flow to the processes of cost accumulation and cost allocation discussed earlier in this chapter. The diagram uses figures in the shape of a large T, called T-accounts, to illustrate the flow of costs. There are T-accounts for Raw Materials Inventory, Work-in-Process Inven-

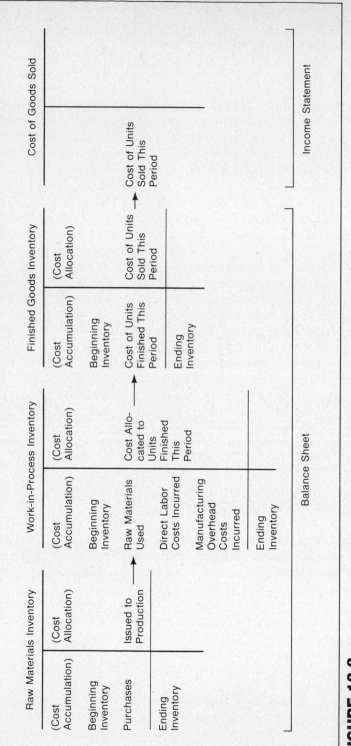

FIGURE 12.2
Flow of Manufacturing Costs

tory, Finished Goods Inventory, and Cost of Goods Sold. The three inventory T-accounts might be viewed as records of accountability for three different responsibility centers: the raw materials storeroom, the factory, and the finished goods storeroom. On the left sides of the inventory T-accounts are shown the costs that have been accumulated for each responsibility center for control purposes. On the right side of the T-accounts are shown the costs allocated to the "output" of each of the responsibility centers (raw materials used, units of product manufactured, units of product sold). Product costs will remain in one of these inventory accounts, depending on their degree of completion, until the units are sold. At this time the costs leave the asset category on the balance sheet and become expenses on the income statement.

The Raw Materials Inventory Account is a record of accountability for the raw materials storeroom. The cost of units on hand at the beginning of the period and the cost of units purchased are shown as cost accumulations. As raw materials are transferred from the storeroom to the factory, part of the accumulated cost of raw materials must be allocated to the units transferred. If raw materials transferred are physically identical to those still on hand, it will be difficult to determine the actual cost of the units transferred. A cost flow assumption will therefore be required. The most common assumptions are first-in, first-out (FIFO), last-in, first-out (LIFO), and weighted average. These cost flow assumptions are discussed in financial accounting texts.

The Work-in-Process Inventory account is a record of accountability for the factory. The costs incurred in prior periods and allocated to units in this period's beginning inventory are shown as the first item under cost accumulation. To this amount is added the manufacturing costs incurred during the current period (direct materials, direct labor, and manufacturing overhead). As units of product are completed and transferred to the finished goods storeroom, part of the accumulated manufacturing costs must be allocated to the units produced. The amount allocated will be equal to the direct materials and direct labor used plus an amount of manufacturing overhead based on a predetermined overhead rate.

The Finished Goods Inventory account is a record of accountability for the finished goods storeroom. Under "cost accumulation" is shown the costs of units in beginning inventory plus the cost of units transferred this period from the factory. A portion of these accumulated costs must be allocated to units sold. Most firms follow a FIFO, LIFO, or weighted average cost flow assumption for making this allocation.

ILLUSTRATION OF PRODUCT COSTING

There are two general types of product cost accounting systems: *job order* systems and *process* systems. Job order systems are useful for firms whose manufacturing operations are designed for specific jobs or orders, such as in a print shop, in custom furniture manufacture, and in construction. In job order systems, actual material and labor costs are accumulated for each specific batch, project, or order. Manufacturing overhead is assigned to each job using a predetermined overhead rate. Process systems are used when the product being manufactured is relatively uniform and where it flows through a series of standardized processes. Process costing is used in industries such as oil refining, chemical production, and automobile manufacture. In process systems,

EXHIBIT 12.1
Custom Manufacturing Corporation
Accounting for Manufacturing Costs in a Job Order System

Raw Materials Inventory

(1) Beginning Inventory	50,000	
(2) Purchases	100,000	110,000
(8) Ending Inventory	40,000	

Manufacturing Overhead Control

(5) Overhead Costs Incurred	140,000	120,000

Work-in-Process Inventory
Job 101

(1) Beginning Inventory	30,000	
(3) Cost of Raw Materials Used	40,000	205,000
(4) Direct Labor Cost Incurred	90,000	
(5) Manufacturing Overhead Applied	45,000	
Ending Inventory	0	

Work-in-Process Inventory
Job 102

(1) Beginning Inventory	0	
(3) Cost of Raw Materials Used	70,000	
(4) Direct Labor Cost Incurred	150,000	
(5) Manufacturing Overhead Applied	75,000	
(4) Ending Inventory	295,000	

Finished Goods Inventory

(1) Beginning Inventory	0	
(6) Cost of Finished Job	205,000	205,000
Ending Inventory	0	

Cost of Goods Sold

(7) Cost of Job Sold	205,000

costs are accumulated during the period by production processes and then assigned at the end of the period to units produced during the period. In this section we present illustrations of job order and process cost accounting systems. These illustrations are based on an actual cost approach. Both systems could be adapted for standard costing as discussed in Chapter Ten. The techniques for this adaptation are discussed in advanced cost accounting texts.

Job Order System

The illustration of a job order system is based on the transactions of Custom Manufacturing Corporation for January 19X0. This company manufactures custom-order heavy equipment. Costs are accumulated in separate accounts for each job or order. Exhibit 12.1 presents the T-accounts for Raw Materials Inventory, Work-in-Process Inventory, Finished Goods Inventory, and Cost of Goods Sold. (The Manufacturing Overhead Control account is discussed below.) Custom Manufacturing Corporation worked on two jobs during January, Job 101 and Job 102. Note that there is a separate Work-in-Process Inventory account for each job. The numbers in parentheses in Exhibit 12.1 correspond to the transactions or events described below.

(1) At the beginning of January 1, 19X0, raw materials costing $50,000 were in the raw materials storeroom. There was one job in the factory, Job 101, that was partially complete. Manufacturing costs accumulated on Job 101 as of the beginning of January were $30,000. Another job, Job 102, was started during the month.

(2) Raw materials costing $100,000 were purchased during January. These purchases are shown on the left side of the Raw Materials Inventory account.

(3) Raw materials costing $110,000 were issued to the factory. The raw materials cost flows from the Raw Materials Inventory account to a Work-in-Process Inventory account. This flow represents an allocation of cost to the raw materials transferred from the viewpoint of the raw materials storeroom and an accumulation of cost from the viewpoint of the factory. A separate Work-in-Process Inventory account is maintained for each job. Records show that raw materials costing $40,000 were used on Job 101 and raw materials costing $70,000 were used on Job 102.

(4) Direct labor costs incurred in the factory during January totaled $240,000, of which $90,000 was attributable to Job 101 and $150,000 was attributable to Job 102.

(5) At the beginning of January, manufacturing overhead costs were estimated for the year. Fixed costs were estimated to be $750,000. Variable overhead costs were estimated to vary with direct labor costs at the rate of $.25 per dollar of direct labor cost. Custom Manufacturing Corporation expected to incur $3,000,000 of direct labor cost for the year. Thus, the total overhead cost expected for the year was $1,500,000 [= $750,000 + (.25 × $3,000,000)]. The predetermined rate for applying manufacturing overhead costs to jobs is 50 percent of direct labor costs (= $1,500,000/$3,000,000). Actual manufacturing overhead costs are accumulated in a separate account. We have called this account Manufacturing Overhead Control. Actual manufacturing overhead costs incurred are entered on the left side of this account. Overhead applied, or allocated, to units produced is entered on the right side of this account. Because overhead costs are typically incurred unevenly during the year whereas production tends to take place relatively evenly, there is likely to be a difference between overhead cost incurred

EXHIBIT 12.2
Frymire Processing Corporation
Accounting for Manufacturing Costs in a Process System

Raw Materials Inventory

(1) Beginning Inventory 200,000	
(2) Purchases 600,000	550,000
(8) Ending Inventory 250,000	

Work-in-Process Inventory

(1) Beginning Inventory 140,600	
(3) Cost of Raw Materials Used 550,000	
(4) Direct Labor Costs Incurred 410,000	1,130,000
(5) Manufacturing Overhead Costs Applied 205,000	
(6) Ending Inventory 175,600	

Finished Goods Inventory

(1) Beginning Inventory 300,000	
(6) Cost of Units Completed 1,130,000	1,030,000
(8) Ending Inventory 400,000	

Cost of Goods Sold

(7) Cost of Units Sold 1,030,000	

Manufacturing Overhead Control

(5) Overhead Costs Incurred 180,000	205,000

CALCULATION OF EQUIVALENT UNITS AND ALLOCATION OF MANUFACTURING COSTS

	Equivalent Units for:					Costs Allocated to:	
	Units Completed (1)	Units Incomplete (2)	Total Equivalent Units (3)	Total Costs (4)	Cost per Equivalent Unit (5)	Units Completed (6)d	Units Incomplete (7)e
Direct Materials	100,000	20,000	120,000	$ 600,000a	$ 5.00	$ 500,000	$100,000
Direct Labor	100,000	12,000	112,000	470,400b	4.20	420,000	50,400
Manufacturing Overhead . . .	100,000	12,000	112,000	235,200c	2.10	210,000	25,200
Total				$1,305,600	$11.30	$1,130,000	$175,600

a Beginning inventory costs + costs incurred = $50,000 + $550,000; see text.
b $60,400 + $410,000; see text.
c $30,200 + $205,000; see text.
d Column (1) × Column (5).
e Column (2) × Column (5).

and overhead cost applied as of any specific time during the year. By the end of the year, the total amounts on the two sides of the account should be approximately the same if the estimates were roughly correct. If there is a difference, it is then allocated, either subtracted or added as appropriate, to the cost of units in production during the period. During January, overhead costs totaling $140,000 were incurred. Overhead costs were allocated to Job 101 and Job 102 at the rate of 50 percent of direct labor cost on each job. These amounts are shown on the right side of the Manufacturing Overhead Control account and on the left side of the Work-in-Process Inventory accounts.

(6) During January, Job 101 was completed and transferred to the finished goods storeroom. The accumulated costs on Job 101 were $205,000. This amount flows, or is transferred, from the Work-in-Process Inventory to the Finished Goods Inventory account.

(7) Job 101 is shipped to the customer. The cost of Job 101 is transferred from Finished Goods Inventory to Cost of Goods Sold.

(8) The Raw Materials Inventory account shows that raw materials costing $40,000 should be in the raw materials storeroom at the end of January. A physical count might be taken to ensure that inventory of this amount is actually on hand.

(9) Job 102 is incomplete as of the end of January. Costs accumulated on this job during the month total $295,000. This amount becomes the beginning inventory for Work-in-Process Inventory, Job 102, for February.

The distinctive feature of a job order system is that costs are accumulated by job. The allocation or assignment of these costs to "output" is relatively simple since the product is a well-defined specific customer's order.

Process System

A process cost system is used when many units of a uniform product are processed continually during the period. That is, at any time there are units at all stages of completion. The illustration that follows is for Frymire Processing Corporation for January 19X0. Frymire's only product passes through a single manufacturing process. Direct labor and manufacturing overhead costs are incurred uniformly over the production process. Exhibit 12.2 presents the T-accounts for Frymire Processing Corporation for January 19X0. Note that there is just one Work-in-Process Inventory T-account for the manufacturing process. The numbers in parentheses correspond to the transactions and events described below.

(1) At the beginning of January, units in inventory had accumulated costs as follows: Raw Materials Inventory, $200,000; Work-in-Process Inventory, $140,600 (composed of $50,000 raw materials, $60,400 direct labor, and $30,200 manufacturing overhead); Finished Goods Inventory, $300,000.

(2) Raw materials purchased during January totaled $600,000.

(3) Raw materials costing $550,000 were issued to the factory by the raw materials storeroom.

(4) Direct labor costs incurred during January totaled $410,000.

(5) Budgeted manufacturing overhead costs for 19X0 were as follows: fixed, $400,000; variable, 40 percent of direct labor costs. Direct labor costs were estimated to be $4,000,000 for the year. Thus, the total overhead cost expected to be incurred during 19X0 was $2,000,000 [= $400,000 + (.40 × $4,000,000)]. The predetermined rate for applying overhead costs to production each month is thus 50 percent of direct labor cost (= $2,000,000/$4,000,000). Actual manufacturing overhead costs are accumulated in a separate Manufacturing Overhead Control account and amounted to $180,000 during January. At the end of each quarter, actual costs are compared with budgeted amounts and significant variances investigated. At the end of the year, the actual overhead costs incurred are compared to the amounts assigned month by month to production. Any differences are reassigned for product costing purposes to units completed and to units in ending inventory on December 31, 19X0. Unusually large excesses of actual over budgeted costs are typically treated as expenses of the period rather than as product costs. During January, direct labor costs were $410,000. Manufacturing overhead cost assigned to January's production is therefore $205,000.

(6) We now come to the aspect of process costing systems that is unique: the assignment or allocation of costs to units completed and to units in ending inventory. During January, 100,000 units were completed and transferred to the finished goods storeroom. At the end of January, 20,000 units were still in the factory at various stages of completion. It was determined that these unfinished units were, on average, 60 percent complete. It would be inappropriate to take the total manufacturing costs (including the cost of beginning inventory) incurred of $1,305,600 (= $140,600 + $550,000 + $410,000 + $205,000) and allocate it 10/12 (= 100,000 units/120,000 units) to units completed and 2/12 (= 20,000 units/120,000 units) to units in ending inventory.

A unit that is incomplete has not received the full production effort that a unit completed has received. The allocation of costs is made by expressing units in ending inventory in terms of equivalent whole or completed units. For example, the units in ending inventory are determined to be 60 percent complete, on average, as of the end of January. The 20,000 partially completed units in ending inventory have therefore received direct labor and overhead effort equal to that of 12,000 (= 60 percent × 20,000) complete units. The total equivalent units for direct labor and manufacturing overhead is therefore 112,000 units (= 100,000 complete + 12,000 partially completed). The direct labor and overhead costs are allocated 100/112 to the units completed and 12/112 to the units in ending inventory.

The calculation of equivalent units for direct material is somewhat different. Direct materials are added at the beginning of processing rather than continuously, as with labor and overhead. Therefore, the 20,000 units in ending inventory have received all of the direct material they will receive. That is, the 20,000 partially completed units have received the same amount of raw materials as 20,000 completed units. With respect to raw materials, there are 120,000 equivalent whole units (= 100,000 units + 20,000 units). The raw materials costs therefore are allocated 100/120 to units completed and 20/120 to units in ending inventory.

The lower panel of Exhibit 12.2 shows the calculation of equivalent units for each of the three elements of manufacturing cost. The total cost in column (4) is the cost in beginning inventory plus the cost incurred during the period. The process costing procedure illustrated here follows a weighted average cost flow assumption. That is, costs from beginning inventory are added to costs incurred during the current period and a weighted average cost per equivalent unit is determined for each element of cost. (An FIFO or LIFO cost flow assumption could also be used. These methods are discussed in cost accounting texts.) For example, the total raw materials inventory cost of $600,000 is composed of $50,000 from beginning inventory (see item **(1)** above) and $550,000 of costs incurred during January. The total cost is expressed in terms of cost per equivalent unit in column (5) by dividing the total cost in column (4) by the equivalent units in column (3). The total costs are then assigned to units completed in column (6) and units in ending inventory in column (7). The basis for the cost allocations in columns (6) and (7) is the equivalent units in columns (1) and (2) and the cost per equivalent unit in column (5).

(7) The cost of units sold during January is determined to be $1,030,000. (The calculation of this amount could follow an FIFO, LIFO, or weighted average cost flow assumption. The calculations are omitted to simplify the illustration.)

(8) Records show that an ending inventory of raw materials costing $250,000 and an ending inventory of finished goods costing $400,000 should be on hand at the end of January.

The distinctive feature of process costing systems is that costs are accumulated by production processes. Because there are a relatively large number of identical units being produced, all in various stages of completion, it is necessary to assign or allocate costs according to equivalent whole units rather than simply to the total number of units being processed.

SUMMARY

The most important product costing concepts discussed in this chapter are summarized below.

1. Manufacturing costs are accumulated by responsibility centers for control purposes. These costs are then allocated to units produced for product costing purposes.

2. Manufacturing, or product, cost includes three elements: direct material, direct labor, and manufacturing overhead. Firms are required to follow absorption costing for purposes of reporting to stockholders and tax authorities. Fixed manufacturing overhead costs are therefore considered to be product costs rather than period expenses.

3. The allocation of direct material and direct labor costs to products is relatively simple because these costs can be traced to particular units manufactured.

4. The allocation of manufacturing overhead costs to products is more difficult because **(a)** these costs are only indirectly associated with particular units produced, and **(b)** these costs tend to be incurred at a nonuniform rate throughout the year. Allocation of overhead cost during a period is accomplished by using a predetermined overhead rate. This rate is based on the budgeted fixed and variable overhead costs for the period and the estimated level of activity (for example, units produced, direct labor hours, direct labor cost). Any difference between the total overhead costs actually incurred during a year and the total amounts assigned to units in production is reassigned at the end of the year to units in production during the year.

5. Manufacturing costs flow through three principal responsibility centers before products are sold to customers: the raw materials storeroom, the factory, and the finished goods storeroom. Three inventory accounts are used to trace the flow of costs through these responsibility centers: Raw Materials Inventory, Work-in-Process Inventory, and Finished Goods Inventory.

6. Job order accounting systems are used when manufacturing operations are designed for specific jobs or customer orders. The distinctive feature of job order systems is that manufacturing costs are accumulated by jobs.

7. Process accounting systems are used when manufacturing operations are designed for production of standardized products that pass through several production processes. The distinctive feature of process systems is the need to express production in terms of equivalent whole units so that costs can be allocated to units finished and to units in ending inventory.

QUESTIONS AND PROBLEMS

1 Review the meaning of the following concepts or terms discussed in this chapter.
   a Cost accumulation versus cost allocation.
   b Product cost versus period expense.
   c Absorption costing.
   d Direct or variable costing.
   e Predetermined overhead rate.
   f Fixed overhead costs incurred.
   g Fixed overhead costs applied.
   h Under- or overapplied overhead.
   i Raw materials inventory.
   j Work-in-process inventory.
   k Finished goods inventory.
   l Manufacturing overhead control.
   m Job order system.
   n Process costing system.
   o Equivalent units.
   p Cost per equivalent unit.

2 Distinguish between absorption costing and direct costing.

3 "It would be a whole lot easier to allocate the actual overhead costs incurred each month to the actual units produced each month than to fool with predetermined overhead rates." Comment.

4 A firm incurred manufacturing overhead costs of $500,000 for the year. Overhead applied to units produced during the year totaled $600,000. What are some of the reasons for this difference?

5 Why is it inaccurate to allocate under- or overapplied overhead for the year to cost of goods sold?

6 What are the essential differences between the process method and the job order method of cost accounting?

7 Manufacturing overhead is sometimes assigned to job orders in proportion to material cost. Do you think this is likely to be a satisfactory procedure? Explain.

8 Assuming that other factors work out as planned, what is the effect on the absorption of overhead of:
   a An excess of actual direct labor cost over estimated direct labor cost, when overhead is allocated as a percentage of direct labor cost.
   b A decrease in the pace of operations so that estimated machine hours exceed actual machine hours, when a machine hour rate of allocating overhead is used.
   c An excess of the actual amount of overhead incurred over the estimated overhead for the period.

9 The Johnson Products Company uses a job order cost accounting system. For 19X0, total overhead is estimated to be $80,000 and the number of direct labor hours is estimated to be 20,000.
   a Based on the above information, what overhead rate might be used?
   b Job 247 is a special order for 100 special-design tables. The Work-in-Process Inventory account for this job shows raw material costs of $4,600 and direct labor costs of $7,600. It is determined that 1,200 direct labor hours have been charged to the job. What is the total cost of Job 247? What is the unit cost of each table on that job?

10 The Facon Manufacturing Company distributes its factory overhead over its job orders as a percentage of direct labor cost. The rate set for the third quarter of the year was 150 percent, based on an estimated total overhead of $75,000 and an estimated total direct labor cost of $50,000.
   Indicate the amount of overabsorbed or underabsorbed overhead for the quarter under each of the following assumptions:
   a Actual overhead, $70,000; actual direct labor, $48,000.
   b Actual overhead, $79,000; actual direct labor, $52,000.
   c Actual overhead, $80,000; actual direct labor, $50,000.
   d Actual overhead, $84,000; actual direct labor, $56,000.
   e Actual overhead, $68,000; actual direct labor, $44,000.
   f Actual overhead, $76,000; actual direct labor, $49,000.

11 The Speed Way Boat Company uses a job order cost accounting system. Factory overhead is allocated to jobs on a direct labor hours basis at the rate of $3 per hour.
   a Job 745 required $8,400 of materials and 1,000 hours of direct labor at an average rate of $4 per hour. What was the total cost shown for Job 745?
   b Job 305 required $6,300 of materials and 3,000 hours of direct labor at an average rate of $4 per hour. Job 305 sold for $30,000. What was the "gross margin" on this sale?
   c During the entire year, total raw material used was $220,000; 70,000 direct labor hours were worked at an average rate of $5 per hour; and total overhead costs incurred were $230,000. (Jobs 745 and 305 are included in these figures.) What is the amount of under- or overapplied overhead for the year?

12 Trapp Electronics Corporation estimated its overhead costs for 19X0 to be as follows: fixed, $400,000; variable, $6 per unit. Trapp expected to produce 100,000 units during the year.
   a Determine the rate to be used to apply overhead costs to products.
   b During 19X0, Trapp incurred overhead costs of $950,000 and produced 90,000 units. Determine the amount of overhead costs applied to units produced.

   c Refer to part **b.** Determine the amount of under- or overapplied overhead for the year.

   d Disaggregate the amount in **c** into a budget variance and a volume variance.

13 Wyman Company uses a predetermined rate for applying overhead costs to production. The rates for 19X0 were as follows: variable, $2 per unit; fixed, $1 per unit. Actual overhead costs incurred were as follows: variable, $95,000; fixed, $45,000. Wyman expected to produce 45,000 units during the year but produced only 40,000 units.

   a What was the amount of budgeted fixed costs for the year?

   b What is the amount of under- or overapplied overhead for the year?

   c Disaggregate the amount in **b** into a budget variance and a volume variance.

14 Hoffman Corporation began business on January 1, 19X0. It expected to incur manufacturing overhead costs during 19X0 as follows: fixed, $300,000; variable, $4 per unit. Hoffman planned to produce 100,000 units during the year. Only 90,000 (in equivalent completed units) were actually produced at the following total manufacturing costs:

	Number of Units	Total Manufacturing Costs
Units Finished and Sold	70,000	$1,050,000
Units Finished But Not Sold	15,000	225,000
Units Incomplete (equivalent whole units)	5,000	45,000
	90,000	$1,320,000

Hoffman incurred overhead costs of $657,000 during the year.

   a Determine the amount of under- or overapplied overhead for the year.

   b Determine the amount of total manufacturing costs allocated to units sold, units finished but not sold, and units incomplete assuming under- or overapplied overhead is allocated to cost of goods sold.

   c Repeat step **b** assuming under- or overapplied overhead is allocated to units in proportion to production during the period.

15 Set up T-accounts for Raw Materials Inventory, Work-in-Process Inventory, Finished Goods Inventory, Cost of Goods Sold, and Manufacturing Overhead Control. Enter the following items in the T-accounts as appropriate for the month of June:

   (1) Beginning inventory accounts were as follows: Raw Materials Inventory, $40,000; Work-in-Process Inventory, $150,000; Finished Goods Inventory, $120,000.

   (2) Raw materials purchased during June were $300,000.

   (3) Raw materials used during June totaled $270,000.

   (4) Direct labor costs incurred during the month were $400,000.

   (5) Manufacturing overhead costs incurred during June totaled $130,000.

   (6) Manufacturing overhead costs applied to units produced totaled $120,000.

   (7) The cost of units completed during June was $910,000.

   (8) The cost of goods sold during June was $850,000.

16 Haskell Company applies overhead costs to products at a rate of 40 percent of direct labor cost. The company uses a separate overhead control account. The following data relate to the manufacturing activities of Haskell Company during March:

	March 1	March 31
Raw Materials Inventory	$32,400	$32,900
Work-in-Process Inventory	55,800	43,200
Finished Goods Inventory	44,200	46,300

Factory costs incurred during the month were as follows:

Raw Materials Purchased	$ 65,700
Direct Labor Cost Incurred	125,000
Factory Heat, Light, and Power	5,000
Factory Rent	10,000
Depreciation on Factory Equipment	25,000

a Determine the cost of raw materials used during March.
b Determine the cost of the units completed during March and transferred to the finished goods storeroom.
c Determine the cost of goods sold during March.

17 Cornell Company applies overhead to products at a rate of 10 percent of direct labor cost. It maintains a separate manufacturing overhead control account during the year. The following data relate to the manufacturing activities of Cornell Company during June:

	June 1	June 30
Raw Materials Inventory	$22,600	$18,900
Work-in-Process Inventory	68,600	76,500
Finished Goods Inventory	54,300	51,900

Factory costs incurred during the month were as follows:

Raw Materials Purchased	$344,000
Labor Services Received	280,300
Factory Heat, Light, and Power	3,300
Factory Insurance	1,800
Depreciation on Factory Equipment	20,800
Factory Rent	2,400

a Determine the cost of raw materials used during June.
b Determine the cost of units completed during June and transferred to the finished goods storeroom.
c Determine the cost of goods sold during June.
d Determine the amount of under- or overapplied overhead for the month of June.

18 The Matron Products Company uses the direct labor hours basis of allocating overhead to jobs. On January 1 it was estimated that total overhead for the coming year would be $400,000 and that 100,000 direct labor hours would be worked.

The actual overhead and direct labor hours for the first five months of the year were as follows:

	Actual Overhead	Actual Direct Labor Hours
January	$ 51,000	12,500
February	40,000	9,600
March	61,000	15,500
April	58,500	14,200
May	50,000	13,000
	$260,500	64,800 hrs.

Determine the amount of overabsorbed or underabsorbed overhead for each month.

19 The Robinson Machine Company uses a job order cost accounting system. Manufacturing overhead is applied to jobs on a direct labor cost basis at a rate of 50 percent of direct labor cost. A Manufacturing Overhead Control account is used to accumulate actual overhead costs.

At August 1, the balance in the Work-in-Process Inventory account was $34,524. The following jobs were in process at August 1:

Job No.	Materials	Direct Labor	Overhead	Total
478	$ 5,100	$ 9,620	$4,810	$19,530
479	3,470	3,960	1,980	9,410
480	4,120	976	488	5,584
Total	$12,690	$14,556	$7,278	$34,524

Selected transactions for the month of August are as follows:

(1) Materials issued: Job 480, $449; Job 481, $3,570; Job 482, $2,100; general factory use, $390; total, $6,509.
(2) Labor costs are assigned as follows: Job 478, $334; Job 479; $2,650; Job 480, $7,800; Job 481, $5,890; Job 482, $1,726; general factory, $853; total, $19,253.
(3) The employer's share of payroll taxes is 8 percent of wages earned. All factory payroll taxes are treated as manufacturing overhead costs.
(4) Depreciation of factory equipment for the month is $3,200.
(5) Building depreciation for the month is $1,200.
(6) Other manufacturing costs for the month include: power, $730; repairs, $520; utility services, $450; fire insurance, $183; property taxes, $317.
(7) Manufacturing overhead for the month is applied to jobs.
(8) Jobs 478 and 479 are completed and transferred to the finished goods warehouse for delivery in September.

Set up T-accounts for Raw Materials Inventory, Work-in-Process Inventory, Finished Goods Inventory, and Manufacturing Overhead Control. The T-account for Work-in-Process Inventory should be set up so as to accumulate the costs of each of the jobs separately. Enter the August 1 amounts plus each of the eight transactions in the T-accounts.

20 Records of the McKinley Machine Company on May 31, before recording the application of factory overhead to products and before recording the transfer of completed units to Finished Goods Inventory, are as follows:

Work-in-Process Inventory $16,842
Factory Overhead Control   3,100

Job order cost records show the following data:

	Job 576	Job 577	Job 578	Job 579	Job 580
Work in Process, May 1					
Material	$ 953	$ 824			
Direct Labor	1,250	1,507			
Factory Overhead	1,075	945			
Direct Costs Incurred in May					
Material	$ 170	$ 520	$1,240	$ 950	$1,312
Direct Labor	1,260	842	2,500	1,302	192

Manufacturing overhead is applied at the rate of 50 percent of direct labor cost. Jobs 576, 577, and 578 were completed during May. Jobs 579 and 580 are still in process at the end of May.

a Determine the total costs allocated to Job 576, to Job 577, and to Job 578.

b Determine the total costs allocated to Job 579 and to Job 580.

21 In the Assembling Department, material A is added at the beginning of processing, material B is added when units reach the 50 percent stage of completion, and direct labor and manufacturing overhead costs are incurred evenly throughout processing. There were no units in Work-in-Process Inventory at the beginning of May. During May, 80,000 units were started and completed. Another 20,000 units were started and are 30 percent complete as of the end of May. Determine the equivalent whole units of work performed during May for material A, material B, direct labor, and manufacturing overhead.

22 Refer to the data in Problem **21.** The Finishing Department receives semifinished products from the Assembling Department. Material C is added at the beginning of processing and material D is added at the end of processing. Direct labor and manufacturing overhead costs are incurred evenly throughout processing. During May, 80,000 units are received from the Assembly Department. Fifty thousand units are completed and transferred to the finished goods storeroom. The remaining 30,000 units are 60 percent complete as of the end of May. Determine the equivalent whole units for transferred in costs, material C, material D, direct labor, and manufacturing overhead.

23 The Homes Metals Company uses a process cost accounting system. Process E is the fifth in their series of seven processes. Material is added proportionately throughout processing. The following data relate to the operations of that process during March:

Work in Process, March 1, none.
Costs Incurred during the Month:
Direct Materials $139,000
Direct Labor   157,000
Factory Overhead Applied   82,000
Units Transferred from Process D, 75,000 at a Cost of $12 per Unit.
Work in Process, March 31, 20,000 Units, 40 Percent Completed.

a Determine the equivalent whole units for transferred in costs, direct material, direct labor, and factory overhead.

b Determine the cost per equivalent unit for each of the costs in **a**.

c Determine the amount of costs allocated to units completed in process E during March and the costs allocated to units incomplete in process E at the end of March.

24 The General Manufacturing Company uses a process cost accounting system. Process C is the third in their series of five processes. The following data relate to the operations of that process during August. There were no goods in process at August 1.

Costs Incurred During August:
Direct Materials. $67,500
Direct Labor 91,000
Manufacturing Overhead Applied 41,500
Units transferred from process B: 65,000, at a cost of $9 per unit. Work in process at August 31: 25,000 units, which are on the average 40 percent complete as to the work of process C. Materials, labor, and overhead are added continuously throughout the process.

a Determine the equivalent whole units for transferred costs, direct material, direct labor, and manufacturing overhead.

b Determine the cost per equivalent unit for each of the costs in **a**.

c Determine the amount of costs allocated to units completed in process C during August and the costs allocated to units incomplete as of the end of August.

25 Wilson Manufacturing Corporation maintains a process cost accounting system. Materials are added at the start of processing, and direct labor and manufacturing overhead costs are incurred evenly over processing. On January 1, there were 5,000 units in process with the following accumulated costs:

Direct Material $50,000
Direct Labor 40,000
Manufacturing Overhead 10,000

During January, 45,000 units were started in process. The following costs were incurred during January:

Direct Material $450,000
Direct Labor 420,000
Manufacturing Overhead 105,000

During January, 40,000 units were completed. The units in ending inventory are, on average, 60 percent complete.

a Prepare an analysis showing the calculation of equivalent whole units for direct material, direct labor, and manufacturing overhead.

b Determine the amount of costs allocated to units completed during January and to units incomplete as of January 31.

26 Denver Products Company maintains a process cost accounting system. Material A is added at the start of processing, and material B is added at the end of processing. Direct labor and manufacturing overhead costs are incurred evenly during processing. On September 1, there were 20,000 units in process with the following accumulated costs:

Material A	$78,000
Material B	0
Direct Labor	40,000
Manufacturing Overhead	30,000

During September, 110,000 units were started in process. The following costs were incurred during September:

Material A	$442,000
Material B	180,000
Direct Labor	490,000
Manufacturing Overhead	367,500

During September, 90,000 units were completed. The units in ending inventory were, on average, 40 percent complete.

a Prepare an analysis showing the calculation of equivalent whole units for material A, material B, direct labor, and manufacturing overhead.

b Determine the amount of cost allocated to units completed during September and to units incomplete as of September 30.

CHAPTER 13
COMMON COST ALLOCATION: THE ACHILLES HEEL OF ACCOUNTANTS

Critics of accounting have suggested that cost allocations made in preparing accounting reports cause more misleading and incorrect interpretations than any other single factor. Many of these same critics go on to suggest that if cost allocations were reduced or eliminated, the need for accountants' services would be substantially lessened. Why are cost allocations made? How can they cause misleading or incorrect interpretations? Are there some cost allocation methods that are better than others? We attempt to answer these questions in this chapter.

THE NATURE OF COMMON COSTS

A distinction is made in accounting between a *direct cost* and a *common cost*. A direct cost is one that can be specifically identified with, or traced to, a particular product, department, or process. For example, direct materials and direct labor costs are direct costs with respect to products manufactured. A departmental manager's salary is a direct cost with respect to the department. A common cost, in contrast, results from the joint use of a facility (for example, plant or machines) or a service (for example, fire insurance) by several products, departments, or processes. There is no way to disaggregate this common, or shared, cost and to attribute its parts directly to particular products, departments, or processes. For some reporting purposes, however, common costs must be disaggregated. It is necessary in these cases to develop some reasonably logical, although imperfect, basis for allocating common costs.

Common costs pervade accounting to a much greater extent than one might initially suppose. In financial accounting, most questions of allocating costs to accounting periods involve common costs. That is, many costs are common, or joint, to more than one reporting period. Several examples follow:

1 The cost of a depreciable asset must be allocated through depreciation to the years of the asset's useful life.
2 The cost of a fire insurance policy providing three years of coverage must be allocated to the periods of benefit.
3 The discount or premium of a bond (the difference between the par value and proceeds of issue) must be allocated to the periods that the bond is outstanding.
4 The revenues and expenses from long-term contracts must be allocated (under the percentage-of-completion method) to the periods during which the income is generated.
5 Costs incurred in making a "basket purchase" (for example, land, building, equipment, and inventory) must be allocated to the individual assets when an entire company is purchased.
6 When quarterly earnings reports are prepared, annual fixed selling and administrative expenses must be allocated to each quarter.

In addition to the above, there are many costs that are common to products manufactured. In order to develop product cost information, these common costs must be allocated. Examples include the following:

1 Manufacturing overhead costs in a factory or department must be allocated to each of the products produced.
2 The cost of operating service departments (for example, employee cafeteria, maintenance department) must be allocated to individual manufacturing departments and then to products.
3 The cost incurred in a manufacturing process that jointly produces several different products simultaneously (for example, beef and hides from a head of cattle) must be allocated to each of the products.

Other examples of common costs include central corporate expenses common to each of the corporate divisions (see the discussion in Chapter Eleven) and costs incurred in paying property taxes (for example, on land, building, and inventory) that must be allocated to the individual assets under certain circumstances.

The purpose of listing these examples is to emphasize the extent to which common cost allocations pervade accounting reports, both internal and external. In order to understand accounting reports and make appropriate interpretations, one must be familiar with the alternative allocation methods used and their effects on the resulting reports.

PURPOSE OF COMMON COST ALLOCATIONS

We have focused on three principal uses of accounting information by management: (1) decision making, (2) planning and control, and (3) product costing. Common cost allocations are typically made for product costing. But using data in which common cost allocations have been made can lead to incorrect decisions, inaccurate plans, and misinterpretations of performance.

Example 1 Technotronics Corporation manufactures a wide line of electronic equipment. One product, a signal detection device, has a unit production cost (raw material, labor, and manufacturing overhead) of $40. Technotronics has been asked to accept a special order for 500 signal detection devices for $35 each. The devices can be produced with capacity that is currently not being used. Acceptance of the order will not affect the regular market for this product. The decision to accept or to reject the order should be based on an assessment of the incremental cash flows from accepting the order. As long as the incremental cash outflows to produce the product (that is, the variable costs) are less than $35, the order should be accepted. Using the $40 unit cost, which includes an allocation of fixed manufacturing overhead cost, could lead to an incorrect decision. As long as the total fixed costs of the company will not change as a result of accepting the order, these costs should not be considered in the decision.

Example 2 Wharton Products Corporation allocates the cost of operating service departments (for example, maintenance department) to each of the manufacturing departments for purposes of product costing. The costs are included in manufacturing overhead. Division A of Wharton Products Corporation is attempting to estimate its overhead cost for the coming year. To develop estimates of fixed and variable overhead costs, it has analyzed past overhead cost behavior using statistical regression and developed the following budget equation: total costs = $100,000 + $5 per unit produced. It has used these estimates in planning for the coming year. In the past, maintenance department costs have been allocated to manufacturing divisions using square footage occupied by each division. This year, corporate management decided to use maintenance hours worked in each division as the basis for allocating maintenance costs in the future. Because the costs allocated under the new rule will differ significantly from those using the old allocation base, using past cost data to construct a budget for total costs can lead to inaccurate plans for the coming year.

Example 3 Diversified Industries, Inc., is organized into 40 autonomous operating divisions. Corporate management uses the divisional rate of return on investment for evaluating the performance of the division managers. In calculating divisional net income, an allocated share of central corporate expenses is deducted. The expenses are allocated to divisions based on divisional sales. Division B increased its sales by 25 percent during the current year. Because of an increase in total central corporate expenses and an increase in the relative share of these expenses allocated to Division B, the 25 percent increase in sales resulted in only a 5 percent increase in Division B's net income and rate of return. Including a share of central corporate expenses in Division B's performance report can give a misleading picture of its operations. Division B has no control over these costs and therefore should not be held accountable for them. More important, allocation of these costs based on sales could lead division managers to reduce sales efforts, to the detriment of the company as a whole.

The message of this section should be fairly clear. Accounting data that include common cost allocations must be interpreted carefully. The cost allocations for the most part are made for product costing purposes. The intention in making the allocations is usually not to aid in decision making, planning, or control.

GENERAL PRINCIPLES OF COST ALLOCATION

The cost allocation process involves three principal steps:

1 Accumulating the costs that relate to the product, department, or division (for example, manufacturing overhead, service department costs, central corporate expenses).
2 Identifying the recipient of the allocated costs (this may be a product, department, or division).
3 Selecting a method or basis for relating the costs in 1 with the recipient in 2.

This third step is the most difficult because common costs cannot be associated directly with a single product, department, or division. The aim therefore is to search for an indirect relationship that might serve as a meaningful allocation base. Some of the guidelines that might be applied in selecting an allocation base are as follows:

1 Does an analysis of past cost behavior suggest a relationship between the incurrence of the cost and an allocation base (for example, manufacturing overhead cost and the number of units produced)?
2 Does knowledge of operations suggest a logical relationship between the incurrence of the cost and an allocation base (for example, the relationship between manufacturing overhead and either the number of labor hours worked or the dollar investment in depreciable assets)?
3 If an allocation base cannot be selected on empirical or logical grounds, is there general acceptance among the parties affected that the allocations must be arbitrary? If not, then perhaps the common costs should not be allocated at all, or if allocated, a concensus of those affected should be reached on the most acceptable base.

ILLUSTRATIONS OF COST ALLOCATION PROCEDURES

In the sections that follow we illustrate allocation procedures for manufacturing overhead, joint product costs, and selling and administrative expenses.

Manufacturing Overhead and Service Department Costs

The illustration that follows will serve to indicate the types of problems involved in allocating manufacturing overhead costs. The manufacturing *division* of Berdan Products Company is composed of five *departments*. Departments A, B, and C are production departments. Departments M and S are service departments (that is, they exist to provide support to the production departments). Records are kept of the direct material and direct labor costs incurred in each of the three production departments. All other manufacturing costs are considered to be overhead and initially accumulated at the level of the manufacturing division. Figure 13.1 summarizes these relationships.

   The accumulation of overhead costs at the divisional level is done for control purposes. For product costing purposes, these overhead costs must be allocated to the

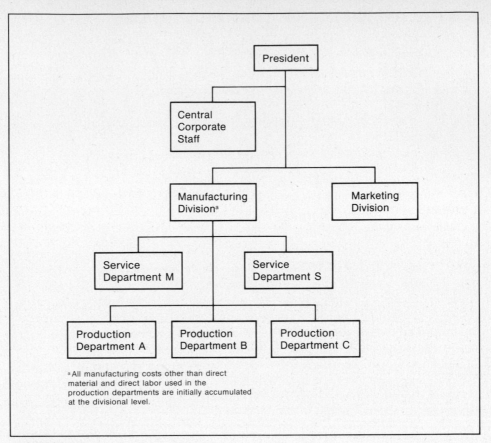

FIGURE 13.1
Berdan Products Company
Organization Chart

production departments and then to individual products. The allocation procedure is outlined below.

1 Any overhead costs that can be attributed directly to a service or production department are allocated first (for example, salary of a foreman in one of the production departments).

2 Next, the remaining manufacturing overhead costs are allocated to the service and production departments using a base selected because of an empirical or logical relationship between the cost and the department.

3 Next, the costs allocated to the service departments in steps 1 and 2 are reallocated to the three production departments.

4 The direct material, direct labor, and share of manufacturing overhead allocated to each production department are then allocated to the units produced during the period.

EXHIBIT 13.1
Berdan Products Company
Manufacturing Overhead Costs
for the Month of March

	Total (1)	Dept. A (2)	Dept. B (3)	Dept. C (4)	Dept. M (5)	Dept. S (6)	Not Directly Allocable (7)
*Foreman's Salary—Dept. A	$ 2,100	$2,100					
*Foreman's Salary—Dept. B	1,950		$1,950				
*Foreman's Salary—Dept. C	1,500			$1,500			
*Foreman's Salary—Dept. M (Maintenance)	2,100				$2,100		
*Maintenance Labor—Dept. M	6,000				6,000		
*Storeroom Labor—Dept. S	2,400					$2,400	
Security Guard's Salary	500						$ 500
*Supplies Used—Dept. A	600	600					
*Supplies Used—Dept. B	900		900				
*Supplies Used—Dept. C	300			300			
*Supplies Used—Dept. S	800					800	
*Supplies Used—Dept. M	450				450		
Property Taxes	1,200						1,200
Fire Insurance	300						300
Workmen's Compensation Insurance	800						800
Payroll Taxes	5,000						5,000
*Depreciation of Equipment—Dept. A	1,200	1,200					
*Depreciation of Equipment—Dept. B	900		900				
*Depreciation of Equipment—Dept. C	330			330			
*Depreciation of Equipment—Dept. S	180					180	
*Depreciation of Equipment—Dept. M	120				120		
Rent—Factory Building	720						720
Electricity, Gas, and Water	600						600
Miscellaneous Factory Costs	750						750
Total	$31,700	$3,900	$3,750	$2,130	$8,670	$3,380	$9,870

* Each item marked with an asterisk can be assigned directly to a department.

Exhibit 13.1, column (1), shows a listing of the manufacturing overhead costs incurred during the month of March for Berdan Products Company. The first step is to allocate overhead costs that can be attributed directly to one of the five departments. Costs in this category include salaries and labor, supplies used, and depreciation. These costs are shown in the appropriate departmental columns of Exhibit 13.1. Technically, these costs are direct rather than common costs with respect to the departments.

The next step is to allocate manufacturing overhead costs that are not directly attributable to one of the departments. These costs are listed in column (7) of Exhibit 13.1 and include the security guard's salary, property taxes, fire insurance, workmen's compensation insurance, payroll taxes, rent, electricity, gas, and water, and miscellaneous factory costs. At this stage it is necessary to select an allocation base. Exhibit 13.2 shows the allocation of each of these costs to the five departments. Note the types of additional information that must be available in order to make these distributions.

(1) The security guard's salary, $500, is distributed in proportion to the number of visits made to each department during a typical night. Section (1) of Exhibit 13.2 shows the distributions of the security guard's salary.

(2) Property taxes and fire insurance are distributed in proportion to the book value of the equipment and inventories in each department. See (2) in Exhibit 13.2.

EXHIBIT 13.2
Berdan Products Company
Distribution of Various Overhead Costs for March

---

(1) SECURITY GUARD'S SALARY

Dept.	No. Visits	Percent	Distribution
A	8	20	$100
B	8	20	100
C	8	20	100
S	16	40	200
M	0	—	—
Totals	40	100	$500

---

(2) PROPERTY TAXES AND FIRE INSURANCE

Dept.	Book Value of Assets	Percent	Distribution of Property Taxes	Distribution of Fire Insurance
A	$100,000	50	$ 600	$150
B	60,000	30	360	90
C	10,000	5	60	15
S	26,000	13	156	39
M	4,000	2	24	6
Totals	$200,000	100	$1,200	$300

EXHIBIT 13.2 (continued)

(3) WORKMEN'S COMPENSATION INSURANCE AND PAYROLL TAXES

Dept.	Direct Labor	Indirect Labor	Total Labor	Percent
A	$17,100	$ 2,200	$ 19,300	19.3
B	37,950	2,050	40,000	40.0
C	28,400	1,600	30,000	30.0
S	—	2,600[a]	2,600	2.6
M	—	8,100[b]	8,100	8.1
Totals	$83,450	$16,550	$100,000	100.0

		Distribution of	
Dept.	Percent	Work. Comp. Ins.	Payroll Taxes
A	19.3	$154	$ 965
B	40.0	320	2,000
C	30.0	240	1,500
S	2.6	21	130
M	8.1	65	405
Totals	100.0	$800	$5,000

(4) RENT—FACTORY BUILDING

Dept.	Square Feet of Floor Space	Percent	Distribution
A	15,000	37.50	$270
B	15,000	37.50	270
C	8,500	21.25	153
S	1,000	2.50	18
M	500	1.25	9
Totals	40,000	100.00	$720

(5) ELECTRICITY, GAS, AND WATER

Dept.	Utility Services (Percent)	Distribution
A	50	$300
B	30	180
C	15	90
S	3	18
M	2	12
Totals	100	$600

[a] $2,600 = $2,400 (storeroom labor from Exhibit 13.1) + $200 (security guard's salary allocated in step **1** above).

[b] $8,100 = $2,100 (foreman's salary—Department M from Exhibit 13.1) + $6,000 (maintenance labor—Department M from Exhibit 13.1).

(3) Workmen's compensation insurance and payroll taxes are distributed in proportion to departmental labor costs. In the schedule the amounts shown for direct labor indicate the amount of compensation earned by production-line workers in each production department. The indirect labor in the production departments is the foreman's salary plus the guard's allocated salary in step (1). In the service departments the indirect labor total is made up of department labor plus the foreman's salary for Department M plus the allocated security guard's salary for Department S. See (3) in Exhibit 13.2.

(4) The rent of the factory building is distributed in proportion to the floor space occupied by each department. See (4) in Exhibit 13.2.

(5) Electricity, gas, and water are distributed according to the capacity of equipment and needs of each department. The distribution results from a study of the departmental requirements. See (5) in Exhibit 13.2.

(6) Miscellaneous factory costs are distributed equally over the five production and service departments because there is no other logical basis for an allocation. Exhibit 13.3 shows the results of these allocations of overhead costs.

When the initial distribution of the overhead accounts to the various departments has been completed, it is then necessary to redistribute the totals of the service departments to the production departments. One logical method, where two or more service departments serve each other as well as the production departments, requires an algebraic solution. This method is beyond the scope of this text. A less exact, but simpler solution, is as follows: (a) distribute the total costs of the service department that receives the smallest dollar amount of service from the other service departments over the other service and production departments; (b) then in the same manner distribute the total costs of the service department receiving the next smallest amount of service from other service departments; and so on, until all service department costs have been allocated to the production departments. Once a given service department's costs have been allocated to other departments, no further costs are allocated to that given service department. This is sometimes called a *step-down* allocation procedure.

In the illustration it is assumed that Department M is the Maintenance Department. It receives little or no service from Department S, the Storeroom Department. The redistribution therefore begins by allocating the total costs of Department M in proportion to the time spent doing work specifically for certain departments.

Allocation of Department M Costs

Department	Chargeable Hours	Percent	Distribution
A	400	40	$3,736
B	200	20	1,868
C	320	32	2,989
S	80	8	748
Totals	1,000	100	$9,341

This allocation is shown in the lower part of Exhibit 13.3.

EXHIBIT 13.3
Allocation of Overhead by Step-Down Allocation Procedure
Berdan Products Company
Overhead Allocation Schedule
Month Ending March 31

	Total	Dept. A	Dept. B	Dept. C	Dept. S Storeroom	Dept. M Maintenance	Reference[a]
Foremen's Salaries	$ 7,650	$ 2,100	$ 1,950	$ 1,500	$ —	$ 2,100	*
Maintenance Labor	6,000	—	—	—	—	6,000	*
Storeroom Labor	2,400	—	—	—	2,400	—	*
Security Guard's Salary	500	100	100	100	200	—	(1)
Supplies Used	3,050	600	900	300	800	450	*
Property Taxes	1,200	600	360	60	156	24	(2)
Fire Insurance	300	150	90	15	39	6	(2)
Workmen's Compensation Insurance	800	154	320	240	21	65	(3)
Payroll Taxes	5,000	965	2,000	1,500	130	405	(3)
Depreciation of Equipment	2,730	1,200	900	330	180	120	*
Rent—Factory Building	720	270	270	153	18	9	(4)
Electricity, Gas, and Water	600	300	180	90	18	12	(5)
Miscellaneous Factory Costs	750	150	150	150	150	150	(6)
Totals	$31,700	$ 6,589	$ 7,220	$ 4,438	$4,112	$ 9,341	
Redistribution—Dept. M	—	3,736	1,868	2,989	748	(9,341)	
	$31,700	$10,325	$ 9,088	$ 7,427	$4,860		
Redistribution—Dept. S	—	1,620	1,620	1,620	(4,860)		
Total Production Department Costs	$31,700	$11,945	$10,708	$ 9,047			

[a] Each item marked with an asterisk is allocated directly to a department. The number in parentheses refers to a section of Exhibit 13.2 or to a discussion reference in the text.

It is difficult to find a logical, and at the same time practical, basis for the spreading of storeroom costs. They should bear some relationship to the quantity of supplies and materials that have been issued, and in part they may be interpreted as a cost of the materials and supplies on hand. The number of requisitions made by each of the departments might be used, but counting numbers of requisitions is probably not worth the effort. If the inventories at the end of the period are small compared to the quantities used during the period, storeroom costs might be allocated on the basis of a physical measure or dollar value of materials issued. If, in the example, materials and supplies are requisitioned in about equal quantities by Departments A, B, and C, the costs of Department S might be apportioned about equally among those departments, as is done in Exhibit 13.3.

As a result of these three allocation steps, that is, (1) allocation of costs directly associated with departments, (2) allocation of costs not directly associated with departments, and (3) allocation of service department costs to the production departments, the total manufacturing overhead of $31,700 is allocated $11,945 to Department A, $10,708 to Department B, and $9,047 to Department C. The next step is to allocate these amounts to the products manufactured in the three production departments. This allocation, as was illustrated in Chapter Twelve, is usually based on the equivalent number of units produced, direct labor hours, direct labor cost, or some other base.

Joint Products and By-Products

A cost allocation problem arises when more than one product emerges from a single production process. The numerous products of meat-packing plants, the variety of metals often found and extracted together in mining operations, the inevitable production of various grades of finished lumber in the operation of a lumber mill, and the several products made from the original material in the dairy and petroleum industries are common examples of jointly produced goods.

The problems of joint production are not limited to manufacturing and mining. For instance, in real estate a similar problem exists in the development of a subdivision. The total cost of developing the tract represents a joint cost of all of the lots that are to be sold. Some reasonable method of allocating this total figure among the lots must be found so that a cost and profit can be calculated for each lot sold and a cost assigned to the unsold lots.

Joint Products Terminology   It will be helpful to understand some terminology before discussing the problems of joint cost allocations. Figure 13.2 summarizes the following information about the joint production process of Trapp Corporation. Raw materials are initially introduced into processing. After the incurrence of some direct labor and manufacturing overhead costs, two identifiable products, product A and product B, emerge from the production process. Product A is processed further. Product B is sold immediately. The point at which the identifiable products emerge is called the *splitoff point*. Costs incurred up to the splitoff point are the *joint costs*. Costs incurred after the splitoff point are called *additional processing costs*.

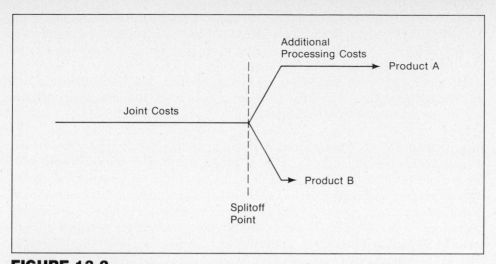

FIGURE 13.2
Trapp Corporation
Diagram of Joint Production
Process

Allocation of Joint Production Costs   Strictly speaking, it is impossible to compute the cost of each product produced under a joint process. Total cost can usually be determined with a satisfactory degree of accuracy, but there is no theoretically correct or objective method of spreading the total cost over the various joint products. The methods used can best be described as feasible, reasonable, or expedient. In spite of this apparently insurmountable barrier, attempts are nevertheless made to allocate joint costs, primarily in order to provide figures that can be used for cost-of-goods-sold and inventory purposes.[1]

Joint costs are usually allocated by either of two methods: the relative sales value method or the physical units method. Both are described in the following illustration

---

[1]   If demand curves, or schedules, are available for the various joint products, then mathematics provides a logical technique for deriving costs to be allocated to the joint products. The technique provides sensible answers, because using them, rather than answers from some other method, will induce management to make decisions that maximize the profits to the firm. For example, beef sold as meat and hides sold for making shoes are both derived from a single cow. So long as the firm must merely cost the hides or beef left over at the end of the period, the economic returns to the firm, as opposed to the accounting profits reported, will be unaffected by a decision to treat the hides as by-products or as joint products with some arbitrary allocation of the cost of the cow. But if management is given the opportunity to purchase hides alone from a separate supplier, it will need to know the economic cost of the hides produced jointly with beef in order to decide whether buying from the outside supplier offers a profitable return. The mathematical technique provides the information management needs to make the correct decision if, to repeat, the demand curves for beef and hides are known. The method is given by Roman L. Weil, "Allocating Joint Costs," *American Economic Review* (December 1968), and is explained in a cost accounting framework in Chapter 14 of Nicholas Dopuch, Jacob G. Birnberg, and Joel Demski, *Cost Accounting*, 2nd ed. (New York: Harcourt Brace Jovanovich, 1974).

based on a real estate development. Sorter Homes Development Company purchases a 2-acre tract of land adjoining a lake for $38,000 and spends $2,000 in legal fees to have the land subdivided into five lots. Houses are built on each of the lots. Exhibit 13.4 shows the various costs and price data.

The differing prices for the half-acre and quarter-acre lots result from differing proximity to the lake. The joint cost problem in this context is to allocate the $40,000 cost of the land to each of the five lots.

Relative Sales Value Method   First, suppose that once the land is legally subdivided, there is a ready market for the lots without houses and that the market prices for the five lots are as shown in column (3) of Exhibit 13.4. If such information is available, then the method of allocating the $40,000 of joint cost is to allocate that cost to the lots in proportion to their relative current market values. Because the cost is 50 percent of the sum of the current market values ($40,000/$80,000), each lot would be assigned a cost of 50 percent of its current market value. The cost allocated to lot 1 would be $8,000. The cost allocated to the other lots would be: lots 2 and 3, $12,500 each; lot 4, $2,000; lot 5, $5,000. Under this method, then, each lot is assigned a portion of the joint cost such that it yields a profit equal to 50 percent of selling price.

Approximate Relative Sales Value Method   To alter the illustration, suppose that the legal agreement allowing subdivision prohibits Sorter Homes from reselling the lots without houses or that for some other reason the information shown in column (3) is not available.

The only information directly available is that shown in columns (4) and (5), from which column (6) is calculated. It would not be logical to make the assignment of the land's cost on the basis of the information in column (4), because those prices include the house as well as the land. For example, the selling price of lot-house combination 4 is $35,000, which is about 11 percent of the total selling prices of $310,000.

EXHIBIT 13.4
Sorter Homes Development Company
Data for Joint Cost Allocations

Lot Number (1)	Size (in acres) (2)	Resale Price After Subdivision (3)	Selling Price for House and Lot (4)	Cost to Build House (5)	Approximate Sales Value of Land at Splitoff (6)
1.	1/2	$16,000	$ 75,000	$ 50,000	$ 25,000
2.	1/2	25,000	80,000	50,000	30,000
3.	1/2	25,000	80,000	50,000	30,000
4.	1/4	4,000	35,000	30,000	5,000
5.	1/4	10,000	40,000	30,000	10,000
	2	$80,000	$310,000	$210,000	$100,000

(3) Market prices given.
(6) = (4) − (5).

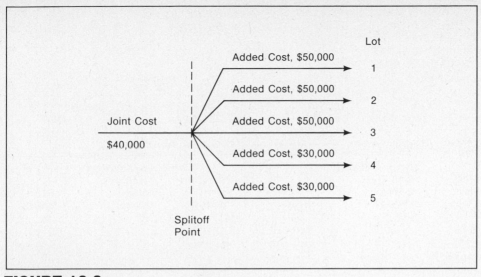

FIGURE 13.3
The Splitoff Point in Allocating
Joint Costs

We can see from the information in column (3) that lot 4 represents only 5 percent (= \$4,000/\$80,000) of the value of the total land package. Using final selling prices of lot-house combinations from column (4) to allocate land costs would intermingle land and house prices and would assign 11 percent of the land costs to lot 4, whereas 5 percent of the cost is more appropriate. The *approximate relative sales value method* is designed to achieve an allocation much like the one obtained from column (3) when the required information is unavailable.

The diagram in Figure 13.3 may help in understanding the nature of the problem. Such a diagram will usually be helpful in analyzing joint cost allocation problems. The splitoff point comes just before the costs of the individual houses are incurred. To use the approximate relative sales value method, relative sales values at the splitoff must be derived, as shown in column (6) of Exhibit 13.4. The approximate sales value of a lot (joint product) is defined to be the selling price of the lot-house combination (final product) less the cost to complete the lot-house combination. Here, the cost to complete is the cost of building the house. The approximate sales value of lot 1 is \$25,000, or the price of the house-lot combination, \$75,000, less the cost of the house, \$50,000. The sum of the approximate sales values of the lots at the splitoff point is \$100,000. Because the cost of the land (\$40,000) is 40 percent of the sum of the approximate sales values, each lot would be assigned a cost of 40 percent (= \$40,000/\$100,000) of its approximate sales value. Lot 1, for example, would be allocated \$10,000 (= .4 × \$25,000).[2] Allocations for the other lots are shown in column (2) of Exhibit 13.5.

EXHIBIT 13.5
Sorter Homes Development Company
Joint Cost Allocation Under
Various Methods with and
without By-Product

	Joint-Product Cost = $40,000			**By-Product Cost = $2,000** **Joint-Product Cost = $38,000**		
	Basis of Allocation			**Basis of Allocation**		
Lot Number	**Relative Sales Values (1)[a]**	**Approximate Relative Sales Values (2)[b]**	**Physical Units (3)[c]**	**Relative Sales Values (4)[d]**	**Approximate Relative Sales Values (5)[e]**	**Physical Units (6)[f]**
1.......	$ 8,000	$10,000	$10,000	$ 7,600	$ 9,500	$ 9,500
2.......	12,500	12,000	10,000	11,875	11,400	9,500
3.......	12,500	12,000	10,000	11,875	11,400	9,500
4.......	2,000	2,000	5,000	1,900	1,900	4,750
5.......	5,000	4,000	5,000	4,750	3,800	4,750
Total ..	$40,000	$40,000	$40,000	$38,000	$38,000	$38,000

[a] (1) = column (3) of Exhibit 13.4 × 40/80.
[b] (2) = column (6) of Exhibit 13.4 × 40/100.
[c] (3) = $40,000 × [column (2) of Exhibit 13.4]/2.
[d] (4) = (1) × 38/40 = column (3) of Exhibit 13.4 × 38/80.
[e] (5) = (2) × 38/40 = column (3) of Exhibit 13.4 × 38/100.
[f] (6) = (3) × 38/40.

Physical Units Method The physical units method is not based on dollar costs but on some obvious physical measure. Here, the obvious measure is area in acres. In other contexts the obvious physical measure might be weight or volume. Because lots 1, 2, and 3 each contain $\frac{1}{2}$ acre out of 2 acres, each would be allocated $(\frac{1}{2})/2 \times \$40,000$ or $10,000. Each $\frac{1}{4}$-acre lot would be allocated $(\frac{1}{4})/2 \times \$40,000$ or $5,000.

The physical units method is usually easy to apply, but its results may not make good sense. For example, if the physical units method using pounds of salable product is used to allocate the cost of a beef cattle to cuts of meat, tenderloin will carry the same cost per pound as liver. Then the sales of tenderloin will appear extraordinarily profitable, whereas liver will seem to be sold at a loss. The relative sales value method will allocate more of the joint costs of beef cattle to a pound of tenderloin than to a pound of liver.

---

[2] In doing the calculations this way, we are ignoring the profit (or markup over cost) that would be added to cost by the contractor in setting the price of the house. It might make sense to use selling prices for houses alone (excluding the price of the lot), not merely the cost of the houses, in column (5) of Exhibit 13.4.

Accounting for By-Products   In accounting for jointly produced products, it is customary to distinguish between by-products and joint products. A by-product is produced as the inevitable result of the production of a main product and is of relatively small value. For example, steel shavings in a machine shop, scraps of lumber in a furniture factory, and buttermilk in a dairy are typical instances of by-products. A joint product is one that is treated as equally significant with other products that emerge from a process. The different grades of lumber in a lumber mill, milk and butter in dairy operations, and subdivision lots are examples of joint products. The difference between by-products and joint products, then, is one of degree; the dividing line is not distinct. A power plant, for instance, that produces both electricity and steam may consider one or the other as a by-product or may treat them both as joint products.

In accounting for by-products, just as for joint products, no processing cost is assigned to the by-product until it is separated from the joint process. The distinctive feature of by-product accounting is that when the by-product is separated from the joint process, the by-product is then assigned a cost equal to its net realizable (or sales) value. The *net realizable sales value* of the by-product is its estimated selling price less any costs yet to be incurred for further processing, handling, and disposal. The cost assigned to by-products is then deducted from the total accumulated joint costs and the remaining joint costs become the cost of the main product or products. By-products are assigned a cost so that the expected gain or loss on their sale is zero. The cost assigned to the by-products reduces the cost of the main product or products and thereby increases the profits of the main product or products.

To illustrate the accounting for by-products, reconsider the Sorter Homes example. Suppose that at the time Sorter Homes arranged for legal subdivision of the land purchase, it also sold to the city the rights for the public to use the lake for $2,000. The rights to the lake probably should be viewed as a by-product in this case, so they would be treated as a reduction in the cost of the land. The joint costs of the land to be allocated to the five lots would be only $38,000. The right-hand panel of Exhibit 13.5 summarizes the allocation of the joint costs.

Selling and Administrative Expenses

Techniques similar to those employed in manufacturing cost analysis are often applied in allocating selling and administrative expenses. A department store, for example, may wish to have its operating expenses and cost of goods sold allocated, as far as possible, by departments; a wholesaler may wish to have information as to the profitability of different territories and types of customers; or a manufacturer may be interested in the cost of handling and selling various products.

Department Store Cost Analysis   The calculation of departmental operating costs in a department store is much the same as the allocation of departmental overhead in a manufacturing plant. Some items, such as salaries and commissions of salespeople, are assignable directly to departments. Others, such as rent, insurance, and supervision, have to be allocated after a preliminary accumulation in an overhead control account. Appropriate bases for the allocation of such costs are adopted, as is done for manufacturing overhead costs. For example, floor space may be used as the basis for the spreading of building service costs, but usually on a weighted basis. The different weights applied to the area occupied by different departments makes allowance for the greater value of certain sections of the store. For example, first-floor space of a given size would be weighted more heavily than the same amount of space on an upper floor.

The complete allocation of all operating costs is not as necessary in a department store as in a manufacturing plant. All manufacturing costs must be completely allocated so that they can be absorbed in the products produced and unit costs for inventories can be derived. In the department store, the results of allocations are used only by management for judging the relative profitability of each department and for comparing the results of the present period with the budget and with past periods. There is good reason for the opinion that such purposes will be served better if the allocation of operating costs is limited to those that can be assigned on some reasonably logical basis without attempting to allocate the more general costs such as office salaries and expenses, executives' salaries, general store advertising, and warehouse expenses, which can be allocated to departments only on an arbitrary basis. None of these costs or other department store operating costs are included in merchandise inventory. The allocations do not affect total net income or inventory valuations but only the amounts of contributions of each department. Although each department should *contribute* toward meeting general overhead, it is often impossible to determine how much it should *absorb* with any useful degree of reliability.

Below, we list some of the bases of allocation that have been suggested for the selling and administrative costs. One striking aspect of the problem of such cost analysis is that extensive data must be accumulated in addition to the regular accounting information. Some of the data can be accumulated regularly; other items, because of the cost of obtaining the information, will be made the subject of occasional studies in order to establish or to correct normal or standard costs of the operation.

For Allocation of	**Basis**
1 Insurance.	Average value of finished goods.
2 Storage and building costs.	Floor space.
3 Cost of sending monthly statements, credit investigations, etc.	Number of customers.
4 Various joint costs such as advertising and supervision of selling activities.	Sales, classified by dealers, territories, or products.
5 Credit investigation, postage, stationery, and other such expenses.	Number of orders received.
6 Handling costs.	Tonnage handled.
7 Salespersons' expenses.	Number of salespersons' calls.
8 Order writing and filling.	Number of items on an order.
9 Stenographic expense.	Number of letters written.
10 Automobile operation, delivery expense, etc.	Number of miles operated.

Fixed Costs and Interim Earnings Reports

The illustrations of common cost allocations considered thus far have been concerned with allocations to products, departments, or processes. An equally perplexing problem arises in allocating costs that are fixed for a year, such as insurance and property taxes, to interim periods within the year. Most firms prepare monthly or quarterly reports for evaluating the performance of departments or divisions. Performance is often judged on the department's or division's net income for the month or quarter. In order to calculate net income for an interim period within a year, a portion of the annual fixed selling and administrative expenses (and perhaps fixed manufacturing expenses if direct costing is used for internal performance evaluation) must be deducted.

The principal problems involved in preparing and interpreting interim reports arise for departments and divisions that have substantial seasonal variations in revenues. Professional sport teams, vacation resorts, and most department stores, for example, sell their goods and services at a nonuniform rate throughout the year. Many operating costs, however, are incurred at a relatively uniform rate throughout the year. Examples include rent, property taxes, insurance, and most salaries. The principal accounting question is how these operating costs are to be assigned to each of the months or quarters during the year. Suppose that a summer resort generates 80 percent of its revenues during the third quarter of the year. Should the interim report for the first quarter of the year, January through March, which shows little or no revenue, show one-fourth of the year's property taxes, insurance, and other similar costs and thereby report a loss? Alternatively, should the interim report for the third quarter, which shows 80 percent of the year's revenues, show 80 percent of the year's costs as expenses and thereby report 80 percent of the anticipated net income for the year?

Illustration of Fixed Cost Allocation to Periods   The illustration that follows demonstrates the issues involved in allocating fixed costs to interim periods. Division C of Montsinger Corporation grows citrus fruits. Exhibit 13.6, column (1), shows the estimated revenues of Division C during each quarter of the coming year. Seasonal sales are expected to occur in the percentages of .10, .60, .20, and .10. That is, 10 percent of the year's sales is expected to occur in the first quarter of the year. Column (2) shows the expected production costs of the citrus fruit sold. Production costs are expected to be 60 percent of selling price. Column (3) shows the expected gross profit. Selling and administrative expenses, which are largely fixed for the year, are expected to be $200,000.

Assume that sales and production costs during the first quarter of the year occur as expected. What is Division C's net income for the first quarter? Two alternative procedures for allocating selling and administrative expenses to the quarters during the year are illustrated in Exhibit 13.6. Column (4) shows an equal allocation to each of the four quarters. Division C therefore shows a net loss of $10,000 for the first quarter. Column (6) shows a seasonal allocation of costs to the four quarters. That is, selling and administrative expenses are allocated according to the proportion of the year's sales expected in each quarter. For example, 10 percent of the year's selling and administrative expenses are allocated to the first quarter.

Before selecting an allocation method, management must decide how it intends to use the interim earnings report. If the report is to be used to evaluate Division C's actual performance during the first quarter and management wishes to view the first quarter as a discrete accounting period, then an equal allocation is reasonable. If management intends to use the interim earnings report to help predict the division's

EXHIBIT 13.6
Montsinger Corporation—Division C
Estimated Revenues, Expenses, and Net
Income for the Next Four Quarters
and Year Based on Two Different
Allocations of Common Costs

| | | | | Method 1 | | Method 2 | |
| | | | | | | | |
Quarter	Estimated Revenues (1)	Production Costs (2)	Gross Profit (3)	Equal Allocation of Other Expenses (4)	Net Income (5)	Seasonal Allocation of Other Expenses (6)	Net Income (7)
1........	$ 100,000	$ 60,000	$ 40,000	$ 50,000	$ (10,000)	$ 20,000	$ 20,000
2........	600,000	360,000	240,000	50,000	190,000	120,000	120,000
3........	200,000	120,000	80,000	50,000	30,000	40,000	40,000
4........	100,000	60,000	40,000	50,000	(10,000)	20,000	20,000
Total..	$1,000,000	$600,000	$400,000	$200,000	$200,000	$200,000	$200,000

(3) = (1) − (2).
(5) = (3) − (4).
(7) = (3) − (6).

net income for the year, then a seasonal allocation of costs makes more sense. The expected divisional net income for the year is $200,000. Using a seasonal assignment of selling and administrative expenses, the first quarter's net income is $20,000. This amount is 10 percent of the expected net income for the year, in direct proportion to the seasonal sales percentage.

The manner in which fixed costs are allocated to interim periods can have a significant effect on reported interim net income. Interpretations of interim earnings reports must therefore be made cautiously, only after knowing the methods used to assign annual fixed costs to the interim periods.[3]

SUMMARY

Common cost allocations permeate accounting reports, both financial and managerial. It would be easy to conclude that, given the arbitrary nature of many of these allocations, accounting reports are meaningless. We think that it is more appropriate to conclude that accounting reports should be read and interpreted carefully, taking into account the effects of common cost allocations that have been made. For most decision-making, planning, and control purposes, accounting reports should be based on a minimum of cost allocations. Cost allocations, however, play a critical role in determinations of net income for individual time periods. Much of financial accounting and advanced cost accounting deals with these cost allocations.

QUESTIONS AND PROBLEMS

1 Review the meaning of the following concepts or terms discussed in this chapter.
   a Common cost.
   b Direct cost.
   c Allocation base.
   d Service department.
   e Step-down allocation procedure.
   f Joint product.
   g By-product.
   h Splitoff point.
   i Relative sales value method.
   j Approximate relative sales value method.
   k Physical units method.
   l Net realizable sales value.
   m Interim report.
   n Seasonal assignment of fixed costs.

2 When service department costs are allocated to production departments, why are these costs first accumulated at the service department level rather than assigned directly to production departments?

---

[3]   For an expanded discussion of interim period accounting problems, see David Green, Jr., "Towards a Theory of Interim Reports," *Journal of Accounting Research*, 2, 1 (Spring 1964), pp. 35–49.

3 Distinguish between a production department and a service department.

4 What is the reasoning behind the opinion that in merchandising (as opposed to manufacturing) enterprises, only those costs that can be assigned on some obviously logical basis should be allocated?

5 Comment on this statement: "The purpose of cost accounting is to determine the cost of producing a unit of product, so that this production cost can be used to determine a sales price that yields the desired gross profit margin."

6 Why are service department costs allocated to production departments?

7 Distinguish between a joint product and a by-product.

8 Comment on the following statement: "The relative sales value method is the best method to use in decisions concerning whether a joint product should be sold at splitoff or processed further."

9 The following estimates for a year were made by the accountants of the Roberts Specialty Company:

	Cutting Department	Assembling Department	Painting Department
Estimated Overhead	$36,000	$50,000	$56,000
Estimated Direct Labor Cost. . .	$60,000	$50,000	$70,000
Estimated Direct Labor Time . .	12,000 hr	12,500 hr	14,000 hr

a Compute the departmental overhead allocation rates using **(1)** direct labor cost and **(2)** direct labor hours as a basis.

b Apply the results obtained in **a** to the data given below for job no. 407. Show the total cost of the job for each basis of overhead allocation.

	Cutting Department	Assembling Department	Painting Department
Direct Material	$ 600	—	$ 80
Direct Labor Cost	$1,500	$2,000	$200
Direct Labor Time	250 hr	400 hr	38 hr

10 The Hamilton Company has two producing departments and a maintenance department. In addition, the upkeep costs for the entire plant are kept in a separate account. The estimated cost data for 19X0 are as follows:

Cost	Producing Dept. 1	Producing Dept. 2	Maintenance	General Plant
Direct Labor	$50,000	$30,000	—	—
Indirect Labor	28,000	14,000	$22,500	$20,000
Indirect Materials . .	9,000	7,000	900	8,000
Miscellaneous	3,000	5,000	1,600	5,000
	$90,000	$56,000	$25,000	$33,000
Maintenance	7,000 hr	13,000 hr	—	—

The "general plant" services the other three departments in the following proportions: 50 percent (Department 1); 30 percent (Department 2); 20 percent (Maintenance). Assume that direct labor cost is the best estimate of activity. Allocate maintenance costs based on maintenance hours.

Compute the overhead allocation rates for Departments 1 and 2, including the allocations of the service department and the general plant center.

11 The Burns Company uses a job order system of cost accounting. The data presented below relate to operations in its plant during January.

There are two production departments and one service department. The factory overhead costs accumulated during the month are $4,000. At the end of the period the overhead costs are allocated as follows: Department A, $2,100; Department B, $1,600; Department C, $300. The service department (Department C) overhead is redistributed as follows: two-thirds to Department A, and one-third to Department B.

Factory overhead is applied to job orders at the following predetermined rates: 60 percent of direct labor costs in Department A, and 80 percent in Department B. The jobs are delivered upon completion. Job orders completed in January are nos. 789, 790, and 791. Complete the job order production record below by filling in appropriate amounts. Be sure to show supporting calculations.

Job Order Production Record

Job Order No.	Jobs in Process Jan. 1	Direct Labor Dept. A	Direct Labor Dept. B	Direct Matl. Dept. A	Direct Matl. Dept. B	Overhead Dept. A	Overhead Dept. B	Total Costs	Jobs in Process Jan. 31	Completed Jobs
788	$1,200	$ 300	$ 150	$ 250	$ 150	$	$	$	$	$
789	850	600	300	450	300					
790		800	450	550	350					
791		1,000	600	600	450					
792										
Totals.	$2,050	$3,900	$2,150	$2,750	$1,650	$	$	$	$	$

12 The Norton Company sells to wholesalers and retailers. The following data are available for 19X0 operations:

Norton Company

	Wholesale	Retail	Total
Sales.	$1,000,000	$1,500,000	$2,500,000
Cost of Goods Sold.	$ 640,000	$1,000,000	$1,640,000
Salespersons' Salaries.			270,000
Advertising.			90,000
Office Costs			140,000
Storage Costs.			70,000
Total Costs for Year			$2,210,000

Data for Allocation

Number of Salespersons' Calls	90	810	900
Number of Invoice Lines	305	1,830	2,135

(continued on following page)

Cost	Allocation Basis
Salespersons' Salaries.	Number of Calls
Advertising.	Gross Sales
Office Costs	Number of Invoice Lines
Storage Costs.	Gross Sales

a Prepare a three-column income statement with columns for wholesale sales, retail sales, and total sales.

b Which channel of trade has the higher ratio of net income to sales?

13 The APCO Company applies manufacturing overhead to all departments by means of allocation ratios. The four departments are (1) Melting, (2) Molding, (3) Coring, (4) Cleaning. From the data shown below, prepare an overhead distribution schedule showing in detail the manufacturing overhead chargeable to each department.

Apco Company
Manufacturing Overhead Costs During the Month

Indirect Labor:	
Melting	$ 6,000
Molding	1,800
Coring.	600
Cleaning	1,800
Supplies Used:	
Melting	300
Molding	300
Coring.	1,200
Cleaning	600
Taxes (Machinery and Equipment, $72; Building, $144)	216
Compensation Insurance	906
Power	300
Heat and Light	480
Depreciation—Building	384
Depreciation—Machinery and Equipment.	360
Total	$15,246

Apco Company
Other Operating Data

Department	Floor Space (sq ft)	Cost of Machinery and Equipment	Direct Labor per Month	Horsepower Rating
Melting	1,000	$20,000	—	60
Molding	4,000	5,000	$ 4,800	—
Coring.	1,000	15,000	2,000	60
Cleaning	2,000	20,000	5,200	180
Total	8,000	$60,000	$12,000	300

14 The Kellermeyer Specialty Shop has three departments: Clothing, Accessories, and Shoes. The operating expenses for the year ending December 31 are shown below.

Kellermeyer Specialty Shop

	Clothing	Accessories	Shoes	Unassigned	Total
Salaries—Clerks	$78,240	$69,360	$50,400	—	$198,000
Salaries—Others.	—	—	—	$48,000	48,000
Supplies Used	3,800	3,200	2,600	1,400	11,000
Depreciation of Equipment	1,600	3,560	2,000	—	7,160
Advertising.	4,000	7,000	1,960	5,200	18,160
Building Rent	—	—	—	19,000	19,000
Payroll Taxes	—	—	—	12,300	12,300
Workmen's Compensation Insurance	—	—	—	2,080	2,080
Fire Insurance	—	—	—	1,000	1,000
Delivery Expense	—	—	—	1,800	1,800
Miscellaneous Expenses	1,000	800	480	900	3,180

Kellermeyer Specialty Shop

	Clothing	Accessories	Shoes	Total
Sales.	$600,000	$400,000	$200,000	$1,200,000
Cost of Goods Sold. . . .	440,000	236,000	124,000	800,000
Equipment	10,080	24,960	12,960	48,000
Inventory (average)	100,800	81,600	57,600	240,000
Floor Space (sq ft)	2,400	2,400	1,200	6,000
Number of Employees . .	8	12	5	25

Kellermeyer Specialty Shop

Expense	Basis of Allocation
Salaries—Other	Gross Margin
Supplies Used (Unassigned).	Sales
Advertising (Unassigned)	Sales
Building Rent	Floor Space
Payroll Taxes	Salaries (including both direct and other allocated salaries)
Workmen's Compensation Insurance	Salaries (including both direct and other allocated salaries)
Fire Insurance	Cost of Equipment and Inventory
Delivery Expense	Sales
Miscellaneous Expenses (Unassigned).	Number of Employees

Merriam Company
Overhead Distribution Schedule
Month of February

	Total	Dept. A	Dept. B	Dept. C	Dept. S Storeroom	Dept. M Maintenance	
Foremen's Salaries	$ 2,550.00	$ 600.00	$ 675.00	$ 637.50		$ 637.50	
Maintenance Wages	1,870.00					1,870.00	
Storeroom Wages	530.00				$ 530.00		
Janitor's Wages	350.00						(1)
Supplies Used	1,350.00	200.00	300.00	100.00	600.00	150.00	(2)
Fire Insurance	150.00						
Workmen's Compensation Insurance	260.00						(3)
Payroll Taxes	1,320.00						(3)
Property Taxes	300.00						(2)
Rent—Factory Building	550.00						(1)
Depreciation of Machinery and Equipment	450.00	202.50	144.00	45.00	36.00	22.50	(4)
Electricity, Gas, and Water	200.00						(4)
Miscellaneous Factory Costs	1,270.00						
Total	$ 11,150.00						

	Total	Dept. A	Dept. B	Dept. C	Storeroom	Maintenance
Direct Labor Costs	$ 44,700.00	$14,000.00	$15,800.00	$14,900.00	—	—
Value of Assets	$100,000.00	$45,000.00	$32,000.00	$10,000.00	$8,000.00	$5,000.00
Floor Space (sq ft)	50,000	16,000	12,000	20,000	1,600	400
Chargeable Maintenance Hours	500	160	200	120	20	—
Requisitions Drawn	200	140	50	10	—	—
Other Distribution Data:						
Electricity, Gas, and Water	100%	40%	30%	20%	6%	4%
Miscellaneous Factory Costs	100%	30%	25%	25%	10%	10%

a Prepare a four-column statement of operating expenses with columns headed as follows: Clothing; Accessories; Shoes; Total. Begin with direct departmental expenses and show a subtotal. Then continue with the allocated expenses, assigning each item to the various departments. Round all values to the nearest dollar. Round all percentages to one decimal place.

b Prepare a condensed income statement with the following columnar headings: Clothing; Accessories; Shoes; Total. Show the total of operating expenses, calculated in part **a** above, as a single deduction from gross margin.

15 The Schneider Spaghetti Company has three production departments: Tubing, Slicing, and Packing. There are also three service departments: Quality Control, Administration, and Maintenance. In June, the Quality Control Department provided 2,000 hours of service: 500 hours each to Tubing and Slicing, 250 hours to Maintenance, and 750 hours to Packing. In the same month, Administration provided 5,000 hours of service, 1,000 to each of the other five departments. Also, in June, Maintenance provided 1,200 hours of service to Tubing, 1,500 hours to Slicing, 1,800 hours to Packing, 300 hours to Quality Control, and 200 hours to Administration. Costs incurred for Quality Control were $20,000, costs incurred for Administration were $60,000, and costs incurred for Maintenance were $75,000.

Use the step-down procedure to allocate service department costs sequentially. Begin with the service department that receives the least benefit from other service departments and continue to allocate the service department costs of the Schneider Spaghetti Company to its three production departments. Start with Administration, then allocate Maintenance, and finally, Quality Control. Check your solution by making certain that $155,000 is finally allocated to the three production departments.

16 The Horton Hose Factory is engaged in the manufacture and sale of garden hoses. The firm's three production departments are Extruding, Slicing, and Nozzles. These departments are served by the Computer, Personnel, and Administration Departments. In January, the Extruding Department consumed the following services: 500 hours from Personnel, 300 from Computer, and 200 from Administration. Slicing used 250 hours from Personnel, 200 from Computer, and 100 from Administration. Nozzles consumed 450 hours from Personnel, 100 from Computer, and 300 from Administration. In addition, Personnel supplied 150 hours each to Computer and Administration and consumed 100 hours from Computer and 200 from Administration. Computer supplied Administration with 600 hours of service and consumed 300 hours from Administration. Costs for the Computer Department were $100,000; for Personnel, $60,000; for Administration, $50,000.

Allocate all service costs using the step-down procedure. Treat service departments in the following order: Personnel, Computer, Administration. Round answers to the nearest dollar.

17 See the partially completed schedule of production overhead distribution for the Merriam Company for February and the additional information to aid in distributing of overhead shown on the facing page. The costs are to be distributed on the following bases.

(1) Janitor's wages and rent of building: on basis of floor space.

(2) Fire insurance and property taxes: on basis of value of assets in each department.

(3) Workmen's compensation insurance and payroll taxes: on basis of proportions of total labor costs, including allocated portion of janitor's wages.

(4) Electricity, gas, and water, and miscellaneous factory costs: on basis of percentages given.

(5) Maintenance costs: on basis of chargeable maintenance hours.

(6) Storeroom costs: on basis of proportions of number of requisitions drawn.

18 The following factory overhead amounts appeared in the Factory Overhead Control account of the Park Manufacturing Company at December 31. Departments A, B, and C are producing departments; Departments 1 and 2 are service departments.

Foreman's Salary—Dept. A	$ 9,450
Foreman's Salary—Dept. B	8,100
Foreman's Salary—Dept. C	9,000
Foreman's Salary—Dept. 1	7,200
Other Wages—Dept. 1	8,925
Wages—Dept. 2	9,150
Night Guard's Salary	3,600
Supplies Used—Dept. A	4,200
Supplies Used—Dept. B	2,900
Supplies Used—Dept. C	2,700
Supplies Used—Dept. 1	2,460
Supplies Used—Dept. 2	2,350
Building Rent	6,000
Property Taxes	1,500
Fire Insurance	1,200
Workmen's Compensation Insurance	1,400
Payroll Taxes	5,840
Depreciation of Machinery—Dept. A	3,600
Depreciation of Machinery—Dept. B	3,200
Depreciation of Machinery—Dept. C	1,700
Depreciation of Machinery—Dept. 1	500
Depreciation of Machinery—Dept. 2	800
Gas, Electricity, and Water	4,900
Miscellaneous Factory Costs	4,620
	$105,295

The following additional information is available:

(1) The night guard visits Departments A and B eight times, Departments C and 1 six times, and Department 2 four times each evening.

(2) Building rent is distributed in proportion to floor space occupied. Departments A and B each occupy 6,000 square feet; Department C, 1,000 square feet; Department 1, 1,800 square feet; and Department 2, 1,200 square feet.

(3) Property taxes and fire insurance are distributed on the basis of the cost of the equipment and inventory in each department: Department A, $45,000; Department B, $35,000; Department C, $12,000; Department 1, $5,000; and Department 2, $3,000.

(4) Total departmental labor costs, including allocated night guard's salary, serve as the basis for distributing workmen's compensation insurance and payroll taxes. The direct labor costs of the productive departments are as follows: Department A, $44,550; Department B, $30,600; Department C, $19,425.

(5) Gas, electricity, and water, and miscellaneous factory costs are distributed as follows: Department A, 35 percent; Department B, 30 percent; Department C, 25 percent; Department 1, 6 percent; Department 2, 4 percent.

(6) Service Department 2 costs are distributed 50 percent to Department A, 25 percent to Department B, 20 percent to Department C, and 5 percent to Department 1.

(7) Service Department 1 costs are allocated 40 percent to Department A and 30 percent each to Departments B and C.

Prepare an overhead distribution schedule for the Park Manufacturing Company.

19 The Roving Eye Cosmetics Company buys bulk flowers and processes them into perfumes. Their highest-grade perfume, Seduction, and a residue that is processed into Romance and Longingly come from a certain mix of petals. In July, the company used 25,000 pounds of petals. Costs involved in Process A, reducing the petals to Seduction and the residue, were

$200,000, direct materials.
$110,000, direct labor.
$ 90,000, overhead and other costs.

The additional costs of producing Romance and Longingly in Process B were

$ 25,000 direct materials.
$ 50,000 direct labor.
$ 40,000 overhead and other costs.

At the end of the month, total completed production was 5,000 ounces of Seduction, 10,000 ounces of Romance, and 18,000 ounces of Longingly. In addition, 5,000 ounces of Seduction, 10,000 ounces of Romance, and 15,000 ounces of Longingly were still in Process B (a continuous process). These units were on the average one-half complete.

Packaging costs incurred for each product as completed were Seduction, $40,000; Romance, $60,000; Longingly, $100,000. The sales price of Seduction is $90 an ounce; of Romance, $50 an ounce; and of Longingly, $20 an ounce.

a Allocate the joint costs using the relative sales value method.
b Allocate the joint costs using the physical units method.
c Is there any inconsistency in using the physical units method in this case?
d Assume that Roving Eye can sell the squeezed petals from Process B to greenhouses for use as fertilizer. In July, there were 12,000 pounds of squeezed petals left over and sold for $8\frac{1}{3}$¢ per pound. With this new information, answer parts **a** and **b**.

20 Up to the point of separation of joint products X, Y, and Z, total production costs amount to $51,500. The following quantities are produced:

Product X: 3,000 units with an estimated sales value of $3 per unit.
Product Y: 4,500 units with an estimated sales value of $4 per unit.
Product Z: 9,700 units with an estimated sales value of $5 per unit.

a Prepare a schedule showing the allocation of production costs to the three joint products and the unit cost of each product.
b Repeat **a** assuming that product X is treated as a by-product.

21 At the conclusion of process 4, the total cost of processing 25,000 gallons of chemical product K is $362,000. At this point, 5,000 gallons of by-product Y emerge and the remaining 20,000 gallons of K are transferred to process 5 for further work. The Y material will require further processing at an estimated cost of $1 per gallon and then it can be sold for $3 per gallon. Determine the cost per gallon of chemical product K transferred to process 5.

22 The Tru-Life Mannequin Company manufactures female, male, and infant mannequins. The process consists of melting, molding, shaping, sanding, assembling, painting, and producing wigs and painted hair.

In October, the following types of costs were incurred and assigned to the classes of products as follows:

Unassigned process costs (other than related to wigs and painted hair): 250,000 pounds of plaster, costing $.10 per pound; labor costs, $90,000; other costs, $35,000.

Assigned processing costs (other than related to wigs and painted hair): female, $8 each; male, $9 each; infant, $2 each.

Wigs for female mannequins: material, $1 each; labor, $10,000; overhead, $7,500.

Painted hair for male and infant mannequins: material, males, $.15 each; material, infants, $.05 each; labor, $18,000; other, $12,000.

Production for October (with no beginning or ending work-in-process inventories): 50,000 female mannequins, 60,000 male mannequins, and 30,000 infant mannequins. Female mannequins sell for $15 each; male mannequins, for $11 each; and infant mannequins, for $8 each.

a Allocate the joint costs using the relative sales value method.

b Allocate the joint costs using the physical units method.

23 A joint production process results in the splitoff of three products: product A, product B, and product C. Joint costs incurred total $100,000. At splitoff, 10,000 units of product A, 10,000 units of product B, and 20,000 units of product C emerge.

a The units can be sold at splitoff at the following prices: product A, $3 each; product B, $6 each; product C, $4.50 each. Using the relative sales value method, determine the net income of each product if they are sold at splitoff.

b By incurring additional processing costs of $1 per unit, product A can be sold for $5 a unit. By incurring additional processing costs of $3 a unit, product C can be sold for $8 a unit. Using the approximate relative sales value at splitoff method, determine the net income of each product if additional processing takes place.

c Which products should be sold at splitoff and which products should be processed further? Explain.

24 Each of the following describes the contents of interim reports or a policy used by a company in preparing its interim reports. On the basis of this information, does it appear that the company is **(1)** treating the interim period as a discrete accounting period, or **(2)** treating the interim period as a component of the annual period and reporting in such a way that valid inferences about annual net income can be made?

a A department store makes 40 percent of its sales in the months of October through December and allocates 40 percent of the annual depreciation charge on the store building to that quarter.

b Payroll taxes are levied on the first $15,000 of the salary earned by an individual during the year. Many of the company's employees earn more than $15,000 per year. The company reports payroll tax expense for employees in interim reports as the salaries are earned and the liability to the government arises.

c The income tax expense was computed as 22 percent of the income before taxes in the first quarter's interim report and 48 percent of the income before taxes in the third quarter's interim report.

d An appliance manufacturer sells most of its television sets in the second half of the year. The company pays bonuses to executives based on income before taxes for the year. The amount of executive bonuses shown as expenses on each of the four quarterly reports for the year is the same.

e A cereal company reports that income for the quarter is 60 percent larger than for the comparable quarter of the preceding year. The increase is attributable to a reduction in advertising expenditures this quarter, relative to expenditures in the corresponding quarter last year. The company expects its advertising expense for this year to be about the same as for last year.

25 Brown Tax Services, Inc., provides income tax preparation services to its customers. Fee revenues are highly seasonal during the four quarters of the calendar year and occur in the following proportions: .60, .20, .10, .10. That is, 60 percent of the firm's revenues are usually generated during the months of January through March. The following operating costs were anticipated and actually incurred evenly throughout the year ended December 31, 19X5.

Salaries	$250,000
Rent	125,000
Insurance	25,000
Total	$400,000

During the first quarter of 19X5, fee revenues totaled $360,000.

a Determine net income for the first quarter assuming that operating costs are assigned equally to each of the four quarters during the year.

b Determine net income for the first quarter assuming that operating costs are assigned to each quarter in proportion to the percentage of the anticipated year's revenues recognized during each quarter.

c If the pattern of fee revenues during 19X5 occurs as anticipated (that is, .60, .20, .10, .10), what is the anticipated net income for the year?

d Which of the interim earnings measures determined in a and b will lead to the more accurate prediction of the annual net income calculated in c?

26 St. Nicholas Tailors rents out a single Santa Claus costume for the months of November and December each year. Its transactions are as follows:

(1) The company commences business on January 1, 19X1.

(2) October 1, 19X1. One Santa Claus costume is purchased for $100. The costume will last for 10 annual rental periods and is depreciated on a straight-line basis. The costume has a zero estimated salvage value. The company takes a full year of depreciation in the first year.

(3) The costume is rented for the months of November and December 19X1, for $70, total.

(4) January 2, 19X2. Cleaning costs of $5 are incurred for the costume, which has been returned to St. Nicholas Tailors.

(5) The costume is stored for the months of January through October 19X2, at a cost of $2 per month.

(6) The costume is rented for the months of November and December 19X2, for $70, total.

(7) The books are closed annually on December 31. Income taxes are to be paid at the rate of 20 percent of the first $5 of taxable income and 40 percent of the rest.

Income statements for the years 19X1 and 19X2 are shown below.

St. Nicholas Tailors
Income Statements for the Years of 19X1 and 19X2

	19X1	19X2
Revenues.	$70	$70
Expenses:		
Storage Costs.	$ 0	$20
Depreciation.	10	10
Cleaning Costs	0	5
Income Taxes.	23	13
Total Expenses.	$33	$48
Net Income.	$37	$22

Prepare interim quarterly reports for March 31, June 30, September 30, and December 31, 19X1 and 19X2. If interim reports would be inadequate or inappropriate, discuss why.

27 Southeast Industries is a conglomerate firm. In the past several years, two matters involving its patents have required analysis. This case illustrates one use of incremental analysis and cost allocations in decision making.

Plywood Division

In its plywood division, Southeast Industries manufactures striated (decorative) plywood that sells in the marketplace for a premium over ordinary plywood. Southeast Industries owns the patent, called the "Deskey patent," on the striation process and currently is the only producer of striated plywood. The machinery required (in addition to the machinery usually required to make plywood) for the striation process costs $15,000 and lasts five years. Southeast Industries is currently operating its plywood manufacturing operation at 80 percent of normal capacity. The specialized machinery currently used for striation is also operating at only 80 percent of normal capacity. The variable (direct) cost of producing 1,000 board feet of striated plywood is $100. The total fixed cost for producing 1,000 board feet of striated plywood at present levels of output is $10. The selling price of 1,000 board feet of striated plywood is $160.

The market demand for striated plywood appears to be increasing. Industry forecasts are that the demand for striated plywood will increase by about 25 percent next year and remain at that level for the next five years. Southeast Industries can acquire additional striating machinery, if necessary, and produce more striated plywood in a plant in South Carolina that currently is able to produce only ordinary plywood. The costs in the South Carolina plant will be comparable to current costs.

A competitor in the ordinary plywood business, Alabama Atlantic Company, has approached Southeast and asked to purchase nonexclusive rights to use the Deskey patent. Alabama Atlantic Company has calculated that, aside from the cost of the patent license to use the Deskey patent, it can make a net incremental profit (after taxes) of $50 per 1,000 board feet of striated plywood produced. Alabama Atlantic has sufficient capacity to match Southeast's production of striated plywood.

a What is the maximum price that Alabama Atlantic should be willing to pay, per 1,000 board feet, as a royalty for the right to use the Deskey patent?

b What is the minimum price that Southeast Industries should be willing to accept from Alabama Atlantic as a royalty to use the Deskey patent?

c Explain why the two companies are, or are not, likely to reach a mutually agreeable price. In your opinion, what is that price likely to be?

Chemical Division

In its chemical division, Southeast Industries manufactures several kinds of flux used in welding. In particular, it owns the patent for flux no. 660; the patent on flux no. 660 expires in four years. At the end of that time, anyone else can manufacture the no. 660 flux without paying a royalty to Southeast Industries.

The Jefferson Electric Company requires a flux in its manufacturing of electric motors. Currently, Jefferson Electric Company owns the right to use both the no. 620 and the no. 650 fluxes, but does not own the right to use the no. 660 flux. Engineers at Jefferson Electric Company state that neither the no. 620 nor the no. 650 flux are suitable for the line of electric motors that Jefferson Electric wishes to build over the next decade. The no. 660 flux is suitable. The engineers are also certain that the Series 700 fluxes, just developed at Jefferson Electric Company, will be ideal for these motors. Unfortunately, the Series 700 fluxes are not scheduled to come off the production line in large quantities until two years from now. All estimates are that the Series 700 fluxes will be substantially cheaper to manufacture than any of the Series 600 fluxes (nos. 620, 650, and 660).

If Jefferson Electric Company were to purchase all of its flux from Southeast Industries, at Southeast's normal selling prices, then Southeast would make a net incremental aftertax profit of $300,000 per year.

The two companies are attempting to negotiate an agreement whereby Jefferson Electric Company pays Southeast Industries for the right to manufacture the no. 660 flux. Assume that the companies consider each year separately in the negotiations.

d Explain why the two companies are, or are not, likely to reach a mutually agreeable royalty payment for each of the next 10 years. In your opinion, what payment is likely to be agreed to for each of the years. Why? What other factors, if any, would you want to consider?

CHAPTER 14

FINANCIAL AND MANAGERIAL ACCOUNTING: CONGENIAL OR UNCONGENIAL TWINS

Chapter One introduced the need for a congenial consistency between effective managerial decisions and good financial reporting. Sound managerial decisions, based on the principles of incremental analysis and proceeding according to plan, should not have the effect of reducing reported net income to stockholders. Likewise, the results of poor management decisions should not be hidden by inappropriate, generally accepted accounting principles.

The wide range of decisions made by management and the multitude of accounting methods considered acceptable for external reporting make it difficult to form any general conclusion on the congeniality versus uncongeniality question. In this chapter, we present illustrations of three important areas where sound managerial decisions and financial reporting are not congenial: (1) accounting for inventories, (2) accounting for partial obsolescence of fixed assets, and (3) accounting for research and development costs. These illustrations provide a synthesis of much of the material covered in this text.

ACCOUNTING FOR INVENTORIES

Could a business possibly report increasing profits year after year and still be approaching bankruptcy? In Chapter Two we saw that a business can become insolvent (or become unable to pay debts when due) because cash and cash-like assets are insufficient to meet obligations even when the business is reporting large net income. In this section, we shall see that if production exceeds sales period after period, a manufacturing business can report increasing profits even though its sales do not increase and it is approaching insolvency. Effective management requires a good understanding of how the methods of accounting for inventories might cause a misleading picture of operating performance.

Methods of Costing Inventories

The manufacturing process consists of converting raw materials into various products ready to be sold. The manufacturing costs of carrying out this conversion can be classified as one of three types: (1) direct material, (2) direct labor, and (3) manufacturing overhead. Direct material and labor costs vary with the number of units produced. Manufacturing overhead consists of some costs that tend to vary with output (for example, indirect labor and supplies) and some costs that are fixed for the period regardless of the number of units produced (for example, factory rent, property taxes, insurance, and depreciation).

As we discussed in Chapter Twelve, there are two approaches to determining which manufacturing costs are to be included in product costs: absorption costing and direct costing. Under *absorption costing*, all manufacturing costs, whether direct or indirect and whether fixed or variable, are included in a product's cost. Absorption costing is required for financial and tax reporting and is used by most businesses for managerial purposes as well. Under *direct costing*, which is sometimes called *variable costing* or *incremental costing*, only the variable manufacturing costs are considered to be product costs. All costs of being a going concern, the ongoing costs of remaining in business, or fixed costs, are treated as expenses of the period when the costs are incurred.

Illustration of Absorption Costing

The transactions of White Products Company for 19X0 and 19X1 will be used to illustrate the calculation of ending inventory, cost of goods sold, and income under absorption and direct costing. White Products Company began business on January 1, 19X0. The following information relates to the events for 19X0 and 19X1.

	19X0	19X1
Units Produced.	100,000	125,000
Units Sold	80,000	100,000
Selling Price (per unit).	$ 20	$ 20
Direct Materials Cost (per unit)	4	4
Direct Labor Cost (per unit)	5	5
Variable Overhead Cost (per unit)	1	1
Fixed Overhead Cost (per period)	500,000	500,000
Fixed Selling and Administrative Expenses (per period)	350,000	350,000

All selling and administrative expenses are assumed to be fixed. The Company uses a first-in, first-out (FIFO) cost flow assumption. Income taxes are ignored in the illustration.

Exhibit 14.1 shows the calculation of income under absorption costing for 19X0 and 19X1. Production exceeded sales in both years. The manufacturing cost per unit during 19X0 is $15.00, comprised of $4.00 of direct material, $5.00 of direct labor, $1.00 of variable overhead, and $5.00 (= $500,000/100,000 units) of fixed overhead. Income for 19X0 is $50,000. During 19X1, the variable manufacturing cost per unit of $10 (= $4.00 + $5.00 + $1.00) and the total fixed overhead costs of $500,000 are the

EXHIBIT 14.1
White Products Company
Illustration of Absorption Costing

	19X0		19X1	
Sales, 80,000 × $20		$1,600,000	100,000 × $20 . . .	$2,000,000
Cost of Goods Sold				
Beginning Inventory	$ 0		. . . .	$ 300,000
Production Costs:				
Direct Material, 100,000 × $4 .	400,000		125,000 × $4	500,000
Direct Labor, 100,000 × $5. . .	500,000		125,000 × $5	625,000
Variable Overhead,				
100,000 × $1	100,000		125,000 × $1	125,000
Fixed Overhead.	500,000		. . . .	500,000
Total	$1,500,000		. . . .	$2,050,000
Less Ending Inventory,				
20,000 × $15[a]	(300,000)		45,000 × $14[b] . . .	(630,000)
Total		(1,200,000)	. . . .	(1,420,000)
Gross Margin		$ 400,000	. . . .	580,000
Selling and Administrative				
Expenses.		(350,000)	. . . .	(350,000)
Income		$ 50,000	. . . .	$ 230,000

[a] Unit cost is $15 (= $1,500,000/100,000 units produced).

[b] Assuming a first-in, first-out cost flow assumption, the 45,000 units in ending inventory come from 19X1 production. The unit production cost during 19X1 is $14 [= ($500,000 + $625,000 + $125,000 + $500,000)/125,000 units produced].

same as in 19X0. However, because a larger number of units were produced during 19X1, the fixed overhead per unit is less. The manufacturing cost per unit during 19X1 is $14 [= $4.00 + $5.00 + $1.00 + ($500,000/125,000 units)]. Based on a FIFO cost flow assumption, the units in ending inventory are assumed to be the last units produced during 19X1. Cost of goods sold is comprised of the units in beginning inventory plus the first units produced during 19X1. Income for 19X1 is $230,000.

Illustration of Direct Costing

Exhibit 14.2 shows the calculation of income for 19X0 and 19X1 under direct costing. The manufacturing cost per unit is $10 in both years, comprised of direct material, direct labor, and variable overhead. The fixed manufacturing costs are considered a period expense rather than a product cost. Note that a net loss of $50,000 is reported for 19X0 under direct costing as compared to an income of $50,000 under absorption costing. Income for 19X1 under direct costing is again less than the amount under absorption costing.

Cumulative income under absorption costing of $280,000 exceeds the cumulative income under direct costing of $100,000. What accounts for this $180,000 difference? The difference is found in the ending inventories on December 31, 19X1. Absorption costing results in an ending inventory of $630,000, whereas direct costing reports an

EXHIBIT 14.2
White Products Company
Illustration of Direct Costing

	19X0		19X1	
Sales, 80,000 × $20		$1,600,000	100,000 × $20 . . .	$2,000,000
Cost of Goods Sold:				
Beginning Inventory	$ 0		. . . .	$ 200,000
Production Costs:				
Direct Material, 100,000 × $4 .	400,000		125,000 × $4	500,000
Direct Labor, 100,000 × $5. . .	500,000		125,000 × $5	625,000
Variable Overhead,				
100,000 × $1.	100,000		125,000 × $1	125,000
Total	$1,000,000		. . . .	$1,450,000
Less Ending Inventory,				
20,000 × $10ᵃ	(200,000)		45,000 × $10ᵇ	(450,000)
Total		(800,000)	. . . .	($1,000,000)
Contribution Margin		$ 800,000	. . . .	$1,000,000
Fixed Manufacturing Expenses		(500,000)	. . . .	(500,000)
Fixed Selling and				
Administrative Expenses . .		(350,000)	. . . .	(350,000)
Net Income		$ (50,000)	. . . .	$ 150,000

ᵃ Unit cost is $10 (= $1,000,000/100,000 units).
ᵇ Unit cost, assuming a first-in, first-out cost flow assumption, is $10 [= ($500,000 + $625,000 + $125,000)/125,000 units].

ending inventory of $450,000. What has happened is that $180,000 of fixed overhead
has accumulated in the ending inventory valuation under absorption costing but was
expensed under direct costing. Fixed manufacturing costs are immediately released
to expense under direct costing, whereas under absorption costing these costs are not
recognized as an expense until the manufactured goods are sold.

Absorption versus Direct Costing: Reporting Effects

The example for White Products Company required including some distracting
details in order to make the example realistic. This section further illustrates the
essence of the distinction between absorption and direct costing.

Consider a simplified situation where either one, two, or three units of a product
are produced each period. Variable costs of production are $30 per *unit* produced and
fixed costs are $120 per *period*. Thus, the total cost per unit under absorption costing
will be $150, $90, or $70 per unit, depending on whether one, two, or three units are
produced during the period. Each unit sells for $100. Exhibit 14.3 shows the income
and the balance sheet amounts for ending inventory under both absorption and direct
costing for each of five cases. In each case, production and sales over the two periods
total four units. Only the timing of production and sales changes. Total income over
the two periods is $40 for each case. This equality of results from absorption and direct
costing over the two periods stems from the fact that inventory at the start of the first

EXHIBIT 14.3
Absorption versus Direct Costing
(Variable Costs Are $30 per Unit; Fixed Costs Are $120 per Period; Units Sell for $100 Each)

	Case I		Case II		Case III		Case IV		Case V	
	Period 1	Period 2	Period 1	Period 2	Period 1	Period 2	Period 1	Period 2	Period 1	Period 2
Production in Units....	2	2	2	2	3	1	3	1	3	1
Sales in Units (at $100).......	2	2	1	3	3	1	2	2	1	3
Absorption Costing										
Average Unit Cost of Production[a]......	$ 90	$ 90	$ 90	$ 90	$ 70	$150	$ 70	$150	$ 70	$150
Sales............	$200	$200	$100	$300	$300	$100	$200	$200	$100	$300
Cost of Goods Sold...	(180)	(180)	(90)	(270)	(210)	(150)	(140)	(220)	(70)	(290)
Income (Loss).......	$ 20	$ 20	$ 10	$ 30	$ 90	$ (50)	$ 60	$ (20)	$ 30	$ 10
Ending Inventory.....	$ 0	$ 0	$ 90	$ 0	$ 0	$ 0	$ 70	$ 0	$140	$ 0
Direct Costing										
Sales............	$200	$200	$100	$300	$300	$100	$200	$200	$100	$300
Variable Cost of Goods Sold.......	(60)	(60)	(30)	(90)	(90)	(30)	(60)	(60)	(30)	(90)
Fixed Expenses......	(120)	(120)	(120)	(120)	(120)	(120)	(120)	(120)	(120)	(120)
Income (Loss).......	$ 20	$ 20	$ (50)	$ 90	$ 90	$ (50)	$ 20	$ 20	$ (50)	$ 90
Ending Inventory.....	$ 0	$ 0	$ 30	$ 0	$ 0	$ 0	$ 30	$ 0	$ 60	$ 0

[a] Equal to $30 + $120/$n$, where n is the number of units produced that period.

period and also at the end of the second period is zero. If the quantity of units in ending inventory is the same as the quantity of units in beginning inventory, then it makes little difference which costs are included in inventory and which costs are treated as period expense. Differences in reported income are matched with differences in changes in inventory amounts. Thus, in cases I and III, where production quantities equal sales quantities each period, there is no difference between the absorption and direct costing amounts.

Firms seek revenues in order to make profits. All else being equal, the larger are revenues in the long run, the larger must be the expenses of producing those revenues. Businesses engage in production only because production is necessary to generate revenue. Thus, the ideal reporting to management will show increased income in periods when there is increased revenue, assuming that costs are under control and are as expected. Notice in cases IV and V that under absorption costing reported income correlates better with production than with sales, whereas under direct costing, reported income correlates with sales. Even in case II the relation between income and sales, though positive for both absorption and direct costing, is stronger under direct costing than under absorption costing.

In our opinion, managers should prefer the results of direct costing reports because direct costing provides a better indication than absorption costing of the overall effectiveness of the firm in generating profits. Profits ultimately stem from increasing sales activity rather than production activity, all other things being approximately equal.

Justification for Direct Costing

In addition to providing a better indication of the overall effectiveness of a firm in generating profit, a strong case can also be made for direct costing on theoretical grounds. One accounting principle is that of matching revenues and expenses. An expense is an expired asset, a "gone asset." The matching principle requires that whenever it is logical to do so, expenses be reported in the same period as that in which the revenue generated by the asset expiration occurred. Why is the salary of a sales manager treated in total as a period expense rather than being allocated to individual sales as they occur? Once the firm decides to be, and remain, in a line of business, it will need a sales manager. The sales manager's salary will have to be paid month after month. Paying the sales manager's salary this month does not remove the need to pay it next month. There will be no reduction in next month's costs as a result of incurring the cost for the sales manager this month. Thus, paying the salary this month does not provide a future benefit. It does not reduce the costs that will have to be incurred next period.

If the salary of the sales manager were not treated as an expense, an expired asset, then it would have to be treated as an asset. An asset is a future benefit. The sales manager's salary is not generally thought to provide a future benefit. Almost all of the benefit occurs during the current month when the manager is working on this month's sales. Thus, virtually all accountants agree that the cost represented by the sales manager's salary is an expense of the period incurred. It does not provide a future benefit, and therefore cannot be an asset. It is an expired asset or expense.

Similarly, fixed manufacturing costs provide the capacity to produce this period and are not saved if for some reason, such as a shut-down of the production line, no product is manufactured. Consider the rent on a factory. A company is obligated to pay that rent whether or not its factory is used to produce anything. Factory rent is a cost of being a going concern. Under absorption costing, factory rent is part of inventory produced. If rent for the month is $500 and 100 parts are produced, then each part will carry $5 (= $500/100 units) of costs for rent; but if 200 units are produced, then each part will probably carry $2.50 (= $500/200 units) of costs for rent. Under absorption costing, we have the puzzling phenomenon that the cost of each unit produced depends on the total number of units produced. If management wants to know what is happening to costs of units produced in the short run, it should probably prefer to know the incremental costs of production—direct labor, direct materials, and variable overhead. In direct costing, only the variable costs of production are included as product costs. All fixed costs are treated as period expenses.

All costs are variable if the time horizon is long enough. Leases need not be renewed, salaried workers can be fired or not replaced as they retire, equipment need not be replaced, and so on. But management is concerned with assessing performance over shorter time horizons. Direct costing often provides information that is more useful to management in the short run. The basic question asked of each cost incurred in direct costing is, "Does incurring this cost today (or this period) keep us from having to incur that cost tomorrow (or in the future)?" If the answer is *yes*, then the cost in question is an incremental cost and is included in product cost. If the answer is *no*, then direct costing treats the cost in question as an expense of the period. Because raw materials used today in producing a unit eliminate the need to use raw materials tomorrow for that unit, raw materials are incremental product costs under direct costing. But factory rent must be paid whether or not any product is made, so direct costing treats factory rent as a period expense rather than as a production cost. Many factory overhead costs—salaries of factory supervisors and guards, depreciation, and property taxes, for example—will not be less next period for having been incurred this period. These costs are therefore period expenses in direct costing.

Selling Profits to Inventory

In the introduction to this section, we pointed out that a firm could report increasing profits year after year and be approaching bankruptcy. We can now see how this might occur. As long as production exceeds sales, income under absorption costing will continue to be greater than income under direct costing. The difference in income will accumulate in the inventory accounts on the balance sheet under absorption costing. If sales level off or decline (and all other factors remain unchanged), then income under direct costing will remain stable or decline. However, income under absorption costing will continue to increase as long as production exceeds sales. Eventually, there will be a staggering amount of inventory, and a firm will become insolvent or bankrupt in spite of its increasing reported income. Absorption costing "sells profits" to ending inventory.

A firm would not normally continue to increase production in the face of stable or declining sales. The moral of the illustration, however, is clear. Inventory valuation, cost of goods sold, and income are affected by the decision as to how much fixed costs are allocated to inventory and how much to expenses for the period. Evaluation of a firm's or a manager's performance can be influenced by the costing method selected. Also, incorrect managerial decisions might be made if managers consider the effects of the decision on absorption costing income. Because direct costing income more closely corresponds to the principles of incremental analysis, it provides a better basis for evaluating the results of management's decisions.

ACCOUNTING FOR PARTIAL OBSOLESCENCE

We live in an era of rapid change in production methods. Automatic factories, nuclear power, and computers get the headlines, but they are only the most eye-catching examples of the many technological changes that are taking place at a rapid rate. Financial accounting has done little to adapt to and report specifically on the effects of technological obsolescence, although managers continually study the impacts of new technology.

As new equipment and processes become available, capable management is on the alert to discover and evaluate them. Chapter Seven described the procedures for making sound decisions on whether or not to replace equipment in the midst of substantial technological change. If the analysis calls for the replacement of old equipment, and the replacement is made, then financial accounting recognizes the complete obsolescence of the old equipment. The financial accounting reports show a loss in the period when the old equipment is retired even though the change in the technical art may have occurred sometime earlier.

In other important cases, the replacement analysis may indicate that the operating cost savings of the new equipment are not sufficient to justify its substitution for the old, even though the economic value of the old equipment has been reduced. So long as the firm holds the older, partially obsolete equipment, financial accounting does not report the loss in economic value from partial obsolescence. Consider the following example.

A machine now owned by the firm has a book value of $20,000. (This means that the original cost of the machine less the depreciation recognized to date, as shown in the accounting records, is $20,000.) The machine has no current salvage or resale value. It is estimated that the machine will be able to produce 100 units of product during each of the next five years if $5,000 cash is spent each year for materials and labor. A new machine has been developed that costs $20,000, that will also last for five years, and that will also produce 100 units of product each year. The yearly costs of materials and labor to use the new machine are, however, only $2,000.

Clearly, it does not make sense to spend $20,000 this year for the new machine in order to save $3,000 (= $5,000 − $2,000) per year for five years. Equally clear, a new firm entering this industry will select the new machine rather than the old one (if their acquisition costs are identical). We must conclude that the old machine is partially obsolete. Financial accounting would not recognize the partial obsolescence of the old machine. If the correct managerial decision is made and the old machine is continued in use, expenses of $4,000 in depreciation (assuming the straight-line method) plus $5,000 for labor and materials, or $9,000 in total, will be reported each year. If the incorrect managerial decision is made and the new machine is purchased, financial accounting will report the same depreciation expense, $4,000, because the new machine costs the same as the book value of the old one. The expenses for labor and materials will be only $2,000, so that total expenses each year will be only $6,000. If the new machine is acquired, reported expenses will be lower and reported income will be higher than if the old machine is kept. Sound managerial analysis, keeping the old machine, results in lower reported income during most of the next five years.

A more logical financial accounting treatment, in our opinion, would be to recognize a loss of $15,000 in the current period when the analysis is made and to reduce the book value of the old machine to $5,000. Then, over the next five years, the depreciation on the old machine will be $1,000 per year and total expenses will be $6,000 (= $1,000 depreciation + $5,000 materials and labor). Reported expenses and income will be the same as that reported if the new machine is acquired. The net result will be to show a loss from obsolescence currently but no lower income over the five-year operating life. This results in a more satisfactory reporting of the correct managerial decision, which is to keep the old machine. Note that the total income over the five-year period is the same whether or not the loss is recognized currently. The alternative treatment better reflects periodic income.

ACCOUNTING FOR RESEARCH AND DEVELOPMENT EXPENDITURES

In this section, we illustrate how generally accepted accounting principles for research and development costs can make a good manager look bad.

The Commercial Division is a 100-percent owned subsidiary of Solomons Company and has $200,000 total assets. The Commercial Division has been earning $20,000 per year and generating $20,000 per year of cash flow from its assets. The cost of capital of Solomons Company is 10 percent per year. Accordingly, the Commercial Division is judged, by both the all-capital earnings rate and discounted cash flow analysis, to be earning average returns for Solomons Company as a whole. Each year the Commercial Division returns its earnings and cash flows of $20,000 to the parent company, so that its total assets remain at $200,000.

Management of the Commercial Division has found a project, involving research and development expenditures now, that will lead to new products that will generate cash flows in the future. Exhibit 14.4 shows the estimated cash outflows during years 1, 2, and 3 to develop the new product and the estimated cash inflows during years 4, 5, and 6 from producing and selling the new product. The new product will have no future excess of cash inflows over cash outflows after year 6. The project involves aftertax cash outflows totaling $30,000 over the first three years and estimated aftertax cash inflows totaling $45,000 over the last three years. Column (4) shows the present value of each of the cash flows discounted at the 10-percent cost of capital. The net

EXHIBIT 14.4
Solomons Company
Commercial Division
Cash Flows and Net Present Value from Research and Development Project
(All Flows Assumed to Occur at Beginning of Year for Discounting Purposes)

Beginning of Year	Estimated Aftertax Cash (Outflows) Inflows for R&D Project	Present Value Factor (10.0%)	Present Value of Cash Flows Discounted at 10.0%	Present Value Factor (16.47%)	Present Value of Cash Flows Discounted at 16.47%
(1)	(2)	(3)	(4)	(5)	(6)
1................	($ 5,000)	1.00000	($ 5,000)	1.00000	($ 5,000)
2................	(10,000)	.90909	(9,091)	.85859	(8,586)
3................	(15,000)	.82645	(12,397)	.73718	(11,058)
4................	15,000	.75131	11,270	.63293	9,494
5................	15,000	.68301	10,245	.54343	8,151
6................	15,000	.62092	9,314	.46658	6,999
Net Present Value as of Beginning of Year 1.....................			$ 4,341		$ 0

present value of the project is $4,341; the project is clearly worthwhile.[1] In fact, the project has a positive net present value for all discount rates up to 16.47 percent per year. Column (6) of Exhibit 14.4 shows the net present value of each of the cash flows discounted at 16.47 percent per year; their sum is zero. Thus, the internal rate of return on this project is 16.47 percent.

For simplicity, we assume that the Commerical Division continues to pay $20,000 from its other activities to the parent company during the first three years while there are cash outflows for the new project. During the last three years of the new project, the Commercial Division retains $10,000 each year of the $15,000 cash inflow so that by the end of the six-year period the total assets are just what they were at the start of the period, $200,000. This payment policy will leave the Commercial Division in exactly the same position at the end of the project as at the beginning. During the six years of the project, an extra $15,000 from the new project will have been paid over to the parent.

Effects of Generally Accepted Accounting for Research and Development

First we examine the financial statements of the Commercial Division if the project is undertaken, as the net present value analysis indicates it should be. Generally accepted accounting principles require the immediate expensing of all expenditures for research

---

[1]   In this discussion we have omitted any considerations of risk. We assume here that the projected cash flows are certain to occur as projected. If the flows were uncertain, we might require a larger discount rate in computing net present values.

EXHIBIT 14.5
Solomons Company
Commercial Division
Summary of Financial Statement
Data, over Six-Year Period of
Research and Development Project

Year (1)	Other Income (2)	+ Revenue from R&D Project (3)[a]	− Expenses for R&D Project (4)	= Income (5)[c]	− Payments to Parent (6)	= Addition to (Subtraction from) Total Assets (7)[d]	Total Assets, Start of Year (8)[e]	Total Assets, End of Year (9)[f]	Average Total Assets (10)[g]	All-Capital Earnings Rate (11)[h]
Generally Accepted Accounting for R&D: Expenditures Expensed as They Occur										
1	$ 20,000	—	($ 5,000)[a]	$ 15,000	$ 20,000	($ 5,000)	$200,000	$195,000	$197,500	7.6%
2	20,000	—	(10,000)[a]	10,000	20,000	(10,000)	195,000	185,000	190,000	5.3
3	20,000	—	(15,000)[a]	5,000	20,000	(15,000)	185,000	170,000	177,500	2.8
4	20,000	$15,000	—	35,000	25,000	10,000	170,000	180,000	175,000	20.0
5	20,000	15,000	—	35,000	25,000	10,000	180,000	190,000	185,000	18.9
6	20,000	15,000	—	35,000	25,000	10,000	190,000	200,000	195,000	17.9
Totals	$120,000	$45,000	($30,000)	$135,000	$135,000	$ 0	Six-Year Average		$186,667	12.1%[i]
R&D Expenditures Capitalized and Amortized (Straight-Line) Over Years 4, 5, and 6										
1	$ 20,000	—	—	$ 20,000	$ 20,000	0	$200,000	$200,000	$200,000	10.0%
2	20,000	—	—	20,000	20,000	0	200,000	200,000	200,000	10.0
3	20,000	—	—	20,000	20,000	0	200,000	200,000	200,000	10.0
4	20,000	$15,000	($10,000)[b]	25,000	25,000	0	200,000	200,000	200,000	12.5
5	20,000	15,000	(10,000)[b]	25,000	25,000	0	200,000	200,000	200,000	12.5
6	20,000	15,000	(10,000)[b]	25,000	25,000	0	200,000	200,000	200,000	12.5
Totals	$120,000	$45,000	($30,000)	$135,000	$135,000	$ 0	Six-Year Average		$200,000	11.25%[i]

[a] See Exhibit 14.4 for cash flow data.
[b] Total R&D costs of $30,000 amortized to expense on straight-line basis over three years; $10,000 = $30,000/3.
[c] Amounts in column (2) + column (3) − column (4).
[d] Amounts in column (5) − column (6).
[e] $200,000 at the start of year 1; amount for any other year equal to end-of-previous-year balance from column (9).
[f] Amounts in column (7) + column (8).
[g] One-half sum of amounts in column (8) + column (9).
[h] Amount in column (5) divided by amount in column (10). This percentage is the conventional rate of return on investment, the so-called "ROI."
[i] Average income over six years of $22,500 (= $135,000/6) divided by six-year average of total assets, column (10).

and development projects.[2] Thus the Commercial Division will prepare financial statements for the six years of the new project as shown in the top panel of Exhibit 14.5. Column (2) shows the other income of the division, $20,000 per year. Column (3) reports the revenues from the R&D project in the last three years. Column (4) shows the expenses for the R&D project; all expenditures are expensed as they occur. Column (5) shows net income, which is the original income of $20,000 per year plus revenues from the new project, if any, less expenses for the new project, if any. Column (6) shows the payments made to the parent, Solomons Company. Column (7) shows the subtraction from or addition to total assets of the Commercial Division for the year. That amount is income minus payments to the parent. In the first three years total assets of the Commercial Division decline, but in the last three years total assets increase. Columns (8) and (9) show total assets at the start and end of each year. Column (10) shows the average of total assets for the year. Column (11) shows the all-capital earnings rate for the Commercial Division each year, which is accounting income divided by average total assets employed during the year. (The all-capital earnings rate, discussed in Chapter Three, is the firm-wide equivalent of the accounting rate of return for a single project.)

Observe that the all-capital earnings rate drops from the 10-percent figure that had been earned to 7.6 percent in the first year and still further to 2.8 percent by the third year. Reported income and total assets both decline by the amount of the cash flows for the new project, but the overall effect on the all-capital earnings rate is a substantial decrease. Then, starting in the fourth year, accounting income is increased by the cash inflows from the new project and total assets start to increase. In the fourth year, the all-capital earnings rate rises by a factor of 7 from 2.8 percent to 20 percent. The all-capital earnings rate in the fifth and sixth years is somewhat less than in the fourth year because reported income stays constant while total assets continue to increase.

If the managers of the Commercial Division are evaluated by top management with a measure based on accounting income and assets, they may be wary of undertaking such a clearly profitable project as this one. A top management that does not understand what is happening would have to be very patient with the declining performance not to fire the management of the Commercial Division. By the fourth year, the income and all-capital earnings rate increase dramatically to offset the reported dismal performance of the early years. It is scant comfort for management of the Commercial Division to be told that, if the new project goes according to plan, reported income will ultimately be higher, indeed higher by an amount that will compensate for the earlier reported decreases in income. Judgments of management performance are made too frequently for managers of the Commercial Division to take much comfort during the first three years from the thought that compensating gains will occur in the future. It is bad enough for the managers of Commercial Division to think of the danger of being replaced by new managers as a result of deficient financial reporting, but even more discouraging to know that the successor managers will look especially good because of the compensating effect for the income decreases reported in the first three years.

---

[2] Financial Accounting Standards Board, *Statement of Financial Accounting Standards No. 2*, 1974.

The Remedy Based on Accounting Theory

Carefully considered and wise managerial action, such as that by the Commercial Division, should not have the immediate impact of reducing income. The remedy for this troublesome financial reporting phenomenon is relatively straightforward and is suggested by accounting theory. An asset is a future benefit. Because the R&D costs incurred in the first three years of the project are estimated to provide future benefits in the form of increased cash flows in the last three years, those costs should be treated as assets until the future benefits expire. They should not be immediately expensed as expenditures are made, but capitalized instead. By the end of the third year, there would be $30,000 of R&D assets. These assets could be amortized over the three years when the project is providing cash flows and the future benefits of the R&D project are expiring.

The bottom panel of Exhibit 14.5 shows the effect on hypothetical financial statements of capitalizing R&D costs. In the first three years, cash is converted into long-term R&D assets, but total assets and income of the Commercial Division are unchanged. Thus, the all-capital earnings rate is unchanged. Then, in the last three years, net income goes up by $5,000 per year—$15,000 of revenues less $10,000 of amortization expense of R&D assets. The all-capital earnings rate increases slightly to 12.5 percent.[3] By the end of the sixth year, reported assets are exactly the same as when R&D expenditures are expensed, but the reporting during the life of the new project is quite different.

Managerial Evaluation of Research and Development Decisions

Top management of Solomons Company should capitalize R&D costs for projects that are proceeding according to schedule when evaluating management of the Commercial Division with measures based on accounting data. If it does not, Commercial Division management may not undertake such projects as the one illustrated here. The problem for decision makers is even more difficult when there are only individual shareholders and the reporting is for them rather than an upper level of management. (This would occur if Commercial Division were a separate, publicly owned company.) Clearly, generally accepted accounting principles make management look unnecessarily bad in the short run and unnecessarily good in later years when a single R&D project is considered. In reality, a growing firm undertakes new and more expensive projects every year. The all-capital earnings rate will constantly be artificially depressed for a company that continues to expand its R&D efforts even when those efforts pay off as planned. Only when the firm stops growing and stops developing new ideas will the accounting measures of performance "catch up" and overcompensate for the prior years' understatement of income. The firm that stops getting new ideas is not the one that is doing best in a real sense, but it is the one that reports larger income.

---

[3]   Some more advanced texts discuss the *compound interest method of amortization* and related matters that allow for asset capitalization and amortization in such a way that the all-capital earnings rate for the entire six-year period is the same each year.

Correct evaluation of managerial decisions about long-term projects should be based on an evaluation of management's proper use of the net present value rule, which is in turn based on accuracy of cash flow estimates. If managerial decisions are to be evaluated on the basis of accounting data, then the accounting principles used in constructing those data should be based on good accounting theory, not necessarily on generally accepted accounting principles. Sound accounting theory should record assets when there are future benefits and should record expenses only when the benefits expire.

SUMMARY

The three illustrations in this chapter indicate some of the more important areas where sound management decisions and financial reporting are uncongenial. There is a common thread running through these examples and others that could be offered. Managerial decisions must rely on estimates of current and future cash flows. Financial reporting focuses on past cash flows and the allocation of those cash flows to periods in accordance with generally accepted accounting principles. These "principles" are more often guided by considerations of conservatism and objectivity than economic reality.

A change, though, is on the horizon for financial reporting. As we discuss in greater depth in Chapter Fifteen, many large firms are now required to present current replacement cost data for inventories, depreciable assets, cost of goods sold, and depreciation expense in addition to the amounts based on historical costs. If this trend toward reporting current value information continues, many of the inconsistencies between managerial and financial accounting will be removed. For example, the reporting of fixed assets at current replacement cost results in the immediate recognition of partial obsolescence. When the current value of the benefits from research and development expenditures are determined in a reasonably accurate manner, then good and poor managerial research and development decisions are properly reflected in the financial statements.

QUESTIONS AND PROBLEMS

1 Review the meaning of the following concepts or terms discussed in this chapter.
   a Absorption (full) costing.
   b Direct (variable) costing.
   c Overhead costs.
   d Production cost.
   e Period expense.
   f Selling profits to inventory.
   g Partial obsolescence.
   h Capitalizing research and development cost.
   i Expensing research and development cost.

2 Assume two years of constant production quantities and rising end-of-year inventory quantities. In year 2, fixed costs are substantially higher than in year 1. Compare the differences in reported income resulting from using absorption costing on the one hand and direct costing on the other in years 1 and 2.

3 Under what circumstances would the shift from absorption costing to direct costing have little effect on the balance sheet and income statement?

4 Inventory valuations appear only on the balance sheet. How is it, then, that inventory valuations affect net income for the period?

5 During its first year of operations, a company produced 1,000 units of product and sold 800 for $80 each. Fixed costs of production for the year were $10,000, and variable costs of production were $25,000.
  a Construct a partial income statement using absorption costing principles.
  b Construct a partial income statement using direct costing principles.

6 Refer to the Standard Products Company illustration in the chapter. Notice that Exhibits 14.1 and 14.2 and the accompanying discussion assume a FIFO cost flow assumption. The purpose of this problem is to demonstrate that the difference between absorption and direct costing effects on financial statements are not substantially affected by the selection of a cost flow assumption. For this problem, make a LIFO (last-in, first-out) cost flow assumption.
  a Reconstruct Exhibits 14.1 and 14.2 as they would appear if a LIFO cost flow assumption were used.
  b Explain the cause of the difference in 19X1 net income computed under absorption costing and direct costing.

7 The Sanlex Company started the year with no inventories on hand. It manufactured two batches of inventory that were identical except that the variable costs of producing the first batch were $120 and the variable costs of producing the second batch were $200 because of rising prices. By the end of the year, Sanlex Company had sold three-fourths of the first batch for $300 and none of the second batch. The ending inventory had a market value of $305. Total fixed manufacturing costs for the year were $160. Under the absorption costing procedure, $100 of fixed manufacturing costs allocated to units produced remained in inventory at the close of the year. Selling and administrative expenses for the year were $30.
  Prepare a statement of pretax income for the Sanlex Company for the year under both of the following sets of assumptions:
  a FIFO, acquisition cost basis and absorption costing.
  b FIFO, acquisition cost basis and direct costing.

8 Copeland Company began operations in 19X0. Its production costs include a substantial component of items that are fixed for relatively long time periods. The following amounts shown in the top panel on the next page were produced and sold over the first six years of operations. Over this six-year period, production costs and selling prices did not change. A FIFO cost flow assumption is used.
  Fill in answers for the question marks in the table shown in the second panel on the next page. Two items are answered as examples.

Copeland Company

Year	Units Produced	Units Sold
19X0	10,000	8,000
19X1	5,000	6,000
19X2	5,000	5,000
19X3	10,000	11,000
19X4	10,000	4,000
19X5	0	6,000

	Absorption Costing Income for the Year Compared to Direct Costing Income for the Year	Absorption Costing Inventory at End of Year Compared to Direct Costing Inventory at End of Year
19X0	Higher	Higher
19X1	?	?
19X2	?	?
19X3	?	?
19X4	?	?
19X5	?	?

9 (This problem and the next are adapted from an article by Raymond P. Marple in *The Accounting Review,* July 1956.)

The All Fixed Costs Company is so named because it has no variable costs—all of its costs are fixed and vary with time rather than output. The All Fixed Costs Company is located on the bank of a river and has its own hydroelectric plant to supply power, light, and heat. The company manufactures a synthetic material from air and river water, and sells its product on a long-term, fixed-price contract. It has a small staff of employees, all hired on an annual salary basis. The output of the plant can be increased or decreased by adjusting a few dials on the control panel. The following data show production, sales, and cost information for the first two months of operations.

All Fixed Costs Company

	Month 1	Month 2
Production	20,000 tons	0 tons
Sales	10,000 tons	10,000 tons
Selling Price per Ton	$ 30	$ 30
Costs (All Fixed):		
Production	$280,000	$280,000
General & Administrative	$ 40,000	$ 40,000

a Prepare income statements for each of the two months using absorption costing.
b Prepare income statements for each of the two months using direct costing.
c Which costing method is management likely to prefer? Why?

10 The Semi-Fixed Cost Company is just like the All Fixed Cost Company (see the preceding problem) except that its production costs are $210,000 per month and $7 per ton. The production, sales, and general and administrative cost data for months 1 and 2 for the All Fixed Cost Company apply to the Semi-Fixed Cost Company as well.

a Prepare income statements for each of the two months using absorption costing.

b Prepare income statements for each of the two months using direct costing.

c Which costing method is management likely to prefer? Why?

11 The following data pertain to operations of the Sikes Company in 19X0 and 19X4.

	19X0	19X4
Opening Inventory in Units.	0	6,000
Units Produced.	50,000	48,000
Units Sold	48,000	50,000
Fixed Overhead Production Costs.	$12,000	$12,000
Variable Overhead Production Costs	12,000	14,000
Fixed Selling Costs	10,000	10,000
Direct Labor.	36,000	40,000
Direct Materials.	48,000	50,000

There are no work-in-process inventories, and a FIFO inventory flow assumption is used.

a Compute the dollar value of ending finished goods inventory in 19X0 under absorption costing.

b Compute the dollar value of ending finished goods inventory in 19X0 under direct costing assuming that all fixed overhead production costs would be incurred even if there were no production.

c Which method, absorption or direct costing, implies larger reported income for 19X0?

12 Refer to the data in the preceding problem for Sikes Company.

a Compute the dollar value of ending finished goods inventory in 19X4 under absorption costing.

b Compute the dollar value of ending finished goods inventory in 19X4 under direct costing assuming that all fixed overhead production costs would be incurred even if there were no production.

c Which method, absorption or direct costing, implies larger reported income for 19X4?

13 The following data relate to the cost and revenue structure of Beel Company.

Variable Costs (per unit):	
Material	$ .90
Labor	1.20
Overhead.	.90
Total	$3.00
Fixed Costs (per period).	$15,000

Assume the following data with respect to sales and production levels (units).

Assumption	Sales	Production
1.	15,000	15,000
2.	15,000	16,000
3.	15,000	14,000
4.	14,000	14,000
5.	14,000	15,000
6.	14,000	16,000
7.	16,000	16,000
8.	16,000	15,000
9.	16,000	14,000

All sales occur at a selling price of $6.00 per unit.

a Under absorption costing, calculate for each set of assumptions the following: Sales; Cost of Goods Sold; Gross Margin; Contribution to Profit.

b Under direct costing, calculate for each assumption the following: Sales; Cost of Goods Sold; Contribution Margin; Fixed Costs; Contribution to Profit.

c Summarize the result of this exercise by explaining how the relationship between sales and production affects net income for the period when absorption and direct costing are used.

14 Lucius Green runs a distillery under the corporate name Green's Distillery. Each year Green distills 10,000 barrels of whiskey, puts the product in barrels, and stores the barrels for four years. Each year Green sells 10,000 barrels of four-year-old whiskey to a retail chain, which bottles the whiskey and puts its own label on the product. The retailer has a long-term, fixed-price contract with Green. The retailer is so pleased with Green's product that it is willing to buy the whiskey at any age. The contract specifies that the retailer will buy a barrel of newly distilled whiskey for $100, a barrel of one-year-old whiskey for $118, a barrel of two-year-old whiskey for $140, a barrel of three-year-old whiskey for $168, and a barrel of four-year-old whiskey for $200. In the past, Green has always sold only four-year-old whiskey. Prices and costs have been stable for several years and are expected to remain so. An income statement for Green's Distillery for a typical year when 10,000 barrels are distilled and 10,000 barrels of four-year-old whiskey are sold appears below.

Green's Distillery
Income Statement for Typical
Year When 10,000 Barrels Are
Produced and 10,000 Barrels
Are Sold

Sales (10,000 Barrels at $200).		$2,000,000
Cost of Goods Sold:		
Variable Costs ($50 per Barrel, 10,000 Barrels)	$500,000	
Depreciation of Distilling Equipment	100,000	
Storage Costs of Aging Whiskey		
($20 per Barrel per Year, 40,000 Barrels).	800,000	(1,400,000)
General and Administrative Expenses		(200,000)
Income before Taxes.		$ 400,000

During 19X0, the retailer suggested to Lucius Green that the distillery be doubled in capacity and that the contract be rewritten so that the retailer would promise to buy as much as Green wanted to produce.

Assume that Green doubled capacity and, starting in 19X1, distilled 20,000 barrels of whiskey each year to be aged. All costs shown on the income statement for 10,000 barrels doubled (that is, *unit* costs including depreciation remained constant) except for general and administrative expenses, which increased $100,000 a year to $300,000 a year. By 19X5 the first batch of extra product was fully aged, and, starting in 19X5, Green sold 20,000 barrels of four-year-old whiskey to the retail chain. During 19X1 through 19X4, 10,000 barrels were sold.

a Prepare income statements for each of the years 19X1 through 19X5 using absorption costing.
b Prepare income statements for each of the years 19X1 through 19X5 using direct costing.
c Which of the costing methods appears to give a better picture of the results of Green's Distillery for the years 19X2–19X4?
d You will probably judge in **c** that absorption costing better reflects the situation. Why is it that direct costing appears to fail in this case, and what should be concluded from this?

15 The Miller Company had sales of $225,000 in 19X1 and $1,800,000 in 19X5. The president of the company has been unhappy because, whereas net income was $15,000 in 19X1, it was only $12,000 in 19X5, when sales volume was 12 times as large. The president expressed concern about the profit decline, pointing out that economic conditions had been favorable in the past five years, sales had grown enormously, and the company had been able to reduce average manufacturing costs by a whopping $66 per unit even though direct material, direct labor, and related costs had increased by 10 percent and fixed costs had doubled since 19X1. The president was also concerned that underapplied overhead of $20,000 for 19X1 and overapplied overhead of $100,000 for 19X5 had not been included in the net income report. The income statements and supplemental information on production and sales for the Miller Company for 19X1 and 19X5 are shown below.

Miller Company
Income Statements for 19X1 and 19X5

	19X1	19X5
Revenues	$225,000	$1,800,000
Expenses:		
Direct Material, Direct Labor, and		
Variable Overhead Costs	$ 40,000	$ 528,000
Fixed Manufacturing Costs	120,000	600,000
Selling and Administrative	50,000	660,000
Total Expenses	$210,000	$1,788,000
Net Income	$ 15,000	$ 12,000
Units Produced during Year	1,500 units	10,000 units
Units Sold during Year	1,000 units	12,000 units

The Company uses absorption costing and a FIFO cost flow assumption for inventories. The total fixed manufacturing costs and the variable manufacturing costs per unit were the same in 19X1 as in 19X0. Also, they were the same in 19X5 as in 19X4.

a Prepare a schedule to show why the president believes that average manufacturing costs per unit have declined by a "whopping $66 per unit" between 19X1 and 19X5.

b Prepare a schedule that correctly shows how average manufacturing costs per unit have actually changed between 19X1 and 19X5.

c Prepare income statements for 19X1 and 19X5 using direct costing.

d Which of the two sets of income statements do you feel provides a better report for management and why?

16 Huefner Company has prepared the following annual flexible budget for use in making decisions relating to product X for the first year of operations.

Huefner Company
Flexible Budget, Product X
First Year of Operations — Produce and Sell

	100,000 Units	150,000 Units	200,000 Units
Sales (at $8 per unit)	$800,000	$1,200,000	$1,600,000
Manufacturing Costs:			
Direct Material	$150,000	$ 225,000	$ 300,000
Direct Labor.	200,000	300,000	400,000
Variable Overhead	50,000	75,000	100,000
Fixed Overhead	100,000	100,000	100,000
Total Manufacturing Costs	$500,000	$ 700,000	$ 900,000
Selling and Other Expenses:			
Variable.	100,000	150,000	200,000
Fixed.	260,000	260,000	260,000
Total Expenses.	$860,000	$1,110,000	$1,360,000
Operating Income (or Loss)	($ 60,000)	$ 90,000	$ 240,000

The 200,000-unit budget was adopted by the management group, and the costs indicated therein were accepted as the goal for the period. This also meant that the 200,000-unit base would be used for allocating the fixed manufacturing costs to units of product X if an absorption costing system were to be used. No decision was made at the outset as to which type of cost accounting system would be selected for internal reporting. Accordingly, complete records were kept with the idea that the necessary data would be available for the subsequent adoption of any of the recognized cost accounting procedures.

All fixed costs are incurred uniformly throughout the year, that is, 1/12 of the annual total each month. Annual sales are expected to have this seasonal pattern, by quarters:

First Quarter.	10 percent
Second Quarter	20 percent
Third Quarter	30 percent
Fourth Quarter	40 percent

Assume that at the end of the first *six months* the following data are available:

Production Completed.	120,000 units
Sales.	60,000 units

All cost incurrences have been identical with those implied by the cost relations in the flexible budget.

a Compute the amount of fixed factory costs applied to product under absorption costing for the first six months.

b Compute reported operating income (or loss) for the first six months under absorption costing.

c Compute reported operating income (or loss) for the first six months under direct costing.

d Compute reported operating income (or loss) for the first six months under direct costing with a seasonalized assignment of fixed manufacturing cost where fixed cost is assigned to a quarter in proportion to sales of that quarter relative to yearly sales. (Prepare an abbreviated income statement.)

e After reviewing the results for the first six months, the management group has changed the projection of its seasonal pattern for the current year to be 20 percent, 20 percent, 20 percent, 40 percent. Using these percentages as a basis, estimate operating income for the current year. (Prepare an abbreviated income statement.)

17 (Adapted from a problem by David O. Green.)

The Utah Specialty Products Company manufactures a stylized product that changes substantially each year. Its fiscal year starts on April 1. Because the product is different each year, the annual production plan calls for no beginning or ending inventory. Historically, the pattern of yearly sales has been as follows:

April 1–June 30	40 percent of annual sales
July 1–September 30	30
October 1–December 31	20
January 1–March 31	10
Total Annual Sales	100 percent

Sales for the quarter beginning April 1, 19X0, were expected to be 140,000 units. Production for the quarter beginning April 1, 19X0, was 150,000 units. During that quarter only 100,000 units were sold. Operating data for the quarter April 1–June 30, 19X0, are given below.

Utah Specialty Products Company
Operating Data for April 1 through June 30, 19X0

Sales: 100,000 Units at $2.50 Each	$250,000
Manufacturing and Operating Costs:	
Variable Manufacturing Costs for 150,000 Units	$135,000
Fixed Manufacturing Costs[a]	43,750
Selling Costs, Variable with Unit Sales	40,000
Fixed Selling and Administrative Costs[a]	32,750

---

[a] Fixed manufacturing, selling, and administrative costs are incurred evenly throughout the year; these amounts represent one-fourth of the expected yearly total.

a Prepare an income statement for the quarter using absorption costing.

b Prepare an income statement for the quarter using direct costing.

c As a basis for evaluating the performance of Utah Specialty Products, what strengths and weaknesses can you find with each of the income statements prepared?

d On July 1, 19X0, the sales manager predicts that 250,000 units will be sold for the entire year starting April 1, 19X0. What do this information and the operating costs for the first quarter suggest will be the annual income of the Company for the year April 1, 19X0, through March 31, 19X1?

e Suggest alterations of the quarterly income statements prepared in **a** or **b** above that would make them more useful as predictors of annual income. (You may find it useful to review the material in Chapter Thirteen on interim reporting.)

18 A manufacturing company segments its operations into two divisions for purposes of internal performance evaluation. Division A assembles the firm's product, whereas Division B conducts the finishing, packing, and selling activities. Quarterly sales during the first year of operations are expected to be seasonal in the following percentages: 20 percent, 30 percent, 30 percent, 20 percent.

Division A plans to produce units at a reasonably uniform rate throughout the year. Units completed by Division A are immediately transferred to Division B on the basis of cost of manufacturing plus a 25-percent markup on cost. A representative market price for the product at this stage is $22. Divisional fixed selling and administrative expenses are allocated equally to each quarter during the year. Central corporate expenses are allocated to divisions on the basis of total sales.

A performance report for the first quarter appears below:

	Division A	Division B
Annual Budgeted Production (Units)	48,000	40,000
Budgeted Production—First Quarter (Units)	12,000	8,000
Units Produced.	10,000	8,000
Units Sold	10,000	5,000
Sales.	$250,000	$500,000
Cost of Goods Sold:		
Variable Expenses	(150,000)	(375,000)
Fixed Expenses[a]	(50,000)	(50,000)
Gross Profit	$ 50,000	$ 75,000
Divisional Fixed Selling and Administrative		
Expenses	(12,000)	(50,000)
Central Corporate Expenses.	(25,000)	(50,000)
Divisional Income (Loss)	$ 13,000	($ 25,000)

[a] Exclusive of any adjustment for under- or overapplied expenses.

a What strengths and weaknesses do you see in this divisional performance report?

b Making whatever changes you feel are appropriate, prepare a divisional performance report for these two divisions for the first quarter. Describe briefly the justification for your treatment of the transfer price, fixed manufacturing expenses, fixed selling and administrative expenses, and central corporate expenses.

19 The Manfin Company uses a cost-of-capital rate of 12 percent in making investment decisions. It currently is considering two projects that are mutually exclusive, each requiring an initial investment of $10 million. The first project has a net present value of $21 million and an internal rate of return of 20 percent. This project will be completed within one year and will raise accounting income and earnings per share almost immediately thereafter. The second project has a net present value of $51 million and an internal rate of return of 30 percent. The second project requires incurring large, noncapitalizable expenses over the next few years before net cash inflows from sales revenue result. Thus accounting income and earnings per share for the next few years will not only be lower than if the first project is accepted but also lower than earnings currently reported.

a Should the short-run effects on accounting income and earnings per share influence the decision as to the choice of projects? Explain.

b Should either of the projects be accepted? If so, which one? Why?

20 Equilibrium Company spends $30,000 on advertising the Company's brand names and trademarks. As a result of the advertising expenditures, gross margin on sales after taxes has been $33,000 larger each year than it would have been without the advertising expenditures. For the purposes of this problem assume that all advertising expenditures are made on the first day of each year and that the $33,000 extra aftertax gross margin on sales occurs on the first day of the next year. Excluding any advertising assets, or profits, Equilibrium Company has $100,000 of other assets which have been producing an aftertax income of $10,000 per year. Equilibrium Company has followed a policy of declaring dividends each year equal to net income, and has a cost of capital of 10 percent per year.

a Is the advertising policy a sensible one? Explain.

b How should the expenditures for advertising be reflected in Equilibrium Company's financial statements in order to reflect accurately the managerial decision of advertising at the rate of $30,000 per year? That is, how can the advertising expenditures be accounted for in such a way that the accounting rate of return for the advertising project and the all-capital earnings rate for the firm reflect the 10-percent return from advertising?

21 Many companies evaluate managerial effectiveness by examining the accounting rate of return of a given manager's division or product lines. If managers think that they are going to be evaluated by an accounting rate of return criterion, they may make decisions in order to increase, or not to decrease, the accounting rate of return. *Statement of Financial Accounting Standards No. 2* requires the immediate expensing of R&D expenditures, whereas capitalization of those expenditures is a reasonable and theoretical alternative. Assume that a manager is contemplating making R&D expenditures that have a positive net present value when cash flows are discounted at the firm's cost of capital. Indicate how generally accepted accounting principles for R&D expenditures are likely to affect the decision making of the manager who is evaluated by the accounting rate of return.

22 The Consumer Division is a 100-percent owned subsidiary of Herzlinger Company and has $300,000 of total assets. The Consumer Division has been earning $45,000 per year and generating $45,000 per year of cash flow from assets. The cost of capital of the Herzlinger Company is 15 percent per year. Each year the Consumer Division distributes its earnings and pays cash of $45,000 to the parent company. Management of the Consumer Division has discovered a project involving research and development costs now that will lead to new products. The anticipated cash flows of the project are as follows:

Beginning of Year	Cash (Outflow) Inflow
1	($24,000)
2, 3, and 4	10,000 each year

Assume that the project is undertaken, that cash flows are as planned, and that the Consumer Division makes payments to the parent of $45,000 at the end of the first year and $47,000 at the end of each of the next three years.

a Compute the all-capital earnings rate of the Consumer Division for each year of the project, assuming that R&D expenditures are expensed as they occur. Use the year-end balance of total assets in the denominator.

b Compute the all-capital earnings rate of the Consumer Division for each year of the project, assuming that R&D costs are capitalized and then amortized on a straight-line basis over the last three years of the project. Use the year-end balance of total assets in the denominator.

c Compute the accounting rate of return for the new project, independent of the other assets and of the income of the Consumer Division, assuming that R&D costs are capitalized and then amortized on a straight-line basis over the entire four years of the project.

d How well has the management of the Consumer Division carried out its responsibility to its owners? On what basis do you make this judgment?

23 This chapter points out how economically sound managerial decisions can often be reported as poor ones and vice versa, at least in the short run. This problem provides an opportunity to explore certain areas where financial accounting rules may impede effective managerial decisions. The financial accounting issues involved in the situations below have not all been discussed in the book. The instructor can provide the student with suitable background, or the student may be asked to do his or her own research in identifying the issues.

For each of the FASB *Statements* described below, describe the required accounting treatment and reasonable alternatives to it. Then describe how the required treatment might alter the behavior of a manager who is to be evaluated by the accounting statements. Assume that the manager wishes to make decisions that are in the long-run best interests of the firm by maximizing the present value of future cash flows, but that the manager is being evaluated currently by reported net income.

a FASB *Statement No. 2,* "Accounting for Research and Development Costs." This statement requires the immediate expensing of research and development costs.

b FASB *Statement No. 5,* "Accounting for Contingencies." In the past, firms often did not carry casualty insurance on some of their assets, but instead spoke of themselves as being "self-insured." They used the following accounting. Each year the firm would charge to income an amount for insurance expense while setting up an estimated liability for losses. Under that practice, firms would later charge catastrophic losses against the estimated liability, rather than against income in the period when the loss occurs. Income under this method would be smoother than when the losses are charged to income in the period of the loss. *Statement No. 5* forbids this practice; it requires that such expense or loss be recognized only in the period when an actual loss occurs.

c FASB *Statement No. 7,* "Accounting and Reporting by Development Stage Enterprises." This statement, in effect, requires expensing of preoperating costs incurred by new businesses. Preoperating costs are those costs incurred before a business has begun its intended operations.

d FASB *Statement No. 8,* "Accounting for the Translation of Foreign Currency Transactions and Foreign Currency Financial Statements." This statement specifies, among other things, the accounting to be followed for changes in the U.S. dollar value of monetary assets and liabilities denominated in foreign currencies. When the exchange rate between the foreign currency and the dollar changes, then there has been a change in the

U.S. dollar equivalent amount for that asset or liability. This statement requires that the result of the change (whether gain or loss) be reflected in income of the current period. Formally, losses were often charged against previously deferred gains, thereby bypassing the income statement.

24 Refer to problems **5** and **6** at the end of Chapter One, on page 16. Using the data given in Problem **5** and the steps outlined in Problem **6,** compute the dollar amount of the partial technological obsolescence for the existing machine that has a current book value of $10,000.

25 Refer to the data in Problem **22** at the end of Chapter Fifteen, on page 389. Assume that the book value (historical cost less accumulated depreciation to date) of the oil-burning plant is now $10 million and that it has a remaining useful life of 20 years.
  a Compute the dollar amount of technological obsolescence using the methods described in this chapter and in Problem **6** at the end of Chapter One (on page 16).
  b Work part **a** of Problem **22** at the end of Chapter Fifteen. Subtract the result from the $11 million dollar cost of the coal-burning plant. Now subtract that result from the $10 million book value of the oil-burning plant to derive another estimate of the dollar amount of the partial technological obsolescence of the oil-burning plant.
  c Which of the estimates of partial technological obsolescence derived in **a** and **b** above do you think provides a better measure under these circumstances? Why?

PART FIVE

SPECIAL TOPICS: MANAGERIAL DECISION MAKING

CHAPTER 15
ACCOUNTING FOR THE EFFECTS OF CHANGING PRICES

The conventional financial accounting model rests on the assumption that a *common* or *uniform measuring* unit is used in recording the results of transactions and events in the accounting records. That is, the measuring unit (the dollar) applied in recording the acquisition of a machine costing $10,000 five years ago is of the same dimension as the measuring unit applied in recording the purchase of merchandise inventory one week ago for $10,000. The conventional accounting model also rests on the *realization convention:* increases in the market prices of individual assets are generally not recognized as gains in determining net income until the assets are sold or otherwise disposed of. Only at the time of sale is the determination of the amount of the gain considered to be sufficiently objective to warrant recognition in the accounts.

During periods when the prices of all goods and services in the economy are relatively stable, the common measuring unit assumption and realization convention are not of particular concern in the analysis and interpretation of financial statements. Market prices of specific goods and services seldom remain stable, however. Since 1945, the general level of prices in the United States has increased at an average rate of approximately 4 percent per year. In recent years, the rate of inflation has been substantially greater. Even during periods when prices in general have remained relatively stable, the prices of some goods and services have increased or decreased significantly. Changing prices, either in general or of specific goods and services, raise serious questions about the appropriateness of the common monetary measuring unit assumption and the realization convention.

This chapter considers the effects of changing prices on the conventional accounting measurements of net income and financial condition. Several procedures for measuring and reporting the effects of changing prices in accounting reports are described briefly and illustrated. An assessment of each of these suggested accounting procedures is then presented.

IMPACT OF CHANGING PRICES ON CONVENTIONAL FINANCIAL STATEMENTS

The accounting problems associated with changing prices should be separated into those related to *changes in general price levels* and those associated with *changes in prices of specific goods and services.* This distinction might be grasped most easily by considering the manner in which a price index is constructed.

Nature and Construction of Price Indices

A *price index* is a measure of the prices of a group, or "basket," of goods and services between two dates. For example, assume that we wished to construct a price index for foods to measure the change in overall prices between January 1 and December 31 of a particular year. We would begin by constructing a typical market basket for food items. To keep the illustration simple, suppose we specify that a typical market basket includes a meat, starch, vegetable, beverage, and bread product. We would determine the price of a specific commodity in each of these food groupings at the beginning and end of the year. The prices of the individual commodities at each date would be summed to obtain the aggregate market price of the basket of goods. The aggregate market price at one date would then be compared to the aggregate price at another date to obtain a price index. Exhibit 15.1 illustrates the construction of such a price index.

Prices for this group of commodities increased an average of 10 percent between the beginning and end of the year. The prices of the individual commodities, however, changed at widely varying rates. The price of bread remained relatively stable, whereas the price of rice decreased slightly. The prices of T-bone steak, frozen vegetables, and beer increased significantly, but only that of beer increased more than the average of 10 percent for the group.

EXHIBIT 15.1
Illustration of the Construction of a Price Index

Commodity	January 1	December 31	Percentage Change in Market Price of Individual Commodities
T-Bone Steak (pound)	$2.40	$2.60	+8%
Rice (32 ounces).	1.30	1.20	−8
Frozen Vegetable (package).	.40	.44	+10
Beer (six-pack)	1.30	1.75	+35
Bread (loaf)	.60	.61	+2
Total	$6.00	$6.60	
Price index, where January 1 prices equal 100.	100	110 (= $6.60/$6.00)	

Price indices are constructed by the federal government for many different groupings, or baskets, of commodities. Some of these indices are based on a wide assortment of goods and services and are intended as measures of price changes in general. The two most important *general price indices* are the Gross National Product Implicit Price Deflator Index and the Consumer Price Index. Numerous indices are constructed for specific groupings of goods and services, such as women's apparel, men's shoes, automobiles, and refrigerators. Even these more *specific price indices,* however, contain an assortment of goods of various qualities, dimensions, and styles within the particular product category.

Accounting Problems Associated with General Price Level Changes

As general price levels change, the purchasing power of the dollar, or its command over goods and services, changes. For example, Exhibit 15.1 indicates that $6.60 was required on December 31 to purchase the same group of foods as $6.00 would have purchased on January 1. The purchasing power of the dollar for this collection of foods declined during the year. Viewed somewhat differently, the December 31 dollar has the equivalent food purchasing power of $.909 January 1 dollars (= $6.00/$6.60 or 100/110).

When the dollar is used as the unit of measurement in preparing financial statements and prices are changing, the purchasing power sacrificed by the firm in acquiring goods and services is not the same over time. The purchasing power sacrificed five years ago to acquire a machine costing $10,000 is not equivalent to the purchasing power sacrificed last week to acquire merchandise inventory for $10,000. When assessed in terms of general purchasing power, therefore, the dollar does not represent a common, or uniform, measuring unit. A technique for making the measuring unit more comparable over time by filtering out the effects of changes in the general purchasing power of the dollar is described and illustrated later in this chapter.

Accounting Problems Associated with Specific Price Changes

An important question in accounting for changes in the market prices of individual assets concerns the period(s) in which gains and losses arising from changing prices of specific commodities are recognized. Under the conventional accounting model, assets such as inventory, land, plant, and equipment are generally stated at acquisition cost on the balance sheet (net of accumulated depreciation in some cases). Any changes in the market prices of these assets while they are held are normally not recognized while they are held (an exception is in the treatment of marketable securities and inventories under the lower-of-cost-or-market valuation basis). When the assets are sold, any difference between the selling price of the asset and its book value is reported as a gain or loss in the period of sale. The conventional market exchange approach results in not recognizing any gains or losses due to changes in market prices during periods while assets are held.

Consider the following example. American Merchandising Corporation regularly purchases parcels of land as possible future sites for retail stores. Most of its tracts of land are ultimately used for stores. If a decision is made not to locate in a particular area, the land is sold. On January 1, 19X0, two parcels of land, tract A and tract B, are acquired in a particular city for $100,000 each. On December 31, 19X0, several competent real estate appraisers estimate the market price of tract A to be $115,000 and of tract B to be $125,000. Late in 19X1, a decision is made to use tract B for a new store. Tract A is then sold for $140,000.

Under the conventional accounting model, a gain of $40,000 (= $140,000 − $100,000) is reported on the sale of tract A during 19X1. This gain, although reported in 19X1, reflects an increase in market price over two accounting periods. Net income for 19X0 would not include the effects of management's decision to hold the parcel of land during 19X0 while its market price increased from $100,000 to $115,000. This increase in market price is reported as part of the gain recognized in 19X1. The increase in market price of tract B will likewise not be reflected in the financial statements until the land is sold. In this case, however, the land is to be used in operations, probably over an extended period of years. The extent to which the recognition of gains or losses is postponed is therefore likely to be even more significant.

The conventional accounting model is subject to several criticisms with respect to the treatment of changes in market prices of the firm's individual assets. First, net income during periods when assets are held does not reflect the effects of management's decisions to hold, rather than sell, assets. Second, assets are not stated on the balance sheet at their current market values, so it is difficult for the statement user to assess the firm's financial condition as of a particular time. Third, net income during periods when assets are sold reflects a biased measure of performance during that period because gains and losses resulting from decisions in prior periods to continue holding the assets are included in the income of the period when the assets are sold.

Several approaches to accounting for specific price changes are discussed later in this chapter. It is important to emphasize at the outset, however, that the accounting problems created by general price level changes (that is, violation of the common monetary measuring unit assumption) are quite different from the accounting problems associated with specific price changes (that is, recognition of holding gains and losses and asset valuation). The procedures designed to deal with general price level changes are not designed to measure the effects of specific price changes.

GENERAL PRICE LEVEL-ADJUSTED FINANCIAL STATEMENTS

The objective of general price level-adjusted financial statements is to state all amounts in dollars of uniform general purchasing power, thereby obtaining a common, or uniform, measuring unit. The purchasing power of the dollar on the date of the most recent balance sheet is usually recommended as the unit of measurement for all financial statements. General price level indices, such as the Gross National Product Implicit

Price Deflator or Consumer Price Index, are used to measure the general purchasing power of the dollar on various dates. The general approach is to convert the number of dollars received or expended at various price levels to an equivalent number of dollars in terms of the price level on the date of the current financial statements.

For example, assume that two parcels of land are held on December 31, 19X9, at which time an index of the general price level is 155. Tract A was acquired during 19X1 for $100,000, when the general price index was 100. Tract B was acquired for $100,000 during 19X3, when the general price index was 106. The acquisition cost of these parcels of land would be restated from 19X1 and 19X3 dollars to an equivalent number of 19X9 dollars as shown in Exhibit 15.2.

EXHIBIT 15.2
Illustration of General Price Level Restatement Procedure for Land

Item	Conventionally Reported Acquisition Cost	Conversion Factor as of 12/31/X9	General Price Level Restated Acquisition Cost as of 12/31/X9
Tract A	$100,000	155/100	$155,000
Tract B	$100,000	155/106	$146,226

The sacrifice in general purchasing power made during 19X1 when tract A was acquired for $100,000 is equivalent to sacrificing $155,000 (= 155/100 × $100,000) in general purchasing power on December 31, 19X9. Likewise, the sacrifice in general purchasing power made during 19X3 when tract B was acquired for $100,000 is equivalent to sacrificing $146,226 (= 155/106 × $100,000) in general purchasing power on December 31, 19X9. The restated amounts in Exhibit 15.2 use a measuring unit of uniform general purchasing power.

Two important aspects of the general price level restatement procedure should be noted in Exhibit 15.2. First, the procedure does not represent a departure from the use of acquisition cost as the principal valuation basis in preparing financial statements. As is illustrated later, the acquisition cost amounts form the basis for the restatements to a common dollar basis. Second, the amounts shown for general price level restated acquisition cost do *not* attempt to reflect the current market prices of these two parcels of land. The market prices of the land could have changed in an entirely different direction and pattern from that of the general price level change. The focus of the general price level restatement procedure is on stating the acquisition cost data in comparable units over time and not on reflecting current market prices of individual assets and equities.

Restatement of Monetary and Nonmonetary Items

An important distinction is made in the general price level restatement procedure between monetary items and nonmonetary items. A *monetary item* is a claim that is receivable or payable in a specified number of dollars regardless of changes in the general purchasing power of the dollar. Examples of monetary items are cash; accounts, notes, and interest receivable; accounts, notes, and interest payable; income taxes payable; and bonds. The valuation of monetary items on the conventional balance sheet at the number of dollars due means that they are automatically stated in terms of the general purchasing power of the dollar at that time. Therefore, no restatement is necessary, and the conventionally reported and restated amounts are the same. For example, assume that a firm has $30,000 of cash on hand on December 31, 19X9. On the conventionally prepared balance sheet, this item would be stated at $30,000, the amount of cash on hand. On the general price level-restated balance sheet, this item would also be reported at $30,000, representing $30,000 of December 31, 19X9, general purchasing power.

Because monetary items are receivable or payable in a specified number of dollars rather than in terms of a given amount of general purchasing power, holding monetary items over time while the general purchasing power of the dollar changes gives rise to *monetary gains and losses.* During a period of inflation, a holder of monetary assets loses general purchasing power. For example, a firm holding notes receivable incurs a monetary loss, because the dollars loaned in the past were worth more in terms of general purchasing power than the dollars to be received when the note is collected. Likewise, a holder of monetary liabilities gains in general purchasing power during periods of inflation. The dollars required to repay the debt command smaller purchasing power than the dollars originally borrowed. The gain or loss from holding monetary items is reported as an element of general price level-restated net income but is not included in conventionally reported net income.

A *nonmonetary item* is an asset or equity that does not represent a claim to or for a specified number of dollars. That is, if an item is not a monetary item, then it must be nonmonetary. Examples of nonmonetary items are inventory, land, buildings, equipment, capital stock, revenues, and expenses. In conventionally prepared financial statements, nonmonetary items are stated in terms of varying amounts of general purchasing power, depending on the date the nonmonetary assets were acquired and nonmonetary equities arose. As illustrated in Exhibit 15.2 with the two parcels of land, the conventionally reported amounts of these items must be restated to an equivalent number of dollars as of the date of the balance sheet. The amount of this restatement does not represent a gain or loss to be included in net income, but is merely an adjustment to equalize the measuring unit.

Illustration of General Price Level-Adjusted Income Statement

Because discussions of the effects of inflation on financial statements focus on the income statement, we will direct our attention to that statement here. Exhibit 15.3 shows the conventional and general price level-adjusted income statements for the General Products Company for the year 19X9, during which the GNP Implicit Price Deflator increased by 12.36 percent. The general price level-adjusted (GPLA) income statement differs in five important ways from the conventional income statement. These differences, or adjustments in determining net income, are explained next. The descriptions of the adjustments are numbered (1) to (5) and the lines of Exhibit 15.3 are keyed to these descriptions.

EXHIBIT 15.3
General Products Company
Income Statements for the Year 19X9
on Both Conventional and General Price Level-Adjusted Bases

	Conventional Basis (Historical Dollars)	Adjustment Number (Keyed to Text)	General Price Level-Adjusted Basis (Dollars of Constant Purchasing Power Dated 12/31/X9)	Percentage Change
Revenues:				
Sales	$13,450,000	(1)	$14,257,000	+6.0%
Equity in Earnings (Losses) of Unconsolidated Subsidiary	50,000	(5)	(25,000)	−150.0
Total Revenues	$13,500,000		$14,232,000	+5.4
Expenses:				
Cost of Goods Sold:				
Items Subject to FIFO Flow Assumption	$ 5,050,000	(2)	$ 5,509,600	+9.1
Items Subject to LIFO Flow Assumption	1,060,000	(2)	1,119,400	+5.6
Depreciation	380,000	(3)	551,000	+45.0
All Other Expenses Including Taxes	6,110,000	(1)	6,476,600	+6.0
Total Expenses	$12,600,000		$13,656,600	+8.4
Income before Gain on Monetary Items	$ 900,000		$ 575,400	−36.1
Gain on Monetary Items	—	(4)	177,400	—
Net Income	$ 900,000		$ 752,800	−16.4

(1) Revenues and Expenses Occurring Evenly during the Year   Most revenues and most expenses, other than cost of goods sold and depreciation, usually occur fairly evenly throughout the year. To restate them in terms of dollars of end-of-year general purchasing power, they are adjusted for half a year of general price change.

If general prices increased at a uniform rate throughout 19X9, so that the year's increase in general prices is 12.36 percent, then the rate of price change for one-half a year is 6 percent, not 6.18 percent as one might first think. Computations involving rates of change in prices are much like computations involving compound interest. The Appendix at the back of this book explains both. For the purpose of this discussion, merely note that if prices go up by 6 percent during six months, then it takes $1.06 at the end of six months to buy what $1.00 would buy at the start of the period. If prices go up by another 6 percent during the second six months, then it takes $1.1236 (= $1.06 × 1.06) at the end of the year to buy what $1.00 would buy at the start of the year.

General Products Company's sales of $13,450,000 occurred evenly throughout 19X9 and are increased by one-half year of general price change, 6 percent, to $14,257,000 of December 31, 19X9, purchasing power. All expenses other than cost of goods sold and depreciation amounted to $6,110,000 in the conventional income statement. These expenses are also increased by one-half year of price change, 6 percent, to $6,476,600 for the GPLA income statement.

(2) Cost of Goods Sold   Cost of goods sold on a conventional income statement is stated in terms of the acquisition cost of the units that were sold during the year. Because it is seldom possible to trace the units sold back to a particular purchase, a cost flow assumption must be used, either FIFO, LIFO, or weighted average. The restatement of conventional cost of goods sold to a GPLA basis is critically affected by the cost flow assumption used.

Consider first the restatement when a FIFO cost flow assumption is used. Figure 15.1 presents a graphical demonstration of the flow of costs into cost of goods sold and ending inventory under FIFO. Cost of goods sold is composed of purchases from the latter part of the previous year plus the first part of this year. The purchases of the previous year that enter the current year's cost of goods sold must be restated for somewhat more than one year of price change. The amount of this "somewhat more" depends on the rate of inventory turnover. The purchases during the current year that enter cost of goods sold must be restated for somewhat less than a year of price change, the amount again depending on the rate of inventory turnover. The historical dollar cost of goods sold for items subject to a FIFO flow assumption is $5,050,000 for General Products Company. After considering rates of inventory turnover, it is determined that the purchases of the previous year and of this year that entered cost of goods sold under FIFO were acquired approximately nine months prior to the end of the current year. The $5,050,000 historical dollar cost of goods sold is therefore restated to $5,509,600 GPLA cost of goods sold, reflecting a price increase of 9.1 percent for the nine months.

Consider next the restatement when a LIFO cost flow assumption is used. Figure 15.2 presents a graphical demonstration of the flow of costs into cost of goods sold and ending inventory under LIFO. Assuming that inventory quantities increased during

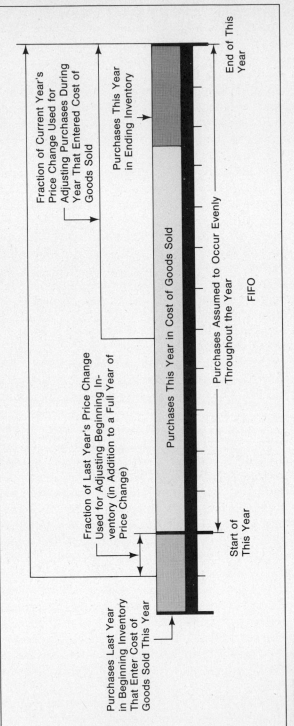

FIGURE 15.1
Illustration of Fractions of Year's
Price Change used in Price Level
Adjustments of Cost of Goods
Sold Assuming FIFO Cost Flow

the year, cost of goods sold is composed entirely of purchases during the current year. The restatement of LIFO cost of goods sold will therefore reflect less than one year of price change. After assessing the rate of inventory turnover for General Products Company, it is determined that the purchases of this year that entered cost of goods sold under LIFO were acquired slightly less than six months before the end of the year. The $1,060,000 historical dollar cost of goods sold is therefore restated to $1,119,400 GPLA cost of goods sold, reflecting a price increase of 5.6 percent.

Observe that GPLA cost of FIFO goods sold is 9.1 percent larger than its conventional amount, whereas cost of LIFO goods sold is only 5.6 percent larger than the conventional amount. This may appear to be a small difference, but cost of goods sold is typically 15 to 25 times larger than net income. A small percentage increase in cost of goods sold makes for a much larger percentage decrease in net income. Thus GPLA net income for firms using a FIFO assumption is likely to be a much smaller percentage of conventional net income than for firms using a LIFO flow assumption.

(3) Depreciation   General price level-adjusted depreciation is almost always much larger than depreciation as conventionally reported. For most firms, depreciable assets typically are acquired many years before the period being reported on, and price levels will have increased substantially since acquisition. It is determined that General Products Company's depreciable assets were acquired, on average, a little over six years before December 31, 19X9. The cumulative price increase over that time has been about 45 percent; the depreciation expense is correspondingly increased.

(4) Gain or Loss on Monetary Items   Price level-adjusted income statements explicitly show the gain in purchasing power captured by a debtor (or the loss suffered by a creditor) during a period of rising general price levels. Because most industrial companies are typically net debtors, they will usually show purchasing power or monetary gains from this debt. (The liabilities will be paid off, or discharged, with dollars of smaller general purchasing power than was originally borrowed. The difference between the purchasing power borrowed and that repaid is the gain on a monetary liability during the term of the loan.) The gain from being in a net monetary liability position, although real in an economic sense, does not produce a current flow of cash.

The gain or loss from holding monetary items is in many ways the most meaningful of the general price level adjustments. To illustrate its significance, consider the monetary gain on long-term debt. The interest expense reported in the conventional income statements is the actual cost of borrowing. It depends on the interest rate negotiated at the time of the loan. That interest rate, in turn, depends in part on the lender's and borrower's anticipations about the rate of inflation during the term of the loan. (Interest rates are increased when the lender expects inflation during the term of the loan. The borrower accepts the higher rate because he or she expects to repay "cheaper" dollars.) Thus the borrower's conventional income statement shows an interest expense that reflects the inflation expected by both the borrower and the lender. The gain from being in a net monetary liability position in a time of rising prices is, in a real sense, an offset to reported interest expense. It reflects a gain from being a debtor during a period of inflation that both parties to the loan expected. After the fact, who benefited, the borrower or the lender, depends on whether the actual rate of inflation

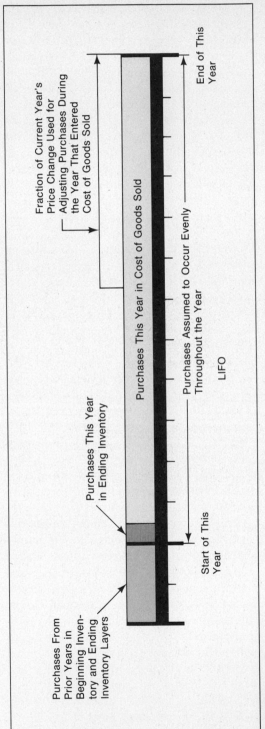

FIGURE 15.2
**Illustration of Fraction of Year's
Price Change Used in Price Level
Adjustments of Cost of Goods
Sold Assuming LIFO Cost Flow**

during the term of the loan differed from the rate anticipated by both parties to the loan at the time the loan was made. If the actual rate of inflation turns out to be less than the anticipated rate, then the lender benefits. If the actual rate turns out to be greater than the anticipated rate, then the borrower benefits. The reporting of both interest expense and the monetary gain provides a better measure of the real cost of borrowing for a firm.

Analysis of General Products Company's balance sheet (not provided here) indicates that during 19X9 the Company had an average excess of monetary liabilities over monetary assets of $1,435,300. That is, on average, the company was borrowing $1,435,300. This is "net" figure; actual borrowings were higher, but holdings of cash and accounts receivable reduced the average net monetary liability. Because the general price level increased by 12.36 percent, the gain on net monetary liabilities is $177,400 (= .1236 × $1,435,300).

The gain is shown as a single-line item on the income statement of General Products Company. The gain on monetary items might better be shown on the income statement as a deduction from reported interest expense. The net amount would represent the "pure" or "real" interest expense after allowing for the inflation actually realized during the period.

(5) Revenue Recognized under the Equity Method   Although the General Products Company consolidates most of its subsidiaries, there are some subsidiaries that are not consolidated because the nature of their operations is significantly different from the main activities of the parent. It is a widespread practice not to consolidate credit companies, banks, and real estate companies. In presenting its conventional income statement, the parent company must then use the equity method and recognize its share of the subsidiaries' net income. Thus the parent's share of the net income of the unconsolidated subsidiaries is shown as a separate item in the parent's statement.

In a price level-adjusted income statement for the parent, the parent's share of the net income of the unconsolidated subsidiary cannot simply be restated for one-half year of price change. Instead, the income statement of the subsidiary must be restated to reflect adjustments **(1)** to **(4)** described above. The parent will then recognize its share of the subsidiary's restated net income.

The unconsolidated subsidiary of General Products Company is a credit company. Virtually all of its assets are monetary so that, on average, the subsidary company is a net lender.

General Products Company's share of the unconsolidated subsidiary's income is reported as $50,000 on a conventional basis; when restated on a general price level-adjusted basis, this is calculated to be a *loss* of $25,000. The large difference between conventional income and adjusted income for the unconsolidated subsidiary is caused almost entirely by its loss on holding net monetary assets during the period of general price increase.

Summary   The difference between conventional and GPLA net income is caused basically by the five adjustments demonstrated in this section. GPLA income before recognizing the gain on monetary items is smaller than conventional net income for virtually all companies. This reduction is caused by the substantial increase in depreciation and, except for LIFO companies, a more than one-half year adjustment to cost of goods sold. Almost all corporations are net borrowers of monetary items, so that the adjustment for monetary items almost always is a gain. In recent years, the GPLA net incomes of many major corporations have been, on average, not much different from conventional net income. Some companies (typically net lenders and capital-intensive firms) have GPLA net income much less than conventional net income, and some companies (typically heavy borrowers with relatively small investments in inventory and depreciable assets) have GPLA net income substantially larger than conventional net income.

Assessment of General Price Level-Adjusted Financial Statements

There is still considerable controversy as to whether or not general price level-adjusted statements provide information that is worth the cost of gathering and reporting it.

The Case for Restatement Proponents of restating financial statements for general price level changes argue that the annual rate of inflation in the United States is now sufficiently large as seriously to violate the common monetary measuring unit assumption. When the annual rate of inflation averaged between 2 and 3 percent, as was the case during the 1950s and early 1960s, the violation of the common monetary measuring unit assumption was considered tolerable. Most assets, other than land and buildings, were not held for a sufficiently long period of time for the cumulative changing general purchasing power of the dollar to distort seriously the conventional measures of earnings and financial position. With an average rate of inflation now substantially higher than had been experienced earlier, serious distortions in accounting measurements can occur over periods of just a few years.

A second argument favoring restatement concerns the highly objective nature of general price level-restated financial statements. The same valuation methods are used as in the conventional financial statements. The general price indices used are prepared by governmental agencies and are widely available. The restated financial statements, therefore, are objective, or verifiable, and hence are easily audited.

A third argument favoring restatement concerns the usefulness of information on the monetary gain or loss reported during the period. This reported gain or loss provides a measure for assessing management's decisions to hold cash, extend credit to customers, and obtain capital from short- and long-term creditors. Firms that do not use long-term debt financing are likely to report small or moderate monetary losses during inflationary periods, assuming that monetary assets exceed current monetary liabilities. Firms making heavy use of long-term debt financing (that is, highly leveraged firms) will report monetary gains during periods of inflation. Information concerning the monetary gain or loss is not available in the conventional financial statements.

The Case against Restatement Critics of restatement argue that the monetary gain or loss reported is of limited usefulness because the price index used to calculate the gain or loss covers too wide a variety of goods and services. Of more importance, it is suggested, is the firm's success or failure in maintaining the purchasing power of its capital for the types of goods and services it normally acquires (that is, merchandise inventory, land, plant, equipment). These items are given relatively little weight in the general price indices, which place heavy weight on the prices of consumer goods and services.

A second argument advanced by critics of restatement concerns the possibly significant measurement biases in the general price indices employed. The general price indices have been criticized for (1) failing to filter out properly the portion of price changes attributable to changes in the quality or other aspects of goods and services; (2) using posted prices for some goods and services (particularly industrial goods) rather than the actual invoice prices, which may include discounts and other price reductions; and (3) failing to update the goods and services included in the market basket on a sufficiently frequent basis, with the result that the price indices do not adequately reflect the items currently being purchased.

Critics of restatement also argue that financial statement users do not understand general price level-restated financial statements, and that an extensive educational effort is required before the statements can be used in investment decisions. An illustration of the misunderstanding concerning general price level statements is the belief by some persons that the general price level-restated amounts for nonmonetary assets, particularly land, buildings, and equipment, represent the current values of these individual assets.

Critics of restatement also point out that several surveys of financial analysts, bankers, and other potential users of the restated accounting reports have indicated that a large proportion of these individuals do not find the statements particularly useful. There is some question, then, as to whether financial statement users would find general price level-adjusted statements helpful in their decisions even after an extensive educational program.

ALTERNATIVE APPROACHES TO ACCOUNTING FOR SPECIFIC PRICE CHANGES

Several approaches to accounting for specific price changes have been suggested. The preceding sections discussed the accounting for changes in the general price level. The remainder of this chapter discusses the accounting for changes in specific prices. One approach, already generally acceptable, adheres to acquisition cost but suggests the use of the last-in, first-out (LIFO) inventory cost flow assumption and accelerated depreciation methods rather than the first-in, first-out (FIFO) cost flow assumption and the straight-line depreciation method. Another alternative approach, not yet generally acceptable, abandons acquisition cost as the valuation basis and substitutes a current valuation basis, either current replacement cost or net realizable value. Each of these approaches is described more fully and evaluated in the sections that follow.

Acquisition Cost with LIFO Inventory and Accelerated Depreciation Methods

The use of the LIFO inventory cost flow assumption and accelerated depreciation methods (double-declining-balance and sum-of-the-years'-digits) are commonly suggested as procedures for giving effect to price changes in financial statements while continuing to adhere to acquisition cost.

LIFO Inventory Cost Flow Assumption   The LIFO inventory cost flow assumption results in cost of goods sold being based on the most recent purchases of inventory items. Net income, therefore, reflects the matching of current selling prices with relatively current costs of acquiring the merchandise. It is suggested that using LIFO provides approximately the same gross profit as if cost of goods sold had been measured by the cost of replacing the goods at the time of sale. The use of LIFO, however, is based on actual inventory purchases and is not subject to the measurement problems inherent in an accounting system based on replacement costs.

As a basis for reflecting changing prices, LIFO is subject to several criticisms. First, whereas the income statement may reflect more current price information under LIFO than other inventory cost flow assumptions, the balance sheet valuation of inventory reflects prices paid during earlier periods, which are typically substantially different from the current prices of inventory items on hand. Second, during periods of a decrease in the quantity of inventory, cost of goods sold under LIFO will reflect prices paid when some inventory layers were added during earlier periods. Under such conditions, net income reflects both current selling prices and perhaps very old inventory acquisition costs. Use of LIFO is, at best, only a partial solution to accounting for changing prices.

Accelerated Depreciation Methods   The more rapid write-down of depreciable assets using the double-declining-balance or sum-of-the-years'-digits depreciation methods rather than the straight-line method is also suggested as a means of recognizing the effects of changing prices. During periods of inflation, the replacement costs of many fixed assets are likely to increase. If depreciation during the period is determined using the replacement costs of the services of fixed assets consumed, depreciation expense would likely be larger than straight-line depreciation on acquisition cost. It is suggested that current replacement cost depreciation can be approximated by using accelerated depreciation methods while remaining on the acquisition-cost basis of valuation.

As with the LIFO inventory cost flow assumption, accelerated depreciation methods are subject to several criticisms as approaches for giving effect to specific price changes. First, even in the early years of an asset's depreciable life, only by coincidence will depreciation expense based on acquisition cost and accelerated depreciation methods equal the amount that would be obtained from determining depreciation using current replacement costs or some other type of current value. Second, because the total amount of depreciation taken on an asset over its life will not exceed acquisition cost, extra depreciation claimed in early years using accelerated depreciation methods means that less depreciation must be charged in later years. Depreciation expense during the later years will probably seriously misstate the current replacement cost of the asset services consumed during those periods. Third, the rapid write-down of depreciable assets using accelerated depreciation methods results in balance sheet amounts that are likely to be significantly different from the current replacement costs for these assets. Use of accelerated depreciation methods is, at best, only a temporary solution to accounting for changing prices. Even at that, accelerated depreciation methods make only the income statement more current. The balance sheet amounts for depreciable assets can be significantly different than the current values of those assets.

Current Valuation Basis

Several approaches to accounting for specific price changes have been suggested that depart from the use of acquisition cost. Among these alternative approaches are proposals for using current replacement cost (entry value) or net realizable value (exit value) as the valuation basis. It should be noted that, in perfectly competitive markets, the spread, or difference, between the current replacement cost and net realizable value of an asset should be relatively small, essentially representing transaction costs. In less active markets, as characterizes the market for many used assets, the spread between entry and exit values could be much larger, reflecting not only transaction costs but also trading advantages by the buyer or the seller.

Current Replacement Cost Valuation Method   When current replacement cost is used as the valuation basis, assets are stated on the balance sheet at the cost of replacing the assets (or their service potential) in their current condition. Changes in the replacement cost of assets held during the period and not sold by the end of the period are reported as *holding gains and losses* in the income statement. Expenses are stated at the cost of replacing the asset services that are consumed during the period.

An example might be helpful in illustrating the use of current replacement cost. Assume that a construction company purchases a crane in new condition on January 1, 19X0, for $50,000. The estimated service life of the crane is 5,000 hours. During 19X0, the crane is used for 1,000 hours. On December 31, 19X0, a similar crane in new condition could be purchased for $60,000, whereas a similar one-year-old crane could be acquired for $48,000. The crane would be stated at a net book value of $48,000 on the December 31, 19X0, balance sheet under the current replacement cost valuation basis. The difference between the acquisition cost on January 1, 19X0, of $50,000 and the valuation at the end of the year of $48,000 would be reflected in net income for 19X0. The $2,000 difference could be disaggregated into a holding gain of $10,000 (= $60,000 − $50,000) and depreciation expense on a replacement cost basis of $12,000 (= $60,000/5).[1]

In determining the replacement cost of various financial statement items, several sources of price data might be used. For merchandise inventory, suppliers' catalogs

---

[1]   There are other procedures for determining the holding gain and depreciation expense on a current replacement cost basis. The procedure illustrated above has the advantage of being simple and should be satisfactory for this introductory discussion of current replacement cost.

could be consulted. For manufacturing firms with work in process and finished goods inventories, it would be necessary to identify the various factor inputs into production (for example, raw material used, direct labor services consumed, depreciation recorded on factory equipment) and determine the replacement cost of each. There is likely to be greater difficulty establishing the replacement costs of manufacturing overhead components than of direct material and direct labor because of the numerous dissimilar indirect cost elements involved in the determination.

In cases where established second-hand markets exist for fixed assets, such as automobiles, furniture, and standardized equipment, replacement cost can be determined from dealers in those markets. In some cases, the federal government prepares specific price indices for certain types of fixed assets. These indices provide information concerning the change in the price of specific assets in a new condition. Some adjustment is necessary to reflect the used condition of the assets on hand. For example, the specific price index for cranes might have increased from 100 to 120 between the beginning and end of 19X0. A new crane purchased for $50,000 on January 1, 19X0, would have a current replacement cost in new condition of $60,000 at year-end. This amount must be adjusted downward, however, to reflect the replacement cost of services consumed during 19X0. The reduction might be based on the replacement cost of the estimated total capacity of the crane that was consumed during the year or on the cost of renting assets that provide similar services.

The current replacement cost of specially designed equipment and buildings is perhaps the most difficult to determine. A combination of suppliers' catalogs, specific price indices, and real estate appraisals is probably required.

Perhaps the major criticism of using current replacement cost in financial accounting reports is the high degree of subjectivity involved in determining replacement cost. Several persons attempting to determine the replacement cost of a specific asset could arrive at widely different replacement cost amounts. Many of these valuations would be difficult to audit effectively, and therefore might not be covered by the opinion of the independent accountant.

Although there are difficulties in measuring replacement cost for fixed assets, there is apparently much less difficulty in the case of marketable securities and inventories. Marketable securities and inventories are written down to replacement cost when the lower-of-cost-or-market valuation basis is used. If replacement cost can be determined in a sufficiently objective manner to make downward adjustments, then replacement cost is also objective enough to be used for upward adjustments (that is, holding gains as well as holding losses should be recognized on marketable securities and inventories). Net holding gains on marketable securities and inventories are not recognized in conventional accounting, however, until the assets are sold.

Net Realizable Value Valuation Basis   Another approach to accounting for changing prices that departs from the use of acquisition cost is to state nonmonetary assets at the net amount at which they could be sold at the end of the year after deducting selling costs (the so-called *net realizable value*). Any difference in the valuation of the asset between the beginning and end of the year would be reflected in the determination of net income for the period.

The net realizable value of assets such as marketable securities and inventories, for which active markets exist, should be relatively easy to determine. Likewise, the net realizable values of some fixed assets are easily determinable if active markets for used machinery, fixtures, and other items are present. Real estate agents might be consulted in determining the net realizable value of land and buildings. For specially designed equipment and similar assets, no second-hand market may exist from which to determine net realizable values.

The use of the net realizable value basis of valuation is subject to the same criticisms as using current replacement cost. The valuations tend to be more subjective than using acquisition cost, and therefore more difficult to audit. The use of net realizable values is subject to several additional criticisms, however. One criticism attacks the rationale for using exit prices. It is argued that assets are acquired so that they can be used in operations. In many cases, selling the assets is not even considered as an alternative. Yet management's performance would be judged on an earnings measure that includes changes in exit prices. A second and somewhat related criticism of using net realizable values is that there may be some specially designed assets that have a significant *value in use* to the firm but that would be stated at zero or relatively small amounts because their *value in exchange* is minimal due to the lack of any interested buyers for the assets or because they are so integrated into permanent structures that their removal costs would be prohibitively high.

Except for the manner of determining the current replacement cost or net realizable value of each asset, the financial statements based on these current valuation approaches are quite similar.

INCOME BASED ON REPLACEMENT COSTS

In 1977, the Securities and Exchange Commission (SEC) began requiring disclosure, in reports filed with the SEC, of certain financial statement information based on replacement cost data.[2] The SEC does not require complete financial statements based on replacement costs but merely disclosure of the following items:

1 Replacement cost of goods sold at the times of sale.
2 Replacement cost of inventory on hand both at the beginning and the end of the year.
3 Replacement cost of plant assets both at the beginning and the end of the year.
4 Depreciation of plant assets based on their average replacement cost during the year.

Exhibit 15.4 illustrates the disclosures required by the SEC for General Products Company discussed earlier in the chapter.

The SEC did not require complete financial statements based on replacement cost, perhaps because the SEC did not want to constrain the uses to which the replacement

---

[2] Securities and Exchange Commission, "Relating to Amendment to Regulation S-X Requiring Disclosure of Replacement Cost Data," Accounting Series Release No. 190, 1976. Disclosure is required of companies with inventory and plant costing $100 million or more.

EXHIBIT 15.4
General Products Company
Replacement Cost Disclosure for 19X9 under SEC Requirements
(ASR No. 190)

---

(1) For items subject to a FIFO cost flow assumption, the cost of goods sold valued at replacement costs on the dates of sale is $5,400,000, which is $350,000 larger than the historical cost of FIFO goods sold of $5,050,000. The replacement cost of goods sold subject to a LIFO cost flow assumption is insignificantly different from the historical cost of $1,060,000.

(2) The inventory at the start of 19X9 valued at replacement costs of that date would have been $100,000 larger than its historical cost.

(3) The inventory at the end of 19X9 valued at replacement costs of that date would have been $220,000 larger than its historical cost.

(4) To replace the productive capacity of plant assets, in new condition, owned at the start of 19X9 would have cost $2,950,000 more than the historical cost amount shown on the balance sheet. The accumulated depreciation based on the replacement cost of productive capacity would have been $1,590,000 larger than the historical amount shown on the balance sheet. The net book value based on replacement costs of the productive capacity of these assets was thus $1,360,000 (= $2,950,000 − $1,590,000) larger than the amount shown on the balance sheet as of the start of 19X9.

(5) To replace the productive capacity of plant assets, in new condition, owned at the end of 19X9 would have cost $3,810,000 more than the historical cost amount shown on the balance sheet. The accumulated depreciation based on replacement cost of productive capacity would have been $1,970,000 larger than the amount shown on the balance sheet. The net book value based on replacement cost of productive capacity of these assets is thus $1,840,000 (= $3,810,000 − $1,970,000) larger than the amount shown on the balance sheet as of the end of 19X9.

(6) If depreciation charges for the year had been based on average replacement cost during 19X9 to reproduce productive capacity [based on the amounts indicated in **(4)** and **(5)**], then depreciation for the year 19X9 would have been $245,000 more than the $380,000 depreciation charges based on historical cost.

---

cost data might be put. In the sections that follow, we demonstrate two possible uses of the replacement cost data: (1) segmentation of the income statement into three measures of income, and (2) disaggregation of the conventionally reported gross margin (sales minus cost of goods sold) into operating margin and realized holding gains.

Three Concepts of Income

Using the replacement cost data, the income statement can be segmented into three measures of income, each much different from the others and each with different meanings. The amounts of these income measures are shown in boldface type in Exhibit 15.5.

EXHIBIT 15.5
General Products Company
Income Statements for the Year 19X9
Based on Both Historical Costs and Replacement Cost Data
Disclosed Because of SEC Requirements

	Conventional Historical Cost Basis	Adjustment	Based on SEC Replacement Cost Disclosure
Revenues:			
Sales	$13,450,000	None	$13,450,000
Equity in Earnings of Unconsolidated Subsidiaries	50,000	None[b]	50,000
Total Revenues	$13,500,000	None	$13,500,000
Expenses:			
Cost of Goods Sold:			
Items Subject to FIFO Flow Assumption	$ 5,050,000	(1)[a] Increased by $350,000	$ 5,400,000
Items Subject to LIFO Flow Assumption	1,060,000	None	1,060,000
Depreciation	380,000	(6)[a] Increased by $245,000	625,000
All Other Expenses Including Taxes	6,110,000	None	6,110,000
Total Expenses	$12,600,000		$13,195,000
Distributable Income	—		$ 305,000
Realized Holding Gains:			
On Inventory	—		$350,000
On Plant Assets	—		245,000
Total Realized Holding Gains	—		595,000
Realized Income (Distributable Income and Realized Holding Gains)	$ 900,000	(= conventional net income)	$ 900,000
Unrealized Holding Gains:			
On Inventory	—	(3) − (2)[a]: $ 220,000 − $ 100,000	$120,000
On Plant Assets	—	(5) − (4)[a]: $1,840,000 − $1,360,000	480,000
Total Unrealized Holding Gains	—		600,000
Economic Income			$ 1,500,000

a See disclosures with these numbers in Exhibit 15.4.
b Parallel disclosure in the annual report of the unconsolidated subsidiaries would make possible parallel adjustments. If the subsidiaries are financial companies, the replacement costs adjustments are not likely to be material.

Distributable Income   If price changes were to stop today but physical operations were to continue without change, what income would we reasonably expect of the firm in the future? To put it another way, what dividends could be declared, at a maximum, without impairing the firm's ability to continue operations at current levels? Distributable income (conventional revenue less expenses based on current replacement costs) measures this capability. General Products Company's distributable income for 19X9 is $305,000.

To take an even simpler example, if a retailer buys one toaster for $30 and sells it for $50 at a time when the replacement cost of a toaster is $38, then pretax distributable income is $12 (= $50 − $38). A retailer who paid out more than $12 in taxes and dividends under these circumstances would not retain sufficient funds to buy the next toaster and could not remain in business at current levels.

Changes in the amount of distributable income over time probably measure the growth capability of a firm better than the changes in any other income figure. This is the income number that financial analysts may study in assessing growth prospects for the company and, hence, in assessing potential for price appreciation of the firm's shares in stock markets. For example, if dividend payments are regularly larger than distributable income, then the firm will likely have to contract operations in the long run or raise new capital just to maintain the current activity levels.

Economic Income   Economists, following the lead of Sir John R. Hicks, often define income during a period as how much better off a firm is at the end of a period than it was at the beginning of the period.[3] That is, economic income is wealth at the end of the period less wealth at the beginning of the period plus any distributions to owners during the period. General Products Company's economic income for 19X9 is $1,500,000. This "well-offness" is measured as conventional income plus all holding gains during the period, both realized and unrealized. Whether or not it makes sense for management or investors to pay attention to the measure is questionable because the degree to which this amount can be earned in the future depends to a large degree on future price changes. It is true, however, that economic income measures the increase in the firm's wealth during the period (but not the change in owners' wealth, which depends upon stock market prices).

Realized Income   Realized income is that portion of economic income that has been realized in transactions with parties outside the firm. It is distributable income plus *realized* holding gains, $900,000 during 19X9 for General Products Company. This income amount is always exactly equal to conventional net income. It is less than economic income by the amount of *unrealized* holding gains during the period. This measure of income has meaning to the extent that the conventional measure has meaning, because they are the same. As managers and investors become accustomed to analyzing distributable income and economic income, this intermediate measure will probably be used less often. Realized income reports only those increments to wealth that have been realized in transactions with outsiders during the period. If replacement

---

[3]   Sir John R. Hicks, *Value and Capital* (Oxford: The Clarendon Press, 1962), p. 176.

costs are properly computed and both inventory and plant are stated at realistic amounts, then the distinction between realized and unrealized—having been involved in a transaction—is artificial.

Operating Margin and Holding Gains on Inventory

A second use of the replacement cost data required by the SEC is in disaggregating the conventional gross margin into operating margins and realized holding gains. Exhibit 15.6 presents this disaggregation for General Products Company.

EXHIBIT 15.6
General Products Company
Disaggregation of Gross Margin
into Operating Margin and Holding
Gains for 19X9

	Conventional Basis	Replacement Cost Basis
Sales Revenue	$13,450,000	$13,450,000
Less Cost of Goods Sold:		
FIFO Items	(5,050,000)	(5,400,000)
LIFO Items	(1,060,000)	(1,060,000)
Conventional Gross Margin	$ 7,340,000	
Operating Margin		$ 6,990,000
Replacement Cost of Goods Sold:		
FIFO Items		$ 5,400,000
LIFO Items		1,060,000
Total Replacement Cost of Goods Sold		$ 6,460,000
Less Acquisition Cost of Goods Sold:		
FIFO Items		$ 5,050,000
LIFO Items		1,060,000
Total Acquisition Cost of Goods Sold		$ 6,110,000
Realized Holding Gain		$ 350,000
Operating Margin Plus Realized Holding Gain		
(= Conventional Gross Margin)		$ 7,340,000

The *operating margin* is the difference between sales and replacement cost of goods sold. For General Products Company, the operating margin is $6,990,000 (= $13,450,000 − $5,400,000 − $1,060,000). The operating margin might be viewed as a measure of management's effectiveness in its operating decisions (pricing policy, production decisions, marketing efficiency, and the like).

The realized holding gain is the difference between cost of goods sold based on replacement cost and cost of goods sold based on acquisition cost. That is, the realized holding gain is measured by the increase in replacement cost between the time goods assumed to be sold were acquired and when they were sold. For General Products Company, the realized holding gain is $350,000.

The realized holding gain is difficult to interpret. It may result partially from skillful forecasting and buying decisions by purchasing management and should be rewarded. It may also result, however, from price increases that all purchasing agents expected, and, therefore, it does not represent superior performance. In addition, the gain is not distributable to owners because, if the firm is to continue operating, it must replace the item at the currently higher replacement cost to remain in business. (Of course, the firm can usually raise new funds with various issues of equity. In measuring distributable income, we assume that future operations at current levels do not require the raising of additional funds.)

INTEGRATION OF ACCOUNTING PROCEDURES FOR GENERAL AND SPECIFIC PRICE CHANGES

In this chapter, we have considered independently the accounting problems associated with general and specific price changes. Changes in the general price level influence the validity of the common monetary measuring unit assumption. Changes in specific prices have consequences for the valuation of assets and the recognition of holding gains and losses. It has been suggested by some accountants that the effects of both general and specific price changes should be recognized in reports to management and, consequently, the accounting procedures designed for both types of price changes should be integrated.

In preparing financial statements adjusted for both general and specific price changes, the general price level methodology would be applied to monetary assets and liabilities and a monetary gain or loss recognized. Nonmonetary assets would be stated using either current replacement costs or net realizable values at the end of the period. The difference between the valuation of nonmonetary assets between the beginning and end of the year would not be entirely reported as a holding gain or loss, however. The replacement cost at the beginning of the period of these assets would be restated to the general purchasing power of the dollar at the end of the period. A distinction would therefore be made between *real* and *nominal* holding gains and losses. For example, consider the treatment of equipment that has a replacement cost of $500 at the beginning of the year and $600 at the end of the year. In replacement cost financial statements a holding gain of $100 would be recognized. Now assume that an index of the general price level increased from 100 to 115 during the year. The real holding gain, stated in dollars of constant purchasing power, is $25. This amount is determined by restating the replacement cost of $500 at the beginning of the year to dollars of equivalent general purchasing power at the end of the year, obtaining $575 (= $500 × 115/100). The difference between the replacement cost at the end of the year of $600 and the general price level-restated replacement cost at the beginning of the year of $575 represents the real holding gain. The remaining $75 (= $575 − $500) is a nominal holding gain.

SUMMARY

This chapter has described the effects of changing prices on conventional accounting measurements of income and financial position. A distinction has been made between changes in the general price level and changes in the prices of specific assets and equities. Changes in the general price level influence the validity of the common monetary measuring unit assumption. Changes in specific prices have consequences for the valuation of assets and the recognition of holding gains and losses. The distinction between these types of price changes and the associated accounting problems should be clearly understood. The techniques for restating financial statements for general price level changes are not designed to reflect changes in the prices of specific assets and equities.

Management is concerned with maintaining the economic position of the firm and is likely to be interested in specific price changes and distributable income. Owners are more likely to be concerned with maintaining and increasing the general purchasing power of their investments. It is not clear, however, that general price level-adjusted financial statements do much to help owners assess their investments.

QUESTIONS AND PROBLEMS

1 Review the meaning of the following concepts or terms discussed in this chapter.
  a Common monetary measuring unit assumption.
  b Realization convention.
  c General price level changes.
  d General price level index.
  e General purchasing power of the dollar.
  f Specific price changes.
  g Specific price index.
  h Monetary item.
  i Nonmonetary item.
  j Monetary gain or loss.
  k Distributable income.
  l Economic income.
  m Operating margin.
  n Realized holding gain or loss.
  o Unrealized holding gain or loss.
  p Current replacement cost.
  q Net realizable value.
  r Real and nominal gains.

2 The accounting problems associated with changing prices have been described as *general* and *specific*. Explain.

3 Distinguish between the pair of terms listed in each of the following cases.
  a General price index and general price level.
  b General price index and general purchasing power of the dollar.
  c General price index and specific price index.

4 "Financial statements prepared under the conventional accounting model reflect dollars of mixed purchasing power." Explain the meaning of the statement in relation to the balance sheet, the income statement, and the statement of changes in financial position.

5 When general price level-adjusted financial statements are prepared, under what conditions will a firm recognize a monetary gain or a monetary loss?

6 For which types of asset and equity structures would you expect:
a Significant differences between earnings as conventionally reported and as restated for general price level changes?
b Insignificant differences between the two earnings measures?

7 Why is there no nonmonetary gain or loss in general price level-restated financial statements?

8 Why is there no monetary gain or loss in financial statements based on replacement costs?

9 In financial statements prepared under the conventional accounting model, some items are stated in terms of the current general purchasing power of the dollar, whereas other items are stated in terms of the general purchasing power of the dollar during prior periods. Give several examples of each type.

10 "The LIFO inventory cost flow assumption and accelerated depreciation methods are not comprehensive means of accounting for specific price changes." Explain.

11 What significant differences would be expected in the balance sheets based on acquisition cost, acquisition cost restated for general price level changes, and replacement cost?

12 What significant differences would be expected in the income statements based on acquisition cost, acquisition cost restated for general price level changes, and replacement cost?

13 On January 1, 19X0, an index of the general price level was 120.0. On December 31, 19X0, the index was 132.3. By what percentage did the general price level increase:
a During the year 19X0?
b During one-half the year 19X0, assuming that prices increased uniformly throughout the year?

14 Indicate whether each of the following accounts is a monetary item (M) or a nonmonetary item (N). State any assumptions you feel are necessary.
a Certificate of Deposit.
b Land.
c Investment in U.S. Treasury Notes.
d Deferred Income Taxes.
e Notes Receivable.
f Bonds Payable.
g Patents.
h Common Stock.
i Investment in Unconsolidated Subsidiaries.
j Allowance for Uncollectible Accounts Receivable.

15 A firm's garage was constructed several decades ago, in part, of a special red cedar wood that today is available only from the Philippine Islands for very high prices. In calculating the replacement cost of the garage, why is the high current price of red cedar wood largely irrelevant?

16 Southside Development Corporation acquired two parcels of land on July 1, 19X0, for $50,000 each. On December 31, 19X0, professional appraisers estimated the current market value, or selling price, of tract A to be $60,000 and of tract B to be $45,000. Tract B was sold on July 1, 19X1, for $38,000. On December 31, 19X1, tract A had a market value of $65,000.

An index of the general price level on various dates is determined to be as follows:

July 1, 19X0	100
December 31, 19X0.	115
July 1, 19X1	125
December 31, 19X1.	140

a Determine the amount of gain or loss recognized during 19X0 and 19X1 relating to these properties under **(1)** the acquisition cost and **(2)** the current market value, or selling price, valuation methods, assuming that changes in the general purchasing power of the dollar are ignored.

b Restate the gain or loss recognized during 19X1 on the sale of tract B from the acquisition cost valuation basis to the general price level-adjusted basis on December 31, 19X1.

c Separate the gain on sale of tract A into real and nominal components.

17 The purpose of this exercise is to provide insight into the potentially enormous impact of the cost flow assumption for inventories in restating net income from a conventional to a general price level-adjusted (GPLA) basis. In a recent year, F. W. Woolworth, the large retailer, had net income of about $65 million from revenues of over $4.20 billion and cost of goods sold, based on a FIFO cost flow assumption, of $2.95 billion. Because Woolworth used FIFO, the average dollar entering cost of goods sold was dated about nine months before year-end. The general price level-adjusted cost of goods sold was 9 percent larger than the historical cost of goods sold.

During the same year, J. C. Penney, another large retailer, had net income of about $125 million from revenues of about $6.94 billion and cost of goods sold, based on a LIFO cost flow assumption, of $4.98 billion. Because Penney used LIFO, the average dollar entering cost of goods sold was dated about six months before year-end. The general price level-adjusted cost of goods sold was about 5.6 percent larger than the historical cost of goods sold.

a By what dollar amount was Woolworth's GPLA cost of goods sold larger than its historical amount? What percentage of conventional net income does this increase represent?

b By what dollar amount was Penney's GPLA cost of goods sold larger than its historical amount? What percentage of net income does this increase represent?

c Explain why such a small difference (3.4 percent = 9.0 percent − 5.6 percent) in the percentage increase in restating conventional to GPLA cost of goods sold makes a much larger difference in restating conventional net income to GPLA net income.

18 The merchandise inventory of Scoggin's Appliance Store on January 1, 19X2, consists of 1,000 units acquired for $250 each. During 19X2, 2,500 units of merchandise are purchased at a unit price of $300, while 2,400 units are sold for $400 each. The average replacement cost per unit during 19X2 is $300, whereas the replacement cost on December 31, 19X2, is $360 per unit.

a Using the acquisition cost valuation method and ignoring general price level changes, determine the gross margin (sales less cost of goods sold) recognized during 19X2 using the FIFO and LIFO cost flow assumptions.

b Using the replacement cost valuation method and ignoring general price level changes, determine the amount of the operating margin and holding gains recognized during 19X2 using the FIFO and LIFO inventory cost flow assumptions.

19 United Manufacturing Corporation purchased a new machine on January 1, 19X3, for $500,000. The machine is to be depreciated using the straight-line method over a 10-year life. Estimated salvage value is zero. An index of the general price level on January 1, 19X3, is 160 and on December 31, 19X3, is 176.

a Determine the amount of depreciation expense for 19X3 and the book value of the machine on December 31, 19X3, using the acquisition cost valuation model (1) as conventionally reported and (2) as restated for general price level changes.

b The replacement cost on December 31, 19X3, of a similar new machine is $560,000 and of a similar one-year-old machine is $504,000. If the replacement cost valuation method is used and changes in the general purchasing power of the dollar are ignored, what is the amount of depreciation expense and holding gain or loss for 19X3?

c Disaggregate the holding gain determined in b into the real gain and the nominal gain.

20 Jones Manufacturing Corporation depreciates its machinery using the straight-line method over a 10-year life with zero estimated salvage value. A full year of depreciation is taken in the year of acquisition and none in the year of disposal. Acquisitions, which took place evenly over the appropriate years, were as follows: 19X1, $500,000; 19X2, $100,000; 19X3, $200,000. An index of the average general price level during 19X1 was 120, during 19X2 was 160, and during 19X3 was 180. The general price index on December 31, 19X3, is 200.

a Determine the amount of depreciation expense for 19X3 and the book value of the machinery on December 31, 19X3, using the acquisition cost valuation method as conventionally reported.

b Repeat a, using the acquisition cost valuation method restated for general price level changes. Round conversion factors used to two decimal places (for example, 200/120 = 1.67).

21 The balance sheet of the Widule Company on January 1, 19X0, is

Cash . . . . $100   Contributed Capital. $100

The following events occur during 19X0.

(1) January 1. The GNP Implicit Price Deflator Index is 100. Current replacement cost of a widule is $50. Two widules are purchased for a total of $100.

(2) June 30. The GNP Implicit Price Deflator Index is 120. Current replacement cost of a widule is $80. One widule is sold for $120.

(3) December 31. The GNP Implicit Price Deflator Index is 132. Current replacement cost of a widule is $90. The books are closed for the year and financial statements are prepared.

Prepare an income statement for 19X0 and a balance sheet as of December 31, 19X0, under each of the following sets of accounting conventions.

a Acquisition cost basis as conventionally prepared.

b Acquisition cost basis as restated to constant dollars dated December 31, 19X0.

c Current replacement cost basis as shown in Exhibit 15.5 (ignoring general price level changes).

d Current replacement cost basis as restated to constant dollars dated December 31, 19X0.

22 The Pepper River Electric Company (PREC) produces electricity. Its current oil-burning plant is several years old and is capable of producing electricity for 20 more years. It can produce 1 million kilowatt-hours of electricity per month by burning 2,000 barrels of fuel oil. Fuel oil now costs $15 per barrel. If PREC were to rebuild a 20-year, oil-burning plant today, the cost would be $10 million. Because of the drastic increases in oil prices since the current plant was built, PREC would not build an oil-burning plant today. Instead, it would build a coal-burning plant. The coal-burning plant would cost $11 million to build. It would have the same life as the oil-burning plant and produce 1 million kilowatt-hours of electricity per month by burning 100 tons of coal at a cost of $80 per ton.

How would you go about determining the current cost to replace the productive capacity of the Pepper River Electric Company's ability to generate 1 million kilowatt-hours of electricity per month? That is, what method of determining current replacement cost of productive capacity should PREC use to derive its footnote disclosure to comply with SEC requirements on current costs? Assume that the current difference in price between a ton of coal and a barrel of oil will not change over the next 20 years, even though both prices may rise.

Assume a cost of capital of 1 percent per month and that all costs are incurred at the beginning of the month.

a What is the present value of the cash savings from using a coal-burning, rather than an oil-burning, plant?

b What is the current replacement cost of the Company's current ability to produce 1 million kilowatt-hours of electricity per month?

c What are the appropriate replacement cost disclosures?

CHAPTER 16
CAPITAL BUDGETING: A CLOSER LOOK

In Chapter Seven we introduced the fundamentals of capital budgeting. We emphasized the importance of separating the investment and financing decisions and focused on the net present value method for evaluating investment projects. In this chapter we describe several other methods for evaluating investment projects and point out their weaknesses. We also consider one type of investment decision where the investment and financing decisions cannot be entirely separated: evaluation of leases.

ALTERNATIVE METHODS FOR EVALUATING PROJECTS

Many methods are used for evaluating projects, but most are conceptually inferior to using the net present value method with a discount rate equal to the cost of capital. Some methods that take the time value of money into account often give the same decision results as the net present value rule and, in practice, prove to be satisfactory. Alternative methods that do not take the time value of money into account are easy to use, because they do not involve present value computations, but this simplicity is their chief virtue.

Excess Present Value Index

The excess present value index is computed as follows:

$$\text{Excess Present Value Index} = \frac{\text{Present Value of Future Cash Flows}}{\text{Initial Investment}}$$

This index indicates the number of present value dollars generated per dollar of investment. For example, if the present value of the *future* cash flows is $17,000 and the initial investment is $12,000, then the excess present value index is 1.42 (= $17,000/ $12,000).

In the absence of capital rationing, the net present value and the excess present value methods result in the same accept/reject decision. Projects with an excess present value index greater than 1.0 (positive net present value) are accepted. Projects with an excess present value index less than 1.0 (negative net present value) are rejected.

When there is capital rationing, constraints are placed on the amount of capital available for investment in a particular period. Under these conditions investment alternatives that have been determined to be desirable (that is, have a positive net present value or excess present value index greater than 1.0) must be ranked in order of desirability. It is at this point that the net present value and excess present value index methods might give conflicting results. Consider the data in Exhibit 16.1. The rankings of the four projects differ depending on whether the rankings are based on net present values or excess present value indexes. The difference in the rankings is caused by the fact that in the excess present value index method, the excess present value is related to the dollars of investment required, rather than to the absolute size of the net present value.

Regardless of which capital budgeting method is used, the procedure for selecting projects when capital rationing is required is the same. As we demonstrated in Exhibit 7.4, the net present value of every combination of projects falling within the budget constraint is calculated. The combination with the largest net present value is selected. In Exhibit 16.1, the best combination with a $20,000 budget constraint is project A and project C (see Exhibit 7.4 for the calculations).

Refer to the discussion in Chapter Seven, on pages 184–185. There we show that capital rationing does not make sense when there is a discount rate to be used in a net present value analysis. If capital is judged to be unavailable to fund all projects with positive net present value, then the discount rate being used is too low.

We prefer the net present value method to the excess present value index method because we often find the latter difficult to interpret. This is particularly a problem

EXHIBIT 16.1
Ranking of Projects According to Net Present Value and Excess Present Value Index Methods

Project (1)	Initial Cash Outlay Required (2)	Present Value of Future Cash Flows (3)	Net Present Value (4)	Ranking by Net Present Value (5)	Excess Present Value Index (6)	Ranking by Excess Present Value Index (7)
A	$12,000	$17,000	$5,000	1	1.42	3
B	11,000	15,000	4,000	2	1.36	4
C	7,000	10,000	3,000	3	1.43	2
D	3,000	5,500	2,500	4	1.83	1

(4) = (3) − (2).
(6) = (3)/(2).

when an investment project requires a relatively small investment. Even a small excess present value can result in a large excess present value index because of the size of the denominator of the index.

Internal Rate of Return

The *internal rate of return,* sometimes called the *time-adjusted rate of return,* of a stream of cash flows is defined as the discount rate that equates the net present value of that stream to zero. Stated another way, it is the rate that discounts the future cash flows to the present so that the present value of the future cash flows is equal to the initial investment.

To illustrate the calculation of the internal rate of return, assume that a proposed project requires an initial investment of $11,059 and is expected to yield net cash inflows for the next four years as follows: year 1, $5,000; year 2, $4,000; year 3, $3,000; year 4, $2,000. To calculate the internal rate of return, we must determine the rate that will discount the net cash inflows during years 1 to 4 so that they have a present value of $11,059 (that is, a net present value equal to zero). Mathematically, this involves solving the following equation for *r,* the discount rate:

$$\$11,059 = \frac{\$5,000}{(1+r)^1} + \frac{\$4,000}{(1+r)^2} + \frac{\$3,000}{(1+r)^3} + \frac{\$2,000}{(1+r)^4}$$

Computers and some pocket calculators can determine this discount rate quickly. Whatever device is used, it is necessary to try various discount rates until the proper one is found. We begin by trying a discount rate of 10 percent. Columns (3) and (4) of Exhibit 16.2 show that at this discount rate the net present value is positive. This suggests that the internal rate of return must be larger than 10 percent. So we try 12 percent. We can see from column (6) of Exhibit 16.2 that 12 percent is the discount rate that equates the net present value to zero. Twelve percent therefore is the internal rate of return for this project. (If the net present value for a given trial rate were *negative,* then we should try a *smaller* rate at the next trial.)

When using the internal rate of return to evaluate investment alternatives, it is necessary to specify a *cutoff rate* (such as 10 percent for Garden Winery Company in Chapter Seven). Projects are accepted if their internal rates of return exceed the cutoff rate and rejected if their internal rates of return are less than the cutoff rate.

Advocates of the internal rate of return argue that the method does not require knowing the firm's cost of capital, and is therefore easier to use in practice than the net present value rule. For the internal rate of return rule to give the correct answers, however, the "cutoff" rate must be the cost of capital. Otherwise, some projects that will increase the value of the firm to its owners will either be rejected when they should be accepted or vice versa. The net present value method does not require more data than the internal rate of return method.

We prefer the net value method to the internal rate of return method for several reasons.

EXHIBIT 16.2
Calculation of Internal Rate of Return

End of Year (1)	Cash Inflow (Outflow) (2)	Present Value Factor at 10% (3)	Present Value of Cash Flows at 10% (4)	Present Value Factor at 12% (5)	Present Value of Cash Flows at 12% (6)
0	$(11,059)	1.00000	$(11,059)	1.00000	$(11,059)
1	5,000	.90909	4,545	.89286	4,464
2	4,000	.82645	3,306	.79719	3,189
3	3,000	.75131	2,254	.71178	2,135
4	2,000	.68301	1,366	.63552	1,271
Net Present Value			$ 412	Net Present Value	$ 0

Simplicity   We find the net present value method easier to calculate and interpret. Both methods require estimates of future cash flows and the cost of capital rate. The internal rate of return requires, however, a "search" for the proper discount rate on each project.

Single Ranking Measure   The net present value method provides a single net present value amount for each project that can be used for making the accept/reject decision. The internal rate of return method, however, may give more than one internal rate of return for a particular project. This mathematical phenomenon can occur when the pattern of yearly net cash flows contains an intermixing of net cash inflows and outflows. For example, if at the end of a project's life, cash expenditures will be made to return the plant site to its original condition, then individual cash flows can be negative both at the beginning and at the end of a project's life, but positive in between. Projects with intermixing of cash inflows and outflows are likely to have multiple internal rates of return. (Solving for the internal rate of return involves finding the roots of a polynomial. Descartes' rule of signs tells how to determine the limit to the number of roots of such a polynomial. See the Glossary for an explanation of this rule. Examples of multiple internal rates of return have been discovered in practice for coal mining companies that use strip mining to generate cash inflows from coal but which are required to spend large amounts of cash at the completion of the mining phase to reclaim the stripped land.)

Better Ranking of Alternatives   Under the net present value rule, projects are either acceptable or unacceptable. When projects are mutually exclusive, then only one of a set of projects can be chosen. Under these conditions the rule tells us to choose the project with the largest net present value. The internal rate of return rule ranks projects in the same way as the net present value rule only when each of the following four conditions is met:

1 If the cutoff rate used for the internal rate of return rate is equal to the cost of capital.
2 If projects are not mutually exclusive.
3 If projects have the same life.
4 If there is only one internal rate of return.

Otherwise, the internal rate of return leads to incorrect decisions about projects, as demonstrated next.

Mutually exclusive projects   Assume that the aftertax cost of capital is 10 percent per year and that only one of the two projects, E or F, as shown in Exhibit 16.3, can be chosen. Project E provides a simple illustration for calculating the internal rate of return. The internal rate of return on project E is the rate r such that

$$\$100 = \frac{\$120}{1 + r}$$

Solving for r gives $r = .20$. The internal rate of return in project F is similarly easy to calculate. The internal rate of return rule would rank project E as better than project F,

EXHIBIT 16.3
Data for Projects E and F

Project Name	Aftertax Cash Flows by Year End of Year 0	1	Internal Rate of Return	Net Present Value at 10 Percent
E	($100)	$120	20%	$ 9.09
F.	(300)	345	15	13.64

whereas the net present value rule prefers project F. To see that project F is better for the firm, consider what the firm must do with the "idle" $200 it will have to invest if project E is chosen. That $200 must be invested, by definition, at the aftertax cost of capital of 10 percent and will provide $220, after taxes, at the end of the first year. So the total flows available at the end of the first year from project E and from the investment of the idle funds at 10 percent will be $120 + $220 = $340, which is less than the $345 available after taxes from project F. The firm will prefer the results from choosing project F as the net present value rule signals.

To better understand why the net present value ranking is better, decide whether you would rather invest $.10 today to get $2 a year from now or invest $1,000 today to get $2,500 a year from now. You may not do both. We presume that you would prefer the second alternative even though the internal rate of return on the first is about 12 times as large as for the second. The internal rate of return rule, applied to mutually exclusive projects, ignores the amount of funds that can be invested at that rate. As we discussed earlier, this shortcoming, sometimes called the *scale effect*, applies to the excess present value index rule as well.

Projects with different lifetimes   Consider projects G and H shown in Exhibit 16.4. The internal rate of return on project H is the rate *r* that satisfies the equation

$$\$100 = \frac{\$50}{(1 + r)} + \frac{\$84}{(1 + r)^2}$$

EXHIBIT 16.4
Data for Projects G and H

Project Name	Cash Flows by Year End of Year 0	1	2	Internal Rate of Return	Net Present Value at 10 Percent
G	($100)	$125	—	25%	$13.64
H	(100)	50	$84	20	14.87

You can verify that the internal rate of return is 20 percent by using the 20-percent column of Table 2 at the back of the book. The internal rate of return rule ranks project G as better than project H, whereas the net present value rule ranks project H better than project G. To see why project H is better for the firm, consider what the firm must do during year 2. If project G is accepted, $125 must be invested in the average investment project available to the firm. The return from such an average project is, by definition, the cost of capital, 10 percent. At the end of the year 2, the firm will have $125 × 1.10 = $137.50. If project H is accepted, the $50 cash inflow at the end of the first year will also be invested at 10 percent and will grow to $50 × 1.10 = $55 by the end of year 2. Thus, the total funds available at the end of the second year are $55 + $84 = $139, which is larger than the $137.50 if project G were accepted. The internal rate of return rule ignores the fact that idle funds must be invested at the cost of capital.

Payback Period

Another method often used in evaluating investment projects involves the payback period. The *payback period* is the length of time that elapses before total cumulative aftertax cash inflows from the project equal the initial cash outlay for the project. Refer to Exhibit 16.2. The proposed project has a payback period of about 2.7 years. By the end of the first year, $5,000 of the initial investment has been "recovered." By the end of the second year, the cumulative cash inflows total $9,000 (= $5,000 + $4,000). The remaining $2,059 (= $11,059 − $9,000) is received approximately two-thirds of the way through the third year. Hence the payback is 2.7 years. The payback period decision rule states that projects be accepted when the payback period is as short as some designated cutoff time period, such as two years, and rejected otherwise.

The weakness in the payback period rule is that both the time value of money and all cash flows subsequent to the payback date are ignored. One project could have a shorter payback period than another but much smaller net present value. The payback period rule is designed to emphasize concern with the firm's liquidity and to facilitate calculations when many small, similar projects are considered. The net present value rule, however, also takes liquidity into account because the cost of capital used for discounting cash flows, by definition, accurately measures the costs of securing additional funds should that become necessary.

If the net cash inflows per year from a project are constant and occur for a number of years at least twice as long as the payback period and when the discount rate is reasonably large, say 10 percent per year or more, then the reciprocal of the payback period is approximately equal to the internal rate of return on the project. Thus the payback period will rank projects in the same way that the internal rate of return does if the stated conditions are met.

Advocates of the payback period argue that the net present value rule, even with its discounting of future cash flows, gives too much weight to cash flows to be received more than three or four years into the future. They point out that many managers have favorite "pet" projects that they would like to see the company invest in. Managers have learned that marginal projects can be made to look acceptable under the net present value method if some of the distant cash inflows are made unrealistically large.

(This might be achieved by making very optimistic projections of future increases in sales revenues or by making optimistic estimates of the rate at which production costs will decline as workers learn new skills.) Such managers might figure that they will not be on the same job by the time top management learns that the cash inflows projected for, say, five years hence were too optimistic. Such managers might reasonably expect to have been promoted or fired by the time five years elapse. Thus, they expect not to be held accountable for their distant projections. Analysts who fear being misled by overly optimistic managers insist on using a payback rule to find out the near-term profitability of a project. Advocates of the net present value method caution about accepting cash flow projections without careful study, but maintain that the method is still superior.

Discounted Payback Period

Given the widespread use[1] of the payback period rule and its inability to yield good decisions for the most general case, some accountants have suggested that firms who want a payback rule should use the discounted payback period. The *discounted pay-back period* is similar to the ordinary payback period, but it is defined as the length of time that elapses before the *present value* of the cumulative cash inflows is at least as large as the initial cash outlay. The discount rate used in this calculation is most often the cost of capital. The discounted payback period gives some recognition to the time value of funds that flow before payback is accomplished. The ordinary payback periods of projects J and K in Exhibit 16.5 are the same, three years, but the discounted payback criteria will properly rank K as better than J.

Either payback rule would improperly prefer both J and K to Project L. Analysts sometimes recommend the discounted payback rule to firms that are wary of applying the net present value rule to projects like project L. As we pointed out above, the manager who made the original forecast for $50,000 cash inflow for year 5 may not be around to be held accountable by the time it is learned that the forecast was too optimistic.

EXHIBIT 16.5
Illustrative Data for Payback Rules, Projects J, K, and L

Project Name	Cash Flow at End of Year					
	0	1	2	3	4	5
J.............	($10,000)	$2,000	$3,000	$5,000	$2,000	—
K	(10,000)	5,000	3,000	2,000	2,000	—
L.............	(10,000)	—	—	—	—	$50,000

---

[1] See the results of the survey reported by Thomas Klammer, "Empirical Evidence of the Adoption of Sophisticated Capital Budgeting Techniques," *Journal of Business*, 45 (July 1972), p. 393.

Bailout and Discounted Bailout Periods

The payback period criteria ignore the cash flows after payback has been achieved and the possible residual value of equipment of a project that for whatever reason does not last its estimated life. The *bailout period* is the shortest elapsed time from the start of the project until the cumulative cash inflows from a project plus the residual value of the equipment at the end of the period equal the cash outflows for the project. Assume, for example, that a project with an initial cash outflow of $100 has cash inflows of $20 at the end of each year. Also assume that the equipment could be sold for $60 at the end of the first year, $50 at the end of the second year, $40 at the end of the third year, $30 at the end of the fourth year, and so on until salvage is zero at the end of the seventh year. The payback period is five years (5 years = $100/$20 per year). Note, however, that by the end of the third year cumulative cash inflows have been $60 and the equipment can be salvaged for $40. Thus, bailout occurs after three periods.

The *discounted bailout period* is calculated from present values of estimated cash flows and residual values. The bailout period (or the discounted bailout period) will always be shorter than the payback period (or the discounted payback period) if the equipment has any residual value at the end of the payback period. The bailout criteria are superior to payback criteria because bailout takes into account the residual value subsequent to the termination date being considered. Because the estimated residual value at any date incorporates an estimate of the present value of the cash flows from the equipment after that date, the bailout criteria use more of the relevant information available than do the payback criteria.

So far as we know, the bailout methods are seldom seen in practice.

Accounting Rate of Return

The *accounting rate of return,* sometimes called the *rate of return on investment* or *ROI,* is defined for a project as

$$\frac{\text{Average Yearly Income from the Project}}{\text{Average Investment in the Project}}$$

Assume that a project requiring an investment of $10,000 is expected to yield total income of $3,300 over four years. The average yearly income is $825. The average investment in the project, assuming straight-line depreciation and no salvage value, is $5,000. Hence, the accounting rate of return is $825/$5,000 = 16.5 percent. The accounting rate of return pays no attention to the time value of money because it uses income, rather than cash flow, data.

We can think of little good to say about the accounting rate of return except that it is easy to compute and sometimes, by coincidence, it gives good answers. Many companies use the accounting rate of return; one survey indicated that it was the most sophisticated investment decision rule used by about 25 percent of the firms surveyed.[2]

---

[2] *Ibid.*

Summary of Evaluation Methods

The methods for evaluating investment projects that do not take the time value of money into account should not be used. All the methods that do take the time value of money into account require a cutoff rate or discount rate. If optimal economic decisions are to result, then the cutoff or discount rate must be set equal to the cost of capital. If the cost of capital rate is to be used at all, then the net present value rule is no more complex than the others. Using the net present value rule will lead to decisions that will make present value of the firm's wealth equal to or larger than that from using any of the other rules.

MANAGERIAL EVALUATION OF LEASES

As we discussed in Chapter Seven, the modern theory of finance suggests that investment decisions be made independently of financing decisions. If a project can earn a return at least as large as the firm's cost of capital, then it should be acquired. The manner in which the specific funds needed for the acquisition will be obtained is a separate question.

It is easy to confuse the investment and financing decisions in the context of making the lease-versus-purchase decision. Certainly, the promotional literature from leasing companies, who have an incentive to encourage businesses to lease rather than purchase, abets the confusion. The confusion arises because many leasing arrangements are in effect installment purchases of the property. Thus, the investment and financing decision are intermingled in the leasing arrangement. In this section we discuss the proper basis for making lease-versus-purchase decisions.

Types of Leases

Leases are of two broad types. Cancelable leases, such as for the use of telephones by the month or of cars rented by the day or week, are generally short-term and can be canceled by either party in the rental transaction. These leases do not present any problems because they are not a form of borrowing and, in any case, would not normally be analyzed as part of a firm's capital budgeting system.

Noncancelable leases, on the other hand, run for much longer periods of time. Under these leases, a firm commits itself to payments over the term of the lease whether or not the leased asset is continued in use. The obligation under a noncancelable lease is, in an economic sense, not significantly different from a loan from a bank or other creditor. The noncancelable lease is a means of financing the acquisition of an asset's service for a specified period of time.

Procedure for Evaluating Leases

To evaluate a leasing proposal properly, the investment and financing decisions must be separated. The procedure we illustrate in this section for evaluating leases is summarized as follows:

1. Determine if acquisition of the asset's services is a desirable investment alternative (the investment decision). To do this, calculate the net present value of the cash flows expected to be generated by the asset *assuming the asset is immediately purchased for cash.* The discount rate used should be the cost of capital. If the net present value is positive, then go to step 2. If the net present value is negative, do not consider the proposal any further.

2. Determine the best means of financing the acquisition of the asset's services (the financing decisions). First, determine the net present value of leasing. To do this, substitute the periodic rental payments for the outright cash payment at the time of the acquisition. Then calculate the net present value of leasing using the firm's cost of capital. Second, determine the net present value assuming the acquisition of the asset is financed by borrowing the necessary funds. It is important that the pattern of amounts to be repaid under the assumed borrowing be roughly equal or the same as the pattern of the assumed lease payments. If they are not, then the method illustrated here may not give the right answer. For example, if the proposed lease requires equal annual payments at the end of the year, then the assumed borrowing should be like a mortgage (with equal annual payments) rather than like a bond (with small interest payments until maturity when the entire principal is repaid). Problem 12 at the end of this chapter explores this requirement. Then, substitute the periodic interest and principal payments for the single outright cash payment at the time of acquisition. Next, determine the net present value of the purchase-borrowing alternative; use the firm's cost of capital in computing discount factors. The financing alternative with the largest net present value should be used.

Illustration of the Lease Evaluation Procedure

Return to the example of the Garden Winery Company discussed in Chapter Seven. The company is contemplating the acquisition of equipment that will permit it to produce a new type of wine. The manufacturer of the equipment is asking an immediate cash price of $10,000 for the equipment. Alternatively, the manufacturer will lease the asset to Garden Winery Company for a rental fee of $3,019 a year for four years. At that time the asset will be scrapped.

Investment Decision   The first step is to determine if acquisition of the asset's services is a desirable investment alternative, as in Exhibit 7.2. The analysis is repeated in the top panel of Exhibit 16.6. The analysis assumes that the asset is purchased outright and that annual cash flows are discounted at the firm's cost of capital of 10 percent per year. If the asset is purchased, then the net present value of the investment project is $1,160. Acquiring the asset is, therefore, a worthwhile undertaking.

Financing Decision   Next we must consider how the investment should be financed. It is necessary that we consider this second question because leasing is a form of financing.

The middle panel of Exhibit 16.6 shows the calculation of the net present value assuming that the asset is acquired through leasing. Instead of a cash outflow of $10,000 at time zero, there is a cash outflow of $3,019 per year for lease payments. To simplify the illustration, we assume that lease payments are made at the end of

EXHIBIT 16.6
Annual Net Cash Flows and Net Present Values of Alternatives Available to Garden Winery Company for Acquiring Use of Asset (Discount Rate Is 10 Percent per Year; Income Taxes Are 40 Percent of Pretax Income)

End of Year (1)	Pretax Cash Inflows Less Cash Outflow Expenses[a] (2)	Depreciation[b] (3)	Lease Payments (4)	Payments to Service Debt — Total (5)	Interest Expense[c] (6)	Principal Repayment[d] (7)	Pretax Income[e] (8)	Income Tax Expense[f] (9)	Net Cash Inflows (Outflows)[g] (10)	Present Value of Net Cash Flows at 10%[h] (11)
Purchase Asset Outright; No Borrowing (See Exhibits 7.1 and 7.2)										
0	—			—	—	—	—	—	($10,000)	($10,000)
1	$ 5,000	$ 2,500	—	—	—	—	$2,500	$1,000	4,000	3,636
2	4,500	2,500	—	—	—	—	2,000	800	3,700	3,058
3	4,000	2,500	—	—	—	—	1,500	600	3,400	2,554
4	3,000	2,500	—	—	—	—	500	200	2,800	1,912
	$16,500	$10,000					$6,500	$2,600	$ 3,900	$ 1,160
Lease Asset; Lease Payment Made at the End of Each Period										
0	—	—	—	—	—	—	—	—	—	—
1	$ 5,000	—	$ 3,019	—	—	—	$1,981	$ 792	$ 1,189	$ 1,081
2	4,500	—	3,019	—	—	—	1,481	592	889	735
3	4,000	—	3,019	—	—	—	981	393[i]	588	442
4	3,000	—	3,019	—	—	—	(19)	(8)	(11)	(8)
	$16,500		$12,076				$4,424	$1,769	$ 2,655	$ 2,250
Purchase Asset; Borrow $10,000 at 8 Percent to Be Repaid in Four Annual Installments										
0	—	—	—	—	—	—	—	—	$ 0[j]	$ 0
1	$ 5,000	$ 2,500	—	$ 3,019 =	$ 800	+ $ 2,219	$1,700	$ 680	1,301	1,183
2	4,500	2,500	—	3,019 =	622	+ 2,397	1,378	551	930	769
3	4,000	2,500	—	3,019 =	431	+ 2,588	1,069	428	553	415
4	3,000	2,500	—	3,019 =	223	+ 2,796	277	110	(129)	(88)
	$16,500	$10,000		$12,076 =	$2,076	+ $10,000	$4,424	$1,769	$ 2,655	$ 2,279

a Refer to Exhibit 7.2; the amounts shown here are the amounts in column (2) less the amounts shown in column (3) of Exhibit 7.2. The initial outlay is not an expense; it appears first in column (10).
b Straight-line method; $10,000 cost/4-year life.
c Eight percent of outstanding loan. Outstanding loan is $10,000 less cumulative principal repayments shown in column (7).
d Lease payment ($3,019) less portion allocated to interest expense from column (6).
e Amount in column (2) less amounts in columns (3), (4), and (6).
f Forty percent of amount in column (8).
g Amount in column (2) less amounts in columns (4), (5), and (9).
h Amount in column (11) multiplied by present value factor for 10-percent discount rate: 1,000 for cash flow at end of year 0; .90909 for cash flows at end of year 1, .82645 for cash flows at end of year 2, .75131 for cash flows at end of year 3, and .66301 for cash flows at end of year 4. See Table 2 at the back of the book and Exhibit 7.2.
i By actual multiplication, this number is $392; rounding to the nearest dollar has caused the sum of number in this column to be in error by $1. This number has been changed to undo the rounding effects.
j At the end of year 0, $10,000 is borrowed and used immediately to acquire asset; this number is +$10,000 − $10,000 = $0.

each year. Because Garden Winery Company is only leasing the asset, it will not deduct depreciation expense in determining taxable income. It does, however, deduct rent expense in calculating taxable income. The net aftertax cash flows are again discounted using the firm's cost of capital of 10 percent. The net present value of acquiring the asset's services through leasing is $2,250. Notice that the net present value of leasing is about twice as large as the net present value of outright purchase.

Some managers would note the much larger net present value for the leasing plan and conclude that leasing is surely better for the firm than buying outright. *Comparing the net present values of buying outright versus leasing is invalid.* The investment decision has been confounded with the financing decision. A noncancelable lease is a form of borrowing. In the first case, the firm is not borrowing; in the second case, it is borrowing. To evaluate the leasing plan, the manager should construct a series of cash flows in which the firm borrows equivalent amounts of funds for equivalent interest rates and then compare a borrow-purchase alternative with the leasing alternative. Correct managerial decisions require comparable financing plans. Because the leasing contract effectively combines the financing and investment decisions, the valid alternative to leasing is a borrow-purchase alternative.

Borrow-purchase alternative   The borrow-purchase alternative is analyzed in the lower panel of Exhibit 16.6. We begin by determining the rate at which Garden Winery Company could borrow $10,000 today, with repayments being made over the next four years. In the illustration we have used an 8 percent rate. This is the rate that the manufacturer/lessor is *implicitly* charging Garden Winery Company in the leasing arrangement. That is, the discount rate that discounts the annual rental payments of $3,019 back to the present so that they have a present value equal to the cost of the asset of $10,000 is 8 percent. If the leasing company is willing to lend to Garden Winery Company at 8 percent, then the Company can presumably borrow from a bank at 8 percent per year. If payments on the loan are made in annual installments at the end of the year, then the payments will be $3,019 for each of the four years, just as for the lease. After all, the same amount is being borrowed and at the same interest rate as in the lease. Part of each payment to the bank is for interest and part is for principal repayment. The separation of the annual payment into interest and principal follows the effective interest method as described in financial accounting texts. This separation is illustrated in Exhibit 16.7. These amounts are shown in columns (6) and (7) of Exhibit 16.6.

Separating the annual payment into interest and principal repayment is required for the computation of income taxes, because the interest expense is a deduction in computing taxable income whereas repayment of the loan principal is not.

If the Company borrows and purchases the asset, it will report depreciation each year identical with that if it purchases without borrowing. Column (3) shows the depreciation charges. In the case of borrow-purchase, pretax income is cash inflows less cash outflows, column (2), less depreciation, column (3), and interest expense, column (5). Column (9) shows income taxes, which are 40 percent of pretax income. Net cash flow for the period shown in column (10) is cash inflows less cash outflows, column (2); less payments to the bank to service the debt, column (5); less income

EXHIBIT 16.7
Separation of Loan Payments into Interest and Principal for a $10,000, Four-Year, 8-Percent Loan; Annual Payment of $3,019

End of Year (1)	Unpaid Liability at Beginning of Period (2)	Interest Expense (3)[a]	Principal Payment (4)[b]	Unpaid Liability at End of Period (5)[c]
0	—	—	—	$10,000
1	$10,000	$ 800	$ 2,219	7,781
2	7,781	622	2,397	5,384
3	5,384	431	2,588	2,796
4	2,796	223	2,796	0
Total . .		$2,076	$10,000	

[a] Column (3) = .08 × column (2).
[b] Column (4) = $3,019 − column (3).
[c] Column (5) = column (2) − column (4).

taxes, column (9). Column (11) shows the present values of each of the net cash flows discounted at 10 percent per year.

The net present value of the borrow-purchase alternative is $2,279, which is somewhat larger than the net present value of the lease alternative ($2,250) because of the timing of income tax payments. In this illustration, borrowing turns out to be slightly superior to leasing as a form of financing.

Why Do Leasing and Borrow-Purchase Appear More Attractive Than Outright Purchase?

Both leasing and borrow-purchase have net present values about twice as large as the net present value of the outright purchase. Why? We can rephrase this question to make the managerial implications clearer. Suppose that the analysis of the outright purchase showed a negative net present value, indicating that the project was not worthwhile for the company but that the analyses of leasing and borrow-purchase showed a positive net present value, indicating that the project is worthwhile when financed with debt. What should the manager conclude?

The answers to both questions involve an understanding of the difference between the interest cost of debt and the cost of capital used in making investment decisions. In the illustration for Garden Winery Company, the aftertax cost of capital is 10 percent, whereas the borrowing rate is 8 percent. (In general, the difference between these two rates can be even larger than in this illustration. A difference of two percentage points is about as small as we would expect to see.) In the net present value of the leasing and borrow-purchase alternatives, the Company is charged with interest on borrowings at 8 percent, but the cash flows are discounted at 10 percent. Any time a series of interest payments is discounted with a higher rate than that specified in the loan contract, the present value of the payments to service the loan will have a lower net present value than the face amount of the borrowing.

Chapter Three discussed the phenomenon of *leverage,* where the rate of return on total capital can be increased if the rate paid to borrow is less than the rate typically earned by the company on its projects. The difference between the net present values of borrowing and outright purchase results from showing the expected returns to leverage as a part of the return to the *specific* project. But, of course, the firm always has the option to borrow at the current market rate of interest. The returns and risks of leverage accrue to the firm's financing policy *as a whole* and should not be attributed to any one investment project.

Thus, we reach the conclusion that if the net present value for outright purchase is negative even though the net present value for one of the borrowing alternatives is positive, then the firm should not undertake the project. Lease contracts by their very nature involve a simultaneous consideration of investment and financing. Because the two aspects cannot easily be separated in general, the manager should first evaluate the project assuming outright purchase. Only after outright purchase appears worthwhile, because the project has a positive net present value, should the form of financing be considered. Once the lease terms are specified, the manager should ascertain the payment schedule for a straight loan that is as similar as possible in terms of amounts borrowed and timing of repayments as are implicit in the lease. Then the borrowing and leasing alternatives can be compared.[3]

SUMMARY

The net present value rule says that a firm should undertake an investment project if the net present value of the cash flows is positive when the cash flows are discounted at the cost of capital rate. This chapter has shown that the rule always leads to at least as good decisions as some other rules often seen in practice: the excess present value index, the internal rate of return rule, the payback rules, and the accounting rate of return (ROI) rules.

The investment decision and the financing decision for investment projects should be kept separate. The use of the net present value rule and the incremental principal for making decisions will enable the manager to choose between various methods of financing only if the contending financing plans involve equal amounts of borrowing for equal amounts of time. Otherwise, the benefits of financial leverage will be confused with the benefits from a particular investment project. The concepts were illustrated in a buy-borrow versus a lease financing decision.

---

[3]   The nature of leasing contracts can be somewhat more complicated than indicated here. For example, lease payments can be made in advance, with the initial lease payment being immediately deductible for tax purposes. It is not usually possible to arrange a straight loan with interest payable in advance that is deductible for tax purposes. (In theory, there is no such thing as interest paid in advance. If payments are made before interest has accrued, then theory says that those payments must be a reduction in the principal amount of the loan, not interest.) Another complication arises when the manufacturer offers a "package deal" where the combined interest payments and asset cost are together smaller than they would be separately. (Automobile dealers often are willing to sell at a lower price when the buyer borrows from the dealer than when the buyer makes an outright purchase.) The advanced questions raised by some leasing contracts are beyond the scope of this introductory, but already sophisticated, discussion. The reader interested in a more advanced discussion is referred to Chapter 8 of the *Handbook of Modern Accounting,* 2nd ed., edited by Sidney Davidson and Roman L. Weil (New York: McGraw-Hill Book Company, 1977).

QUESTIONS AND PROBLEMS

1 Review the meaning of the following concepts or terms discussed in this chapter.
 a Excess present value index.
 b Internal rate of return.
 c Cutoff rate.
 d Payback period.
 e Reciprocal of payback period.
 f Discounted payback period.
 g Bailout period.
 h Discounted bailout period.
 i Accounting rate of return.
 j Cancelable lease.
 k Noncancelable lease.
 l Separating the investment and financing decisions for leases.

2 The internal rate of return rule and the net present value rule both take the time value of money into account and usually give the same decision. When may they give different decisions?

3 What are the weaknesses of using the payback period as a device for capital budgeting decisions?

4 For mutually exclusive projects, the project with the lowest net present value of cash inflow per dollar of initial cash outlay can be the best alternative for the firm. How can this be?

5 The Larson Company must choose between two mutually exclusive projects. The cost of capital is 12 percent. Given the data below, which project should Larson choose and why?

	After Tax Cash Flows End of Year			
Project Label	**0**	**1**	**2**	**3**
M	($500,000)	$175,000	$287,500	$400,000
N	(450,000)	477,000	195,000	60,000

6 What is the internal rate of return on the following projects, each of which requires a $10,000 cash outlay now and returns the cash flows indicated?
 a $5,530.67 at the end of years 1 and 2.
 b $1,627.45 at the end of years 1 through 10.
 c $1,556.66 at the end of years 1 through 13.
 d $2,053.39 at the end of years 1 through 20.
 e $2,921.46 at the end of years 3 through 7.
 f $2,101.77 at the end of years 2 through 10.
 g $24,883.20 at the end of year 5 only.

7 What is the payback period of the projects in Problem **6, a** through **g?**

8 Compare the internal rate of return on the projects in Problem **6, a** through **d,** with the *reciprocal* of the payback period for those projects computed in Problem **7.** Notice that the internal rate of return on **d** is exactly equal to the reciprocal of its payback period, but this relation does not hold for the other projects. Explain.

9 What is the payback period of the projects in Problem **6, a** through **g,** assuming that cash flows occur uniformly throughout the year?

10 Carlo Company is considering the acquisition of a machine that costs $40,000 and that is expected to save $8,000 in cash outlays per year, after taxes, at the end of each of the next 12 years. The new machine is estimated to have no salvage value at the end of its useful life.
a Compute the approximate internal rate of return for this project.
b Compute the approximate internal rate of return, assuming that the cash savings were to last only 6, instead of 12, years.
c Compute the approximate internal rate of return, assuming that the cash savings were to last 20, rather than 12, years.
d Compute the approximate internal rate of return, assuming that the cash savings will be $6,000, rather than $8,000, per year for 12 years.

11 The Lessee Company must acquire a computer that has a three-year life, costs $30,000, and will save $25,000 per year before taxes in cash operating costs over the present data-processing system. Lessee Company can borrow for three years at 8 percent per year. The computer manufacturer is willing to sell the computer for $30,000 or to lease it for three years on a noncancelable basis—that is, on the basis that Lessee Company must make payments for the three years no matter what happens. The annual lease payment will be $11,641. The income tax rate is 40 percent. If purchased, the computer will be depreciated on a straight-line basis. Prepare an analysis that will help Lessee Company decide what it should do. The cost of capital is 10 percent.

12 The Carom Company plans to acquire, as of January 1, 19X0, a computerized cash register system that costs $100,000 and that has a five-year life and no salvage value. The new computerized system will save $35,000 in cash operating costs per year. The company is considering two plans for acquiring the system:
(1) Outright purchase. To finance the purchase, $100,000 of par value 8-percent annual coupon bonds will be issued January 1, 19X0, at par.
(2) Lease. The lease requires five annual payments to be made on December 31, 19X0, 19X1, 19X2, 19X3, and 19X4. The lease payments are to be $25,046 and they have a present value of $100,000 on January 1, 19X0, when discounted at 8 percent per year, and the firm's cost of capital is 12 percent.
Straight-line depreciation will be used if the computerized system is acquired. The income tax rate is 40 percent.
a Construct an exhibit similar to Exhibit 16.6. Use three panels, one for each of the following alternatives:
    i   Outright purchase for cash.
    ii Outright purchase with borrowing as explained in (1), above.
    iii Lease under terms as explained in (2), above.
b Should the services of the asset be acquired? How do you reach this conclusion?
c Which of the financing plans, borrowing via a bond issue or leasing, appears preferable? How can one financing plan with an interest cost of 8 percent per year (bond issue) appear preferable to another financing plan with an interest cost of 8 percent per year (lease)? What can you conclude from the answers to these two questions?
d Now assume that the lease contract calls for payments of $24,400 per year (an implicit

interest rate of 7 percent). Construct a fourth panel in the exhibit called for in **a,** above. Which financing plan, leasing at 7 percent or borrowing at 8 percent, appears preferable? How can one plan of financing with an interest cost of 8 percent per year (bond issue) appear preferable to another plan of financing with an interest cost of 7 percent per year (lease)? What can you conclude from the answers to these two questions?

e   Should Carom Company lease the asset or purchase it? How can you tell? If you judge that purchase is preferable, what is the minimum aftertax payment that the lessor could offer to make Carom Company indifferent to leasing?

13 Xenophon Company has undertaken an investment project that has a net present value of zero when cash flows are discounted at its cost of capital of 12 percent per year. The investment project has a five-year life. The initial investment to undertake this project is $100,000. Suppose that Xenophon Company finances the project by borrowing $100,000 at a rate of 8 percent per year. It will make $8,000 interest payments at the end of each of the next five years and repay the $100,000 at the end of the fifth year.

a   What is the present value at the start of the project of the benefits of financial leverage? That is, compute the net present value of the debt service payments, including principal repayment, using the 12-percent discount rate, and subtract that amount from the $100,000 borrowed.

b   Repeat the requirements of **a** assuming that the investment project has a 10-year life and that the $100,000 is borrowed for 10 years with interest paid annually and the principal repaid at maturity.

14 Eichenfield offers to sell a mass spectrometer with a useful life of five years to David Scientific Systems, Inc., for $45,000 or to lease (noncancelable) it for five years for $11,300 per year, payable *in advance.* That is, each lease payment is made at the start of each year. After five years, the spectrometer will be obsolete and assumed to be worthless. David Scientific's cost of capital is 12 percent, it can borrow from the bank at an 8-percent rate, and it pays taxes at the rate of 40 percent.

Eichenfield's Analysis

	Leasing Alternative			Purchase Alternative		
End of Year	Lease Payment (1)	Taxes Saved (2)	Present Value at 12% of Taxes Saved (3)	D.D.B. Depre-ciation Expense (4)	Taxes Saved (5)	Present Value at 12% of Taxes Saved (6)
0.	$11,300	$4,520	$ 4,520	—	—	—
1.	11,300	4,520	4,036	$18,000	$7,200	$ 6,429
2.	11,300	4,520	3,603	10,800	4,320	3,444
3.	11,300	4,520	3,217	6,480	2,592	1,845
4.	11,300	4,520	2,873	4,860	1,944	1,235
5.	0	—	—	4,860	1,944	1,103
			$18,249	$45,000		$14,056

(1) Given.
(2) .40 × (1).
(3) Present value at 12 percent × (2).
(4) Double-declining-balance provides for a larger present value of tax deductions than does sum-of-the-year's-digit × (2).
(5) .40 × (4).
(6) Present values at 12 percent × (5).

Eichenfield says that the present value of the tax savings from leasing is almost $4,200 larger than the present value of the tax savings from purchasing. Because the cash purchase price is only $3,726 less than the present value of the lease payments, leasing is superior when all factors are considered.

b Eichenfield is incorrect. Why? Present calculations to support your conclusions.

15 A manager's favorite project requires an aftertax cash outflow on January 1 of $4,000 and promises to return $1,000 of aftertax cash inflows at the end of each of the next five years. The aftertax cost of capital is 10 percent per year.

a Use the net present value method to decide whether or not this favorite project is a good investment.

b How much would the projected cash inflow for the end of year 5 have to be increased for the project to be acceptable?

c How much would the projected cash inflow for the end of year 5 have to be increased for the project to have a net present value of +$100?

CHAPTER 17
THE INCREMENTAL PRINCIPLE AND THE IMPACT OF INCOME TAXES ON BUSINESS DECISIONS

Many capital investment proposals were rejected by business firms in the Fall of 1970 because the anticipated rates of return from the investments were less than the minimum required. The income tax laws were changed late in 1970 to permit a faster write-off of certain depreciable assets. As a result of the change, many of these investment proposals became immediately acceptable. Likewise, the tax credit granted for investments in certain depreciable assets was increased early in 1975 from 7 to 10 percent of acquisition cost. As a result, many projects not previously meeting minimum required rates of return suddenly became acceptable. These two cases illustrate the impact that income taxes can have on business decisions. Chapters Seventeen and Eighteen summarize some of the more important income tax provisions affecting business decisions and illustrate how these income tax factors might be assessed analytically. In this chapter, consideration is given to selecting accounting methods for computing taxable income and to income tax factors affecting the acquisition, use, and disposal of depreciable assets. In Chapter Eighteen, we consider decisions about compensation, intercorporate investments, capital structure, and organizational form.

ROLE OF INCOME TAXES IN BUSINESS DECISIONS

The amount and timing of income taxes payable under various alternatives affect the cash flows from those alternatives and therefore their relative desirability. The impact of income taxes on decisions can be assessed with the same analytic methods as are used for any other cash flows. In capital investment decisions, for example, the present value of the income taxes payable (or saved) can be incorporated into the calculation of the net present value of each investment proposal. In compensation package decisions, the present value of the income tax savings from deducting various forms of compensation paid to employees can be incorporated into the calculation of the net present value of each alternative compensation package.

In some cases, income taxes play a dominant role in making decisions. For example, when selecting the optimum depreciation method for tax purposes, the decision is based almost entirely on an assessment of the tax savings from alternative depreciation methods. Little concern is likely to be given to nontax factors such as consistency with the method used for financial reporting or ease in computation. In other cases, income taxes play a relatively minor role in making decisions. For example, the nontax benefits of the corporate form of organization for a large multinational firm are so large that such a firm would be unlikely to consider the tax advantages of operating in some other form, such as a partnership. In other cases, significant trade-offs are required between tax and nontax factors. For example, in designing a compensation package for employees, consideration must be given to employees' current and future needs for cash, their retirement plans, and other factors, in addition to the income taxes that will be payable under alternative compensation packages.

TAXATION OF BUSINESS FIRMS

Business firms are typically organized in one of three forms: sole proprietorship, partnership, or corporation. In this section, a brief description is presented of the taxation of each of these forms of organization.

Sole Proprietorship

The most frequently used form of organization in the United States is the sole proprietorship. It is generally used by small, single-owner businesses. For tax purposes, a business firm operated as a sole proprietorship is not considered a separate taxable entity. Instead, the income of the business is combined with the nonbusiness income of the owner in determining the tax liability. Income taxes are assessed on the combined business and nonbusiness income at graduated rates ranging from 14 percent to 70 percent. If a net loss results, the loss can be carried back three years and a refund received for any prior taxes paid. The loss can also be carried forward seven years to offset income generated in those years.

Partnership

A partnership is essentially the same as a sole proprietorship except that there is more than one owner. The partnership form is used by businesses ranging from small grocery stores to large national and multinational public accounting firms. Like a sole proprietorship, a partnership is not a separate taxable entity. The income of the partnership passes through to the individual partners according to their agreement as to the division of income. The partners combine their share of partnership income with their nonbusiness income in determining their tax liabilities. Because the income of the partnership is subjected to taxation at the level of the individual partners, it is taxed at the same graduated rates as a sole proprietorship. Net losses of a partnership pass through to the individual partners and can offset their nonbusiness income similarly to those of a sole proprietorship.

Corporation

The dominant form of business organization in terms of aggregate sales, income, and assets is the corporation.[1] For tax purposes, a corporation is viewed as a separate taxable entity. The taxable income of a corporation is taxed at a statutory rate of 20 percent of the first $25,000, 22 percent of the next $25,000, and 48 percent of taxable income in excess of $50,000. Periodically, as in some recent years, these rates have been temporarily changed in an effort to stimulate corporate investments or achieve other fiscal objectives. Note that corporate taxable income is not subject to graduated rates to the same extent as a sole proprietorship or a partner. Net losses of a corporation are treated the same as those of a sole proprietor or partner. They can be carried back three years and forward seven years.

When a corporation pays dividends, the dividends are included in the taxable income of the stockholders and taxed at the usual graduated rates for individuals. Thus, the income of a corporation is subject to taxation at the corporate level when earned and a second time at the individual level when distributed as a dividend. The income of a sole proprietorship or partnership, in contrast, is taxed only once, as it is earned. Distributions to sole proprietors and partners are much like withdrawals from a checking account and are not subject to income taxation.

The preceding paragraphs are intended merely as an introduction to business taxation. Other important provisions relating to these forms of organization are discussed later in Chapter Eighteen.

SELECTION OF ACCOUNTING METHODS

Business firms are granted relatively wide latitude in selecting the methods of accounting that will be used in determining taxable income. With the exception of the use of the LIFO cost flow assumption for inventories, a firm can in almost all situations use different methods of accounting for tax and financial reporting purposes.

In selecting accounting methods for tax purposes, the objective is to choose those methods that minimize the present value of the stream of income tax payments (or maximize the present value of income tax deductions and credits). This objective is sometimes expressed as the *least and latest rule*. Business firms should pay the least amount of taxes as late as possible within the law. For corporations, this rule suggests postponing the recognition of revenue as long as possible and recognizing expenses as quickly as possible. For sole proprietorships and partnerships, the least and latest rule may require trade-offs. Because the income of these forms of business is taxed at graduated rates, it may be preferable in some cases to recognize income in an earlier, low-income year rather than postpone recognition to a later, high-income year. These trade-offs can be analyzed by expressing the stream of cash payments for taxes in terms of present values.

---

[1]   This is not to say that corporations pay the majority of income taxes collected by the federal government. In recent years, only about 25 percent of federal income tax collections were from corporations. The remainder came from individuals.

In the sections that follow, we consider some of the more important areas where business firms can select from among alternative accounting methods.

Recognition of Income[2]

The sequence of activities in producing and selling a product might be depicted as in Figure 17.1. The income from this sequence of activities is the difference between the cash received from customers and the cash payments made in producing and selling the product. This income could conceivably be recognized at any one or a combination of the five times indicated in Figure 17.1. For tax purposes, some of these recognition times are preferable to others, depending on the circumstances.

Cash Basis of Accounting   In almost all cases, the cash basis of accounting, when permitted, is preferable for tax purposes. Under a cash basis, revenue is recognized when cash is collected and expenses are recognized, or deducted, when cash expenditures are made. The cash basis is desirable because it generally permits the earliest deduction of expenses and the longest postponement of revenue recognition. The Internal Revenue Code, however, prohibits a firm from using the cash basis if inventories are a significant factor in generating its income. The reason for this provision should be fairly obvious. A firm engaged in production activities may acquire a factory and manufacturing equipment many years before the assets are fully used up in manufacturing products. If such a firm were permitted to use the cash basis, it would deduct significant portions of the cost of manufacturing several years prior to the time when revenues would be recognized from the sale of products. This may be desirable from the standpoint of the business firm, but not from the standpoint of the government attempting to assess and collect taxes. In cases where the time elapsed from point (1) to point (3) in Figure 17.1 is long or the costs involved are significant, a firm is required to use the accrual basis of accounting.

Example 1   Management Consultants, Incorporated, provides management advisory services to clients. The firm should use the cash basis of accounting in determining its taxable income. Cash expenditures for salaries, utilities, and other costs can be deducted when made, whereas revenue is not recognized until cash is received from clients. There are, however, restrictions on the deductibility of some prepaid costs, especially for depreciable assets.

Example 2   Miller Manufacturing Corporation is engaged in the production and sale of heavy construction equipment. The firm cannot use the cash basis because inventories are a significant factor in generating its income.

Accrual Basis of Accounting   Under the accrual basis of accounting, the costs incurred in generating revenues are deducted as expenses in the same period as the revenue is recognized. There is some effort, then, to match expenses with revenues.

---

[2]   The income tax law generally uses the terms "income" and "revenue" interchangeably. We use the term "income" in this section more broadly to refer to the recognition of both revenues and expenses.

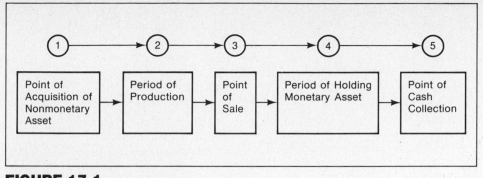

FIGURE 17.1
Sequence of Activities in
Producing and Selling a Product

Most firms are required to use the accrual basis for tax purposes because of the significance of inventories and are required to recognize income at the point of sale. A few types of businesses have the option of recognizing income at some point in the earnings process other than the point of sale.

Firms engaged in long-term contract work can recognize income as production progresses (percentage-of-completion method) or at the time of sale or delivery (completed-contract method). Because postponement of taxes is desirable whenever permitted, the completed-contract method would appear to be best. This is likely to be true for a corporation that has sufficient taxable income to be taxed at a marginal rate of 48 percent each year. The completed-contract method may not be best for a sole proprietorship or partnership. These noncorporate businesses may find a conflict between "least" and "latest." The lumping of all of the income from the contract in the year completed may result, because of the graduated rate structure, in larger present value of taxes being paid than if the income were recognized earlier but spread over each year of the contract.[3]

Example 3   Diversified Construction Company operates as a corporation. On January 1, 19X0, it contracted to construct a bridge for $1,800,000. Costs were incurred as follows: 19X0—$500,000; 19X1—$500,000; 19X2—$500,000. The bridge was completed at the end of 19X2. The present values (assuming a discount rate of 10 percent) of the taxes payable by this firm under the percentage-of-completion and completed-contract methods are shown in the top panel of Exhibit 17.1. Because the marginal tax rate is 48 percent regardless of when the income is recognized, it is preferable to use the completed-contract method and postpone the payment of the tax.

Example 4   Assume that the construction company in Example 3 is operated as a sole proprietorship. The present values of the taxes payable under the two income recogni-

---

[3]   The effect of a sharp increase in marginal tax rates due to irregular flows of income is lessened somewhat for sole proprietorships and partnerships by special income averaging provisions, a subject beyond the scope of this text.

EXHIBIT 17.1
Present Value of the Tax Payments under Percentage-of-Completion and Completed-Contract Methods (assuming a discount rate of 10 percent)

Year	Income Recognized (1)	Income Tax Rate[a] (2)	Taxes Payable (3)	Present Value Factor (4)	Present Value of Tax Payments (5)
BUSINESS OPERATED AS A CORPORATION					
Percentage-of-Completion Method					
19X0	($500,000/$1,500,000) × $300,000 = $100,000	.48	$ 48,000	.91	$ 43,680
19X1	($500,000/$1,500,000) × $300,000 = 100,000	.48	48,000	.83	39,840
19X2	($500,000/$1,500,000) × $300,000 = 100,000	.48	48,000	.75	36,000
Total—Percentage-of-Completion Method	$300,000		$144,000		$119,520
Completed-Contract Method					
19X2	$1,800,000 − $1,500,000 = $300,000	.48	$144,000	.75	$108,000[b]
BUSINESS OPERATED AS A SOLE PROPRIETORSHIP					
Percentage-of-Completion Method					
19X0	($500,000/$1,500,000) × $300,000 = $100,000	.50	$ 50,000	.91	$ 45,500
19X1	($500,000/$1,500,000) × $300,000 = 100,000	.52	52,000	.83	43,160
19X2	($500,000/$1,500,000) × $300,000 = 100,000	.46	46,000	.75	34,500
Total—Percentage-of-Completion Method	$300,000		$148,000		$123,160[b]
Completed-Contract Method					
19X2	$1,800,000 − $1,500,000 = $300,000	.60	$180,000	.75	$135,000

(3) = (1) × (2).
(5) = (3) × (4).

[a] These rates are assumed for purposes of illustration.
[b] The completed-contract method results in a lower present value of tax payments in this case if the corporate form is used, whereas the percentage-of-completion method results in a lower present value for a sole proprietorship.

tion methods are shown in the lower panel of Exhibit 17.1. Even though the completed-contract method permits postponing the recognition of income until 19X2, it is subject to a higher tax rate and produces, under the assumed graduated rates, a higher present value of the tax payments. The percentage-of-completion method is therefore preferable in this case for the sole proprietorship.

An analysis similar to that in the lower panel of Exhibit 17.1 is necessary for businesses operated as sole proprietorships or partnerships to determine which income recognition method is preferable in its activities. The critical variable that must be predicted is the marginal tax rate during future years. Note that a firm is generally not permitted to choose the best method for each contract individually. It can only select the method that, for all of its contract work in total, is expected to minimize the present value of income tax payments.

Firms that sell products on an installment basis (that is, cash is periodically collected from customers over some time period after the products are sold) can generally recognize income for tax purposes either at the time of sale or at the time cash is collected (installment method). In almost all cases the installment method is preferable. For a corporation with sufficient taxable income to be subject to a 48-percent marginal tax rate each year, postponing income recognition until cash is collected minimizes the present value of the income tax payments. For a sole proprietorship or partnership, use of the installment method not only postpones the tax payments, but also spreads the income over several periods.

Example 5   Jones Department Store operates as a sole proprietorship. During 19X0, products costing $15,000 were sold under an installment plan for $20,000. Installment collections were as follows: 19X0—$10,000; 19X1—$5,000; 19X2—$5,000. Exhibit 17.2 shows the calculation of the present value of the income tax payments assuming that income is recognized at the time of sale and at the times cash is collected under the installment method. Note that the installment method both postpones payment of the taxes and, because of the smoothing effect on income, results in a lower tax rate.

Example 6   Sears, Roebuck, and Company recognizes income using the installment method for tax purposes. Use of the installment method saved Sears $93 million in taxes during the year ended January 31, 1977, over the amount that would have been paid if income had been recognized at the time of sale. As of the end of 1977, approximately 10 years after having adopted the installment method, Sears has postponed, perhaps indefinitely, approximately $900 million in taxes.

Summary of Income Recognition   Most business firms do not have wide latitude in selecting a method of income recognition. For firms in service-type businesses, the cash basis is preferable. When inventories are a significant income-generating factor, an accrual method must be used. The only firms with much choice as to when income is recognized are those operating with long-term contracts or selling on an installment basis.

EXHIBIT 17.2
Present Value of the Tax Payments When Income Is Recognized at the Time of Sale and as Cash Is Collected (assuming a discount rate of 10 percent)

Year		Income Tax Rate[a]	Taxes Payable	Present Value Factor	Present Value of Tax Payments
Income Recognized at Time of Sale					
19X0	$20,000 − $15,000 = $5,000	.34	$1,700	.91	$1,547
Income Recognized at Time of Cash Collection (Installment Method)					
19X0	$10,000/$20,000 × $5,000 = $2,500	.28	$ 700	.91	$ 637
19X1	$ 5,000/$20,000 × $5,000 = 1,250	.26	325	.83	270
19X2	$ 5,000/$20,000 × $5,000 = 1,250	.24	300	.75	225
Total—Installment Method	$5,000				$1,132

a These income tax rates are assumed for purposes of illustration.

Inventory Cost Flow Assumption

In terms of the dollar impact on income taxes paid, the most important decision for most firms is whether or not to use the last-in, first-out (LIFO) cost flow assumption for inventories. The decision to use LIFO for tax purposes is complicated by the requirement that, if used for tax reporting, it must also be used for financial reporting to stockholders. In this section, we discuss several of the more important factors that a firm should consider in the LIFO-versus-FIFO (or average cost) decision.

Factors to Consider in the LIFO-Versus-FIFO Decision   Perhaps the most important factor to be considered in adopting LIFO is the anticipated direction of future price changes for the inventory items. If prices are expected to rise, LIFO is preferable for tax purposes because the more recent higher costs of purchases are used in determining cost of goods sold. If prices are expected to fall, FIFO is preferable because the older, higher costs are used in determining cost of goods sold.

Example 7   United Manufacturing Corporation produces standardized heavy equipment. Production requires more than a year from start to finish and an additional year to market the equipment. Raw material and labor costs have been increasing steadily in recent years and are expected to continue increasing in the foreseeable future. This is a classic example of where LIFO is preferable to FIFO. Acquisition costs are steadily increasing and the production and distribution period is relatively long.

Example 8   American Electronics Corporation manufactures and sells a patented new electronic device for continually monitoring automobile engine performance. The potential market for this device is extensive. In anticipation of substantial growth, the firm has recently constructed several capital-intensive plants to manufacture the electronic device. At the current time, the firm is producing at less than optimum capacity because demand is somewhat limited. Economies of scale are likely to be realized as the level of production increases and the capital-intensive plants become fully used. If these expectations are realized, then the firm should be able to produce the device at a decreasing cost per unit (that is, depreciation and other fixed manufacturing costs will be spread over a larger number of units). With decreasing costs anticipated in the future, FIFO is likely to be preferable.

Suppose, however, that the prices of inventory items are expected to fluctuate widely for several years in the future. Should a firm adopt LIFO or FIFO? In order to respond to this question, an illustration will be helpful. Figure 17.2 presents graphically the relationship between the selling price of a particular product and the cost of goods sold under LIFO and FIFO. LIFO cost of goods sold tends to approximate the replacement cost of products sold. Because selling prices are generally changed in response to changes in replacement costs, the gross margin per unit under LIFO (selling price less LIFO cost of goods sold) tends to remain fairly constant. On the other hand, the gross margin per unit under FIFO tends to fluctuate significantly from period to period as prices change. Selling prices during period 2 are matched against the

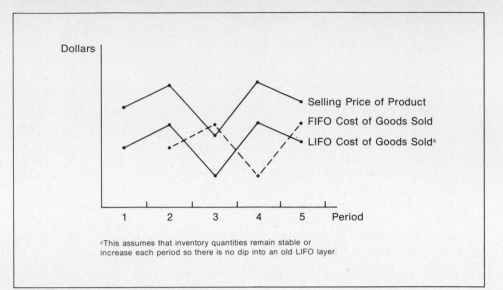

FIGURE 17.2
Diagram of Gross Margins under
LIFO and FIFO over Several
Periods of Fluctuating Prices

costs of purchases of period 1.[4] Under FIFO, the gross margin includes a one-period holding gain or loss. Under LIFO, most of the holding gain or loss is "buried" in the valuation of inventories on the balance sheet. Gross margins and incomes under LIFO, therefore, tend to be more stable than under FIFO during periods when prices fluctuate.

What are the implications of the more stable income stream in the LIFO versus FIFO decision? If a firm operates as a corporation and is subject to a 48 percent marginal tax rate each period, it is difficult to generalize as to whether LIFO or FIFO is better. If the trend in long-term prices is expected to be reasonably stable, as illustrated in Figure 17.2, then the decision will likely revolve around the anticipated price changes during the first few periods. This is because the tax savings during the early periods have a more significant impact on present values than do those of later periods. On the other hand, if the long-term price trend is upward (downward), even though in a fluctuating pattern, LIFO (FIFO) is better.

If a firm operates as a sole proprietorship or partnership, an additional factor enters the decision. Because of the graduated rate structure, the more stable income under LIFO might be preferable. For example, note the large increase in the gross margin under FIFO during period 4. This increase could lead to a significantly higher marginal tax rate than if LIFO had been used.

---

[4]   The length of the "period" depends on the rate of inventory turnover. If inventory turns over four times each year, the period is three months.

A second factor to consider in the LIFO-versus-FIFO decision is the extent to which inventory quantities fluctuate each year. If inventory quantities decrease between the beginning and end of a year for a firm using LIFO, a portion of the cost of goods sold will be based on an old LIFO layer. If prices have been increasing over time, the dip into an old LIFO layer can result in the recognition of a large holding gain.

For a corporation subject to a 48 percent tax rate, LIFO is still preferable in this situation. Under LIFO, the holding gain is recognized in a later period than if FIFO had been used, and it is not taxed at a higher rate. For a sole proprietorship or partnership, however, the recognition of a large holding gain can push the owner into a higher graduated tax rate category. Some trade-offs are therefore necessary for noncorporate businesses between the more stable income under LIFO when quantities increase and the recognition of possibly large holding gains when quantities decrease.

One additional factor affecting the LIFO-versus-FIFO decision is the rate of inventory turnover. The more slowly inventory turns over, the longer will be the period of accumulating price changes and, therefore, the larger will be the difference between LIFO and FIFO cost of goods sold. The production and selling period of United Manufacturing Corporation in Example 7 spanned two years. Greater differences in cost of goods sold between LIFO and FIFO would be expected here than in Example 8, where the time span would be probably just a few months.

Example 9 United Bakers, Incorporated, is a wholesale distributor of baked goods. Inventory turns over approximately once every two days. The decision between LIFO and FIFO is relatively unimportant for this firm, because cost of goods sold under the two methods will be about the same.

Factors to Consider in Applying LIFO Several factors should be considered once a decision has been made to adopt LIFO. First, LIFO should be adopted at a time when prices are expected to increase. In this way the base layers will be priced at the lower current prices and cost of goods sold will be priced at the higher future prices. This is particularly a concern for firms that experience fluctuating prices for their products. Second, LIFO is preferably adopted when inventory quantities are either relatively low or at normal levels. If LIFO is adopted when inventory quantities are unusually high, there is an increased probability that a dip into the base layer will be required in future years. This is more of a concern for a sole proprietorship or partnership than for a corporation because of the different degrees of progressions in the tax rate structure.

A third factor to consider in adopting LIFO is whether a quantity-based or a dollar-based LIFO system should be used. Most illustrations of LIFO to which you have been previously exposed have used a quantity-based LIFO system. That is, LIFO layers are maintained in terms of the quantity of inventory items (for example, pounds of steel, barrels of oil). To determine if there has been an increase or decrease in the LIFO layers during a period, a comparison is made of the quantity of items on hand at the beginning and end of the period. It is possible, however, to base LIFO on dollar investments in inventory items. For example, LIFO may be applied to the dollar investment in men's suits, furniture, or appliances. Dollar-value LIFO is particularly useful for firms whose products are subject to a high degree of style change or obsolescence. Without dollar-value LIFO, base LIFO layers would be continuously eliminated as specific products were discontinued or substantially changed. With dollar-value LIFO, the base inventory layers will not be eliminated as long as the discontinued or improved products are replaced by newer, similar goods. The accounting procedures employed in applying dollar-value LIFO are beyond the scope of this book. We merely point out that the risk of depleting old LIFO layers is lower with dollar-based as compared to quantity-based LIFO. Also, it should be noted that the layers, or pools, under dollar-value LIFO should be defined as broadly as possible (that is, one pool for men's clothing rather than two—men's shirts and men's shoes) to minimize the risk of depleting dollar-value LIFO layers.

Effects of LIFO-Versus-FIFO Decision   The importance of the LIFO-versus-FIFO decision for tax purposes can be reemphasized by considering the magnitude of the possible tax savings. General Electric has been using LIFO for several years and has deferred more than half a *billion* dollars in taxes since it switched to LIFO in the 1940s. In a recent year, Caterpillar Tractor Company, by using LIFO, saved income taxes equal in amount to net income for the year. Similar examples of significant tax savings are easily found for other firms.

Depreciation Method

In discussing the statement of changes in financial position in Chapter Two, we emphasized that depreciation expense is not a source (or a use) of funds. By itself, depreciation is merely a "book" entry reducing a noncurrent asset and reducing net income and retained earnings. Business firms are permitted, however, to deduct depreciation charges in determining their taxable income. By reducing the amount of taxes otherwise payable, depreciation expense has an effect on cash flows. To illustrate this, consider the following example. A firm has sales minus cash operating expenses (expenses other than depreciation) during 19X0 of $100,000. Depreciation expense is $20,000, and the income tax rate is 48 percent. Exhibit 17.3 illustrates the effect on taxes payable and net income of not deducting versus deducting depreciation charges.

EXHIBIT 17.3
Illustration Showing the Incremental Effect on Cash Flows and Net Income of Depreciation Deductions

	Net Income Assuming That Depreciation Is Not Deducted	Net Income Assuming That Depreciation Is Deducted	Incremental Effect
Sales Minus Operating Expenses			
Other Than Depreciation (a cash flow).	$100,000	$100,000	—
Less Depreciation (not a cash flow).	—	20,000	($20,000)
Net Income before Taxes	$100,000	$ 80,000	($20,000)
Income Taxes at 48 Percent (a cash flow).	48,000	38,400	9,600
Net Income	$ 52,000	$ 41,600	($10,400)

By deducting depreciation, the cash outflow for income taxes is reduced from $48,000 to $38,400. Depreciation expense, therefore, leads to a cash savings of $9,600.

In selecting a depreciation method for tax purposes, the firm should select the method that maximizes the present value of the income tax savings by minimizing the present value of the tax payments. This generally means that the cost of depreciable assets should be written off as quickly as possible. The double-declining-balance (DDB) and sum-of-the-years'-digits (SYD) methods are preferable to the straight-line method. The critical choice then narrows to DDB versus SYD. Which of these two methods is better depends on the depreciable life used and two other choices that must be made under a depreciation accounting system called the Asset Depreciation Range (ADR) system. Because the optimum depreciation method is so heavily influenced by these other choices, we shall defer consideration of the depreciation method decision until we discuss the ADR system later in this chapter.

Capitalization Policy

There are several provisions in the Internal Revenue Code that permit firms either to capitalize and subsequently amortize certain costs or to deduct them immediately during the period in which they are incurred. For example, research and development costs can be capitalized and amortized over five years or immediately expensed when incurred. Similar provisions apply to certain storage costs for inventories and setup costs for depreciable assets. Whenever possible, a corporation should deduct these costs as they are incurred for tax purposes to minimize the present value of income tax payments.

INVESTMENTS IN DEPRECIABLE ASSETS

There are numerous provisions in the Internal Revenue Code relating to investments in depreciable assets. Many of these provisions are aimed at encouraging firms to invest in depreciable assets and thereby stimulate technological progress and aggregate economic activity. Our purpose in this section is to summarize some of the more important provisions relating to the acquisition, use, and disposition of depreciable assets. These provisions can play a critical role in evaluating investment alternatives in a firm's capital budgeting system. At the end of this section, we present a comprehensive example which shows how the income tax factors can be integrated into the capital budgeting models discussed in Chapters Seven and Sixteen.

The Internal Revenue Code makes frequent references to *real* and *personal* property. Real property includes land, buildings, and other structures more or less permanently fixed to the land. Personal property includes equipment, fixtures, automobiles, and similar items not permanently fixed to the land. Our principal concern in this section is with *depreciable* property.

Acquisition of Depreciable Property

Firms are granted an investment tax credit (ITC) for investments in certain types of depreciable property. The credit is equal to a stated percentage times the acquisition cost of qualifying property. The ITC offsets the income taxes otherwise due each year on a dollar-for-dollar basis (that is, an ITC of $20,000 offsets $20,000 of taxes otherwise payable). In effect, the federal government pays for a share of the cost of the property equal to the amount of credit allowed. The principal ITC provisions are summarized below:

1 Rate—The statutory ITC rate is currently 10 percent of the cost of qualifying property, although this rate has been changed several times in recent years.
2 Qualifying Property—Investments in depreciable personal and real property (except buildings) qualify for the credit. No investment credit is allowed if the depreciable life is less than three years. If the depreciable life of the property is at least three and under five years, only one-third of the cost of the property qualifies for the credit. If the depreciable life is at least five and under seven years, two-thirds of the cost qualifies for the credit. With a depreciable life of seven or more years, all of the asset's cost qualifies. There are some restrictions placed on investments in used property.
3 Limit—The maximum ITC allowed in any year is $25,000 plus one-half of the tax liability in excess of $25,000. Any excess ITC can be carried back three years and forward seven years.

Example 10   The income tax liability of the Bell Corporation for 19X0 before claiming the ITC is $225,000. During 19X0 it purchased equipment as follows:

Item	Cost	Depreciable Life (years)
X	$300,000	4
Y	900,000	6
Z	500,000	8

The qualifying investment is $1,200,000 [$= (\frac{1}{3} \times \$300,000) + (\frac{2}{3} \times \$900,000) + (1.00 \times \$500,000)$]. The ITC at 10 percent is $120,000 ($= .10 \times \$1,200,000$). Because this amount is less than the maximum credit allowed of $125,000 [$= \$25,000 + (.50 \times \$200,000)$], the full credit of $120,000 can be claimed for 19X0.

Use of Depreciable Property

A firm is allowed to deduct a portion of the cost of depreciable property each year of its useful life. As illustrated in this chapter, depreciation charges reduce taxable income and thereby the amount of income taxes that would otherwise be payable. We indicated earlier that the optimum depreciation method decision cannot be made independently of other choices, such as the depreciable life employed. In fact, an initial decision must be made regarding the manner in which the depreciable life will be determined before deciding which specific life and depreciation method is best.

The depreciable life may be based on either (1) a "facts-and-circumstances" approach, or (2) the Asset Depreciation Range (ADR) system. Under a facts-and-circumstances approach, a firm uses its past experience and other information to decide which depreciable life is appropriate. This approach leads to many administrative difficulties. Corporations attempt to use as short a life as possible to maximize the present value of the income tax savings from depreciation deductions. The Internal Revenue Service often questions the depreciable life selected and the issue ends up in the courts. Thus, this approach to determining a depreciable life involves initial costs to choose a life and perhaps subsequent legal and other costs of having to justify the life selected.

To overcome some of these difficulties, the ADR system was instituted in 1970. Under this system, the Internal Revenue Service specifies a range of acceptable lives for various types of property. As long as the depreciable life selected falls within that range, the Internal Revenue Service will not question the life selected. There are several additional advantages of using the ADR system rather than the facts and circumstances approach that are beyond the scope of this book.[5] In most cases, firms should follow the ADR system in selecting a depreciable life.

We shall concentrate our attention on two of the important decisions that a firm must make under the ADR system:

1 What depreciable life within the asset depreciation range should be used?
2 What is the optimum depreciation method for the depreciable life selected?

Optimum Depreciable Life We indicated earlier that the present value of the tax savings from depreciation deductions can be maximized by depreciating assets as quickly as possible. This suggests using the depreciable life at the lower end of the asset depreciation range. For example, a three-year life would be used for an asset having a range of three to five years. The depreciable life decision becomes more complex when considered in conjunction with the investment tax credit. Recall that the credit is reduced for assets having a depreciable life of less than seven years. Trade-offs are required, therefore, between shorter lives to maximize the present value of the tax savings from depreciation deductions and longer lives to obtain the full investment tax credit. We return to this question shortly.

Optimum Depreciation Method The Internal Revenue Code designates the allowable depreciation methods for various types of real and personal property. The methods allowed depend on the asset's condition when acquired (new or used), depreciable life, and other factors. The allowable methods are periodically changed to attain certain governmental policy objectives. It is difficult, therefore, to generalize on the optimum method for all types of property. Usually the choice is between the two accelerated methods—the double-declining-balance (DDB) method and the sum-of-the-years'-digits (SYD) method.[6] The DDB method provides the largest depreciation charges during the first few years of an asset's life. After that, the SYD method provides larger

---

[5] The interested reader may refer to Clyde P. Stickney and Jeffrey B. Wallace, *A Practical Guide to the Class Life (ADR) System.* Lawyers & Judges Publishing Company, Tucson, Arizona, 1977.
[6] Under the ADR system, a firm can use a combination of DDB and SYD under some circumstances. This combination method is generally better than either DDB or SYD independently. Due to the complexities involved, we shall not consider further the DDB/SYD combination method. See Stickney and Wallace, *ibid.,* for additional discussion of this method.

depreciation charges. As with the optimum life decision, trade-offs are required between the early superiority of DDB and the later superiority of SYD. The trade-offs can be assessed analytically by determining the present value of the tax savings for all combinations of depreciable lives and depreciation methods and selecting the combination providing the largest present value. We illustrate the approach to this type of analysis in the comprehensive example at the end of this section.

Disposition of Depreciable Property

A firm may dispose of depreciable assets by selling them or by trading them in. Let us first consider the tax consequences of trading in.

Tax Consequences of Trading In   If a firm trades in an asset for another asset that has a similar use, no gain or loss is recognized for tax purposes. The new asset simply assumes the tax basis (that is, remaining undepreciated cost) of the asset traded in. In most trade-in transactions, however, some cash passes hands in addition to the assets exchanged. If cash is given, no gain or loss is recognized. The tax basis of the asset received is equal to the tax basis of the asset given up plus the cash given. If cash is received, any realized gain (market value of consideration received minus tax basis of the asset given up) is recognized to the extent cash is received. A loss is not recognized. The tax basis of the asset received is equal to the tax basis of the old property plus the taxable gain recognized and minus the cash received. These seemingly complicated rules can be illustrated with several examples as shown in Exhibit 17.4.

Tax Consequences of Selling   If a firm sells a depreciable asset, any gain or loss on the sale is fully recognized for tax purposes (that is, gain is taxable and loss is deductible).

EXHIBIT 17.4
Illustration of the Tax Consequences of Trade-In Transactions

	(A)	(B)	(C)	(D)	(E)
(1) Market Value of Asset Received. . .	$20,000	$20,000	$20,000	$20,000	$20,000
(2) Cash Received	—	—	$ 2,000	$ 2,000	$15,000
(3) Tax Basis of Asset Given Up	$10,000	$10,000	$15,000	$25,000	$30,000
(4) Cash Given	—	$ 8,000	—	—	—
(5) Realized Gain (Loss)					
(1 + 2) − (3 + 4)	$10,000	$ 2,000	$ 7,000	$(3,000)	$ 5,000
(6) Taxable Gain.	-0-	-0-	$ 2,000	-0-	$ 5,000
(7) Tax Basis of Asset Received	$10,000	$18,000[a]	$15,000[b]	$23,000[c]	$20,000[d]

[a] $10,000 + $8,000.
[b] $15,000 + $2,000 − $2,000.
[c] $25,000 − $2,000.
[d] $30,000 + $5,000 − $15,000.

Depreciable assets are specifically excluded from the definition of capital assets in the Internal Revenue Code. In most cases then, the gain or loss is subject to the "ordinary income" tax rates of the firm—graduated individual tax rates for sole proprietorships and partnerships and a maximum rate of 48 percent for corporations. In a few special instances, special capital gain and loss rates may apply.

If a firm is planning to dispose of an asset, should the asset be traded in on a new one or should the old asset be sold and a new one acquired? The present value of income tax payments can be minimized by recognizing losses as quickly as possible and postponing or avoiding the recognition of gains. It is clear, then, that if a gain is anticipated, the old asset should be traded in. This avoids the recognition of all or a part of the gain, depending on whether or not cash is received. If a loss is anticipated, the old asset should be sold and the new one then acquired. In this way the loss can be deducted immediately in determining the current year's taxable income.

Comprehensive Illustration

The Green Typing and Office Supply Company has recently initiated purchase orders for $10,000 of new office equipment, including typewriters, calculators, and copiers. This equipment has an asset depreciation range of five to seven years. Regardless of the depreciable life selected, Green expects to use the equipment for seven years. The equipment is expected to reduce annual cash operating costs by $1,500 per year after taxes [$2,885 of pretax cash savings less $1,385 (= .48 × $2,885) of taxes]. The salvage value for the equipment is expected to be equal to the cost of disposal. The rate for the investment tax credit is 10 percent. Assume that the discount rate is 12 percent per year, all cash flows occur at the end of each period, and the income tax rate is 48 percent. Green must decide whether a five-, six-, or seven-year depreciable life should be selected and whether the DDB method—with an appropriate switch to straight-line (SL) so as to depreciate the assets fully by the end of the seventh year—or the SYD method should be used. In order to make this decision, an analysis is required to determine the present value of the tax savings for each of these three depreciable lives under both DDB and SYD. Such analyses are presented in Exhibits 17.5, 17.6, and 17.7.

As indicated in these analyses, a seven-year life and the SYD method provide the maximum present value of the tax savings. This is the optimum combination from among the six alternatives. The critical trade-off is between a five-year life to accelerate the depreciation deductions and a seven-year life to claim the full investment tax credit. In this case, the incremental benefits of a full ITC are greater than the loss in tax savings from depreciating over a seven-year rather than a five-year life ($11,213 from Exhibit 17.7 as compared to $11,185 in Exhibit 17.5). Note that the six-year life could have been eliminated immediately as an alternative. The five-year life provides the same ITC but a faster write-off of the cost of the assets. It is interesting to note that with a five-year life, DDB produces the greater present value of tax savings ($3,749 as compared to $3,722 for SYD), but for a seven-year life SYD yields the greater tax savings ($3,483 as compared to $3,457 for DDB).

EXHIBIT 17.5
Green Typing and Office Supply Company
Net Present Value Calculation for Assets Depreciated on a Five-Year Life

Item	Amount	Factor	1	2	3	4	5	6	7
	Present Value								
(1) Cash Operating Savings after Taxes	$ 6,840	4.56[a]	$1,500	$1,500	$1,500	$1,500	$1,500	$1,500	$1,500
(2) Investment Tax Credit (.10 × 2/3 × $10,000)	$ 596	.89	670						
(3) DDB/SL Depreciation Tax Savings:									
$10,000 × 2 × 1/5 = $4,000 × .48	$ 1,709	.89	1,920						
$ 6,000 × 2 × 1/5 = $2,400 × .48	922	.80		1,152					
$ 3,600 × 2 × 1/5 = $1,440 × .48	491	.71			691				
$ 2,160/2 × .48 = $1,080 × .48	332	.64				518			
$ 1,080 × .48	295	.57					518		
Total	$ 3,749								
(4) SYD Depreciation Tax Savings:									
$10,000 × 5/15 × .48 = $3,333 × .48	$ 1,424	.89	1,600						
$10,000 × 4/15 × .48 = $2,667 × .48	1,024	.80		1,280					
$10,000 × 3/15 × .48 = $2,000 × .48	682	.71			960				
$10,000 × 2/15 × .48 = $1,333 × .48	410	.64				610			
$10,000 × 1/15 × .48 = $ 667 × .48	182	.57					320		
Total	$ 3,722								
(5) Present Value Using DDB/SL Depreciation, (1) + (2) + (3)	$11,185								
(6) Present Value Using SYD Depreciation, (1) + (2) + (4)	$11,158								

a This is the factor for the present value of an annuity for seven periods at 12 percent. See Table 4 at the back of the book.

EXHIBIT 17.6
Green Typing and Office Supply Company
Present Value Calculation for Assets Depreciated on a Six-Year Life

Item	Present Value Amount	Factor	1	2	3	4	5	6	7
(1) Cash Operating Savings after Taxes	$ 6,840	4.56	$1,500	$1,500	$1,500	$1,500	$1,500	$1,500	$1,500
(2) Investment Tax Credit (.10 × 2/3 × $10,000)	$ 596	.89	670						
(3) DDB/SL Depreciation Tax Savings:									
$10,000 × 1/3 × .48 = $3,333 × .48	$ 1,424	.89	1,600						
$ 6,667 × 1/3 × .48 = $2,222 × .48	854	.80		1,067					
$ 4,445 × 1/3 × .48 = $1,482 × .48	505	.71			711				
$ 2,963 × 1/3 × .48 = $ 988 × .48	303	.64				474			
$ 1,975/2 × .48 = $987 × .48	270	.57					474		
$987 × .48	242	.51						474	
Total	$ 3,598								
(4) SYD Depreciation Tax Savings:									
$10,000 × 6/21 × .48 = $2,857 × .48	$ 1,220	.89	1,371						
$10,000 × 5/21 × .48 = $2,381 × .48	914	.80		1,143					
$10,000 × 4/21 × .48 = $1,905 × .48	649	.71			914				
$10,000 × 3/21 × .48 = $1,429 × .48	439	.64				686			
$10,000 × 2/21 × .48 = $ 952 × .48	260	.57					457		
$10,000 × 1/21 × .48 = $ 476 × .48	116	.51						228	
Total	$ 3,598								
(5) Present Value Using DDB/SL Depreciation, (1) + (2) + (3)	$11,034								
(6) Present Value Using SYD Depreciation, (1) + (2) + (4)	$11,034								

EXHIBIT 17.7
Green Typing and Office Supply Company
Present Value Calculation for Assets Depreciated on a Seven-Year Life

Item	Amount	Factor	1	2	3	4	5	6	7
			$1,500	$1,500	$1,500	$1,500	$1,500	$1,500	$1,500
(1) Cash Operating Savings After Taxes	$ 6,840	4.56							
(2) Investment Tax Credit (.10 × $10,000)	$ 890	.89	1,000						
(3) DDB/SL Depreciation Tax Savings:									
$10,000 × 2/7 × .48 = $2,850 × .48	$ 1,218	.89	1,368						
$ 7,150 × 2/7 × .48 = $2,036 × .48	782	.80		977					
$ 5,114 × 2/7 × .48 = $1,457 × .48	496	.71			699				
$ 3,657 × 2/7 × .48 = $1,042 × .48	320	.64				500			
$ 2,615/3 × .48 = $872 × .48	239	.57					419		
$872 × .48	214	.51						419	
$871 × .48	188	.45							418
Total	$ 3,457								
(4) SYD Depreciation Tax Savings:									
$10,000 × 7/28 × .48 = $2,500 × .48	$ 1,068	.89	1,200						
$10,000 × 6/28 × .48 = $2,143 × .48	823	.80		1,029					
$10,000 × 5/28 × .48 = $1,786 × .48	608	.71			857				
$10,000 × 4/28 × .48 = $1,429 × .48	439	.64				686			
$10,000 × 3/28 × .48 = $1,071 × .48	293	.57					514		
$10,000 × 2/28 × .48 = $ 714 × .48	175	.51						343	
$10,000 × 1/28 × .48 = $ 357 × .48	77	.45							171
Total	$ 3,483								
(5) Present Value Using DDB/SL Depreciation, (1) + (2) + (3)	$11,187								
(6) Present Value Using SYD Depreciation, (1) + (2) + (4)	$11,213								

SUMMARY

Income taxes can have a significant impact on certain business decisions. In this chapter we have discussed the factors to be considered in selecting accounting methods for calculating taxable income and the important role of income taxes in evaluating alternative capital investment proposals. In Chapter Eighteen, we discuss several other decisions where income taxes can play a significant role.

QUESTIONS AND PROBLEMS

1 Review the meaning of the following concepts or terms discussed in this chapter.
  a Statutory tax rate.
  b Marginal tax rate.
  c Average (effective) tax rate.
  d Graduated tax rates.
  e Least and latest rule.
  f Quantity LIFO versus dollar-value LIFO.
  g Nontaxable exchange.
  h Investment tax credit.
  i Tax savings from depreciation deductions.
  j Asset Depreciation Range (ADR) system.

2 The text states: "Business firms should pay the least amount of taxes as late as possible within the law." Evaluate this statement, taking into consideration your opinion of the social and economic responsibilities of business firms.

3 Why is the "least and latest" rule more difficult to apply in the case of a sole proprietorship or partnership than for a corporation?

4 Support or refute the following statement: "Income taxes can be ignored in most business decisions, because proposals expected to generate a positive aftertax net income will also produce a positive pretax net income."

5 The text states: "For sole proprietorships and partnerships, the least and latest rule may require trade-offs." Develop a numerical illustration where similar trade-offs may be required of a corporation.

6 The text states: "Gross margins under LIFO tend to be more stable than under FIFO during periods when prices fluctuate." Explain.

7 Refer to Question 6. Is this statement correct when prices steadily increase or steadily decrease?

8 Distinguish between quantity LIFO and dollar-value LIFO. Why is dollar-value LIFO generally preferable for tax purposes?

9 Why are broad layers or pools preferable to more narrow ones in applying dollar-value LIFO?

10 To determine the net effect on cash flows of salary expense, the amount of salary expense is multiplied by the complement (for example, 1.00 − .48) of the tax rate. To determine the net effect on cash flows of depreciation expense, the amount of depreciation expense is multiplied by the tax rate (for example, .48). Why is there a difference in procedure?

11 "A business firm should prefer direct costing over absorption costing (see Chapter Fourteen) for tax purposes." Explain.

12 In 1971, the Internal Revenue Code was amended to provide for depreciable lives for tax purposes from 20 percent less than the guideline lives previously established to 20 percent more than the guideline lives. The Secretary of the Treasury announced that depreciable lives had been extended by 40 percent. A noted accountant remarked that the government could have extended depreciable lives by 100 percent (from 20 percent less to 80 percent more) with the same effects on tax collections by the Treasury as the 40 percent extension. What was the basis for the accountant's statement?

13 The statutory tax rate for General Electric during a recent year was 22 percent of the first $25,000 of taxable income and 48 percent of any excess. The effective (average) tax rate (income taxes payable/net income before taxes) was 35.6 percent. Assume that these same rates are anticipated for the following year. What tax rate should General Electric use in determining the tax savings from depreciation deductions in its capital budgeting program for the following year?

14 A business firm had net income before taxes of $100,000 during 19X0 and made distributions totaling $40,000 to owners. The firm used the same methods of accounting for tax and financial reporting purposes. Determine the taxable income of each taxable entity under the assumptions below:
  a Assume that the business firm is a sole proprietorship. Its owner, Charles Terrell, had $15,000 of nonbusiness-related taxable income during 19X0.
  b Assume that the business firm is a partnership. John Michaels and Jill Conrad, equal partners, had nonbusiness-related taxable income of $15,000 each during 19X0.
  c Assume that the business firm is a corporation. Four sisters each own 25 percent of the common stock and each had $15,000 of nonbusiness-related taxable income during 19X0.

15 Andersen Corporation had the following amounts of gross income (loss) before any carryforwards or carrybacks of operating losses between 19X0, its first year of operations, and 19X4.

19X0:   ($20,000)
19X1:   30,000
19X2:   50,000
19X3:   (80,000)
19X4:   30,000

Assuming that an income tax rate of 48 percent applies, determine the amount of taxes paid or refund received for each year.

16 Discuss when income should be recognized for tax purposes in each of the independent cases below:
  a Little Construction Company is organized as a corporation. Its business involves many small contracts that average two months from start to completion.

b Large Construction Company is organized as a corporation. Its business involves a few large contracts that average three years from start to completion.

c Same as **a,** except that the firm is organized as a sole proprietorship.

d Same as **b,** except that the firm is organized as a sole proprietorship.

e Symonds and Grey are organized as a professional corporation to conduct a regional public accounting practice.

f Retirement Development Corporation sells undeveloped lots to future retirees. Development work takes approximately five years to complete after the signing of a sales contract. Payments are received monthly from the buyers over a period of 20 years.

g Same as **f,** except that the firm is organized as a partnership.

h Johnson Travel Agency is organized as a sole proprietorship to provide travel and entertainment services to clients.

i Pickin Chicken, Incorporated, is a national franchisor of short-order food restaurants. Upon the signing of the franchise agreement, 25 percent of the franchise fee of $30,000 is received. The remaining 75 percent is received from the franchisee over the next 10 years. Be concerned here with when the initial franchise fee income should be recognized for tax purposes.

17 Durham Construction Company contracted on January 1, 19X0, to construct a large office building for $4,000,000. Costs were incurred as follows: 19X0—$850,000; 19X1—$1,700,000; 19X2—$850,000. The building was completed during 19X2. The discount rate to be used in each part below is 10 percent. Round present value factors used to two decimal places.

a Assume that this firm is operated as a corporation and is subject to a marginal tax rate of 48 percent during each year. Determine the present value of the tax payments from using **(1)** the percentage-of-completion method and **(2)** the completed-contract method.

b Assume that this firm is operated as a sole proprietorship. The appropriate marginal tax rates are as follows: 19X0—45 percent; 19X1—55 percent; 19X2—49 percent if the percentage-of-completion method is used and 60 percent if the completed-contract method is used. Determine the present value of the tax payments from using **(1)** the percentage-of-completion method and **(2)** the completed-contract method.

c Repeat step **b,** but assume that the appropriate marginal tax rates are as follows: 19X0—55 percent; 19X1—45 percent; 19X2—38 percent if the percentage-of-completion method is used and 42 percent if the completed-contract method is used.

d Summarize the conditions when the percentage-of-completion and completed-contract methods are preferable for **(1)** a corporation and **(2)** a sole proprietorship, making reference to the calculations in parts **a** to **c** where appropriate.

18 Fields Department Store sold products during 19X0 costing $500,000 for $750,000. Installment payments were received as follows: 19X0—$375,000; 19X1—$225,000; 19X2—$150,000. The discount rate to be used in each part below is 10 percent. Round present value factors used to two decimal places.

a Assume that this firm is operated as a corporation and is subject to a marginal tax rate of 48 percent during each year. Determine the present value of the tax payments from recognizing income **(1)** at the time of sale and **(2)** on an installment basis as collections are received.

b Assume that this firm is operated as a sole proprietorship. Determine the present value of the tax payments assuming that income is recognized at the time of sale and that the marginal tax rate is 50 percent.

c Repeat step **b** assuming that income is recognized on an installment basis as cash is received. The appropriate marginal tax rates are as follows: 19X0—40 percent; 19X1—36 percent; 19X2—34 percent.

  d Repeat steps **b** and **c** but assume that the appropriate marginal tax rates are as follows: 19X0—60 percent if income is recognized at time of sale and 50 percent if income is recognized on an installment basis as collections are received; 19X1—46 percent; 19X2—44 percent.

  e Summarize the conditions under which recognition of income at the point of sale or as cash is collected on an installment basis are preferable for **(1)** a corporation and **(2)** a sole proprietorship.

19 Discuss whether the LIFO or FIFO cost flow assumption should be used in each of the independent cases below. Assume that the firm operates as a corporation in each case.

  a A firm sells room air conditioning units. The cost (purchase price) of this product has decreased during the past decade. Physical inventory quantities fluctuate widely during the year but are reasonably constant at the end of each year.

  b A firm purchases corn, beans, and other farm goods and processes them into various preserved vegetable products (for example, canned corn, frozen beans). The physical inventory and price of unprocessed farm goods fluctuate widely from year to year in response to supply and demand.

  c A firm produces ready-to-order paper products such as stationery and envelopes. The production cycle typically takes one week, and raw materials are purchased only for specific customers' orders.

  d A steel producer is operating at capacity on old and technically obsolete equipment. The old equipment is continually being replaced by more expensive but more efficient new equipment, but the replacement process is likely to take several years. The costs of raw materials and labor are expected to remain relatively stable over the next decade.

  e A firm publishes paperback books that seldom require a second printing. Inventories of each book are generally maintained for three years. Manufacturing costs have been increasing slightly in recent years.

20 The data shown below were taken from a recent edition of *Accounting Trends and Techniques (ATT)*. The data indicate the percentage of firms in each industry in the *ATT* sample that used LIFO. For each pair of industries, suggest reasons for the significant difference in the percentage of firms using LIFO.

  a Department stores—75 percent; grocery stores—12 percent.

  b Petroleum products—64 percent; shoes—25 percent.

  c Paper products—63 percent; meat products—18 percent.

21 Wallace Corporation acquired a new machine on January 1, 19X0. The machine cost $12,000, has a six-year estimated life, and zero salvage value.

  a Determine the present value of the tax savings from depreciation deductions under each of the following depreciation methods, assuming that the discount rate is 10 percent and the marginal income tax rate is 48 percent. Round present value factors used to two decimal places.

    (1) Straight-line (SL) method.

    (2) Double-declining-balance (DDB) method (with switch to straight-line).

    (3) Sum-of-the-years'-digits (SYD) method.

  b Repeat step **a** using a discount rate of 4 percent.

  c Repeat step **a** using a discount rate of 16 percent. The factors for the present value of $1 at 16 percent are as follows: 1 period, .86; 2 periods, .74; 3 periods, .64; 4 periods, .55; 5 periods, .48; 6 periods, .41.

d Using the results of the calculations in parts **a** and **c,** summarize the conditions when SL, DDB, and SYD are preferable for tax purposes.

22 Standard Electronics Corporation is engaged primarily in research and development work in the field of electronics. It was organized in 19X0 by two ex-college roommates. The firm expects to receive substantial government contracts in the future. However, it will take approximately four years for the firm to develop the necessary capital and reputation to compete effectively with more established firms for government contract awards. What should be this firm's capitalization policy for tax purposes with respect to research and development costs?

23 The summary of significant accounting policies reproduced below was taken from a recent annual report of Fuqua Industries, Incorporated. The summary describes the accounting methods used by this firm for *financial reporting* purposes. Evaluate each of the methods described from the standpoint of income tax reporting.

Fuqua Industries, Incorporated
Summary of Significant Accounting Policies

The accompanying financial statements have been prepared in accordance with generally accepted accounting principles applied on a consistent basis. Operating results of discontinued operations have been reclassified in the statement of income for last year to conform with changes in accounting rules regarding such transactions.

Principles of Consolidation   The consolidated financial statements include the accounts of Fuqua and its subsidiaries. All significant inter-company transactions and accounts have been eliminated in consolidation.

Currency Translation   The amounts recorded for Canadian assets and liabilities have been translated into United States dollars, generally at exchange rates prevailing at year-end. Fixed and other assets not subject to exchange fluctuations have been reflected at the exchange rates prevailing when acquired. Operating results, other than depreciation of fixed assets, have been translated at rates of exchange during the year. Translation adjustments which are included in income when they occur are not material.

Inventories   Inventories of finished goods, work in process and raw materials are stated at the lower of cost or market, generally on the first-in, first-out method (FIFO). Condominium units and land under development are valued at the lower of specific costs of land, development and construction (including interest and overhead during development or construction) or market.

Property and Depreciation   Property, plant and equipment are recorded at cost at the time of purchase. For financial reporting purposes, depreciation is computed over the expected useful service lives of depreciable assets using the straight-line method.

Intangibles   Motor carrier operating rights and broadcast licenses, which are fundamental to the operation of the respective businesses, are not being amortized. Such franchises are not considered to decrease in value as may be the case for depreciable assets.

The excess of the purchase price over net assets of businesses acquired prior to 1971 is not being amortized because, in the opinion of management, they represent assets with continuing value. For acquisitions since 1971, new accounting rules require that such excess or "goodwill" be amortized on the straight-line method not to exceed 40 years.

Research and Development Costs   Research and development costs are substantially all charged to operations as expense when incurred.

Real Estate Accounting   Interest and other costs associated with the acquisition and development of land and the construction of condominium units for sale are capitalized until development or construction is completed or when the property is committed to productive use or made available for sale. Capitalized costs are included in the cost of sales when the property is sold.

Revenues at Arizona Valley Development Corporation are recognized from the sale of property after the time has elapsed in which the buyer can cancel his contract with a full refund (up to one year). When the cancellation period elapses, the sale is recorded and reserves are established for the estimated cost of future development work. Also, a portion of the gross profit is deferred until the Company's development obligations (such as streets, water and sewer facilities) have been completed. Appropriate reserves are also established for possible failure by customers to make full payment of the purchase contracts.

At the Haft-Gaines development, "Inverrary," sales of condominium units are recognized when title is passed to the buyer and full cash payment is received (Fuqua does not finance the purchase of condominiums). Sales of land to other builders, resulting in net income of approximately $854,000 in this year, are recognized when it is determined that the buyer has made sufficient down payment to reasonably assure full payment for the property.

24 The income tax liability of Wyman Corporation for 19X0 before claiming the investment tax credit is $125,000. During 19X0, the following items of equipment were acquired:

Item	Cost	Depreciable Life (years)
X	$600,000	3
Y	450,000	6
Z	500,000	10

a Determine the allowable amount of the investment tax credit if the rate is 7 percent.
b Determine the allowable amount of the investment tax credit if the rate is 10 percent.

25 (Prepared by Professor David O. Green.) The Blackstone Company, located in the country of Neverland, is contemplating the purchase of a highly specialized new machine which is available from two vendors: one is a domestic producer and the other is in a country with which Neverland has terminated diplomatic relations.

If the Blackstone Company buys from the domestic producer, it is entitled to receive an investment tax credit of 10 percent, which is paid to the company by a check from the Neverland government two years after the investment is made. Depreciation for tax purposes is calculated by the sum-of-the-years'-digits method.

If the Blackstone Company buys from the foreign producer, it will not be entitled to the investment credit or to depreciation deductions. Any proceeds from selling the asset at the end of its useful life will be fully subject to tax.

The corporate income tax rate in Neverland is 25 percent. The discount rate is 10 percent and all cash flows are assumed to take place at the end of the year (except the initial investment). Round present value factors used to two decimal places. Other relevant information is as follows:

	Domestic Producer	Foreign Producer
Cost of Machine	$300,000	$200,000
Expected Useful Life	5 years	5 years
Expected Salvage Value after 5 Years	-0-	$ 30,000
Expected Annual Operating Costs	$ 10,000	$ 20,000

a Determine the net present value of each investment alternative.
b Which alternative should be chosen by the Blackstone Company?

26 The Putnam Corporation acquired a high-speed printing press on January 1, 19X0, for $120,000. The printing press was depreciated during 19X0 using the double-declining-balance method, a six-year useful life, and zero estimated salvage value.

Early in 19X1, Putnam is thinking of replacing the high-speed printing press with a smaller press more suitable to its needs. The new equipment will be depreciated over a five-year life using the double-declining-balance method. Salvage value at the end of five years is estimated to be zero. Three alternatives are under consideration:

Alternative A—Keep the high-speed press. Operating costs will be $15,000 each year if the high-speed press is retained.
Alternative B—Trade in the high-speed press for the smaller press. Putnam will also receive $40,000 in cash. Operating costs on the smaller press are expected to be $12,000 each year.
Alternative C—Sell the high-speed press for $85,000. The smaller press will then be purchased for $50,000.

Determine the net present value of each alternative. The marginal income tax rate for Putnam Corporation is 48 percent. The firm's aftertax cost of capital is 10 percent. Ignore the investment tax credit provisions in this problem. Round present value factors to two decimal places.

27 (Prepared by Professor David O. Green.) The production manager of the Precision Gear Company has submitted the same proposal to the Capital Budgeting Committee on several occasions, starting with a first submission in 1953. Each time there is a change in the relevant income tax laws, the Capital Budgeting Committee invites the resubmission of proposals rejected earlier. Accordingly, the production manager requested an appropriation in 1953, 1954, 1962, 1964, and 1971 without success. Another change in the tax laws occurred recently, but the production manager wants to avoid the embarrassment of another refusal. You have been asked to calculate the net present value of the proposal under the new legislation as well as under earlier tax laws. You want to determine the impact of the tax law changes on the proposal itself, which has not required modification over the years. The aftertax cost of capital is 12 percent, the income tax rate is 48 percent, and all cash flows (except the initial investment) occur at the end of each year. Round present value factors used to two decimal places.

The production manager's proposal is for a machine costing $10,000. The machine is expected to have a four-year useful life and zero net salvage value. The savings in direct costs attributable to the machine are $3,000 a year for four years.

The relevant income tax laws at the time of each submission are summarized below:

1 In 1953, at the time of the first submission, the tax laws provided for straight-line depreciation only.

2 In 1954, at the time of the second submission, the tax laws provided for sum-of-the-years'-digits depreciation.

3 In 1962, at the time of the third submission, the tax laws provided for sum-of-the-years'-digits and a 7 percent investment tax credit. For purposes of the remaining parts of this problem, assume that the entire acquisition cost qualifies for the investment tax credit (that is, .07 × $10,000 = $700). The investment credit claimed, however, must be deducted from the asset's cost in determining the tax basis for depreciation (that is, depreciation is based on 93 percent of the asset's cost).

4 In 1964, at the time of the fourth submission, the same conditions applied as in 1962 except that depreciation was based on 100 percent of acquisition cost, unreduced by the investment credit.

5 In 1971, at the time of the fifth submission, the Asset Depreciation Range System was instituted. The range for this machine was three to five years. The production manager selected a three-year life in an effort to make the proposal most attractive. It is anticipated that the machine will be used for four years.

6 Now, the same conditions apply as in 1964 and 1971 except that the investment tax credit is increased to 10 percent of acquisition cost.

28 Stickney and Wallace (*Taxation for Accountants*, July 1975) have developed a set of coefficients that, when multiplied by the cost of an asset, equals the present value of the tax savings from depreciation deductions and the investment tax credits. One set of these coefficients is presented below, using a discount rate of 10 percent.

Depreciable Life in Years	Double-Declining Balance/Straight-Line[a]	Sum-of-the-Years'-Digits[a]	Investment Tax Credit at 7 Percent[b]	Investment Tax Credit at 10 Percent[b]
3	.4176	.4112	.0233	.0333
4	.4038	.3988	.0233	.0333
5	.3896	.3948	.0467	.0667
6	.3754	.3760	.0467	.0667
7	.3631	.3653	.0700	.1000

[a] These coefficients are based on the "regular first-year convention," which assumes that one-half year of depreciation is taken in the year of acquisition.
[b] Assuming tax savings from investment credits are realized immediately.

a Determine the optimum depreciation method and depreciable life for each of the items below:

Item	Asset Depreciation Range in Years	Applicable Rate for Investment Credit
u	3–5	7%
v	4–6	7
w	5–7	7
x	3–5	10
y	4–6	10
z	5–7	10

b Comment on the results obtained in a.

29 The Internal Revenue Code describes five principal methods of depreciation:

1. Double-declining-balance (DDB).
2. Sum-of-the-years'-digits (SYD).
3. Limited declining balance at 1.5 times the straight-line rate (1.5DB).
4. Limited declining balance at 1.25 times the straight-line rate (1.25DB).
5. Straight line (SL).

The methods of depreciation that can be used for various types of property are summarized below:

New personal property—DDB, SYD, 1.5DB, 1.25DB, SL.
Used personal property—1.5DB, 1.25DB, SL.
New real property:
   Residential rental—DDB, SYD, 1.5DB, 1.25DB, SL.
   Buildings and structural components—1.5DB, 1.25DB, SL.
   Other new real property—1.5DB, 1.25DB, SL.
Used real property:
   Residential rental—1.25DB, SL.
   Buildings and structural components—SL.
   Other used real property SL.

Using logic only, indicate the optimum depreciation method for each type of property. Where a clear-cut choice cannot be made, indicate the most likely candidates. Indicate the reasoning behind your choice in each case.

30 In each of the independent trade-in transactions below, determine **(1)** the amount of the gain or loss recognized for tax purposes and **(2)** the tax basis of the new asset acquired. In each case, the asset received is similar in use to the asset traded in, and the nontaxable exchange provisions apply.

	a	b	c	d	e	f
Market Value of						
Asset Received	$10,000	$10,000	$10,000	$10,000	$10,000	$10,000
Cash Received	—	—	$ 2,000	$ 2,000	—	$ 5,000
Tax Basis of Asset						
Traded In	$ 8,000	$ 8,000	$ 8,000	$13,000	$ 8,000	$12,000
Cash Given	—	$ 1,000	—	—	$ 3,000	—

31 John Medicine, M.D., opened his general medical practice on January 1, 19X0. Expecting to make numerous house calls, he purchased an automobile on January 1 for $9,000. Because the automobile is used exclusively in his business, he can claim depreciation deductions. John used a three-year estimated life and the straight-line depreciation method.

a Determine the amount of depreciation claimed for 19X0 and the tax basis of the automobile on December 31, 19X0.

b In an effort to maintain a good appearance, John traded in his 19X0 automobile on January 1, 19X1, for a 19X1 model. He also gave $5,000 in cash. Determine the amount of gain or loss recognized on the trade-in and the tax basis of the new automobile on January 1, 19X1.

c On January 1, 19X2, John again traded in his one-year-old automobile on a new 19X2 model and gave $5,000 in cash. Determine the amount of gain or loss recognized on the trade-in and the tax basis of the new automobile on January 1, 19X2.

d Repeat steps **a** through **c** assuming that the double-declining-balance method is used instead of the straight-line method.

e Assume that John continued to trade in on each January 1 and continued to give $5,000 in cash each time. Estimate the amount of the tax basis of the new automobile 30 years after the first one was acquired, **(1)** assuming that straight-line depreciation is used and **(2)** assuming that the double-declining-balance method is used.

32 Sunder (*The Accounting Review,* April 1976) has developed a model for measuring the relative effect of using LIFO rather than FIFO on the present value of a firm during periods of inflation. The model can also be used to measure the relative benefit of FIFO over LIFO during periods of deflation. Sunder states:

During times of inflation, the use of the last-in-first-out (LIFO) method of inventory valuation has the effect of lowering the reported earnings by excluding inventory holding gains from this number. Current income tax payments due on the reduced earnings are also lower. Taxes payable on inventory holding gains, therefore, are postponed until some future period when the inventory is liquidated. Thus, the economic consequence of using LIFO in the presence of inflation is to increase the net cash flow to the firm. Since the value of a business entity can be represented as the discounted net present value of future cash flows, a change to LIFO also implies a change in the value of the firm, which is positive during inflation and negative during deflation.

The economic impact of adopting LIFO during inflation depends on four variables: **(1)** the dollar amount of inventory under FIFO before the switch to LIFO, **(2)** the firm's cost of capital, or discount rate, **(3)** the expected rate of inflation for the inventory items, and **(4)** the firm's marginal tax rate. The larger the amount of inventory relative to other assets of the firm, the more significant will be the impact on present value of a switch to LIFO. In general, the lower the discount rate (r) and the higher the rate of price change (i), the more significant will be the effects of the switch. Sunder expresses the relationship between the discount rate and price change in a ratio: rate of discount/rate of price change. The smaller

Net Present Value of Differences in Cash Flows under LIFO and FIFO for $1 Carried in Inventory

Ratio of Discount Rate to the Rate of Price Change r/i, $r > i$	Marginal Tax Rate						
	0%	10%	20%	30%	40%	50%	60%
1.1	$0	$1.00	$2.00	$3.00	$4.00	$5.00	$6.00
1.2	0	.50	1.00	1.50	2.00	2.50	3.00
1.3	0	.33	.67	1.00	1.33	1.67	2.00
1.4	0	.25	.50	.75	1.00	1.25	1.50
1.5	0	.20	.40	.60	.80	1.00	1.20
1.8	0	.125	.25	.375	.50	.625	.75
2.0	0	.10	.20	.30	.40	.50	.60
2.5	0	.067	.13	.20	.27	.33	.40
3.0	0	.05	.10	.15	.20	.25	.30
3.5	0	.04	.08	.12	.16	.20	.24
4.0	0	.033	.067	.10	.13	.17	.20
4.5	0	.03	.06	.09	.11	.14	.17
5.0	0	.025	.05	.075	.10	.125	.15

is this ratio, the more significant is the economic impact. Finally, the effects of the switch to LIFO will be greater for higher, as compared to lower, marginal tax rates.

The model used to measure the effect of a switch to LIFO rests on three important assumptions: **(1)** the switch to LIFO is permanent, **(2)** inventory quantities remain stable each year, and **(3)** the discount rate, rate of price change, and marginal tax rate are known with certainty. (In subsequent research, Sunder has adapted this deterministic model for probabilistic, or stochastic, settings.)

The table below indicates the effect on the present value of the firm of a switch to LIFO during inflation for each dollar of preswitch FIFO inventory. The present value effect is a function of **(1)** the ratio of the discount rate to the rate of price change and **(2)** the marginal tax rate.

a   Explain why the benefits of a switch to LIFO become greater as the ratio of discount rate to price change becomes smaller.
b   Explain the reason why the benefits of a switch to LIFO increase as the marginal tax rate is increased.
c   Determine the effect of a switch to LIFO on the present value of a firm in each of the independent cases below.

Number	Preswitch FIFO Inventory Value	Discount Rate = r	Anticipated Annual Rate of Price Change = i	Marginal Tax Rate
i.	$ 50,000	12%	8%	40%
ii.	500,000	12	8	40
iii.	5,000,000	12	8	40
iv.	50,000	12	8	20
v.	500,000	12	8	20
vi.	5,000,000	12	8	20
vii.	500,000	16	8	40
viii.	500,000	16	10	40
ix.	500,000	16	12	40
x.	500,000	16	14	40

d   Shamula Manufacturing Company has used FIFO for several years in measuring cost of goods sold and ending inventory. At December 31, 19X1, its inventory under FIFO amounts to $100,000. The company has decided to make a permanent switch to LIFO as of January 1, 19X2. The switch will require an immediate tax-deductible expenditure of $20,000 to convert to LIFO. In addition, the incremental cost of maintaining LIFO records, as compared to FIFO, will be $5,000 per year. This amount can be deducted each year in determining taxable income. The firm's cost of capital is 12 percent, and its marginal tax rate is 40 percent. The replacement cost of the firm's products will increase at a rate of 8 percent annually. Should the switch to LIFO be made?
e   Refer to part **d.** Assuming that the discount rate remains unchanged at 12 percent and that the rate of price change remains unchanged at 8 percent, determine the marginal tax rate at which the switch to LIFO becomes undesirable.
f   Refer to part **d.** Assuming that the marginal tax rate remains at 40 percent and that the discount rate remains at 12 percent, determine the ratio of discount rate to price change at which the switch to LIFO becomes undesirable.

CHAPTER 18
I COME TAXES A D BUSINESS DECISIONS: A CLOSER LOOK

In this chapter we consider further the impact that income taxes can have on certain business decisions. In particular, we focus on decisions concerning employee compensation, intercorporate investments, capital structure, and organizational form.

COMPENSATION DECISION

In what form and in what amounts should employees' compensation be paid? This is a question continually faced by both employers and employees. It is often the subject of extensive bargaining, especially when employees are represented by well-organized unions.

There are numerous factors to be considered in such negotiations. From the employer's side, there is a need for a qualified, stable work force. From the employees' side, there are concerns for the work environment, adequate time for leisure, and other factors. Another important consideration by both parties is the income tax consequences of various compensation packages. In this section, we discuss briefly the taxation of some of the more important forms of compensation and then present an analytical framework that may be used for evaluating alternative compensation packages.

Income Tax Objectives

Other things being equal, employers would like to minimize the present value of their aftertax compensation payments to employees. With respect to the tax consequences of various forms of compensation, the employer's ordering of preferences is as follows:

1 Item is deductible during the current period.
2 Item is deductible during a future period.
3 Item is never deductible.

The employees would like to maximize the present value of their aftertax compensation payments received. The employees' order of preferences with respect to the tax consequences of various forms of compensation is as follows:

1 Item is never taxable.
2 Item is taxable during a future period.
3 Item is taxable during the current period.

As is evident, the tax objectives and ordering of preferences of employers and employees directly conflict. Exhibit 18.1 presents a matrix of the nine possible combinations of employer and employee preferences. Within the cells of the matrix are lists of some of the more common forms of compensation that satisfy the particular combination of tax effects. These are discussed more fully in the next section.

EXHIBIT 18.1
Taxation of Various Forms of Compensation

Tax Effect on Employee	Tax Effect on Employer		
	Deductible in Current Year	**Deductible in a Future Year**	**Never Deductible**
Taxable during Current Year	Salaries and Bonuses. Contributions Made by Employers under Non-qualified Pension Plans. Benefit Element in a Stock Option Plan If Measurable at Date of Grant.		Bribes and Other Illegal Payments.
Taxable during a Future Year	Contributions Made by Employers and Payments Received by Employees under Qualified Pension Plans. Payments Received by Employees under Non-qualified Pension Plans.	Benefit Element in a Stock Option Plan If Not Measurable until Date of Exercise.	
Never Taxed	Premiums Paid on Group Health and Hospitalization Insurance. Premium Paid on Group Term Life Insurance. Employee Courtesy Discounts (May Reduce Revenue for Firm).		Premiums on Life Insurance Where Company Is Beneficiary.

Taxation of Various Forms of Compensation

Salaries and Bonuses   Salaries, wages, bonuses, and other types of direct cash compensation paid during the current year are immediately deductible by the employer and immediately taxable to the employee. Although the maximum income tax rate for individuals is 70 percent, the maximum rate at which earned income can be taxed is 50 percent. That is, once salary and bonus income reach the point when they are taxed at a marginal rate of 50 percent, any additional such income is taxed at 50 percent rather than at some higher marginal rate. Because of the need for a certain amount of cash for living expenses, virtually all compensation packages contain a considerable portion of salary, bonuses, and the like.

Pension Plans   Pension plans provide for payments to be made to employees during their retirement. Employers are required to set aside sufficient funds each year to ensure that the pension payments can be made when required.

Pension plans may be qualified or nonqualified. Qualified plans must meet certain requirements as to types of employees included, funding and vesting provisions, and reporting requirements. Since the Pension Reform Act of 1974 (ERISA), most pension plans are qualified. Within limits, amounts contributed by employers under qualified pension plans are immediately deductible. The employee is not taxed on these contributions until pension payments are received during retirement. Because the income level of most employees is lower during retirement than during working years, the taxation of pension payments under qualified plans is both postponed and taxed at lower marginal rates.

Pension plans not meeting the requirements of a qualified plan are nonqualified plans for tax purposes. Employer contributions to a pension fund are deductible when made, the same as with a qualified plan. The important difference is that the employee is immediately taxed on these contributions. Then, during retirement, the employee is taxed on pension payments received to the extent that they exceed the amounts on which the employee was taxed during working years (that is, the employer's contributions). Other things being equal, an employee would demand larger pension benefits from a nonqualified, as compared to a qualified, plan for two reasons: employer contributions are taxed at the personal level both sooner and very likely at higher marginal rates in a nonqualified plan.

Stock Option Plans   Most stock option plans permit employees to purchase shares of a corporation's stock for prices less than they would have to pay on the open market. This discount or benefit element in stock option plans is a form of compensation.

Employees are taxed at ordinary income rates on the benefit element in a stock option as soon as it is reasonably quantifiable. Depending on the specific arrangements of a plan, this may be as soon as the date the option is granted or as late as when the option is exercised. Employers can deduct the same amount as compensation expense.

Illustration of the Compensation Package Decision

The compensation package and capital budgeting decisions are similar in that both involve analysis of a series of future cash flows under various alternatives. The compensation decision requires somewhat different analysis from that described in previous chapters for capital budgeting problems. An example will help illustrate the nature of the difference in analysis.

Suppose that you are offered two alternative compensation packages for the current year. Under alternative A you will receive a salary of $20,000. Under alternative B you will receive a salary of $15,000 plus accrue rights to receive a pension of $10,000 per year beginning at age 65. However, in order to receive that pension, you must work for the company for at least 10 years. We cannot, as in previous capital budgeting problems, simply calculate the present value of these alternative sets of cash flows and then make a decision. This is because these two mutually exclusive alternatives (selection of one automatically precludes selection of the other) do not cover similar time periods. Alternative A covers only the current period. Alternative B is a combination of current and future compensation. We need some mechanism for putting both alternatives in an equivalent time frame. That is, either we express the salary amounts in terms of an average annual salary from now through retirement, or we express the pension in terms of equivalent salary for the current period. In this way we express both alternatives in terms of either the alternative with the longest time frame or the alternative with the shortest time frame. Given uncertainties as to future salaries and continued employment, it is easier to express both alternatives in terms of the shorter time span. The approach is to determine the aftertax salary for the current year that is equivalant to the future pension benefits accruing during the year.[1]

The following data will be used to illustrate the analysis involved in a compensation decision. Lewellan Corporation's only employee, Ms. Stiefeld, is 55 years old. Three compensation packages have surfaced as alternatives for the current year.

Alternative A—Salary of $100,000.

Alternative B—Salary of $85,000 and a pension of $15,000 per year for 15 years[2] beginning at age 65, payable whether or not she is living.

Alternative C—Salary of $60,000, a pension of $15,000 per year for 15 years beginning at age 65, and deferred compensation of $25,000 per year for 10 years beginning at age 65, payable whether or not she is living.

The pension and deferred compensation plans are qualified. Amounts that the firm contributes each year to fund the pension and deferred compensation obligations are deductible by Lewellan Corporation when made but not taxed to the employee until received. The firm expects to earn 10 percent each year on amounts invested. Lewellan Corporation is subject to a marginal tax rate of 48 percent and has a 10 percent cost of capital. All cash flows are assumed to occur at the end of each period.

Exhibit 18.2 presents an analysis of the three compensation packages from the standpoint of Lewellan Corporation. Each package is expressed in terms of the present value of aftertax equivalent salary payments for the current year. Because the firm would select the package that minimizes the present value of cash outflows for com-

---

[1]   This approach is discussed more fully in Wilbur G. Lewellan, *Executive Compensation in Large Industrial Corporations* (National Bureau of Economic Research, 1968).

[2]   Pensions are normally payable until death. Specifying a 15-year payment period avoids the complexities introduced with contingent annuities, the analytical approach required when the date of death is uncertain. For a discussion of contingent pension annuities, see the Appendix.

EXHIBIT 18.2
Present Value of Compensation Package Alternatives
—from Standpoint of Employer

Salary	Alternative A	Alternative B	Alternative C
Cash Outflow for Salary	$100,000	$ 85,000	$ 60,000
Less Tax Savings at .48	48,000	40,800	28,800
Net Cash Outflow	$ 52,000	$ 44,200	$ 31,200
Factor for the Present Value of $1 for 1 Period at .10	× .9091	× .9091	× .9091
Present Value of Aftertax Cash Outflow for Salary	$ 47,273	$ 40,182	$ 28,364
Pension			
Required Annual Pension Payment to Employee Beginning at Age 65		$ 15,000	$ 15,000
Factor for Present Value of an Annuity for 15 Periods at .10		× 7.6061	× 7.6061
Present Value of Pension Payments at Age 65 .		$114,092	$114,092
Factor for the Future Value of an Annuity for 10 Periods at .10		÷ 15.9374	÷ 15.9374
Amount That Must Be Funded Annually for Next 10 Years		$ 7,159	$ 7,159
Less Tax Savings at .48		3,436	3,436
Present Value of Equivalent Aftertax Salary for Pension per Year		$ 3,723	$ 3,723
Deferred Compensation			
Required Annual Deferred Compensation Payment to Employee Beginning at Age 65 .			$ 25,000
Factor for the Present Value of an Annuity for 10 Periods at .10			× 6.1446
Present Value of Deferred Compensation at Age 65			$153,615
Factor for the Future Value of an Annuity for 10 Periods at .10			÷ 15.9374
Amount That Must Be Funded Annually for Next 10 Years			$ 9,639
Less Tax Savings at .48			4,627
Present Value of Equivalent Aftertax Salary for Deferred Compensation per Year			$ 5,012
Summary			
Salary	$ 47,273	$ 40,182	$ 28,364
Pension		3,723	3,723
Deferred Compensation			5,012
Total	$ 47,273	$ 43,905	$ 37,099
Ranking from Employer's Standpoint . . .	3	2	1

EXHIBIT 18.3
Present Value of Compensation Package Alternatives
—from Standpoint of Employee

Salary	Alternative A	Alternative B	Alternative C
Cash Inflow for Salary	$100,000	$85,000	$ 60,000
Tax on Salary Based on Maximum Tax on			
Earned Income (calculations not shown)[a] . .	46,000	38,270	25,370
Net Cash Inflow	$ 54,000	$46,730	$ 34,630
Factor for the Present Value of $1			
for 1 Period at .03	× .9709	× .9709	× .9709
Present Value of Aftertax Cash			
Inflow for Salary	$ 52,429	$45,370	$ 33,622
Pension and Deferred Compensation			
Cash Inflow from Ages 65 to 75		$15,000	$ 40,000
Less Tax on Pension and Deferred			
Compensation (calculations not shown)[a] . . .		3,520	14,390
Net Cash Inflow		$11,480	$ 25,610
Factor for Present Value of Annuity			
for 10 Periods at .05		× 7.7217	× 7.7217
Present Value of Pension and Deferred			
Compensation Payments at Age 65		$88,645	$197,753
Factor for the Future Value of an			
Annuity for 10 Periods at .05		÷ 12.5779	÷ 12.5779
Present Value of Equivalent Aftertax Salary			
for Pension and Deferred Compensation			
per Year—Ages 65 to 75		$ 7,048	$ 15,722
Cash Inflow from Ages 76 to 80		$15,000	$ 15,000
Less Tax on Pension			
(calculations not shown)		3,520	3,520
Net Cash Inflow		$11,480	$ 11,480
Factor for Present Value of Annuity			
For 5 Periods at .05		× 4.3295	× 4.3295
Present Value of Pension at Age 75		$49,703	$ 49,703
Factor for Present Value of $1			
for 10 Periods at .05		× .6139	× .6139
Present Value of Pension at Age 65		$30,513	$ 30,513
Factor for the Future Value of an Annuity			
for 10 Periods at .05		÷ 12.5779	÷ 12.5779
Present Value of Equivalent Aftertax Salary			
for Pension per Year—Ages 76 to 80		$ 2,426	$ 2,426
Summary			
Salary	$ 52,429	$45,370	$ 33,622
Pension and Deferred Compensation—			
Ages 65 to 75		7,048	15,722
Pension—Ages 76 to 80		2,426	2,426
Total	$ 52,429	$54,844	$ 51,770
Ranking from Employee's Standpoint . . .	2	1	3

[a] These amounts approximate the results of applying the tax law and regulations; such things as extra credits or deductions available to the elderly have been ignored for simplicity.

pensation, its preference ordering would be (1) alternative C, (2) alternative B, and (3) alternative A.

Now look at this decision from the standpoint of Ms. Stiefeld. She is single and files an individual income tax return. Her income from other sources is such that it exactly offsets her deductible expenses and exemptions. Thus, her taxable salary, pension, and deferred compensation benefits are equal to her taxable income. These forms of compensation are ordinary income and are subject to the usual graduated rates for individuals. However, the provisions for a maximum tax rate on earned income of 50 percent apply. Ms. Stiefeld feels that appropriate aftertax discount rates are 3 percent for salary income and 5 percent for pension and deferred compensation income.

Exhibit 18.3 presents an analysis of the three compensation packages from the standpoint of Ms. Stiefeld. Each package is again expressed in terms of the present value of aftertax equivalent salary payments for the current year. These present value amounts differ for the employer and employee because of different tax rates and discount rates. Because Ms. Stiefeld would select the package that maximizes the present value of cash inflows for compensation, her preference ordering would be (1) alternative B, (2) alternative A, and (3) alternative C. Note that the preference ordering of the employee does not necessarily have to be the opposite of the employer. In fact, it is desirable to design a package that ranks first from the standpoint of both parties. Where the rankings do not coincide, as in this case, further bargaining must take place.

The preceding analyses can be altered for other compensation packages. For example, if the pension plan was nonqualified, the employer's contributions would be taxable to Ms. Stiefeld when made. They would therefore be subject to a higher tax rate and taxed currently rather than during retirement. If stock options were included in the package, estimates of the benefit element in the stock option and the amount taxed at ordinary income rates would have to be made.

INTERCORPORATE INVESTMENTS

Business firms may invest in the common stock of other firms either as temporary investments of excess cash or as long-term investments aimed at improved integration or diversification of operations. In this section, we consider several income tax provisions that should be considered by a firm in making such investments. Attention is directed to (1) corporate acquisitions, (2) recognition of income subsequent to acquisition, and (3) recognition of gain or loss at the time the investment is sold.

Corporate Acquisitions

The acquisition of one firm by another is treated for tax purposes either as a taxable or a nontaxable exchange. To illustrate these methods, assume that P Company gives shares of its common stock with a market value of $1,000,000 to the stockholders of S Company in exchange for all of their S Company common stock. Their S Company shares were acquired several years previously for $100,000. The net assets of S Company have a book value of $400,000.

Unless the acquisition qualifies for special nontaxable exchange provisions discussed below, the acquisition will be viewed for tax purposes as a purchase of net assets by P Company and a sale of common stock by the shareholders of S Company (that is, a taxable exchange). P Company will record the net assets received at their cost to P Company, $1,000,000. From a tax standpoint, this treatment of the acquisition is desirable for P Company. It can base future cost of goods sold, depreciation, and other charges on a portion of the $1,000,000 valuation. This will provide greater future tax savings than if the $400,000 book values were used. The shareholders of S Company are viewed as having received consideration of $1,000,000 for common stock having a tax basis of $100,000. They would recognize a gain of $900,000 and be taxed on the entire increase in the value of their investment in the year of sale. Taxation of such a large gain in one year, even at capital gains rates, could have significant effects on the willingness of shareholders to sell out or at least on the price they would be willing to accept for their shares.

To overcome these tax disadvantages to selling shareholders, special nontaxable exchange provisions have been placed in the tax law. If an acquisition has a sound business purpose other than tax avoidance (for example, more effective integration or diversification of operations) and meets certain criteria as to the form of consideration given, then it can qualify as a nontaxable exchange. Under the nontaxable exchange provisions, the net assets acquired by P Company will have a tax basis of only $400,000, equal to their tax basis and book value to S Company. Most important, however, the shareholders of S Company will not recognize a gain on the exchange. The stock received from P Company will have the same tax basis as their old S Company shares, $100,000. Any gain will be postponed until the owners of the old S Company shares sell their new P Company shares.

There are greater tax advantages to P Company if the acquisition is treated as a taxable exchange. There are greater tax advantages to the shareholders of S Company if the acquisition is treated as a nontaxable exchange. The tax law provides, however, that both parties to the transaction must account for it in the same manner. Thus, one of the factors to be considered in the negotiations between the parties is the manner in which the transaction will be treated for tax purposes. P Company will attempt to keep the price as low as possible and aim for treatment as a taxable exchange. The shareholders of S Company will seek as high a price as possible and aim for treatment as a nontaxable exchange. If an agreement is reached that the transaction will be treated as a taxable exchange, the shareholders of S Company will likely demand a higher price to offset the income tax that must be paid immediately on the gain.

Income Recognition

The requirements for recognizing income from intercorporate investments in common stock differ significantly between financial and income tax reporting. The lower-of-cost-or-market method is required for financial reporting when less than 20 percent of the voting stock is owned,[3] the equity method is required for investments between

---

[3] Financial Accounting Standards Board, *Statement of Financial Accounting Standards No. 12*, 1975.

20 percent and 50 percent, and either the equity method or consolidated statements are required for investments greater than 50 percent.

For income tax purposes, a firm owning less than 80 percent of another firm's common stock must use the cost method. That is, it recognizes its share of dividends received, but not its share of undistributed earnings. Corporations get a deduction, however, for 85 percent of the dividends received from other U.S. corporations. Only 15 percent of the dividends received are effectively taxed. Because the maximum corporate tax is 48 percent, the dividends received are taxed at a maximum rate of only 7.2 percent (= .48 × .15). The dividends-received deduction was placed in the tax law to relieve the effects of triple taxation—once when earned, once when distributed as a dividend to the investor corporation, and once when distributed to the investor corporation's stockholders. Because income taxes are not imposed directly on sole proprietorships and partnerships, they cannot claim the 85 percent deduction for dividends received.

Example 1   Investor Corporation has $100,000 to invest and is considering two alternatives. It can purchase corporate bonds yielding 8 percent, or it can acquire shares of common stock that will pay an annual dividend of $5,000, a 5-percent yield. The aftertax return on the bonds each year will be $4,160 [= $8,000 − (.48 × $8,000)]. The aftertax return on the common stock will be $4,640 [= $5,000 − (.48 × .15 × $5,000)]. The dividends-received deduction more than offsets the differential pretax rate of return on the two investment alternatives. This investment decision would, of course, be based on additional considerations besides the annual rates of return, such as any gain or loss on subsequent sale and differences in the risk of the two investments.

If a firm owns at least 80 percent of another firm's voting stock, it can either file a consolidated tax return with that other corporation, or the two firms can file separate returns. In a consolidated tax return, the incomes of the two corporations are combined, and any intercompany items are eliminated. Among the advantages of filing a consolidated tax return are the following:

1 Operating losses of one corporation can be offset against operating profits of another corporation in determining consolidated taxable income.
2 Dividends received by one corporation from another member of the consolidated group of companies are excluded entirely (not just 85 percent) from taxable income.
3 The recognition of any gains (and losses) from intercompany sales is postponed until the item is sold outside of the consolidated entity.
4 Greater advantage can be taken of certain deductions subject to limits (for example, charitable contributions, investment tax credits) in that amounts in excess of the limits for one corporation can offset unused amounts allowed another corporation.

Among the disadvantages of filing a consolidated tax return are the following:

1 Costly record keeping may be required in order to keep track of intercompany profits and losses on sales of goods between corporations.
2 All corporations must have the same tax year. This might produce operating difficulties if the year-end selected occurs at a time when one corporation is at a peak in its business activities.

3 Once the decision is made to file a consolidated tax return, it is difficult to terminate the election.

The careful reader may suppose that it would be advantageous for a firm to organize itself into as many separate corporations as possible, file separate tax returns, and thereby have its income taxed at 20 and at 22 percent instead of at 48 percent. Prior to the early 1970s, this could be done and was an important advantage of filing separate tax returns. The income tax laws have been revised, however, and this is no longer permitted.

On balance, it would appear that the advantages of filing a consolidated return outweigh the disadvantages in most cases.

Recognition of Gain or Loss on Sale

Investments in a corporation's bonds, preferred stock, and common stock are considered capital assets as defined by the Internal Revenue Code. As a result, any gain or loss on the sale of such securities is taxed at capital gain or loss rates rather than the "ordinary income" rates described earlier in this chapter. Capital gains and losses of businesses operated as sole proprietorships or partnerships pass through to the firm's owners. They are taxed at maximum rates from 25 percent to 35 percent depending on the amount of the capital gain. Net capital gains of businesses operated as corporations are taxed at a maximum rate of 30 percent. The procedures for calculating the tax on net capital gains are beyond the scope of this book. (Net capital losses are not deductible by corporations.) It is sufficient here to point out that it is generally desirable to have gains qualify for capital gains rates, because those rates are less than for ordinary income.

CAPITAL STRUCTURE DECISION

In the preceding two sections, we have been concerned with the tax implications of investments in common stock and employee compensation. In this section, we consider tax factors to be considered in raising capital from various sources. In particular, we focus on the tax implications of raising new capital from debt, preferred stock, and common stock. To facilitate discussion, an example is presented in Exhibit 18.4. This firm is currently earning a rate of return on common stockholders' equity of 10 percent. It now needs $1,000 (the actual amount is $1,000,000 but the 000's are omitted to simplify the presentation) of new capital. Three alternatives are under consideration: (1) to issue bonds yielding 8 percent, (2) to issue preferred stock yielding 9 percent, and (3) to issue additional common stock. The last three columns of Exhibit 18.4 indicate the amount of additional pretax income that must be generated from the $1,000 of new capital in order to maintain the rate of return on common stockholders' equity. Let us consider each of the three alternatives.

If the capital is obtained through the issuance of debt, only $80 of additional pretax income needs to be generated in order to maintain the 10 percent return to common stockholders. Because interest on the debt is deductible in determining taxable income, the additional funds need only generate earnings at a rate equal to the interest rate.

EXHIBIT 18.4

Illustration of the Effect of $1,000 of New Debt versus New Equity Capital on Rate of Return on Common Stockholders' Equity

		If Assumed Financing Is		
	Currently	New 8% Bonds	New 9% Preferred Stock	New Common Stock
Required Net Income before Interest and Income Taxes	$ 2,000	$ 2,080	$ 2,173	$ 2,192
Interest Expense.	—	(80)	—	—
Taxable Income	$ 2,000	$ 2,000	$ 2,173	$ 2,192
Income Taxes at 48 Percent	(960)	(960)	(1,043)	(1,052)
Net Income	$ 1,040	$ 1,040	$ 1,130	$ 1,140
Preferred Dividend	—	—	(90)	—
Net Income to Common Stockholders . . .	$ 1,040	$ 1,040	$ 1,040	$ 1,140
Average Common Stockholders' Equity.	$10,400	$10,400	$10,400	$11,400
Rate of Return on Common Stockholders' Equity	10%	10%	10%	10%

(Of course, the business would hope to generate more than $80, so that the project does more than merely break even.)

If the capital is obtained through issuing preferred stock, $173 of additional pretax income must be generated. Because dividends on preferred stock are not tax deductible, additional funds obtained from this source must earn approximately twice the required preferred dividend rate in order to maintain the rate of return on common stockholders' equity.

If the capital is obtained through issuing common stock, $192 of additional pretax income must be generated. Dividends on common stock are not deductible, so additional funds must earn approximately twice the current rate of return on common stockholders' equity.

This illustration is overly simplified in that the required rates of return were based on the book values of common stockholders' equity. Moreover, we have ignored changes in the riskiness of the firm that occur when a firm issues new debt rather than stock. The common stockholders are more concerned that the issuance of new debt or stock does not reduce the market value of their investments. There is seldom a precise relationship between changes in book values and market values of the common stockholders' equities. The illustration does serve to illustrate, however, that the tax law favors debt as compared to equity financing.

ORGANIZATIONAL FORM DECISION

Three principal forms of organization were discussed in Chapter Seventeen: sole proprietorship, partnership, and corporation. For large, multinational firms, the benefits of limited liability, ability to raise large amounts of funds, and ease in transferring ownership heavily favor the corporate form. Any income tax advantages of operating such firms as sole proprietorships or partnerships are of little consequence. On the other hand, income tax considerations play an important role in the choice of organizational form for a small, closely held business. The nontax advantages of the corporate form for large firms listed above are not nearly as important for smaller firms. In this section, we discuss some of the more important tax considerations in selecting (1) the sole proprietorship or partnership form versus (2) the corporate form. Sole proprietorships and partnerships are taxed so similarly that we can consider them as one alternative (the choice between them depends essentially on the number of individuals that will be designated as owners).

Tax Rates

You will recall that the income of a sole proprietorship or partnership is not taxed at the level of the business entity. Instead, it is combined with the nonbusiness income of the owner(s) and taxed at graduated rates ranging from 14 percent to 70 percent. The income of a corporation is taxed when earned at a rate of 20 percent of the first $25,000 of taxable income, 22 percent of the next $25,000, and 48 percent of any excess.[4]

The corporate income is effectively taxed a second time when distributed to stockholders as a dividend. When the average tax rates[5] of owners are less than approximately 48 percent, the sole proprietorship or partnership is favored. These forms may even be favored when the owners' average tax rates exceed 48 percent. This is because the maximum effective tax rate on income generated from the corporate form must include both the 48 percent corporate tax rate plus the rate on amounts that owners receive as dividends. The income level at which the corporate form becomes preferred to the sole proprietorship or partnership form depends on the amount of nonbusiness income of the owners.

Stability of Income

If a firm is engaged in a type of business subject to significant fluctuations in earnings, the corporate form may be preferable.[6] This is because the corporation is not subject to graduated tax rates to the same extent as the sole proprietorship or partnership. On the other hand, if a firm incurs net losses, the sole proprietorship or partnership form is better. Net losses of these businesses immediately pass through to the owners and can offset their nonbusiness income. Net losses of a corporation do not pass to their owners.[7] If they cannot be carried back or carried forward to offset corporate taxable income in other years, then their benefits to the owners are largely lost.

---

[4] Corporate tax rates change from time to time; these are the rates in effect as this book goes to press.
[5] The average tax rate is determined by dividing income taxes payable by net income before taxes. Because of the differing degrees of progression in the rate structure for corporations and individuals, it is the average rather than the marginal tax rate that is important.
[6] Income averaging provisions for earned incomes of individuals may provide some tax relief for non-corporate taxpayers.
[7] The rules are somewhat different for Subchapter S corporations, but we do not discuss those rules in this book.

Fringe Benefits

The income tax law permits more liberal deductions for fringe benefits for employees when the corporate form is adopted as compared to when the sole proprietorship or partnership form is used. Included in the more favored treatment are deductions for life insurance policies, pensions, profit sharing, and stock option arrangements.

Retention of Earnings

A growing firm desiring to retain earnings will be able to so do more easily if it operates as a sole proprietorship or partnership. There are no specific taxes imposed on owners of these firms when distributions are made. Thus, the Internal Revenue Service is not particularly concerned with whether sole proprietorship or partnership earnings are distributed or retained. On the other hand, stockholders are taxed when dividends are received from their corporations. In an effort to avoid this double tax, many corporations attempt to retain as much earnings as possible. The Internal Revenue Service has the power effectively to force dividend distributions by imposing a relatively steep accumulated earnings tax. This tax is imposed when the Internal Revenue Service feels that a corporation, particularly a small, closely held firm, is retaining more earnings than the business reasonably needs and is merely retaining earnings to avoid the double tax. Thus, retentions of earnings when the corporate form is used may have to be justified.

Another Alternative—Subchapter S Corporation

The discussion in the preceding sections did not indicate any clear preference for either the sole proprietorship/partnership form or the corporate form. Many firms faced with the organization form decision thereby find the decision difficult to make. One additional alternative, however, has been placed in the tax law—a Subchapter S corporation. This is a firm legally organized as a corporation and, therefore, enjoying the nontax benefits described earlier. The corporation is taxed each year, however, as if it were a partnership. That is, the income of the corporation is not taxed at the corporate level but as part of the income of the individual stockholders. Operating losses of such a corporation pass to the stockholders and can offset their nonbusiness income. The deductions for fringe benefits of a Subchapter S corporation are more like a regular corporation than like a partnership. Thus, a Subchapter S corporation can enjoy many of the tax benefits of both partnership and corporate organizational forms, while losing only a few tax benefits available to one or the other.

There are several criteria that must be met in order for a corporation to qualify as a Subchapter S corporation, including restrictions on the source and type of income. Most important, there cannot be more than 15 stockholders in the firm. Only relatively small firms, therefore, have the option of being treated as a Subchapter S corporation for tax purposes.

SUMMARY

We have considered several of the many income tax factors affecting various types of business decisions in Chapters Seventeen and Eighteen. The old adage, "a little knowledge can be dangerous," is certainly appropriate with respect to our coverage of this important topic. We have merely scratched the surface in an effort to create an awareness of the significance of income taxes in business decisions. Partly as an indication of the magnitude of income tax effects in certain kinds of decisions and partly as a synthesis of the material discussed in this chapter, we present in Exhibit 18.5 an analysis of the statutory and effective corporate tax rates for the General Electric Company for 1976. This analysis indicates the tax savings realized by General Electric during the year from several permanent and timing differences between book income and taxable income. Similar tax savings are realized by many other large as well as small firms every year.

EXHIBIT 18.5

General Electric Company and Consolidated Affiliates Reconciliation of Statutory and Effective Corporate Tax Rates for the Year 1976 (in millions of dollars)

	Income Tax Expense	Income Taxes Payable	Percentage of Net Income before Taxes
I. Income Taxes on "Net Income before Taxes" at Statutory Rate	$781.2	$781.2	48.0%
II. Permanent Differences:			
A. Income of Consolidated Affiliates Subject to Effective Tax Rates Less Than 48%	(63.5)	(63.5)	(3.9)
B. Income of Unconsolidated Affiliates Subject to Effective Tax Rates Less Than 48%	(27.7)	(27.7)	(1.7)
C. Savings from Investment Tax Credit	(31.4)	(31.4)	(1.9)
D. Income Taxed at Capital Gains Rates	(14.6)	(14.6)	(.9)
E. Other Permanent Differences—Net	24.6	24.6	1.5
	$668.6	$668.6	41.1%
III. Timing Differences:			
A. Tax over Book Depreciation		(7.8)	(.5)
B. Undistributed Earnings of Affiliate		(4.3)	(.3)
C. Margin on Installment Sales		(2.1)	(.1)
D. Provision for Warranties and Other Costs		21.6	1.3
E. Other Timing Differences—Net		15.1	1.0
Total	$668.6	$691.1	42.5%

QUESTIONS AND PROBLEMS

1 Review the meaning of the following concepts or terms discussed in this chapter.
  a Double taxation of corporate earnings.
  b Triple taxation of corporate earnings.
  c Consolidated tax return.
  d Ordinary income versus capital gain.
  e Qualified versus nonqualified pension plans.
  f Stock option plans.
  g Subchapter S corporation.

2 Distinguish between the taxation of a qualified and a nonqualified pension plan to both the employer and employee.

3 What are the advantages of a stock option plan to the employee? To the employer?

4 What is a Subchapter S corporation? Describe the principal advantages of being taxed as a Subchapter S corporation rather than as a partnership or a regular corporation.

5 Howard Hoffman is employed by Carolina Copiers, Incorporated. He has been offered a choice of three alternative compensation packages for 19X0:

Alternative A—salary of $20,000.
Alternative B—salary of $18,000 and bonuses of $1,500 to be paid at the end of both 19X1 and 19X2.
Alternative C—salary of $17,000 and a bonus of $4,000 to be paid at the end of 19X1.

Prepare an analysis to indicate which alternative Hoffman should select. Hoffman's marginal tax rate is expected to be as follows: 19X0—30 percent; 19X1—32 percent; 19X2—34 percent. He feels that 4 percent is an appropriate discount rate for salaries and bonuses. All cash flows occur at the end of each year. Round present value factors used to two decimal places. The bonuses in alternatives B and C are guaranteed to Hoffman regardless of whether or not he continues to work for Carolina Copiers after 19X0.

6 Jill Lawson, who is 55 years old, was recently hired by Medical Consultants, Incorporated. In addition to her salary, Jill will accrue benefits to a pension of $10,000 per year during retirement. The mandatory retirement age is 65. The pension plan is qualified. Her employer will contribute $6,000 per year to the plan for the next 10 years. Jill (or her estate) will receive the annual pension for 15 years, regardless of whether or not she is living. She feels that a discount rate of 6 percent is appropriate for pension benefits. Her marginal tax rate during the next 10 years is expected to be 30 percent, and during retirement it is expected to be 20 percent. Round present value factors used to two decimal places. Note that Jill must continue working for Medical Consultants until retirement in order to receive the pension benefits.
  a Determine the present value of the aftertax pension benefits to Jill as of the time of her employment.
  b For this part, assume that the pension plan is nonqualified. All other information given above still applies. Because her employer will make contributions of $60,000 (= $6,000 × 10 years) on Jill's behalf, she will not be taxed on the first $4,000 received each year

during retirement (= \$60,000/15 years = \$4,000). Determine the amount of the annual pension that Jill must receive under this nonqualified pension plan such that the present value of all aftertax cash flows is equivalent to the corresponding amount determined in part **a** for the qualified pension plan.

7 Lee Reynolds, 30 years old, is employed by MTA, Incorporated. Three alternative compensation packages for 19X0 have surfaced from initial discussions.

Alternative A—Salary of \$30,000.

Alternative B—Salary of \$25,000 and rights to a pension of \$10,000 per year during retirement, beginning at age 60. The pension plan is qualified. MTA will contribute \$756 per year for the next 30 years on Lee's behalf.

Alternative C—Salary of \$25,000 and rights to a pension of \$12,000 per year during retirement, beginning at age 60. The pension plan is nonqualified. MTA will contribute \$907 per year for the next 30 years on Lee's behalf.

Lee's marginal tax rate for 19X0 under each alternative is as follows: Alternative A—32 percent; alternatives B and C—28 percent. His marginal tax rate during retirement is expected to be 20 percent. Lee (or his estate) will receive the pension for 15 years regardless of whether or not Lee is living. Lee feels that an appropriate discount rate for salary is 3 percent and for pension benefits is 6 percent. Assume that all cash flows occur at the end of each period. Round present value factors used to two decimal places.

Prepare an analysis that will assist Lee in choosing a compensation package for 19X0. Note that Lee must continue working for MTA until retirement in order to receive the pension benefits under alternatives B and C.

8 Refer to Problem **7**. MTA is subject to a marginal tax rate of 48 percent. The firm's cost of capital is 8 percent. Round present value factors used to two decimal places. Prepare an analysis that will assist MTA in deciding which of the three alternative compensation packages is optimum from its standpoint.

9 John Hanson owns all of the common stock of Hanson Electric Corporation. The stock was acquired for \$50,000 when the firm was organized. The net assets of Hanson Electric Corporation on January 1, 19X0, have a book value and tax basis of \$300,000. John Hanson has agreed to exchange all of his shares in Hanson Electric for shares of common stock in Diversified Electronics Corporation. The shares received have a market value of \$500,000.

a Determine the amount of gain or loss recognized on this exchange by all parties involved, assuming that it is treated as a taxable exchange.

b Repeat step **a** assuming that the transaction is treated as a nontaxable exchange.

c Determine the tax basis of the Diversified Electronics Corporation's shares issued to John Hanson, assuming that the transaction is treated as a taxable exchange.

d Repeat step **c** assuming that the transaction is treated as a nontaxable exchange.

e Determine the tax basis of the net assets of Hanson Electric Corporation transferred to Diversified Electronics Corporation, assuming that the transaction is treated as a taxable exchange.

f Repeat step **e** assuming that the transaction is treated as a nontaxable exchange.

g Is a nontaxable exchange really nontaxable?

10 Joan Williams owns all of the common stock of Williams' Consultants, Incorporated. She acquired the shares for \$10,000 when the firm was organized several years ago. A tentative agreement has been reached in which she will exchange all of her common stock in Williams' Consultants for shares of common stock of Diversified Investors, Incorporated. The only remaining questions between the parties are (1) the tax treatment of the transaction (that is, a taxable or a nontaxable exchange) and (2) the market value of Diversified Investors shares to be exchanged.

Joan Williams has stated that she would be willing to accept shares having a market value of $100,000 if the transaction were accounted for as a nontaxable exchange. What minimum amount should she be willing to accept if the transaction were accounted for as a taxable exchange and:

a Any gain on the exchange were immediately taxed at a rate of 25 percent?

b Any gain on the exchange were immediately taxed at a rate of 35 percent?

c Any gain on the exchange were taxed one year later at a rate of 25 percent? Use a discount rate of 6 percent.

d Any gain on the exchange were taxed one year later at a rate of 35 percent? Use a discount rate of 6 percent.

11 At the beginning of 19X0, General Investment Company (GIC) is considering two alternatives for the investment of $50,000 in excess funds:

Alternative A—Purchase 1,000 shares of common stock of Standard Products, Inc., for $50 per share. GIC expects to receive dividends of $3,000 at the end of 19X0 and $3,200 at the end of 19X1. The firm plans to sell the shares at the end of 19X1 (after receiving the dividend for 19X1) for an estimated $58,000.

Alternative B—Purchase at par value $50,000 of 20-year bonds of Standard Products, Inc. The bonds have a coupon rate of 12 percent and pay interest on December 31 of each year. GIC plans to sell the bond at the end of 19X1 (after receiving the interest payment for 19X1) for an estimated $51,000.

The marginal tax rate on ordinary income of GIC is 48 percent. Capital gains are taxed at 30 percent. The firm's discount rate is 10 percent for both of these alternatives.

a Determine the net present value of alternative A and of alternative B as of January 1, 19X0.

b Assume that GIC is a sole proprietorship. Ordinary income is taxed at a marginal rate of 35 percent and capital gains are taxed at a marginal rate of 17.5 percent. Determine the net present value of alternative A and of alternative B as of January 1, 19X0.

12 Brooks Products, Incorporated, has $15,000 of taxable income for 19X0 before selling a particular asset. It can sell either marketable securities (gain is taxed at 30 percent) or a machine (gain taxed at ordinary income rate of 22 percent). Which asset should be sold if the gain, regardless of the asset sold, will be

a $ 5,000?

b $ 20,000?

c $100,000?

13 Langenderfer Corporation is considering two investment alternatives as of January 1, 19X0.

Alternative A—Purchase shares of common stock of General Products Corporation for $90,000. Langenderfer expects to receive dividends of $20,000 per year for three years. After receiving the third dividend, the shares will be sold for an estimated $96,000.

Alternative B—Purchase new equipment for $90,000. The equipment is expected to save $20,000 in pretax cash operating cost per year for three years. Depreciation for book purposes is to be on the straight-line method and for tax purposes is to be on the double-declining-balance method (with appropriate switch to straight-line at the optimum point). Depreciation is to be calculated using a three-year life. Actual salvage value at the end of three years is expected to be $5,000. Because of various tax provisions, this salvage value can be ignored entirely in calculating depreciation for tax purposes. The 10 percent investment tax credit provision applies to this equipment. Use a 48 percent tax rate for all ordinary corporate income.

a Determine the net present value of alternative A and of alternative B. Assume that all cash flows, except the initial investments, occur at the end of the year. The firm uses a 12 percent aftertax cost of capital. Round present value factors used to two decimal places.

b Discuss briefly several additional factors that Langenderfer Corporation should consider before making a decision.

14 Rockness Manufacturing Corporation is currently earning a rate of return on common stockholders' equity of 15 percent (= $150,000/$1,000,000). It is subject to an income tax rate of 48 percent. It now needs to raise $100,000 of new capital. Three alternatives are under consideration:

Alternative A—Issue $100,000 of 10 percent bonds at par value.
Alternative B—Issue $100,000 of 12 percent preferred stock at par value.
Alternative C—Issue 10,000 shares of common stock for $10 per share. Each share is to receive an annual dividend of $3.

Determine the amount of net income before interest and income taxes that must be generated from each of these alternatives in order to maintain the 15 percent rate of return on the common stockholders' equity.

15 Stanley Manufacturing Company is solely owned by John Stanley. John is attempting to determine whether the firm should be operated as a sole proprietorship or a corporation. One of the factors to be considered is the amount of income taxes that will be payable at various levels of income. John's nonbusiness income is such that it exactly offsets his deductible expenses and exemptions. Thus, if the firm is operated as a sole proprietorship, his taxable income will be equal to the net income of the manufacturing business. If the firm is operated as a corporation, his taxable income will be equal to the amount of dividends received from the corporation.

The amount of income taxes that will be payable at various levels of income if the firm operates as a sole proprietorship are listed below (assuming that John Stanley is single):

Pretax Income Level	Income Taxes Payable	Marginal Tax Rate
$ 10,000	$ 2,090	27%
20,000	5,230	38
30,000	9,390	45
40,000	14,390	55
50,000	20,190	62
75,000	36,090	66
100,000	53,090	70

The amount of income taxes that will be payable at various income levels if the firm operates as a corporation are listed below. Also shown are the amounts of income taxes payable by John Stanley on amounts received as dividends.

Income Level	Corporate Income Taxes Payable	Taxes Payable on Dividends for Various Percentages of Pretax Income Distributed		
		20%	40%	60%
$ 10,000	$ 2,200	$ 310	$ 690	$ 1,110
20,000	4,400	690	1,590	2,630
30,000	7,900	1,110	2,630	4,510
40,000	12,700	1,590	3,830	6,790
50,000	17,500	2,090	5,230	9,390
75,000	29,500	3,520	9,390	17,190
100,000	41,500	5,230	14,390	26,390

a Prepare a graph as follows. The horizontal axis should be labeled "Income Level" and should provide space for the seven income levels indicated above. The vertical axis should be labeled "Income Taxes Payable" and should provide space for amounts up to $70,000.

b Using the graph prepared in part **a,** plot the amounts of income taxes payable for each income level for the sole proprietorship form and for the corporate form assuming that 20 percent, 40 percent, and 60 percent of pretax corporate net income is distributed as a dividend.

c After carefully studying the graph, prepare a written analysis of the effect of income taxes on the sole proprietorship versus corporate organizational form decision across income levels.

16 Leisure Products Company is in an industry that experiences significant fluctuations in net income over the business cycle. Listed below are the estimated amounts of net income before taxes for 19X0 through 19X3 and the corresponding amounts of income taxes payable assuming that the firm is operated as a sole proprietorship.

Year	Net Income before Taxes	Income Taxes as a Sole Proprietorship	Marginal Tax Rate
19X0	$20,000	$ 5,230	38%
19X1	50,000	20,190	62
19X2	10,000	2,090	27
19X3	70,000	32,790	66

The amounts of income taxes payable for these years if the firm operates as a corporation and 25 percent of its pretax income is paid out in dividends are shown below:

Year	Net Income before Taxes	Income Taxes on Corporation	Income Taxes on Dividends	Total
19X0	$20,000	$ 4,400	$ 900	$ 5,300
19X1	50,000	17,500	2,775	20,275
19X2	10,000	2,200	405	2,605
19X3	70,000	27,100	4,340	31,440

a Assuming that income taxes are paid at the end of each year, determine the present value of the income taxes payable for 19X0 through 19X3 for the sole proprietorship and for the corporate forms. Use a discount rate of 10 percent.

b After studying your results in part **a,** summarize briefly the effect of fluctuating income levels on the choice of organizational form.

APPENDIX
COMPOUND-INTEREST CONCEPTS AND APPLICATIONS

Money is a scarce resource, which its owner can use to command other resources. Like owners of other scarce resources, owners of money can permit others (borrowers) to rent the use of their money for a period of time. Payment for the use of money differs little from other rental payments, such as those made to a landlord for the use of property or to a car rental agency for the use of a car. Payment for the use of money is called *interest*. Accounting is concerned with interest because it must record transactions where the use of money is bought and sold.

Managers are concerned with interest calculations for another, equally important, reason. Expenditures for an asset most often do not occur at the same time as the receipts for services produced by that asset. Money received sooner is more valuable than money received later. The difference in timing can affect whether or not acquiring an asset is profitable. Amounts of money received at different times are different commodities. Managers use interest calculations to make amounts of money to be paid or received at different times comparable. For example, an analyst might compare two amounts to be received at two different times by using interest calculations to find the equivalent value of one amount at the time the other is due. Money contracts involving a series of money payments over time, such as bonds, mortgages, notes, and leases, are evaluated by finding the *present value* of the stream of payments. The present value of a stream of payments is a single amount of money at the present time that is the economic equivalent of the entire stream.

COMPOUND INTEREST

The quotation of interest "cost" is typically specified as a percentage of the amount borrowed per unit of time. Examples are 6 percent per year and 1 percent per month. Another example occurs in the context of discounts on purchases. The terms of sale "2/10, net/30" is equivalent to 2 percent for 20 days, because if the discount is not taken, the money can be used for an extra 20 days. The amount borrowed or loaned is called the *principal.* Compound interest means either to pay to the lender at the end of the period the interest accumulated during the period or to add the interest to the principal at the end of the period so that the principal for the next interest period is larger. The period between interest calculations, during which the principal accumulates interest, is called the *compounding* period.

If you deposit $1,000 in a savings account that pays compound interest at the rate of 6 percent per year, you will earn $60 by the end of one year. Thus, $1,060 will be earning interest during the second year. During the second year your principal of $1,060 will earn $63.60 interest, $60 on the initial deposit of $1,000 and $3.60 on the $60 earned the previous year. By the end of the second year, you will have $1,123.60.

The "force," or effect of compound interest is more substantial than many people realize. For example, compounded annually at 6 percent, money "doubles itself" in less than 12 years. Put another way, if you invest $49.70 in a savings account that pays 6 percent compounded annually, you will have $100 in 12 years. If the Indians who sold Manhattan Island for $24 in May 1626 had been able to invest that principal at 8 percent compounded annually, the principal would have grown to almost $12 trillion by May 1976, 350 years later. The rate of interest affects the amount of accumulation more than you might expect. If the Indians invested at 6 percent rather than 8 percent, the $24 would have grown to $17 billion in 350 years; if the rate were 4 percent, the $24 would have grown to a mere $22 million.

When only the original principal earns interest during the entire life of the loan, the interest due at the time the loan is repaid is called *simple* interest. Simple interest is computed as the principal multiplied by the rate multiplied by the elapsed time. At simple interest of 6 percent per year, the Indians' $24 would have grown to only $528 in 350 years, $24 of principal and $504 of simple interest ($24 × .06 × 350). Nearly all economic calculations involve compound interest.

Problems involving compound interest generally fall into two groups with respect to time: first, there are the problems for which we want to know the future value of money invested or loaned today; second, there are the problems for which we want to know the present value, or today's value, of money to be received or paid at later dates.

Future Value

When $1.00 is invested today at 6 percent compounded annually, it will grow to $1.0600 at the end of 1 year, $1.1236 at the end of 2 years, $1.1910 at the end of 3 years, and so on according to the formula

$$F_n = P(1 + r)^n$$

where

F_n represents the accumulation or future value,
P represents the one-time investment today,
r is the interest rate per period, and
n is the number of periods from today.

The amount F_n is the future value of the present payment, P, compounded at r percent per period for n periods. Table 1, on page 484, shows the future values of $P = \$1$ for various numbers of periods and for various interest rates. Extracts from that table, rounded to five decimal places, are shown here in Table A.1.

TABLE A.1 (Excerpt from Table 1)
Future Value of $1 at 6 Percent and 8 Percent per Period
$F_n = (1 + r)^n$

Number of Periods = n	Rate = r	
	6%	8%
1	1.06000	1.08000
2	1.12360	1.16640
3	1.19102	1.25971
10	1.79085	2.15892
20	3.20714	4.66096

Example Problems in Determining Future Value

1 How much will $1,000 deposited today at 6 percent compounded annually be worth 10 years from now?

One dollar deposited today at 6 percent will grow to $1.79085; therefore $1,000 will grow to $1,000(1.06)^{10} = $1,000 \times 1.79085 = $1,790.85$.

2 How much will $500 deposited today at 8 percent compounded annually be worth 23 years from today?

The tables do not show values for 23 periods. Interpolation between the numbers shown in tables is imprecise; rather, notice that $F_{23} = P(1.08)^{23} = P(1.08)^{20} \times (1.08)^3$. Calculate the future value for 23 years in two steps: first, determine the amount that $1 will grow to in 20 years at 8 percent, or $4.66096. Then let $4.66096 be the principal that grows for 3 (more) years. One dollar invested for 3 years at 8 percent grows to $1.25971. Therefore, $4.66096 invested for 3 years grows to $4.66096 \times 1.25971 = 5.8715. (Note that factors for any two periods that sum to 23 can be used to produce the same answer. For example, factors from the compound interest tables can be used to compute: $(1.08)^{23} = (1.08)^{11} \times (1.08)^{12} = 2.33164 \times 2.51817 = 5.8715$.) So $1 invested for 23 years at 8 percent has a future value of $5.8715, and $500 invested for 23 years at 8 percent grows to $500 \times 5.8715 = $2,935.75$.

A rule of thumb worth remembering for rough calculations is the *Rule of 72*. For interest rates between 3 percent and 12 percent per period, the number of periods required for an amount to double in value when invested at i percent per period is $72/i$. The Rule of 72 says, for example, that money invested at 4 percent per period doubles in $72/4 = 18$ periods; the exact answer is slightly more than 17.67 periods. At 10 percent, the Rule of 72 suggests that money doubles in 7.2 periods, which is reasonably close to the correct answer, approximately 7.27 periods.[1]

---

[1] An even better rule, one that works for interest rates between $\frac{1}{4}$ percent and 100 percent, is the Rule of 69: compounded at i percent per period, money doubles in $69/i + .35$ periods. See John P. Gould and Roman L. Weil, "The Rule of 69," *Journal of Business*, 47 (July 1974), pp. 397–398.

Present Value

The preceding section developed the tools for computing the future value, F_n, of a sum of money, P, deposited or invested today. P is known; F_n is calculated. This section deals with the problems of calculating how much principal, P, has to be invested today in order to have a specified amount, F_n, at the end of n periods. The future amount, F_n, the interest rate, r, and the number of periods, n, are known; P is to be found. In order to have \$1 one year from today when interest is earned at 6 percent, P of \$.94340 must be invested today. That is, $F_1 = P(1.06)^1$ or $\$1 = \$.94340 \times 1.06$. Because $F_n = P(1 + r)^n$, dividing both sides of the equation by $(1 + r)^n$ yields

$$\frac{F_n}{(1 + r)^n} = P$$

or

$$P = \frac{F_n}{(1 + r)^n} = F_n(1 + r)^{-n}$$

To have $F_2 = \$1$ two years from today, the amount P that must be invested at 6 percent is $P = \$1/(1.06)^2$. The value of $(1.06)^2$ can be read from Table A.1 (2-period row, under the $r = 6$ percent column) as 1.12360. The quotient is $1/1.12360 = .89000$. In order to accumulate \$1 at the end of two periods, \$.89 must be invested when the interest rate is 6 percent.

The number $(1 + r)^{-n}$ is the present value of \$1 to be received after n periods when interest is earned at r percent per period. The term *discount* is used in this context as follows: the *discounted* present value of \$1 to be received n periods in the future is $(1 + r)^{-n}$ when the *discount* rate is r percent per period for n periods. The number r is the discount *rate* and the number $(1 + r)^{-n}$ is the discount *factor* for n periods. A discount factor $(1 + r)^{-n}$ is merely the reciprocal, or inverse, of a number, $(1 + r)^n$, in Table A.1. Therefore, tables of discount factors are not necessary for present value calculations if tables of future values are at hand. But present value calculations are so frequently needed, and division is so onerous, that tables of discount factors are as widely available as tables of future values. Portions of Table 2 (on page 485), which shows discount factors or, equivalently, present values of \$1 for various interest (or discount) rates for various numbers of periods, are shown in Table A.2.

Example Problems in Determining Present Values

3 What is the present value of \$1 due 10 years from now if the interest (equivalently, the discount) rate r is 6 percent per year?

From Table A.2, 6-percent column, 10-period row, the present value of \$1 to be received 10 periods hence at 6 percent is \$.55839.

4 You issue a non-interest-bearing note that promises to pay \$13,500 three years from today in exchange for undeveloped land. How much is that promise worth today if the discount rate is 8 percent per period?

One dollar received 3 years hence discounted at 8 percent has a present value of \$.79383. Thus the promise is worth $\$13,500 \times .79383 = \$10,717$.

TABLE A.2 (Excerpt from Table 2)
Present Value of $1 at 6 Percent and 8 Percent per Period
$$P = F_n(1 + r)^{-n}$$

Number of Periods = n	Rate = r	
	6%	8%
1	.94340	.92593
2	.89000	.85734
3	.83962	.79383
10	.55839	.46319
20	.31180	.21455

5 What is the present value of $5,000 to be received 23 years hence when the discount rate is 6 percent per year?

The tables do not show values for 23 periods. Interpolation is not precise; rather, note that $P = F_{23}(1.06)^{-23} = F_{23}(1.06)^{-20}(1.06)^{-3}$. Calculate the present value in two steps: first, discount $1 back 20 periods, from year 23 to year 3. At 6 percent, this is $.31180. Then discount $.31180 back 3 more periods, from year 3 to the present. At 6 percent, this is $.2618 (= $.31180 × .83962). [Factors for any two periods that sum to 23 could be used: for example, $(1.06)^{-23} = (1.06)^{-11} \times (1.06)^{-12} = .52679 \times .49697 = .2618$.] So $1 received 23 years from now is currently worth $.2618, and $5,000 received 23 years from now is worth $5,000 × .2618 = $1,309 today, when the discount rate is 6 percent per year.

CHANGING THE COMPOUNDING PERIOD: NOMINAL AND EFFECTIVE RATES

"Six percent, compounded annually" is the price for a loan; this means that interest is added to or *converted* into principal once a year at the rate of 6 percent. Often, however, the price for a loan states that compounding is to take place more than once a year. A savings bank may advertise that it pays 6 percent, compounded quarterly. This means that at the end of each quarter the bank credits savings accounts with interest calculated at the rate 1.5 percent (= 6 percent/4). Corporate bonds usually pay interest twice a year. This section examines the effect of changing the compounding period from one year.

If $1,000 is invested today at 12 percent compounded annually, its future value one year later is $1,120. If the rate of interest is stated as 12 percent compounded semiannually, then 6 percent interest is added to the principal every six months. At the end of the first six months, $1,000 will have grown to $1,060. At the end of the second six months, interest at 6 percent is computed on a principal of $1,060 so that the accumulation will be $1,060 × 1.06 = $1,123.60 by the end of the year. Notice that 12 percent compounded *semiannually* is equivalent to 12.36 percent compounded *annually*.

Suppose that the price is quoted as 12 percent, compounded quarterly. Then an additional 3 percent of the principal will be added to, or converted into, principal every three months. By the end of the year, $1,000 will grow to $1,000 × $(1.03)^4$ = $1,000 × 1.12551 = $1,125.51. Twelve percent compounded quarterly is equivalent to 12.55 percent compounded annually. If 12 percent is compounded monthly, then $1 will grow to $1 × $(1.01)^{12}$ = $1.12683. Thus, 12 percent compounded monthly is equivalent to 12.68 percent compounded annually.

For a given *nominal* rate, such as the 12 percent in the examples above, the more often interest is compounded or converted into principal, the higher the *effective* rate of interest paid. If a nominal rate, r, is compounded m times per year, then the effective rate is $(1 + r/m)^m - 1$.

Some savings banks advertise that they compound interest daily or even continuously. The mathematics of calculus provides a mechanism for finding the effective rate when interest is compounded continuously. We shall not go into details but merely state that if interest is compounded continuously at nominal rate r per year, then the effective annual rate is $e^r - 1$, where e is the base of the natural logarithms. Tables of values of e^r are widely available.[2] Six percent per year compounded continuously is equivalent to 6.1837 percent compounded annually; 12 percent per year compounded continuously is equivalent to 12.75 percent compounded annually. Do not confuse the compounding period with the payment period. Some banks, for example, compound interest daily but pay interest quarterly. You can be sure that such banks do not employ clerks or even computers to calculate interest every day. They merely use tables to derive an equivalent effective rate to apply at the end of each quarter.

In practice, to solve problems that require computation of interest quoted at a nominal rate of r percent per period compounded m times per period for n periods, merely use the tables for rate r/m and $m × n$ periods. For example, 8 percent compounded quarterly for 7 years is equivalent to the rate found in the interest tables for $r = 8/4 = 2$ percent for $m × n = 4 × 7 = 28$ periods.

Sample Problems in Changing the Compounding Period

6 What is the future value five years hence of $600 invested at 8 percent compounded quarterly?

Eight percent compounded four times per year for 5 years is equivalent to 2 percent per period compounded for 20 periods. Table 1 shows the value of $F_{20} = (1.02)^{20}$ to be 1.48595. Six hundred dollars, then, would grow to $600 × 1.48595 = $891.57.

7 How much money must be invested today at 6 percent compounded semiannually in order to have $1,000 four years from today?

Six percent compounded two times a year for 4 years is equivalent to 3 percent per period compounded for 8 periods. The *present* value, Table 2, of $1 received 8 periods

---

[2] See, for example, Sidney Davidson and Roman L. Weil (eds.), *Handbook of Modern Accounting,* 2nd ed. (New York: McGraw-Hill Book Company, 1977), chap. 8, Exhibit 1.

hence at 3 percent per period is $.78941, so that to have $1,000 in 4 years, $1,000 × .78941 = $789.41 must be invested today.

8 If prices increased at the rate of 6 percent during each of two consecutive six-month periods, how much did prices increase during the entire year?

If a price index is 100.00 at the start of the year, it will be $100.00 × (1.06)^2 = 112.36$ at the end of the year. The price change for the entire year is $(112.36/100.00) - 1 = 12.36$ percent.

ANNUITIES

An *annuity* is a series of equal payments made at the beginning or end of equal periods of time. Examples of annuities include monthly rental payments, semiannual corporate bond coupon (or interest) payments, and annual payments to a retired employee under a pension plan. Armed with an understanding of the tables for future and present values, you can solve any annuity problem. Annuities arise so often, however, and their solution is so tedious without special tables that annuity problems warrant special study and the use of special tables.

Terminology

The terminology used for annuities can be confusing because not all writers use the same terms. Definitions of the terms used in this text follow.

An annuity whose payments occur at the *end* of each period is called an *ordinary annuity* or an *annuity in arrears*. Corporate bond coupon payments are usually paid in arrears, or, equivalently, the first payment does not occur until after the bond has been outstanding for six months.

An annuity whose payments occur at the *beginning* of each period is called an *annuity due* or an *annuity in advance*. Rent is usually paid in advance, so that a series of rental payments is an annuity due.

A *deferred* annuity is one whose first payment is at some time later than the end of the first period.

Annuities can be paid forever. Such annuities are called *perpetuities*. Bonds that promise payments forever are called *consols*. The British and Canadian governments have, from time to time, issued consols. A perpetuity can be in arrears or in advance. The only difference between the two is the timing of the first payment.

Annuities can be confusing. Their study is made easier with a *time line* such as the one shown below.

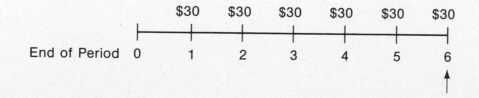

A time line marks the end of each period, numbers the periods, shows the payments to be received or paid, and shows the time at which the annuity is valued. The time line just pictured represents an ordinary annuity (in arrears) for six periods of $30 to be valued at the end of period 6. The end of period 0 is "now." The first payment is to be received one period from now.

Annuities in Arrears (Ordinary Annuities)

The future values of ordinary annuities are shown in the back of the book in Table 3, portions of which are reproduced in Table A.3.

TABLE A.3 (Excerpt from Table 3)
Future Value of an Ordinary Annuity of $1 per Period at 6 Percent and 8 Percent

$$F_A = \frac{[(1 + r)^n - 1]}{r}$$

Number of Periods = n	Rate = r	
	6%	**8%**
1	1.00000	1.00000
2	2.06000	2.08000
3	3.18360	3.24640
5	5.63709	5.86660
10	13.18079	14.48656
20	36.78559	45.76196

Consider an ordinary annuity for three periods at 6 percent. The time line for the future value of such an annuity is

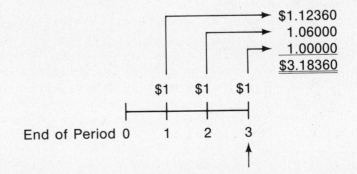

The $1 received at the end of the first period earns interest for two periods, so it is worth $1.12360 at the end of period 3. (See Table A.1.) The $1 received at the end of the second period grows to $1.06 by the end of period 3, and the $1 received at the end of period 3 is, of course, worth $1 at the end of period 3. The entire annuity is worth

$3.18360 at the end of period 3. This is the amount shown in Table A.3 for the future value of an ordinary annuity for three periods at 6 percent. The mathematical expression for the future value, F_A, of an annuity of A per period compounded at r percent per period for n periods is

$$F_A = \frac{A[(1 + r)^n - 1]}{r}$$

The present values of ordinary annuities are shown on page 487, in Table 4, portions of which are reproduced in Table A.4.

TABLE A.4 (Excerpt from Table 4)
Present Value of an Ordinary Annuity of $1 per Period at 6 Percent and 8 Percent

$$P_A = \frac{[1 - (1 + r)^{-n}]}{r}$$

Number of Periods = n	Rate = r	
	6%	8%
1	.94340	.92593
2	1.83339	1.78326
3	2.67301	2.57710
5	4.21236	3.99271
10	7.36009	6.71008
20	11.46992	9.81815

The time line for the present value of an ordinary annuity of $1 per period for three periods, discounted at 6 percent, is

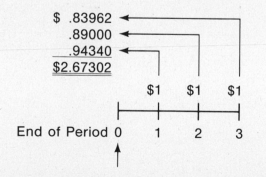

The $1 to be received at the end of period 1 has a present value of $.94340, the $1 to be received at the end of period 2 has a present value of $.89000, and the dollar to

be received at the end of the third period has a present value of $.83962. Each of these numbers comes from Table A.2. The present value of the annuity is the sum of these individual present values, $2.67302, shown in Table A.4 as 2.67301 (our calculation differs because of roundings).

The present value of an ordinary annuity for n periods is the sum of the present values of $1 received 1 period from now plus $1 received two periods from now, . . . plus $1 received n periods from now. The mathematical expression for the present value, P_A, of an annuity of A per period, for n periods, compounded at r percent per period, is

$$P_A = \frac{A[1 - (1 + r)^{-n}]}{r}$$

Sample Problems Involving Ordinary Annuities

9 What is the present value of an annuity in arrears of $30 to be received every six months for 10 years if interest is 6 percent compounded semiannually?

Six percent compounded semiannually for 10 years is equivalent to 3 percent per period compounded for 20 periods. From Table 4, 3-percent column and 20-payment row, $1 received at the end of each period has a present value of $14.87747. So the $30 semiannual annuity has a present value of $30 × 14.87747 = $446.32.

10 What is the future value of $1 invested each year for 23 years and earning 6 percent compound interest if the first dollar is invested one year from now (an ordinary annuity for 23 periods)?

The time line is

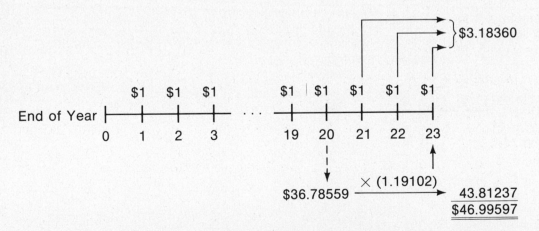

The tables do not show future values for 23 years. At the end of year 20, the annuity will have grown to $36.78559 (Table A.3). That accumulation will grow for three more years at 6 percent, so (from Table A.1 future value of $1 compounded at 6 percent for 3 periods) it will grow to $36.78559 × 1.19102 = $43.81237. In addition, as of the end of year 20, the payments from the ends of years 21, 22, and 23 are an ordinary annuity for three years with a future value of $3.18360. The entire annuity has a future value of $43.81237 + $3.18360 = $46.99597. Note that the future value of the first 20 payments is *added* to the future value of the last three payments.

11 What is the present value of an ordinary annuity of $1 per year for 23 years at 6 percent?

The time line for this problem is

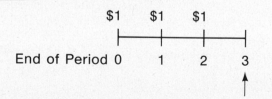

The first 20 payments have a present value of $11.46992 shown in Table A.4. As of the end of year 20, the final three payments have a present value of $2.67301. One dollar received in 20 years is worth $.31180 at the start of year zero (Table 2), so $2.67301 is worth $2.67301 × .31180 = $.83344 at the start of year zero. The entire annuity is worth $11.46992 + $.83344 = $12.30336.

Annuities in Advance (Annuities Due)

The time line for the future value of a three-period annuity in advance is

Notice that the future value is defined for the *end* of the period at the start of which the last payment is made. When tables of ordinary annuities are available, tables for annuities due are unnecessary.

Compare the time line for the future value of an annuity in advance for three periods *with the time axis relabeled to show start of period* and the time line for the future value of an ordinary annuity (in arrears) for four periods.

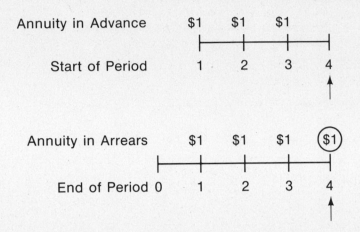

A $1 annuity in advance for *n* periods has a future value equal to the future value of a $1 annuity in arrears for *n* + 1 periods *minus* $1. The $1 circled in the time line for the annuity in arrears is the $1 that must be subtracted to calculate the future value of an annuity in advance. The "note" at the foot of Table 3 states: "To convert from this table to values of an annuity in advance, determine the annuity in arrears above for one more period and subtract 1.00000."

The time line for the present value of an annuity in advance for three periods is

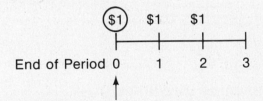

Notice that except for the first, circled payment it looks just like the present value of an ordinary annuity for two periods. A $1 annuity in advance for *n* periods has a present value equal to the present value of a $1 annuity in arrears for *n* − 1 periods *plus* $1. The "note" at the foot of Table 4 states: "To convert from this table to values of an annuity in advance, determine the annuity in arrears above for one less period and add 1.00000."

Sample Problems Involving Annuities Due

12 What is the present value of rents of $350 to be paid monthly, in advance, for one year when the discount rate is 1 percent per month?

The present value of $1 per period *in arrears* for 11 periods at 1 percent per period is $10.36763; the present value of $1 per period in advance for 12 periods is $10.36763 + $1.00 = $11.36763, and the present value of this year's rent is $350 × 11.36763 = $3,978.67.

13 Mr. Mason is 62 years old today. He wishes to invest an amount today and equal amounts on his sixty-third, sixty-fourth, and sixty-fifth birthdays so that starting on his sixty-sixth birthday he can withdraw $5,000 on each birthday for 11 years. His investments will earn 8 percent per year. How much should be invested on the sixty-second through sixty-fifth birthdays?

The time line for this problem is

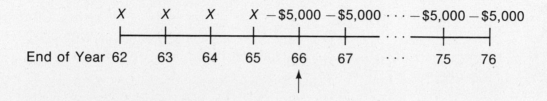

For each $1 that Mr. Mason invests on his sixty-second, sixty-third, sixty-fourth, and sixty-fifth birthdays, he will have $4.86660 = $5.86660 − $1 (see Table 3 for 5 periods at 8 percent) on his sixty-sixth birthday. On his sixty-sixth birthday Mr. Mason needs to have accumulated an amount large enough to fund an 11-year, $5,000 annuity in advance. An 11-year, $1 annuity in advance has a present value of $7.71008 = $6.71008 + $1 (Table 4, 10 periods, 8 percent). Mr. Mason then needs on his sixty-sixth birthday an accumulation of $5,000 × 7.71008 = $38,550.40. Because each $1 deposited on the sixty-second through sixty-fifth birthdays grows to $4.86660, Mr. Mason must deposit $38,550.40/4.86660 = $7,921.42 on each of the sixty-second through sixty-fifth birthdays to accumulate $38,550.40.

Deferred Annuities

When the first payment of an annuity occurs some time after the end of the first period, the annuity is *deferred*. The time line for an ordinary annuity of $1 per period for four periods deferred for two periods is

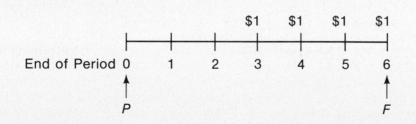

The arrow marked *"P"* shows the time for which the present value is calculated; the arrow marked *"F"* shows when the future value is calculated. The *future* value is not

affected by the deferral and equals the future value of an ordinary annuity for four periods.

Notice that the time line for the present value looks like one for an ordinary annuity for six periods *minus* an ordinary annuity for two periods:

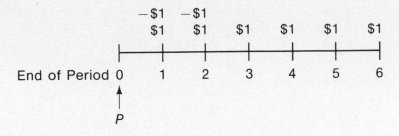

Calculate the present value of an annuity of n payments deferred for d periods by subtracting the present value of an annuity for d periods from the present value of an annuity for $n + d$ periods.

An Example of a Deferred Annuity

14 What is the present value at the sixty-second birthday of Mr. Mason's *withdrawals?* Recall that Mr. Mason is 62 years old, and will receive $5,000 on his sixty-sixth through seventy-sixth birthdays, and his investment earns 8 percent.

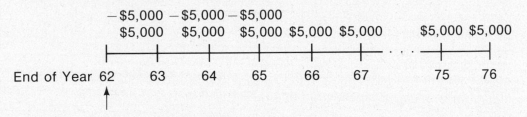

The present value at 8 percent of $5,000 received for 14 years, starting one year hence, is $5,000 × 8.24424 = $41,221 (Table 4, 14 periods, 8 percent). The present value at age 62 of the $5,000 he will *not* receive on birthdays 63 through 65 is − $5,000 × 2.57710 = − $12,885. The present value of the actual payments to Mr. Mason is $41,221 − $12,885 = $28,336.

Perpetuities

A periodic payment to be received forever is called a *perpetuity*. Future values of perpetuities are undefined. If $1 is to be received at the end of every period and the discount rate is r percent, then the present value of the perpetuity is $1/r$. This expression can be derived with algebra or by observing what happens in the expression for the present value of an ordinary annuity of A per payment as n, the number of payments, approaches infinity:

$$P_A = \frac{A[1 - (1 + r)^{-n}]}{r}$$

As n approaches infinity $(1 + r)^{-n}$ approaches zero, so that P_A approaches $A(1/r)$. If the first payment of the perpetuity occurs now, the present value is $A[1 + 1/r]$.

Examples of Perpetuities

15 The Canadian government offers to pay $30 every six months forever. What is that promise worth if the discount rate is 8 percent compounded semiannually?

Eight percent compounded semiannually is equivalent to 4 percent per six-month period. If the first payment occurs six months from now, the present value is $30/.04 = $750. If the first payment occurs today, the present value is $30 + $750 = $780.

16 Every two years, Ms. Lane gives $6,000 to the University to provide a scholarship for an entering student in a two-year business administration course. If the University earns 6 percent per year on its investments, how much must Ms. Lane give to the University to provide such a scholarship every two years forever, starting two years hence?

A perpetuity in arrears assumes one payment at the end of each period. Here, the period is two years; 6 percent compounded once a year over two years is equivalent to a rate of $(1.06)^2 - 1 = .1236$ or 12.36 percent compounded once per two-year period. Consequently, the present value of the perpetuity paid in arrears every two years is $6,000/.1236 = $48,544. A gift of $48,544 will be sufficient to provide a $6,000 scholarship forever. A gift of $54,544 is required if the first scholarship is to be awarded now.

Combinations of Cash Flows

Financial instruments may combine annuities and single payments. Bonds typically pay a specified sum every six months and a single, lump-sum payment along with the final periodic payment. Here is a simple example: the U.S. government promises to pay $30 every six months for 10 years, the first payment to occur six months from now, and an additional $1,000 ten years from now. If payments are discounted at 6 percent, compounded semiannually, then the $1,000 single payment has a present value of $1,000 × .55368 = $553.68 (Table 2, 20 periods, 3 percent) and the present value of the annuity is $30 × 14.87747 = $446.32 (Table 4, 20 periods, 3 percent). The sum of the two components is $1,000. (This is a $1,000 par-value, 10-year bond with 6-percent semiannual coupons issued at par to yield 6 percent compounded semiannually.)

Life-Contingent Annuities

The annuities discussed above all last for a certain or specified number of payments. Such annuities are sometimes called *certain annuities* to distinguish them from *contingent annuities,* for which the number of payments depends on an event to occur at an uncertain date. For example, businesses often want to know the cost of an annuity (pension) that will be paid only so long as the annuitant (retired employee) lives. Such annuities are called *life-contingent* or *life annuities.* Some texts show an incorrect calculation for the cost of a life annuity. The details of life-annuity calculations are beyond the scope of this text, but an unrealistic, hypothetical example is shown below so that our readers will be properly warned about the subtleties of life annuities.

Mr. Caplan is 65 years old today, and he has an unusual disease. He will die either $1\frac{1}{2}$ years from today or $10\frac{1}{2}$ years from today. Mr. Caplan has no family, and his employer wishes to purchase an ordinary life annuity for Mr. Caplan that will pay him $10,000 on his sixty-sixth birthday and $10,000 on every birthday thereafter on which Mr. Caplan is still alive. Funds invested in the annuity will earn 10 percent per year. How much should Mr. Caplan's life annuity cost?

The Wrong Calculation Mr. Caplan's life expectancy is 6 years: one-half chance of his living $1\frac{1}{2}$ years plus one-half chance of his living $10\frac{1}{2}$ years. The employer expects that six payments will be made to Mr. Caplan. The present value of an ordinary annuity of $1 for 6 years at 10 percent is $4.35526 (Table 4). Therefore the annuity will cost $43,553.

The Right Calculation Mr. Caplan will receive one payment for certain. The present value of that payment of $10,000 at 10 percent is $9,091 (Table 2). Mr. Caplan will receive nine further payments if he survives the critical second year. Those nine payments have present value $52,355, which is equal to the present value of a nine-year ordinary annuity that is deferred for one year, $61,446 − $9,091 (Table 4). The probability is one-half that Mr. Caplan will survive to receive those nine payments. Thus, their *expected* present value is $26,178 (= .5 × $52,355), and the *expected* present value of the entire life annuity is $9,091 + $26,178 = $35,269.

Mr. Caplan's life annuity, correctly calculated, costs only 81 percent as much as is found by the incorrect calculation. Actuaries for insurance companies use mortality tables to estimate probabilities of an annuitant's receiving each payment and, from those data, calculate the expected cost of a life annuity. Different mortality tables are used for men and women because of the well-documented difference in life expectancies.

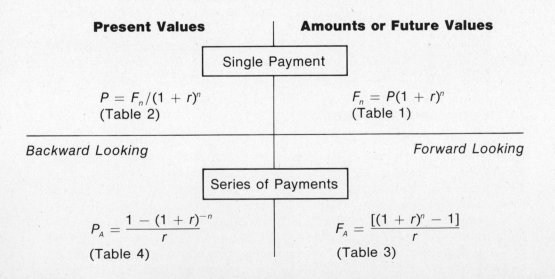

Present Values | **Amounts or Future Values**

Single Payment

$$P = F_n/(1 + r)^n$$
(Table 2)

$$F_n = P(1 + r)^n$$
(Table 1)

Backward Looking   *Forward Looking*

Series of Payments

$$P_A = \frac{1 - (1 + r)^{-n}}{r}$$
(Table 4)

$$F_A = \frac{[(1 + r)^n - 1]}{r}$$
(Table 3)

SUMMARY

Accountants typically use one of four kinds of compound interest calculations: the present or future value of a single payment or of a series of payments. These four calculations are pictured in the following diagram.[3]

The table numbers shown correspond to the table numbers on pages 484–487, which give the appropriate factors. As is apparent from a study of the formulas, all the compound interest factors in Tables 2, 3, and 4 can be derived from numbers in Table 1. Nevertheless, the other tables are given because the calculations are done relatively often and having all the tables makes for fewer odious calculations.

In working annuity problems, you will find drawing a time line helpful in deciding which particular kind of annuity is involved. The following time lines summarize the various kinds of annuities that accountants must understand. In each case, except for the perpetuity, an annuity for four periods is illustrated.

FIGURE A.1
Summary of Compound Interest Calculations

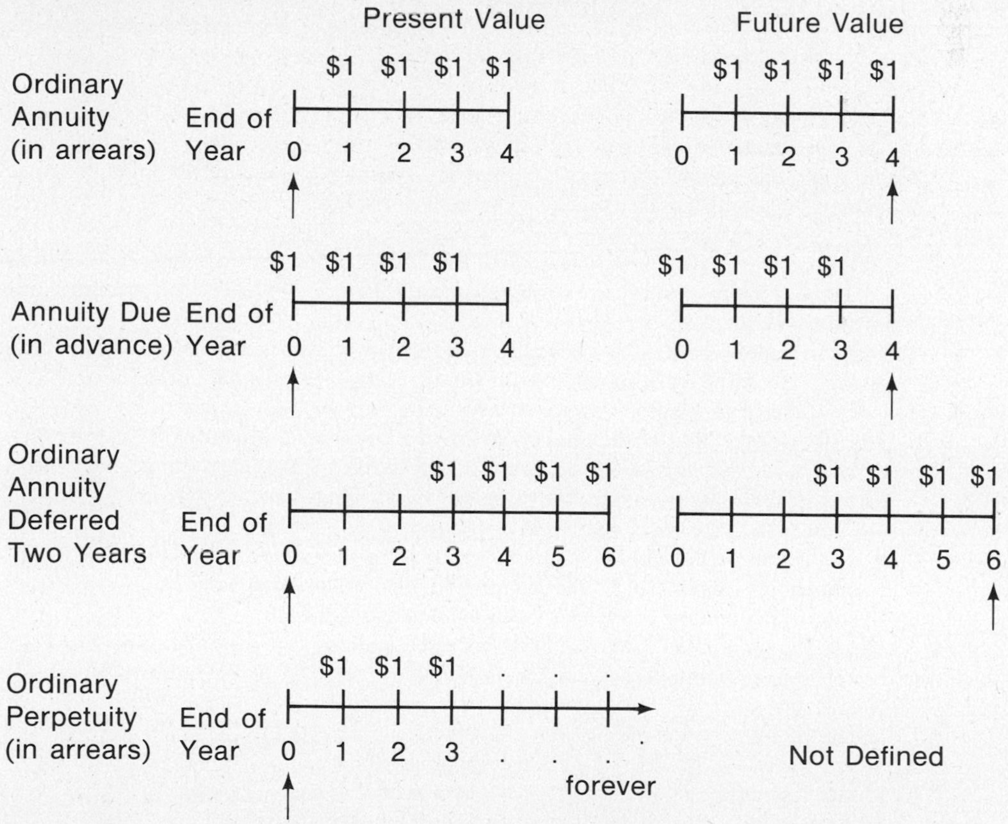

[3]   David O. Green of the University of Chicago was, to our knowledge, the first to present this diagram.

QUESTIONS AND PROBLEMS

1 Review the following concepts or terms discussed in this appendix.
  a Compound interest.
  b Principal.
  c Simple interest.
  d Future value.
  e Present value.
  f Discounted value.
  g Discount factor.
  h Discount rate.
  i Rule of 72 and Rule of 69.
  j Ordinary annuity (annuity in arrears).
  k Annuity in advance (annuity due).
  l Contingent annuity.
  m Perpetuity.
  n Deferred annuity.

2 Does the present value of a given amount to be paid in 10 years increase or decrease if the interest rate increases? Suppose that the amount were due in 5 years? 20 years? Does the present value of an annuity to be paid for 10 years increase or decrease if the discount rate decreases? Suppose that the annuity were for 5 years? 20 years?

3 Rather than pay you $100 a month for the next 20 years, the person who injured you in an automobile accident is willing to pay a single amount now to settle your claim for injuries. Would you rather an interest rate of 6 percent or 12 percent be used in computing the present value of the lump sum settlement? Comment or explain.

4 The terms of sale "2/10, net/30" mean that a discount of 2 percent from gross invoice price can be taken if the invoice is paid within 10 days and that otherwise the full amount is due within 30 days.
  a Write an expression for the implied annual rate of interest being offered, if the entire discount is viewed as being interest for funds received sooner rather than later. (Note that 98 percent of the gross invoice price is being borrowed for 20 days.)
  b The tables at the back of the book do not permit the exact evaluation of the expression derived in **a.** The rate of interest implied is 44.59 percent per year. Use the tables to convince yourself that this astounding (to some) answer must be close to correct.

5 State the rate per period and the number of periods, in each of the following:
  a 12 percent per annum, for 5 years, compounded annually.
  b 12 percent per annum, for 5 years, compounded semiannually.
  c 12 percent per annum, for 5 years, compounded quarterly.
  d 12 percent per annum, for 5 years, compounded monthly.

6 Compute the future value of:
  a $100 invested for 5 years at 4 percent compounded annually.
  b $500 invested for 15 periods at 2 percent compounded once per period.
  c $200 invested for 8 years at 3 percent compounded semiannually.
  d $2,500 invested for 14 years at 8 percent compounded quarterly.
  e $600 invested for 3 years at 12 percent compounded monthly.

7 Compute the present value of:
  a $100 due in 33 years at 4 percent compounded annually.
  b $50 due in 27 years at 6 percent compounded semiannually.
  c $250 due in 8 years at 8 percent compounded quarterly.
  d $1,000 due in 2 years at 12 percent compounded monthly.

8 Compute the amount (future value) of an ordinary annuity (an annuity in arrears) of:
  a 13 rents of $100 at $1\frac{1}{2}$ percent per period.
  b 8 rents of $850 at 6 percent per period.
  c 27 rents of $375 at 4 percent per period.
  d 35 rents of $1,400 at 3 percent per period.

9 What is the amount (future value) of an annuity due (in advance) of:
  a 13 rents of $200 each at 6 percent per period.
  b 9 rents of $75 each at 4 percent per period.
  c 24 rents of $100 each at 2 percent per period.

10 Compute the present value of an ordinary annuity (an annuity in arrears) of:
  a $1,000 for 29 years at 4 percent per year.
  b $1,500 for 31 years at 6 percent per year.
  c $400 for 41 years at 8 percent per year.
  d $750 for 75 years at 10 percent per year.

11 What is the present value of an annuity due (in advance) of:
  a 28 rents of $50 at 12 percent per period.
  b 32 rents of $45 at 10 percent per period.

12 Mr. Adams has $500 to invest. He wishes to know how much it will amount to if he invests it at:
  a 6 percent per year for 21 years.
  b 8 percent per year for 33 years.

13 Ms. Black wishes to have $15,000 at the end of 8 years. How much must she invest today to accomplish this purpose if the interest rate is
  a 6 percent per year.
  b 8 percent per year.

14 Mr. Case plans to set aside $4,000 each year, the first payment to be made on January 1, 1973, and the last on January 1, 1983. How much will he have accumulated by January 1, 1983, if the interest rate is
  a 6 percent per year.
  b 8 percent per year.

15 Ms. David wants to have $450,000 on her sixty-fifth birthday. She asks you to tell her how much she must deposit on each birthday from her fifty-eighth to sixty-fifth, inclusive, in order to receive this amount. Assume an interest rate of:
  a 4 percent per year.
  b 6 percent per year.

16 If Mr. Edwards invests $900 on June 1 of each year from 1978 to 1988, inclusive, how much will he have accumulated on June 1, 1989 (note that one year elapses after last payment) if the interest rate is

a 5 percent per year?

b 10 percent per year?

17 How much must Ms. Frank invest on July 1 of each of the years 1978 to 1985, inclusive, to have $300,000 on July 1, 1986? Assume an interest rate of:

a 8 percent per year.

b 10 percent per year.

18 Mr. Grady has $145,000 with which he purchases an annuity on February 1, 1978. The annuity consists of six annual payments, the first to be made on February 1, 1979. How much will he receive in each payment? Assume an interest rate of:

a 4 percent per year.

b 6 percent per year.

19 Ms. Howe wishes to provide her two sons with an income of $7,500 each for five years. How much must she invest on January 1, 1978, to provide for five such payments, the first to be made on January 1, 1981? Assume interest rates of:

a 6 percent per year.

b 10 percent per year.

20 Mr. Irons borrowed money from a friend, and he agreed to repay $8,000 on March 1, 1978. On that date he was unable to pay his friend, so he made the following arrangement with the Regional Loan Company: the loan company paid the friend the $8,000 on March 1, 1978, and Mr. Irons agreed to repay the loan in a series of five equal annual payments. Assume an interest rate of 8 percent per year. How much must Mr. Irons pay each year if he makes the first payment on March 1,

a 1978?

b 1979?

c 1980?

21 Ms. Jones bought a car for $4,500, and agreed to pay for it in 12 equal monthly installments with interest at 12 percent per year, the first payment to be made immediately. What is the monthly payment?

22 Mr. Karls agrees to lease a certain property for 10 years at the following annual rentals, payable in advance:

Years 1 and 2—$1,000 per year.

Years 3 to 6—$2,000 per year.

Years 7 to 10—$2,500 per year.

What single immediate sum will pay all of these rents if they are discounted at:

a 6 percent per year?

b 8 percent per year?

c 10 percent per year?

23 In order to establish a fund that will provide a scholarship of $3,000 a year indefinitely, with the first award to occur now, how much must be deposited if the fund earns:

a 6 percent per period?

b 8 percent per period?

24 Consider the scholarship fund in Problem **23**. Suppose that the first scholarship is not to be awarded until one year from now. How much should be deposited if the fund earns:
a 6 percent per period.
b 8 percent per period.
Suppose that the first scholarship is not to be awarded until five years from now. How much should be deposited if the fund earns:
c 6 percent per year?
d 8 percent per year?

25 The state helps a rural county maintain a bridge and has agreed to pay $6,000 now and every two years thereafter forever toward the expenses. The state wishes to discharge its obligation by paying a single sum to the county now in lieu of the payment due and all future payments. How much should the state pay the county if the discount rate is
a 4 percent per year?
b 6 percent per year?

26 Mr. and Mrs. Clark want to establish a fund that will pay a $25,000 prize to an outstanding academic accountant. The first prize is to be awarded 5 years from now, and the prize is to be awarded every 10 years thereafter. How much should be deposited if the fund earns:
a 8 percent per year?
b 10 percent per year?

27 An oil-drilling company figures that $300 must be spent for an initial supply of drill bits and that $100 must be spent every month to replace the worn-out bits. What is the present value of the cost of the bits if the company plans to be in business indefinitely and discounts payments at 1 percent per month?

28 If you promise to leave $25,000 on deposit at the Quarter Savings Bank for four years, the bank will give you a new car and your $25,000 back at the end of four years. How much are you, in effect, paying today for the car if the bank pays 8 percent interest compounded quarterly (2 percent paid four times per year)?

29 When Mr. Shafer died, his estate after taxes amounted to $300,000. His will provided that Widow Shafer would receive $24,000 per year starting immediately from the principal of the estate and that the balance of the principal would pass to the Shafer's son on Widow Shafer's death. The state law governing this estate provided for a *dower* option. If Widow Shafer elects the dower option, she renounces the will and can have one-third of the estate in cash now. The remainder will then immediately pass to their son. Widow Shafer wants to maximize the present value of her bequest. Should she take the annuity or elect the dower option if she will receive five payments and discounts payments at:
a 8 percent per year?
b 12 percent per year?

30 Mrs. Heileman occasionally drinks beer. She consumes one case in 20 weeks. She can buy beer in disposable bottles for $6.60 per case or for $6.00 a case of returnable bottles if a $1.50 refundable deposit is paid at the time of purchase. If her discount rate is $\frac{1}{4}$ percent per week, how much in present value dollars does she save by buying the returnables and thereby losing the use of the $1.50 deposit for 20 weeks?

31 When the General Electric Company first introduced the Lucalox ceramic, screw-in light bulb, the bulb cost $3\frac{1}{2}$ times as much as an ordinary bulb but lasted 5 times as long. An ordinary bulb cost $.50 and lasted about 8 months. If a firm has a discount rate of 12 percent compounded three times a year, how much would it save in present value dollars by using one Lucalox bulb?

32 The Roberts Dairy Company switched from delivery trucks with regular gasoline engines to ones with diesel engines. The diesel trucks cost $2,000 more than the ordinary gasoline trucks, but $600 per year less to operate. Assume that the operating costs are saved at the end of each month. If Roberts Dairy uses a discount rate of 1 percent per month, approximately how many months, at a minimum, must the diesel trucks remain in service for the switch to save money?

33 In the mid-1950s, International Business Machines Corporation (IBM) entered into a consent judgment with the U.S. Justice Department by agreeing to offer its business machines for sale. Prior to that time IBM would only rent its machines.
a Assume that the type 402 accounting machine had been renting for $5,220 per year, paid in advance, and the selling price of $27,950 was set so that it was equal to the present value of seven rental payments. What annual discount rate did IBM use in determining the selling price?
b If a type 82 card sorter had been rented for $55 a month, paid in advance, and the purchase price had been set at $3,400, what number of rental payments is equivalent to the purchase price? Assume that the rental payments were discounted at $\frac{1}{2}$ percent per month.
c If a type 24 keypunch machine had been rented for $40 per month, paid in advance, and if IBM wanted to set a purchase price so that the price would be equal to the discounted present value of 48 months' rent discounted at $\frac{1}{2}$ percent per month, what should the purchase price be?

34 When Warner & Swasey Company first decided to allow its customers to lease as well as buy its machine tools, it offered the following rental plans:

Under	Customer Pays This Percent of the Purchase Price as Rent in Advance	Each Year for This Many Years[a]
Plan A	36%	2
Plan B	24%	3
Plan C	18%	4

[a] Lease payments due for 7 years in total; see text.

In addition, lease payments were due for a total of seven years in amounts such that the total lease payments were equal to 114 percent of the purchase price. Assume that the payments required for each of the remaining years were constant under a given plan. For example, under plan C, rents for each of the last three years would be 14 [= (114 − 4 × 18)/3] percent per year.

Should a customer buy outright or lease under one of the plans? If leasing is preferred, which plan should be elected? Assume that the machine tool costs $1,000 if purchased and that there is a discount rate of:
a 5 percent per year.
b 10 percent per year.
c 12 percent per year.
Certain preferred customers who decide to rent under Plan C are also given a purchase option. At the end of the second, third, and fourth years, such customers can purchase the

machine for 105 percent of the original purchase price plus 5 percent for each year during which the machine was rented, less the sum of the lease payments already made. That is, for example, at the end of year 3, the price would be 1.20 times the original price less three years of payments.

Assume that the machine tool costs $1,000 if purchased. What strategy has the lowest present value of cost for a preferred customer? Assume a discount rate of:

d 5 percent per year.
e 10 percent per year.
f 12 percent per year.

35 (This problem is the basis of the major illustration of Chapter Seven.) The Garden Winery Company invests $10,000 at the end of year 0 so that it may receive the following stream of payments (initial investment also shown):

End of Year	Cash Payment
0	−$10,000
1	4,000
2	3,400
3	3,100
4	2,800

What is the present value at the end of year zero of that stream of payments if the discount rate is:

a 0 percent per year?
b 2 percent per year?
c 6 percent per year?
d 10 percent per year?
e 14 percent per year?
f Construct a graph that shows the discount rate on the horizontal axis and the net present value for the Garden Winery payment on the vertical axis. Plot the points derived in **a–e.**
g Is the line connecting the plotted points a straight line?

36 On January 1, 19X0, Outergarments, Inc., opened a new textile plant for the production of synthetic fabrics. The plant is on leased land; 20 years remain on the nonrenewable lease.

The cost of the plant was $2 million. Net cash flow to be derived from the project is estimated to be $300,000 per year. The company does not normally invest in such projects unless the anticipated yield is at least 12 percent.

On December 31, 19X0, the company finds cash flows from the plant to be $280,000 for the year. On the same day, farm experts predict cotton production to be unusually low for the next two years. Outergarments estimates the resulting increase in demand for synthetic fabrics to boost cash flows to $350,000 for each of the next two years. Subsequent years' estimates remain unchanged. Ignore tax considerations.

a Calculate the present value of the future expected cash flows from the plant when it was opened.
b What is the present value of the plant on January 1, 19X1, after the reestimation of future incomes?
c On January 1, 19X1, the day following the cotton production news release, Overalls Company announces plans to build a synthetic fabrics plant to be opened in three years. Outergarments, Inc., keeps its 19X1–19X3 estimates, but reduces the estimated annual

cash flows for subsequent years to $200,000. What is the value of the Outergarments' present plant on January 1, 19X1, after the new projections?

d On January 2, 19X1, an investor contacts Outergarments about purchasing a 20-percent share of the plant. If the investor expects to earn at least a 12-percent annual return on the investment, what is the maximum amount that the investor can pay? Assume that the investor and Outergarments, Inc., use the same estimates of annual cash flows.

37 A group of investors has decided to purchase a large herd of beef cattle, to sell cattle as calves are born, and to sell the entire herd after six years. They have also agreed that no investment of the syndicate should return less than 10 percent per year. They purchase the cattle on January 1, 19X0, for a price of $1,200,000, and they expect to sell the herd remaining on December 31, 19X5, for the same price. The projected net cash flows from sale of beef during the six years is $200,000 per year.

On December 31, 19X0, the syndicate finds that its cash flow from the herd is $210,000. But during December, the herd was stricken with a disease and 20 percent of the cattle died. The syndicate wants to rebuild the herd, and they decide to sell only enough beef to cover expenses until the herd grows to its original size. They anticipate that this process will result in zero cash flow for 19X1, and $200,000 for each of the remaining four years.

Ignore tax considerations in your calculations.

a Calculate the present value of the herd to the syndicate at time of purchase.

b If there had been no disease, what would have been the value of the herd on January 1, 19X1? Use only future cash flows for this and subsequent computations.

c What was the value of the herd on January 1, 19X1, after the disease and the decision to rebuild?

d What was the cost to the syndicate of the disease?

e On January 1, 19X1, an investor who has a 25-percent interest in the herd decides to sell out. What is the least amount that the investor should be willing to accept for the 25-percent share? Assume that the investor is looking at alternative investments that would yield 10 percent per year.

COMPOUND
INTEREST
AND
ANNUITY
TABLES

TABLE 1
Future Value of $1

$$F_n = P(1 + r)^n$$

r = interest rate; n = number of periods until valuation; $P = \$1$

Periods $= n$	¼%	½%	⅔%	¾%	1%	1½%	2%	3%	4%	5%	6%	7%	8%	10%	12%	20%
1	1.00250	1.00500	1.00667	1.00750	1.01000	1.01500	1.02000	1.03000	1.04000	1.05000	1.06000	1.07000	1.08000	1.10000	1.12000	1.20000
2	1.00501	1.01003	1.01338	1.01506	1.02010	1.03023	1.04040	1.06090	1.08160	1.10250	1.12360	1.14490	1.16640	1.21000	1.25440	1.44000
3	1.00752	1.01508	1.02013	1.02267	1.03030	1.04568	1.06121	1.09273	1.12486	1.15763	1.19102	1.22504	1.25971	1.33100	1.40493	1.72800
4	1.01004	1.02015	1.02693	1.03034	1.04060	1.06136	1.08243	1.12551	1.16986	1.21551	1.26248	1.31080	1.36049	1.46410	1.57352	2.07360
5	1.01256	1.02525	1.03378	1.03807	1.05101	1.07728	1.10408	1.15927	1.21665	1.27628	1.33823	1.40255	1.46933	1.61051	1.76234	2.48832
6	1.01509	1.03038	1.04067	1.04585	1.06152	1.09344	1.12616	1.19405	1.26532	1.34010	1.41852	1.50073	1.58687	1.77156	1.97382	2.98598
7	1.01763	1.03553	1.04761	1.05370	1.07214	1.10984	1.14869	1.22987	1.31593	1.40710	1.50363	1.60578	1.71382	1.94872	2.21068	3.58318
8	1.02018	1.04071	1.05459	1.06160	1.08286	1.12649	1.17166	1.26677	1.36857	1.47746	1.59385	1.71819	1.85093	2.14359	2.47596	4.29982
9	1.02273	1.04591	1.06163	1.06956	1.09369	1.14339	1.19509	1.30477	1.42331	1.55133	1.68948	1.83846	1.99900	2.35795	2.77308	5.15978
10	1.02528	1.05114	1.06870	1.07758	1.10462	1.16054	1.21899	1.34392	1.48024	1.62889	1.79085	1.96715	2.15892	2.59374	3.10585	6.19174
11	1.02785	1.05640	1.07583	1.08566	1.11567	1.17795	1.24337	1.38423	1.53945	1.71034	1.89830	2.10485	2.33164	2.85312	3.47855	7.43008
12	1.03042	1.06168	1.08300	1.09381	1.12683	1.19562	1.26824	1.42576	1.60103	1.79586	2.01220	2.25219	2.51817	3.13843	3.89598	8.91610
13	1.03299	1.06699	1.09022	1.10201	1.13809	1.21355	1.29361	1.46853	1.66507	1.88565	2.13293	2.40985	2.71962	3.45227	4.36349	10.69932
14	1.03557	1.07232	1.09749	1.11028	1.14947	1.23176	1.31948	1.51259	1.73168	1.97993	2.26090	2.57853	2.93719	3.79750	4.88711	12.83918
15	1.03816	1.07768	1.10480	1.11860	1.16097	1.25023	1.34587	1.55797	1.80094	2.07893	2.39656	2.75903	3.17217	4.17725	5.47357	15.40702
16	1.04076	1.08307	1.11217	1.12699	1.17258	1.26899	1.37279	1.60471	1.87298	2.18287	2.54035	2.95216	3.42594	4.59497	6.13039	18.48843
17	1.04336	1.08849	1.11958	1.13544	1.18430	1.28802	1.40024	1.65285	1.94790	2.29202	2.69277	3.15882	3.70002	5.05447	6.86604	22.18611
18	1.04597	1.09393	1.12705	1.14396	1.19615	1.30734	1.42825	1.70243	2.02582	2.40662	2.85434	3.37993	3.99602	5.55992	7.68997	26.62333
19	1.04858	1.09940	1.13456	1.15254	1.20811	1.32695	1.45681	1.75351	2.10685	2.52695	3.02560	3.61653	4.31570	6.11591	8.61276	31.94800
20	1.05121	1.10490	1.14213	1.16118	1.22019	1.34686	1.48595	1.80611	2.19112	2.65330	3.20714	3.86968	4.66096	6.72750	9.64629	38.33760
22	1.05647	1.11597	1.15740	1.17867	1.24472	1.38756	1.54598	1.91610	2.36992	2.92526	3.60354	4.43040	5.43654	8.14027	12.10031	55.20614
24	1.06176	1.12716	1.17289	1.19641	1.26973	1.42950	1.60844	2.03279	2.56330	3.22510	4.04893	5.07237	6.34118	9.84973	15.17863	79.49685
26	1.06707	1.13846	1.18858	1.21443	1.29526	1.47271	1.67342	2.15659	2.77247	3.55567	4.54938	5.80735	7.39635	11.91818	19.04007	114.4755
28	1.07241	1.14987	1.20448	1.23271	1.32129	1.51722	1.74102	2.28793	2.99870	3.92013	5.11169	6.64884	8.62711	14.42099	23.88387	164.8447
30	1.07778	1.16140	1.22059	1.25127	1.34785	1.56308	1.81136	2.42726	3.24340	4.32194	5.74349	7.61226	10.06266	17.44940	29.95992	237.3763
32	1.08318	1.17304	1.23692	1.27011	1.37494	1.61032	1.88454	2.57508	3.50806	4.76494	6.15339	8.71527	11.73708	21.11378	37.58173	341.8219
34	1.08860	1.18480	1.25347	1.28923	1.40258	1.65900	1.96068	2.73191	3.79432	5.25335	7.25103	9.97811	13.69013	25.54767	47.14252	492.2235
36	1.09405	1.19668	1.27024	1.30865	1.43077	1.70914	2.03989	2.89828	4.10393	5.79182	8.14725	11.42394	15.96817	30.91268	59.13557	708.8019
38	1.09953	1.20868	1.28723	1.32835	1.45953	1.76080	2.12230	3.07478	4.43881	6.38548	9.15425	13.07927	18.62528	37.40434	74.17966	1020.675
40	1.10503	1.22079	1.30445	1.34835	1.48886	1.81402	2.20804	3.26204	4.80102	7.03999	10.28572	14.97446	21.72452	45.25926	93.05097	1469.772
45	1.11892	1.25162	1.34852	1.39968	1.56481	1.95421	2.43785	3.78160	5.84118	8.98501	13.76461	21.00245	31.92045	72.89048	163.9876	3657.262
50	1.13297	1.28323	1.39407	1.45296	1.64463	2.10524	2.69159	4.38391	7.10668	11.46740	18.42015	29.45703	46.90161	117.3909	289.0022	9100.438
100	1.28362	1.64667	1.94343	2.11108	2.70481	4.43205	7.24465	19.21863	50.50495	131.5013	339.3021	867.7163	2199.761	13780.61	83522.27	828×10^5

TABLE 2
Present Value of $1

$$P = F_n(1 + r)^{-n}$$

r = discount rate; n = number of periods until payment; F_n = $1

Periods = n	¼%	½%	⅔%	¾%	1%	1½%	2%	3%	4%	5%	6%	7%	8%	10%	12%	20%
1	.99751	.99502	.99338	.99256	.99010	.98522	.98039	.97087	.96154	.95238	.94340	.93458	.92593	.90909	.89286	.83333
2	.99502	.99007	.98680	.98517	.98030	.97066	.96117	.94260	.92456	.90703	.89000	.87344	.85734	.82645	.79719	.69444
3	.99254	.98515	.98026	.97783	.97059	.95632	.94232	.91514	.88900	.86384	.83962	.81630	.79383	.75131	.71178	.57870
4	.99006	.98025	.97377	.97055	.96098	.94218	.92385	.88849	.85480	.82270	.79209	.76290	.73503	.68301	.63552	.48225
5	.98759	.97537	.96732	.96333	.95147	.92826	.90573	.86261	.82193	.78353	.74726	.71299	.68058	.62092	.56743	.40188
6	.98513	.97052	.96092	.95616	.94205	.91454	.88797	.83748	.79031	.74622	.70496	.66634	.63017	.56447	.50663	.33490
7	.98267	.96569	.95455	.94904	.93272	.90103	.87056	.81309	.75992	.71068	.66506	.62275	.58349	.51316	.45235	.27908
8	.98022	.96089	.94823	.94198	.92348	.88771	.85349	.78941	.73069	.67684	.62741	.58201	.54027	.46651	.40388	.23257
9	.97778	.95610	.94195	.93496	.91434	.87459	.83676	.76642	.70259	.64461	.59190	.54393	.50025	.42410	.36061	.19381
10	.97534	.95135	.93571	.92800	.90529	.86167	.82035	.74409	.67556	.61391	.55839	.50835	.46319	.38554	.32197	.16151
11	.97291	.94661	.92952	.92109	.89632	.84893	.80426	.72242	.64958	.58468	.52679	.47509	.42888	.35049	.28748	.13459
12	.97048	.94191	.92336	.91424	.88745	.83639	.78849	.70138	.62460	.55684	.49697	.44401	.39711	.31863	.25668	.11216
13	.96806	.93722	.91725	.90743	.87866	.82403	.77303	.68095	.60057	.53032	.46884	.41496	.36770	.28966	.22917	.09346
14	.96565	.93256	.91117	.90068	.86996	.81185	.75788	.66112	.57748	.50507	.44230	.38782	.34046	.26333	.20462	.07789
15	.96324	.92792	.90514	.89397	.86135	.79985	.74301	.64186	.55526	.48102	.41727	.36245	.31524	.23939	.18270	.06491
16	.96084	.92330	.89914	.88732	.85282	.78803	.72845	.62317	.53391	.45811	.39365	.33873	.29189	.21763	.16312	.05409
17	.95844	.91871	.89319	.88071	.84438	.77639	.71416	.60502	.51337	.43630	.37136	.31657	.27027	.19784	.14564	.04507
18	.95605	.91414	.88727	.87416	.83602	.76491	.70016	.58739	.49363	.41552	.35034	.29586	.25025	.17986	.13004	.03756
19	.95367	.90959	.88140	.86765	.82774	.75361	.68643	.57029	.47464	.39573	.33051	.27651	.23171	.16351	.11611	.03130
20	.95129	.90506	.87556	.86119	.81954	.74247	.67297	.55368	.45639	.37689	.31180	.25842	.21455	.14864	.10367	.02608
22	.94655	.89608	.86400	.84842	.80340	.72069	.64684	.52189	.42196	.34185	.27751	.22571	.18394	.12285	.08264	.01811
24	.94184	.88719	.85260	.83583	.78757	.69954	.62172	.49193	.39012	.31007	.24698	.19715	.15770	.10153	.06588	.01258
26	.93714	.87838	.84134	.82343	.77205	.67902	.59758	.46369	.36069	.28124	.21981	.17220	.13520	.08391	.05252	.00874
28	.93248	.86966	.83023	.81122	.75684	.65910	.57437	.43708	.33348	.25509	.19563	.15040	.11591	.06934	.04187	.00607
30	.92783	.86103	.81927	.79919	.74192	.63976	.55207	.41199	.30832	.23138	.17411	.13137	.09938	.05731	.03338	.00421
32	.92321	.85248	.80846	.78733	.72730	.62099	.53063	.38834	.28506	.20987	.15496	.11474	.08520	.04736	.02661	.00293
34	.91861	.84402	.79779	.77565	.71297	.60277	.51003	.36604	.26355	.19035	.13791	.10022	.07305	.03914	.02121	.00203
36	.91403	.83564	.78725	.76415	.69892	.58509	.49022	.34503	.24367	.17266	.12274	.08754	.06262	.03235	.01691	.00141
38	.90948	.82735	.77686	.75281	.68515	.56792	.47119	.32523	.22529	.15661	.10924	.07646	.05369	.02673	.01348	.00098
40	.90495	.81914	.76661	.74165	.67165	.55126	.45289	.30656	.20829	.14205	.09722	.06678	.04603	.02209	.01075	.00068
45	.89372	.79896	.74156	.71445	.63905	.51171	.41020	.26444	.17120	.11130	.07265	.04761	.03133	.01372	.00610	.00027
50	.88263	.77929	.71732	.68825	.60804	.47500	.37153	.22811	.14071	.08720	.05429	.03395	.02132	.00852	.00346	.00011
100	.77904	.60729	.51455	.47369	.36971	.22563	.13803	.05203	.01980	.00760	.00295	.00115	.00045	.00007	.00001	.00000

TABLE 3
Future Value of Annuity of $1 in Arrears

$$F_A = \frac{(1+r)^n - 1}{r}$$

r = interest rate; n = number of payments

No. of Payments = n	¼%	½%	⅔%	¾%	1%	1½%	2%	3%	4%	5%	6%	7%	8%	10%	12%	20%
1	1.00000	1.00000	1.00000	1.00000	1.00000	1.00000	1.00000	1.00000	1.00000	1.00000	1.00000	1.00000	1.00000	1.00000	1.00000	1.00000
2	2.00250	2.00500	2.00667	2.00750	2.01000	2.01500	2.02000	2.03000	2.04000	2.05000	2.06000	2.07000	2.08000	2.10000	2.12000	2.20000
3	3.00751	3.01503	3.02004	3.02256	3.03010	3.04523	3.06040	3.09090	3.12160	3.15250	3.18360	3.21490	3.24640	3.31000	3.37440	3.64000
4	4.01503	4.03010	4.04018	4.04523	4.06040	4.09090	4.12161	4.18363	4.24646	4.31013	4.37462	4.43994	4.50611	4.64100	4.77933	5.36800
5	5.02506	5.05025	5.06711	5.07556	5.10101	5.15227	5.20404	5.30914	5.41632	5.52563	5.63709	5.75074	5.86660	6.10510	6.35285	7.44160
6	6.03763	6.07550	6.10089	6.11363	6.15202	6.22955	6.30812	6.46841	6.63298	6.80191	6.97532	7.15329	7.33593	7.71561	8.11519	9.92992
7	7.05272	7.10588	7.14157	7.15948	7.21354	7.32299	7.43428	7.66246	7.89829	8.14201	8.39384	8.65402	8.92280	9.48717	10.08901	12.91590
8	8.07035	8.14141	8.18918	8.21318	8.28567	8.43284	8.58297	8.89234	9.21423	9.54911	9.89747	10.25980	10.63663	11.43589	12.29969	16.49908
9	9.09053	9.18212	9.24377	9.27478	9.36853	9.55933	9.75463	10.15911	10.58280	11.02656	11.49132	11.97799	12.48756	13.57948	14.77566	20.79890
10	10.11325	10.22803	10.30540	10.34434	10.46221	10.70272	10.94972	11.46388	12.00611	12.57789	13.18079	13.81645	14.48656	15.93742	17.54874	25.95868
11	11.13854	11.27917	11.37410	11.42192	11.56683	11.86326	12.16872	12.80780	13.48635	14.20679	14.97164	15.78360	16.64549	18.53117	20.65458	32.15042
12	12.16638	12.33556	12.44993	12.50759	12.68250	13.04121	13.41209	14.19203	15.02581	15.91713	16.86994	17.88845	18.97713	21.38428	24.13313	39.58050
13	13.19680	13.39724	13.53293	13.60139	13.80933	14.23683	14.68033	15.61779	16.62684	17.71298	18.88214	20.14064	21.49530	24.52271	28.02911	48.49660
14	14.22979	14.46423	14.62315	14.70340	14.94742	15.45038	15.97394	17.08632	18.29191	19.59863	21.01507	22.55049	24.21492	27.97498	32.39260	59.19592
15	15.26537	15.53655	15.72063	15.81368	16.09690	16.68214	17.29342	18.59891	20.02359	21.57856	23.27597	25.12902	27.15211	31.77248	37.27971	72.03511
16	16.30353	16.61423	16.82544	16.93228	17.25786	17.93237	18.63929	20.15688	21.82453	23.65749	25.67253	27.88805	30.32428	35.94973	42.75328	87.44213
17	17.34429	17.69730	17.93761	18.05927	18.43044	19.20136	20.01207	21.76159	23.69751	25.84037	28.21288	30.84022	33.75023	40.54470	48.88367	105.9306
18	18.38765	18.78579	19.05719	19.19472	19.61475	20.48938	21.41231	23.41444	25.64541	28.13238	30.90565	33.99903	37.45024	45.59917	55.74971	128.1167
19	19.43362	19.87972	20.18424	20.33868	20.81090	21.79672	22.84056	25.11687	27.67123	30.53900	33.75999	37.37896	41.44626	51.15909	63.43968	154.7400
20	20.48220	20.97912	21.31880	21.49122	22.01900	23.12367	24.29737	26.87037	29.77808	33.06595	36.78559	40.99549	45.76196	57.27500	72.05244	186.6880
22	22.58724	23.19443	23.61066	23.82230	24.47159	25.83758	27.29898	30.53678	34.24797	38.50521	43.39229	49.00574	55.45676	71.40275	92.50258	271.0307
24	24.70282	25.43196	25.93319	26.18847	26.97346	28.63352	30.42186	34.42647	39.08260	44.50200	50.81558	58.17667	66.76476	88.49733	118.1552	392.4842
26	26.82899	27.69191	28.28678	28.59027	29.52563	31.51397	33.67091	38.55304	44.31174	51.11345	59.15638	68.67647	79.95442	109.1818	150.3339	567.3773
28	28.96580	29.97452	30.67187	31.02823	32.12910	34.48148	37.05121	42.93092	49.96758	58.40258	68.52811	80.69769	95.33853	134.2099	190.6989	819.2233
30	31.11331	32.28002	33.08885	33.50290	34.78489	37.53868	40.56808	47.57542	56.08494	66.43885	79.05819	94.46079	113.2832	164.4940	241.3327	1181.881
32	33.27157	34.60862	35.53818	36.01483	37.49407	40.68829	44.22703	52.50276	62.70147	75.29883	90.88978	110.2181	134.2135	201.1378	304.8477	1704.109
34	35.44064	36.96058	38.02026	38.56458	40.25770	43.93309	48.03380	57.73018	69.85791	85.06696	104.1838	128.2588	158.6267	245.4767	384.5210	2456.118
36	37.62056	39.33610	40.53556	41.15272	43.07688	47.27597	51.99437	63.27594	77.59831	95.83632	119.1209	148.9135	187.1022	299.1268	484.4631	3539.009
38	39.81140	41.73545	43.08450	43.77982	45.95272	50.71989	56.11494	69.15945	85.97034	107.7095	135.9042	172.5610	220.3159	364.0434	609.8305	5098.373
40	42.01320	44.15885	45.66754	46.44648	48.88637	54.26789	60.40198	75.40126	95.02552	120.7998	154.7620	199.6351	259.0565	442.5926	767.0914	7343.858
45	47.56606	50.32416	52.27734	53.29011	56.48107	63.61420	71.89271	92.71986	121.0294	159.7002	212.7435	285.7493	386.5056	718.9048	1358.230	18281.31
50	53.18868	56.64516	59.11042	60.39426	64.46318	73.68283	84.57940	112.7969	152.6671	209.3480	290.3359	406.5289	573.7702	1163.909	2400.018	45497.19
100	113.44996	129.33370	141.51445	148.14451	170.4814	228.8030	312.2323	607.2877	1237.624	2610.025	5638.368	12381.66	27484.52	137796.1	696010.5	414×10⁶

Note: To convert from this table to values of an annuity in advance, determine the annuity in arrears above for one more period and subtract 1.00000.

TABLE 4
Present Value of an Annuity of $1 in Arrears

$$P_A = \frac{1-(1+r)^{-n}}{r}$$

r = discount rate; n = number of payments

No. of Payments = n	¼%	½%	⅔%	¾%	1%	1½%	2%	3%	4%	5%	6%	7%	8%	10%	12%	20%
1	0.99751	0.99502	0.99338	0.99256	.99010	.98522	.98039	.97087	.96154	.95238	.94340	.93458	.92593	.90909	.89286	.83333
2	1.99252	1.98510	1.98018	1.97772	1.97040	1.95588	1.94156	1.91347	1.88609	1.85941	1.83339	1.80802	1.78326	1.73554	1.69005	1.52778
3	2.98806	2.97025	2.96044	2.95556	2.94099	2.91220	2.88388	2.82861	2.77509	2.72325	2.67301	2.62432	2.57710	2.48685	2.40183	2.10648
4	3.97512	3.95050	3.93421	3.92611	3.90197	3.85438	3.80773	3.71710	3.62990	3.54595	3.46511	3.38721	3.31213	3.16987	3.03735	2.58873
5	4.96272	4.92587	4.90154	4.88944	4.85343	4.78264	4.71346	4.57971	4.45182	4.32948	4.21236	4.10020	3.99271	3.79079	3.60478	2.99061
6	5.94785	5.89638	5.86245	5.84560	5.79548	5.69719	5.60143	5.41719	5.24212	5.07569	4.91732	4.76654	4.62288	4.35526	4.11141	3.32551
7	6.93052	6.86207	6.81701	6.79464	6.72819	6.59821	6.47199	6.23028	6.00205	5.78637	5.58238	5.38929	5.20637	4.86842	4.56376	3.60459
8	7.91074	7.82296	7.76524	7.73661	7.65168	7.48593	7.32548	7.01969	6.73274	6.46321	6.20979	5.97130	5.74664	5.33493	4.96764	3.83716
9	8.88852	8.77906	8.70719	8.67158	8.56602	8.36052	8.16224	7.78611	7.43533	7.10782	6.80169	6.51523	6.24689	5.75902	5.32825	4.03097
10	9.86386	9.73041	9.64290	9.59958	9.47130	9.22218	8.98259	8.53020	8.11090	7.72173	7.36009	7.02358	6.71008	6.14457	5.65022	4.19247
11	10.83677	10.67703	10.57242	10.52067	10.36763	10.07112	9.78685	9.25262	8.76048	8.30641	7.88687	7.49867	7.13896	6.49506	5.93770	4.32706
12	11.80725	11.61893	11.49578	11.43491	11.25508	10.90751	10.57534	9.95400	9.38507	8.86325	8.38384	7.94269	7.53608	6.81369	6.19437	4.43922
13	12.77532	12.55615	12.41303	12.34237	12.13374	11.73153	11.34837	10.63496	9.98565	9.39357	8.85268	8.35765	7.90378	7.10336	6.42355	4.53268
14	13.74096	13.48871	13.32420	13.24302	13.00370	12.54338	12.10625	11.29607	10.56312	9.89864	9.29498	8.74547	8.24424	7.36669	6.62817	4.61057
15	14.70420	14.41662	14.22934	14.13699	13.86505	13.34323	12.84926	11.93794	11.11839	10.37966	9.71225	9.10791	8.55948	7.60608	6.81086	4.67547
16	15.66504	15.33993	15.12848	15.02431	14.71787	14.13126	13.57771	12.56110	11.65230	10.83777	10.10590	9.44665	8.85137	7.82371	6.97399	4.72956
17	16.62348	16.25863	16.02167	15.90502	15.56225	14.90765	14.29187	13.16612	12.16567	11.27407	10.47726	9.76322	9.12164	8.02155	7.11963	4.77463
18	17.57953	17.17277	16.90894	16.77918	16.39827	15.67256	14.99203	13.75351	12.65930	11.68959	10.82760	10.05909	9.37189	8.20141	7.24967	4.81219
19	18.53320	18.08236	17.79034	17.64683	17.22601	16.42617	15.67846	14.32380	13.13394	12.08532	11.15812	10.33560	9.60360	8.36492	7.36578	4.84350
20	19.48449	18.98742	18.66590	18.50802	18.04555	17.16864	16.35143	14.87747	13.59033	12.46221	11.46992	10.59401	9.81815	8.51356	7.46944	4.86958
22	21.37995	20.78406	20.39967	20.21121	19.66038	18.62082	17.65805	15.93692	14.45112	13.16300	12.04158	11.06124	10.20074	8.77154	7.64465	4.90943
24	23.26598	22.56287	22.11054	21.88915	21.24339	20.03041	18.91393	16.93554	15.24696	13.79864	12.55036	11.46933	10.52876	8.98474	7.78432	4.93710
26	25.14261	24.32402	23.79883	23.54219	22.79520	21.39863	20.12104	17.87684	15.98277	14.37519	13.00317	11.82578	10.80998	9.16095	7.89566	4.95632
28	27.00989	26.06769	25.46484	25.17071	24.31644	22.72672	21.28127	18.76411	16.66306	14.89813	13.40616	12.13711	11.05108	9.30657	7.98442	4.96967
30	28.86787	27.79405	27.10885	26.77508	25.80771	24.01584	22.39646	19.60044	17.29203	15.37245	13.76483	12.40904	11.25778	9.42691	8.05518	4.97894
32	30.71660	29.50328	28.73116	28.35565	27.26959	25.26714	23.46833	20.38877	17.87355	15.80268	14.08404	12.64656	11.43500	9.52638	8.11159	4.98537
34	32.55611	31.19555	30.33205	29.91278	28.70267	26.48173	24.49859	21.13184	18.41120	16.19290	14.36814	12.85401	11.58693	9.60857	8.15656	4.98984
36	34.38647	32.87102	31.91181	31.44681	30.10751	27.66068	25.48884	21.83225	18.90828	16.54685	14.62099	13.03521	11.71719	9.67651	8.19241	4.99295
38	36.20770	34.52985	33.47071	32.95808	31.48466	28.80505	26.44064	22.49246	19.36786	16.86789	14.84602	13.19347	11.82887	9.73265	8.22099	4.99510
40	38.01986	36.17223	35.00903	34.44694	32.83469	29.91585	27.35548	23.11477	19.79277	17.15909	15.04630	13.33171	11.92461	9.77905	8.24378	4.99660
45	42.51088	40.20720	38.76658	38.07318	36.09451	32.55234	29.49016	24.51871	20.72004	17.77407	15.45583	13.60552	12.10840	9.86281	8.28252	4.99863
50	46.94617	44.14279	42.40134	41.56645	39.19612	34.99969	31.42361	25.72976	21.48218	18.25593	15.76186	13.80075	12.23348	9.91481	8.30450	4.99945
100	88.38248	78.54264	72.81686	70.17462	63.02888	51.62470	43.09835	31.59891	24.50500	19.84791	16.61755	14.26925	12.49432	9.99927	8.33323	5.00000

Note: To convert from this table to values of an annuity in advance, determine the annuity in arrears above for one less period and add 1.00000.

GLOSSARY[1]

A

AAA. *American Accounting Association.*

abnormal spoilage. Actual spoilage exceeding that expected to occur under normal operating efficiency. Spoilage that should not occur if operations are normally efficient. Usual practice treats this cost as an *expense* of the period rather than as a *product cost.* Contrast with *normal spoilage.*

absorption costing. The generally accepted method of *costing* that assigns all types of *manufacturing costs* (direct material and labor as well as fixed and variable overhead) to units produced. Sometimes called "full costing." Contrast with *direct costing.*

accelerated depreciation. Any method of calculating *depreciation* charges where the charges become progressively smaller each period. Examples are *double-declining-balance* and *sum-of-the-years'-digits* methods.

account. Any device for accumulating additions and subtractions relating to a single *asset, liability, owners' equity* item, *revenue, expense,* and other items.

account form. The form of *balance sheet* where *assets* are shown on the left and *equities* are shown on the right. Contrast with *report form.*

account payable. A *liability* representing an amount owed to a *creditor,* usually arising from purchase of *merchandise* or materials and supplies; not necessarily due or past due. Normally, a *current* liability.

account receivable. A claim against a *debtor* usually arising from sales or services rendered; not necessarily due or past due. Normally, a *current asset.*

accountancy. The British word for *accounting.* In the United States; it means the theory and practice of accounting.

Accountants' Index. A publication of the *AICPA* that indexes, in detail, the accounting literature of the period. Issued quarterly and annually since 1974.

accountant's opinion. *Auditor's report.*

accountant's report. *Auditor's report.*

accounting. An *information system* conveying information about a specific *entity.* The information is in financial terms and is restricted to information that can be made reasonably precise. The *AICPA* defines accounting as a service activity whose "function is to provide quantitative information, primarily financial in nature, about economic entities that is intended to be useful in making economic decisions."

accounting changes. As defined by *APB Opinion* No. 20, a change in (a) an *accounting principle* (such as a switch from *FIFO* to *LIFO* or from *sum-of-the-years'-digits* to *straight-line depreciation*), (b) an accounting estimate (such as estimated useful lives or salvage value of depreciable assets and estimates of *warranty* costs or *uncollectible accounts*), and (c) the reporting *entity.* Changes of type (a) should be disclosed. The cumulative effect of the change on

---

[1] Certain terms in the definitions are *italicized.* The italicized terms, or variants of them, are themselves explained in the glossary. This glossary contains terms that are not used in the text. Explanations of such terms are included to make the glossary more useful.

retained earnings at the start of the period during which the change was made should be included in reported earnings for the period of change. Changes of type (b) should be treated as affecting only the period of change and, if necessary, future periods. The reasons for changes of type (c) should be disclosed and, in statements reporting on operations of the period of change, the effect of the change on all other periods reported on for comparative purposes should also be shown. In some cases (such as a change from *LIFO* to other inventory *flow assumptions* or in the method of accounting for long-term construction contracts), changes of type (a) are treated like changes of type (c). That is, for these changes all statements shown for prior periods must be restated to show the effect of adopting the change for those periods as well. See *all-inclusive concept.*

accounting conventions. Methods or procedures used in accounting. This term tends to be used when the method or procedure has not been given official authoritative sanction by a pronouncement of a group such as the *APB, FASB,* or *SEC.* Contrast with *accounting principles.*

accounting cycle. The sequence of accounting procedures starting with *journal entries* for various transactions and events and ending with the *financial statements* or, perhaps, the *postclosing trial balance.*

accounting entity. See *entity.*

accounting equation. *Assets = Equities. Assets = Liabilities + Owners' Equity.*

accounting errors. Arithmetic errors and misapplications of *accounting principles* in previously published financial statements that are corrected in the current period with direct *debits* or *credits* to *retained earnings.* In this regard, they are treated like *prior-period adjustments,* but, technically, they are not classified by *APB Opinion* No. 9 as prior-period adjustments. See *accounting changes* and contrast with changes in accounting estimates as described there.

accounting event. Any occurrence that is recorded as a transaction in the accounting records.

accounting methods. *Accounting principles.* Procedures for carrying out accounting principles.

accounting period. The time period for which *financial statements* that measure *flows,* such as the *income statement* and the *statement of changes in financial position,* are prepared. Should be clearly identified on the financial statements. See *interim statements.*

accounting policies. *Accounting principles* adopted by a specific *entity.* See *summary of significant accounting policies.*

accounting principles. The concepts that determine methods or procedures used in accounting for *transactions* or events reported in the *financial statements.* This term tends to be used when the method or procedure has been given official authoritative sanction by a pronouncement of a group such as the *APB, FASB,* or *SEC.* Contrast with *accounting conventions.*

Accounting Principles Board. See *APB.*

accounting procedures. See *accounting principles,* but usually this term refers to the methods required to implement accounting principles.

accounting rate of return. Income for a period divided by average investment during the period. Based on income, rather than discounted cash and, hence, is a poor decision-making aid or tool. See *ratio.*

Accounting Research Bulletin (ARB). The name of the official pronouncements of the former *Committee on Accounting Procedure* of the *AICPA.* Fifty-one bulletins were issued between 1939 and 1959. ARB No. 43 summarizes the first forty-two bulletins.

Accounting Series Release. See *SEC.*

accounting standards. *Accounting principles.*

Accounting Trends and Techniques. An annual publication of the *AICPA* that surveys the reporting practices of 600 large corporations. It presents tabulations of specific practices, terminology, and disclosures along with illustrations taken from individual annual reports.

accounts receivable turnover. *Net sales* on account for a period divided by the average balance of net accounts receivable. See *ratio.*

accretion. Increase in economic worth through physical change, usually said of a natural resource such as an orchard, caused by natural growth. Contrast with *appreciation.*

accrual. Recognition of an *expense* (or *revenue*) and the related *liability* (or *asset*) that is caused by an *accounting event,* frequently by the passage of time, and that is not signaled by an explicit cash transaction. For example, the recognition of interest expense or revenue (or wages, salaries, or rent) at the end of a period even though no explicit cash transaction is made at that time. See *accrued.*

accrual basis of accounting. The method of recognizing *revenues* as *goods* are sold (or delivered) and as *services* are rendered, independent of the time when cash is received. *Expenses* are recognized in the period when the related revenue is recognized independent of the time when cash is paid out. Contrast with the *cash basis of accounting.*

accrued. Said of a *revenue (expense)* that has been earned (recognized) even though the related *receivable (payable)* is not yet due. This adjective should not be used as part of an account title. Thus, we prefer to use Interest Receivable (Payable) as the account title rather than Accrued Interest Receivable (Payable). See *matching convention.* See *accrual.*

accrued receivable. A *receivable* usually resulting from the passage of time. See *accrued.*

accumulated depreciation. A preferred title for the *contra-asset* account that shows the sum of *depreciation* charges on an asset since it was acquired. Other titles used are *allowance* for *depreciation* (acceptable term) and *reserve* for *depreciation* (unacceptable term).

accurate presentation. The qualitative accounting objective suggesting that information reported in financial statements should correspond as precisely as possible with the economic effects underlying transactions and events. See *fair presentation* and *full disclosure.*

acid test ratio. Sum of *(cash, current marketable securities,* and *receivables)* divided by *current liabilities.* Some nonliquid receivables may be excluded from the numerator. Often called the *quick ratio.* See *ratio.*

acquisition cost. Of an *asset,* the net *invoice* price plus all *expenditures* to place and ready the asset for its intended use. The other expenditures might include legal fees, transportation charges, and installation costs.

activity accounting. *Responsibility accounting.*

activity-based depreciation. *Production method of depreciation.*

actual cost (basis). *Acquisition* or *historical cost.* Also, contrast with *standard cost.*

actuarial. Usually said of computations or analyses that involve both *compound interest* and probabilities. Sometimes the term is used if only one of the two is involved.

additional paid-in capital. An alternative acceptable title for the *capital contributed in excess of par (or stated) value account.*

adequate disclosure. *Fair presentation* of *financial statements* requires *disclosure* of *material* items. This *auditing standard* does not, however, require publicizing all information detrimental to a company. For example, the company may be threatened with a lawsuit and disclosure might seem to require a *debit* to a *loss* account and a *credit* to an *estimated liability.*

But the mere making of this entry might adversely affect the actual outcome of the suit. Such entries need not be made although impending suits should be disclosed.

adjunct account. An *account* that accumulates additions to another account. For example, Premium on Bonds Payable is adjunct to the liability Bonds Payable; the effective liability is the sum of the two account balances at a given date. Contrast with *contra account.*

adjusted acquisition (historical) cost. Cost adjusted for *general* or *specific price level changes.* See also *book value.*

adjusted bank balance of cash. The *balance* shown on the statement from the bank plus or minus appropriate adjustments, such as for unrecorded deposits or outstanding checks, to reconcile the bank's balance with the correct cash balance. See *adjusted book balance of cash.*

adjusted basis. The *basis* used to compute gain or loss on disposition of an *asset* for tax purposes. Also, see *book value.*

adjusted book balance of cash. The *balance* shown in the firm's account for cash in bank plus or minus appropriate adjustments, such as for *notes* collected by the bank or bank service charges, to reconcile the account balance with the correct cash balance. See *adjusted bank balance of cash.*

adjusted trial balance. *Trial balance* taken after *adjusting entries* but before *closing entries.* Contrast with *pre-* and *postclosing trial balances.* See *unadjusted trial balance.*

adjusting entry. An entry made at the end of an *accounting period* to record a *transaction* or other *accounting event,* which for some reason has not been recorded or has been improperly recorded during the accounting period. An entry to update the accounts. See *worksheet.*

adjustment. A change in an *account* produced by an *adjusting* entry. Sometimes the term is used to refer to the process of restating *financial statements* for general price level changes.

administrative expense. An *expense* related to the enterprise as a whole as contrasted to expenses related to more specific functions such as manufacturing or selling.

ADR. See *asset depreciation range.*

advances from (by) customers. A preferred term for the *liability* account representing *receipts* of *cash* in advance of delivering the *goods* or rendering the *service* (that will cause *revenue* to be recognized). Sometimes called "deferred revenue" or "deferred income."

advances to affiliates. *Loans* by a parent company to a *subsidiary.* Frequently combined with "investment in subsidiary" as "investments and advances to subsidiary" and shown as a *noncurrent asset* on the parent's *balance sheet.* These advances are eliminated in *consolidated financial statements.*

advances to suppliers. A preferred term for *disbursements* of cash in advance of receiving *assets* or *services.*

adverse opinion. An *auditor's report* stating that the financial statements are not fair or are not in accord with *GAAP.*

affiliated company. Said of a company controlling or controlled by another company.

after closing. *Postclosing;* said of a *trial balance* at the end of the period.

aging accounts receivable. The process of classifying *accounts receivable* by the time elapsed since the claim came into existence for the purpose of estimating the amount of uncollectible accounts receivable as of a given date. See *sales, uncollectible accounts adjustment* and *allowance for uncollectibles.*

aging schedule. A listing of *accounts receivable* classified by age used in *aging accounts receivable.*

AICPA. American Institute of Certified Public Accountants. The national organization that represents *CPA*s. It oversees the writing and grading of the Uniform CPA Examination. Each state, however, sets its own requirements for becoming a CPA in that state. See *certified public accountant.*

all-capital earnings rate. Net *income* (plus interest charges net of tax effects) plus minority interest in income divided by average total assets. Perhaps the single most useful ratio for assessing management's overall operating performance. See *ratio.*

all-inclusive (income) concept. Under this concept, no distinction is drawn between *operating* and *nonoperating revenues* and *expenses;* thus the only entries to retained earnings are for *net income* and *dividends.* Under this concept, all income, *gains,* and *losses* are reported in the *income statement;* thus, events usually reported as *prior-period adjustments* and as *corrections of errors* are included in net income. This concept in its pure form is not the basis of *GAAP,* but *APB Opinions* Nos. 9 and 30 move very far in this direction. They do permit retained earnings entries for prior-period adjustments and correction of errors.

all financial resources. All *assets* less all *liabilities.* Sometimes the *statement of changes in financial position* explains the changes in all financial resources rather than only the changes in *working capital.*

allocate. To spread a *cost* from one *account* to several accounts, to several products or activities, or to several periods.

allocation of income taxes. See *deferred income tax.*

allowance. A balance sheet *contra account* generally used for *receivables* and depreciable assets. See *sales* (or *purchase) allowance* for another use of this term.

allowance for uncollectibles (accounts receivable). A *contra* to Accounts Receivable that shows the estimated amount of *accounts receivable* that will not be collected. When such an allowance is used, the actual *write-off* of specific accounts receivable (*debit* allowance, *credit* specific account) does not affect *revenue* or *expense* at the time of the write-off. The revenue reduction is recognized when the allowance is credited; the amount of the credit to the allowance may be based on a percentage of sales on account for a period of time determined from *aging accounts receivable.* This contra account enables an estimate to be shown of the amount of receivables that will be collected without identifying specific uncollectible accounts. See *allowance method.*

allowance method. A method of attempting to *match* all *expenses* of a transaction with its associated *revenues.* Usually involves a debit to expense and credit to an *estimated liability,* such as for estimated warranty expenditures, or a debit to a revenue (*contra)* account and a credit to an asset (*contra)* account, such as for uncollectible accounts. See *allowance for uncollectibles* for further explanation. When the allowance method is used for *sales discounts,* sales are recorded at *gross invoice* prices (not reduced by the amounts of discounts made available). An estimate of the amount of discounts to be taken is debited to a *revenue contra account* and *credited* to an allowance account, shown contra to *accounts receivable.*

American Accounting Association. An organization primarily for academic accountants, but open to all interested in accounting. *AAA.*

American Institute of Certified Public Accountants. See *AICPA.*

amortization. The general process of *allocating acquisition cost* of assets to either the periods of benefit as *expenses* or to *inventory* accounts as *product costs.* Called *depreciation* for *plant assets,* *depletion* for *wasting assets* (natural resources), and *amortization* for *intangibles.* Also used for the process of allocating *premium* or *discount* on *bonds* and other *liabilities* to the periods during which the liability is outstanding.

analysis of changes in working capital accounts. The *statement of changes in financial postion* explains the causes of the changes in *working capital* during a period. This part of the statement, which may appear in footnotes, shows the net changes in the specific working capital accounts that have been explained in the main section of the statement.

analysis of variances. See *variance analysis.*

annual report. A report for stockholders and other interested parties prepared once a year; includes a *balance sheet,* an *income statement,* a *statement of changes in financial position,* a reconciliation of changes in *owners' equity* accounts, a *summary of significant accounting principles,* other explanatory *notes,* the *auditor's report,* and perhaps, comments from management about the year's events. See *10-K* and *financial statements.*

annuitant. One who receives an *annuity.*

annuity. A series of payments, usually made at equally spaced time intervals.

annuity certain. An *annuity* payable for a definite number of periods. Contrast with *contingent annuity.*

annuity due. An *annuity* whose first payment is made at the start of period 1 (or at the end of period 0). Contrast with *annuity in arrears.*

annuity in advance. An *annuity due.*

annuity in arrears. An *ordinary annuity* whose first payment occurs at the end of the first period.

annuity method of depreciation. See *compound interest depreciation.*

APB. Accounting Principles Board of the *AICPA.* It set *accounting principles* from 1959 through 1973, issuing 31 *APB Opinions.* It was superseded by the *FASB.*

APB Opinion. The name given to pronouncements of the APB that make up much of *generally accepted accounting principles;* there are 31 APB Opinions, issued from 1962 through 1973.

APBs. An abbreviation used for *APB Opinions.*

APB Statement. The APB issued four Statements between 1962 and 1970. The Statements were approved by at least two-thirds of the Board, but they are recommendations, not requirements. For example, Statement No. 3 (1969) suggested the publication of *general price level-adjusted statements* but did not require them.

application of funds. Any transaction that reduces *funds* (however "funds" is defined). A *use of funds.*

applied cost. A *cost* that has been *allocated* to a department, product, or activity; need not be based on actual costs incurred.

applied overhead. *Overhead costs* charged to departments, products, or activities.

appraisal. The process of obtaining a valuation for an *asset* or *liability* that involves expert opinion rather than explicit market transactions.

appraisal method of depreciation. The periodic *depreciation* charge is the difference between the beginning and end-of-period appraised value of the *asset* if that difference is positive. If negative, there is no charge. Not generally accepted.

appreciation. An increase in economic worth caused by rising marked prices for an *asset.* Contrast with *accretion.*

ARB. *Accounting Research Bulletin.*

arm's length. Said of a transaction negotiated by unrelated parties, each acting in his or her own self-interest; the basis for a *fair market value* determination.

arrears. Said of *cumulative preferred stock dividends* that have not been declared up to the current date. See *annuity in arrears* for another context.

articles of incorporation. Document filed with state authorities by persons forming a corporation. When the document is returned with a certificate of incorporation, it becomes the corporation's *charter.*

articulate. Said of the relationship between any operating statement (for example, *income statement* or *statement of changes in financial position*) and *comparative balance sheets,* where the operating statement explains (or reconciles) the change in some major balance sheet category (for example, *retained earnings* or *working capital*).

ASR. *Accounting Series Release* of the *SEC.*

asset. A future benefit or service potential, recognized in accounting only when a transaction has occurred. May be *tangible* or *intangible, short-term* (current) or *long-term* (noncurrent).

asset depreciation range. ADR. The range of *depreciable lives* allowed by the *Internal Revenue Service* for a specific depreciable *asset.*

asset turnover. Ratio of net sales to average assets. See *ratio.*

at par. Said of a *bond* or *preferred stock* issued or selling at its *face amount.*

attest. Rendering of an *opinion* by an auditor that the *financial statements* are fair. This procedure is called the "attest function" of the CPA. See *fair presentation.*

audit. Systematic inspection of accounting records involving analyses, tests, and *confirmations.* See *internal audit.*

audit committee. A committee of the board of directors of a *corporation* usually consisting of outside directors who nominate the independent auditors and discuss the auditors' work with them. If the auditors believe certain matters should be brought to the attention of stockholders, the auditors first bring these matters to the attention of the audit committee.

audit program. The procedures followed by the *auditor* in carrying out the *audit.*

audit trail. A reference accompanying an *entry,* or *posting,* to an underlying source record or document. A good audit trail is essential for efficiently checking the accuracy of accounting entries.

auditing standards. A set of 10 standards promulgated by the *AICPA,* including three general standards, three standards of field work, and four standards of reporting. According to the AICPA, these standards "deal with the measures of the quality of the performance and the objectives to be attained," rather than with specific auditing procedures.

auditor. One who checks the accuracy, fairness, and general acceptability of accounting records and statements and then *attests* to them.

auditor's opinion. *Auditor's report.*

auditor's report. The auditor's statement of the work done and an opinion of the *financial statements.* Opinions are usually unqualified ("clean"), but may be *qualified,* or the auditor may disclaim an opinion in the report. Often called the "accountant's report." See *adverse opinion.*

authorized capital stock. The number of *shares* of stock that can be issued by a corporation; specified by the *articles of incorporation.*

average. The arithmetic mean of a set of numbers; obtained by summing the items and dividing by the number of items.

average tax rate. The rate found by dividing *income tax expense* by *net income* before taxes. Contrast with *marginal tax rate, statutory tax rate.*

average-cost flow assumption. An *inventory flow assumption* where the cost of units is the *weighted average* cost of the *beginning inventory* and purchases. See *inventory equation.*

avoidable cost. An *incremental* or *variable cost.* See *programmed cost.*

B

bad debt. An *uncollectible account receivable;* see *sales, uncollectible accounts adjustment.*

bad debt expense. See *sales, uncollectible accounts adjustment.*

bad debt recovery. Collection, perhaps partial, of a specific account receivable previously written off as uncollectible. If the *allowance method* is used, the *credit* is usually to the *allowance* account. If the direct write-off method is used, the credit is to a *revenue account.*

bailout period. In a *capital budgeting* context, the total time that must elapse before net accumulated cash inflows from a project including potential *salvage value* of assets at various times equal or exceed the accumulated cash outflows. Contrast with *payback period,* which assumes completion of the project and uses terminal salvage value. Bailout is superior to payback because bailout takes into account, at least to some degree, the *present value* of the cash flows after the termination date being considered. The potential salvage value at any time includes some estimate of the flows that can occur after that time.

balance. The difference between the sum of *debit* entries minus the sum of *credit* entries in an *account.* If positive, the difference is called a debit balance; if negative, a credit balance.

balance sheet. Statement of financial position that shows *total assets = total liabilities + owners' equity.*

balance sheet account. An account that can appear on a balance sheet. A *permanent account;* contrast with *temporary account.*

bank balance. The amount of the balance in a checking account shown on the *bank statement.* Compare with *adjusted bank balance* and see *bank reconciliation schedule.*

bank reconciliation schedule. A schedule that shows how the difference between the book balance of the cash in bank account and the bank's statement can be explained. Takes into account the amount of such items as checks issued that have not cleared or deposits that have not been recorded by the bank as well as errors made by the bank or the firm.

bank statement. A statement sent by the bank to a checking account customer showing deposits, checks cleared, and service charges for a period, usually one month.

bankrupt. Said of a company whose *liabilities* exceed its *assets* where a legal petition has been filed and accepted under the bankruptcy law. A bankrupt firm is usually, but need not be, *insolvent.*

base stock method. A method of inventory valuation that assumes that there is a minimum normal or base stock of goods that must be kept on hand at all times for effective continuity of operations. This base quantity is valued at *acquisition cost* of the earliest period. The method is not allowable for income tax purposes and is no longer used, but is generally considered to be the forerunner of the *LIFO* method.

basis. *Acquisition cost,* or some substitute therefor, of an asset used in computing gain or loss on disposition or retirement.

basket purchase. Purchase of a group of assets for a single price; *costs* must be assigned to each of the assets so that the individual items can be recorded in the *accounts.*

beginning inventory. Valuation of *inventory* on hand at the beginning of the accounting period.

bid. An offer to purchase; or the amount of the offer.

big bath. A *write-off* of a substantial amount of costs previously treated as *assets.* Usually caused when a corporation drops a line of business that required a large investment but that proved to be unprofitable. Sometimes used to describe a situation where a corporation takes a large write-off in one period in order to free later periods of gradual write-offs of those amounts. In this sense it frequently occurs when there is a change in top management.

Big Eight. The eight largest *public accounting (CPA)* partnerships; in alphabetical order: Arthur Andersen & Co.; Coopers & Lybrand; Deloitte, Haskins & Sells; Ernst & Ernst; Peat, Marwick, Mitchell & Co.; Price Waterhouse & Co.; Touche Ross & Co.; and Arthur Young & Company.

bill. An *invoice* of charges and *terms of sale* for *goods and services.* Also, a piece of currency.

bill of materials. A specification of the quantities of *direct materials* expected to be used to produce a given job or quantity of output.

board of directors. The governing body of a corporation elected by the stockholders.

bond. A certificate to show evidence of debt. The *par value* is the *principal* or face amount of the bond payable at maturity. The *coupon rate* is the amount of interest payable in one year divided by the principal amount. Coupon bonds have attached to them coupons that can be redeemed at stated dates for interest payments. Normally, bonds are issued in $1,000 units and carry semiannual coupons.

bond conversion. The act of exchanging *convertible bonds* for *preferred* or *common stock.*

bond discount. From the standpoint of the issuer of a *bond* at the issue date, the excess of the *par value* of a bond over its initial sales price; at later dates the excess of par over the sum of (initial issue price plus the portion of discount already amortized). From the standpoint of a bondholder, the difference between par value and selling price when the bond sells below par.

bond indenture. The contract between an issuer of *bonds* and the bondholders.

bond premium. Exactly parallel to *bond discount* except that the issue price (or current selling price) is higher than *par value.*

bond redemption. Retirement of *bonds.*

bond refunding. To incur *debt,* usually through the issue of new *bonds,* intending to use the proceeds to retire an *outstanding* bond *issue.*

book. As a verb, to record a transaction. As a noun, usually plural, the *journals* and *ledgers. As an adjective, see book value.*

book inventory. An *inventory* amount that results, not from physical count, but from the amount of initial inventory plus *invoice* amounts of purchases less invoice amounts of *requisitions* or withdrawals; implies a *perpetual method.*

book of original entry. A *journal.*

book value. The amount shown in the books or in the *accounts* for any *asset, liability,* or *owners' equity* item. Generally used to refer to the net amount of an *asset* or group of assets shown in the accounts which record the asset and reductions, such as for *amortization,* in its cost. Of a firm, the excess of total assets over total liabilities. *Net assets.*

book value per share of common stock. Common *stockholders' equity* divided by the number of shares of *common stock outstanding.* See *ratio.*

bookkeeping. The process of analyzing and recording transactions in the accounting records.

boot. The additional money paid or received along with a used item in a trade-in or exchange transaction for another item. See *trade-in transaction.*

borrower. See *loan.*

breakeven analysis. See *breakeven chart.*

breakeven chart. Two kinds of breakeven charts are shown in Figure 6.1 on page 150. The cost-volume-profit graph presents the relationship of changes in volume to the amount of *profit,* or *income.* On such a graph, total *revenue* and total *costs* for each volume level are indicated and profit or loss at any volume can be read directly from the chart. The profit-volume graph does not show revenues and costs but more readily indicates profit (or loss) at various output levels. For a multiproduct firm, the horizontal axis would have to be stated in dollars rather than in physical units of output. Breakeven charts for multiproduct firms necessarily assume that constant proportions of the several products are sold and changes in this mixture as well as in costs or selling prices would invalidate such a chart.

breakeven point. The volume of sales required so that total *revenues* and total *costs* are equal. May be expressed in units *(fixed costs/contribution per unit)* or in sales dollars [selling price per unit × (fixed costs/contribution per unit)]. See example at *breakeven chart*, Figure 6.1, page 150.

budget. A financial plan that is used to estimate the results of future operations. Frequently used to help control future operations.

budgetary control. Management of governmental (nongovernmental) unit in accordance with an official (approved) *budget* in order to keep total expenditures within authorized (planned) limits.

budgeted statements. *Pro forma* statements prepared before the event or period occurs.

burden. See *overhead costs*.

business combination. As defined by the *APB* in Opinion No. 16, the bringing together into a single accounting *entity* of two or more incorporated or unincorporated businesses. The *merger* will be accounted for either with the *purchase method* or the *pooling of interests method*. See *conglomerate*.

business entity. *Entity*. *Accounting entity*.

bylaws. The rules adopted by the stockholders of a corporation that specify the general methods for carrying out the functions of the corporation.

by-product. A *joint product* whose value is so small relative to the value of the other joint product(s) that it does not receive normal accounting treatment. The costs assigned to by-products reduce the costs of the main product(s). By-products are allocated a share of joint costs such that the expected gain or loss upon their sale is zero. Thus, by-products are shown in the *accounts* at *net realizable value*.

C

CA. *Chartered Accountant*.

call premium. See *callable bond*.

call price. See *callable bond*.

callable bond. A *bond* for which the issuer reserves the right to pay a specific amount, the call price, to retire the obligation before *maturity* date. If the issuer agrees to pay more than the *face amount* of the bond when called, the excess of the payment over the face amount is the call premium.

Canadian Institute of Chartered Accountants. The national organization that represents *Chartered Accountants* in Canada.

cancelable lease. See *lease*.

capacity. Stated in units of product, the amount that can be produced per unit of time. Stated in units of input, such as *direct labor* hours, the amount of input that can be used in production per unit of time. This measure of output or input is used in allocating *fixed costs* if the amounts producible are normal, rather than maximum, amounts.

capacity cost. A *fixed cost* incurred to provide a firm with the capability to produce or to sell. Consists of *standby costs* and *enabling costs*. Contrast with *programmed costs*.

capacity variance. Standard fixed *overhead* rate per unit of normal *capacity* (or base activity) times (units of base activity budgeted or planned for a period minus actual units of base activity worked or assigned to product during the period). Often called a "volume variance."

capital. *Owners' equity* in a business. Often used, equally correctly, to mean the total assets of a business. Sometimes used to mean *capital assets*.

capital asset. Properly used, a designation for income tax purposes that describes property held by a taxpayer, except *cash*, inventoriable *assets*, goods held primarily for sale, most depreciable property, *real estate, receivables*, certain *intangibles*, and a few other items. Sometimes this term is imprecisely used to describe *plant* and *equipment*, which are clearly not capital assets under the income tax definition. Often the term is used to refer to an *investment* in *securities*.

capital budget. Plan of proposed outlays for acquiring long-term *assets* and the means of *financing* the acquisition.

capital budgeting. The process of choosing *investment* projects for an enterprise by considering the *present value* of cash flows and deciding how to raise the funds required by the investment.

capital contributed in excess of par (or stated) value. A preferred title for the account that shows the amount received by the issuer for *capital stock* in excess of *par* (or *stated*) *value*.

capital expenditure (outlay). An *expenditure* to acquire long-term *assets*.

capital gain. The excess of proceeds over *cost,* or other *basis,* from the sale of a *capital asset* as defined by the Internal Revenue Code. If the capital asset is held more than nine months before sale, then the tax on the gain is computed at a rate lower than is used for gains and ordinary income.

capital lease. See *financing lease.*

capital loss. A negative capital gain; see *capital gain.*

capital rationing. In a *capital budgeting* context, the imposing of constraints on the amounts of total capital expenditures in each period.

capital stock. The ownership shares of a corporation. Consists of all classes of *common* and *preferred stock.*

capital structure. The composition of a corporation's equities; the relative proportions of *short-term debt, long-term debt,* and *owners' equity.*

capitalization of a corporation. A term used by investment analysts to indicate *stockholders' equity* plus *bonds outstanding.*

capitalization rate. An *interest rate* used to convert a series of payments or receipts or earnings into a single *present value.*

capitalize. To record an *expenditure* that may benefit a future period as an *asset* rather than to treat the expenditure as an *expense* of the period of its occurrence. Whether or not expenditures for advertising or for research and development should be capitalized is controversial, but *FASB Statement* No. 2 requires expensing of *R&D* costs. We believe expenditures should be capitalized if they lead to future benefits and thus meet the criterion to be an asset.

carryback, carryforward, carryover. The use of losses or tax credits in one period to reduce income taxes payable in other periods. There are three common kinds of carrybacks: for net operating losses, for *capital losses,* and for the *investment tax credit.* The first two are applied against taxable income and the third against the actual tax. In general, carrybacks are for three years with the earliest year first. Operating losses, the investment tax credit, and the capital loss for corporations, can generally be carried forward for five years. The capital loss for individuals can be carried forward indefinitely.

carrying cost. Costs (such as property taxes and insurance) of holding, or storing, *inventory* from the time of purchase until the time of sale or use.

CASB. Cost Accounting Standards Board. A board of five members authorized by the U.S. Congress to "promulgate cost-accounting standards designed to achieve uniformity and consistency in the cost-accounting principles followed by defense contractors and subcontractors under federal contracts." The

principles promulgated by the CASB are likely to have considerable weight in practice where the *FASB* has not established a standard.

cash. Currency and coins, negotiable checks, and balances in bank accounts.

cash basis of accounting. In contrast to the *accrual basis of accounting,* a system of accounting in which *revenues* are recognized when *cash* is received and *expenses* are recognized as *disbursements* are made. No attempt is made to *match revenues* and *expenses* in determining *income.*

cash budget. A schedule of expected cash *receipts* and *disbursements.*

cash collection basis. The *installment method* for recognizing *revenue.* Not to be confused with the *cash basis of accounting.*

cash cycle. The period of time that elapses during which *cash* is converted into *inventories,* inventories are converted into *accounts receivable,* and receivables are converted back into cash. *Earnings cycle.*

cash discount. A reduction in sales or purchase price allowed for prompt payment.

cash dividend. See *dividend.*

cash flow. Cash *receipts* minus *disbursements* from a given *asset,* or group of assets, for a given period.

cash flow statement. A statement similar to the typical *statement of changes in financial position* where the flows of cash, rather than of *working capital,* are explained.

cash receipts journal. A specialized *journal* used to record all *receipts* of *cash.*

cash yield. See *yield.*

cash-equivalent value. A term used to describe the amount for which an *asset* could be sold. *Market value. Fair market price (value).*

central corporate expenses. General *overhead expenses* incurred in running the corporate headquarters and related supporting activities of a corporation. These expenses are treated as *period expenses.* Contrast with *manufacturing overhead.* A major problem in *line-of-business reporting* is the treatment of these expenses.

certificate. The document that is the physical embodiment of a *bond* or a *share of stock.* A term sometimes used for the *auditor's report.*

certified financial statement. A financial statement attested to by an independent *auditor* who is a *CPA.*

certified internal auditor. See *CIA.*

certified public accountant (CPA). An accountant who has satisfied the statutory and administrative requirements of his or her jurisdiction to be registered or licensed as a public accountant. In addition to passing the Uniform CPA Examination administered by the *AICPA*, the CPA must meet certain educational, experience, and moral requirements that differ from jurisdiction to jurisdiction. The jurisdictions are the 50 states, the District of Columbia, Guam, Puerto Rico, and the Virgin Islands.

changes, accounting. See *accounting changes*.

changes in financial position. See *statement of changes in financial position*.

charge. As a noun, a *debit* to an account; as a verb, to debit.

charge off. To treat as a *loss* or *expense* an amount originally recorded as an *asset;* usually the term is used when the charge is not in accord with original expectations.

chart of accounts. A list of names and numbers of *accounts* systematically organized.

charter. Document issued by a state government authorizing the creation of a corporation.

chartered accountant (CA). The title used in Australia, Canada, and the United Kingdom for an accountant who has satisfied the requirements of the institute of his or her jurisdiction to be qualified to serve as a *public accountant*. In Canada, each provincial institute or order has the right to administer the examination and set the standards of performance and ethics for Chartered Accountants in its province. For a number of years, however, the provincial organizations have pooled their rights to qualify new members through the Inter-provincial Education Committee and the result is that there are nationally set and graded examinations given in English and French. The pass/fail grade awarded by the Board of Examiners (a subcommittee of the Interprovincial Education Committee) is rarely deviated from.

check. The Federal Reserve Board defines a check as "a *draft* or order upon a bank or banking house purporting to be drawn upon a deposit of funds for the payment at all events of a certain sum of money to a certain person therein named or to him or his order or to bearer and payable instantly on demand." It must contain the phrase "pay to the order of." The amount shown on the check's face must be clearly readable, and it must have the signature of the drawer. Checks need not be dated, although they usually are. The *balance* in the *cash account* is usually reduced when a check is issued, not later when it clears the bank and reduces cash in bank.

CIA. Certified Internal Auditor. One who has satisfied certain requirements of the *Institute of Internal Auditors*, including experience, ethics, education, and examinations.

CICA. *Canadian Institute of Chartered Accountants.*

CIF. A term used in contracts along with the name of a given port to indicate that the quoted price includes insurance, handling, and freight charges up to delivery by the seller at the given port.

clean opinion. See *auditor's report*.

clean surplus concept. The notion that the only entries to the *retained earnings* account are to record net earnings and dividends. Contrast with *current operating performance concept*. This concept, with minor exceptions, is now controlling in *GAAP*. (See *APB Opinions* Nos. 9 and 30.)

close. As a verb, to transfer the *balance* of a *temporary* or *contra* or *adjunct* account to the main account to which it relates; for example, to transfer *revenue* and *expense* accounts directly, or through the *income summary* account, to an *owners' equity* account, or to transfer *purchase discounts* to purchases.

closed account. An account with equal debits and credits, usually as a result of a closing entry.

closing entries. The entries that accomplish the transfer of balances in temporary accounts to the related balance sheet accounts. See *worksheet*.

closing inventory. *Ending inventory.*

CMA. Certificate in Management Accounting. Awarded by the Institute of Management Accounting of the *National Association of Accountants* to those who pass a set of examinations and meet certain experience and continuing education requirements.

collectible. Capable of being converted into cash; now, if due; later, otherwise.

commission. Remuneration, usually expressed as a percentage, to employees based upon an activity rate, such as sales.

Committee on Accounting Procedure. Predecessor of the *APB*. The *AICPA's* principle-promulgating body from 1939 through 1959. Its 51 pronouncements are called *Accounting Research Bulletins*.

common cost. *Cost* resulting from use of *raw materials,* a facility (for example, plant or machines), or a service (for example, fire insurance) that benefits several products or departments and must be allocated to those products or departments. Common costs result when multiple products are produced together although they could be produced separately; joint costs occur when multiple products are of necessity produced together. Many writers use common costs and *joint costs* synonymously. See *joint costs, indirect costs,* and *overhead.*

common monetary measuring unit. For U.S. corporations, the dollar. See also *stable monetary unit assumption.*

common stock. *Stock* representing the class of owners who have residual claims on the assets and earnings of a corporation after all debt and preferred stockholders' claims have been met.

common-dollar accounting. General *price level-adjusted* accounting.

company-wide control. See *control system.*

comparative (financial) statements. Financial statements showing information for the same company for different times, usually two successive years. Nearly all published financial statements are in this form. Contrast with *historical summary.*

compensating balance. When a bank lends funds to a customer, it often requires that the customer keep on deposit in his or her checking account an amount equal to some percentage, say 20 percent, of the loan. The amount required to be left on deposit is the compensating balance. Such amounts effectively increase the *interest rate.* The amounts of such balances must be disclosed in *notes* to the *financial statements.*

completed-contract method. Recognizing *revenues* and *expenses* for a job or order only when it is finished, except that when a loss on the contract is expected, revenues and expenses are recognized in the period when the loss is first forecast.

completed-sales basis. See *sales basis of revenue recognition.*

compound entry. A *journal entry* with more than one *debit* or more than one *credit,* or both. See *trade-in transaction* for an example.

compound interest. *Interest* calculated on *principal* plus previously undistributed interest.

compound interest depreciation. A method designed to hold the *rate of return* on an asset constant. First find the *internal rate of return* on the cash inflows and outflows of the asset. The periodic depreciation charge is the cash flow for the period less the internal rate of return multiplied by the asset's book value at the beginning of the period. When the cash flows from the asset are constant over time, the method is sometimes called the "annuity method" of depreciation.

compounding period. The time period for which *interest* is calculated. At the end of the period, the interest may be paid to the lender or added (that is, converted) to principal for the next interest-earning period, which is usually a year or some portion of a year.

comprehensive budget. *Master budget.*

comptroller. Same meaning and pronunciation as *controller.*

confirmation. A formal memorandum delivered by the customers or suppliers of a company to its independent *auditor* verifying the amounts shown as receivable or payable. The confirmation document is originally sent by the auditor to the customer. If the auditor asks that the document be returned whether the *balance* is correct or incorrect, then it is called a "positive confirmation." If the auditor asks that the document be returned only if there is an error, it is called a "negative confirmation."

conglomerate. *Holding company.* This term is used when the owned companies are in dissimilar lines of business.

conservatism. A *reporting objective* that calls for anticipation of all *losses* and *expenses* but defers recognition of *gains* or *profits* until they are *realized* in *arm's length* transactions. In the absence of certainty, events are to be reported in a way that tends to minimize current income.

consistency. Treatment of like *transactions* in the same way in consecutive periods so that financial statements will be more comparable than otherwise. The reporting policy implying that procedures, once adopted, should be followed from period to period by a reporting *entity.* See *accounting changes* for the treatment of inconsistencies.

consolidated financial statements. Statements issued by legally separate companies that show financial position and income as they would appear if the companies were one legal *entity.* Such statements reflect an economic, rather than a legal, concept of the *entity.*

constructive receipt. An item is included in taxable income when the taxpayer can control funds whether or not cash has been received. For example, *interest* added to *principal* in a savings account is deemed to be constructively received.

consumer price index (CPI). A *price index* computed and issued monthly by the Bureau of Labor Statistics of the U.S. Department of Labor. The index attempts to track the price level of a group of goods and services purchased by the average consumer. Contrast with *GNP Implicit Price Deflator.*

contingent annuity. An *annuity* whose number of payments depends upon the outcome of an event whose timing is uncertain at the time the annuity is set up; for example, an annuity payable for the life of the *annuitant.* Contrast with *annuity certain.*

contingent liability. A potential *liability;* if a specified event were to occur, such as losing a lawsuit, a liability would be recognized. Until the outcome is known, the contingency is merely disclosed in notes rather than shown in the balance sheet accounts. A *material* contingency may lead to a qualified, *"subject to,"* auditor's opinion.

continuing operations. See *income from continuing operations.*

continuity of operations. The assumption in accounting that the business *entity* will continue to operate long enough for current plans to be carried out. The *going-concern assumption.*

continuous compounding. *Compound interest* where the *compounding period* is every instant of time. See *e* for the computation of the equivalent annual or periodic rate.

continuous inventory method. The *perpetual inventory* method.

contra account. An *account,* such as *accumulated depreciation,* that accumulates subtractions from another account, such as machinery. Contrast with *adjunct account.*

contributed capital. The sum of the balances in *capital stock accounts* plus *capital contributed in excess of par (or stated) value* accounts. Contrast with *donated capital.*

contributed surplus. An inferior term for *capital contributed in excess of par value.*

contribution margin. *Revenue* from *sales* less all variable *expenses.* See *gross margin.*

contribution per unit. Selling price less *variable costs* per unit.

contributory. Said of a *pension plan* where employees, as well as employers, make payments to a pension *fund.* Note that the provisions for *vesting* are applicable to the employer's payments. Whatever the degree of vesting of the employer's payments, the employee typically gets back his or her payments, with interest, in case of death, or other cessation of employment, before retirement.

control (controlling) account. A summary *account* with totals equal to those of entries and balances that appear in individual accounts in a *subsidiary ledger.* Accounts Receivable is a control account backed up with accounts for each customer. The balance in a control account should not be changed unless a corresponding change is made in the subsidiary accounts.

control system. A device for ensuring that actions are carried out according to plan or for safeguarding *assets.* A system for ensuring that actions are carried out according to plan can be designed for single functions within the firm, called "operational control," for autonomous segments within the firm that generally have responsibility for both revenues and costs, called "divisional control," or for activities of the firm as a whole, called "company-wide control." Systems designed for safeguarding *assets* are called "internal control" systems.

controllable cost. A *cost* whose amount can be influenced by the way in which operations are carried out, such as advertising costs. These costs can be *fixed* or *variable.* See *programmed costs.*

controlled company. A company, a majority of whose voting stock is held by an individual or corporation. Effective control can sometimes be exercised when less than 50 percent of the stock is owned.

controller. The title often used for the chief accountant of an organization. Often spelled *comptroller.*

conversion. The act of exchanging a convertible security for another security.

conversion cost. *Direct labor* costs plus factory *overhead* costs incurred in producing a product. That is, the cost to convert raw materials to finished products. *Manufacturing cost.*

conversion period. *Compounding period.* Period during which a *convertible bond* or *preferred stock* can be converted into *common stock.*

convertible bond. A *bond* that may be converted into a specified number of shares of *capital stock.*

convertible preferred stock. *Preferred stock* that may be converted into a specified number of shares of *common stock.*

copyright. Exclusive right granted by the government to an individual author, composer, playwright and the like for 28 years (renewable for another 28 years) to enjoy the benefit of a piece of written work. Commencing January 1, 1978, copyrights extend for the life of the individual plus 50 years. If the copyright is granted to a firm, then the right extends 75 years after the original publication. The *economic life* of a copyright may be considerably less than the legal life as, for example, the copyright of this book.

corporation. A legal entity authorized by a state to operate under the rules of the entity's *charter.*

correction of errors. See *accounting errors.*

cost. The sacrifice, measured by the *price* paid or required to be paid, to acquire *goods* or *services.* See *acquisition cost* and *replacement cost.* The term "cost" is often used when referring to the valuation of a good or service acquired. When "cost" is used in this sense, a cost is an *asset*. When the benefits of the acquisition (the goods or services acquired) expire, the cost becomes an expense or *loss*. Some writers, however, use cost and expense as synonyms. Contrast with *expense*.

cost accounting. Classifying, summarizing, recording, reporting, and allocating current or predicted *costs*. A subset of *managerial accounting*.

Cost Accounting Standards Board. See *CASB*.

cost center. A unit of activity for which *expenditures* and *expenses* are accumulated.

cost effective. Among alternatives, the one whose benefit, or payoff, divided by cost is highest. Sometimes said of an action whose expected benefits exceed expected costs whether or not there are other alternatives with larger benefit/cost ratios.

cost flow assumption. See *flow assumption*.

cost flows. Costs passing through various classifications within an entity. See *flow of costs* for a diagram.

cost method (for investments). Accounting for an investment in the *capital stock* of another company where the investment is shown at *acquisition cost*, and only *dividends* declared are treated as *revenue*. Used if less than 20 percent of the voting stock is held by the investor.

cost method (for treasury stock). The method of showing *treasury stock* as a *contra* to all other items of *stockholders' equity* in an amount equal to that paid to reacquire the stock.

cost of capital. The average rate per year a company must pay for its *equities*. In efficient capital markets, the *discount rate* that equates the expected *present value* of all future cash flows to common stockholders with the market value of common stock at a given time.

cost of goods manufactured. The sum of all costs allocated to products completed during a period; includes materials, labor, and *overhead*.

cost of goods purchased. Net purchase price of goods acquired plus costs of storage and delivery to the place where the items can be productively used.

cost of goods sold. Inventoriable *costs* that are expensed because the units are sold; equals beginning inventory plus cost of goods purchased or manufactured minus ending inventory.

cost of sales. Generally refers to *cost of goods sold;* occasionally, to *selling expenses*.

cost or market, whichever is lower. See *lower of cost or market*.

cost principle. The *principle* that requires reporting assets at *historical* or *acquisition cost*, less accumulated *amortization*. This principle is based on the assumption that cost is equal to *fair market value* at the date of acquisition and subsequent changes are not likely to be significant.

cost sheet. Statement that shows all the elements comprising the total cost of an item.

costing. The process of determining the cost of activities, products, or services. The British word for *cost accounting*.

cost-volume-profit graph (chart). A graph that shows the relation between *fixed costs, contribution per unit, breakeven point,* and *sales*. See *breakeven chart*.

coupon. That portion of a *bond* document redeemable at a specified date for *interest* payments. Its physical form is much like a ticket; each coupon is dated and is deposited at a bank, just like a check, for collection or is mailed to the issuer's agent for collection.

coupon rate. Of a *bond*, the amount of annual coupons divided by par value. Contrast with *effective rate*.

CPA. See *certified public accountant*. The *AICPA* suggests that no periods be shown in the abbreviation.

CPI. *Consumer price index*.

Cr. Abbreviation for *credit*.

credit. As a noun, an entry on the right-hand side of an *account*. As a verb, to make an entry on the right-hand side of an account. Records increases in *liabilities, owners' equity, revenues,* and *gains;* records decreases in *assets* and *expenses*. Also the ability or right to buy or borrow in return for a promise to pay later.

credit loss. The amount of *accounts receivable* that is, or is expected to become, *uncollectible*.

creditor. One who lends.

cross-section analysis. Analysis of *financial statements* of various firms for a single period of time, as opposed to time series analysis where statements of a given firm are analyzed over several periods of time.

cumulative dividend. Preferred stock *dividends* that, if not paid, accrue as a commitment which must be paid before dividends to common stockholders can be declared.

cumulative preferred stock. *Preferred* stock with *cumulative dividend* rights.

current asset. *Cash* and other *assets* that are expected to be turned into cash, sold, or exchanged within the normal operating cycle of the firm, usually one year. Current assets include *cash, marketable securities, receivables, inventory,* and *current prepayments*.

current cost. *Cost* stated in terms of current market prices rather than in terms of *acquisition cost. Current replacement cost.* See *net realizable value, current selling price.*

current funds. *Cash* and other assets readily convertible into cash. In governmental accounting, funds spent for operating purposes during the current period. Includes *general, special revenue, debt service,* and enterprise funds.

current (gross) margin. See *operating margin (based on replacement costs).*

current liability. A debt or other obligation that must be discharged within a short time, usually the *earnings cycle* or one year, normally by expending *current assets.*

current operating performance concept. The notion that reported *income* for a period ought to reflect only ordinary, normal, and recurring operations of that period. A consequence is that *extraordinary* and nonrecurring items are entered directly in the Retained Earnings account. Contrast with *clean surplus concept.* This concept is no longer acceptable. (See *APB Opinions* Nos. 9 and 30.)

current ratio. Sum of *current assets* divided by sum of *current liabilities.* See *ratio.*

current replacement cost. Of an *asset,* the amount currently required to acquire an identical asset (in the same condition and with the same service potential) or an asset capable of rendering the same service at a current *fair market price.* If these two amounts differ, the lower is usually used. See *reproduction cost.*

current selling price. The amount for which an *asset* could be sold as of a given time in an *arm's-length* transaction, rather than in a forced sale.

current value accounting. The form of accounting where all assets are shown at *current replacement cost (entry value)* or *current selling price* or *net realizable value (exit value)* and all *liabilities* are shown at *present value.* Entry and exit values may be quite different from each other so there is no general agreement on the precise meaning of current value accounting.

currently attainable standard cost. *Normal standard cost.*

customers' ledger. The *ledger* that shows accounts receivable of individual customers. It is the *subsidiary ledger* for the *controlling account.* Accounts Receivable.

D

days of average inventory on hand. See *ratio.*

DDB. *Double-declining-balance depreciation.*

debit. As a noun, an entry on the left-hand side of an *account.* As a verb, to make an entry on the left-hand side of an account. Records increases in *assets* and *expenses;* records decreases in *liabilities, owners' equity,* and *revenues.*

debt. An amount owed. The general name for *notes, bonds, mortgages,* and the like that are evidence of amounts owed and have definite payment dates.

debt financing. Raising *funds* by issuing *bonds, mortgages,* or *notes.* Contrast with *equity financing. Leverage.*

debt ratio. *Debt-equity ratio.*

debt-equity ratio. Total *liabilities* divided by total *equities.* See *ratio.* Sometimes the denominator is merely total *stockholders' equity.* Sometimes the numerator is restricted to long-term *debt.*

debtor. One who borrows.

declaration date. Time when a *dividend* is declared by the *board of directors.*

declining-balance depreciation. The method of calculating the periodic *depreciation* charge by multiplying the *book value* at the start of the period by a constant percentage. In pure declining balance depreciation the constant percentage is $1 - \sqrt[n]{s/c}$, where n is the *depreciable life,* s is *salvage value,* and c is *acquisition cost.* See *double-declining-balance depreciation.*

default. Failure to pay *interest* or *principal* on a *debt* when due.

deferral method. See *flow-through method* (of accounting for the *investment tax credit*) for definition and contrast.

deferred annuity. An *annuity* whose first payment is made sometime after the end of the first period.

deferred asset. *Deferred charge.*

deferred charge. *Expenditure* not recognized as an *expense* of the period when made but carried forward as an *asset* to be *written off* in future periods, such as for advance rent payments or insurance premiums.

deferred cost. *Deferred charge.*

deferred credit. Sometimes used to indicate *advances from customers.* Also sometimes used to describe the *deferred income tax liability.*

deferred debit. *Deferred charge.*

deferred expense. *Deferred charge.*

deferred gross margin. *Unrealized gross margin.*

deferred income. *Advances from customers.*

deferred income tax (liability). An *indeterminate-term liability* that arises when the pretax income shown on the tax return is less than what it would have been had the same *accounting principles* been used in tax returns as used for financial reporting. *APB Opinion No. 11* requires that the firm debit income tax *expense* and credit deferred income tax with the amount of the taxes delayed by using different accounting principles in tax returns from those used in financial reports. See *timing difference* and *permanent difference*. See *installment sales*. If, as a result of timing differences, cumulative taxable income exceeds cumulative reported income before taxes, the deferred income tax account will have a *debit* balance and will be reported as a *deferred charge*.

deferred revenue. Sometimes used to indicate *advances from customers*.

deficit. A *debit balance* in the Retained Earnings account; presented on the balance sheet as a *contra* to stockholders' equity.

defined-benefit plan. A *pension plan* where the employer promises specific benefits to each employee. The employer's cash contributions and pension expense are adjusted in relation to investment performance of the pension *fund*. Sometimes called a "fixed-benefit" pension plan. Contrast with *money-purchase plan*.

defined-contribution plan. A *money-purchase (pension) plan*.

deflation. A period of declining general prices.

demand deposit. *Funds* in a *checking account* at a bank.

denominator volume. Capacity measured in expected number of units to be produced this period; divided into *budgeted fixed costs* to obtain fixed costs applied per unit of product.

depletion. Exhaustion or *amortization* of a *wasting asset,* or natural resource. Also see *percentage depletion*.

depletion allowance. See *percentage depletion*.

depreciable cost. That part of the *cost* of an asset, usually *acquisition cost* less *salvage value,* that is to be charged off over the life of the asset through the process of *depreciation*.

depreciable life. For an *asset,* the time period or units of activity (such as miles driven for a truck) over which *depreciable cost* is to be allocated. For tax returns, depreciable life may be shorter than estimated *service life*.

depreciation. *Amortization* of *plant assets;* the process of allocating the cost of an asset to the periods of benefit—the *depreciable life*. Classified as a *production cost* or a *period expense*, depending upon the asset and whether *absorption* or *direct costing* is used.

depreciation reserve. An inferior term for *accumulated depreciation*. See *reserve*. Do not confuse with a replacement *fund*.

Descartes' rule of signs. In a *capital budgeting* context, the rule says that a series of cash flows will have a nonnegative number of *internal rates of return*. The number is equal to the number of variations in the sign of the cash flow series or is less than that number by an even integer. Consider the following series of cash flows, the first occurring now and the others at subsequent yearly intervals: -100, -100, $+50$, $+175$, -50, $+100$. The internal rates of return are the numbers for r that satisfy the equation

$$-100 - \frac{100}{(1+r)} + \frac{50}{(1+r)^2} + \frac{175}{(1+r)^3}$$
$$- \frac{50}{(1+r)^4} + \frac{100}{(1+r)^5} = 0$$

The series of cash flows has three variations in sign: a change from minus to plus, a change from plus to minus, and a change from minus to plus. The rule says that this series must have either three or one internal rates of return; in fact, it has only one, about 12 percent. But also see *reinvestment rate*.

differential analysis. Analysis of *incremental costs*.

differential cost. *Incremental cost*.

dilution. A potential reduction in *earnings per share* or *book value* per share by the potential *conversion* of securities or by the potential exercise of *warrants* or *options*.

dipping into LIFO layers. See *LIFO inventory layer*.

direct cost. Cost of *direct material, direct labor,* and *variable overhead* incurred in producing a product. See *prime cost*.

direct costing. This method of allocating costs assigns only *variable manufacturing costs* to product and treats *fixed manufacturing costs* as *period* expenses. Sometimes called "variable costing."

direct labor (material) cost. Cost of labor (material) applied and assigned directly to a product; contrast with *indirect labor (material)*.

disbursement. Payment by *cash* or by a *check*. See *expenditure*.

DISC. Domestic International Sales Corporation. A U.S. *corporation,* usually a *subsidiary,* whose *income* is primarily attributable to exports. *Income tax* on 50 percent of a DISC's income is usually deferred for a long period. Generally, this results in a lower overall corporate tax for the *parent* than would otherwise be incurred.

disclosure. The showing of facts in *financial statements, notes* thereto, or the *auditor's report.*

discontinued operations. See *income from discontinued operations.*

discount. In the context of *compound interest, bonds,* and *notes,* the difference between *face* or *future value* and *present value* of a payment. In the context of *sales* and *purchases,* a reduction in price granted for prompt payment.

discount factor. The reciprocal of one plus the *discount rate.* If the discount rate is 10 percent per period, the discount factor for three periods is $(1.10)^{-3} = 0.75131.$

discount rate. *Interest rate* used to convert future payments to *present values.*

discounted bailout period. In a *capital budgeting* context, the total time that must elapse before discounted value of net accumulated cash flows from a project, including potential *salvage value* at various times of assets, equals or exceeds the *present value* of net accumulated cash outflows. Contrast with *discounted payback period.*

discounted payback period. Amount of time over which the discounted present value of cash inflows from a project equals the discounted *present value* of the cash outflows.

discovery value accounting. In exploration for natural resources, there is the problem of what to do with the expenditures for exploration. Suppose that $10 million is spent to drill 10 holes ($1 million each) and that nine of them are dry whereas one is a gusher containing oil with a *net realizable value* of $40 million. Dry-hole, or successful-efforts, accounting would *expense* $9 million and *capitalize* $1 million to be *depleted* as the oil was lifted from the ground. Full costing would expense nothing but capitalize the $10 million of drilling costs to be depleted as the oil is lifted from the single productive well. Discovery value accounting would capitalize $40 million to be depleted as the oil is lifted, with a $30 million *credit* to *income* or *contributed capital.*

Discussion Memorandum. A neutral discussion of all the issues concerning an accounting problem of current concern to the *FASB.* The publication of such a document usually implies that the FASB is considering issuing a *Statement of Financial Accounting Standards* on this particular problem. The discussion memorandum brings together material about the particular problem to facilitate interaction and comment by those interested in the matter. It may lead to an *Exposure Draft.*

distributable income. The portion of conventional accounting net income that can be distributed to owners (usually in the form of *dividends*) without impairing the physical capacity of the firm to continue operations at current levels. Pretax distributable income is conventional pretax income less the excess of *replacement cost* of goods sold and *depreciation* charges based on the replacement cost of *productive capacity* over cost of goods sold and depreciation on an *acquisition-cost basis.* Since *SEC Accounting Series Release* No. 190 became effective, annual reports of large manufacturing and retailing companies disclose information sufficient for calculation of distributable income. Contrast with *sustainable income.* See *inventory profit.*

distribution expense. *Expense* of selling, advertising, and delivery activities.

dividend. A distribution of *earnings* to owners of a corporation; it may be paid in cash (cash dividend), with stock (stock dividend), with property, or with other securities (dividend in kind). Dividends, except stock dividends, become a legal liability of the corporation when they are declared. Hence, the owner of stock ordinarily recognizes *revenue* when a dividend, other than a stock dividend, is declared. See also *stock dividend.*

dividend yield. *Dividends* declared for the year divided by market price of the stock as of a given time of the year.

dividends in arrears. Dividends on *cumulative preferred stock* that have not been declared in accordance with the preferred stock contract. Such arrearages must usually be cleared before dividends on *common stock* can be declared.

dividends in kind. See *Dividend.*

divisional control. See *control system.*

divisional reporting. *Line-of-business reporting.*

dollar-value LIFO method. A form of *LIFO* inventory accounting with inventory quantities *(layers)* measured in dollar, rather than physical, terms. Adjustments to account for changing prices are made by use of a specific price index appropriate for the kinds of items in the inventory.

Domestic International Sales Corporation. See *DISC.*

donated capital. A *stockholders' equity* account credited when contributions, such as land or buildings, are freely given to the company. Do not confuse with *contributed capital.*

double entry. The system of recording transactions that maintains the equality of the accounting equation; each entry results in recording equal amounts of *debits* and *credits.*

double T-account. *T-account* with an extra horizontal line showing a change in the account balance to be explained by the subsequent entries into the account, such as:

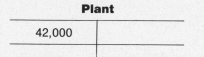

Plant

42,000	

This account shows an increase in the plant asset account, of $42,000 to be explained. Such accounts are useful in preparing the *statement of changes in financial position;* they are not a part of the formal record keeping process.

double taxation. Corporate income is subject to the corporate income tax and the aftertax income, when distributed to owners, is subject to the personal income tax.

double-declining-balance depreciation (DDB). *Declining-balance depreciation,* which see, where the constant percentage used to multiply by book value in determining the depreciation charge for the year is $2/n$ and n is the *depreciable life* in periods. Maximum declining-balance rate permitted in the *income tax*

laws. *Salvage value* is omitted from the depreciable amount. Thus if the asset cost $100 and has a depreciable life of five years, the depreciation in the first year would be $40 = \frac{2}{5} \times 100, in the second would be $24 = \frac{2}{5} \times ($100 - $40)$, and in the third year would be $14.40 = \frac{2}{5} \times ($100 - $40 - $24)$. By the fourth year, the remaining undepreciated cost could be depreciated under the straight-line method at $10.80 = \frac{1}{2} \times ($100 - $40 - $24 - $14.40)$ per year for tax purposes.

doubtful accounts. *Accounts receivable* estimated to be *uncollectible.*

Dr. The abbreviation for *debit.*

dry-hole accounting. See *discovery value accounting* for definition and contrast.

dual transactions assumption (fiction). In presenting the *statement of changes in financial position,* some transactions not involving *working capital* accounts are reported as though working capital was generated and then used. For example, the issue of *capital stock* in return for the *asset,* land, is reported in the statement of changes in financial position as though stock were issued for *cash* and cash were used to acquire land. Other examples of transactions that require the dual transaction fiction are the issue of a *mortgage* in return for a noncurrent asset and the

E

e. The base of natural logarithms: 2.7182818284-59045. . . . If *interest* is compounded continuously during a period at stated rate of *r* per period, then the effective *interest rate* is equivalent to interest compounded once per period at rate *i* where $i = e^r - 1$. Tables of e^r are widely available. If 12 percent annual interest is compounded continuously, the effective rate is $e^{.12} - 1 = 12.75$ percent.

earnings. *Income,* or sometimes *profit.*

earnings cycle. The period of time that elapses for a given firm, or the series of transactions, during which *cash* is converted into *goods* and *services,* goods and services are sold to customers, and customers pay for their purchases with cash. *Cash cycle.*

earnings per share (of common stock). *Net income* to common stockholders (net income minus *preferred dividends*) divided by the average number of *common shares* outstanding. See *ratio.*

earnings per share (of preferred stock). *Net income* divided by the average number of *preferred shares* outstanding during the period. This ratio indicates how well the preferred dividends are covered or protected; it does not indicate a legal share of *earnings.* See *ratio.*

earnings, retained. See *retained earnings.*

easement. The acquired right or privilege of one person to use, or have access to, certain property of another. For example, a public utility's right to lay pipes or lines under property of another and to service those facilities.

economic entity. See *entity.*

economic life. The time span over which the benefits of an *asset* are expected to be received. The economic life of a *patent, copyright,* or *franchise* may be less than the legal life. *Service life.*

economic order quantity. In mathematical *inventory* analysis, the optimal amount of stock to order when inventory is reduced to a level called the "reorder point." If A represents the *incremental cost* of placing a single order, D represents the total demand for a period of time in units, and H represents the incremental holding cost during the period per unit of inventory, then the economic order quantity $Q = \sqrt{2AD/H}$. Q is sometimes called the "optimal lot size."

effective (interest) rate. Of a bond, the *internal rate of return* or *yield to maturity* at the time of issue. Contrast with *coupon rate.* If the bond is issued for a price below *par,* the effective rate is higher than the coupon rate; if it is issued for a price greater than par, then the effective rate is lower than the coupon rate.

In the context of *compound interest,* when the *compounding period* on a *loan* is different from one year, such as a nominal interest rate of 12 percent compounded monthly, then the single payment that could be made at the end of a year that is economically equivalent to the series of interest payments is larger than an amount equal to the quoted nominal rate multiplied by the *principal.* If 12 percent per year is compounded monthly, the effective interest rate is 12.683 percent. In general, if the nominal rate is r percent per year and is compounded m times per year, then the effective rate is $(1 + r/m)^m - 1$.

efficiency variance. A term used for the *quantity variance* for labor or *variable overhead* in a *standard cost system.*

efficient market hypothesis. The supposition in finance that securities' prices reflect all available information and react nearly instantaneously and in an unbiased fashion to new information.

eliminations. *Worksheet* entries to prepare *consolidated statements* that are made to avoid duplicating the amounts of *assets, liabilities, owners' equity, revenues,* and *expenses* of the consolidated *entity* when the accounts of the *parent* and *subsidiaries* are summed.

employee stock option. See *stock option.*

employer, employee payroll taxes. See *payroll taxes.*

enabling costs. A type of *capacity cost* that will stop being incurred if operations are shut down completely but must be incurred in full if operations are carried out at any level. Costs of a security force or of a quality control inspector for an assembly line might be examples. Contrast with *standby costs.*

ending inventory. The *cost of inventory* on hand at the end of the *accounting period,* often called "closing inventory." The dollar amount of inventory to be carried to the subsequent period.

entity. A person, *partnership, corporation,* or other organization. The *accounting entity* for which accounting statements are prepared may not be the same as the entity defined by law. For example, a *sole proprietorship* is an accounting entity, but the individual's combined business and personal assets are the legal entity in most jurisdictions. Several affiliated corporations may be separate legal entities while *consolidated financial statements* are prepared for the group of companies operating as a single economic entity.

entity theory. The view of the corporation that emphasizes the form of the *accounting equation* that says *assets = equities.* Contrast with *proprietorship theory.* The entity theory is less concerned with a distinct line between *liabilities* and *stockholders' equity* than is the proprietorship theory. Rather, all equities are provided to the corporation by outsiders who merely have claims of differing legal standings. The entity theory implies using a *multiple-step* income statement.

entry value. The current *cost* of acquiring an asset or service at a *fair market price. Replacement cost.*

EOQ. *Economic order quantity.*

EPS. *Earnings per share.*

EPVI. *Excess present value index.*

equities. *Liabilities* plus *owners' equity.*

equity. A claim to *assets;* a source of assets.

equity financing. Raising *funds* by issuance of *capital stock.* Contrast with *debt financing.*

equity method. A method of accounting for an *investment* in the stock of another company in which the proportionate share of the earnings of the other company is debited to the investment account and credited to a *revenue* account as earned. When *dividends* are received, *cash* is debited and the investment account is credited. Used in reporting when the investor owns twenty percent or more of the stock of an unconsolidated company. One of the few instances where revenue is recognized without a change in *working capital.*

equity ratio. *Stockholders' equity* divided by total *assets.*

equivalent production. *Equivalent units.*

equivalent units (of work). The number of units of completed output that would require the same costs as were actually incurred for production during a period. Used primarily in *process costing* calculations to measure in uniform terms the output of a continuous process.

ERISA. Employee Retirement Income Security Act of 1974. The federal law that sets *pension plan* requirements.

estimated liability. The preferred terminology for estimated costs to be incurred for such uncertain things as repairs under *warranty.* An estimated liability is shown in the *balance sheet.* Contrast with *contingent liability.*

estimated salvage value. Synonymous with *salvage value* of an *asset* before its retirement.

estimates, changes in. See *accounting changes.*

except for. Qualification in *auditor's report,* usually caused by a change, approved by the auditor, from one acceptable accounting principle or procedure to another.

excess present value. In a *capital budgeting* context, *present value* of (anticipated net cash inflows minus cash outflows including initial cash outflow) for a project.

excess present value index. *Present value* of future *cash* inflows divided by initial cash outlay.

exchange. The generic term for a transaction (or more technically, a reciprocal transfer) between one entity and another. In another context, the name for a market, such as the New York Stock Exchange.

exchange gain or loss. The phrase used by the *FASB* for *foreign exchange gain or loss.*

exchange rate. The *price* of one country's currency in terms of another country's currency. For example, the British pound might be worth \$1.80 at a given time. The exchange rate would be stated as "one pound is worth one dollar and eighty cents" or "one dollar is worth .5556 (= £1/\$1.80) pounds."

excise tax. Tax on the manufacture, sale, or consumption of a commodity.

ex-dividend. Said of stock at the time when the declared *dividend* becomes the property of the person who owned the stock on the *record date.* The payment date follows the ex-dividend date.

exemption. A term used for various amounts subtracted from gross income to determine taxable income. Not all such subtractions are called "exemptions." See *tax deduction.*

exercise. When the owner of an *option* or *warrant* purchases the security that the option entitles him or her to purchase, he or she has exercised the option or warrant.

exercise price. See *option.*

exit value. The proceeds that would be received if assets were disposed of in an *arm's-length transaction. Current selling price. Net realizable value.*

expected value. The mean or arithmetic *average* of a statistical distribution or series of numbers.

expenditure. Payment of *cash.* Virtually synonymous with *disbursement,* except that some use "expenditure" as a narrower term and exclude from its definition all payments to discharge liabilities.

expense. As a noun, the *cost* of *assets* used up in producing *revenue.* A "gone" asset; an expired cost. Do not confuse with *expenditure* or *disbursement,* which may occur before, when, or after the related expense is recognized. Use the word cost to refer to an item that still has service potential and is an asset. Use the word expense after the asset's service potential has been used. As a verb, to designate a past or current expenditure as a current expense.

expense account. An *account* to accumulate *expenses;* such accounts are closed at the end of the accounting period. A *temporary owners' equity* account. Also used to describe a listing of expenses by an employee submitted to the employer for reimbursement.

expired cost. An *expense* or a *loss.*

Exposure Draft. A preliminary statement of the *FASB* (or *APB* between 1962 and 1973) which shows the contents of a pronouncement the Board is considering making effective.

external reporting. Reporting to stockholders and the public, as opposed to internal reporting for management's benefit. See *financial accounting* and contrast with *managerial accounting.*

extraordinary item. A *material expense* or *revenue* item characterized both by its unusual nature and infrequency of occurrence that is shown along with its income tax effects separately from ordinary income and *income from discontinued operations* on the *income statement.* A *loss* from an earthquake would probably be classified as an extraordinary item. Gain (or loss) on retirement of *bonds* is treated as an extraordinary item under the terms of *FASB Statement* No. 4.

F

face amount (value). The nominal amount due at *maturity* from a *bond* or *note* not including contractual interest that may also be due on the same date. The corresponding amount of a stock certificate is best called the *par* or *stated value,* whichever is applicable.

factory. Used synonymously with *manufacturing* as an adjective.

factory burden. *Manufacturing overhead.*

factory cost. *Manufacturing cost.*

factory expense. *Manufacturing overhead. Expense* is a poor term in this context because the item is a *product cost.*

factory overhead. Usually an item of *manufacturing cost* other than *direct labor* or *direct materials.*

fair market price (value). Price (value) determined at *arm's length* between a willing buyer and a willing seller, each acting rationally in their own self interest. May be estimated in the absence of a monetary transaction.

fair presentation (fairness). When the *auditor's report* says that the *financial statements* "present fairly . . . ," the auditor means that the accounting alternatives used by the entity are all in accordance with *GAAP.* In recent years, however, courts are finding that conformity with *generally accepted accounting principles* may be insufficient grounds for an opinion that the statements are fair. *SAS* No. 5

requires that the auditor judge the accounting principles used "appropriate in the circumstances" before attesting to fair presentation.

FASB. Financial Accounting Standards Board. An independent board responsible, since 1973, for establishing *generally accepted accounting principles.* Its official pronouncements are called "Statements of Financial Accounting Standards" and "Interpretations of Financial Accounting Standards." See *Discussion Memorandum.*

FASB Interpretation. An official statement of the *FASB* interpreting the meaning of *Accounting Research Bulletins, APB Opinions,* and *Statements of Financial Accounting Standards.*

favorable variance. An excess of actual *revenues* over expected revenues; an excess of *standard cost* over actual cost.

federal income tax. *Income tax* levied by the U.S. government on individuals and corporations.

Federal Unemployment Tax Act. see *FUTA.*

feedback. The process of informing employees about how their actual performance compares with the expected or desired level of performance in the hope that the information will reinforce desired behavior and reduce unproductive behavior.

FEI. *Financial Executives Institute.*

FICA. Federal Insurance Contributions Act. The law that sets *"Social Security" taxes* and benefits.

FIFO. First-in, first-out; an *inventory flow assumption* by which *ending inventory* cost is determined from most recent purchases and *cost of goods sold* is determined from oldest purchases including beginning inventory. See *LISH.* Contrast with *LIFO.*

finance. As a verb, to supply with *funds* through the *issue* of stocks, bonds, notes, or mortgages, or through the retention of earnings.

financial accounting. The accounting for *assets, equities, revenues,* and *expenses* of a business. Primarily concerned with the historical reporting of the *financial position* and operations of an *entity* to external users on a regular, periodic basis. Contrast with *managerial accounting.*

Financial Accounting Standards Board. *FASB.*

Financial Executives Institute. An organization of financial executives, such as chief accountants, *controllers,* and treasurers of large businesses.

financial expense. An *expense* incurred in raising or managing *funds.*

financial position (condition). Statement of the *assets* and *equities* of a firm displayed on the *balance sheet* statement.

financial ratio. See *ratio.*

financial statements. The *balance sheet, income statement, statement of retained earnings, statement of changes in financial position,* statement of changes in *owners' equity accounts,* and *notes* thereto.

financial structure. *Capital structure.*

financing lease. A *lease* treated by the lessee as both the borrowing of funds and the acquisition of an *asset* to be *amortized.* Both the *liability* and the asset are recognized on the balance sheet. Expenses consist of *interest* on the *debt* and *amortization* of the asset. The lessor treats the lease as the sale of the asset in return for a series of future cash receipts. Contrast with *operating lease.* Called a "capital lease" by the *FASB* in Statement No. 13.

finished goods. Manufactured product ready for sale; a *current asset (inventory) account.*

firm. Informally, any business entity. (Strictly speaking, a firm is a *partnership.*)

first-in, first-out. See *FIFO.*

fiscal year. A period of 12 consecutive months chosen by a business as the *accounting period* for annual reports. May or may not be a *natural business year* or a calendar year.

FISH. An acronym, conceived by George H. Sorter, for *first-in, still-here. FISH* is the same cost flow assumption as *LIFO.* Many readers of accounting statements find it easier to think about inventory questions in terms of items still on hand. Think of LIFO in connection with *cost of goods sold* but of FISH in connection with *ending inventory.* See *LISH.*

fixed assets. *Plant assets.*

fixed budget. A plan that provides for specified amounts of *expenditures* and *receipts* that do not vary with activity levels. Sometimes called a "static budget." Contrast with *flexible budget.*

fixed cost (expense). An *expenditure* or *expense* that does not vary with volume of activity, at least in the short run. See *capacity costs,* which include *enabling costs* and *standby costs,* and *programmed costs* for various subdivisions of fixed costs.

fixed liability. *Long-term* liability.

fixed manufacturing overhead applied. The portion of *fixed manufacturing overhead cost* allocated to units produced during a period.

fixed-benefit plan. A *defined benefit (pension) plan.*

flexible budget. *Budget* that projects receipts and expenditures as a function of activity levels. Contrast with *fixed budget.*

flexible budget allowance. With respect to manufacturing overhead, the total cost that should have been incurred at the level of activity actually experienced during the period.

flow. The change in the amount of an item over time. Contrast with *stock*.

flow assumption. When a *withdrawal* is made from *inventory*, the cost of the withdrawal must be determined by a flow assumption if *specific identification* of units is not used. The usual flow assumptions are *FIFO, LIFO,* and *weighted-average*.

flow of costs. *Costs* passing through various classifications within an *entity*. The diagram on the next page summarizes *product* and *period cost* flows.

flow-through method. Accounting for the *investment tax credit* to show all income statement benefits of the credit in the year of acquisition, rather than spreading them over the life of the asset acquired, called the "deferral method." The *APB* preferred the deferral method in Opinion No. 2 (1962) but accepted the flow-through method in Opinion No. 4 (1964). Sometimes also used in connection with *depreciation* accounting where *straight-line method* is used for financial reporting and an *accelerated* method for tax reporting. Followers of the flow-through method would not recognize a *deferred tax liability*. APB Opinion No. 11 prohibited the use of the flow-through approach in this connection.

FOB. Free on board some location (for example, FOB shipping point; FOB destination); the *invoice* price includes delivery at seller's expense to that location. Title to goods usually passes from seller to buyer at the FOB location.

footnotes. More detailed information than that provided in the *income statement, balance sheet, statement of retained earnings,* and *statement of changes in financial position;* these are considered an integral part of the statements and are covered by the *auditor's report.* Sometimes called "notes."

forecast. An estimate or projection of costs or revenues or both.

foreign exchange gain or loss. Gain or loss from holding *net* foreign *monetary items* during a period when the *exchange rate* changes.

Form 10-K. See *10-K*.

franchise. A privilege granted or sold, such as to use a name or to sell products or services.

free on board. *FOB.*

freight-in. The *cost* of freight or shipping in acquiring *inventory*, preferably treated as a part of the cost of *inventory*. Often shown temporarily in an *adjunct account* that is closed by the acquirer at the end of the period with other purchase accounts to the inventory account.

freight-out. The *cost* of freight or shipping in selling *inventory*, treated by the seller as a selling *expense* in the period of sale.

full costing. *Absorption costing*. See *discovery value accounting* for another definition in the context of accounting for natural resources.

full disclosure. The reporting policy requiring that all significant or *material* information is to be presented in the financial statements. See *fair presentation*.

fully vested. Said of a *pension plan* when an employee (or his or her estate) has rights to all the benefits purchased with the employer's contributions to the plan even if the employee is not employed by this employer at the time of retirement.

functional classification. *Income statement* reporting form in which *expenses* are reported by functions, that is, cost of goods sold, administrative expenses, financing expenses, selling expenses; contrast with *natural classification*.

fund. An *asset* or group of assets set aside for a specific purpose. See also *fund accounting*.

fund accounting. The accounting for resources, obligations, and *capital* balances, usually of a not-for-profit or governmental *entity*, which have been segregated into *accounts* representing logical groupings based on legal, donor, or administrative restrictions or requirements. The groupings are described as "funds." The accounts of each fund are *self-balancing* and from them a *balance sheet* and an operating statement for each fund can be prepared. See *fund*.

funded. Said of a *pension plan* or other obligation when *funds* have been set aside for meeting the obligation when it becomes due. The federal law for pension plans requires that all *normal costs* be funded as recognized. In addition, *past and prior service costs* of pension plans must be funded over 30 or 40 years, depending on the circumstances.

funding. Replacing *short-term* liabilities with *long-term* debt.

funds. Generally *working capital;* current assets less current liabilities. Sometimes used to refer to *cash* or to cash and *marketable securities*.

funds provided by operations. An important subtotal in the *statement of changes in financial position*. This amount is the total of revenues producing *funds* less *expenses* requiring funds. Often, the amount is shown as *net income* plus expenses not requiring funds (such as depreciation charges) minus revenues not producing funds (such as revenues recognized under the *equity method* of accounting for a long-term investment). The statement of changes in financial position maintains the same distinctions between *continuing*

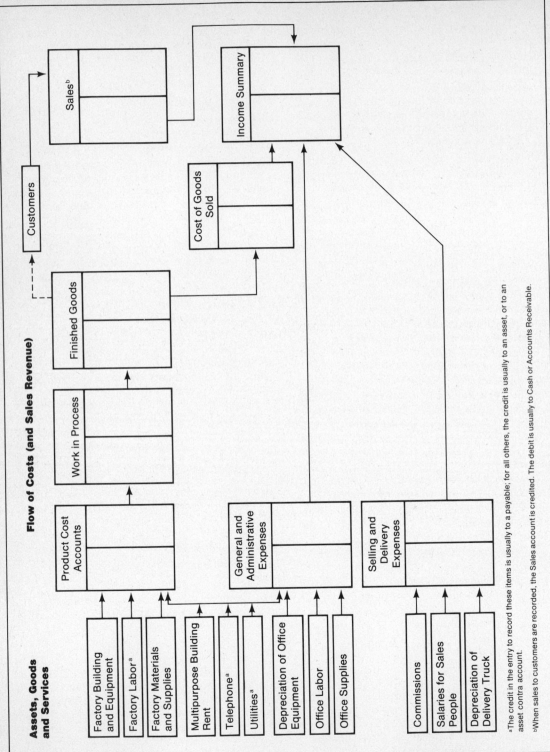

operations, discontinued operations, and *income* or *loss* from *extraordinary items* as in the *income statement.*

funds statement. An informal name often used for the *statement of changes in financial position.*

FUTA. Federal Unemployment Tax Act, which provides for taxes to be collected at the federal level, to help subsidize the individual states' administration of their unemployment compensation programs.

G

GAAP. *Generally accepted accounting principles.* A plural noun.

gain. Excess of *revenues* over *expenses* from a specific transaction. Frequently used in the context of describing a transaction not part of a firm's typical, day-to-day operations.

general expenses. *Operating expenses* other than those specifically assigned to cost of goods sold, selling, and administration.

general journal. The formal record where transactions, or summaries of similar transactions, are recorded in *journal entry* form as they occur.

general ledger. The name for the formal *ledger* containing all of the financial statement accounts. It has equal debits and credits as evidenced by the *trial balance.* Some of the accounts in the general ledger may be *controlling accounts,* supported by details contained in *subsidiary ledgers.*

general price index. A measure of the aggregate prices of a wide range of goods and services in the economy at one time relative to the prices during a base period. See *consumer price index* and *GNP Implicit Price Deflator.* Contrast with *specific price index.*

general price level changes. Changes in the aggregate prices of a wide range of goods and services in the economy. These price changes are measured using a *general price index.* Contrast with *specific price changes.*

general price level-adjusted statements. See *price level-adjusted statements.*

general purchasing power of the dollar. The command of the dollar over a wide range of goods and services in the economy. The general purchasing power of the dollar is inversely related to changes in a general price index. See *general price index.*

generally accepted accounting principles (GAAP). As previously defined by the *APB* and now by the *FASB,* the conventions, rules, and procedures necessary to define accepted accounting practice at a particular time; includes both broad guidelines and relatively detailed practices and procedures.

generally accepted auditing standards. The standards, as opposed to particular procedures, promulgated by the *AICPA* (in *Statements on Auditing Standards*), that concern "the auditor's professional qualities" and "the judgment exercised by him in the performance of his examination and in his report." Currently, there are 10 such standards, three general ones (concerned with proficiency, independence, and degree of care to be exercised), three standards of field work, and four standards of reporting. The first standard of reporting requires that the *auditor's report* state whether or not the *financial statements* are prepared in accordance with *generally accepted accounting principles.* Thus the typical auditor's report says that the examination was conducted in accordance with generally accepted accounting principles and that the statements are prepared in accordance with generally accepted accounting principles. See *auditor's report.*

GNP Implicit Price Deflator (Index). A *price index* issued quarterly by the Office of Business Economics of the U.S. Department of Commerce. This index attempts to trace the price level of all *goods and services* comprising the *gross national product.* Contrast with *consumer price index.*

going-concern assumption. For accounting purposes a business is assumed to remain in operation long enough for all its current plans to be carried out. This assumption is part of the justification for the *acquisition cost* basis, rather than a *liquidation* or *exit value* basis, of accounting.

goods. Items of merchandise, supplies, raw materials, or finished goods. Sometimes the meaning of "goods" is extended to include all *tangible* items, as in the phrase "goods and services."

goods available for sale. The sum of *beginning inventory* plus all acquisitions, or purchases, of merchandise or finished goods during an *accounting period.*

goods in process. *Work in process.*

goodwill. The excess of cost of an acquired firm or operating unit over the current or *fair market value* of *net assets* of the acquired unit. Informally used to indicate the value of good customer relations, high employee morale, a well-respected business name, and so on, that are expected to result in greater than normal earning power.

goodwill method. A method of accounting for the *admission* of a new partner to a *partnership* when the new partner is to be credited with a portion of capital different from the value of the *tangible* assets contributed as a fraction of tangible assets of the partnership.

graded vesting. Said of a *pension plan* where not all employee benefits are currently *vested*. By law, the benefits must become vested according to one of several formulas as time passes.

gross. Not adjusted or reduced by deductions or subtractions. Contrast with *net*.

gross margin. *Net sales* minus *cost of goods sold*.

gross margin percentage. $100 \times (1 - cost\ of\ goods\ sold/net\ sales) = 100 \times (gross\ margin/net\ sales)$.

gross national product (GNP). The market value within a nation for a year of all goods and services produced as measured by final sales of goods and services to individuals, corporations, and governments plus the excess of exports over imports.

gross profit. *Gross margin.*

gross profit ratio. *Gross margin* divided by *net sales*.

gross sales. All *sales* at *invoice* prices, not reduced by *discounts, allowances, returns,* or other adjustments.

group depreciation. A method of calculating *depreciation* charges where similar assets are combined, rather than depreciated separately. No gain or loss is recognized on retirement of items from the group until the last item in the group is sold or retired.

H

historical cost. *Acquisition cost; original cost;* a *sunk cost.*

historical summary. A part of the *annual report* to stockholders that shows important items, such as *net income, revenues, expenses, asset* and *equity* totals, *earnings per share,* and the like, for five or ten periods including the current one. Usually not as much detail is shown in the historical summary as in *comparative statements,* which typically report as much detail for the immediately preceding year as for the current year. Annual reports may contain both comparative statements and a historical summary.

holding company. A company that confines its activities to owning *stock* in, and supervising management of, other companies. A holding company usually owns a controlling interest in, that is, more than 50 percent of the voting stock of, the companies whose stock it holds. Contrast with *mutual fund*. See *conglomerate*.

holding gain or loss. Difference between end-of-period price and beginning-of-period price of an asset held during the period. Ordinarily, realized holding gains and losses are not separately reported in financial statements. Unrealized gains are not usually reflected in income at all. Some unrealized losses, such as on inventory or marketable securities, are reflected in income or *owners' equity* as the losses occur. See *inventory profit* for further refinement, including *gains* on *assets* sold during the period.

horizontal analysis. *Time series analysis.*

human resource accounting. A term used to describe a variety of proposals that seek to report and emphasize the importance of human resources—knowledgeable, trained, and loyal employees—in a company's earning process and total assets.

I

ideal standard costs. *Standard costs* set equal to those that would be incurred under the best possible conditions.

IIA. *Institute of Internal Auditors.*

IMA. *Institute of Management Accounting.* See *CMA* and *National Association of Accountants.*

improvement. An *expenditure* to extend the useful life of an *asset* or to improve its performance (rate of output, cost) over that of the original asset. Such expenditures are *capitalized* as part of the asset's cost. Contrast with *maintenance* and *repair*.

imputed cost. A cost that does not appear in accounting records, such as the *interest* that could be earned on cash spent to acquire inventories rather than, say, government bonds. Or, consider a firm that owns the buildings it occupies. This firm has an imputed cost for rent in an amount equal to what it would have to pay to use similar buildings owned by another.

imputed interest. See *interest, imputed*.

in the black (red). Operating at a profit (loss).

income. Excess of *revenues* and *gains* over *expenses* and *losses* for a period; *net income*. Sometimes used with an appropriate modifier to refer to the various intermediate amounts shown in a *multiple-step income statement*. Sometimes used to refer to revenues, as in "rental income."

income accounts. *Revenue* and *expense accounts.*

income distribution account. *Temporary account* sometimes debited when *dividends* are declared; closed to *retained earnings*.

income from continuing operations. As defined by *APB Opinion* No. 30, all *revenues* less all *expenses* except for the following: results of operations, including income tax effects, that have been or will be discontinued; *gains* or *losses,* including income tax effects, on disposal of segments of the business; gains or losses, including income tax effects, from *extraordinary items;* and the cumulative effect of *accounting changes.*

income from discontinued operations. *Income,* net of tax effects, from parts of the business that have been discontinued during the period or are to be discontinued in the near future. Such items are reported on a separate line of the *income statement* after *income from continuing operations* but before *extraordinary items.*

income (revenue) bond. See *special revenue debt.*

income statement. The statement of *revenues, expenses, gains,* and *losses* for the period ending with *net income* for the period. The *earnings per share* amount is usually shown on the income statement; the *reconciliation* of beginning and ending balances of *retained earnings* may also be shown in a combined statement of income and retained earnings. See *income from continuing operations, income from discontinued operations, extraordinary items.*

income summary. An *account* used in problem solving that serves as a surrogate for the *income statement.* All *revenues* are closed to the Income Summary as *credits* and all *expenses,* as *debits.* The *balance* in the account, after all other *closing entries* are made, is then closed to the retained earnings or other *owners' equity* account and represents *net income* for the period.

income tax. An annual tax levied by the federal and other governments on the income of an entity. An *expense;* if not yet paid, a *liability.*

income tax allocation. See *deferred tax liability* and *tax allocation: intrastatement.*

incremental. An adjective used to describe the change in *cost, expense, investment, cash flow, revenue, profit,* and the like if one more unit is produced or sold or if an activity is undertaken.

indenture. See *bond indenture.*

independence. The mental attitude required of the *CPA* in performing the *attest* function. It implies impartiality and that the members of the auditing CPA firm own no stock in the corporation being audited.

independent accountant. The *CPA* who performs the *attest* function for a firm.

indeterminate-term liability. A *liability* lacking the criterion of being due at a definite time. This term is our own coinage to encompass the *deferred income tax liability* and *minority interest.*

indexation. An attempt by lawmakers or parties to a contract, to cope with the effects of *inflation.* Amounts fixed in law or contracts are "indexed" when these amounts change as a given measure of price changes. For example, a so-called escalator clause in a labor contract might provide that hourly wages will be increased as the *consumer price index* increases. Many economists have suggested the indexation of numbers fixed in the *income tax* laws. If, for example, the personal *exemption* is $750 at the start of the period, prices rise by 10 percent during the period, and the personal exemption is indexed, then the personal exemption would automatically rise to $825 ($= \$750 + .10 \times \$750$) at the end of the period.

indirect costs. Costs of production not easily associated with the production of specific goods and services; *overhead costs.* May be *allocated* on some arbitrary basis to specific products or departments.

indirect labor (material) cost. An *indirect cost* for labor (material) such as for supervisors (supplies).

inflation. A time of generally rising prices.

information system. A system, sometimes formal and sometimes informal, for collecting, processing, and communicating data that are useful for the managerial functions of decision making, planning, and control, and for financial reporting under the *attest* requirement.

insolvent. Unable to pay debts when due. Said of a company even though *assets* exceed *liabilities.*

installment. Partial payment of a debt or collection of a receivable, usually according to a contract.

installment contracts receivable. The name used for *accounts receivable* when the *installment method* of recognizing revenue is used. Its *contra, unrealized gross margin,* is shown on the balance sheet as a subtraction from the amount receivable.

installment sales. Sales on account where the buyer promises to pay in several separate payments, called *installments.* Sometimes are, but need not be, accounted for on the *installment method.* If installment sales are accounted for with the sales *basis of revenue recognition* for financial reporting but with the installment method for income tax returns, then a *deferred income tax liability* arises.

installment (sales) method. Recognizing *revenue* and *expense* (or *gross margin*) from a sales transaction in proportion to the fraction of the selling price collected during a period. Allowed by the *IRS* for income tax reporting, but acceptable in *GAAP* (*APB Opinion* No. 10) only when cash collections are sufficiently uncertain.

Institute of Internal Auditors. The national association of accountants who are engaged in internal auditing and are employed by business firms. See *CIA.*

Institute of Management Accounting. See *CMA.*

insurance. A contract for reimbursement of specific losses; purchased with insurance premiums. Self-insurance is not insurance but merely the willingness to assume risk of incurring losses while saving the premium.

intangible asset. A nonphysical, *noncurrent* asset such as a *copyright, patent, trademark, goodwill, organization cost, capitalized* advertising cost, computer program, license for any of the preceding, government license (e.g., broadcasting or the right to sell liquor), *lease, franchise,* mailing list, exploration permit, import and export permit, construction permit, marketing quota, and other right that gives a firm an exclusive or preferred position in the marketplace.

intercompany elimination. See *eliminations.*

intercompany profit. If one *affiliated company* sells to another, and the goods remain in the second company's *inventory* at the end of the period, then the first company's *profit* has not been realized by a sale to an outsider. That profit is called "intercompany profit" and is eliminated from net *income* in *consolidated income statements* or when the *equity method* is used.

interest. The charge or cost for using money; expressed as a rate per period, usually one year, called the interest rate. See *effective interest rate* and *nominal interest rate.*

interest factor. One plus the *interest* rate.

interest, imputed. If a borrower merely promises to pay a single amount, sometime later than the present, then the present value (computed at a *fair market* interest rate, called the "imputed interest rate") of the promise is less than the *face amount* to be paid at *maturity.* The difference between the face amount and the present value of a promise is called imputed interest. See also *imputed cost.*

interest rate. See *interest.*

interim statements. Statements issued for periods less than the regular, annual *accounting period.* Most corporations are required to issue interim statements on a quarterly basis. The basic issue in preparing interim reports is whether their purpose is to report on the interim period (1) as a self-contained accounting period, or (2) as an integral part of the year of which they are a part so that forecasts of annual performance can be made. *APB Opinion* No. 28 and the *SEC* require that interim reports be constructed largely to satisfy the second purpose.

internal audit. An *audit* conducted by employees to ascertain whether or not *internal control* procedures are working, as opposed to an external audit conducted by a *CPA.*

internal control. See *control system.*

internal rate of return. The discount rate that equates the net *present value* of a stream of cash outflows and inflows to zero.

Internal Revenue Service (IRS). Agency of the U.S. Treasury Department responsible for administering the Internal Revenue Code and collecting income, and certain other, taxes.

internal reporting. Reporting for management's use in planning and control; contrast with *external reporting* for financial statement users.

International Accounting Standards Committee. An organization that promotes the establishment of international accounting standards.

interperiod tax allocation. See *deferred income tax liability.*

interpolation. The estimation of an unknown number intermediate between two (or more) known numbers.

intrastatement tax allocation. See *tax allocation: intrastatement.*

inventoriable costs. *Costs* that "attach" to products. *Product costs (assets)* as opposed to *period expenses.*

inventory. As a noun, the *balance* in an asset *account* such as raw materials, supplies, work in process, and finished goods. As a verb, to calculate the *cost* of goods on hand at a given time or to physically count items on hand.

inventory equation. *Beginning inventory + net additions − withdrawals = ending inventory.* Ordinarily, additions are net purchases and withdrawals are *cost of goods sold.* Notice that ending inventory, to be shown on the balance sheet, and cost of goods sold, to be shown on the income statement, are not independent of each other. The larger is one; the smaller must be the other. In valuing inventories, beginning inventory and net purchases are usually known. In some inventory methods (for example, some applications of the *retail inventory method*), cost of goods sold is measured and the equation is used to find the cost of ending inventory. In most methods, cost of ending inventory is measured and the equation is used to find the cost of goods sold (withdrawals). In *replacement cost* (in contrast to *historical cost*) accounting, *additions* (in the equation) include holding gains, whether realized or not. Thus the replacement cost inventory equation is

> *beginning inventory* (at replacement cost)
> + *purchases* (where replacement cost is historical cost)
> + *holding gains* (whether realized or not)
> − *ending inventory* (at replacement cost)
> = *cost of goods sold* (replacement cost)

inventory holding gains. See *inventory profit.*

inventory layer. See LIFO *inventory layer.*

inventory profit. This term has several possible meanings. Consider the data in the accompanying illustration. The *historical cost* data are derived in the conventional manner; the firm uses a *FIFO cost flow assumption.* The *replacement cost* data are assumed, but are of the kind that the *SEC* requires in *ASR* No. 190.

We use the term *distributable income* to refer to revenues less expenses based on replacement, rather than historical, costs. To that subtotal add realized holding gains to arrive at realized (conventional) income. To that, add unrealized holding gains to arrive at *economic income.*

The SEC, in its *Accounting Series Releases,* uses the term "inventory profit" to refer to the realized holding gain, $110 in the illustration. The amount of inventory profit will usually be material when FIFO is used and prices are rising.

Others, including us, prefer to use the term "inventory profit" to refer to the total *holding gain,* $300 (= $110 + $190, both realized and unrealized), but this appears to be a lost cause.

In periods of rising prices and increasing inventories, the realized holding gains under a FIFO cost flow assumption will be substantially larger than under LIFO. In the illustration, for example, assume under LIFO that the historical cost of goods sold is $4,800, that historical LIFO cost of beginning inventory is $600, and that historical LIFO cost of ending inventory is $800. Then distributable income, based on replacement costs, remains $350 (= $5,200 − $4,850), realized holding gains are $50 (= $4,850 − $4,800), realized income is $400 (= $350 + $50), the unrealized holding gain for the year is $250 [= ($1,550 − $800) − ($1,100 − $600)], and economic income is $650 (= $350 + $50 + $250). Because the only real effect of the cost flow assumption is to split the total holding gain into realized and unrealized portions, economic income is the same, independent of the cost flow assumption. The total of holding gains is $300 in the illustration. The choice of cost flow assumption governs how much holding gain is conventionally reported as realized (SEC "inventory profit") and how much is not.

inventory turnover. Number of times the average *inventory* has been sold during a period; *cost of goods sold* for a period divided by average inventory for the period. See *ratio.*

invested capital. *Contributed capital.*

investee. A company whose *stock* is owned by another.

Inventory Profit Illustration

Assumed Data	(Historical) Acquisition Cost Assuming FIFO	Replacement Cost
Inventory, 1/1/X0	$ 900	$1,100
Inventory, 12/31/X0	1,160	1,550
Cost of Goods Sold for 19X0	4,740	4,850
Sales for 19X0 . . . . $5,200		
Income Statement for 19X0		
Sales.	$5,200	$5,200
Cost of Goods Sold	4,740	4,850
(1) **Distributable Income**.		$ 350
Realized Holding Gains		110[a]
(2) **Realized Income** = Conventional Net Income (Under FIFO)	$ 460	$ 460
Unrealized Holding Gain		190[b]
(3) **Economic Income**		$ 650

[a] Realized holding gain during a period is replacement cost of goods sold less historical cost of goods sold; for 19X0 the realized holding gain under FIFO is $110 = $4,850 − $4,740. The SEC refers to this as "inventory profit".

[b] The total unrealized holding gain at any time is replacement cost of inventory on hand at that time less historical cost of that inventory. The unrealized holding gain during a period is unrealized holding gain at the end of the period less the unrealized holding gain at the beginning of the period. Unrealized holding gain prior to 19X0 is $200 = $1,100 − $900. Unrealized holding gain during 19X0 = ($1,550 − $1,160) − ($1,100 − $900) = $390 − $200 = $190.

investment. An *expenditure* to acquire property or other assets in order to produce *revenue;* the *asset* so acquired; hence, a *current* expenditure made in anticipation of future income. Said of *securities* of other companies held for the long term and shown in a separate section of the *balance sheet;* in this context, contrast with *marketable securities.*

investment tax credit. A reduction in income tax liability granted by the federal government to firms that buy new equipment. This item is a credit, in that it is deducted from the tax bill, not from pretax income. The tax credit has been a given percentage of the purchase price of certain assets purchased. The actual rules and rates have changed over the years. See *flow-through method* and *carry forward.*

invoice. A document showing the details of a sale or purchase transaction.

issue. When a corporation exchanges its stock (or bonds) for cash or other assets, the corporation is said to issue, not sell, that stock (or bonds). Also used in the context of withdrawing supplies or materials from inventory for use in operations and drawing of a *check.*

issued shares. Those shares of *authorized capital stock* of a *corporation* that have been distributed to the stockholders. See *issue.* Shares of *treasury stock* are legally issued but are not considered to be *outstanding* for the purposes of voting, *dividend declarations,* and *earnings per share* calculations.

J

job cost sheet. A schedule showing actual or budgeted inputs for a special order.

job development credit. The name used for the *investment tax credit* in the 1971 tax law on this subject.

job order costing. Accumulation of *costs* for a particular identifiable batch of product, known as a job, as it moves through production.

joint cost. Cost of simultaneously producing or otherwise acquiring two or more products, called joint products, that must, by the nature of the process, be produced or acquired together, such as the cost of beef and hides of cattle. Other examples include central *corporate expenses, overhead* of a department when several products are manufactured, and *basket purchases.* See *common cost.*

joint product. One of two or more outputs from a process that must be produced or acquired simultaneously. See *by-product* and *joint cost.*

journal. The place where transactions are recorded as they occur. The book of original entry.

journal entry. A recording in a *journal,* of equal *debits* and *credits,* with an explanation of the *transaction,* if necessary.

journalize. To make an entry in a *journal.*

L

labor variances. The *price* (or *rate*) and *quantity* (or *usage*) *variances* for *direct labor* inputs in a *standard cost system.*

land. An *asset shown at acquisition cost* plus the *cost* of any nondepreciable *improvements.* In accounting, implies use as a plant or office site, rather than as a *natural resource,* such as timberland or farm land.

last-in, first-out. See *LIFO.*

layer. See *LIFO inventory layer.*

lead time. The time that elapses between order placing and receipt of the ordered *goods or services.*

lease. A contract calling for the lessee (user) to pay the lessor (owner) for the use of an asset. A cancelable lease is one the lessee can cancel at any time. A noncancelable lease requires payments from the lessee for the life of the lease and usually has many of the economic characteristics of *debt financing.* A noncancelable lease meets the usual criteria to be classified as a *liability* but some leases entered into before 1977 need not be shown as a liability. *FASB* Statement No. 13 and the *SEC* requires disclosure in notes to the financial statements of the commitments for noncancelable leases. See *financing lease* and *operating lease.*

leasehold. The *asset* representing the right of the *lessee* to use leased property. See *lease* and *leasehold improvement.*

leasehold improvement. An *improvement* to leased property. Should be *amortized* over *service life* or the life of the lease, whichever is shorter.

least and latest rule. Pay the least amount of taxes as late as possible within the law to minimize the *present value* of tax payments for a given set of operations.

ledger. A book of accounts. Contrast with *journal.*

legal capital. *Par* or *stated value* of issued *capital stock.* The amount of *contributed capital* that, according to state law, must remain permanently in the firm as protection for creditors.

legal entity. See *entity.*

lender. See *loan.*

lessee. See *lease.*

lessor. See *lease.*

leverage. Operating leverage refers to the tendency of *net income* to rise at a faster rate than sales when there are *fixed costs*. A doubling of sales, for example, usually implies a more than doubling of net income. This phenomenon can be studied at *breakeven chart*. Capital leverage refers to the increased rate of return on owners' equity (see *ratio*) when an investment earns a return larger than the *interest rate* paid for *debt* financing. Because the interest charges on debt are usually fixed, any *incremental* income benefits owners and none benefits debtors. When this term is used without a qualifying adjective, it usually refers to the capital leverage and means the use of *long-term* debt in securing *funds* for the *entity*.

liability. Usually, a legal obligation to pay a definite or reasonably certain amount at a definite or reasonably certain time in return for a current benefit. Some of the criteria are not met by items classified as liabilities where there are special circumstances. Examples are *pension* liabilities, estimates of future *warranty* expenditures, and *deferred tax liabilities*. See *indeterminate-term liability*. Other items meet the criteria to be a liability but are not shown as such. For example, noncancelable leases, which are sometimes disclosed only in footnotes; see *lease*.

life annuity. A *contingent annuity* in which payments cease at death of a specified person(s), usually the *annuitant(s)*.

LIFO. An *inventory* flow assumption where the *cost of goods sold* is the cost of the most recently acquired units and the *ending inventory cost* is determined from costs of the oldest units. Contrast with *FIFO*. In periods of rising prices and increasing inventories, LIFO leads to higher reported expenses and therefore lower reported income and lower balance sheet inventories than does FIFO. See also *FISH* and *inventory profit*.

LIFO inventory layer. The *ending inventory* for a period is likely to be larger than the *beginning inventory*. Under a *LIFO cost flow assumption*, this increase in physical quantities is given a value determined by the prices of the earliest purchases during the year. The LIFO inventory, then, consists of layers, sometimes called "slices," which typically consist of relatively small amounts of physical quantities from each of the past several years. Each layer carries the prices from near the beginning of the period when it was acquired. The earliest layers will typically (in periods of rising prices) have prices very much less than current prices. If inventory quantities should decline in a subsequent period, the latest layers enter cost of goods sold first.

limited liability. Stockholders of corporations are not personally liable for debts of the company.

line of business reporting. See *segment reporting*.

line of credit. An agreement with a bank or set of banks for short-term borrowings on demand.

liquid. Said of a business with a substantial amount (the amount is unspecified) of *working capital*, especially *quick assets*.

liquid assets. *Cash*, current *marketable securities*, and, sometimes, *current receivables*.

LISH. An acronym, conceived by George H. Sorter, for *last-in, still-here*. LISH is the same cost flow assumption as *FIFO*. Many readers of accounting statements find it easier to think about inventory questions in terms of items still on hand. Think of FIFO in connection with *cost of goods sold* but of LISH in connection with *ending inventory*. See *FISH*.

list price. The published or nominally quoted price for goods.

list price method. See *trade-in transaction*.

long-lived (term) asset. An asset whose benefits are expected to be received over several years. A *noncurrent* asset, usually includes *investments, plant assets*, and *intangibles*.

loss. Excess of *cost* over net proceeds for a single transaction; negative *income* for a period. A cost expiration that produced no *revenue*.

lower of cost or market. A basis for *inventory* and *marketable securities* valuation where the inventory value is set at the lower of *acquisition cost* or *current*

M

maintenance. *Expenditures* undertaken to preserve an *asset's* service potential for its originally intended life; these expenditures are treated as *period expenses* or *product costs*. Contrast with *improvement*. See *repair*.

make-or-buy decision. A managerial decision about whether the firm should produce a product internally or purchase it from others. Proper make-or-buy decisions in the short run result only when *opportunity costs* are the only costs considered in decision making.

management. Executive authority that operates a business.

management audit. An audit conducted to determine whether the objectives, policies, and procedures for a firm or one of its operating units are properly carried out. Generally applies only to activities for which qualitative standards can be specified. See *audit* and *internal audit*.

management by exception. A principle of management where attention is focused only on performance that is significantly different from that expected.

management (managerial) accounting. Reporting designed to enhance the ability of management to do its job of decision making, planning, and control; contrast with *financial accounting*.

managerial accounting. See *management accounting*.

manufacturing cost. Costs of producing goods, usually in a factory.

manufacturing expense. Another, less useful title for *manufacturing overhead*.

manufacturing overhead. General manufacturing *costs* incurred in providing a capacity to carry on productive activities but that are not directly associated with identifiable units of product. *Fixed* manufacturing overhead costs are treated as a *product cost* under *absorption costing* but as an *expense* of the period under *direct costing*.

margin. *Revenue* less specified expenses. See *contribution margin*, *gross margin* and *current margin*.

margin of safety. Excess of actual, or budgeted, sales over *breakeven* sales. Usually expressed in dollars; may be expressed in units of product.

marginal cost. *Incremental cost* per unit.

marginal costing. *Direct costing*.

marginal revenue. The increment in *revenue* from sale of one additional unit of product.

marginal tax rate. The tax imposed on the next dollar of taxable income generated. Contrast with *statutory tax rate* and *average tax rate*.

market price. See *fair market price*.

market rate. The rate of *interest* a company must pay to borrow *funds* currently. See *effective rate*.

marketable securities. *Stocks* and *bonds* of other companies held that can be readily sold on stock exchanges or over-the-counter markets and that the company plans to sell as cash is needed. Classified as *current assets* and as part of *working capital*. The same securities held for *long-term* purposes would be classified as *noncurrent assets*. *FASB Statement* No. 12 requires the *lower-of-cost-or-market* valuation basis for all marketable equity securities but different accounting treatments (with differing effects on income) depending upon whether the security is a *current* or a *noncurrent asset*.

master budget. A *budget* projecting all *financial statements* and their components.

matching convention. The concept of recognizing cost expirations *(expenses)* in the same accounting period when the related *revenues* are recognized.

material. As an adjective, it means relatively important. See *materiality*. Currently, no operational definition exists. As a noun, *raw material*.

material variances. *Price* and *quantity variances* for *direct materials* in *standard cost systems*. Sometimes used to mean variances that are significant; see *materiality*.

materiality. The concept that accounting should disclose separately only those events that are relatively important (no operable definition yet exists) for the business or for understanding its statements.

maturity. The date at which an obligation, such as the *principal* of a *bond* or a *note*, becomes due.

maturity value. The amount expected to be collected when a loan reaches *maturity*. Depending upon the context, the amount may be *principal* or principal and *interest*.

merchandise. *Finished goods* bought by a retailer or wholesaler for resale. Contrast with finished goods of a manufacturing business.

merchandise turnover. *Inventory turnover* for merchandise; see *ratio*.

merchandising business. As opposed to a manufacturing or service business, one that purchases (rather than manufactures) *finished goods* for resale.

merger. The joining of two or more businesses into a single *economic entity*. See *holding company*.

minority interest. A *balance sheet account* on *consolidated statements* showing the *equity* in a *subsidiary* company allocable to those who are not part of the controlling (majority) interest. May be classified either as stockholders' equity or as a liability of *indeterminate term* on the consolidated balance sheet. On the *income statement*, the minority's interest in current income must be subtracted to arrive at consolidated *net income* for the period.

minority investment. A holding of less than 50 percent of the *voting stock* in another corporation. Accounted for with the *cost method* when less than 20 percent is held, and with the *equity method* otherwise. See *mutual fund*.

mixed cost. A *semifixed* or a *semivariable* cost.

modified cash basis. The *cash basis of accounting* with long-term assets accounted for with the *accrual basis of accounting*.

monetary assets, liabilities. See *monetary items*.

monetary gain or loss. The *gain* or *loss* in general purchasing power as a result of holding *monetary assets* or liabilities during a period when the *general purchasing power of the dollar* changes. During periods of *inflation*, holders of net monetary assets lose, and holders of net monetary liabilities gain, general purchasing power. During periods of *deflation,* holders of net monetary assets gain, and holders of net monetary liabilities lose, general purchasing power.

monetary items. Amounts fixed in terms of dollars by statute or contract. *Cash, accounts receivable, accounts payable,* and *debt.* The distinction between monetary and nonmonetary items is important for general *price level-adjusted statements* and for *foreign exchange gain or loss* computations. In the foreign exchange context, account amounts denominated in dollars are not monetary items, whereas amounts denominated in any other currency are monetary.

money. A word seldom used with precision in accounting, at least in part because economists have not yet agreed on its definition. Economists use the term to refer to both a medium of exchange and a unit of value. See *cash* and *monetary items.*

money-purchase plan. A *pension plan* where the employer contributes a specified amount of cash each year to each employee's pension fund. Benefits ultimately received by the employee are not specifically defined but depend on the rate of return on the cash invested. Sometimes called a "defined-contribution" pension plan. Contrast with *defined-benefit plan.* As of the mid-1970s, most corporate pension plans were defined-benefit plans because both the law and *generally accepted accounting principles* for pensions made defined-benefit plans more attractive than money-purchase plans. The federal pension law of 1974 makes money-purchase plans relatively more attractive than they had been. We expect the number of money-purchase plans to increase. See *ERISA.*

mortgage. A claim given by the borrower (mortgagor) to the lender (mortgagee) against the borrower's property in return for a loan.

moving average. An *average* computed on observations over time. As a new observation becomes available, the oldest one is dropped so that the average is always computed for the same number of observations and only the most recent ones. Sometimes, however, this term is used synonymously with *weighted average.*

mutual fund. An investment company that issues its own stock to the public and uses the proceeds to invest in securities of other companies. A mutual fund usually owns less than five or ten percent of the stock of any one company and accounts for its investments using current *market values.* Contrast with *holding company.*

mutually exclusive projects. Competing investment projects, where accepting one project eliminates the possibility of undertaking the remaining projects.

N

National Association of Accountants (NAA). A national society generally open to all engaged in activities closely associated with *managerial accounting.* Oversees the administration of the *CMA* Examinations through the Institute of Management Accounting.

natural business year. A 12-month period chosen as the reporting period so that the end of the period coincides with a low point in activity or inventories. See *ratio* for a discussion of analyses of financial statements of companies using a natural business year.

natural classification. *Income statement* reporting form in which *expenses* are classified by nature of items as acquired, that is, materials, wages, salaries, insurance, and taxes, as well as depreciation. Contrast with *functional classification.*

natural resources. Timberland, oil and gas wells, ore deposits, and other products of nature that have economic value. The cost of natural resources is subject to *depletion.* Often called "wasting assets." See also *discovery value accounting* and *percentage depletion.*

negative confirmation. See *confirmation.*

net. Reduced by all relevant deductions.

net assets. *Owners' equity;* total *assets* minus total *liabilities.*

net current assets. *Working capital = current assets − current liabilities.*

net income. The excess of all *revenues* and *gains* for a period over all *expenses* and *losses* of the period. Negative net income.

net loss. The excess of all *expenses* and *losses* for a period over all *revenues* and *gains* of the period. Negative *net income.*

net of tax reporting. Reporting, such as for *income from discontinued operations, extraordinary items,* and *prior-period adjustments,* where the amounts presented in *financial statements* have been adjusted for all income tax effects. For example, if an extraordinary loss amounted to $10,000 and the marginal tax rate were 40 percent, then the extraordinary item would be reported "net of taxes" as a $6,000 loss. Hence, all income taxes may not be reported on one line of the income statement. The taxes will be allocated to *income from continuing operations,* income from discontinued operations, extraordinary items, cumulative effects of an accounting change, and prior-period adjustments.

net present value. Discounted or *present value* of all cash inflows and outflows of a project or from an *investment* at a given *discount rate.*

net realizable value. Selling price of an item less reasonable further costs to make the item ready for sale and to sell it.

net sales. Sales (at gross invoice amount) less *returns, allowances,* freight paid for customers, and *discounts* taken.

net working capital. *Working capital;* the "net" is redundant in accounting. Financial analysts sometimes mean *current* assets when they speak of working capital, so for them the "net" is not redundant.

net worth. A misleading term, to be avoided, that means the same as *owners' equity.*

next-in, first-out. See *NIFO.*

NIFO. *next-in, first-out.* In making decisions, many managers consider *replacement costs* (rather than *historical costs*) and refer to them as NIFO costs.

no par. Said of *stock* without a *par value.*

nominal accounts. *Temporary accounts* as opposed to *balance sheet accounts.* All nominal accounts are *closed* at the end of each *accounting period.*

nominal interest rate. A rate specified on a *debt* instrument, which usually differs from the market or *effective rate.* Also, a rate of *interest* quoted for a year. If the interest is compounded more often than annually, then the *effective interest rate* is higher than the nominal rate.

noncancelable. See *lease.*

noncontributory. Said of a *pension plan* where only the employer makes payments to a pension *fund.* Contrast with *contributory.*

noncurrent. Due more than one year (or more than one *operating cycle*) hence.

nonmonetary items. All items that are not monetary; see *montary items.*

nonoperating. In the *income statement* context, said of revenues and expenses arising from transactions incidental to the company's main line(s) of business. In the *statement of changes in financial position* context, said of all sources or uses of *working capital* other than working capital provided by operations.

nonprofit corporation. An incorporated *entity,* such as a hospital, with no owners who share in the earnings. It usually emphasizes providing services rather than maximizing income.

nonrecurring. Said of an event that is not expected to happen often for a given firm. Under *APB* Opinion No. 30, the effects of such events should be disclosed

separately, but as part of *ordinary* items unless the event is also unusual. See *extraordinary item.*

normal cost. *Pension plan* expenses incurred during an *accounting period* for employment services performed during that period. Contrast with *past* and *prior service cost* and see *funded.*

normal spoilage. Costs incurred because of ordinary amounts of spoilage; such costs should be prorated to units produced as *product costs.* Contrast with *abnormal spoilage.*

normal standard cost. The *cost* expected to be incurred under reasonably efficient operating conditions with adequate provision for an average amount of rework, spoilage, and the like.

normal volume. The level of production over a time span, usually one year, that will satisfy demand by purchasers.

note. An unconditional written promise by the maker (borrower) to pay a certain amount on demand or at a certain future time. See *footnotes* for another context.

number of days sales in inventory (or receivable). Days of average inventory on hand (or average collection period for receivables). See *ratio.*

O

OASD(H)I. *Old Age, Survivors, Disability, and (Hospital) Insurance.*

objective. See *reporting objectives* and *objectivity.*

objectivity. The reporting policy implying that formal recognition will not be given to an event in financial statements until the magnitude of the events can be measured with reasonable accuracy and is subject to independent verification.

obsolescence. A decline in *market value* of an *asset* caused by improved alternatives becoming available that will be more *cost-effective;* the decline in market value is unrelated to physical changes in the asset itself. See *partial obsolescence.*

off-balance-sheet financing. A description often used for a *long-term, noncancelable lease* accounted for as an *operating lease.*

Old Age, Survivors, Disability and (Hospital) Insurance. The technical name for Social Security under the Federal Insurance Contribution Act (FICA).

open account. Any *account* with a nonzero debit or credit *balance.*

operating. An adjective used to refer to *revenue* and *expense* items relating to the company's main line(s) of business.

operating accounts. *Revenue, expense,* and *production cost accounts.* Contrast with *balance sheet account.*

operating cycle. *Earnings cycle.*

operating expenses. *Expenses* incurred in the course of *ordinary* activities of an *entity.* Frequently, a narrower classification including only *selling, general,* and *administrative expenses,* thereby excluding *cost of goods sold, interest,* and *income tax* expenses.

operating lease. A *lease* accounted for by the *lessee* without showing an *asset* for the lease rights *(leasehold)* or a *liability* for the lease payment obligations. Rental payments of the lessee are merely shown as *expenses* of the period. The lessor keeps the asset on his or her *books* and shows the rental payments as *revenues.* Contrast with *financing lease.* Note that the same lease may have been, in some cases prior to *FASB Statement* No. 13, treated as a financing lease by the lessor and an operating lease by the lessee.

operating margin (based on replacement costs). *Revenues* from *sales* minus current *replacement cost* of goods sold. A measure of operating efficiency that is independent of the *cost flow assumption* for *inventory.* Sometimes called "current (gross) margin." See *inventory profit* for example computations.

operating ratio. See *ratio.*

operational control. See *control system.*

opinion. The *auditor's report* containing an attestation or lack thereof. Also, *APB Opinion.*

opportunity cost. The *present value* of the *income* (or *costs*) that could be earned (or saved) from using an *asset* in its best alternative use to the one being considered.

option. The legal right to buy something during a specified period at a specified price, called the *exercise* price. Employee stock options should not be confused with put and call options traded in various public markets.

ordinary annuity. An *annuity in arrears.*

ordinary income. For income tax purposes, reportable *income* not qualifying as *capital gains.*

organization costs. The *costs* incurred in planning and establishing an *entity;* example of an *intangible* asset. Often, since the amounts are not *material,* the costs are treated as *expenses* in the period incurred even though the *expenditures* clearly provide future benefits and should be treated as *assets.*

original cost. *Acquisition cost.* In public-utility accounting, the acquisition cost to the *entity* first devoting the asset to public use.

original entry. Entry in a *journal.*

outlay. The amount of an *expenditure.*

out-of-pocket. Said of an *expenditure* usually paid for with cash. An *incremental* cost.

out-of-stock cost. The estimated decrease in future *profit* as a result of losing customers because insufficient quantities of *inventory* are currently on hand to meet customers' demands.

output. Physical quantity or monetary measurement of *goods* and *services* produced.

outstanding. Unpaid or uncollected. When said of *stock,* the shares issued less *treasury stock.* When said of checks, it means a check issued that did not clear the *drawer's* bank prior to the *bank statement* date.

overapplied (overabsorbed) overhead. An excess of costs applied, or *charged,* to product for a period over actual *overhead* costs during the period. A *credit balance* in an overhead account after overhead is assigned to product.

overdraft. A check written on a checking account that contains less funds than the amount of the check.

overhead costs. Any *cost* not specifically or directly associated with the production or sale of identifiable goods and services. Sometimes called "burden" or "indirect costs" and, in Britain, "oncosts." Frequently limited to manufacturing overhead. See *central corporate expenses* and *manufacturing overhead.*

overhead rate. Standard, or other predetermined, rate at which *overhead costs* are applied to products or to services.

owners' equity. *Proprietorship; assets* minus *liabilities; paid-in capital* plus *retained earnings* of a corporation; partners' capital accounts in a *partnership;* owner's capital account in a *sole proprietorship.*

P

paid-in capital. Sum of balances in *capital stock* and *capital contributed in excess of par (or stated) value* accounts. Same as *contributed capital* (minus *donated capital*).

paper profit. A *gain* not yet realized through a *transaction.* An *unrealized holding gain.*

par. See *at par* and *face amount.*

par value. *Face amount* of a *security.*

par value method. The method of accounting for *treasury stock* that *debits* a common stock account with the *par value* of the shares reacquired and allocates the remaining debits between the *additional paid-in capital* and *retained earnings* accounts. Contrast with *cost method.*

parent company. Company owning more than 50 percent of the voting shares of another company, called the *subsidiary.*

partial obsolescence. As technology improves, the economic value of existing *assets* declines. In many cases, however, it will not pay a firm to replace the existing asset with a new one even though the new type, rather than the old, would be acquired if the acquisition were to be made currently. In these cases, the accountant should theoretically recognize a loss from partial obsolescence from the firm's owning an old, out-of-date asset, but *GAAP* does not permit recognition of partial obsolescence. The old asset will be carried at *cost* less *accumulated depreciation* until it is retired from service. See *obsolescence.*

partially funded. Said of a *pension plan* where not all earned benefits have been funded. See *funded* for funding requirements.

partially vested. Said of a *pension plan* where not all employee benefits are *vested.* See *graded vesting.*

past service cost. *Present value* at a given time of a *pension plan's* unrecognized, and usually unfunded, benefits assigned to employees for their service before the inception of the plan. A part of *prior service cost.* See *prior service cost* for disclosure rules. See *funded.* Contrast with *normal cost.*

patent. A right granted for up to 17 years by the federal government to exclude others from manufacturing, using, or selling a claimed design, product, or plant (e.g., a new breed of rose) or from using a claimed process or method of manufacture. An asset if acquired by purchase. If developed internally, the development costs are *expensed* when incurred under current *GAAP.*

payable. Unpaid but not necessarily due or past due.

payback period. Amount of time that must elapse before the cash inflows from a project equal the cash outflows.

payback reciprocal. One divided by the *payback period.* This number approximates the *internal rate of return* on a project when the project life is more than twice the payback period and the cash inflows are identical in every period after the initial investment.

payout ratio. *Common stock dividends* declared for a year divided by net *income* to common stock for the year. A term used by financial analysts. Contrast with *dividend yield.*

payroll taxes. Taxes levied because salaries or wages are paid; for example, *FICA* and unemployment compensation insurance taxes. Typically, the employer pays a portion and withholds part of the employee's wages for the other portion.

P/E ratio. Price-earnings ratio.

pension fund. *Fund,* the assets of which are to be paid to retired ex-employees, usually as a *life annuity.* Usually held by an independent trustee and then not an *asset* of the firm.

pension plan. Details or provisions of employer's contract with employees for paying retirement *annuities* or other benefits. See *funded, vested, normal cost, past service cost, prior service cost, money-purchase plan,* and *defined-benefit plan.*

percentage depletion (allowance). Deductible *expense* allowed in some cases by the federal *income tax* regulations; computed as a percentage of gross income from a *natural resource* independent of the unamortized cost of the asset. Because the amount of the total deductions for tax purposes is usually greater than the cost of the asset being *depleted,* many people think the deduction is an unfair tax advantage or "loophole."

percentage-of-completion method. Recognizing *revenues* and *expenses* on a job, order, or contract (a) in proportion to the *costs* incurred for the period divided by total costs expected to be incurred for the job or order, or (b) in proportion to engineers' estimates of the incremental degree of completion of the job, order, or contract during the period. Contrast with *completed-contract method.*

period. *Accounting period.*

period cost. An inferior term for *period expense.*

period expense (charge). *Expenditure,* usually based upon the passage of time, charged to operations of the accounting period rather than *capitalized* as an asset. Contrast with *product cost.*

periodic inventory. A method of recording *inventory* that uses data on beginning inventory, additions to inventories, and ending inventory in order to find the cost of withdrawals from inventory.

permanent account. An account that appears on the *balance sheet;* contrast with *temporary account.*

permanent difference. Difference between reported income and taxable income that will never be reversed and, hence, requires no entry in the *deferred income tax (liability)* account. An example is the difference between taxable and reportable income from interest earned on state and municipal bonds. Contrast with *timing difference* and *see deferred income tax liability.*

perpetual annuity. *Perpetuity.*

perpetual inventory. Records on quantities and amounts of *inventory* that are changed or made current with each physical addition to or withdrawal from the stock of goods; an inventory so recorded. The records will show the physical quantities and, frequently, the dollar valuations that should be on hand at any time. A perpetual inventory facilitates *control;* contrast with *periodic inventory.*

perpetuity. An *annuity* whose payments continue forever. The *present value* of a perpetuity in *arrears* is p/r, where p is the periodic payment and r is the *interest rate* per period.

petty cash fund. Currency and coins maintained for expenditures that are conveniently made with cash on hand.

physical verification. *Verification,* by an *auditor,* performed by actually inspecting items in *inventory, plant assets,* and the like. May be based on statistical sampling procedures. Contrasted with mere checking of written records.

plant. *Plant assets.*

plant assets. Buildings, machinery, equipment, land, and natural resources. The phrase "property, plant, and equipment" is, therefore, a redundancy. In this context, "plant" means buildings.

plug. For any *account,* beginning balance + additions − deductions = ending balance; if any three of the four items are known, the fourth can be found by algebra, which accountants often call "plugging." In making a *journal entry,* often all *debits* are known, as are all but one of the *credits* (or vice versa). Because *double-entry* bookkeeping requires equal debits and credits, the unknown quantity can be determined by subtracting the sum of the known credits from the sum of all the debits (or vice versa). This process is also known as plugging. The unknown found is called the plug. For example, if a *discount* on *bonds payable* is being *amortized* with the *straight-line method,* then *interest expense* is a plug: interest expense = interest payable + discount amortization. See *trade-in transaction* for an example.

pooling-of-interests method. Accounting for a *business combination* by merely adding together the *book value* of the *assets* and *equities* of the combined firms. Contrast with *purchase method.* Generally leads to a higher reported *net income* for the combined firms than would be reported had the business combination been accounted for as a purchase. See *APB Opinion* No. 16 for the conditions that must be met before the pooling of interests treatment is acceptable.

positive confirmation. See *confirmation.*

post. To record entries in an *account* in a *ledger;* usually the entries are transferred from a *journal.*

postclosing trial balance. *Trial balance* taken after all *temporary accounts* have been closed.

preclosing trial balance. *Trial balance* taken at the end of the period before *closing entries.* In this sense, an *adjusted trial balance.* Sometimes taken before *adjusting entries* and then is synonymous with *unadjusted trial balance.*

predetermined (factory) overhead rate. Rate used in applying *overhead* to products or departments developed at the start of a period by dividing estimated overhead cost by the estimated number of units of the overhead allocation base (or *denominator volume*) activity.

preemptive right. The privilege of a stockholder to maintain a proportionate share of ownership by purchasing a proportionate share of any new stock issues.

preferred stock. *Capital stock* with a claim to income or assets after bondholders but before *common stock. Dividends* on preferred stock are income distributions, not expenses. See *cumulative preferred stock.*

premium. The excess of issue (or market) price over *par value.* For a different context, see *insurance.*

prepaid expense. An *expenditure* that leads to a *deferred charge* or *prepayment;* strictly speaking, a contradiction in terms for an *expense* is a gone asset and this title refers to past *expenditures,* such as for rent or insurance premiums, that still have future benefits and thus are *assets.*

prepaid income. An inferior alternative title for *advances from customers.* An item should not be called *revenue* or *income* until earned, when goods are delivered or services are rendered.

prepayments. *Deferred charges. Assets* representing *expenditures* for future benefits. Rent and insurance premiums paid in advance are usually classified as *current* prepayments.

present value. Value today of an amount or amounts to be paid or received later, discounted at some *interest* or *discount rate.*

price. The quantity of one *good* or *service,* usually *cash,* asked in return for a unit of another good or service. See *fair market price.*

price index. A series of numbers, one for each period, that purports to represent some *average* of prices for a series of periods, relative to a base period. See, for example, the *CPI* and the *GNP Deflator.*

price level. The number from a *price index* series for a given period or date.

price level-adjusted statements. *Financial statements* expressed in terms of dollars of uniform purchasing power. *Nonmonetary* items are restated to reflect changes in general *price levels* since the time specific *assets* were acquired and *liabilities* were incurred. A *gain* or *loss* is recognized on *monetary items* as they are held over time periods when the general *price level* changes. Conventional financial statements show *hisorical costs* and ignore differences in purchasing power in different periods.

price variance. In accounting for *standard costs*, (actual cost per unit − standard cost per unit) times quantity purchased.

price-earnings ratio. At a given time, the market value of a company's *common stock*, per share, divided by the *earnings per* common *share* for the past year. See *ratio*.

prime cost. Sum of *direct materials* plus *direct labor* costs assigned to product.

principal. An amount on which *interest* is charged or earned.

principle. See *generally accepted accounting principles*.

prior service cost. *Present value* at a given time of a *pension plan's* unrecognized benefits assigned to employees for their service before that given time. Includes *past service cost*. Such obligations are not recognized as liabilities in the accounting records, but must be disclosed in the notes of the financial statements. Contrast with *normal cost*. See *funded*.

prior-period adjustment. A *debit* or *credit* made directly to *retained earnings* (that does not affect *income* for the period) to adjust retained earnings for such things as lawsuit settlements and changes in *income tax expense* of prior periods. Theory would suggest that corrections of errors in accounting estimates (such as the *depreciable life* or *salvage value* of an asset) should be treated as adjustments to retained earnings. But *GAAP* require that corrections of such estimates flow through current, and perhaps future, *income statements*. See *accounting changes* and *accounting errors*.

pro forma statements. Hypothetical statements. Financial statements as they would appear if some event, such as a *merger* or increased production and sales, had occurred or were to occur. Pro forma is often spelled as one word.

process costing. A method of *cost accounting* based on average costs (total cost divided by the *equivalent units* of work done in a period). Typically used for assembly lines or for products that are produced in a series of steps that are more continuous than discrete.

product. *Goods* or *services* produced.

product cost. Any *manufacturing cost* that can be inventoried. See *flow of costs* for example and contrast with *period expenses*.

production cost. *Manufacturing cost.*

production cost account. A *temporary account* for collecting *manufacturing costs* during a period.

production department. A department producing salable *goods* or *services;* contrast with *service department*.

production method (depreciation). The depreciable asset is given a *depreciable life* measured, not in elapsed time, but in units of output or perhaps in units of time of actual use. Then the *depreciation* charge for a period is a portion of depreciable cost equal to a fraction determined by dividing the actual output produced during the period by the expected total output to be produced over the life of the asset. Sometimes called the "units-of-production (or output) method."

productive capacity. In computing *replacement costs* of *long-term assets*, we are interested in the cost of reproducing the productive capacity (for example, the ability to manufacture 1 million units a year), not the cost of reproducing the actual physical assets currently used (see *reproduction cost*). Replacement cost of productive capacity will be the same as reproduction cost of assets only in the unusual case when there has been no technological improvement in production processes and the relative prices of goods and services used in production have remained approximately the same as when the currently used ones were acquired.

profit. Excess of *revenues* over *expenses* for a *transaction;* sometimes used synonymously with *net income* for the period.

profit and loss statement. *Income statement.*

profit center. A unit of activity for which both *revenue* and *expenses* are accumulated. Contrast with *cost center.*

profit margin. Sales minus all expenses as a single amount. Frequently used to mean the ratio of sales minus all *operating* expenses divided by sales.

profit maximization. The doctrine that a given set of operations should be accounted for so as to make reported *net income* as large as possible. Contrast with *conservatism*. This concept in accounting is slightly different from the profit maximizing concept in economics where the doctrine states that businesses should be run to maximize the present value of the firm's wealth, generally by equating *marginal costs* and *marginal revenues*.

profitability accounting. *Responsibility accounting*.

profit-volume graph. See *breakeven chart*.

profit-volume ratio. Net *income* divided by net sales in dollars.

programmed costs. A *fixed cost* not essential for carrying out operations. Research and development and advertising designed to generate new business are controllable, but once a commitment is made to incur them, they become fixed costs. Sometimes called *managed costs* or *discretionary costs.* Contrast with *capacity costs.*

progressive tax. Tax for which the rate increases as the taxed base, such as income, increases. Contrast with *regressive tax.*

projected financial statement. *Pro forma* financial statement.

proprietorship. *Assets* minus *liabilities* of an *entity;* equals *contributed capital* plus *retained earnings.*

proprietorship theory. The view of the corporation that emphasizes the form of the *accounting equation* that says *assets − liabilities = owners' equity.* Contrast with *entity theory.* The major implication of a choice between these theories deals with the treatment of *subsidiaries.* For example, the view that *minority interest* is an *indeterminate-term liability* is based on the proprietorship theory. The proprietorship theory implies using a *single-step income statement.*

prorate. To *allocate* in proportion to some base; for example, to allocate *service department* costs in proportion to hours of service used by the benefited departments.

provision. Often the exact amount of an *expense* is uncertain, but must be recognized currently anyway. The entry for the estimated expense, such as for *income taxes* or expected costs under *warranty,* is

Expense (Estimated) X
   Liability (Estimated) X

In American usage, the term "provision" is often used in the expense account title of the above entry. Thus, Provision for Income Taxes is used to mean the estimate of income tax expense. (In British usage, the term "provision" is used in the title for the estimated liability of the above entry, so that Provision for Income Taxes is a balance sheet account.)

public accounting. That portion of accounting primarily involving the *attest* function, culminating in the *auditor's report.*

PuPU. An acronym for *p*urchasing *p*ower *u*nit. Some, including a former Chief Accountant of the *SEC,* who think *general price level-adjusted* accounting is not particularly useful, poke fun at it by calling it "PuPu accounting."

purchase method. Accounting for a *business combination* by adding the acquired company's assets at the price paid for them to the acquiring company's assets. Contrast with *pooling-of-interests method.* Because the acquired assets are put on the books at current rather than original costs, the *amortization expenses* are usually larger (and reported income, smaller) than for the same business combination accounted for as a pooling of interests. The purchase method is required unless all criteria to be a pooling are met.

purchase order. Document authorizing a seller to deliver goods with payment to be made later.

Q

qualified report (opinion). *Auditor's report* containing a statement that the auditor was unable to complete a satisfactory examination of all things considered relevant or that the auditor has doubts about the financial impact of some material item reported in the financial statements. See *except for* and *subject to.*

qualified (stock) option (plan). Said of a compensation scheme in which *options* to purchase *stock* are granted to employees and in which the implicit compensation is neither tax deductible as an *expense* by the employer nor taxable *income* to the employee.

quantity variance. In *standard cost* systems, the standard price per unit times (actual quantity used minus standard quantity that should be used).

quick assets. *Assets* readily convertible into *cash;* includes cash, *current marketable securities,* and *current receivables.*

quick ratio. *Acid test* ratio. See *ratio.*

R

R&D. See *research and development.*

rate of return on common stock equity. See *ratio.*

rate of return on stockholders' equity. See *ratio.*

rate of return (on total capital). See *ratio* and *all capital earnings rate.*

rate variance. *Price variance,* usually for *direct labor costs.*

ratio. The number resulting when one number is divided by another. Ratios are generally used to assess aspects of profitability, solvency, and liquidity. The commonly used financial ratios are of essentially two kinds: (1) those that summarize some aspect of operations for a period, usually a year, and (2) those that summarize some aspect of *financial position* at a given moment—the moment for which a balance sheet has been prepared. Exhibit 3.5 on page 81 lists the most common financial ratios and shows separately both the numerator and denominator used to calculate the ratio.

raw material. Goods purchased for use in manufacturing a product.

real accounts. *Balance sheet accounts;* as opposed to *nominal accounts.* See *permanent account.*

real estate. *Land* and its *improvements,* such as landscaping and roads but not buildings.

realizable value. *Market value* or, sometimes, *net realizable value.*

realization convention. The accounting practice of delaying the recognition of *gains* and *losses* from changes in the market price of *assets* until the assets are sold. However, unrealized losses on *inventory* and *marketable securities* classified as *current assets* are recognized prior to sale when the *lower-of-cost-or-market* valuation basis is used.

realize. To convert into *funds.* See *recognize.*

realized holding gain. See *inventory profit* for definition and an example.

receipt. Acquisition of *cash.*

receivable. Any *collectible* whether or not it is currently due.

recognize. To enter a transaction in the books. Some writers use "recognize" to indicate that an event has been *journalized* and use "realize" only for those events that affect the *income statement.*

reconciliation. A calculation that shows how one balance or figure is derived systematically from another, such as a *reconciliation of retained earnings* or a *bank reconciliation schedule.* See *articulate.*

redemption. Retirement by the issuer, usually by a purchase or *call,* of stocks or *bonds.*

regressive tax. Tax for which the rate decreases as the taxed base, such as income, increases. Contrast with *progressive tax.*

Regulation S-X. The *SEC* regulation specifying the form and content of financial reports to the SEC.

reinvestment rate. In a *capital budgeting* context, the rate at which cash inflows from a project occurring before the project's completion are invested. Once such a rate is assumed, there will never be multiple *internal rates of return.* See *Descartes' rule of signs.*

relative sales value method. A method for *allocating joint costs* in proportion to *net realizable values* of the joint products. For example, joint products A and B together cost $100 and A sells for $60 whereas B sells for $90. Then A would be allocated ($60/$150) × $100 = .40 × $100 = $40 of cost whereas B would be allocated ($90/$150) × $100 = $60 of cost.

relevant cost. *Incremental cost. Opportunity cost.*

relevant range. Activity levels over which costs are linear or for which *flexible budget* estimates and *breakeven charts* will remain valid.

rent. A charge for the use of land, buildings, or other assets.

reorder point. See *economic order quantity.*

repair. An *expenditure* to restore an *asset's* service potential after damage or after prolonged use. In the second sense, after prolonged use, the difference between repairs and maintenance is one of degree and not of kind. Treated as an *expense* of the period when incurred. Because repairs and maintenance are treated similarly in this regard, the distinction is not important. A repair helps to maintain capacity intact at levels planned when the *asset* was acquired. Contrast with *improvement.*

replacement cost. For an asset, the current fair market price to purchase another, similar asset (with the same future benefit or service potential). *Current cost. SEC ASR* No. 190 requires certain large firms to disclose replacement cost data. See *reproduction cost* and *productive capacity.* See also *distributable income* and *inventory profit.*

report. *Financial statement; auditor's report.*

report form. The form of balance sheet where *equities* are shown below *assets.* Contrast with *account form.*

reporting objectives (policies). The general doctrines underlying accounting. These include *full disclosure, objectivity, consistency, conservatism,* the assumption of *continuity of operations,* and *materiality.*

reproduction cost. The *cost* necessary to acquire an *asset* similar in all important physical respects to another asset for which a *current value* is wanted. See *replacement cost* and *productive capacity* for further contrast.

research and development. Research is activity aimed at discovering new knowledge in hopes that such activity will be useful in creating a new product, process, or service or improving a present product, process, or service. Development is the translation of research findings or other knowledge into a new or improved product, process, or service. The *FASB* requires that costs of such activities be *expensed* as incurred on the grounds that the future benefits are too uncertain to warrant *capitalization* as an *asset.* This treatment seems questionable to us because we wonder why firms would continue to undertake R&D if there were no expectation of future benefit; if future benefits exist, then the *costs* should be assets.

reserve. When properly used in accounting, the term refers to an account that appropriates *retained earnings* and restricts dividend declarations. Appropriating retained earnings is itself a poor and slowly vanishing practice, so the word should seldom be used in accounting. In addition, used in the past to indicate an asset *contra* (for example, "reserve for depreciation") or an *estimated liability* (for example, "reserve for warranty costs"). In any case, reserve accounts have credit balances and are not pools of *funds* as the unwary reader might infer. If a company has set aside a pool of *cash* (or *marketable securities*), then that cash will be called a *fund.*

residual income. In an *external reporting* context, this term refers to *net income* to *common stock* = net income less *preferred stock dividends.* In *managerial accounting,* this term refers to the excess of income for a division or *segment* of a company over the product of the *cost of capital* for the company multiplied by the average amount of capital invested in the division during the period over which the income was earned. See Exhibit 11.2.

residual value. At any time, the estimated, or actual, *net realizable value* (that is, proceeds less removal costs) of an *asset,* usually a depreciable *plant asset.* In the context of depreciation accounting, this term is equivalent to *salvage value* and is preferable to *scrap value,* because the asset need not be scrapped. Sometimes used to mean net *book value.* In the context of a *noncancelable* lease, the estimated value of the leased asset at the end of the lease period. See *lease.*

responsibility accounting. Accounting for a business by considering various units as separate entities, or *profit centers,* giving management of each unit responsibility for the unit's *revenues* and *expenses.* Sometimes called "activity accounting." See *transfer price.*

restricted retained earnings. That part of *retained earnings* not legally available for *dividends.* See *retained earnings, appropriated. Bond indentures* and other loan contracts can curtail the legal ability of the corporation to declare dividends without formally requiring a retained earnings appropriation, but disclosure is required.

retail inventory method. Ascertaining *inventory* amounts for financial statements by using ratios of cost to selling price. That is, *cost of sales* = (1 − *markup percentage*) × *sales;* and *ending inventory* = (1 − *markup percentage*) × *ending inventory* at retail prices.

retained earnings. Net *income* over the life of a corporation less all income distributions (including capitalization through stock dividends); *owners' equity* less *contributed capital.*

retained earnings, appropriated. An *account* set up by crediting it and debiting *retained earnings.* Used to

indicate that a portion of retained earnings is not available for dividends. The practice of appropriating retained earnings is misleading unless all capital is earmarked with its use, which is not practical. Use of formal retained earnings appropriations is declining.

retained earnings statement. *Generally accepted accounting principles* require that whenever *comparative balance sheets* and an *income statement* are presented, there must also be presented a *reconciliation* of the beginning and ending balances in the *retained earnings account.* This reconciliation can appear in a separate statement, in a combined statement of income and retained earnings, or in the balance sheet.

retirement plan. *Pension plan.*

return. A schedule of information required by governmental bodies, such as the tax return required by the *Internal Revenue Service.* Also the physical return of merchandise. See also *return on investment.*

return of capital (investment). A payment to owners *debited* to an *owners' equity account* other than *retained earnings.*

return on investment (capital). *Income* (before distributions to suppliers of capital) for a period. As a rate, this amount divided by average total assets. *Interest,* net of tax effects, should be added back to *net income* for the numerator. See *ratio.*

revenue. The monetary measure of a service rendered. Do not confuse with *receipt* of funds, which may occur before, when, or after revenue is recognized.

revenue center. A *responsibility center* with a firm that has control only over revenues generated. Contrast with *cost center.* See *profit center.*

revenue expenditure. A phrase sometimes used to mean *expense* in contrast to a capital *expenditure* to acquire an *asset* or to discharge a *liability.* Avoid using this phrase; use *period expense* instead.

revenue received in advance. An inferior term for *advances from customers.*

revenue-cost graph. See *breakeven chart.*

reversal (reversing) entry. An *entry* in which all *debits* and *credits* are the credits and debits, respectively, of another entry, and in the same amounts. It is usually made on the first day of an *accounting period* to reverse a previous *adjusting entry,* usually an *accrual.* The purpose of such entries is to make the bookkeeper's tasks easier.

right. The privilege to subscribe to new *stock* issues or to purchase stock. Usually, rights are contained in securities called *warrants* and the warrants may be sold to others. See also *preemptive right.*

risk. A measure of the variability of the *return on investment.* For a given expected amount of return, most people prefer less risk to more risk. Therefore, in rational markets, investments with more risk usually promise, or are expected to yield, a higher rate of return than investments with lower risk. Most people use "risk" and "uncertainty" as synonyms. In technical language, however, these terms have different meanings. "Risk" is used when the probabilities attached to the various outcomes are known, such as the probabilities of heads or tails in the flip of a fair coin. "Uncertainty" refers to an event where the probabilities of the outcomes, such as winning or losing a lawsuit, can only be estimated.

risk premium. Extra compensation paid to an employee or extra interest paid to a lender, over amounts usually considered normal, in return for their undertaking to engage in activities more risky than normal.

risk-adjusted discount rate. In a *capital budgeting* context, a decision maker compares projects by comparing their *net present values* for a given *interest* rate, usually the *cost of capital.* If a given project's outcome is considered to be much more or much less risky than the normal undertakings of the company, then the interest rate will be increased (if the project is more risky) or decreased (if less risky) and the rate used is said to be risk-adjusted.

ROI. *Return on investment,* but usually used to refer to a single project and expressed as a *ratio: income* divided by average *cost* of *assets* devoted to the project.

royalty. Compensation for the use of property, usually copyrighted material or natural resources, expressed as a percentage of receipts from using the property or as an amount per unit produced.

rule of 69. An amount of money invested at r percent per period will double in $69/r + .35$ periods. This approximation is accurate to one-tenth of a period for interest rates between $\frac{1}{4}$ and 100 percent per period. For example, at 10 percent per period, the rule says that a given sum will double in $69/10 + .35 = 7.25$ periods. At 10 percent per period, a given sum doubles in $7.27+$ periods.

rule of 72. An amount of money invested at r percent per period will double in $72/r$ periods. A reasonable approximation but not nearly as accurate as the *rule of 69.* For example, at 10 percent per period, the rule says that a given sum will double in $72/10 = 7.2$ periods.

S

SAB. *Staff Accounting Bulletin* of the *SEC.*

salary. Compensation earned by managers, administrators, professionals, not based on an hourly rate. Contrast with *wage.*

sale. A *revenue* transaction where *goods* or *services* are delivered to a customer in return for cash or a contractual obligation to pay.

sales basis of revenue recognition. *Revenue* is recognized, not as goods are produced nor as orders are received, but only when the sale (delivery) has been consummated and cash or a legal receivable obtained. Most revenue is recognized on this basis. Compare with the *percentage-of-completion method* and the *installment method.* Identical with the *completed-contract method,* but this latter term is ordinarily used only for *long-term* construction projects.

sales discount. Reduction in sales *invoice* price usually offered for prompt payment. See *terms of sale* and *2/10, n/30.*

sales, uncollectible accounts adjustment. The preferred title for the *contra-revenue account* to recognize estimated reductions in income caused by accounts receivable that will not be collected. Called *bad debt expense* and treated as an expense, rather than an adjustment to revenue, when the write-off method is used. See *allowance for uncollectibles* and *allowance method.*

sales value method. *Relative sales value method.*

salvage value. Actual or estimated selling price, net of removal or disposal costs, of a used *plant asset* to be sold or otherwise retired. See *residual value.*

SAS. *Statement on Auditing Standards* of the *AICPA.*

schedule. Supporting set of calculations that show how figures in a statement or tax return are derived.

scrap value. *Salvage value* assuming item is to be junked. A *net realizable value. Residual value.*

SEC. Securities and Exchange Commission, an agency authorized by the U.S. Congress to regulate, among other things, the financial reporting practices of most public corporations. The SEC has indicated that it will usually allow the *FASB* to set accounting principles but it reserves the right to require more disclosure than required by the FASB. The SEC's accounting requirements are stated in its *Accounting Series Releases (ASR)* and *Regulation S-X.*

Securities and Exchange Commission. *SEC.*

security. Document that indicates ownership or indebtedness or potential ownership, such as an *option* or *warrant.*

segment (of a business). As defined by *APB Opinion* No. 30, "a component of an *entity* whose activities represent a separate major line of business or class of customer. . . . [It may be] a *subsidiary,* a division, or a department, . . . provided that its *assets,* results of *operations,* and activities can be clearly distinguished, physically and operationally for financial reporting purposes, from the other assets, results of operations, and activities of the entity." In *FASB Statement* No. 14, a segment is defined as "A component of an enterprise engaged in promoting a product or service or a group of related products and services primarily to unaffiliated customers . . . for a profit."

segment reporting. Reporting of *income* and *assets* by *segments of a business,* usually classified by nature of products sold but sometimes by geographical area where goods are produced or sold. Sometimes called "line of business reporting." *Central corporate expenses* are usually allocated to the segments, although these reports may be more useful when such expenses are separately disclosed.

self-insurance. See *insurance.*

selling and administrative expenses. *Expenses* not specifically identifiable with, nor assigned to, production.

semifixed costs. *Costs* that increase with activity as a step function.

semivariable costs. *Costs* that increase strictly linearly with activity but that are positive at zero activity level. Royalty fees of 2 percent of sales are variable; royalty fees of $1,000 per year plus 2 percent of sales are semivariable.

service department. A department, such as the personnel or computer department, that provides services to other departments, rather than direct work on salable product. Contrast with *production department.*

service life. Period of expected usefulness of an asset; may not coincide with *depreciable life* for income tax purposes.

service potential. The future benefits embodied in an item that cause the item to be classified as an *asset.* Without service potential, there are no future benefits and the item should not be classified as an asset.

services. Useful work done by a person, a machine, or an organization. See *goods.*

setup. The time or costs required to prepare production equipment for doing a job.

share. A unit of *stock* representing ownership in a corporation.

shareholders' equity. See *stockholders' equity.*

short-term. Current; ordinarily, due within one year.

shrinkage. An excess of *inventory* shown on the *books* over actual physical quantities on hand. Can result from theft or shoplifting as well as from evaporation or general wear and tear.

simple interest. *Interest* calculated on *principal* where interest earned during periods before maturity of the loan is neither added to the principal nor paid to the lender. *Interest = principal × interest rate × time.* Seldom used in economic calculations except for periods less than one year. Contrast with *compound interest.*

single proprietorship. *Sole proprietorship.*

Social Security taxes. Taxes levied by the federal government on both employers and employees to provide *funds* to pay retired persons (or their survivors) who are entitled to receive such payments, either because they paid Social Security taxes themselves or because the Congress has declared them eligible. See *Old Age, Survivors, Disability,* and *(Hospital) Insurance.*

sole proprietorship. All *owners' equity* belongs to one person.

solvent. Able to meet debts when due.

source of funds. Any *transaction* that increases *working capital.*

sources and uses statement. *Statement of changes in financial position.*

SOYD. *sum-of-the-years'-digits depreciation. SYD.*

special journal. A *journal,* such as a sales journal or cash disbursements journal, to record *transactions* of a similar nature that occur frequently.

special revenue debt. Debt of a governmental unit backed only by revenues from specific sources such as tolls from a bridge.

specific identificiation method. Method for valuing *ending inventory* and *cost of goods sold* by identifying actual units sold and in inventory and summing the actual costs of those individual units. Usually used for items with large unit value, such as jewelry, automobiles, and fur coats.

specific price changes. Changes in the market prices of specific *goods and services.* Contrast with *general price level changes.*

specific price index. A measure of the price of a specific good or service, or a small group of similar goods or services, at one time relative to the price during a base period. Contrast with *general price index.* See *dollar-value LIFO method.*

spending variance. In *standard cost systems,* the *rate* or *price variance* for *overhead costs.*

split. *Stock split.* Sometimes called "splitup."

splitoff point. The point where all costs are no longer *joint costs* but can be identified with individual products or perhaps with a smaller number of *joint products.*

spoilage. See *abnormal spoilage* and *normal spoilage.*

stable monetary unit assumption. In spite of *inflation* that appears to be a way of life, the assumption that underlies *historical cost* accounting—namely that current dollars and dollars of previous years can be meaningfully added together. No specific recognition is given to changing values of the dollar in the usual *financial statements.* See *price level-adjusted statements.*

Staff Accounting Bulletin. An interpretation issued by the Staff of the Chief Accountant of the *SEC* "suggesting" how the various *Accounting Series Releases* should be applied in practice. A substantial fraction of the first 20 or so SABs are concerned with the implementation of *replacement cost* accounting, as required by *ASR* No. 190.

standard cost. Anticipated *cost* of producing a unit of output; a predetermined cost to be assigned to products produced.

standard cost system. *Product costing* using *standard costs* rather than actual costs. May be based on either *absorption* or *direct costing* principles.

standard price (rate). Unit price established for materials or labor used in *standard cost systems.*

standard quantity allowed. The quantity of direct material or direct labor (inputs) that should have been used if the units of output had been produced in accordance with preset *standards.*

standby costs. A type of *capacity cost,* such as property taxes, incurred even if operations are shut down completely. Contrast with *enabling costs.*

stated capital. Amount of capital contributed by stockholders. Sometimes used to mean *legal capital.*

stated value. A term sometimes used for the *face amount* of *capital stock,* when no *par value* is indicated. Where there is a stated value per share, it may be set by the directors (in which case, capital *contributed in excess of stated value* may come into being).

statement of changes in financial position. As defined by *APB Opinion* No. 19, a statement which explains the changes in *working capital* (or cash) balances during a period and shows the changes in the working capital (or cash) accounts themselves. Sometimes called the "funds statement." See *dual transactions assumption* and *all financial resources.*

Statement of Financial Accounting Standards. See *FASB.*

statement of financial position. *Balance sheet.*

statement of retained earnings (income). A statement that reconciles the beginning-of-period and end-of-period balances in the *retained earnings* account. It shows the effects of *earnings, dividend declarations,* and *prior-period adjustments.*

Statements on Auditing Standards. No. 1 of this series (1973) codifies all statements on auditing standards previously promulgated by the *AICPA.* Later numbers deal with specific auditing standards and procedures.

static budget. *Fixed budget.*

statutory tax rate. The tax rate specified in the *income tax* law for each type of income (for example, *ordinary income, capital gain or loss*).

step cost. *Semifixed cost.*

step-down method. The method for *allocating service department* costs that starts by allocating one service department's costs to *production departments* and to all other service departments. Then a second service department's costs, including costs allocated from the first, are allocated to production departments and to all other service departments except the first one. In this fashion, the costs of all service departments, including previous allocations, are allocated to production departments and to those service departments whose costs have not yet been allocated.

stock. *Inventory. Capital stock.* A measure of the amount of something on hand at a specific time; in this sense, contrast with *flow.*

stock dividend. A so-called *dividend* where additional *shares* of *capital stock* are distributed, without cash payments, to existing shareholders. It results in a *debit* to *retained earnings* in the amount of the market value of the shares issued and a *credit* to *capital stock* accounts. It is ordinarily used to indicate that earnings retained have been permanently reinvested in the business. Contrast with a *stock split,* which requires no entry in the capital stock accounts other than a notation that the *par* or *stated value* per share has been changed.

stock option. The right to purchase a specified number of shares of *stock* for a specified price at specified times, usually granted to employees. Contrast with *warrant.*

stock right. See *right.*

stock split. Increase in the number of common shares outstanding resulting from the issuance of additional shares to existing stockholders without additional capital contributions by them. Does not increase the total *par* (or *stated*) *value* of *common stock* outstanding because par (or stated) value per share is reduced in inverse proportion. A three-for-one stock split reduces par (or stated) value per share to one-third of its former amount. Stock splits are usually limited to distributions that increase the number of shares outstanding by 20 percent or more. Compare with *stock dividend.*

stock warrant. See *warrant.*

stockholders' equity. *Proprietorship* or *owners' equity* of a corporation. Because *stock* means inventory in Australian, British, and Canadian usage, the term *shareholders' equity* is usually used by Australian, British, and Canadian writers.

stores. *Raw materials,* parts, and supplies.

straight debt value. An estimate of what the *market value* of a *convertible bond* would be if the bond did not contain a conversion privilege.

straight-line depreciation. If the *depreciable life* is *n* periods, then the periodic *depreciation* charge is $1/n$ of the *depreciable cost.* Results in equal periodic charges and is sometimes called "straight-time depreciation."

Subchapter S corporation. A firm legally organized as a *corporation* but taxed as if it were a *partnership.*

subject to. Qualifications in an *auditor's report* usually caused by a *material* uncertainty in the valuation of an item, such as future promised payments from a foreign government or outcome of pending litigation.

subsidiary. Said of a company more than 50 percent of whose voting stock is owned by another.

successful-efforts accounting. In petroleum accounting, the *capitalization* of the drilling costs of only those wells which contain oil. See *discovery value accounting* for an example.

summary of significant accounting principles. *APB* Opinion No. 22 requires that every *annual report* summarize the significant *accounting principles* used in compiling the annual report. This summary may be a separate exhibit or the first *note* to the financial statements.

sum-of-the-years'-digits depreciation. SYD. SOYD. An *accelerated depreciation* method of an asset with *depreciable life* of *n* years where the charge in period i ($i = 1, \ldots, n$) is the fraction $(n + 1 - i)/[n(n + 1)/2]$ of the *depreciable cost.* If an asset has a depreciable cost of \$15,000 and a five-year depreciable life, for example, the depreciation charges would be \$5,000 ($= 5/15 \times \$15,000$) in the first year, \$4,000 in the second, \$3,000 in the third, \$2,000 in the fourth, and \$1,000 in the fifth.

sunk cost. *Costs* incurred in the past that are not affected by, and hence irrelevant for, current deci-

sions aside from *income tax* effects. Contrast with *incremental costs* and *imputed costs.* For example, the *acquisition cost* of machinery is irrelevant to a decision of whether or not to scrap the machinery. The current *exit value* of the machine is the imputed cost of continuing to own it and the cost of, say, electricity to run the machine is an incremental cost of its operation.

supplementary statements (schedules). Statements (schedules) in addition to the four basic *financial statements* (including the retained earnings reconciliation as a basic statement).

surplus. A word once used but now considered poor terminology; prefaced by "earned" to mean *retained earnings* and prefaced by "capital" to mean *capital contributed in exess of par* (or *stated*) *value.*

sustainable income. The part of *distributable income* (computed from *replacement cost* data) that the firm can be expected to earn in the next accounting period if operations are continued at the same levels as during the current period. *Income from discontinued operations,* for example, may be distributable but not sustainable.

S-X. See *Regulation S-X.*

SYD. *Sum-of-the-years'-digits depreciation. SOYD.*

T

T-account. Account form shaped like the letter T with the title above the horizontal line. *Debits* are shown to the left of the vertical line; *credits,* to the right.

tangible. Having physical form. Accounting has never satisfactorily defined the distinction between tangible and *intangible assets.* Typically, tangibles are defined by giving an exhaustive list and everything not on the list is defined as intangible.

tax. A nonpenal, but compulsory, charge levied by a government on income, consumption, wealth, or other bases for the benefit of all those governed. The term does not include fines or specific charges for benefits accruing only to those paying the charges, such as licenses, permits, special assessments, admissions fees, and tolls.

tax allocation: interperiod. See *deferred income tax liability.*

tax allocation: intrastatement. The showing of income tax effects on *extraordinary items, income from discontinued operations,* and *prior period adjustments* along with these items, separately from income taxes on other income. See *net of tax reporting.*

tax avoidance. See *tax shelter.*

tax credit. A subtraction from taxes otherwise payable, contrast with *tax deduction.*

tax deduction. A subraction from *revenues* and *gains* to arrive at taxable income. Tax deductions are technically different from tax *exemptions,* but the effect of both is to reduce gross income in computing taxable income. Both are different from *tax credits,* which are subtracted from the computed tax itself in determining taxes payable. If the tax rate is *t* percent of pretax income, then a *tax credit* of $1 is worth $1/$t$ of *tax deductions.*

tax evasion. The fraudulent understatement of taxable income or overstatement of deductions and expenses or both. Contrast with *tax shelter.*

tax exempts. See *municipal bonds.*

tax shelter. The legal avoidance of, or reduction in, *income taxes* resulting from a careful reading of the complex income tax regulations and the subsequent rearrangement of financial affairs to take advantage of the regulations. Often the term is used pejoratively, but the courts have long held that an individual or corporation has no obligation to pay taxes any larger than the legal minimum. If the public concludes that a given tax shelter is "unfair," then the laws and regulations can be changed. Sometimes used to refer to the investment that permits tax avoidance.

tax shield. The amount of an *expense* that reduces taxable income but does not require *working capital,* such as *depreciation.* Sometimes this term is expanded to include expenses that reduce taxable income and use working capital. A depreciation deduction (or *R&D expense* in the expanded sense) of $10,000 provides a tax shield of $4,800 when the marginal tax rate is 48 percent.

temporary account. *Account* that does not appear on the *balance sheet. Revenue* and *expense* accounts, their *adjuncts* and *contras, production cost accounts, income distribution accounts,* and purchases-related accounts (which are closed to the various inventories). Sometimes called a "nominal account."

temporary difference. See *timing difference.*

temporary investments. Investments in *marketable securities* that the owner intends to sell within a short time, usually one year, and hence classified as *current assets.*

10-K. The name of the annual report required by the *SEC* of nearly all publicly held corporations. This report contains more information than the *annual report* to stockholders. Corporations must send a copy of the 10-K to those stockholders who request it.

terms of sale. The conditions governing payment for a sale. For example, the terms *2/10, n(et)/30* mean that if payment is made within 10 days of the invoice date, a *discount* of 2 percent from *invoice* price can be taken; the invoice amount must be paid, in any event, within 30 days or it becomes overdue.

time cost. *Period cost.*

time deposit. Cash in a bank earning interest; contrast with *demand deposit.*

time series analysis. See *cross-section analysis* for definition and contrast.

time-adjusted rate of return. *Internal rate of return.*

times-interest earned. Ratio of pretax *income* plus *interest* charges to interest charges. See *ratio.*

timing difference. A difference between taxable income and pretax income reported to stockholders that will be reversed in a subsequent period and requires an entry in the *deferred income tax* account. For example, the use of *accelerated depreciation* for tax returns and *straight-line depreciation* for financial reporting.

trade-in. Acquiring a new *asset* in exchange for a used one and perhaps additional cash. See *boot* and *trade-in transaction.*

trade-in transaction. The accounting for a trade-in depends upon whether or not the asset received is "similar" to the asset traded in and whether the accounting is for *financial statements* or for *income tax* returns. Assume that an old asset cost $5,000, has $3,000 of *accumulated depreciation* (after recording depreciation to the date of the trade-in), and hence has a *book value* of $2,000. The old asset appears to have a market value of $1,500, according to price quotations in used-asset markets. The old asset is traded in on a new asset with a list price of $10,000. The old asset and $5,500 cash *(boot)* are given for the new asset. The generic entry for the trade-in transaction is

New Asset	A		
Accumulated Depreciation			
(Old Asset)	3,000		
Adjustment on Exchange			
of Asset	B	or	B
Old Asset			5,000
Cash			5,500

(1) the *list price* method of accounting for trade-ins rests on the assumption that the list price of the new asset closely approximates its market value. The new asset is recorded at its list price (A = $10,000 in the example); B is a *plug* (= $2,500 credit in the example). If B requires a *debit* plug, the Adjustment on Exchange of Asset is a *loss;* if a *credit* plug is

required (as in the example), the adjustment is a *gain*.

(2) Another theoretically sound method of accounting for trade-ins rests on the assumption that the price quotation from used-asset markets gives a more reliable measure of the market value of the old asset than is the list price a reliable measure of the market value of the new asset. This method uses the *fair market value* of the old asset, $1,500 in the example, to determine B (= $2,000 book value − $1,500 assumed proceeds on disposition = $500 debit or loss). The exchange results in a loss if the book value of the old asset exceeds its market value and in a gain if the market value exceeds the book value. The new asset is recorded on the books by plugging for A (= $7,000 in the example.)

(3) For income tax reporting, no gain or loss may be recognized on the trade-in. Thus, the new asset is recorded on the books by assuming B is zero and plugging for A (= $7,500 in the example). In practice, firms that wish to recognize the loss currently will sell the old asset directly, rather than trading it in, and acquire the new asset entirely for cash.

(4) *Generally accepted accounting principles (APB Opinion No. 29)* require a variant of these methods. The basic method is (1) or (2), depending upon whether the list price of the new asset (1) or the quotation of the old asset's market value (2) is the more reliable indication of market value. If, when applying the basic method, a debit entry, or loss, is required for the Adjustment on Exchange of Asset, then the trade-in is recorded as described in (1) or (2) and the full amount of the loss is recognized currently. If, however, a credit entry, or gain, is required for the Adjustment on Exchange of Asset, then the amount of gain recognized currently depends upon whether or not the old asset and the new asset are "similar." If the assets are not similar, then the entire gain is recognized currently. If the assets are similar and cash is not received by the party trading in, then no gain is recognized and the treatment is like that in (3); i.e., B = O, plug for A. If the assets are similar and cash is received by the party trading in—a rare case—then a portion of the gain is recognized currently. The portion of the gain recognized currently is the fraction *cash received/market value of old asset*. (When the list price method, (1), is used, the market value of the old asset is assumed to be the list price of the new asset plus the amount of cash received by the party trading in.)

The results of applying GAAP to the example can be summarized as follows:

More Reliable Information as to Fair Market Value	Old Asset Compared with New Asset	
	Similar	**Not Similar**
New Asset List Price	A = $7,500	A = $10,000
	B = 0	B = 2,500 gain
Old Asset Market Price	A = $7,000	A = $ 7,000
	B = 500 loss	B = 500 loss

trademark. A distinctive word or symbol affixed to a product, its package or dispenser, which uniquely identifies the firm's products and services. See *trademark right.*

trademark right. The right to exclude competitors in sales or advertising from using words or symbols that may be confusingly similar to the firm's *trademarks.* Trademark rights last as long as the firm continues to use the trademarks in question. In the U.S., trademark rights arise from use and not from government registration. They therefore have a legal life independent of the life of a registration. Registrations last 20 years and are renewable as long as the trademark is being used. Thus, as an asset, purchased trademark rights might, like land, not be subject to amortization if management believes that the life of the trademark is indefinite. In practice, accountants usually amortize a trademark right over some estimate of its life, not to exceed 40 years. Under *FASB Statement* No. 2, internally developed trademark rights must be *expensed.*

trading on the equity. Said of a firm engaging in *debt financing;* frequently said of a firm doing so to a degree considered abnormal for a firm of its kind. *Leverage.*

transaction. An exchange between the accounting *entity* and another party, or parties, that leads to an accounting entry. Sometimes used to describe any event that requires a *journal entry.*

transfer price. A substitute for a *market,* or *arm's-length, price* used in *profit center,* or *responsibility,* *accounting* when one segment of the business "sells" to another segment. Incentives of profit center managers will not coincide with the best interests of the entire business unless transfer prices are properly set.

translation gain (or loss). *Foreign exchange gain (or loss).*

treasury bond. A bond issued by a corporation and then reacquired; such bonds are treated as retired when reacquired and an *extraordinary gain* or *loss* on reacquisition is recognized. Also, a *bond* issued by the U.S. Treasury Department.

treasury stock. *Capital stock* issued and then reacquired by the corporation. Such reacquisitions result in a reduction of *stockholders' equity,* and are usually shown on the balance sheet as *contra* to stockholders' equity. Neither *gain* nor *loss* is recognized on transactions involving treasury stock. Any difference between the amounts paid and received for treasury stock transactions is debited (if positive) or credited (if negative) to *additional paid-in capital.* See *cost method* and *par value method.*

trial balance. A listing of *account balances;* all accounts with *debit* balances are totaled separately from accounts with *credit* balances. The two totals should be equal. Trial balances are taken as a partial check of the arithmetic accuracy of the entries previously made. See *adjusted, preclosing, postclosing, unadjusted trial balance.*

turnover. The number of times that *assets,* such as *inventory* or *accounts receivable,* are replaced on average during the period. Accounts receivable turnover, for example, is total sales on account for a period divided by average accounts receivable balance for the period. See *ratio.*

2/10, n(et)/30. See *terms of sale.*

U

unadjusted trial balance. Trial balance before *adjusting* and *closing entries* are made at the end of the period.

uncertainty. See *risk* for definition and contrast.

uncollectible account. An *account receivable* that will not be paid by the *debtor.* If the preferable *allowance method* is used, the entry on judging a specific account to be uncollectible is to *debit* the allowance for uncollectibles accounts and to *credit* the specific account receivable. See *sales, uncollectible accounts adjustment.*

unconsolidated subsidiary. A *subsidiary* not consolidated and, hence, accounted for on the *equity method.*

uncontrollable cost. The opposite of *controllable cost.*

underapplied (underabsorbed) overhead. An excess of actual *overhead costs* for a period over costs applied, or charged, to products produced during the period. A *debit balance* remaining in an overhead account after overhead is assigned to product.

unearned income (revenue). *Advances from customers;* strictly speaking, a contradiction in terms.

unemployment tax. See *FUTA.*

unexpired cost. An *asset.*

unfavorable variance. In *standard cost* accounting, an excess of actual cost over standard cost assigned to product.

unfunded. Not *funded.* An obligation or *liability,* usually for *pension costs,* exists, but no *funds* have been set aside to discharge the obligation or liability.

unqualified opinion. See *auditor's report.*

unrealized appreciation. An *unrealized holding gain;* frequently used in the context of *marketable securities.*

unrealized holding gain. See *inventory profit* for definition and an example.

usage variance. *Quantity variance.*

use of funds. Any *transaction* that reduces *funds* (however "funds" is defined).

useful life. *Service life.*

V

value. Monetary worth; the term is usually so subjective that it ought not be used without a modifying adjective unless most people would agree on the amount; not to be confused with *cost.* See *fair market-value.*

value variance. *Price variance.*

variable budget. *Flexible budget.*

variable costing. *Direct costing.*

variable costs. *Costs* that change as activity levels change. Strictly speaking, variable costs are zero when the activity level is zero. See *semivariable costs.*

variance. Difference between actual and *standard costs* or between *budgeted* and actual *expenditures* or, sometimes, *expenses.* In accounting, the word has a completely different meaning from its meaning in statistics, where it is a measure of dispersion of a distribution.

variance analysis. The investigation of the causes of *variances* in a *standard cost system.* This term has a different meaning in statistics.

verifiable. A qualitative *objective* of financial reporting specifying that items in *financial statements* can be checked by tracing back to supporting *invoices,* cancelled *checks,* and other physical pieces of evidence.

verification. The auditor's act of reviewing or checking items in *financial statements* by tracing back to supporting *invoices,* canceled *checks,* and other business documents, or sending out *confirmations* to be returned. Compare with *physical verification.*

vested. Said of *pension plan* benefits that are not contingent on the employee continuing to work for the employer.

volume variance. *Capacity variance.*

voucher. A document that serves to recognize a *liability* and authorize the disbursement of cash. Sometimes used to refer to the written evidence documenting an *accounting entry,* as in the term *journal voucher.*

W

wage. Compensation of employees based on time worked or output of product for manual labor.

warrant. A certificate entitling the owner to buy a specified amount of stock at a specified time(s) for a specified price. Differs from a *stock option* only in that options are granted to employees and warrants are issued to the public. See *right.*

warranty. A promise by a seller to correct deficiencies in products sold. When warranties are given, good accounting practice recognizes an estimate of warranty *expense* and an *estimated liability* at the time of sale.

wasting asset. A *natural resource* having a limited *useful life* and, hence, subject to *amortization* called *depletion.* Examples are timberland, oil and gas wells, and ore deposits.

weighted average. An average computed by counting each occurrence of each value, not merely a single occurrence of each value. For example, if one unit is purchased for $1 and two units are purchased for $2 each, then the simple average of the purchase prices is $1.50, but the weighted average price per unit is $5/3 = $1.67. Contrast with *moving average.*

weighted-average inventory method. Valuing either *withdrawals* or *ending inventory* at the *weighted average* purchase price of all units on hand at the time of withdrawal or of computing ending inventory. The *inventory equation* is used to calculate the other quantity. If the *perpetual inventory* method is in use, often called the "moving-average method."

withholding. Deductions from *salaries* or *wages,* usually for *income taxes,* to be remitted by the employer, in the employee's name, to the taxing authority.

work in process. Partially completed product; an *asset* which is classified as *inventory.*

working capital. *Current assets* minus *current liabilities.* The *statement of changes in financial position* usually explains the changes in working capital for a period.

working capital provided by operations. See *funds provided by operations.*

working papers. The schedules and analyses prepared by the *auditor* in carrying out investigations prior to issuing an *opinion* on *financial statements.*

worksheet. A tabular schedule for convenient summary of *adjusting* and *closing entries.*

worth. *Value.* See *net worth.*

worth-debt ratio. Reciprocal of the *debt-equity ratio.* See *ratio.*

write down. *Write off,* except that not all the asset's cost is charged to expense or *loss.* Generally used for nonrecurring items.

write off. *Charge* an *asset* to *expense* or *loss;* that is, *debit* expense (or loss) and *credit* asset.

write-off method. A method for treating *uncollectible accounts* that charges *bad debt expense* and credits accounts receivable of specific customers as uncollectible amounts are identified. May not be used when uncollectible amounts are significant and can be estimated. See *sales, uncollectible accounts adjustment,* and the *allowance method* for contrast.

write up. To increase the recorded *cost* of an *asset* with no corresponding *disbursement* of *funds;* that is, *debit* asset and *credit revenue* or, perhaps, *owners' equity.* Seldom done because currently accepted accounting principles are based on actual transactions.

Y

yield. *Internal rate of return* on a stream of cash flows. Cash yield is cash flow divided by book value. See also *dividend yield.*

yield to maturity. At a given time, the *internal rate of return* of a series of cash flows, usually said of a *bond.* Sometimes called the "effective rate."

Z

zero based(d) budgeting (ZBB). In preparing an ordinary *budget* for the next period, a manager starts with the budget for the current period and makes adjustments as seem necessary, because of changed conditions, for the next period. Since most managers like to increase the scope of the activities managed and since most prices increase most of the time, amounts in budgets prepared in the ordinary, incremental way seem to increase period after period. The authority approving the budget assumes operations will be carried out in the same way as in the past and that next period's expenditures will have to be at least as large as the current period's. Thus, this authority tends to study only the increments to the current period's budget. In ZBB, the authority questions the process for carrying out a program and the entire budget for next period: every dollar in the budget is studied, not just the dollars incremental to the previous period's amounts. The advocates of ZBB claim that in this way: (1) programs or divisions of marginal benefit to the business or governmental unit will more likely be deleted from the program, rather than being continued with costs at least as large as the present ones, and (2) alternative, more cost-effective ways of carrying out programs are more likely to be discovered and implemented. ZBB implies questioning the existence of programs, and the fundamental nature of the way they are carried out, not merely the amounts used to fund them. Experts appear to be evenly divided as to whether the middle word should be "base" or "based."

zero salvage value. If the *salvage value* of a *depreciable asset* is estimated to be less than 10 percent of its *cost,* then the tax regulations permit an assumption of zero salvage value in computing *depreciation* for federal *income tax* purposes. This convention is often used in financial reporting as well.

INDEX